Praise for
IMMOVABLE OBJECT

"A.B. Abrams tells the history of the fraught relationship between the United States and North Korea with care. His undertaking explains how the two countries, from Kim Il Sung and Harry Truman to Kim Jong Un and Donald J. Trump, have managed a difficult coexistence. To understand where the Korean Peninsula might go in the rest of the 21st century, Abrams' telling of the story of how the two countries got to where they are today is essential."

Ankit Panda, senior editor, *The Diplomat* and Adjunct Senior Fellow in the Defense Posture Project at the Federation of American Scientists

"Timely and profound....Paying due attention to the historical origins of the U.S.–DPRK conflict in the Korean War period, as well as the Cold War confrontation and post-Cold War nuclear crises, the author also explores new frontiers of conflict in the economy, ideology, and information. An excellent and informed introduction to North Korea and to America's unending confrontation with that poorly-understood country."

Charles K. Armstrong, author of *The North Korean Revolution, 1945–1950*

"If North Korea were ever to publish its own view of the history of its relationship with the USA, the result might well look something like this book. While controversial, Abrams is careful to support his assertions with footnotes and references, so that even those who find his conclusions unpalatable will be forced to weigh them carefully."

John Everard, British Ambassador to North Korea from 2006–2008 and former Coordinator UNSC Panel of Experts on sanctions on North Korea

"A.B. Abrams has written a most [illegible] of the various ways the United States h[illegible]lture and sovereignty of the people [illegible]ding this historical treatise will pr[illegible]ible, yet intriguing details of this ve[illegible]ting greatly to the reader's understan[illegible]

S. Brian Willson, J.D. LL.D., Viet Nam veteran 1966–1970, U.S. Air Force Captain (ret.), author of *Don't Thank Me For My Service: My Viet Nam Awakening to the Long History of U.S. Lies*

IMMOVABLE OBJECT

North Korea's 70 Years at War with American Power

A.B. ABRAMS

Clarity Press, Inc.

ISBN: 978-1-949762-30-3
EBOOK ISBN: 978-1-949762-31-0

In-house editor: Diana G. Collier
Cover design: A.B. Abrams and R. Jordan Santos

Library of Congress Control Number: 2020942813

Clarity Press, Inc.
2625 Piedmont Rd. NE, Ste. 56
Atlanta, GA 30324, USA
https://www.claritypress.com

TABLE OF CONTENTS

Part Four: New Battlefronts and the Evolving Nature of Conflict

Appendices: Major Incidents in the 2010s

ABBREVIATIONS

AEC – (United States) Atomic Energy Commission
ANC – African National Congress
A2AD – Anti-Access Area Denial
CFR – Council on Foreign Relations
CIA – Central Intelligence Agency
CIC – Counter Intelligence Corps
CIVD – Complete Irreversible Verifiable Denuclearisation
COMCON – Council for Mutual Economic Assistance
CSIS – Center For Strategic and International Studies
DIU – Down with Imperialism Union
DPRK – Democratic People's Republic of Korea
ECOSOC – United Nations Economic and Social Council
FAO – (United Nations') Food and Agricultural Organization
GDP – Gross Domestic Product
GNP – Gross National Product
HQ – Headquarters
IAEA – International Atomic Energy Agency
ICBM – Intercontinental Range Ballistic Missile
IDF – Israeli Defence Force
ISR – Intelligence, Surveillance and Reconnaissance
INF Treaty – Intermediate Range Nuclear Forces Treaty
JCPOA – Joint Comprehensive Plan of Action
JCS – (United States) Joint Chiefs of Staff
JSA – Joint Security Area
KCIA – (South) Korean Central Intelligence Agency
KMAG – Korean Military Advisory Group
KMDTC – Korea Mining Development Trading Corporation
KPA – Korean People's Army
MAD – Mutually Assured Destruction
MaRV – Manoeuvring Re-Entry Vehicle
MENA – Middle East and North Africa
MPLA – People's Movement for the Liberation of Angola
NATO – North Atlantic Treaty Organisation

NPT – Treaty on the Non-Proliferation of Nuclear Weapons
NSA – National Security Agency
NWYMA – North West Young Men's Association
OSS – Office for Strategic Services
PATRIOT Act – Providing Appropriate Tools Required to Intercept and Obstruct Terrorism Act
PLA – People's Liberation Army
POW – Prisoner of War
PPC – Provisional People's Committee
PRC – People's Republic of China
PSB – Psychological Strategy Board
PVA – People's Volunteer Army
ROK – Republic of Korea
ROKAF – Republic of Korea Armed Forces
SWAPO – South West African People's Organization
UMDH – Unsymmetrical Dimethylhydrazine
UN – United Nations
UNCOK – United Nations Commission on Korea
UNESCO – United Nations Educational, Scientific and Cultural Organization
UNICEF – United Nations Children's Fund
UNITA – National Union for the Total Independence of Angola
UNSC – United Nations Security Council
US – United States
USAMGIK – United States Army Military Government in Korea
USFJ – United States Forces Japan
USFK – United States Forces Korea
USSR – Union of Soviet Socialist Republics
WHO – World Health Organisation
WIDF – Women's International Democratic Federation
WMD – Weapons of Mass Destruction
ZANLA – Zimbabwean African National Liberation Army

TERMS

Asia-Pacific: Collective term for East and Southeast Asia.

China: Unless otherwise specified will from 1949 in political contexts refer to the Beijing-based People's Republic of China rather than the Taipei-based Republic of China. The Republic of China will from 1949 be referred to as Taiwan.

East Asia: The region encompassing China—including Taiwan, the Koreas and Japan. Geographically also includes the Russian Far East.

Korea: As this work primarily covers conflict between the Democratic People's Republic of Korea and the United States, referring to the state of "Korea" after the partition of the country in 1945 will, unless otherwise specified, refer to the DPRK rather than the Republic of Korea.

Southeast Asia: Members and observers in the ASEAN including Brunei, Cambodia, East Timor, Indonesia, Laos, Malaysia, Myanmar, Papua New Guinea, the Philippines, Singapore, Thailand and Vietnam.

Soviet Bloc: Soviet-led alliance of socialist states including Warsaw Pact members Bulgaria, Czechoslovakia, East Germany, Hungary, Poland and Romania as well as the USSR itself and the Mongolian People's Republic. All but the USSR had seen socialist parties initially placed in power by Moscow, received considerable Soviet aid and would later collapse with the Cold War's end.

Western Bloc: Alliance of leading Western powers established in the early Cold War and led by the United States. The founding members of the North Atlantic Treaty Organisation including Belgium, Britain, Canada, Denmark, France, Germany, Italy, Norway, the Netherlands, Luxembourg, Portugal and the United States. All but Canada, Luxemburg and Norway were major colonial powers—with these three having spent extended periods incorporated into larger European empires.

THE KOREAN PENINSULA

INTRODUCTION

The year 2020 marks the 70th year of an ongoing war between the Democratic People's Republic of Korea (DPRK—otherwise North Korea) and the United States of America, which from its outset in June 1950 saw three years of open hostilities and has continued under a fragile armistice for 67 years since. This conflict is the longest between any two modern industrial nations in history, and by far the longest war in U.S. history—beginning just months after the outbreak of the Cold War with the Soviet Union and the formation of the People's Republic of China and continuing long after hostilities with both these larger states subsided. The U.S. has since 1950 waged well over a dozen other hot wars from Panama and Grenada to Iraq and Somalia, all of which were very distinct in their nature from that which took place in Korea and could be concluded far more quickly.

The period of open hostilities between North Korea and the United States from 1950 to 1953 represented the only major conventional ground war waged between Western and East Asian powers since the mid-19th Century. To a greater extent than any other Cold War conflict, its legacy continues to have reverberations for the entire Asia-Pacific region and the wider world. A unique aspect of the U.S.-North Korean conflict from its outset has been its comprehensive nature—and the considerable ideological and cultural disparity between the two actors. The northern half of Korea is one of very few inhabited parts of the world never to have been placed under Western rule, and has evolved to present one of the most consistent challenges to Western dominated order not only politically and militarily but also ideologically. The identity of the Korean state north of the 38th parallel and its deep cultural and ideological roots—Confucian, socialist and otherwise—means it represents an entirely unique form of adversary for America which has proven considerably more difficult to tackle than almost any other. While conflict has been continuous over seven decades, the way it has been waged has changed considerably over time—from open warfare in the early 1950s to low level provocations and brinkmanship the following decade and a greater focus on economic and information warfare today.

This work will attempt to comprehensively explore the nature of conflict between the United States and the DPRK, the way it has been waged and evolved over seven decades, and the intentions of both actors towards the other. The first section will explore the origins of conflict—namely the formation of separate states on the Korean Peninsula and the outbreak, conduct during, and conclusion of the Korean War. Some key aspects include both parties' conduct towards civilians and treatment of prisoners of war, America's strategic bombing campaign and use of unconventional weapons, and both parties' incentives for initiating, continuing and ending hostilities. The legacies of this conflict on the bilateral relationship today, and in particular how historical memory and identity were shaped and have since influenced North Korea's state and society, are also covered.

The second section of this work will assess the Korean War's aftermath and the continuation of hostilities primarily during the Cold War period. This will include the evolving nature of the conflict in the context of the wider Cold War, shifting economic and technological balances of power, and the circumstances surrounding and conduct during major military incidents. The emergence during this period of war by proxy as a major aspect of the conflict between the two parties is also explored in depth—with both sides having repeatedly provided significant material assistance and in many cases manpower contributions to opposing sides of several major conflicts from the Vietnam War in the 1960s to the conflict in Syria in the 2010s. The nature of U.S.-South Korean relations in the Korean War's aftermath, and the conduct of the U.S. Military towards South Korean civilians, is also elaborated primarily to provide a contrast to America's relationship with the DPRK. Assessment of U.S. interactions with the South Korean population in parallel to its conflict with the DPRK shows a potential alternative fate for the Korean people to that under Pyongyang's rule, providing context critical to understanding the nature of the U.S.-North Korean conflict.

The third section of this work covers the evolution of U.S.-North Korean relations from the end of the Cold War to the present day. Pyongyang's prioritisation of a nuclear deterrence program following the Soviet collapse, the leveraging of economic crisis in the DPRK by Washington and Seoul to press Pyongyang for concessions, and the Bill Clinton administration's Agreed Framework deal are among the phenomena and events explored. The differences in policy between U.S. administrations is also assessed, as is Pyongyang's leveraging of the increasingly overstretched nature of American defence commitments to its own ends from 2002. Growing use of alternative means of warfare such as cyber and information warfare are also covered—as are the implications of gradual progress made by North Korea in seeking a longer ranged and more sophisticated nuclear delivery capability. This section concludes with an assessment of conflict from 2017 and U.S. relations with the DPRK under the Donald Trump administration—the first year of which coincided with the DPRK's successful development of both a fully miniaturised thermonuclear warhead and intercontinental ranged ballistic missiles. The crisis which brought both states near the brink of war that year, and the potential evolution of both bilateral relations and of North Korean capabilities, is then explored further.

The fourth and final section of this work focuses on the non-military forms of conflict between the DPRK and the U.S. in the present day which continue to be waged and will increasingly be relied on as developments in both states' military capabilities make kinetic attacks by either increasingly unthinkable. Economic warfare and U.S. attempts to constrain economic growth and place downward pressure on living standards in the DPRK through a number of means, from economic sanctions to pressure on Korean trading partners, are explored in detail. An assessment of North Korea's ideological foundations, and the factors which have set it apart from other American adversaries, are also made. The work further sheds light on the growing consensus in the West on the need to use information warfare to force societal change and westernisation of the Korean state as a means of undermining its identity from within—and the measures undertaken by Pyongyang to prevent this. The means of waging information warfare and the objectives of both parties in doing so are also explored.

Part One
THE KOREAN WAR

Chapter 1
THE BEGINNING

The New America: Superpower and Emerging Global Hegemon

The United States emerged in August 1945 as the undisputed hegemonic power in the Pacific. The claims of its only two rivals, Britain and Japan, had been quashed by four years of extremely costly total war in the region. Of the three parties to the Washington Naval Treaty and London Naval Treaty, America was the last standing. Britain was on the brink of bankruptcy and heavily dependent on U.S. support as a result of wartime expenses on multiple fronts (Western Europe, Africa, South Asia, and the Pacific) while the Japanese Empire, the most assertive challenger, was thoroughly ravaged and forcefully dismantled. Japan's modernity and sovereignty had long been an abnormality in the Asia-Pacific, where Western imperial rule and a state of "colonial underdevelopment" among Asian nations were the norm. The Asian Empire's defeat appeared at the time to have corrected this irregularity, and a regional order dictated almost exclusively in accordance with Western interests—namely those of the United States as the new leader of the Western world—could thus prevail indefinitely. So it was that the commander of U.S. Army Forces in the Far East, General Douglas MacArthur, a chief architect of the campaign which brought about Japan's surrender, proclaimed upon America's victory: "the Pacific is now an Anglo-Saxon lake."[1]

While the Soviet Union balanced the power of the American-led Western Bloc in Europe, the Asia-Pacific had long been the domain of maritime rather than continental powers, which played to the strengths of the West and the U.S. in particular. America's vast and undisputed naval superiority and power projection capabilities could thus ensure Western dominance of this region remained unchallenged. While Imperial Japan had invested heavily in maritime power projection capabilities sufficient to contest Western control of the seas, the Soviet Union would not begin to seriously do so until the 1980s grand project involving at least two 80,000 ton high-endurance supercarriers,[2] multiple 28,000 ton nuclear powered cruisers[3] and other heavyweight assets. Most of these were never completed, however, due to the state's collapse. U.S. maritime dominance has thus remained undisputed to this day.

America's wartime mobilisation and military successes had given the emerging superpower a new level of confidence in its ability to effectively govern not only the Western hemisphere, which had been policy for well over a century under the Monroe Doctrine, but also Eurasia where its intervention had been key to shifting the balance of power against the Rome–Berlin–Tokyo Axis. With Tokyo's surrender in 1945 the United States Navy would rule the waves from the Mediterranean to the East China Sea, and with 350,000 troops in Japan[4] and hundreds of thousands more in Europe, China and Korea, an American world order was in the making.

American global leadership could itself be recognised as a new and distinctive phase in a several hundred-year old global order centred on the dominant might of the West. Under this order the mantle of the leading Western hegemon had shifted between the Western powers as newer models for empire building and sustaining hegemony replaced older ones. The American hegemon inherited considerable assets from its predecessors, from the empires of Portugal and Spain which relied almost purely on brute force and terror to dominate overseas territories in the 15th century[5] to the British Empire which predominated in the 19th and introduced many more sophisticated and subtle means to administer and assert control.[6] The U.S. improved on preceding Western models for building and maintaining overseas empire with more modern concepts and strategies. Subjugation to this new hegemon was to be less direct than to those beforehand, and nominal self-rule was widely granted to American client states under this new order.[7]

Perhaps the greatest facilitator of America's newfound hegemonic position, more critical than its recently achieved global military reach or its weapons of mass destruction, was the sheer size of its economy—which in 1945 amounted to approximately half of global GDP.[8] With the economies of major rival powers without exception devastated, from Germany and Japan to the Soviet Union and Britain, it seemed as if most of the world with the exception of the USSR was dependant on American aid and loans. Wartime mobilisation in the U.S. had seen the country's economy double in size within four years from December 1941[9] and, in part due to technological transfers from Britain[10] and the flow of scientists from Germany,[11] its defence sector was without compare.

The clout economic primacy provided the United States was compounded by the technological primacy of its armed forces, and by its unique ability through long range bombers, overseas bases and high endurance naval assets to project power far from its own shores and across Eurasia. No rival power could similarly hope to threaten the American mainland. British intelligence officer Peter Calvocoressi notably observed of the state of affairs after the U.S. detonated its first nuclear bomb over a Japanese city: "For the first time in the history of the world one state had become more powerful than all other states put together."[12] While the number of nuclear warheads available was limited at the time, the sheer size of the American war economy, the safety of its mainland effectively out of reach of all challengers, and the sophistication of its defence sector, meant that even if this statement were an exaggeration it may have only been a slight one.

The sheer power that a massive and fully mobilised wartime economy had bestowed upon the U.S. was perhaps best epitomised by the B-29 Superfortress bomber program and its role in bringing about a Japanese defeat. This entirely unique aircraft was by far the heaviest ever to be mass produced, with approximately 4,000 of the 60,000kg bombers manufactured using components from across the United States. No remotely comparable aircraft existed anywhere in the world—with rival German[13] and Japanese[14] programs brought to an end by the Axis' defeat.

Far more so than the atom bomb, the Superfortress was responsible for the ravaging of the Japanese mainland in a brutal and intensive firebombing campaign targeting 67 population centres over several months. Estimates for the death toll vary widely, with the number killed in the single bloodiest incident, the firebombing of Tokyo on the night of March 9th 1945, estimated at 100,000–120,000 residents within hours[15]—with some estimates placing the death toll at closer to half a million.[16] Deployed to bases overseas, this asset had a near global reach and allowed the United States to destroy population and industrial centres while its own mainland remained relatively safe. It was indicative of the state of the Soviet Union's strategic deterrent at the time that it relied on the much older and lighter American-built 11,000kg A-20 bombers provided as part of U.S. Lend Lease assistance, which had a very short range and low payload relative to the B-29 and were considered obsolete by 1945. The destructive capacity of the United States Military as a result of both the scale at which it could manufacture advanced armaments and their sophistication was thus wholly unrivalled in 1945—even without considering the atom bomb which was an exclusively American asset.

Post-Colonial State and the New Korea

While the United States had emerged in 1945 more certain of its position than ever, Korea's place following the Japanese Empire's defeat was highly uncertain. The country had last known independence under the Choson dynasty in 1905, a state which had invested heavily in economic modernisation with its capital the first in East Asia to have street lights, electricity, trolley cars, telephone systems and running water.[17] Korea under Choson had been an effective protectorate of the United States and Britain. Citizens of both Western states had been granted extraterritoriality—effective immunity to Korean law—and the U.S. had been provided with a most favoured nation status including extensive trade privileges. Privileges were formalised under the Shufeldt Treaty signed with the United States in 1882 and the United Kingdom-Korea Treaty of 1883. Under Article 1 of the former Washington was expected to come to the country's aid in the event of "unjust or oppressive" treatment by a third party. When news of Japan's intentions to annex Korea emerged in the 1890s King Gojong, the last Choson king, sent multiple requests through his emissaries for assistance to ensure Korea's independence.

Washington for its part saw greater benefit in reaching an accord with the Japanese Empire, and agreed to recognise Tokyo's sovereignty over the Korean Peninsula if American sovereignty over the Philippines was in turn acknowledged—which Tokyo accepted under the Taft-Katsura agreement.[18] Britain too reached a similar accord, with Article 3 of the treaty signed by ambassador to London Hayashi Tadasu and the British Foreign Ministry stating: "Japan reserves special interests, political, military and economic, in Korea the United Kingdom acquiesces to the right of Japan to take measures in Korea for guidance, administration and protection and promotion of these interests."[19] Japan reciprocated by recognizing British sovereignty over India. Adding insult to injury in Korean eyes, the settlement of the Russo-Japanese War, which left Korea a Japanese protectorate, was mediated by U.S. President Theodore Roosevelt, who was awarded the Nobel Peace Prize for his contribution. As a protectorate from 1905 Korea's sovereignty was seriously compromised, with the size of the Korean army forcibly reduced by 95%, all police work transferred to the Japanese Gendarmerie and a Japanese military presence set to remain indefinitely.[20] Less than five years later, in 1910, Korea was officially annexed and placed under Japanese rule.

Japan's rule over Korea would see a harsh suppression of the country's language and traditional culture, both of which would be illegalised under a "Japanification" program. Tens of thousands of Korean sexual slaves, known as comfort women, were forced to serve the Japanese military. A generally accepted figure in South Korea today is "up to 200,000 women, mostly from Korea, but also from other parts of Asia"—meaning under 200,000 from Korea itself.[21] The highest estimates place the number at approximately 200,000 Koreans exclusively.[22]

A further 450,000 Korean male labourers were sent to Japan involuntarily.[23] Including Koreans relocated for forced labour to northern Korea and Manchuria for work in mines and factories, scholars have placed the numbers effectively enslaved under Japanese rule at over one million.[24] Unlike Western colonies in the Asia-Pacific such as French Indochina, however, under Japanese administration there was no policy of "colonial non-industrialisation" or the "development of underdevelopment"—the intentional retardation of economic development and of education in a colonised state to sustain poverty and subsistence living among Asian subjects.[25] Japan by contrast went to great lengths to increase agricultural[26] and industrial[27] outputs in its overseas colonies, primarily enriching the Japanese mainland, but also positively affecting living standards for the populations in Korea, Taiwan, Manchuria and elsewhere. One prominent example was the construction of one of the world's largest irrigation damming networks to increase agricultural output in northern Korea. By the end of the Japanese occupation period 75 percent of the rice production of what became North Korea relied on this efficient dam-based irrigation system. The Sui Ho dam built as part of this Korean system was the second largest in the world after the Hoover Dam in the United States.[28]

Korea had been an independent nation within well-recognized territorial confines for over a millennium which, combined with its pronounced ethnic, linguistic and cultural differences from neighboring states and near unique level of ethnic homogeneity, provided considerable basis for nationalism and the rejection of external subjugation. The idea of a struggle for a modern and independent Korea was thus popular among the country's intelligentsia both domestically and in Japan during the colonial period, and concepts of a first Korean republic were heavily influenced by both nationalism and Marxism.

The surrender of the Japanese Empire on August 15, 1945 led to renewed hopes for Korean independence, with nationalists across the peninsula quickly moving to organize a new government—the People's Republic of Korea. The republic was proclaimed less than a month after Japan's surrender, and was responsible for managing rice collection and food stock and redistributing land formerly held by Japan and its collaborators. By inclusion of the entire population, this republican movement gained a great deal of legitimacy and popularity. The People's Republic was, according to U.S. military reports, operating successfully before the first Americans arrived in the country.[29] The republic was governed by a network of people's committees across Korea under the leadership of Lyuh Woon Hyung, a former member of the Goryeo Communist Party and vocal activist against Japanese rule. Lyuh had been a member of China's Guomindang nationalist party and had affiliated closely with the Communist Party of the Soviet Union, paying a visit to Moscow in an official capacity in 1921. Having anticipated Japan's defeat, Lyuh had played a leading role from 1944 in laying the ground for a new independent Korean state—forming the Korean Restoration Brotherhood and the Committee for Preparation of Korean Independence. Lyuh aimed through his movement to unify the political left and right under the cause of national independence—which he was largely successful in achieving with the People's Republic of Korea receiving broad support from across the political spectrum.

Professor of history at New York University and expert on Korean history Monica Kim noted regarding the independent establishment of a sovereign Korean state: "Using the network of People's Committees already in place on the ground, the Korean populace had clearly decided to act on the structural change they wanted to see happen, which was the immediate replacement of markers of Japanese colonial sovereignty with local Korean authority. The Korean populace was not waiting for the U.S. Military to 'grant' them their independence."[30]

A Memorandum to Public Safety Officer would later note on November 7, 1945 the following observations by U.S. officers in Korea:

> The People's Committee in the more rural districts is well organized and has a large and influential membership…they do not appear to be gangsters, hoodlums or [a] "bad element" organization, but on the contrary a representative group of Korean people.[31]

Edward Grant Meade, who worked under and later wrote extensively on the U.S. Military Government in Korea, referred to the People's Republic of Korea as the "de facto government" on the Korean peninsula—the positions of which "represented with reasonable accuracy the views of the Korean majority."[32]

Lyuh Woon Hyung's efforts were key to the initial success of the People's Republic of Korea as a viable state, which was highly popular for its provision of inalienable individual rights and freedoms for the first time in Korean history—including rights for peasants to own land, its redistribution of the properties of the Japanese and their collaborators, and its nationalisation of major industries. The state's 27-Point Program laid out the following guidelines:

> the confiscation without compensation of lands held by the Japanese and collaborators; free distribution of that land to the peasants; rent limits on the non-redistributed land; nationalization of such major industries as mining, transportation, banking, and communication; state supervision of small and mid-sized companies; …guaranteed basic human rights and freedoms, including those of speech, press, assembly, and faith; universal suffrage to adults over the age of eighteen; equality for women; labour law reforms including an eight-hour day, a minimum wage, and prohibition of child labour… [and] establishment of close relations with the United States, USSR, Britain, and China, and positive opposition to any foreign influences interfering with the domestic affairs of the state.[33]

The People's Republic and hopes that it would provide a fully sovereign, genuinely nationalist and progressive government would be short lived in southern Korea, with U.S. forces arriving in the country in September 1945 and forcibly dismantling the state. The republic was outlawed on December 12th under the newly declared United States Army Military Government in Korea (USAMGIK), which under Lieutenant-General John R. Hodge would rule southern Korea in accordance with Washington's designs for the territory.[34] This ended prospects for genuine self-rule in southern Korea for decades to come—arguably indefinitely, with American rule imposed in its place and all subsequent

South Korean governments, though to varying degrees, beholden to the U.S. in many areas of their policymaking.[35]

Despite having demonstrated effective governance and popular support the republic was deemed illegitimate by the Americans. This was on the basis that Korea could not yet be a nation state and the Koreans not yet citizens—as political authenticity lay exclusively with the United States.[36] The independence and nationalist character of the People's Republic was seen as a threat to American designs for the Korean nation, and although the state's land redistribution efforts were primarily aimed at righting the perceived injustices of the Japanese imperial period, they were nevertheless sufficient to label the state a Communist government in the eyes of the Americans. As General Hodge, later referring to the People's Republic, stated: "one of our missions was to break down this Communist government."[37] The nature of land redistribution efforts strongly indicates they were a product of nationalist rather than Marxist ideology, and although the republic included communist elements it represented a united front of nationalists which collectively did not have any obvious Communist leanings.

The People's Republic of Korea was not only dissolved, but participation in the people's committees which comprised it was outlawed—as was the publication or circulation of, or intent to publish or circulate, materials printed by or on behalf of them. Displays of the Republic's insignia, flags or uniforms were also prohibited by decree of the U.S. Military Government.[38] These decrees were accompanied by considerable restrictions on the rights of Koreans to political assembly or to freely criticise American military rule—which were issued in response to the low popularity of USAMGIK.[39] A state of emergency was declared and the American Counter Intelligence Corps (CIC) was put into action, undermining opposition and enforcing the ban on independent assembly of political groups deemed undesirable by the U.S. Military. The South Korean Labour Party and other political parties were also banned. Criminalisation of political activities critical of American rule amounted to criminalisation of peaceful opposition to the imposition of foreign authority over Korea and of all leftist or genuinely nationalist political activity.

The CIC for its part was widely likened by the Korean population to the notorious Japanese secret police, the Kempei Tai, as a result of its actions.[40] The corps was, according to Captain Kenneth MacDougall who served under USAMGIK, "well known by the local populace" and "took a hand in manipulating local politics." This included raids on the headquarters of undesirable political parties,[41] and infiltration of undesirable political organisations using trained informants.[42] William J. Tigue, a CIC agent in Korea during the occupation, noted regarding the organization's power and authority over the Korean population: "For the early months of the occupation, CIC was God in Korea as far as the police and the general populace was concerned."[43] Fear of the CIC was key to establishing the rule of the U.S. military, and later of the American appointed South Korean government, over the Korean populace. It did so despite the former's lack of public support or popular legitimacy, and in spite of the gross unpopularity of the latter among the Korean population.[44] As First Lieutenant Jack Sells of the 11th CIC Detachment noted: "The letters 'CIC' strike fear into the hearts of all Koreans." Referring to the South Korean CIC later established and trained by the Americans to carry out the same tasks, he noted "Korean CIC is an utterly ruthless organization. American CIC is generally regarded in the same light."[45] CIC Master Sergeant Joseph Gorman similarly described the corps as "very much feared."[46]

An American Trusteeship

An American trusteeship over Korea, under which the authority of the People's Republic had been forcibly dissolved, had been strongly opposed both by nationalists in the country and by the Korean Provisional Government based in Shanghai. At the Cairo Conference in 1943 the American, British and Guomindang Chinese[i] leaders Franklin D. Roosevelt, Winston Churchill and Chiang Kaishek had drafted the Cairo Declaration in which they laid out plans for the dismantling of the Japanese empire and the fate of its overseas territories including Korea. The first version read that Korea should be granted its independence "at the earliest moment"—but President Roosevelt replaced the word "earliest" with "proper" on November 25, which had significantly different implications for Korea's fate. Prime Minister Churchill soon afterwards suggested changing the phrase "at the proper moment" to "in due course"—which was fixed in the final version of the declaration. "In due course" was open to interpretation and highly ambiguous, leaving the

i China was at the time ruled by three major rival governments each with separate capitals all competing for support and territory, including the Western aligned Guomindang, the Yan'an based Communist government and the Reorganized National Government of the Republic of China formed with Japanese support.

Western powers with room to manoeuvre in their policymaking to avoid binding them to granting Korea its independence. On December 4, 1943, three days after the declaration was issued, members of the Provisional Government of Korea visited the American embassy in China. They asked for clarification as to the meaning of the term "in due course." The embassy did not provide an answer but reported their inquiry to Washington. The United States, Britain and Guomindang China all declined to comment in any official capacity.

Later statements by Roosevelt referencing the Korean issue boded ill for the nation's independence, confirming many of the worst apprehensions of Korean nationalists, with the President announcing that Korea's independence would take the same course as the Philippines—specifically a "forty-year tutelage."[47] At the Yalta Conference in February 1945 he put the figure at "about fifty years," although the Soviet leader Joseph Stalin strongly urged his ally to consider a shorter period.[48] Regarding the "Philippines model," the Southeast Asian archipelago had seen its own nationalist movement, the First Philippine Republic, brutally quashed by American military action. The resulting Philippine-American War had lasted three years from 1899 and saw resistance fighters frequently tortured to death by "water cure" among other means.[49] Much of the population were forced into poorly sanitised concentration camps—referred to as the "suburbs of Hell" by American commanders.[50] An estimated 1.4 million[51] or more[52,53] of the population of 6–8 million[54] Filipinos were killed. When the Philippines eventually did attain independence, it did so granting extensive concessions to the United States politically, militarily and in terms of trade—while the American CIA continued to play a very considerable role in influencing the country's political processes.[55] The independence the United States planned to grant Korea was nominal only—and arguably left the nation in a worse position than the Japanese Empire had beforehand.[ii]

On August 14, 1945, in anticipation of the Japanese surrender which came later that day, two lower level officials from the Pentagon's Strategy Policy Committee, Dean Rusk and Charles Bonesteel were tasked with splitting the Korean Peninsula into American and Soviet

ii The "development of underdevelopment" was common to Western empires in the Asia-Pacific, and strongly discouraged economic modernisation of the colonies or client states of which the Philippines was a key example and French Indochina another. Japanese rule, for all its faults, had as previously mentioned invested in education, modernisation and industrialisation in Korea in a way Western empires did not in their own East Asian colonies.

trusteeships. Reportedly using only a National Geographic map, without an idea of the landmarks which could be used to partition the peninsula, they opted to use the circles of latitude on the equatorial plane. The two initially considered the 39th parallel but thought this would be unacceptable for the Soviets as it would grant the Americans the vast majority of the peninsula. They thus opted for the lower 38th, granting themselves the southern half and the Soviets the northern half. The Soviet Red Army had already taken Japanese-held Manchuria and was well positioned to take all of Korea. Moscow's concession of the southern half of the peninsula, which the Americans would reach over a month after the Red Army arrived in the north, was made in good faith to ensure a post-war balance between the world's two leading powers—and possibly in hope that the Americans would reciprocate with a joint trusteeship over Japan, which they did not.[56]

Following the dissolution of the People's Republic, the actions of the U.S. Military Government indicated plans for application of the "Philippines model" to Korea. The first American civilian officers selected for deployment to the peninsula had received nine months of training for the Philippines "with no more than a single hour's lecture on Korea"—according to the vice consul for the American Military Government in Korea, Gregory Henderson.[57] The nature of the Korean military subsequently established by USAMGIK closely resembled the American-established military forces in the Philippines—with both set up primarily to ensure internal security against groups opposing the occupation.[58]

Where Korean nationalists had sought the dismantling of the Japanese colonial administration, General Hodge announced that this administration would remain in place, including Japanese bureau chiefs and the governor general—prompting a massive public outcry.[59] USAMGIK would later further decree that the laws and regulations of the Japanese colonial period, previously abolished by the Korean People's Republic with considerable public support, would remain in place in full force under American rule.[60] Under public pressure the governor general, Abe Nobuyuki, was replaced by an American and the bureau chiefs removed. The Japanese administration overall remained largely intact however, from Japanese bureaucrats to the collaborators who retained their material privileges and the officers who would command the armed forces. Japanese collaborators would thus remain a central force in the politics of southern Korea for decades to come, with a study conducted by the

South Korean government in the early 2000s finding that over 90 percent of pre-1990 South Korean elites had ties to collaborationist families or individuals.[61]

In the Korean armed forces set up under American rule the presence of Japanese collaborators was even more pronounced, and almost all officers were graduates either from the Imperial Japanese Military Academy in Tokyo or the Manchukuo army's military academy. Military historian Alan Millet, a colonel in U.S. Marine Corps and former president of the Marine Corps' officer association, described them as: "veterans of Japanese service and 'class enemies' of the North Korean Communists; they tended to be Christians, educated, and middle class."[62] On November 5, 1945 the USAMGIK ordered: "any former officers, regardless of their background—Japanese Army, Manchurian, or Chinese—were to register so they could form the Korean Army."[63]

The United States' Office for Strategic Services (OSS), the predecessor to the CIA, selected Dr. Syngman Rhee, a Korean dissident who had resided in the United States for 25 years, for the presidency of the new American-established Korean government. Rhee was previously impeached by the Provisional Government of Korea for misuse of power, and while his vision for the peninsula closely aligned with Western interests, he had little standing in the country itself.[64] The Princeton-educated politician was strongly pro-American and pro-Western, a devout Christian and a staunch anti-communist. He was considered an ideal candidate by head of the United States Pacific Command General MacArthur to head a new Korean government, and was flown to Tokyo from his home in Washington D.C. to meet with the General in mid-October 1945 before being dropped in Seoul on MacArthur's personal plane. The CIA's personality assessment of Rhee had described him as having "devoted his whole life" to "the ultimate objective of controlling that country [Korea]. In pursuing this end he has shown few scruples about the elements which he has been willing to utilize for his personal advancement, with the important exception that he has always refused to deal with communists…Rhee's vanity has made him highly susceptible to contrived flattery or self-seeking interests in the U.S. and Korea. His intellect is a shallow one, and his behaviour is often irrational and even childish."[65]

Appointed to positions of considerable power at Rhee's side were a number of the most notorious collaborationist officers from the Japanese Imperial era, who proved invaluable in suppressing dissent against

American military rule. These collaborators owed their positions to the United States' intervention, having otherwise been set to lose power and in many cases face trial. They came to form an invaluable apparatus vital to governing southern Korea in accordance with American designs.[66] Former Japanese collaborator Pak Hung Sik, a later advisor to the United States' Korean Economic Mission, testified that the military in southern Korea was primarily led by former Japanese commanders, stating to this effect: "the central figures in charge of national defence are mostly graduates of the former Military College of Japan."[67] An example was the first Chief of Staff General Yi Ung Jun, who had previously pledged fealty to the Emperor of Japan in blood, and Kim Chong Won, former Japanese officer in the Philippines and New Guinea, who was prized as a military commander by the new government for his brutal tactics. American Ambassador John Muccio called him "ruthless and effective."[68] According to both South Korean and American reports, such individuals were responsible for numerous atrocities against the population in southern Korea—from massacres of political prisoners to brutal beatings of civilians including women and children.[69] They enforced the will of the U.S. Military Government and later the U.S. installed Rhee government.[70]

Despite statements by Supreme Commander MacArthur that the American occupation would be "guided by a nation whose long heritage of democracy has fostered kindly feelings for peoples less fortunate," and strong American rhetoric professing their democratising influence, USAMGIK not only disbanded the democratic republic previously in place but also appeared to have had a strong preference for a non-representative system which denied the Korean people self-rule.[71] Creation of a racialised theorisation of the Korean population provided a vital pretext for the bypassing of the rules of law in governance by the USMGIK and the CIC and dismissing the political structures developed by Koreans in favour of those chosen by Americans.[72]

The idea that Koreans were unfit for self-rule suited American interests, providing a pretext for imposition of their own will and the overthrow of the republic previously in place. Similar conclusions by Western powers that non-Western peoples across the world were "not ready for self-rule" had been used as pretexts for asserting Western dominance for over a century in much the same way.[73] A report by CIC agent in Korea Theodore Griemann stated to this effect regarding observations of the Korean population: "They were not trained in any skills and that included the art of governing themselves. A very few were able to function at all if someone were not telling them what to do and how to do it. A democratic government or any government other than a dictatorship of some kind would have brought chaos."[74] The aforementioned first-hand reports by Western observers attesting to the People's Republic's effective rule, and the considerable economic and social progress made by the Democratic People's Republic in northern Korea, strongly contradicted these claims and demonstrated that Koreans were fully capable of governing themselves as they had been for millennia—although it was contrary to the American interest to admit it.

Captain James Hausman, serving under USAMGIK, concluded to much the same effect: "We had no illusions about forming a true democracy. Benevolent dictatorship would do for starters."[75] Second Lieutenant Joseph Farell gave a similar assessment of the Korean population supporting the imposition of American will, stating: "to describe the average mentality of the South Korean ROK [citizen]…I would judge the [level of the] average ROK as being that of at least a seven year old boy."[76] Officials in the Rhee government itself appeared to have a similar discriminating attitude towards their population—believing that they were "unfit for the responsibilities of government" and that "only those who have lived abroad…can be counted upon to have the proper attitude."[77] Effectively, only those coming from the Japanese imperial system and thoroughly westernised Korean exiles such as Rhee himself were considered fit to rule the new Korea being remade in America's image, with paucity of the latter leading to a heavy reliance on the former. The vast majority of the Korean populace would have no say in the matter.

The effective quashing of the popular People's Republic and the governance to which the population of southern Korea was subsequently subjected, described as ineffective and corrupt[78] even by its Western allies,[79] led to rebellion against both the U.S. Military Government and the apparatus it had put in place. Rebellion escalated as this apparatus increasingly took responsibility for governance in the stead of direct American rule. "Benevolent dictatorship" ultimately amounted to brutal suppression of nationalist and leftist forces in Korea, with the U.S. directly sponsoring extremist youth groups—often described by the Americans themselves as terrorists[80] —in full knowledge of the means they would employ to undermine resistance to American designs. American scholar and later prominent CIA consultant Chalmers Johnson referred to one such group, the Northwest Youth League (NYL), as "a paramilitary vigilante organisation...whom the U.S. Army tolerated with full knowledge of their reputation for brutality."[81] The NYL, and to a lesser extent the Tai Han Youth Corps and North West Young Men's Association, were the most prominent of these groups. These youth groups were critical to the survival of U.S. military rule and later the Rhee government, and the American Counter Intelligence Corps described them as having "exercised police power more than the police itself and their cruel behavior has invited the deep resentment of the inhabitants."[82] The value of these youth groups as a paramilitary force went beyond the employment of violence—although this was critical—and they were vital to gathering intelligence for the CIC and creating blacklists of targets. Target lists were comprised of those individuals whose political affiliations made them a threat to USAMGIK.[83]

American reports repeatedly indicated that USAMGIK was aware of and tacitly approved of the methods of youth groups to suppress dissent. Indeed, many of the youth groups derived their authority from association and close cooperation with the American CIC.[84] Donald Nichols, a commander in the American CIC, noted in reference to the conduct of these youth groups: "on many occasions, I had to accept the methods used during interrogation by our Allies... I had to maintain an air of detachment—even approval." He described some of these incidents in gruesome detail, noting that there were some he would "never be able to erase" from his memory due to the severity of the brutalities committed.[85] American historian and renowned Korea expert Bruce Cumings noted regarding the conduct of the American aligned youth groups towards civilians suspected of supporting leftist or nationalist activities against the occupation: "In Hagui village, for example, right-wing youths captured a pregnant twenty-one-year-old woman named Mun, whose husband was allegedly an insurgent, dragged her from her home, and stabbed her thirteen times with spears, causing her to abort. She was left to die with her baby half-delivered. Other women were serially raped, often in front of villagers, and then blown up with a grenade in the vagina."[86]

Noting the endorsement the leaders of terrorist youth groups received both from the CIC and from the Rhee government—even when found to have killed and brutally tortured civilians with leftist leanings—Professor of history at New York University, Monica Kim, concluded in her own study: "these very brutal, very public acts of violence were integral to the anti-Communist politics practiced and developed on the southern half of the Korean peninsula in the post-1945 era. In other words, the North West Young Men's Association's practice and mobilization of violence were a part of the everyday political landscape created under the USAMGIK-supported regime."[87] The conduct of the youth groups towards the population thus reflected the nature of U.S. governance and the system the U.S. Military imposed to replace the People's Republic of Korea.

Among the most notorious single incidents of rebellion against American rule was the insurrection on Cheju island. There extreme political repression and massacres of political protestors at the hands of youth groups, namely the NYL, and the police force, sparked open rebellion among its rural population in 1948.[88] The U.S. military referred to the ensuing conflict as the Cheju Civil War, with American public sources claiming 15,000–20,000 islanders were massacred in the thirteen-month clashes which ended in May 1949. South Korea's own official figure for the death toll stood at 27,719, while North Korea claimed over 30,000 islanders had been "butchered" in the government's response. South Korean scholarly sources have more recently put the death toll at 38,000, although according to declassified intelligence reports the military governor of Cheju had himself privately told American intelligence that 60,000 islanders had died and up to 40,000 had been forced to flee to Japan. Officially 39,285 homes had been demolished and, according to the governor, "most of the houses on the hills" were gone. Only 170 of 400 villages remained, with up to a fifth of the population killed.[89] The U.S. reportedly arranged for former Imperial Japanese counterinsurgency forces to return to Korea from American-occupied Japan for operations against the Cheju islanders.[90] Scholar Hwang Su Kyoung referred to the "disciplining" actions against Cheju's population carried out primarily by the American CIC and associated youth groups with police support as "one of the most violent events in twentieth century Korean history."[91]

Another prominent rebellion was the Daegu Uprising of September 1946, which started in the city of Pusan on the southern coast and spread across southern Korea from Gyeongsangbuk Do in the northeast to Jeollanam Do in the southwest—also reaching the capital, Seoul. The protests demanded political and workers' rights which had been abolished with the end of the People's Republic and the release of political prisoners. While the response was far less bloody than the Cheju incident, the U.S. Army Military Government relied on battle tanks and a number of radicalised youth groups to put down the rebellion—staging mass arrests and often brutally torturing the participants. Homes and property of the protestors were permanently confiscated in many cases, leaving them destitute as a warning to future dissenters.[92]

On August 15, 1948 the government of Syngman Rhee unilaterally declared the Republic of Korea with the full authorisation of USAMGIK. This was done without consulting with the governing people's committees in the north or the USSR. It effectively ended prospects for a Korean unification process overseen by the two superpowers as had been initially planned. Rhee's government very soon faced full-scale rebellion across the country for its highly unpopular policies, against which the response was a reign of terror targeting those with communist or socialist leanings and nationalist sympathisers of the preceding Korean People's Republic. Government forces led by former officers in the Imperial Japanese Army and affiliated militarised youth groups were estimated to have killed 100,000 civilians in South Korea by 1950—2 percent of the population at the time.[93] According a report published many decades later by the South Korean government-funded Truth and Reconciliation Commission, these figures were "highly conservative." Kim Dong Choon, a leading member of the South Korean government commission, who had investigated these killings for two years, stated that he estimated the death toll was at minimum half of the 300,000 South Koreans who were imprisoned in concentration camps by the Rhee government.[94] South Korean reports from the early 2000s indicate a far higher death toll of between 600,000 and 1.2 million.[95]

New York Times correspondent Walter Sullivan wrote in early 1950 that large parts of southern Korea "are darkened today by a cloud of terror that is probably unparalleled in the world." The persistence of guerrillas "puzzles many Americans here," as does "the extreme brutality" of the conflict. He went on to argue that "there is a great divergence of wealth" in the country leaving even those previously relatively better off among the peasant population living "a marginal existence." Exactions from the peasants, not only on Cheju but throughout southern Korea from both the government and the landlords was up to 70 percent of the annual crop. Sullivan believed that it was this oppression and exploitation of the majority of the population that was the primary cause of unrest, not only on Cheju but throughout the country.[96]

While Rhee had the support of the United States, and his government inherited much of the colonial apparatus of Imperial Japan, his extreme lack of popularity led to poor electoral performances. Although he won the 1948 presidential election, these were hardly an indicator of his popularity and could not be considered free or fair. This was not only due to the intimidation of political opposition widely reported by American sources, but also because there was no opposition candidate running against the one the American OSS and General MacArthur had chosen. Rhee's rival, Kim Koo from the Korean Independence Party, a nationalist who had headed the Provisional Government of Korea, refused to take part in the election as it was conducted on the premise of forming a separate South Korean state and dividing the peninsula in two. Although Kim viewed growing communist influence in the country with much apprehension, he had opposed the joint Soviet-American trusteeship of Korea and had met with the northern Korean leadership and its president, Kim Il Sung, to discuss prospects for a peaceful reunification independently of the United States or Soviet Union. Unlike Rhee, Kim prioritized Korean reunification and opposed foreign intervention in the country's affairs. He would be targeted for assassination by the CIA and killed within a year of the election.[97]

Eyewitness testimony collected by the U.S. Military's psychological warfare section was one of many sources shedding light on the conduct of the Rhee government during elections. An example was the following testimony by a university student: "The government mobilised youth groups at election places. If men refused to vote for the right people, they were beaten up… I saw goon squads all around with sticks at election time… [There] was an atmosphere of terror all around there." He added, regarding means of ensuring political control, that the "Rhee government put terrorists in the schools, not to study, but to keep surveillance on all other students… Anyone talking about politics was sure to be regarded as a communist." Members of the youth groups had engaged in a wide array of activities—which according to the psychological warfare section's report included covering for the killings of politically suspect professors. Accounts from other sources on the ground painted much the same picture. Such actions served to alienate much of the population, and as a direct result much of the public was moved to support the coming of North Korea's armed forces in 1950 as a liberation from the rule of the Americans and of Rhee.[98] According to CIA intelligence reports, even in the capital Seoul most of the student population actively worked with and welcomed the arrival of the North Koreans—a direct result of the conduct of both USAMGIK and the Rhee government.[99]

The unpopularity of Rhee's administration forced it to rely heavily on intimidation to contest elections. An example was the treatment of representatives who had opposed constitutional amendments to increase the powers of Rhee's presidency—who were subsequently detained and charged with "communist connections" to ensure a favourable outcome.[100] Two United Nations Commissions reported on the Rhee government's mishandling of elections and heavy reliance on threats to gain votes. Threats to confiscate rice ration cards on which much of the population relied to subsist was a milder form of coercion, according to UN observers.[101] The CIA had a similar view of Rhee's administration, reporting in 1950: "Syngman Rhee and his regime are unpopular among many if not the majority of non-communist Koreans."[102]

During the Republic of Korea's first parliamentary elections, held two years after the presidential election on May 30, 1950, the results for Rhee's ruling Liberal Party proved disastrous with 128 of the 210 seats won by independents and Rhee's party retaining only 22 seats.[103] The fact that Rhee's administration used violence to intimidate its political opponents and gain votes, and had lost overwhelmingly regardless, was testament to the intense public disapproval. The failure of Rhee's party in the first parliamentary elections came just a month before the outbreak of the Korean War.

Democratic People's Republic of Korea: Salvaging Korean Independence

Where the rule of the United States Army Military Government in southern Korea, and arguably more so the Sygnman Rhee government under the Republic of Korea from 1948, represented the frustration of the Korean nationalist movement's aspirations for the nation's future, this future was at least in part realised in northern Korea where a very different form of government came to power. When the Soviet armed forces arrived in northern Korea on August 24, 1945 to exercise governance over their own mandated half of the peninsula, they too found the nation under the governance of several people's committees under the People's Republic of Korea. While there was widespread opposition to the Soviet trusteeship in the north, Moscow did not impose a military government as the Americans had in the south. Moreover, the Soviet Civil Administration did not abolish the People's Republic outright nor illegalise the people's committees as the U.S. Military Government did in the south, but rather incorporated this governing apparatus into the Provisional People's Committee (PPC). Under this committee, with the full endorsement of the USSR, abolishment of the Japanese colonial system continued with the collaborationists tried and their assets and privileges gained under Tokyo's rule redistributed and removed.[104]

Perhaps the most significant contrast between the Soviet and American trusteeships in Korea, which would lead to the major differences between the two Korean governments that emerged under them, was that the USSR allowed the Korean nationalist project to continue with minimal interference whereas the American military government went to great lengths to suppress it. As prominent Korea expert, Colombia University Professor Charles Armstrong, concluded: "The Soviet occupation authorities in Eastern Europe were much more heavy-handed than their American counterparts; the opposite is true in Korea." He further noted the scarcity of "Soviet manipulating of North Korea's internal affairs," in sharp contrast to Soviet client states in Europe and Mongolia or to the American client state south of the 38th parallel.[105] The governing people's committees in northern Korea were neither established nor run under Soviet direction,[106] and had already began to organise governing institutions including a police force before the Soviets arrived.[107]

The lack of Soviet influence on Korean internal politics[108] would become particularly evident in the 1950s, with Pyongyang purging overly "pro-Soviet" Koreans from government and making an ideological and political break with Moscow after the superpower revised its previous positions under the Premiership of Nikita Khrushchev.[109] No similar break from the U.S. would ever have been possible in South Korea due to the far greater penetration the Americans had achieved and would maintain indefinitely. The distinct nature of the North Korean state as a continuation of the prior Korean nationalist movement, rather than an artificial creation of Moscow, was further attested to by its separate ideology, very much distinct from the USSR and that which Moscow imposed on Mongolia and the Warsaw Pact nations,[110] and ultimately by the state's survival where the Soviet decline and eventual collapse saw the artificial client states fall with it. As Kim Namsik, a South Korean scholar who witnessed this period in North Korea first hand, observed regarding the independent nature of state formation north of the 38th parallel: "The People's Regime of North Korea was founded on the basis of the People's Committees spontaneously organised after liberation.... The People's Committees were not created from the centre but organised from the bottom up."[111]

Although forced to accept a three-year Soviet military presence, the Provisional People's Committee in northern Korea was able to carry out much of the mandate of the Korean People's Republic leading to widespread admiration and support from nationalists in the south and among the overseas Korean community. The earlier Twenty-Seven Point Program of the People's Republic was effectively fulfilled entirely under this government, with the exception of the final two points: "establishment of close relations with the United States, USSR, Britain, and China, and positive opposition to any foreign influences interfering with the domestic affairs of the state." The Soviet Civil Administration ensured that the new government in northern Korea, which made its temporary capital in Pyongyang, would remain locked into the Soviet alliance system—meaning while interference in domestic affairs was limited the formation of close ties to the Western Bloc and a position of neutrality in the emerging Cold War were effectively ruled out. The independent nature and leftist leanings of the PPC however meant that, like the People's Republic of Korea that preceded it, hostility from the Western powers and the United States in particular was guaranteed even if this new government in Pyongyang had been allowed to make diplomatic overtures—as other leftist and nationalist groups in the region and beyond would come to learn in the early Cold War years.[112]

The leadership of the PPC, much like that of the People's Republic, had its roots in the anti-Japanese struggle for independence. The body's chairman, Kim Il Sung, was the leader of an anti-Japanese guerrilla movement and the son of prominent Korean nationalists Kim Hyong Jik and Kang Pan Sok. The chairman's parents had, according to North Korean sources, run secret Korean language classes at a time when Korean was banned and the Japanese language was imposed, and were involved in the founding of the armed guerilla movement against Japanese rule. Whether Kim and Kang's movement was affiliated with communist ideology or with a basic Korean nationalism remains uncertain, but their eldest son Kim Il Sung was heavily influenced by their activities. He went on to found the Down with Imperialism Union (DIU) in 1926 in what was then Manchuria—today a part of China with a high population of ethnic Koreans. The union was intended to promote resistance to Japanese occupation and was heavily influenced by Marxist thought, which was increasingly gaining traction as the wave of the future for the Korean nation to replace the feudal monarchical system which had preceded Japanese rule.[113] DIU was, according to the North Korean leadership of later years, a "fresh start for the Korean communist movement and the Korean revolution…the beginning of the struggle to found a new type of party"—referred to as a means for "anti-Japanese national-liberation struggle relying on the masses."[114, iii]

Regarding Kim Il Sung's rise to assume leadership, this process too presents a strong contrast to that of Sygnman Rhee in southern Korea. Japanese sources indicate that Kim was elected as the leader of Korean guerrillas over older and more experienced partisans,[115] and was already well known across the peninsula for his activities and those of his parents against the empire. This paved the way for his leadership of the post-colonial government. As Charles Armstrong emphasized in his own study of the immediate post-Japanese period: "at the time of liberation thirty-three-year-old Captain Kim Il Sung was the leading Korean among the Manchurian partisan exiles in the Soviet Far East. Kim's emergence as leader of the Korean group does not arise from his being the handpicked choice of the Soviets for their occupation government, which was the assumption of many Western observers, both at the time and since."[116]

The PPC was organised at a meeting in February 1946 of 137 representatives, most of whom had comprised the leadership of the People's Republic of Korea, including two representatives each from the Democratic Party of Korea, the Independence Alliance, the Communist Party of Korea, the General Federation of Labour Unions, the General Federation of Peasant Unions and one each from the Women's League and the Democratic Youth League. [117] On the second day of the meeting on February 9, 23 members of the Provisional People's Committee were elected, including six from the Communist Party, five from the Democratic Party and two from the Independence Alliance. On March 23, committee chairman Kim Il Sung, also now chairman of the Communist Party of Korea, issued a 20-Point Platform for reform and decolonisation of northern Korea. This very closely resembled the 27-Point Program

iii It was and remains difficult to equate the two governments in respect to their legitimacy because one represented a continuation of the republican system Koreans had chosen and overwhelmingly supported before foreign intervention in the country—while the other was very conspicuous in its artificial imposition by a foreign power leading to widespread resistance and civil war south of the 38th parallel. While the government in southern Korea had a support base in the north as well as domestically, this was overwhelmingly comprised of devout Christians who identified with Rhee and Japanese collaborators who relied on his and America's protection to survive. This support base represented a small minority as evidenced by numerous aforementioned American reports from the time contrasting strongly with the far more widespread appeal of the northern government's nationalist vision. The image of Syngman Rhee, a westernised exile with a European wife flown in from Washington on an American military plane, contrasted strongly to that of Kim Il Sung—a much renowned freedom fighter who had led guerrillas against Japanese rule for decades.

of the People's Republic of Korea, fulfilling the mandate of ending the legacies of Japanese rule, providing the people with inalienable rights and modernising the nation's economy. This program was implemented across northern Korea under the PPC's jurisdiction, and stipulated the following:

1. Completely purge all remnants of the former Japanese imperialist rule in the political and economic life in Korea.
2. Open a merciless struggle against reactionary and anti-democratic elements within the country, and absolutely prohibit activities by fascist and anti-democratic parties, groups and individuals.
3. Guarantee the freedoms of speech, press, assembly and faith to all people. Guarantee the conditions for the free activities of democratic political parties, working associations, peasant associations, and other democratic social organizations.
4. Have the entire Korean people possess the duty and the right to organize people's committees, the unified local administrative institutions, through elections based on a universal, direct, equal and secret ballot.
5. Guarantee equal rights to all citizens regardless of gender, faith and possession of property.
6. Insist on the inviolability of residence and person, and the lawful guarantee of property and personal possessions of citizens.
7. Abolish all legal and judicial institutions used during the time of the former Japanese imperialist rule and also influenced by it, and elect people's judicial institutions on democratic principles and guarantee equal rights under the law for all citizens.
8. Develop industries, farms, transportation and commerce for increasing the well-being of the people.
9. Nationalize large enterprises, transport institutions, banks, mines and forests.
10. Allow and encourage freedom in private handicraft and commerce.

11. Confiscate land from Japanese persons, Japanese nationals, traitors, and landowners who practice tenant farming, scrap the tenant farming system, and transfer all confiscated land into properties of peasants, free of charge. Have the state manage all irrigation facilities free of charge.
12. Struggle against speculators and loan sharks by enacting market prices for daily necessities.
13. Enact a single and fair tax system and implement a progressive income tax system.
14. Implement an 8-hour work system for workers and office clerks and regulate minimum wages. Prohibit work for males below the age of 13 and implement a 6-hour work system for males aged 13 to 16.
15. Implement life insurance for workers and office clerks, and implement an insurance system for workers and enterprises.
16. Implement a universal compulsory education system, and extensively expand primary schools, middle schools, high schools and universities under state management. Reform the people's education system in accordance with the democratic system of the state.
17. Actively develop the national culture, science and art, and expand the number of theatres, libraries, radio broadcasting stations and movie theatres.
18. Extensively install special schools for cultivating the talent being required in all sectors of state institutions and people's economy.
19. Encourage people and enterprises engaged in science and art, and give aid to them.
20. Expand the number of state hospitals, eradicate infectious diseases, and treat poor people for free.

The 20-Point Program was implemented gradually over the following year, beginning with the confiscation of land from Japanese nationals and collaborators on March 8. On June 24, an eight-hour workday was implemented, and work for those under 14 years old was prohibited. On July 22, a law on gender equality was enacted. On August 10, over 1000 major industrial facilities, or 90% of industry in northern Korea, were nationalised. Reforms under the 20-Point Program, from inalienable rights to the right to form people's committees and gender equality, were unprecedented in Korean history.[iv]

To raise revenues for the new state, the PPC decided on 27 December that farmers were to provide 25% of their harvest as agricultural tax. While high, this paled in comparison to the reported 70% exactions from peasants in southern Korea from both the government and landlords.[118] The result of the PPC's successful implementation of its policies, and the gross economic mismanagement south of the 38th parallel under Syngman Rhee, was a considerable discrepancy in the quality of life between the two by 1948. On August 15 of that year, the provisional southern government declared the formation of the Republic of Korea in the south with Rhee as its President. While the partitioning of Korea into Soviet and American spheres of influence had occurred in 1945 on the basis that nationwide elections be carried out to reunify the peninsula within five years, the Rhee government's extremely poor electoral prospects led both U.S. and South Korean sources to predict a major loss if these were carried out freely and fairly.[119] The U.S. was thus adamant that elections be carried out under the UN Temporary Commission on Korea, which the Soviets for reasons later elaborated believed would show a strongly pro-Western bias and would allow the Western Bloc to manipulate results in their favour. Later counterproposals from North Korea for reunifying elections held under an unspecified framework, to be decided on by both Koreas together, were in turn flatly rejected by the south with the U.S. also threatening penalties against Seoul should it accept them.[120]

Washington's apprehensions towards unifying elections were strongly in line with a wider Cold War trend—namely that the democratic process could only be endorsed if it produced candidates favourable to the interests of the Western Bloc.[121] This was far from the case for the expected outcome of a free and fair unifying election in Korea. An almost exact reoccurrence of this would occur in Vietnam where the South Vietnamese government, proving itself highly repressive and carrying forward many of the policies of the French colonial period, was expected to overwhelmingly lose unifying elections which were scheduled for 1954 under the Geneva Accords. The U.S. prompted a South Vietnamese

---

iv It is notable that following the forced abolition of the People's Republic by the U.S. Military Government, no similar decolonisation program could ever be implemented south of the 38th parallel, which would form the crux of the major contrast which emerged between the two states.

withdrawal because, in the words of President Eisenhower: "had elections been held…a possible 80 per cent of the population would have voted for the communist Ho Chi Minh as their leader."[122] The CIA had predicted in their own report: "if scheduled national elections are held in July 1956…the Viet Minh will almost certainly win."[123] Preventing unifying elections was thus the only means by which the two Western client regimes could retain power in the divided East Asian states.

The Rhee government's unpopularity was not without cause, and other than severe abuses of the population, mass killings, and Seoul's economic ineptitude, it bore a strong contrast to the rapid economic and social progress in the north. In his twelve years as president Rhee would never institute a national economic policy and his country made negligible economic gains as a result. While Seoul could rely on U.S. aid for one third its budget, a lifeline seen as critical to maintaining what integrity the state had, little was done to monitor its use and much of these funds were diverted by officials for personal use. [124] As professors Uk Heo and Terrence Roehrig noted in their study of South Korean political history, alongside rampant corruption "Rhee also had little expertise or interest in economic development, and his economic ministers were similarly inexperienced and untrained in economic policy making."[125] *Time* magazine thus referred to southern Korea under Rhee as "an economic wasteland…really one of the poorest places in the world."[126] A further result of the Rhee government's economic failings was the promotion and strong encouragement of prostitution servicing the U.S. Military,[127] a means for Seoul to earn much needed foreign currency which by the end of Rhee's rule accounted for nearly 25% of Gross National Product (GNP).[128] This and the accompanying rise in human trafficking and sexual slavery was abhorred in Korean society,[129] and further undermined the popularity of Rhee's government as well as the United States.

The considerable discrepancy in the achievements of the two Korean governments meant that it was widely expected that had nationwide reunifying elections been carried out, the PPC would have won overwhelmingly. Thus American sources, from the CIA[130] to the *New York Times,*[131] widely reported[132] that a reunified Korea with free elections would almost certainly lead to Rhee's fall and a form of governance similar to that in place in the north. Pyongyang's adherence to the nationalist mandate of the People's Republic of Korea, in contrast to the southern government's continuation of many prominent aspects of the Japanese colonial system from land distribution to military structure and civil administration, guaranteed it widespread support in southern Korea. Such an electoral outcome would not only see Rhee removed from power and likely tried, alongside the Japanese collaborators forming much of his political and military leadership, but it would reverse the considerable investments the U.S. had made to undermine the People's Republic of Korea and establish a Western-aligned client state. The northern government integrated several aspects of the People's Republic, from its leadership to its ideals, into its own governance, meaning its rule of southern Korea would closely resemble that of the people's committees which preceded imposition of American military governance below the 38th parallel.

With the American backed southern government declaring a Seoul based Republic of Korea (ROK) and unilaterally claiming jurisdiction over the entire Korean nation, the Pyongyang-based Provisional People's Committee declared its own republic, the Democratic People's Republic of Korea (DPRK), to protect its claim to sovereignty against Rhee's government. The result was the formation of two separate Korean states—each claiming to represent the entire Korean nation. One was nationalist, progressive, decolonised and fast modernising. The other was in a state of effective civil war and suffering from the results of severe corruption and economic mismanagement, heavily reliant on and largely subservient to the United States, and governing through an apparatus inherited from the Japanese colonial period.

NOTES

1 Hopkins, William B., *The Pacific War: The Strategy, Politics, and Players that Won the War*, Minneapolis, MN, Zenith Press, 2011 (p. 345).
James, Doris Clayton, *The Years Of MacArthur, Volume III*, Boston, Houghton Mifflin, 1985 (p. 401).

2 Huard, Richard, 'Meet the Ulyanovsk: Russia's 85,000 Ton Monster Aircraft Carrier,' *National Interest,* September 28, 2019.

3 Farley, Robert, 'Russia's Kirov-Class Battlecruiser Might Be The World's Last Living Battleship,' *National Interest,* November 21, 2019.

4 Talmdage, Eric, 'U.S. troops used Japan brothels after WWII,' *Seattle Times,* April 26, 2007.

5 Adamson, John, 'The Reign of Spain was Mainly Brutal,' *Telegraph,* December 2, 2002.
Goodwin, Robert, *Spain: The Centre of the World 1519–1682,* London, Bloomsbury, 2015.
Gady, Franz-Stefan, 'How Portugal Forged an Empire in Asia,' *The Diplomat,* July 11, 2019.
'"Colonial-era mass grave" found in Potosi, Bolivia,' *BBC,* July 27, 2014.

6 Kaul, Chandrika, *Communications, Media and the Imperial Experience: Britain and India in the Twentieth Century*, London, Palgrave MacMillan, 2014.
Darwin, John, *Unfinished Empire: The Global Expansion of Britain,'* London, Penguin Books, 2012.
Bowen, H. V., *The Business of Empire: The East India Company and Imperial Britain, 1756–1833,'* New York, Cambridge University Press, 2006.
7 'The Philippines: Early Years of the Republic,' Background, Office of Public Affairs, Department of State, June 1951.
Morgan, Gordon D., *Toward an American Sociology: Questioning the European Construct*, Westport, Praeger, 1997 (p. 160).
8 *The Development Dimension Fostering Development in a Global Economy*, Paris, Organisation for Economic Co-Operation and Development, 2005 (p. 49).
9 Harrison, Mark, *The Economics of World War II: Six Great Powers in International Comparison*, Cambridge, Cambridge University Press, 2000 (pp. 1–42).
10 Ellis, Guy, *Britain's Jet Age: From the Meteor to the Sea Vixen,* Stroud, Amberley, 2016 (Chapter 3: Ignored, Rejected and Given Away).
Wade, Andrew, 'September 1946: the Miles 52, the supersonic aircraft that never was,' *The Engineer*, September 19, 2016.
11 O'Reagan, Douglas M., *Taking Nazi Technology: Allied Exploitation of German Science after the Second World War*, Baltimore, John Hopkins University Press, 2019.
Gibel, John, 'Project Paperclip: German Scientists, American Policy, and the Cold War,' *Diplomatic History,* vol. 14, no. 3, Summer 1990 (pp. 343–365).
12 Calvocoressi, Peter, *World Politics Since 1945*, Abingdon, Routledge, 2008 (p. 5).
13 Wulf, Dieter, 'Hitler's "Amerikabomber,"' *The Atlantic,* May 2004.
14 'Nakajima G10N Fukagu; Imperial Japan's Intercontinental Bomber Made to Strike America,' *Military Watch Magazine*, April 24, 2019.
15 Wilson, Ward, 'The Bomb Didn't Beat Japan…Stalin Did,' *Foreign Policy*, May 30, 2017.
16 Selden, Mark, 'A Forgotten Holocaust: U.S. Bombing Strategy, the Destruction of Japanese Cities & the American Way of War from World War II to Iraq,' *The Asia-Pacific Journal*, vol. 5, issue 5, 2007.
17 Cumings, Bruce, *Parallax Visions: Making Sense of American-East Asian Relations*, Chapel Hill, NC, Duke University Press, 2002 (p. 72).
18 Sung Chol, Ryo, *Korea; The 38th Parallel North*, University Press of the Pacific, 2004 (p.10).
19 Ibid. (p.10).
Paine, S.C.M., *The Japanese Empire: Grand Strategy from the Meiji Restoration to the Pacific War*, Cambridge, Cambridge University Press, 2017 (pp. 79–80).
20 *Railroads in Korea: From United States Consul-General Paddock, Seoul, Korea* (p. 4) in: *Daily Consular Reports,* Department of Commerce and Labour, no. 2147, January 3, 1905.
21 'Japan PM urges S. Korea to remove "comfort woman" statue,' *The Korea Herald*, January 8, 2017.
22 Moon, Katherine H. S., *Sex Among Allies*, New York, Colombia University Press, 1997 (pp. 15–16).
23 Kim, Seong-hwan, 일제의 침략 전쟁과 병참기지화, (Japanese War of Aggression and Logistics Base), Paju, SaKyejul, 2004 (p. 173).
24 Cumings, Bruce, *Parallax Visions: Making Sense of American-East Asian Relations*, Chapel Hill, NC, Duke University Press, 2002 (p. 74).
25 Ngô, Vĩnh Long, *Before the Revolution: The Vietnamese Peasants under the French*, Cambridge, MA, The MIT Press, 1973 (pp. 73–74).
Cumings, Bruce, *Parallax Visions: Making Sense of American-East Asian Relations*, Chapel Hill, NC, Duke University Press, 2002 (pp. 83–86).

26 Hsiao, Mei-Chu W. and Hsiao, Frank S. T., *Taiwan in the Global Economy—Past, Present and Future* in: Chow, Peter C., *Taiwan in the Global Economy: From an Agrarian Economy to an Exporter of High-Tech Products*, Westport, Praeger, 2002 (Section V: 'Taiwan in the Global Economy During the Japanese Period').

27 '朝鮮総督府統計年報 昭和17年 [Governor-General of Korea Statistical Yearbook 1942],' Governor-General of Korea, March 1944.

28 Williams, Christopher, *Leadership Accountability in a Globalizing World*, London, Palgrave Macmillan, 2006 (p. 185).

29 *History of the United States Armed Forces in Korea, Volume III*, United States Far East Command, 1948 (Chapter 4, Part I, p. 50).
Cumings, Bruce, *Origins of the Korean War, Volume 1: Liberation and the Emergence of Separate Regimes, 1945–1947, Volume One*, Yeogsabipyeongsa Publishing Co, 2004 (pp. 702–703).

30 Kim, Monica, *The Interrogation Rooms of the Korean War; The Untold History*, Princeton, NJ, Princeton University Press, 2019 (p. 58).

31 Meade, Edward Grant, *American Military Government in Korea,* New York, King's Crown Press, 1952 (p. 188).

32 Ibid. (pp. 56, 72).

33 Hart-Landsberg, Martin, *Korea: Division, Reunification, & U.S. Foreign Policy,* New York, Monthly Review Press, 1998 (pp. 65–66).

34 Henderson, Gregory, *Korea: The Politics of Vortex*, Cambridge, MA, Harvard University Press, 1968 (p. 126).
Kim, Monica, *The Interrogation Rooms of the Korean War; The Untold History*, Princeton, NJ, Princeton University Press, 2019 (p. 48).

35 Henderson, Gregory, *Korea: The Politics of Vortex*, Cambridge, MA, Harvard University Press, 1968 (p. 127).

36 Kim, Monica, *The Interrogation Rooms of the Korean War; The Untold History*, Princeton, NJ, Princeton University Press, 2019 (p. 55).

37 Cumings, Bruce, *Korea's Place in the Sun: A Modern History*, New York, W. W. Norton & Company, 1997 (p.202).

38 Mi Kunjongch'ong kwanbo: Official Gazette, United States Army Military Government in Korea, Seoul, Wonju Munhwasa, Ordinance 72.

39 Kim, Jinwung, 'A Policy of Amateurism: The Rice Policy of the U.S. Army Military Government in Korea, 1945–1948,' *Korea Journal*, vol. 47, no. 2, Summer 2007 (pp. 208–231).
Kim, Inhan, 'Land Reform in South Korea under the U.S. Military Occupation, 1945–1948,' *Journal of Cold War Studies,* vol. 18, no. 2, Spring 2016 (pp. 111, 117).

40 Kim, Monica, 'The Intelligence of Fools: Reading the US Military Archive of the Korean War,' *Positions Asia Critique,* vol. 23, issue 4, November 2015 (p. 708).
Kim, Monica, *The Interrogation Rooms of the Korean War; The Untold History*, Princeton, NJ, Princeton University Press, 2019. (pp. 61–63, 66).
CIC 1945.9–1949.1, vol. 1, report dated April 19, 1946, included in 971st Counter Intelligence Corps Detachment Annual Progress Report for 1947 (p. 386).

41 'Interview with Kenneth E. MacDougall, Capt, MPC, October 5, 1954, Bldg 22, Ft Holabird,' Folder 228–01 Macdougall, Kenneth E.—CIC during Occupation of Korea—(1947–1948) Box 6, Counter Intelligence Corps Collection, Assistaint Chief of Staff, G-2 (Intelligence), RG 319, NARA, College Park, Maryland.
Kim, Monica, *The Interrogation Rooms of the Korean War; The Untold History*, Princeton, NJ, Princeton University Press, 2019 (pp. 61–63, 66).

42 1948 Annual Progress Report of the 971st CIC Detachment in Korea, Box 14856, WWII Operations Report, 1941–48, Central Intelligence, RG 407, NARA, College Park, Maryland.

43 Tigue, William J., Box 6, Records of the Army Staff, Assistant Chief of Staff, G-2 (Intelligence), Counter Intelligence Collection, Record Group 319, NARA, College Park, Maryland.

44 Foreign Relations of the United States, 1950, vol. VII, Korea, Washington D.C., Government Printing Office, 1976 (p. 602).
Laurie, Clayton, *Baptism by Fire: CIA Analysis of the Korean War: a Collection of Previously Released and Recently Declassified Intelligence Documents*, CIA Historical Review Program (p. 41).

45 Interview with 1st Lt. Jack D. Sells, 111th Counter Intelligence Corps Detachment, Folder: 228–01 EEI: CIC Operations in Korea, 1952, Box 6, Counter Intelligence Corps Collection, Assistant Chief of Staff, G-2 (Intelligence), RG 319, NARA, College Park, Maryland, Folder 228.

46 Interview with M/Sgt. Joseph P. Gorman, 111th Counter Intelligence Corps Detachment, Folder: 228–01 EEI: CIC Operations in Korea, 1952, Box 6, Counter Intelligence Corps Collection, Assistant Chief of Staff, G-2 (Intelligence), RG 319, NARA, College Park, Maryland, Folder 228.

47 Pacific War Council Minutes, January 12, 1944, Roosevelt Paper (cited in: Louis, William Roger Louis, *Imperialism at Bay: The United States and the Decolonization of the British Empire, 1941–1945,* Oxford, Clarendon Press, 1944 (p. 355).)

48 *'Bohlen Minutes,' in:* Foreign Relations of the United States, Diplomatic Papers, Conferences at Malta and Yalta, 1945, ed. Barron, Bryton, Washingotn D. C., United States Government Printing Office, 1955, (Document 393).

49 Tucker, Spencer, *Almanac of American Military History, Volume 1*, Santa Barbara, CA, ABC-CLIO, 2012 (p. 1248).
Palitto, Robert M., *Torture and State Violence in the United States: A Short Documentary History*, 3.12 Letter from Secretary of War Elihu Root to Henry Cabot Lodge, February 27, 1906.
Lens, Sydney, and Zinn, Howard, *The Forging of the American Empire: From the Revolution to Vietnam: A History of American Imperialism*, London, Pluto Press, 2003 (p. 189).

50 Welman, Frans, *Face of the New Peoples Army of the Philippines: Volume Two*, Booksmango, 2012 (pp. 138–139).

51 Francisco, Luzviminda, *The End of an Illusion*, London, AREAS, 1973.

52 Ahmed, Eqbal, 'The Theory and Fallacies of Counter-Insurgency,' *The Nation*, August 2, 1971.

53 San Juan, Epifanio, 'U.S. Genocide in the Philippines: A Case of Guilt, Shame, or Amnesia?,' *Medium*, March 22, 2005.

54 Boot, Max, *The Savage Wars Of Peace: Small Wars And The Rise Of American Power*, New York, Basic Books, 2002 (p. 125).

55 Burkholder Smith, Joseph, *Portrait of a Cold Warrior*, New York, Putnam, 1976 (p. 95).
Blum, William, *Killing Hope: U.S. Military and C.I.A. Interventions Since World War II*, London, Zed Books, 2003 (p. 43).
Bonner, Raymond, *Waltzing With a Dictator: The Marcoses and the Making of American Policy*, New York, Times Books, 1987 (pp. 39–41).

56 Kim, Monica, *The Interrogation Rooms of the Korean War; The Untold History*, Princeton, NJ, Princeton University Press, 2019 (pp. 43–44).

57 Henderson, Gregory, *Korea: The Politics of the Vortex*, Cambridge, MA, Harvard University Press, 1968 (p. 124).

58 Man, Simeon, *Soldiering through Empire: Race and the Making of the Decolonizing Pacific,* Oakland, University of California Press, 2018 (p. 23).

59 Kim, Monica, *The Interrogation Rooms of the Korean War; The Untold History*, Princeton, NJ, Princeton University Press, 2019 (p. 48).
G-2 Periodic Report/ United States Army Forces in Korea, Headquarters, G-2,

1945–1948, vol. 1, September 12, 1945.
G-2 Periodic Report/ United States Army Forces in Korea, Headquarters, G-2, 1945–1948, vol. 1, October 23, 1945.

60 Kim, Monica, *The Interrogation Rooms of the Korean War; The Untold History*, Princeton, NJ, Princeton University Press, 2019 (p. 55).

61 Cumings, Bruce, *The Korean War: A History*, New York, Modern Library, 2010 (p. 58).

62 Millett, Alan R., 'Captain James H. Hausman and the Formation of the Korean War, 1945–1950,' *Armed Forces and Society 23*, no. 4, 1997 (p. 515).

63 Ibid. (p. 506)

64 Breen, Michael, 'Syngman Rhee: president who could have done more,' *The Korea Times*, 2 November, 2011.

65 CIA, *Prospects for the Survival of the Republic of Korea*, ORE 44–48, October 28, 1948, Appendix A, 'Personality of Syngman Rhee.'

66 Cumings, Bruce, *The Korean War: A History*, New York, Modern Library, 2010 (p. 58).

67 Rozman, Gilbert, and Armstrong, Charles K., *Korea at the Center: Dynamics of Regionalism in Northeast Asia*, Abingdon, Routledge, 2005.

68 Cumings, Bruce, *The Korean War: A History*, New York, Modern Library, 2010 (Chapter 7: Part 5, 'Mr. Massacre').

69 Ibid. (p. 172).

70 Shaines, Robert A., *Command Influence: A Story of Korea and the Politics of Injustice*, Parker, Outskirts Press, 2010 (p. 395).

71 Kim, Monica, *The Interrogation Rooms of the Korean War; The Untold History*, Princeton, NJ, Princeton University Press, 2019 (p. 44).

72 Ibid. (pp. 67–68).

73 United States Philippines Commission (1899–1900), *Report of the Philippine Commission to the President, Volume II, Testimony and Exhibits,* Washington, Government Printing Office, 1900 (p. 352).
Liddle, Joanna and Joshi, Rama, 'Gender and Imperialism in British India,' *Economic and Political Weekly*, vol. 20, no. 43, October 1985 (pp. WS72–WS78).

74 Folder 228–01, Griemann, Theodore E., CIC during Occupation of Korea—1947–49, Box 6, Counter Intelligence Corps Collection, Assistant Chief of Staff, G-2 (Intelligence), RG 319, NARA, College Park, Maryland.

75 Interview with James Hausman, Box 141, Series VI, 'In Mortal Combat,' Toland Papers, Franklin D. Roosevelt Presidential Library and Archives.

76 Second Lieutenant Joseph H. Farell of the 116th CIC Detachment, Folder : 228–01 EEI: CIC Operations in Korea, 1952, Box 6, Counter Intelligence Corps Collection, Assistant Chief of Staff, G-2 (Intelligence), RG 319, NARA, College Park, Maryland.

77 'Memorandum for the Ambassador, date December 27, 1948, by Bertel, Kuniholm,' Reel XIII, 'Internal Affairs of Korea, 195–1949' Microfilm. Department of State Decimal File 895. Records of the U.S. Department of State relating to the Internal Affairs of Korea, 1945–9.

78 Heo, Uk and Roehrig, Terence, *South Korea Since 1980*, Cambridge, Cambridge University Press, 2010 (p. 18).

79 Cumings, Bruce, *The Korean War: A History*, New York, Modern Library, 2010 (p. 179).

80 Meyers, Samuel M., and Biderman, Albert D., *Mass Behaviour in Battle and Captivity: The Communist Soldier in the Korean War*, Chicago, University of Chicago Press, 1968 (pp. 280–281).

81 Johnson, Chalmers, *Blowback: The Costs and Consequences of American Empire*, New York, Henry Holt, 2004 (p. 99).

82 G-2 Weekly Summary no. 116, November 23–30, 1947.
Seoul Times, June 15, 1950.

Seoul Times, June 18, 1950.

83 Kim, Monica, *The Interrogation Rooms of the Korean War; The Untold History,* Princeton, NJ, Princeton University Press, 2019 (pp. 231–232, 236).

84 Ibid. (p. 229).

85 Nichols, Donald, *How Many Times Can I Die?,* Brooksville, FL, Brooksville Printing, 1981 (pp. 119–120).

86 Cumings, Bruce, *The Korean War: A History*, New York, Modern Library, 2010 (p. 119).
Kim, Seong Nae, 'The Cheju April Third Incident and Women: Trauma and Solidarity of Pain,' paper presented at the Cheju 4.3 Conference, Harvard University, April 24–26, 2003.

87 Kim, Monica, *The Interrogation Rooms of the Korean War; The Untold History,* Princeton, NJ, Princeton University Press, 2019 (p. 231).

88 United States Forces in Korea (USFIK) G-2 Intelligence Summaries nos. 134–142, April 2–June 4, 1948.
Seoul Times, April 7 and April 8, 1948.
Office of the Chief of Military History, History of United States Army Forces in Korea (HUSAFIK), vol. 2, part 2, 'Police and National Events, 1947–1948.'

89 'The Background of the Present War in Korea,' *Far Eastern Economic Review*, August 31, 1950 (pp. 233–237).
Cumings, Bruce, *Korea's Place in the Sun: A Modern History*, New York, W. W. Norton & Company, 1997 (p. 221).
Hwang, Su Kyoung, *Korea's Grievous War*, Philadelphia, University of Pennsylvania Press, 2016 (p. 29).

90 Cumings, Bruce, *Korea's Place in the Sun: A Modern History*, New York, W. W. Norton & Company, 1997 (p. 221).

91 Hwang, Su Kyoung, *Korea's Grievous War,* Philadelphia, University of Pennsylvania Press, 2016 (p. 29).

92 'We must properly understand and define the 1946 Daegu uprising,' *Hankyoreh,* January 22, 2013.

93 Cumings, Bruce, *The Korean War: A History*, New York, Modern Library, 2010 (pp. 70, 133).
McCann, David R. and Strauss, Barry S., *War and Democracy: A Comparative Study of the Korean War and the Peloponnesian War,* Abingdon, Routledge, 2015 (p. 59).

94 Hanley, Charles J., and Change, Jae-Soon, 'Summer of Terror: At least 100,000 said executed by Korean ally of U.S. in 1950,' *The Asia-Pacific Journal*, vol. 7, issue 7, July 2, 2008.

95 '최소 60만명, 최대 120만명!,' ['More than 600,000, less than 1,200,000!,'] *Hankyoreh,* June 20, 2001.

96 *New York Times,* March 6, 1950.

97 Blum, William, *Killing Hope: U.S. Military and C.I.A. Interventions Since World War II*, London, Zed Books, 2003 (Appendix III).
Chambliss, William J., *Power, Politics and Crime,* Abingdon, Routledge, 2018 (Part 3: Implications, Chapter 7: Crime Myths and Smoke Screens, Section 5: State Organized Crime).

98 Meyers, Samuel M. and Biderman, Albert D., *Mass Behaviour in Battle and Captivity: The Communist Soldier in the Korean War*, Chicago, University of Chicago Press, 1968 (pp. 280–281).

99 Hanley, Charles J. and Choe, Sang Hun, and Mendoza, Martha, *The Bridge at No Gun Ri: A Hidden Nightmare from the Korean War*, New York, Henry Holt and Company, 2001 (pp. 195–196).

100 Heo, Uk, and Roehrig, Terence, *South Korea Since 1980,* Cambridge, Cambridge University Press, 2010 (p. 17).

101 Stone, I. F., *Hidden History of the Korean War*, Amazon Media, 2014 (Chapter 17, 'Free Elections?').

102 Foreign Relations of the United States, 1950, vol. VII, Korea, Washington D.C., Government Printing Office, 1976 (p. 602).
Hanley, Charles J. and Choe, Sang Hun and Mendoza, Martha, *The Bridge at No Gun Ri: A Hidden Nightmare from the Korean War*, New York, Henry Holt and Company, 2001 (p. 170).

103 Gunther, John, *The Riddle of MacArthur*, New York, Harper and Row, 1951 (p. 163).

104 *New York Times,* February 20, 1946.

105 Armstrong, Charles, *The North Korean Revolution, 1945–1950,* Ithaca, Cornell University Press, 2003 (Chapter 2: Liberation, Occupation and the Emerging New Order).

106 Chŏn'guk inmin wiwonhoe taep'yoja taehoe ŭisarok [Record of the National People's Committee Representative Conference], Seoul, Chosŏn chongp'ansa, 1946 (pp. 68–70).

107 Van Ree, Eric, *Socialism in One Zone: Stalin's Policy in Korea, 1945–1947*, Oxford, Berg, 1989 (p. 89).

108 Cumings, Bruce, *The Origins of the Korean War, Volume 1: Liberation and the Emergence of Separate Regimes, 1945–1947*, Princeton, NJ, Princeton University Press, 1981.

109 Szalontai, Balazs, *The Failure of De-Stalinization in North Korea, 1953–1964: The DPRK in a Comparative Perspective*, Budapest, Central European University, 2003.
Radchenko, Sergey S., *The Soviet Union and the North Korean Seizure of the USS Pueblo: Evidence from Russian Archives*, Washington D.C., Woodrow Wilson International Center for Scholars.
David-West, Alzo, 'Between Confucianism and Marxism-Leninism: Juche and the Case of Chŏng Tasan,' *Korean Studies*, vol. 35, 2011 (pp. 93–121).
Buzo, Adrian, *The Guerilla Dynasty: Politics and Leadership in North Korea,* Boulder, CO, Westview Press, 1999 (p. 67).

110 David-West, Alzo, 'Between Confucianism and Marxism-Leninism: Juche and the Case of Chŏng Tasan,' *Korean Studies*, vol. 35, 2011 (pp. 93–121).

111 Kim, Namsik, 'Rethinking the Pre- and Post-Liberation North Korean History,' *Haebang chŏnhusa ŏi insik [Understanding Pre-and Post-Liberation History]*, vol. 5 (pp. 21–22).

112 Abrams, A. B., *Power and Primacy: The History of Western Intervention in the Asia-Pacific*, Oxford, Peter Lang, 2019 (pp. 119–120).

113 Matray, James K., *The Reluctant Crusade: American Foreign Policy in Korea, 1941–1950,* Honolulu, University of Hawaii Press, 1985 (p. 7).

114 Kim, Jong Il, *The Workers' Party of Korea is a Juche-Type Revolutionary Party Which Inherited the Glorious Tradition of the DIU,* Pyongyang, Foreign Languages Publishing House, 1982.

115 Wada, Haruki, *Kin Nichisei to Manshu konichi senso* [Kim Il Sung and the Anti-Japanese War in Manchuria], Tokyo, Heibonsha, 1992 (pp. 337–38).

116 Armstrong, Charles, *The North Korean Revolution, 1945–1950,* Ithaca, Cornell University Press, 2003 (Chapter 2: Liberation, Occupation and the Emerging New Order).

117 'Establishment of the Provisional People's Committee of North Korea,' *National Institute of Korean History.*

118 Sullivan, Walter, *New York Times,* March 6, 1950.

119 Hanley, Charles J. and Choe, Sang Hun and Mendoza, Martha, *The Bridge at No Gun Ri: A Hidden Nightmare from the Korean War*, New York, Henry Holt and Company, 2001 (p. 170).

Stone, I. F., *Hidden History of the Korean War*, Amazon Media, 2014 (Chapter 17, 'Free Elections?').

120 Gupta, Karunakar, 'How Did the Korean War Begin?,' *The China Quarterly*, no. 52, October–December 1972 (pp. 699–716).

121 'The Kissinger Doctrine,' *New York Times*, February 27, 1975.

122 Eisenhower, Dwight, *Mandate for Change, 1953–1956; The White House Years*, New York, Doubleday, 1963 (p. 372).

123 Kolko, Gabriel, *Vietnam: Anatomy of a War, 1940–1975*, New York, Harper Collins Publishers, 1987 (p. 85).

124 Heo, Uk, and Roehrig, Terence, *South Korea Since 1980,* Cambridge, Cambridge University Press, 2010 (p. 18).

125 Ibid. (p. 18).

Henderson, Gregory, *The Politics of the Vortex*, Cambridge, MA, Harvard University Press, 1968 (pp. 348–349).

126 'Is South Korea the greatest success story of the last century,' *Time,* December 6, 2012.

127 Choe, Sang-Hun, 'After Korean War, brothels and an alliance,' *New York Times,* January 8, 2009.

Lee, Na Young, 'The Construction of U.S. Camptown Prostitution in South Korea: Trans/Formation and Resistance,' University of Maryland, Department of Women's Studies, 2006.

Cho, Hyoung, and Chang, P'ilhwa, 'Perspectives on Prostitution in the Korean Legislature: 1948–1989,' *Women's Studies Review,* vol. 7, 1990 (p. 95).

Moon, Katherine H. S., *Sex Among Allies*, New York, Colombia University Press, 1997 (pp. 44–45).

128 Ibid. (p. 44).

129 Maynes, Katrin, 'Korean Perceptions of Chastity, Gender Roles, and Libido; From Kisaengs to the Twenty First Century,' *Grand Valley Journal of History*, vol. 1, issue 1, article 2, February 2012.

130 Hanley, Charles J., Choe, Sang Hun and Mendoza, Martha, *The Bridge at No Gun Ri: A Hidden Nightmare from the Korean War*, New York, Henry Holt and Company, 2001 (p. 170).

131 Stone, I. F., *Hidden History of the Korean War*, Amazon Media, 2014 (Chapter 17, 'Free Elections?').

132 Weathersby, Kathryn, '"Should We Fear This?" Stalin and the Danger of War with America,' *Cold War International History Project*, Working Paper No. 39, 2002.

Chapter 2
STRATEGIC IMPLICATIONS OF THE KOREAN WAR'S OUTBREAK

Two Koreas and the Outbreak of War

The result of the declaration of the Republic of Korea (ROK) on August 15th, 1948 was the emergence of two neighbouring states with overlapping claims to sovereignty over the Korean nation. With the new South Korean state under Syngman Rhee unilaterally laying claim to all of Korea, the provisional government and constituent people's committees in northern Korea had little choice but to contest this by declaring its own state—the Pyongyang-based Democratic People's Republic of Korea (DPRK). This was declared within a month of the Rhee government's declaration on September 9th, and the DPRK also claimed sovereignty over the entire peninsula. The nature of the two states' competing mandates, and above all their clashing roots and identities in either the Japanese and American imperial projects or the Korean nationalist movement, meant that peaceful coexistence between them remained unlikely.

The Rhee government's near complete lack of interest in economic affairs, as attested to by a range of American sources, combined with severe corruption, continued to negatively affect living standards leaving many in desperate poverty. The DPRK's economic situation was very different. According to reports from the CIA, while North Korea faced issues from labour shortages and struggled to meet its extremely ambitious state planning goals for expanded industrial and agricultural output by 1949, living standards nevertheless saw a very substantial increase by the end of the decade.[1] Despite significant wartime damage to the Japanese industrial infrastructure, manufacturing had significantly exceeded previous levels by 1949. Industrial output and state industry in 1949 were 340% and 420% of the levels in 1946—representing not only a recovery but also a 20% increase over the Japanese imperial period.[2] The rural economy had also seen considerable improvements, with gross output of agricultural and animal products increasing by 40% from 1944 to 1949—despite a wartime slump in 1945. The average salaries of factory and officer workers increased by 83%.[3] Thus the discrepancy in living standards between the two Koreas appeared to be fast growing and strongly favoured the DPRK.

In light of the fragility of the southern government, ongoing internal conflict and the poor electoral performance of Syngman Rhee's Liberal Party, it appeared that all Pyongyang needed to do to prevail was to wait out its rival's downfall. The passage of time would only widen the economic discrepancy between the two states and strengthen the DPRK position relative to the ROK. Rhee's government was confronted not only with an active insurgency, but also with widespread dissatisfaction among the population and a strong movement demanding peaceful reunification which the president vehemently opposed. The disastrous performance of Rhee's Liberal Party in the ROK's first parliamentary elections on May 30, 1950, less than a month before the outbreak of the Korean War, and considerable pressure from both the public and rival parties to begin peaceful reunification, gave Pyongyang further cause to perceive a favourable resolution to be forthcoming via peaceful means.

Although the United States threatened a withdrawal of aid should a peaceful merger of the two Korean states take place, passing the Korean Aid Bill to this effect through Congress in February 1950, the vast majority of political forces in the ROK strongly favoured immediate steps towards peaceful unification. Electoral fraud and American support could only take Rhee so far, and with his government enjoying so little public backing[4] Pyongyang had considerable grounds to expect major political change in South Korea particularly after the elections in May. There was little need for a military solution, either directly or by proxy, and Pyongyang's awareness of this was perhaps best indicated by that fact it did not provide armaments to anti-government guerrillas in the south despite the permeability of the inter-Korean border at the time. Had it done so, the outcome of insurgencies such as that on Cheju may have been very different. The election of an assembly in Seoul strongly in favour of co-operation and peaceful reunification on terms similar to those proposed by Pyongyang made a bloodless reunification appear likely—a far more desirable outcome than what could ever be achieved by force. Reports from the CIA and the *New York Times* among other sources all indicated that a reunifying election would yield a result strongly favouring the northern political system.[5]

With Rhee's administration faced with a loosening grip on power after the election, a stagnant and aid-dependent economy mired by corruption,[6] little public support[7] and a sizeable ongoing insurgency, military force was only means of ensuring its survival. This included the threatening of political opposition, the establishment of concentration camps, mass arrest and torture of political prisoners, and the killing of over 2 percent of the population to quash dissent. [8] This also materialised in the Rhee government's approach to North Korea, with the president dismissing the potential for negotiation as "concessions" and a "road to disaster" and strongly advocating forceful reunification. When on June 7, 1950 North Korean President Kim Il Sung called for nationwide elections to be held in August, and for a consultative conference in Haeju from June 15 to 17, this was strongly opposed by both Rhee and the United States. When four days later the DPRK sent three delegates to the south in a peace overture to begin talks on reunification, this too was rejected outright by Rhee.[9]

Rhee's government had strongly prioritized militarization which it could ill afford, increasing the size of the armed forces to 100,000 personnel in the summer of 1949 to gain a considerable numerical advantage over the north. Reports from Western and international observers indicated that the president and much of the ROK's military leadership appeared strongly inclined to initiate a conflict against the DPRK, staging frequent provocations across the 38th parallel for this purpose.[10] William Mathews, a reporter accompanying prominent statesman and later Secretary of State John Foster Dulles to a meeting with Rhee, reported immediately afterwards that the president was "militantly for the unification of Korea. Openly says it must be brought about soon... Rhee pleads justice of going into North country. Thinks it could succeed in a few days...if he can do it with our help he will do it." Mathews further warned that the South Korean president was willing to initiate an attack on the DPRK even if "it brought on a general war."[11]

Reports of the ROK leadership's offensive designs appeared to be strongly reflected in its actions. Several skirmishes along the 38th parallel took place from May to December 1949 between the Republic of Korea Armed Forces (ROKAF) and the Korean People's Army (KPA), which according to internal American accounts were almost all initiated by the South Koreans. The head of United States' Korean Military Advisory Group (KMAG), General William L. Roberts, observed of the border clashes that the ROK was the more belligerent party, stating: "almost every incident has been provoked by the South Korean security forces."[12] The general reported separately on multiple attacks on border villages in the DPRK, saying that "each was in our opinion brought on by the presence of a small South Korean salient north of the parallel… The South Koreans wish to invade the North."[13] Sources from the DPRK claim that thousands of South Korean troops led by Brigadier General Kim Suk Won, a close confidant of Syngman Rhee, led units from the ROKAF across the border on multiple unprovoked assaults—initiating six months of border fighting. Kim was a former captain in the Imperial Japanese Army's mechanised artillery who had played a leading role in the invasion of Manchuria. These claims are supported by the general's calls for war with the north to bring forceful reunification under ROK rule. He had said to this effect: "We should have a program to recover our lost land, North Korea, by breaking through the 38th border which has existed since 1945." Kim told the United Nations Commission on Korea (UNCOK) shortly before the outbreak of the war that the moment of major battles was "rapidly approaching."[14] Had the southern general's months long incursions into North Korea not been met with staunch KPA resistance, it is far from unlikely that the ROKAF under his command would have pressed further and perhaps sought to take Pyongyang itself with a full scale invasion.

General Kim was far from alone in calling for attacks on the DPRK with the intent of debellatio against the northern state and imposition of ROK rule. British sources reported just weeks before the outbreak of the war that KMAG advisers had raised concerns that the ROKAF's "over-aggressive officers in command positions along the parallel" presented a significant risk that "a border incident…could precipitate civil war."[15] Other British intelligence sources similarly concluded that the leadership in the south was willing to initiate a war of aggression, with one stating that South Korean commanders' heads "are full of ideas of recovering the North by conquest."[16]

Prominent UN diplomat and expert from the United Nations Commission on Korea Egon Ranshofen-Wertheimer observed similar dangers to peace on the Korean peninsula posed by South Korea's apparent willingness to initiate a full-scale war. He wrote to this effect in September 1949:

> the ROK might feel that its chances of absorbing the North are diminished from month to month in view of the growing strength of Kim Il Sung's armies… The temptation for Rhee to invade the North and the pressure exerted upon him to

> do so might, therefore, become irresistible. The top military authorities of the Republic…are exerting continual pressure upon Rhee to take the initiative and cross the parallel.[17]

Thus, as both short- and long-term power trajectories strongly favoured the north, only the south could have benefitted from initiating a conflict.

While Rhee and much of the military leadership appeared by all accounts to be eager to initiate a war to impose their rule over the DPRK, it was in their interest to ensure the full support of the United States and if possible American participation in such an offensive. A number of high-level American reports shed light on the means by which this could be done. Col. M. Preston Goodfellow, former deputy director of the OSS and a personal friend of Syngman Rhee, had previously paid many visits to the president in Seoul and had been recommended for stationing in Korea.[18] In his discussion with the Guomindang Chinese ambassador it was made clear that an outcome favourable to both the Rhee government and hardline anti-communist factions in U.S. would be a North Korean attack on South Korea. This would provide pretext for American military intervention, which could be used to launch a full-scale joint invasion of North Korea to realise Rhee's designs. Goodfellow told the Chinese ambassador that the momentum for attack had shifted, and the ambassador reported from their meeting:

> it was the South Koreans anxious to go into N. K., because they were feeling sharp with their army of well-trained 100,000 strong. But U.S. Govt was most anxious to restrain any provocation by the S. K. and Goodfellow had gone there lately to do just that. I asked how great was the possibility or danger of war breaking out in Korea. Goodfellow said U.S. Govt. position is this: avoid any initiative on S. Korea's part in attacking N. K., but if N. K. should invade S. K. then S. K. should resist and march right into N. K.…in such a case, the aggression came from N. K. and the American people would understand it.[19]

To gain American support for an invasion of North Korea, it was vital for the Rhee government to somehow achieve a North Korean attack, perhaps through the border incidents which international observers reported his forces were continuously provoking, or at least to create the impression that the KPA had started a war.

While South Korea had by all accounts been the more belligerent party and carried out multiple attacks on the north, some continuing for several months, Goodfellow's statement elucidates the strong incentive for the more aggressive parties in the ROK to attempt to provoke a North Korean attack or counterattack—to win support for their own invasion plans. Rhee was personally said to have "lobbied forcefully for U.S. backing for a military solution to the division of the peninsula," and himself hinted that a KPA attack on the border could be used as a pretext to launch a full-scale invasion to forcefully topple the DPRK. In the event of a KPA border attack, Rhee said, U.S. support would be needed to "hurl them back, but also to attack their retreating forces and in so doing to liberate our enslaved fellow countrymen in the north."[20]

A potential North Korean attack was seen as highly favourable to both the expansionist goals of the Rhee government and the interests of hardline American anti-communists, who sought a pretext to directly confront the "red menace." In the eyes of many in the U.S. leadership, General MacArthur included, war in Korea was an effective means of bringing about a greater confrontation with the communist powers in East Asia—reversing the communist victory in neighbouring China and restoring the Western-aligned Guomindang client government to power in Beijing. U.S. Ambassador John Muccio thus observed from Seoul:

> There is increasing confidence in the army. An aggressive, offensive spirit is emerging. Nerves that were frayed and jittery the past few months may now give way to this new spirit. A good portion of the Army is eager to get going. More and more people feel that the only way unification can be brought about is by moving north by force…Chiang Kaishek told Rhee that the Nationalist [Chinese Guomindang] air force could support a move North and that they discussed the possibility of the Nationalists starting an offensive move against Manchuria through Korea! There is some feeling that now is the time to move north while the Chinese communists are preoccupied. I doubt whether Rhee would actually order a move North in his saner moments… However, should we have another Kaesong or Ongjin flare-up, a counter-attack might lead to all sorts of unpredictable developments.[21]

Rhee's government had everything to gain from provoking a war and if possible the impression of a northern invasion. This would guarantee Seoul the support of the United States, the sizeable Chinese Guomindang forces on Taiwan and most likely other powers of the Western Bloc as well—saving Rhee's ailing government and facilitating realisation of its expansionist designs. The outbreak of open war in Korea in late June can be attributed at least in part to this motivation.

When hostilities broke out on June 25, 1950 international observers present could not determine which party fired first—neither could the U.S. ambassador in Seoul. South Korean state radio did report a successful ROKAF attack on the border city of Haeju however, something the North Koreans confirmed but Seoul later retracted, which indicates that an ROKAF border provocation could have sparked the conflict.[22] The South Koreans would later amend their claim to state that they had in fact attacked Haeju at a later date—long after announcing the successful capture of the city. As shown in a detailed study by historian Karunakar Gupta at the University of London, this was effectively impossible, given the positions and largely disordered nature of their fast retreating forces at the time. If there was an ROKAF attack on Haeju, it had to have been in the war's opening hours.[23] Preceding British and U.S. reports indicating it was the south which had initiated almost all border clashes strongly supports this, and gives a strong indication that it was most likely the ROK which first initiated hostilities. The conflict subsequently intensified as North Korea responded with a major counterattack, escalating in a way that it never had before, with the leadership giving the order to launch a full-scale attack on the ROK in response to the attack of Haeju.

American Interests and the Outbreak of the Korean War

While the outbreak of war in Korea was key to saving Syngman Rhee's government, the United States itself had a great deal to gain from the conflict. Implications of a war against a communist power in response to an alleged communist aggression, even that by a small developing nation of under 10 million people, would provide ample pretext to remobilise the U.S. economy against a new threat and turn the previously unfavourable tide of the Cold War in favour of the Western Bloc. President Harry Truman thus stated within hours of the war's outbreak, despite no evidence regarding which party had initiated it, that "communism has now passed beyond the use of subversion to conquer independent nations, and will now use armed invasion and war"—a claim which would facilitate a wide range of measures to escalate the Cold War and engineer a Western advantage.[24] After initial clashes which both Koreas blamed the other for initiating, North Korean forces were able to gain a decisive advantage and press an offensive southwards (the war's and early offensives are detailed in the following chapter). While tactically its allies, the South Koreans, were losing ground, strategically America's position was strengthened considerably vis-à-vis the Soviet Union—allowing it to partially recover following the disastrous "loss of China" a year prior. State Secretary Dean Acheson noted in this regard that the Korean War "came along and saved us."[25]

The outbreak of the war facilitated the drafting of NSC 68, the key National Security Council report that became one of the most important statements of American foreign policy, and "provided the blueprint for the militarization of the Cold War from 1950 to the collapse of the Soviet Union at the beginning of the 1990s."[26] NSC 68 advocated prioritising the development and large scale deployment of thermonuclear weapons and the means to deliver them across Soviet territory. It further called for a significant expansion in military expenditure, which would quadruple following the war's outbreak. A peacetime military draft was established for the first time, along with a permanent standing army of three million American personnel deployed across the world. The rearmament of West Germany[27] and Japan[28] despite considerable prior controversy was also enabled under the new imperative of fighting communism—a part of the response to the Korean War's outbreak. The United States further moved to escalate its involvement in Vietnam in support of French colonial forces, sowing the seeds for further conflict yet to come.[29] The strengthening and expansion of the recently formed U.S.-led NATO military alliance unifying the powers of the Western Bloc was a further result of the war in Korea.[30]

By the end of the year President Truman had used the war as a pretext to declare an indefinite state of emergency, mobilizing the U.S. for a permanent state of Cold War. In the president's words, he summoned "our farmers, our workers in industry, and our businessmen to make a mighty production effort to meet the defence requirements of the Nation…every person and every community to make, with a spirit of neighbourliness, whatever sacrifices are necessary for the welfare of the Nation…all State and local leaders and officials to cooperate fully with the military and civilian defence agencies of the United States in the national defence program."[31] The United States, and to some extent the entire Western

Bloc, devoted itself fully to a state of war against the communist world. The microcosm that was conflict between two visions for Korea's future, one as a nationalist, independent and post-colonial continuation of the Korean republican project and the other as an externally imposed client regime with little vision for economic or social progress, was used as a pretext for an initiative with truly global implications.

In Europe, at the time seen as the most vital Cold War theatre, the American position was bolstered considerably by the outbreak of war in Korea to the detriment of Soviet interests. The war began just nine months after the USSR tested its first nuclear device, had yet to widely deploy the munitions, and was far from achieving nuclear parity with the United States. This American advantage was emphasized by both General MacArthur and by CIA reports, the latter of which noted: "The Soviets had fewer than 25 atomic bombs," a fraction of the U.S. arsenal of "over 500 atomic bombs and at least 264 nuclear-capable aircraft."[32] The pretext of a communist threat based on events in Korea was instrumental in allowing the United States to press its nuclear advantage to the fullest—deploying large numbers of nuclear weapons to Europe at a rate which the Soviets could not match at the time—thereby shifting the balance of power in the strategically vital theatre strongly in their favour. A report from the prominent neoconservative think tank Project for the New American Century was among the sources which strongly alluded to the Korean War's role in facilitating America's ability to press its nuclear advantage in Europe.[33]

While hardline anti-communist factions in the U.S. government and military achieved the remobilisation of American resources to fight the Cold War which they had long advocated,[34] an equally significant beneficiary of open war in Korea was the formerly struggling American economy. Although it had thrived and doubled in size during the Second World War,[35] there were considerable fears among the U.S. leadership for the potentially catastrophic consequences peace could have on the country's heavily war-oriented economy. A heavy reliance on wartime production had developed during the conflict with the Axis Powers, leading to a hard recession in the five subsequent years. Thus, the dominant trend in American economic and military thinking, according to a number of highly placed sources, was a fear of genuine peace due to its negative implications for the country's economic wellbeing. This concept of the need for a "permanent war economy" to avoid economic contraction and retain high employment rates emerged in 1944 as wartime production peaked. Sustainment of high defence spending to maintain high employment and stimulate economic growth has since been referred to as "military Keynesianism" or "weaponized Keynesianism" by a number of prominent experts, politicians[36] and scholars.[37] The importance of this was further highlighted in 1954, when the U.S. economy would again dip into recession after the Korean War armistice ended hostilities.

Examples of the importance of wartime demand in stimulating key industries included the rise in annual production of aircraft, ships, rubber, steel and aluminium. These sectors boomed from 1940, the year before American entered the war, to 1944 when wartime production peaked—respectively rising by 1045%, 1175%, 276%, 89% and 50%. Production booms in these sectors, and an even larger boom in munitions production, led an overall trend throughout the U.S. economy.[38] Unemployment as percentages of the population and labour force respectively dropped drastically during this period from highs of 8.1% and 14.6% in 1940 to just 0.7% and 1.2% in 1944, with both again rising from 1945 as arms production wound down which continued until 1950.[39] Defence production, more so than production of civilian goods, was and is today considered not only more profitable, but capable of generating more jobs.[40]

The U.S. economy had sharply contracted in the aftermath of the Second World War and, following peak arms production in 1944 GDP, the following year was 4% lower. In 1946, a year of almost total peace which preceded the Cold War, real GDP fell by 20.6%—the worst fall in American history far exceeding that of the Great Depression.[41] Although the U.S. economy was contracting in 1949, albeit at a slower rate, it saw significant expansion from 1950 with growth rates at 8.7 percent that year.[42] The needs of the Korean front, preparations for a greater war against the Soviet Bloc and the resulting boom in armaments production for the United States served as a highly potent stimulant. Several large-scale armaments projects which faced imminent closure due to loss of funding were saved by the outbreak of war in Korea. The Bell Aircraft Company, for example, had employed over 28,000 workers for the B-29 bomber program alone—despite its sole plant in Georgia manufacturing under 17% of the total fleet. Employment at the Bell plant fell from 1945 but would rise again from 1950 as refurbishment contracts for old B-29s were signed. The acceleration and expansion of new bomber programs with more funding further stimulated manufacturing and raised employment levels.[43]

In Southern California alone projects developing "strategic bombers, supercarriers, and…a previously cancelled Convair contract to develop an intercontinental rocket for the Air Force" were resumed. The colossal wartime aircraft production industry was again booming in 1952, and these defence projects sourcing labour and components from across the United States were vital to the country's economic wellbeing. Los Angeles County, for example, had 160,000 people employed in aircraft production, with defence and aerospace accounting for 55 percent of employment. In San Diego this figure was nearly 80 percent. Defence industries, reliant on war to stimulate demand, kept hundreds of thousands of factories running throughout the United States.[44]

Award winning journalist I. F. Stone gave an insightful assessment of the relationship between war and the orientation of the American economy, writing shortly after the Korean War's outbreak:

> With the arms race and the rampant inflation and costs piling up, American leadership was still gripped by dread of the consequences of peace upon the economy. This dread was dictating the actions of the politicians and mega business leaders. An economy accustomed to injections of inflationary narcotic trembled at the thought that its deadly stimulant might be shut off… The dominant trend in American political, economic and military thinking was, and is, a fear of peace.[45]

With the economy heavily reliant on stimulation from military expenditure, war or an ever-present threat of war was highly favourable. General MacArthur was one of many in the U.S. leadership who attested to America's fear of peace and overreliance on its war economy, stating four years after the Korean War began: "It is part of the general pattern of misguided policy that our country is now geared to an arms economy which was bred in an artificially induced psychosis of war hysteria and nurtured upon an incessant propaganda of fear." He warned that this economic orientation "renders among our political leaders almost a greater fear of peace than is their fear of war."[46] The highly skewed orientation of the U.S. economy towards war production, and reliance on high military expenditure to a far greater extent than other industrial nations,[47] was also attested to by U.S. President Eisenhower. The president, who would take office in 1953, would state to this effect:

> Our military organization today bears little relation to that known by any of my predecessors in peacetime… We have been compelled to create a permanent armaments industry of vast proportions. Added to this, three and a half million men and women are directly engaged in the defense establishment. We annually spend on military security more than the net income of all United States corporations. This conjunction of an immense military establishment and a large arms industry is new in the American experience. The total influence—economic, political, even spiritual—is felt in every city, every Statehouse, every office of the Federal government.

Having himself served as 1st Supreme Allied Commander Europe, Eisenhower warned that such a heavy reliance on military industries for America's economic wellbeing threatened to compromise democratic processes. State policy could be substantially influenced by the indefinite need to continue the large scale manufacture of war materials.[48] There was thus a strong incentive not only to intervene militarily in Korea, but also to engineer circumstances under which hostilities between the two Koreas were likely to break out in the first place. Tolerance of overly aggressive officers in the ROKAF who frequently launched incursions into North Korea was an example. Another was the emphasis placed in January 1950 that South Korea was outside America's defensive perimeter in East Asia,[49] giving Pyongyang room if not a green light to respond to future provocations with overwhelming force.[50]

The outbreak of the Korean War put America's vast war economy back to work, and it would continue to work indefinitely thereafter to arm the United States and its allies from Iran to Japan. Now fearing "communist aggression" based on allegations of a North Korean attack, America's defence clients across the world were driven to maintain far larger standing armies and navies and to adopt far more interventionist foreign policies to contain the "Red Menace"—providing a further boost to U.S. defence manufacturing.[51] By far the largest permanent military industrial complex thus grew and thrived in the United States, with government spending providing a significant boost to GDP growth from 1950.[52] This indefinitely postponed the post-war recession which had seemed inevitable before the war.

Chinese and Soviet Interests and the Outbreak of War in Korea

While the outbreak of war in Korea was key to ensuring the survival of the Rhee government in the south and had considerable strategic and economic benefits for the United States, the conflict created immense difficulties for both Moscow and Beijing. The newly formed People's Republic of China (PRC), then less than a year old, saw its window for the recapture of the last major Guomindang-held territory of Taiwan quickly close—and with it the chance lost to recover the national treasures and substantial gold reserves[53] which had been taken to Taipei and bring the civil war to a final conclusion. What British and American intelligence termed "the last battle" of the Chinese Civil War was expected to occur within weeks, with the PRC expected to win an overwhelming victory. War in Korea justified American intervention in the Taiwan Strait—providing protection to the remnants of the Western-aligned Guomindang which lasted throughout the Cold War.[54] American journalist and reporter John Gunther thus reported from Tokyo on Beijing's attitude towards the outbreak of the Korean War and the alleged North Korean attack: "they deplored it—strange as it may seem now. For the North Korean aggression had, for the moment at least, cost Mao Tsetung a prize he coveted above all—Formosa [Taiwan]."[55]

Denial of the strategically critical territory to China, with the protection of Guomindang remnants becoming official U.S. policy from June 1950 as General MacArthur among other hardliners had long advocated, played well into the hands of more extremist anti-communist elements in the American leadership. PRC control of Taiwan would, according to prior statements by the general, allow American adversaries to deploy ten or twenty air groups, serve as a major forward operating base for submarines, and allow enemy forces to increase air efforts against American bases such as those on Okinawa by 100% as well as against Western-controlled shipping lanes. He further warned that Beijing could provide bases on the territory to the Soviet Red Army, compensating for the latter's overall weakness at sea and complementing its already predominant power on land, stating: "Formosa in the hands of the Communists can be compared to an unsinkable aircraft carrier and submarine tender ideally located to accomplish Soviet offensive strategy and at the same time checkmate counteroffensive operations by United States Forces based on Okinawa and the Philippines." He equated the importance of this asset as a base for aircraft alone to "ten or twenty aircraft carriers."[56] Denial of this territory to the PRC was thus a major strategic benefit gained from the Korean War's outbreak and a major loss for China and the communist world.

Taipei was further allowed to hold the Chinese seat at the United Nations Security Council as one of only five permeant members—a considerable asset lost to Beijing for over twenty years. The continued existence of the Taipei-based Guomindang government further bolstered American efforts to isolate PRC, with Washington pressing many of its client states not to recognize the new republic. This practice continues to some extent to this day, with a number of Western client states continuing to recognise Taipei as the government of all of China and threatened with repercussions by the U.S. should they shift to form ties with Beijing.[57] Had there been no alternative Western-aligned Chinese government in Taipei to contest Beijing's claim, the Western Bloc would have lacked a pretext upon which to campaign for the denying of recognition to the PRC.

Arguably more so than China, the Soviet Union suffered a major setback to its interests not only in Northeast Asia but globally as a result of the outbreak of war in Korea. Moscow had at the time been seeking peace and improved relations with Washington, with General Secretary Joseph Stalin indicating that he wished to personally meet with President Truman. In contrast to the United States it was the continuation of the peaceful status quo, rather than the outbreak of war, which benefitted Moscow's interests and strengthened its Cold War position. As more nations gained independence from European colonial rule, and with Soviet ideology holding widespread appeal at the time due to the considerable successes of the Stalinist industrialisation and development program, the Soviet Union was in a strong position to win a soft war in which its ideals and in particular its model for economic modernisation would win over developing nations as allies.[58] The fact that the USSR was enjoying considerable economic growth,[59] where the U.S. was sliding deeper into recession, further strengthened the appeal of continued peace to the Soviet leadership—a trend which the outbreak of war would end.

John Foster Dulles, author of the influential American containment policy analysis *War and Peace* and soon to be Secretary of State, dismissed what he termed Soviet "Peace Offensives" as "deceptive Cold War strategy" which posed an imminent threat to U.S. interests. In terms of prestige and influence in the third world, economic growth and military modernisation, the USSR was seriously undermining the formerly overwhelming advantages the Western Bloc had enjoyed—and was doing so without firing a shot. Shedding light on the Soviet favouring trend in global power trajectories preceding the Korean War, Dulles declared: "as things are going now…we must develop better techniques… They [the USSR] can win everything by the cold war they could win by a hot war."[60] The outbreak of the war quickly blunted these previously successful "peace offensives," seriously undermining the Soviet position.

War in Korea further provided the United States with the pretext it needed to retain naval and air bases in Japan indefinitely, which were perfectly situated to housing strategic nuclear capable bombers for targeting Vladivostok, the Soviet Far East and cities across East Asia. This opened a second permanent front for Soviet air defences which would require considerable investment to shore up, and also placed China permanently in the firing line. This occurred alongside expanded deployments of nuclear assets to Europe, and allowed the U.S. administration to dismiss considerable Japanese pressure to withdraw its assets at the time of Japan's scheduled independence in 1952.[61] Calls in Japan for peace treaties with the USSR were postponed indefinitely on American authority, which have affected relations[i] until today.[62]

The USSR had gone to considerable lengths to prevent the outbreak of war on the Korean Peninsula and would subsequently take measures to prevent its escalation. When addressing the Soviet military mission in Korea before the war's outbreak Soviet Chief of General Staff Marshal Matvei Zakharov had informed them that although it was easy to organize an air force of 1,000 planes or so for the Korean People's Army, and there were no shortages of trained Korean pilots, it was necessary for political reasons to refrain from doing so. The Marshal feared that the presence of a potent KPA air wing would escalate regional tensions and lead to an arms race, which could in turn "bring war with the United States, and we are not interested in provoking such a war." The USSR for this reason ensured that they supplied North Korea with only what was necessary for defence to retain a balance of power with the south, and not more.[63] The private report of Senator H. Alexander Smith to the Senate Foreign Relations Committee stated to much the same effect regarding the Soviet stance towards tensions on the Korean Peninsula and measures taken by Moscow to avert war: "they did not wish to initiate World War 3 by creating an incident in a minor area like Korea."[64]

i The Russian Federation has yet to sign a peace treaty with Japan, with territorial disputes from the Second World War remaining unresolved.

With hostilities on the peninsula seriously undermining both Beijing and Moscow's interests, the lack of Chinese or Soviet complicity in initiating war in Korea was perhaps best demonstrated by their lack of support for the Korean People's Army even after the outbreak of hostilities. In the opening months of the war when engaging a growing and heavily armed coalition of primarily Western powers led by the United States, the vastly outnumbered KPA did not receive much needed material support from either the USSR or China.[65] A stalemate at what came to be known as the Pusan Perimeter near the southernmost tip of Korea and a halt in the KPA advance southwards was a direct result of its extremely strained logistics and lack of supplies. Had this not been a constraining factor, the KPA would have likely controlled the entire peninsula by the end of July 1950 despite initial American and European reinforcements, and the calculus for any further landings of Western troops would have been entirely different.[66] Although the Western Bloc depicted the "Kim Il Sung regime" as proxies of the "International Communist Conspiracy," and as aggressors acting at the behest of Moscow and Beijing, the absence of much needed material assistance to the KPA which likely would have turned the tide of the war strongly undermines this narrative.

Time magazine noted on October 6, 1950, regarding the lack of Soviet and Chinese support for the DPRK's war effort: "If Russia [USSR] or China intended to intervene in Korea, they should have done so earlier when they could have pushed U.N. forces into the sea."[67] Supreme Commander of the Korean War effort, U.S. General Douglas MacArthur stated to much the same effect following the turning back of the KPA in September: "had they [Chinese or Soviets] interfered in the first or second months [of the war] it would have been decisive. We are no longer fearful of their intervention."[68] The state of the KPA's inventory strongly indicated that it did not enjoy support from the world's second largest military industrial economy—forced to abandon tanks due to lack of fuel and press obsolete First World War-era rifles the into service. Beijing and Moscow's unwillingness to provide support to North Korean forces was a strong testament to the importance they attached by both to avoiding confrontation with the Western Bloc or escalation of the conflict in Korea.

At a Tokyo HQ Korean War briefing the speaker for the military's Far East Command explained that the KPA was suffering shortages of men and equipment, which would not have been the case had they been receiving external material support. The speaker also explained that "there was no indication that the North Korean tank losses were being replaced by further supplies from the Soviet Union, which furnished the original armour and lent instructors who taught the North Koreans how to use it."[69] Furthering this point, Tokyo HQ reported later on the same day that "the weapons captured from the North Koreans have been a wide assortment, even including some World War 1 rifles... The latest estimates...are that neither the North Korean army nor the air force has any post-war Soviet weapons." Further dismissing reports of Soviet material assistance, the announcement confirmed that the recent report "that Communist-flown jet planes have been sighted over South Korea now is evaluated as an error in identification."[70]

Complementing the briefings from Tokyo HQ, intelligence sources later reported to the *New York Times* that they had "no knowledge that the North Korean invaders actually received new supplies from the Soviet Union since the war began." Not only were the Soviets not sending weapons, but none of their military advisers were assisting the Korean People's Army in their advance.[71] These reports discredit the notion that the KPA offensive was part of a Soviet conspiracy, or that North Korean forces were acting under orders from Moscow.

Had the Soviets backed a North Korean invasion, they not only would have been expected to adequately arm their allies—but also to support similar provocations across the world against the Western Bloc once the Western powers were bogged down in the theatre. On the basis of claims that North Korea had carried out an unprovoked invasion at Moscow's direction, Western leaders had widely expected such moves to be taken.[72] Soviet actions, however, continued to demonstrate their need to avoid confrontation at almost any cost. According to CIA reports from November 1952 the Soviets did not back leftist or anti-colonial insurgent groups elsewhere in the world as would be logical had Moscow orchestrated the Korean attack, nor had it or any of its clients taken to the offensive elsewhere in the world despite the concentration of Western forces in Korea providing an excellent opportunity.[73] This would hardly be the case had Moscow engineered the whole conflict for the purpose of tying up Western forces in Korea, as was widely claimed in the West at the time. Soviet measures to avoid escalation or further conflict, at a time when months of near continuous KPA victories over U.S. forces had stunned the Western Bloc (see following chapter) and raised the prestige of national liberation movements to new heights, demonstrated the extent to which the USSR sought to avoid conflict.[74] In retrospect, failure to press their advantage may well have been a mistake on Moscow's part, when considering the highly offensive actions the Western Bloc would itself take in the Korean War's aftermath against both the Soviet Bloc[75] and non-aligned nations which refused to join the Western-led anti-Soviet alliance—Indonesia,[76] Iran[77] and Ghana[78] being among the prime examples.

A Continued Civil War: Was June 1950 Really the Beginning?

It is important to consider that the outbreak of war in Korea between the two newly formed states north and south of the 38th parallel—neither of them UN members or enjoying significant international recognition and neither recognizing the other's sovereignty or right to exist—was perceived in many circles at the time as a continuation of the brutal civil war which had been ongoing in South Korea for five years. A push north under orders from ROKAF officers could be seen as a continuation of the campaign to eradicate communism and anti-American nationalism from the Korean peninsula in line with the aspirations of Syngman Rhee and his associates. A push south by the Korean People's Army meanwhile could be perceived as an intervention—perhaps a humanitarian one—to bring an end to the slaughter of the Korean people under the American installed government which enjoyed little legitimacy in the eyes of the populations[79] on either side of the parallel. The first shot of the Korean War, some may argue, was not the crossing of the parallel by the ROKAF or KPA—most likely the former based on the preceding circumstances—but rather an incident which had started war in southern Korea almost five years prior. This was the forceful abolishment of the Korean People's Republic and later extremely brutal suppression of its remnants under the United States Military Government with the assistance of youth groups—described as terrorists even by their American allies[80]—and with the backing of the Rhee government itself. Doing so was not only a denial of the right of the Korean population to self-determination by the forceful overthrow of their republic and its institutions, but also a denial of the right of the Korean nation to decolonize given the forced sustainment of the Japanese colonial administrative system and the protection of the immense privileges of Japanese collaborators by the U.S. at the expense of the vast majority of the population.

The Counter Intelligence Corps itself furthered this interpretation with its own report, stating: "In many respects, the armed conflict that broke out in Korea in June 1950 was simply a new phase of a war that had been going on silently, insidiously, for five years. In its earlier phases, this war made few headlines and drew little attention. But CIC agents in the Korean occupation had known the quiet struggle. It was a war of espionage."[81] There was a strong though often unseen logic to this.

Prominent American historian and Korea expert Bruce Cumings noted that assessment of the Korean War as part of an ongoing civil war within one nation since 1945, and drawing of analogies to the American civil war, seriously undermined "the official American view that Kim [Il Sung] committed international aggression: say it and the logic collapses, the interpretation loses its power." He observed regarding the possibly artificial distinction between the war from June 1950 and that which had begun in September 1945:

> For Americans a discrete encapsulation limits this war to the time frame of June 1950 to July 1953. This construction relegates all that went before to mere prehistory. [Alleged North Korean invasion on] June 25 is the original sin, all that comes after is postbellum. It also presumes to demarcate the period of active American involvement.... The American focus on "who started it" is a political and often an ideological position, a point of honor that abstracts from and makes easy and comprehensible the politically shaped verdicts that began with Washington's official story on June 25, 1950. The Korean War was (and is) a civil war; only this conception can account for the 100,000 lives lost in the South before June 1950 and the continuity of the conflict down to the present, in spite of assumptions that Moscow's puppets in Pyongyang would surely collapse after the USSR itself met oblivion in 1991.[82]

Operations by the American Counter Intelligence Corps and its local allies had from late 1945 targeted remnants of the People's Republic of Korea and other nationalist and leftist elements in southern Korea, with the members of political parties and polities killed, tortured or placed in concentration camps. Their families, including children, frequently shared the same fate. The Democratic People's Republic of Korea was an amalgamation of nationalist and leftist forces which had formed the People's Republic and its constituent People's Committees—a direct successor to the state the Americans had abolished in southern Korea. War against the DPRK was thus a continuation of the war against both Korean nationalist and leftist forces in southern Korea which had opposed American rule—a conflict which the Americans themselves had started in 1945 through their actions against the People's Republic, the people's committees and "undesirable" political parties. This was despite the republic and the committees having been deemed even by American reports to be representative of the will of the Korean population.[83]

While the Soviet Union had occupied northern Korea itself, it had not forcefully interfered in domestic politics in a comparable way[84] nor had it sought to abolish the existing de facto government of Korea or its people's committees. Thus while Korean nationalism had no significant cause for conflict with the USSR, the U.S. had effectively initiated a conflict in final months of 1945 by abolishing the Korean republic and brutally imposing its will, and this conflict had continued to escalate it since. Forms of escalation ranged from ever harsher crackdowns on nationalist and leftist groups in South Korea and imposition of Syngman Rhee to the actions of the Rhee government including its armed forces' regular and unprovoked incursions north of the 38th parallel. The conflict between American dominance and Korean nationalists' assertion of their right to self-rule and self-determination first emerged in September 1945—and would continue throughout the Cold War and well into the 21st century through the conflict between the DPRK and the United States.

NOTES

1 United States Central Intelligence Agency, *Current Capabilities of the North Korean Regime*, ORE 18-50, June 1950 (p. 10).
Armstrong, Charles, *The North Korean Revolution, 1945–1950,* Ithaca, Cornell University Press, 2003 (Chapter 5: Planning the Economy).

2 Kuark, Yoon T., 'North Korea's Industrial Development during the Post-War Period,' *The China Quarterly,* no. 14, April 1963 (p. 52).
United States Armed Forces in Korea, Assistant Chief of Staff, G-2, Record Group 332, box 57, North Korea Today (pp. 21–23).

3 Kuark, Yoon T., 'North Korea's Industrial Development during the Post-War Period,' *The China Quarterly,* no. 14, April 1963 (p. 52).

4 Hanley, Charles J. and Choe, Sang Hun and Mendoza, Martha, *The Bridge at No Gun Ri: A Hidden Nightmare from the Korean War*, New York, Henry Holt and Company, 2001 (p. 170).
Graham, Edward M., *Reforming Korea's Industrial Conglomerates*, Washington D.C., Peterson Institute for International Economics, 2003 (p. 12).

5 Hanley, Charles J. and Choe, Sang Hun and Mendoza, Martha, *The Bridge at No Gun Ri: A Hidden Nightmare from the Korean War*, New York, Henry Holt and Company, 2001 (p. 170).

Stone, I. F., *Hidden History of the Korean War*, Amazon Media, 2014 (Chapter 17, 'Free Elections?').

6 Heo, Uk, and Roehrig, Terence, *South Korea Since 1980*, Cambridge, Cambridge University Press, 2010 (p. 18).
Henderson, Gregory, *The Politics of the Vortex*, Cambridge, MA, Harvard University Press, 1968 (pp. 348–349).

7 Foreign Relations of the United States, 1950, vol. VII, Korea, Washington D.C., Government Printing Office, 1976 (p. 602).
Hanley, Charles J. and Choe, Sang Hun and Mendoza, Martha, *The Bridge at No Gun Ri: A Hidden Nightmare from the Korean War*, New York, Henry Holt and Company, 2001 (p. 170).

8 Cumings, Bruce, *The Korean War: A History*, New York, Modern Library, 2010 (pp. 70, 133).
McCann, David R. and Strauss, Barry S., *War and Democracy: A Comparative Study of the Korean War and the Peloponnesian War,* Abingdon, Routledge, 2015 (p. 59).

9 Gupta, Karunakar, 'How Did the Korean War Begin?,' *The China Quarterly*, no. 52, OctoberDecember 1972 (p. 699).

10 Did You Know, Land of the Morning Calm, The Korean War, Veterans Affairs Canada, Government of Canada. (http://www.veterans.gc.ca/eng/remembrance/history/korean-war/land-morning-calm/didyouknow).
Cumings, Bruce, *Korea's Place in the Sun: A Modern History*, New York, W. W. Norton & Company, 1997 (p. 247).
Boose, Donald W., Jr., and Matray, James I., *The Ashgate Research Companion to the Korean War*, Farnham Ashgate, 2015 (p. 28).

11 Mathews Papers, box 90, *Korea with the John Foster Dulles Mission*, June 14–29, 1950.

12 National Records Center, USFIK 11071 file, box 62/96, G-2 'Staff Study,' February 1949, signed by Lieutenant Colonel B. W. Heckemeyer of Army G-2.

13 Cumings, Bruce, *Korea's Place in the Sun: A Modern History,* New York, W. W. Norton & Company, 1997 (Chapter 5).

14 UN Archives, BOX DAG-1/2.1.2, box 3, account of briefing on June 15, 1949.

15 Cumings, Bruce, *Korea's Place in the Sun: A Modern History*, New York, W. W. Norton & Company, 1997 (p. 257).

16 British Foreign Office (FO 317), piece no. 76259, Holt to FO, Sept. 2, 1949.
Washington to Canberra, memorandum 953, August 17, 1949.

17 National Archives, 895.00 file, box 7127, Ranshofen-Wertheimer to Jessup, September 22, 1949.

18 United States of America Department of State, Office of the Historian, Foreign Relations of the United States, 1946, The Far East, vol. 7, *The Political Adviser in Korea (Benninghoff) to the Secretary of State*, January 28, 1946.

19 Cumings, Bruce, *The Korean War: A History*, New York City, Modern Library, 2010 (p. 140).
Wellington Koo Papers, Colombia University, box 217, Koo Diaries, entry for Jan. 4, 1950.

20 Lee, Steven Hugh, *Outposts of Empire: Korea, Vietnam, and the Origins of the Cold War in Asia, 1949–1954*, Quebec, McGill-Queen's University Press, 1995 (p. 33).

21 National Archives, 895.00 file, box 946, Muccio to Butterworth, August 27, 1949.

22 Cotton, James and Neary, Ian, *The Korean War in History,* Manchester, Manchester University Press, 1989 (pp. 49–50).
Kim, Han Gil, *Modern History of Korea,* Pyongyang, Foreign Languages Publishing House, 1979 (pp. 306–307).
Blum, William, *Killing Hope: U.S. Military and C.I.A. Interventions Since World War II*, London, Zed Books, 2003 (p. 48).

23 Gupta, Karunakar, 'How Did the Korean War Begin?,' *The China Quarterly*, no. 52, October–December 1972 (pp. 699–716).
24 Ibid. (p. 699).
25 LaFeber, Walter, *America, Russia, and the Cold War*, New York, John Wiley, 1976 (p. 100).
26 Heale, Michael, *The United States in the Long Twentieth Century: Politics and Society Since 1900*, London, Bloomsbury, 2015 (p. 174).
27 Acheson, Dean, *Present at the Creation,* New York, Norton, 1969 (p. 437)
Warner, Geoffrey, 'The United States and the Rearmament of West Germany, 1950–4,' *Royal Institute of International Affairs,* vol. 61, no. 2, Spring 1985 (pp. 279–286).
28 Kowalski, Frank, *An Inoffensive Rearmament: The Making of the Postwar Japanese Army*, Annapolis, MD, Naval Institute Press, 2014 (Chapter 3: 'Basic Plan').
29 Hanley, Charles J. and Choe, Sang Hun and Mendoza, Martha, *The Bridge at No Gun Ri: A Hidden Nightmare from the Korean War*, New York, Henry Holt and Company, 2001 (p. 222).
30 Lafeber, Walter, 'NATO and the Korean War: A Context,' *Diplomatic History*, vol. 13, no. 4, Fall 1989 (pp. 461–477).
31 Truman, Harry S., 'Proclaiming the Existence of a National Emergency,' December 16, 1950.
32 Leffler, Melvyn P, *A Preponderance of Power*, Stanford, Stanford University Press, 1992 (p. 369).
Cumings, Bruce, *Origins of the Korean War: The Roaring of the Cataract, 1947–1950, Volume Two*, Princeton, NJ, Princeton University Press, 1990 (p. 749).
Scott, Daniel, 'An Old Soldier's View Of The Early Cold War, 1949–1953,' Theses and Dissertations, Illinois State University, 2015.
33 *Rebuilding America's Defenses, A Report of The Project for the New American Century*, September 2000 (p. 20).
34 Lacey, Michael James, *The Truman Presidency,* Cambridge, Cambridge University Press, 1989 (p. 390).
United States State Department, *Foreign Relations of the United States*, U.S. G.P.O., 1948, vol. 6: Asia and the Pacific (p. 711).
35 Harrison, Mark, *The Economics of World War II: Six Great Powers in International Comparison*, Cambridge, Cambridge University Press, 2000 (pp. 1–42).
36 Krugman, Paul, 'Weaponized Keynesianism,' *New York Times*, June 24, 2009.
37 Cypher, James M., 'The origins and evolution of military Keynesianism in the United States,' *Journal of Post Keynesian Economics*, vol. 38, no. 3, 2015.
38 Milward, Alan S. *War, Economy, and Society, 1939–1945*, Berkeley, University of California Press, 1979 (p. 69).
39 Bureau of Labor Statistics, 'Employment status of the civilian noninstitutional population, 1940 to date.' (http://www.bls.gov/cps/cpsaat1.pdf).
40 Uchitelle, Louis, 'The U.S. Still Leans on the Military-Industrial Complex,' *New York Times*, September 22, 2017.
41 Higgs, Robert, *Depression, War, and Cold War: Studies in Political Economy,* Oxford, Oxford University Press, 2006 (pp. 102–103).
Carroll, Richard J., *An Economic Record of Presidential Performance: From Truman to Bush,* Westport, Praeger, 1995 (p. 41).
42 The Balance, *Unemployment Rate by Year Since 1929 Compared to Inflation and GDP, U.S. Unemployment Rate History* (<https://www.thebalance.com/ unemployment-rate-by-year-3305506>).
43 'Boeing B-29 Superfortress Assembly Plants, & Production Numbers,' *b29-superfortress.com.*
44 Cumings, Bruce, *The Korean War: A History*, New York, Modern Library, 2010 (pp. 199–200).

45 Stone, I. F., *Hidden History of the Korean War*, Amazon Media, 2014 (pp. 347–348).
46 Speech to the Michigan legislature, in Lansing, Michigan, May 15, 1952, published in: Imparato, Edward T., *General MacArthur Speeches and Reports 1908–1964*, Nashville, Turner, 2000 (p. 206).
47 'Economic Consequences of War on the U.S. Economy,' *Institute for Economics and Peace*, 2011.
48 *Farewell Address of President Dwight D. Eisenhower*, January 17, 1961.
49 Acheson, Dean, *Speech on the Far East*, January 12, 1950.
50 Stone, I. F., *Hidden History of the Korean War*, Amazon Media, 2014 (Introduction: Korea is Near).
51 December 22, 1950, *New York Times*.
Kowalski, Frank, *An Inoffensive Rearmament: The Making of the Postwar Japanese Army*, Annapolis, Naval Institute Press, 2014 (Chapter 3: Basic Plan).
52 'Economic Consequences of War on the U.S. Economy,' *Institute for Economics and Peace*, 2011.
53 O'Neill, Mark, 'How Chiang spirited China's gold away from the Reds,' *South China Morning Post*, June 6, 2010.
54 FO317, piece no. 83297, comment or 'minute' on Gascoigne to FO, Jan. 13, 1950; piece no. 83243, memo on invasion of Formosa, Jan. 25, 1950, minute by Burgess; piece no. 83247, report on Formosa, April 14, 1950, minute by Burgess.
55 Stone, I. F., *Hidden History of the Korean War*, Amazon Media, 2014 (Chapter 10: The Best Army in Asia).
56 United States State Department, *Foreign Relations of the United States*, U.S. G.P.O., 1948, vol. 7: The Far East and Australasia (pp. 162–163).
MacArthur, Douglas, *A Soldier Speaks: Public Papers and Speeches of General of the Army Douglas MacArthur*, New York, Praeger, 1965 (pp. 218–222).
57 Harris, Gardiner, 'U.S. Weighed Penalizing El Salvador Over Support for China, Then Backed Off,' *New York Times*, September 29, 2018.
'U.S. recalls diplomats in El Salvador, Panama, Dominican Republic over Taiwan,' *Reuters*, September 8, 2018.
58 Paine, S.C.M., *The Japanese Empire: Grand Strategy from the Meiji Restoration to the Pacific War*, Cambridge, Cambridge University Press, 2017 (p. 111).
Levine, Alan J., *Stalin's Last War; Korea and the Approach to World War III*, Jefferson, McFarland & Company, 2005 (pp. 10–11).
59 Khanin, Grigorii Isaakovich, 'The 1950s: The Triumph of the Soviet Economy,' *Europe-Asia Studies*, vol. 55, no. 8, 2003 (pp. 1187–1211).
60 Stone, I. F., *Hidden History of the Korean War*, Amazon Media, 2014 (Chapter 4: The Role of John Foster Dulles).
61 Ibid. (Chapter 7: The Stage Was Set).
62 'Stationing American troops in Japan will lead to bloody tragedy—ex-PM of Japan,' *RT*, (televised interview), November 6, 2016.
63 Stone, I. F., *Hidden History of the Korean War*, Amazon Media, 2014 (Chapter 7: The Stage Was Set).
64 Ibid. (Chapter 7: The Stage Was Set).
65 Cumings, Bruce, *Korea's Place in the Sun: A Modern History*, W. W. Norton and Company, New York, 1997 (p. 266).
66 Hastings, Max, *Korean War*, London, Michael Joseph, 1988 (p. 98).
67 *Time Magazine*, October 6, 1950.
68 *The Truman-MacArthur Wake Island Conference*, October 15, 1950.
Hopkins, William B., *One Bugle, No Drums: The Marines at Chosin Reservoir*, Chapel Hill, Algonquin Books, 1986 (p. 46).
69 Stone, I. F., *Hidden History of the Korean War*, Amazon Media, 2014 (Chapter 13: MacArthur's Blank Check).

70 Ibid. (Chapter 13: MacArthur's Blank Check).
71 Cumings, Bruce, *Korea's Place in the Sun: A Modern History*, New York, W. W. Norton & Company, 1997 (p. 266).
72 Dockrill, Saki, *Britain's Policy for West German Rearmament, 1950–1955,* Cambridge, Cambridge University Press, 1991 (p. 32).
Sandler, Stanley, *The Korean War: An Interpretative History,* London, UCL Press, 1999 (p. 4).
73 Kalic, Sean N., *Spies: The U.S. and Russian Espionage Game from the Cold War to the 21st Century,* Santa Barbara, Praeger, 2019 (pp. 61–62).
74 Ibid. (pp. 61–62).
75 Blum, William, *Killing Hope: U.S. Military and C.I.A. Interventions Since World War II*, London, Zed Books, 2003 (Chapter 17: Soviet Union late 1940s to 1960s: From spy planes to book publishing).
Ibid. (Chapter 7: Eastern Europe 1948–1956: Operation Splinter Factor).
76 Ibid. (Chapter 14: Indonesia 1957–1958: War and pornography).
Abrams, A. B., *Power and Primacy: The History of Western Intervention in the Asia-Pacific*, Oxford, Peter Lang, 2019 (Chapter 4: Chapter 4: Sukarnoism and the Rise and Fall of an Independent Indonesia: Wars both Overt and Covert to Return an Asian Power to Western Clienthood).
77 Blum, William, *Killing Hope: U.S. Military and C.I.A. Interventions Since World War II*, London, Zed Books, 2003 (Chapter 9: Iran 1953: Making it safe for the King of Kings).
Allen-Ebrahimian, Bethany, '64 Years Later, CIA Finally Releases Details of Iranian Coup,' *Foreign Policy,* June 20, 2017.
78 Stockwell, John, *In Search of Enemies: A CIA Story*, New York, W. W. Norton & Company, 1978 (p. 201).
Prados, John, *Safe For Democracy: The Secret Wars of the CIA*, Chicago, Ivan R. Dee, 2006 (p. 329).
Hersh, Seymour, 'CIA Said to Have Aided Plotters Who Overthrew Nkrumah in Ghana,' *New York Times*, May 9, 1978.
79 Foreign Relations of the United States, 1950, vol. VII, Korea, Washington D.C., Government Printing Office, 1976 (p. 602).
Hanley, Charles J. and Choe, Sang Hun and Mendoza, Martha, *The Bridge at No Gun Ri: A Hidden Nightmare from the Korean War*, New York, Henry Holt and Company, 2001 (p. 170).
80 Meyers, Samuel M., and Biderman, Albert D., *Mass Behaviour in Battle and Captivity: The Communist Soldier in the Korean War*, Chicago, University of Chicago Press, 1968 (pp. 280–281).
81 Counter Intelligence Corps, 1945.9—1949.1, vol. 1, CIC, vol. 1, U.S. Army Intelligence Centre, History of the Counter Intelligence Corps Volume XXX, 'CIC during the Occupation of Korea, March 1959 (p. 24).
82 Cumings, Bruce, *The Korean War: A History*, New York, Modern Library, 2010 (pp. 65–66).
83 Meade, Edward Grant, *American Military Government in Korea,* New York, King's Crown Press, 1952 (pp. 56, 72, 188).
84 Armstrong, Charles, *The North Korean Revolution, 1945–1950,* Ithaca, Cornell University Press, 2003 (Chapter 2: Liberation, Occupation and the Emerging New Order).

Chapter 3
THE KOREAN WAR

Ground War in Northeast Asia

The Korean War remains the only major conventional ground war waged between Western and East Asian powers since the mid-19th century, and at the time of its outbreak it was the first major conventional war since Imperial Japan's surrender—ending hopes for a peaceful new era of inter-state cooperation. For the United States the war remains the bloodiest it has fought since the dismantling of the Japanese Empire, with over four times the casualty rate of the Vietnam War and, according to the a wide range of testimonies, surpassing even the excesses of the Second World War in either the European or the Pacific theatres in the destruction wrought and the brutalities committed. Supreme Commander of U.S. and UN forces in Korea General Douglas MacArthur, who had previously led the war effort against Imperial Japan as Commander of U.S. Army Forces in the Far East, testified to this effect after witnessing the war in Korea: "I have never seen such devastation. I have seen, I guess, as much blood and disaster as any living man, and it just curdled my stomach the last time I was there." He referred to the war as "a slaughter never heard of in the history of mankind."[1] Similar sentiments were expressed by a number of prominent figures in the American leadership who witnessed both wars first-hand.[2]

The losses North Korea suffered during the war have few parallels in history, with conservative estimates placing the death toll at 20 percent of the population[3] and some estimates ranging as high as 30 percent.[4] The extent of the damage surpasses that of any other nation's wartime experience in modern history—with 635,000–698,000 tons of bombs dropped on the country[5] compared to 503,000 tons dropped on the Japanese Empire in its entirety during the Pacific War.[6] To put the intensity of this campaign in perspective, the small Korean republic of 120,000 square kilometres was subjected to bombardment with more ordinance in three years by the United States Military than the entire Japanese Empire at well over 3 million square kilometres over four years—even if including the nuclear attacks on Hiroshima and Nagasaki.[7] Although fewer bombs were dropped on North Korea than would be dropped in the Vietnam War, the significantly smaller size of the country, the shorter time period over which the attacks were carried out, and the far greater concentration of the population in major settlements, between them by some estimates, makes the bombardment of Korea the most intense in world military history. The war exerts a major influence on Korean identity particularly in the DPRK, the results of which can be seen to manifest widely from its education and popular art to its foreign policy and more recently its pursuit of a nuclear deterrent.

The consequences of the conflict both for the Korean nation and for the wider world remain significant today, from the ongoing clean-up operation for unexploded American ordinance, which is expected to continue to endanger North Korean civilians for at least 100 years,[8] to the Korean People's Army's current defence doctrine. The evolution of the U.S. nuclear and chemical weapons[9] programs and associated delivery systems, Western perceptions of Chinese and North Korean military capabilities, and the indefinite American military presence globally are other examples of the war's profound and lasting influence. The nature of the war's outbreak remains far more obscure however, and while Washington and many of its allies from the outset declared Pyongyang's sole responsibility for initiating hostilities an undisputed fact, an assessment of the circumstances under which this conclusion was reached and how the U.S. came to lead a broad coalition into war provides context key to understanding the conflict's place in the global Cold War and its importance.

Determining the Aggressor: Building of a United Nations Coalition Against North Korea

Almost immediately after the outbreak of hostilities the United States moved to form a military coalition through the recently formed United Nations with the purpose of gaining both material and diplomatic support for an armed intervention against North Korea. The American representative alleged that the "unprovoked assault" by the Korean People's Army was an attack on "the vital interest which all members of the United Nations have in the organization."[10] The overwhelming influence of the United States and its allies at the UN at the time, an organisation first conceptualised by the U.S. State Department near the end of the Second World War and based in New York City, meant that Washington had little trouble projecting its own narrative of the events in Korea and gaining the UN support. The United Nations Security Council's (UNSC) four permanent members in attendance at the time were the United States, the United Kingdom, France and the Taipei-based Republic of China—all anticommunist states with the latter three close U.S. partners heavily reliant on American aid. The UN Secretary General of Norwegian origin Trygve Lie himself was no neutral outsider, but a staunch anti-communist as made very clear in his later memoirs which reveal his maneuvering in the UN to best assure Western interests were served against those of the USSR, the DPRK and other non-Western actors.[11] It was later revealed that in 1949 Lie had entered into an agreement with the U.S. State Department to dismiss those whose political leanings were not favored by Washington from employment at the UN.[12]

The Soviet Union, which previously held the UNSC's fifth permanent seat, had boycotted the council in protest at the United Nations' refusal to recognize the People's Republic of China or provide Beijing with a seat at the Council or the General Assembly. This refusal was seen in Moscow and much of the non-Western world as a politicized decision by the Western powers and a sign of their disproportionate influence in the organization, given that the Western client government in Taipei which held the Chinese seat was in control of significantly less than 0.5% of Chinese territory. The USSR's absence meant it was unable to veto Western-drafted resolutions against North Korea. Due in part to the nature of the accession process at the time, only four Soviet Bloc nations were UN members when these resolutions were passed—none of them Security Council members.[13] As a result of these factors, the United States was able to dominate and effectively set the agenda at the UN.

Despite overwhelming American influence at the organisation, the United Nations investigative team could not bring itself to condemn North Korea as the aggressor—lacking verifiable evidence implicating the Korean People's Army as the initiator of hostilities. The cable from the United Nations mission in Seoul confirmed that observers at the inter-Korean border were unable to determine which of the Koreas had initiated hostilities. The UN commission merely reported that the South Koreans alleged they had been attacked and that Seoul denied the North Korean radio account that claimed the south had attacked first and that northern forces had repelled the invaders and then gone over on to launch a counteroffensive. The commission itself expressed no opinion as to who had started the war.[14]

North Korean official sources claimed that the ROKAF troops had attacked and captured their assets on the 38th parallel and seized the small city of Haeju near the border.[15] These claims were initially substantiated by South Korean sources, with the ROK Office of Public Information announcing the capture of the northern city by the ROKAF.[16] According to North Korean sources, KPA forces moved to reclaim the city and repel other attacks which had occurred simultaneously on the border, and proceeded to launch a counterattack. With the capture of Haeju undermining the South Korean narrative of an unprovoked northern attack, Seoul later denied that the successful attack on the city had ever taken place—retracting the earlier report by the Office of Public Information which had supported the DPRK's claim.[17] The frequency of major ROKAF attacks on northern border settlements preceding the war, which as previously mentioned were confirmed by U.S. and British intelligence,[18] and the significant aforementioned gains Seoul had from provoking a KPA counterattack, lend credibility to Pyongyang's claim that it had come under attack without provocation.

The U.S. State Department for its part purposefully withheld evidence from the United Nations Security Council when calling for a military intervention against the DPRK. The 171-word cable received from Seoul by the U.S. differed considerably from the 38-word and highly paraphrased sentence it presented to the Security Council.[19] The full text of the cable and the early reports which could have further elaborated on how hostilities broke out were all withheld without explanation. U.S. Ambassador Muccio reported from Seoul that he could only "partly confirm" the ROK's accusation of North Korean aggression. Even weeks later Muccio never gave evidence or tried to claim that the DPRK had been responsible for the opening of hostilities, let alone that they were the sole initiator of aggression as the U.S. was claiming before the Security Council. American military advisers serving alongside the South Korean forces on the border were not cited as sources to confirm the ROK's claims.[20]

The United States not only asked the Security Council to brand the DPRK the sole aggressor despite a complete lack of evidence, but the resolution it introduced, UNSC Resolution 82, also asked for a ceasefire directed solely at the KPA. India's delegation raised questions "over the use of the term 'act of aggression'" citing insufficient evidence provided by the accusers. Delhi thus refused to contribute to the Western-led war effort.[21] The Yugoslav delegation, representing a country with hostile relations with the USSR and highly dependent on American aid and political support, nevertheless insisted that although the U.S. asked for North Korea to be declared the aggressor, "there seemed to be lack of precise information that could enable the Security Council to pin responsibility."[22] Yugoslavia instead proposed that representatives from the DPRK be invited to present Pyongyang's side of the story which, had the Council been seeking an objective assessment of the causes of the war, would have been a sensible course given the scarcity of evidence or intelligence implicating the country. Such a course of action would not have been in the interests of the Council's permanent members, however, and would have undermined their ability to dictate the narrative of the war's outbreak to facilitate an armed intervention on the Asian mainland. It appeared neither the U.S. nor its allies could present evidence implicating North Korea, and while it is uncertain whether Pyongyang could have proven its purported innocence had it been allowed to make a case at the Council, a lack of evidence by both sides would not have given cause to an international intervention supporting either party.

When the Soviet Union returned to the Security Council three months after the war's outbreak Foreign Minister Vyacheslav Molotov put forward a motion for representatives from both the DPRK and ROK to be heard at the United Nations. This was met with the same staunch opposition from Taipei and the Western powers, and the Western-dominated Security Council decided to invite representatives from South Korea alone.[23] The U.S. and its allies thus maintained a monopoly on the narratives put forth at the United Nations. Many cables and documents in U.S. possession on the subject of the war's outbreak were denied as evidence to the Security Council—likely because they did not point to North Korea as the sole aggressor.[24] Although UN investigators had no proof that North Korea was the aggressor, and had never made such a claim, "peacekeeping" actions were initiated at the behest of the Western powers against the DPRK. This amounted to a United Nations military taskforce being placed under the direct command of the U.S. Military's Pacific Command in Tokyo and its Supreme Commander General MacArthur, which itself was accountable only to Washington and not to the UN.

UNSC Resolution 84, which passed on July 7, established the UN military coalition as an asset to assist U.S. goals on the peninsula. It stipulated "that all members providing military forces and other assistance…make sure such forces and other assistance available to a unified command under the United States," adding that the U.S. was itself free "to designate the commander of such forces," for which MacArthur was chosen.[25] The nature of the UN intervention as an auxiliary force to the United States Military, under direct American command, led President Eisenhower to later conclude that the UN coalition's true purpose was to provide the U.S. with a means to intervene without the appearance of acting unilaterally. He stated: "the *token forces* supplied by other nations, as in Korea, would lend real moral standing to a venture that otherwise could be made to appear as a brutal example of imperialism."[26] The United States thus gained substantial diplomatic cover and manpower contributions to its war effort against the small Northeast Asian republic,[27] and would seek nothing less than the complete destruction of the state and imposition of the client government of Syngman Rhee in its place.

The Korean People's Army Meets the United States Military: Offensives and Counteroffensives

The outbreak of the Korean War saw the fighting capacity of South Korea's armed forces almost immediately collapse in the face of a KPA counteroffensive—with North Korean forces pressing southwards after the recapture of Haeju in an attempt to reunify the peninsula by force. Despite its numerical superiority, within days the South Korean military faced mass defections to the KPA. Those that weren't defecting were retreating.[28] Within a week Supreme Commander General MacArthur cabled Washington that only a quarter of the ROKAF's personnel could even be located.[29] Within a month fully half of the ROKAF were dead, captured or otherwise missing. Only two divisions maintained their equipment while the remainder, around 70 percent, had lost or abandoned it.[30] The ROKAF's near collapse resembled that of the Chinese Guomindang forces five years prior during the Chinese Civil War[31] and South Vietnamese forces two decades later—all armed and trained by the United States and retaining significant material advantages but crippled by corrupt leadership and poor morale leading to mass defections and desertions when facing a better motivated adversary.[32]

British journalist Philip Knightly was told by an American colonel regarding the performance of the ROKAF, and the poor impression they made on the Americans in combat: "South Koreans and North Koreans are identical. Why then do North Koreans fight like tigers and South Koreans run like sheep?"[33] This contrast can be attributed to the discrepancy in the morale and leadership of the two armies and the perceived legitimacy of their governments and causes. The head of the South Korean CIA, Brigadier General Kim Hyong Uk, confirmed that this was the primary factor allowing North Korean troops to defeat South Korean forces despite their considerable disadvantages in numbers and armaments. The nature of the government in ROK meant few were willing to die for it.[34] It is notable, as an example of this, that every ROKAF division in 1950 without exception was under the command of former officers from the Imperial Japanese Armed Forces.[35] The Morse code "HA" was used across the front to indicate South Korean forces "hauling ass"—that is, retreating. Even in later stages of the war after the tide had turned against the Korean People's Army, South Korean units would continue to prove highly unreliable.

American General Matthew B. Ridgway noted in 1951 his dismay that the South Koreans were unwilling to fight a war supposedly being waged for their own freedom. He wrote: "I drove out north of Seoul and into a dismaying spectacle. ROK soldiers by truckloads were streaming south, without orders, without arms, without leaders, in full retreat… They had thrown away their rifles and pistols and had abandoned all artillery, mortars, machine guns, every crew-serviced weapon."[36] With the benefit of hindsight, mass defections and the collapse of the ROKAF could have been predicted. In a single incident in 1949 two whole Army battalions and a South Korean warship had defected to the north—and due to the nature of governance under Rhee this was hardly an isolated event. A year prior at Yosu on the south-western coast 2000 South Korean soldiers and much of the local population staged a major armed rebellion. While ROKAF units led by U.S. officers succeeded in putting down the revolt, guerilla activity by surviving soldiers and civilians was ongoing at the time of the Korean War's outbreak. The Rhee government's extreme and indiscriminate response to the Yosu rebellion had, alongside massive casualties, left over 20,000 homeless—further embittering the local population.[37]

Where the South Koreans failed to successfully engage the Korean People's Army, the United States Military was expected to perform considerably better. Pulitzer prize winning American journalist David Halberstam noted regarding the prevalent attitude in the U.S. Military towards the North Koreans, and the expectation that they would yield at the very sight of Western soldiers in the field: "almost everyone, from top to bottom, seemed to share the view that the moment the North Koreans saw they were fighting Americans rather than the ROKs they would cut and run. It was arrogance born of racial prejudice."[38] Such attitudes prevailed even at the highest levels of command, with the KPA by virtue of their East Asian ethnicity assumed to be incompetents who would not dare fight Westerners. Supreme Commander General Douglas MacArthur for one had an intuitive approach to military intelligence, mingling hard facts with the enemy's presumed racial qualities. "Chinamen can't fight," he had once said, and he didn't expect Koreans to fight much better. On the day of the war's outbreak the general demonstrated complacency and overconfidence, stating regarding the KPA: "I can handle it with one arm tied behind my back." The following day he told John Foster Dulles that if he only deployed U.S. 1st Cavalry Division to Korea, "why, heavens, you'd see these fellows [KPA] scuttle up to the Manchurian border so quick, you would see no more of them."[39]

Within ten days of the war's outbreak the United States Military had seen its first major engagements with the Korean People's Army—the first open battles in a conflict which would last over seventy years. The Battle of Osan saw the U.S. Army's 1st Battalion, 21st Infantry regiment and supporting 52nd Field Artillery Battalion, surprised by the professionalism and training of the KPA, forced into a swift retreat and taking heavy casualties. Positions were abandoned prematurely, leaving considerable stashes of equipment behind alongside wounded soldiers and allowing the KPA to capture 82 Americans.[40] The battle was over within three hours—the first of a string of defeats over several months which saw U.S. and allied forces pressed into a fast-contracting perimeter in the southeast corner of the Korean Peninsula. The U.S. Army 34th Infantry Regiment the following day deployed a force of 2000 men to face the KPA in the Battle of Pyongtek, with the Americans failing to stall Korean forces or cause significant delays, and again facing heavy casualties and retreating.[41] The battle's aftermath saw the regiment's commander replaced and the units again sent north—but according to American reports, the 34th immediately became disorganised and again retreated when facing KPA resistance.[42] The Battle of Cheonan the following night again saw the 34th Infantry routed, taking heavy casualties and forced into a disorderly retreat by the KPA—again abandoning considerable quantities of equipment and seeing many of its number taken prisoner.[43]

North Korean forces continued to advance southwards in the face of a crumbling and almost entirely ineffective South Korean force—and an American force which fared little better. As one British report stated regarding the performance of U.S. troops: "In their very first contact with the North Koreans they were outmanoeuvred and soundly defeated. Retreat was the only option."[44] On July 14, a week after the victory at Cheonan, the KPA faced a large American force at the city of Taejon comprised of the U.S. Army's 19th, 21st and 34th infantry regiments under the command of Major General William F. Dean—approximately 9000 U.S. personnel with some limited support from reorganised South Korean units. Able to retreat into the Taejon, U.S. forces succeeded in stalling the KPA in a series of intensive street battles which caused considerable damage to the city. They were forced to retreat within a week, suffering over 1000 casualties with 922 killed and 228 wounded. Almost 2,400 men were declared missing in action, and given the low probability of defection and the Army's inability to locate the vast majority of them, a total casualty number of over 3000 men remains likely.[45] General Dean for his part, after reportedly abandoning his command post to personally hunt down and destroy a Korean T-34 tank, was apprehended as a prisoner of war.[46]

The trend towards a constant U.S. retreat, heavy losses and a seemingly unstoppable Korean advance would continue for several months. In an attempt to turn the tide, and blaming the poor equipment of its existing Army regiments for their failures on the battlefield, the U.S. Military deployed superior and better armed Cavalry regiments.[i] These elite reinforcing units were active in the theatre by the end of July, but they too proved incapable of defeating the KPA on the ground and quickly fell into disorder. Coalition wartime reports revealed that within two days of engaging North Korean forces the 7th Cavalry regiment had shot several of their own men by accident. "On the next (third) night, July the 25, elements were positioned on a hillside a few miles behind the front line. Rumours went around that the North Koreans had made a breakthrough causing mass panic. In the morning 119 cavalrymen were unaccounted for, along with many of the unit's heavy weapons." A soldier interviewed said: "It was just nothing but mass confusion. You didn't. You stop here. You dig in. You just wait. You're gonna have to

i While U.S. sources frequently blamed insufficient armaments for their early failures, Army regiments were equipped with munitions which were nothing less than state of the art to engage the KPA. The 3.5 inch M20 'Super Bazooka' was a key example, and was used extensively at the battle of Taejon. The weapon had entered production in June 1950 just two weeks before the beginning of the war, and was considered the most advanced munition of its kind in the world at the time. Some KPA units by contrast were using rifles over 30 years old.

leave. Nobody knew what was going on. Matter of fact I didn't even know if we had a platoon leader, majority of the time. I didn't know if we had a platoon sergeant. There was nobody in charge."[47]

In the face of overwhelming KPA victories, Supreme Commander MacArthur and the American leadership were faced with the reality that they had seriously underestimated the capabilities of the North Koreans—who despite limited armaments and supplies and a lack of overseas support had soundly outmatched the U.S. Army in the field. MacArthur at first wanted an American regimental combat team in Korea, then two divisions. Within a week he cabled Washington that the KPA was "operating under excellent top-level guidance and had demonstrated superior command of strategic and tactical principles." By the beginning of July MacArthur wanted a minimum of 30,000 American combat personnel, meaning more than four infantry divisions, three tank battalions and assorted artillery. A week later he asked for eight whole divisions.[48]

By the end of July, with a continued inflow of reinforcements and supplies, the United States and their allies retained an overwhelming numerical advantage with 140,000 men on the front facing the KPA's 70,000. The U.S. Navy and newly formed U.S. Air Force were able to supplement this already vast advantage with uncontested naval and air superiority, while supporting elements bringing in supplies from overseas could provide significant technological and logistical advantages.[49] Despite every material advantage the U.S. would continue to retreat and see its perimeter contract, albeit at a slower rate, over the following month of August. The fighting stabilised at the Pusan Perimeter, a 130km by 80km right angled front in the south east of the peninsula. North Korean Premier Kim Il Sung, who on July 5 was declared Supreme Commander of the Korean People's Army, later recalled that the military leadership had planned to end the war by the end of July—a goal very nearly achieved had it not been for the vastness of the inflow of American reinforcements and their concentration at Pusan.[50] Engagements near this perimeter were often within range of the guns of U.S. warships, which combined with carrier based aircraft and bombers based in Japan provided a tremendous further advantage in firepower which the KPA would struggle to overcome. Korean firepower, limited to handheld weapons and a scattering of light artillery and tanks, was negligible by comparison.

Two months after the war's outbreak in late August the U.S. and their allies were still pressed on the defensive, with the KPA making "startling gains" for two consecutive weeks which placed a serious strain on their enemy's heavily fortified perimeter. Korean forces simultaneously pressed their adversaries on three points at once, Kyongju, Masan and Taegu, bringing the perimeter "near breaking point." As U.S. forces were pushed closer to the coast the benefit of naval bombardments continued to grow. Even a small number of American warships could boast more firepower than the entire KPA, and combined with air and artillery strikes, they inflicted considerable casualties. American warships including gargantuan 58,000 ton Iowa Class battleships—the heaviest and most powerful in the world at the time—would on several occasions during the war serve as mobile artillery, striking the KPA from well beyond retaliation range with massive firepower.[51] It was a total mismatch of the greatest firepower in the world against a well-trained but relatively small and scantly armed ground force fighting primarily with light man-portable weapons. Nevertheless, even the fire laid down from the sea, sky and from artillery assets, paired with the coalition's significant numerical, logistical and other armament advantages, could not initially halt the North Korean advance at Pusan.

The KPA crossed the Naktong River and captured the cities of Pohang and Chinju in the first two weeks of September, breaking enemy lines and again forcing a retreat[52] but simultaneously placing greater pressure on its own supply lines. American historian Roy Appleman noted in regard to the situation in Pusan following the capture of these two cities: "After two weeks of the heaviest fighting of the war," he wrote, UN forces "had just barely turned back the great North Korean offensive." By September 15, U.S. forces, which were doing the bulk of the fighting, had alone suffered 20,000 casualties.[53] On September 9, KPA Supreme Commander Kim Il Sung said the war had reached an "extremely harsh, decisive stage,"[54] with Commander of the U.S. Eighth Army General Walton Walker reporting two days later that the frontline situation was the most dangerous since the perimeter had been established.[55]

Although the Western powers widely depicted the KPA as a proxy of the "International Communist Conspiracy" the pinning of the U.S. Military at Pusan, when Washington viewed defeat and withdrawal from the peninsula as a very real prospect, had provided the perfect opportunity for either Beijing or Moscow to intervene with material or manpower support to turn the tide and rout remaining Western forces from Korea.

Such action would, according to General MacArthur among others, have proven decisive. [56] They refrained from doing so however, forcing the North Koreans to contest with a massive manpower and material disadvantages and increasingly strained logistics which prevented them from bringing about a decisive routing of their adversaries. [57] Indeed, in a later study the U.S. Army's institute for strategic and national security research and analysis, the U.S. Army War College Strategic Studies Institute, would attribute the halting of the KPA advance and North Korea's inability to take complete control of the peninsula to serious logistical issues.[58] These could have easily been circumvented by Chinese or Soviet material support.

With almost half of global GDP, a population fifteen times that of North Korea, and growing support from across the Western world with British and Australian troops and warships already arriving, the U.S. and its coalition benefitted from tremendous material advantages which only grew as more and more assets were diverted to the front. So great was the threat the KPA was seen to pose that all of United States' combat ready divisions, with the exception of the 82nd Airborne Division in Germany, would be deployed to Korea.[59] Against the increasingly undersupplied KPA, which was forced to abandon its battle tanks due to a lack of fuel, America's vast military industrial base was tasked with providing its forces with any equipment they could possibly need. This ensured that U.S. forces would enjoy considerable advantages not only in quantity of arms deployed, but also in quality. While the U.S. put its most capable battle tank, the M26 Pershing, into service in Korea, the most capable Soviet tanks of the time, the T-55 and IS-3, were never supplied to the KPA. This left Korean forces to make do with a very small number of older and lighter T-34 tanks—a design which dated back to 1940. The American M26 was 60% heavier and considerably more modern. By early September over 500 of these superior tanks were deployed at Pusan—outnumbering KPA armour by more than 5:1.[60] The case of battle tanks provides an exemplar of a general trend which disadvantaged the KPA, which, as reported by Tokyo HQ, were forced to rely on obsolete "World War 1 rifles" and did not receive "any post-war Soviet weapons."[61]

The performance of the Korean People's Army was such as to leave a lasting impression on the U.S. Military leadership, achieving what had been thought impossible against impossible odds. As a victor of the Second World War, which had less than five years prior placed Tokyo under occupation and dismantled both the Japanese Empire and the German Third Reich—the leading Empires of East Asia and Europe respectively—the U.S. had since considered itself near invincible. This made three months of constant retreat in the face of repeated Korean victories a particularly staggering and astonishing phenomenon. Major General Dean, who led the 24th Infantry against the KPA in the war's opening stages, reported to Supreme Commander MacArthur: "I am convinced that the North Korean Army, the North Korean solider and his status and training and the quality of his equipment have been underestimated."[62] U.S. Army General Matthew Ridgway, the commander of the Eighth Army, later appointed Supreme Allied Commander Europe and Chief of Staff of the U.S. Army, was himself taken aback by the KPA's performance stating: "we had never…imagined that the NKPA [North Korean People's Army—same as KPA] was a force so well-trained, so superbly disciplined, so battle-ready."[63] Even Supreme Commander MacArthur, after having done so himself, warned of the dangers of underestimating the capabilities of North Korean soldiers and its military leaders.[64] He stated to this effect: "The North Korean soldier must not be underestimated. He is a tough opponent, well-led, and has combined the infiltration tactic of the Japanese with the tank tactics of the Russian of World War II. He is able to march and manoeuvre and to attack at night with cohesion…tank work is extremely efficient and skilful."[65]

U.S. Marines Land at Inchon: The Tide Turns

By mid-August KPA supply lines were stretched thin and coming under increasing pressure from American air attacks as more American bombers were deployed to the Korean front. With North Korea lacking naval capabilities of any significance, a blockade of Pusan or interdiction of supplies and reinforcements was impossible—allowing growing numbers of U.S. and other Western forces to deploy behind the perimeter. The Korean numerical and material disadvantages thus grew more dire by the day, but were still insufficient to reverse the tide in favour of the U.S. and its allies.[66] It was only when General MacArthur staged and personally oversaw an amphibious landing of 80,000 U.S. troops behind KPA lines that North Korean forces were, for the first time in the three month war, forced onto the defensive by the overwhelming capabilities of their enemy.

Landings at the port city of Inchon were preceded by an intensive bombardment of KPA positions by U.S. and British naval assets. From September 10, suspected KPA defensive positions and nearby villages with a suspected North Korean presence, such as Wolmi and Tanyang, were doused with napalm and subsequently strafed by American aircraft. According to a later investigation by a South Korean government commission, these attacks purposefully targeted villagers and caused hundreds of civilian casualties.[67] On the 13th a fleet of two British heavy cruisers and six American destroyers fired almost 1000 127mm shells to eradicate the limited Korean coastal fortifications in place at Inchon and nearby Wolmi Island, crippling KPA defences in preparation for the massive amphibious assault which would follow.[68] Lacking any significant naval or air assets of their own, KPA forces near Inchon were unable to retaliate against such strikes.

The vast majority of U.S. troops landing at Inchon were elite Marines from the 1st Division, although the U.S. Army 7th Infantry and other supporting units also participated alongside a massive Joint Task Force from the U.S. Navy of 270 warships. Inchon's location was ideal, less than 100km south of the 38th parallel and under 200km from Pyongyang, which was within a day's strike distance for American mechanised units, and over 300km from Pusan where the main KPA force was located. The introduction of such large numbers of additional U.S. personnel left the KPA impossibly outnumbered, and with a third of the enemy force in a position to march northwards on its cities the North Koreans were forced to withdraw from the Pusan Perimeter to protect their own territory.

While the relief of the Pusan Perimeter was widely portrayed as a tactical defeat of the Korean People's Army, the increasingly scantly-armed but battle hardened contingent in south-eastern Korea were not defeated in battle but rather conducted an orderly withdrawal of their assets without significant losses. Fuel shortages and the T-34's poor suitability for mountainous terrain and forests, however, meant that much of North Korea's armour was completely abandoned. Shortages were exacerbated when the air wing of the American carrier *USS Valley Forge* destroyed a large oil refinery at Wonsan—and with it, thousands of tons of petroleum products. As the bulk of the KPA withdrew north, guerrilla forces including the entire KPA 10th Division abandoned their artillery and disappeared into the mountains south of the 38th parallel from where they would continue to harass U.S. forces for much of the war. The cadre had been formed of veteran officers in early 1950 and had spearheaded the offensive across the Naktong River in September.

Although the Inchon landings succeeded in turning the tide against the KPA, bringing the vast American advantages in the quantity of its manpower and its armaments fully to bear against the small East Asian state, the highly optimistic early reports that North Korea's military power had been neutralised were later proven false. Had the UN forces under U.S. command fulfilled their mandate to restore the Republic of Korea, returning Syngman Rhee and his associates to power and re-establishing the 38th parallel as the dividing line between the two Koreas, they likely would have seen no more of the Korean People's Army after the Inchon landings and subsequent recapture of Seoul. The latter occurred on September 25 and saw an American force of over 40,000 take over 1,500 casualties against a small and lightly armed KPA garrison of under 8000 men. Supreme Commander MacArthur's decision to press northwards indefinitely with the intention of bringing debellatio to the DPRK and imposing the Rhee government's rule in its place, however, forced the withdrawing North Korean forces to regroup from mid-October and continue the fight. This regrouping took place near the country's northern border, where the climate was extremely harsh. The speed and effectiveness with which the KPA did so surprised and impressed not only their enemies, but the armed forces of neighboring China as well.

British correspondent and writer Russel Spurr himself observed that "The North Koreans had in fact astonished the Chinese by the speed at which they had reconstituted their shattered forces."[69] American pilots began to observe large and intact North Korean formations in October at a time when the KPA's fighting capacity was considered almost completely spent. As reporter Hugh Deane, former Coordinator of Information and naval intelligence officer on General MacArthur's staff, reported, the general had "announced that the Korean People's Army had been destroyed when in fact a number of reconstituted divisions were about to take the field against him."[70]

North Korean officers themselves claimed that withdrawal north was part of a strategy adopted after Inchon to draw out the U.S. Military and then envelop them. How aware the KPA military leadership was of General MacArthur's intentions to invade and destroy their state, rather than halting the coalition's advance at the 38th parallel, remains uncertain. Chief of political intelligence for the KPA's 8th division Pak Ki Song stated regarding the post-Inchon withdrawal: "The main force of the enemy still remained intact, not having been fully damaged. When they were not fully aware of the power of our forces, they pushed their infantry far forward…to the Yalu River. This indicated that they underestimated us. All these conditions were favorable to lure them near."[71] A KPA officer captured later in the war explained what he alleged was the true nature of the organized withdrawal, stating:

> One may think that going down all the way to the Pusan perimeter and then withdrawing all the way to the Yalu River was a complete defeat. But that is not so. That was a planned withdrawal. We withdrew because we knew that UN troops would follow us up here, and that they would spread their troops thinly all over the vast area. Now, the time has come for us to envelop these troops and annihilate them.[72]

The officers' claims could well have been made in order to avoid admitting defeat or demoralizing their soldiers, but they were consistent with Western reports from the time. Reginald Thompson, a British reporter present at Inchon, reported that 2000 KPA soldiers present were quickly defeated by a landing force over 20 times their size with the majority taken captive. These Korean troops had turned out to be young wholly inexperienced decoys, while the bulk of KPA, including their more experienced personnel and officers, "had disappeared like wraiths into the hills." MacArthur's trap "had closed, and it was empty." The KPA appeared to have mastered the art of strategic withdrawal, escaping a massive U.S. offensive without serious losses.[73]

The tactics described by the KPA officers were notably prominent in the strategic thought of the Chinese People's Liberation Army (PLA)—an organization in which at least three Korean divisions had served during the Chinese Civil War before returning home to form the KPA's hardened elite. In particular, the PLA strategy of "luring the enemy in deep" closely resembled the KPA's strategic withdrawal, which was described by Chinese communist leader Mao Zedong as follows: "We have always advocated the policy of 'luring the enemy in deep,' precisely because it is the most effective military policy for a weak army strategically on the defensive to employ against a strong army."[74] Supreme Commander Kim Il Sung and much of the KPA leadership had fought alongside Mao and PLA, and many strategic concepts were thus shared. The idea that the KPA was applying this same strategy, luring UN forces deep into their territory before revealing their reconstituted divisions, thus remains plausible.

Impossible Terms: What America's Conditions for Ending Hostilities Meant for North Korea and Why this Guaranteed the War Would Continue

Following the reconquest of Seoul on September 25 and swift withdrawal of North Korean assets above the 38th parallel, the question remained whether U.S. and allied forces would halt at the original inter-Korean border or whether either the White House or Tokyo HQ would seek to press northwards and impose Seoul's and their own authority beyond South Korea's previous borders. The latter, though strongly advocated by Rhee and anti-communist hardliners in the West, was beyond the mandate of UNSC Resolution 84 and risked bringing U.S. forces to the borders of China and the Soviet Union—the former which lay little over 300km beyond the 38th parallel.

At a press conference on September 21, the day before the Second Battle of Seoul began, President Truman was asked if he had come to a decision regarding a potential move of American troops beyond the 38th parallel. United Press reported the followed day:

> He said he had reached no decision and that after all it is up to the United Nations to decide, as American troops are only part of the overall UN Army opposing the North Koreans. He promised to abide by any decisions reached by the United Nations.

With Truman under considerable pressure from prominent hardliners including MacArthur himself, his official position on invasion quickly changed. At the following week's press conference Truman "said he could not say publicly whether General Douglas MacArthur's forces would cross the 38th parallel." The word "publicly" implied that while the decision was still under debate at the UN, the president had some knowledge of the course MacArthur would take.[75] When asked whether MacArthur had the authority to order a crossing of the parallel, "Mr Truman remarked…that General MacArthur was under direct orders of the President and the Chiefs of Staff and that he would follow those orders." This fuelled speculation that the President was avoiding answering the question directly to mislead the press. A three paragraph dispatch from Washington at around the same time quoted "responsible informants" stating the Supreme Commander had been authorised by Washington "to send United Nations troops into North Korea if necessary as a military measure to destroy the power of the fleeing North Korean Army."[76] Whether coalition forces would invade the DPRK was not only not put to the United Nations, but appears to have been left to the discretion of an outstandingly hawkish general with hard-line ideological opposition to the North Korean state. MacArthur would eventually receive authorisation to cross the 38th parallel on September 27, but by this time the invasion was a *fait accompli* with U.S. troops having already deployed across the parallel on the Supreme Commander's own authority.[77]

General MacArthur's masterstroke, which decisively ended prospects for an early peace in Korea, was his pre-emption of any possible United Nations negotiation of a settlement by unilaterally demanding Pyongyang's unconditional surrender.[78] Such terms were wholly inappropriate to the situation, and it was clear from the outset that it was effectively impossible for Pyongyang to accede to them. This made the war's continuation and a U.S.-led invasion of the DPRK inevitable. As chairman of the U.S. Department of the Army's Historical Advisory Subcommittee Robert Citino noted regarding the nature of unconditional surrender and why it prolonged wars: "no self-respecting military or self-respecting state could ever submit to unconditional surrender. It's like the end of your national existence"—a consensus widely shared by military historians.[79] The United Nations could have offered to negotiate with Pyongyang directly, request a surrender on specific terms, or even sought a change in government through countrywide elections under international supervision. All these terms were more likely to have been accepted by Pyongyang than the blank cheque MacArthur had demanded they sign, which placed the future of the recently liberated nation in his hands and in those of Syngman Rhee.

MacArthur would later confirm that the American objective from the outset was not status quo ante bellum, but rather that the "mission was to clear out all North Korea, to unify it and to liberalise it."[80] The General had pledged in an impassioned speech two years prior, made at Rhee's inauguration, that the "artificial barrier" dividing Korea "must and shall be torn down,"[81] and he appeared to consistently favour offensive "rollback" action against rather than containment of communist states. As early as July, when American forces were still retreating and taking heavy losses, the General saw the final goal of a U.S. counteroffensive as being to "compose and unite Korea"—this at a time when politicians had yet to publicly voice any approval for such a move.[82] General Omar

Bradley would later insist that Washington had never issued orders of a political nature and that MacArthur's sole mission was to destroy North Korea's armed forces.[83] MacArthur thus appeared to have taken matters largely into his own hands in pursuing political objectives.

While MacArthur acted on his own accord in drafting surrender terms and sending troops into North Korea, the invasion was far from unpopular in the United States and received significant support both from both politicians and the general public. As American historian and Korea expert professor James Matray noted:

> Few Americans raised any words of opposition to MacArthur's offensive into North Korea. In fact, most commentators demanded a "final" settlement in Korea. In one senate speech the Democratic chairman of the Senate Foreign Relations Committee, Tom Connally, called upon the United Nations to reaffirm its commitment to the creation of a united Korea. Republicans were even more enthusiastic about the prospects for victory in Korea. [John Foster] Dulles explained in one private letter that "if we have the power to do otherwise, it would be folly to go back to the division of Korea at the 38th Parallel." Dulles conveyed his opinion to the administration in a memorandum to [head of the Policy Planning Staff Paul] Nitze. "If we have the opportunity to obliterate the line as a political division," he reasoned, "certainly we should do so in the interest of peace and security in the area."[84]

Another prominent advocate for invasion was the director of the Office of Northeast Asian Affairs, John M. Allison.[85] American leftists were similarly vocal in their support,[86] as were the Pentagon and State Department.[87] Thus support for what Matray referred to as the "decision to pursue the complete destruction of North Korea" notably came from across the American political spectrum.[88]

Announcing the surrender terms, General MacArthur proclaimed: "I…call upon you [the North Korean commander] and the forces under your command, in whatever part of Korea situated, forthwith to lay down your arms and cease hostilities *under such military supervisions as I may direct*." Regarding what an unconditional surrender would have meant for the North Koreans, it would have facilitated an American occupation under a client dictatorship known to massacre its own people en-masse,[89] the one which America had installed in the south under Syngman Rhee. The Rhee government had killed 2 percent of its population at the most conservative estimate over the past five years,[90] with later South Korean studies placing the death toll between 600,000 and 1.2 million.[91] The government and associated youth groups had targeted suspected leftist and nationalist sympathisers and their families indiscriminately in southern Korea, and had a vendetta against the Korean Workers Party, their families and their wide support base in the north. Rhee's government claimed sovereignty over the whole of Korea and his soldiers and militant youth groups were widely known to massacre possible communist sympathizers—let alone communists themselves—often using extremely brutal methods.[92] Rhee had made his intentions in occupying the north very clear, stating:

> I can handle the Communists. The Reds can bury their guns and burn their uniforms, but we know how to find them. With bulldozers we will dig huge excavations and trenches, and fill them with Communists. Then cover them over. And they will be really underground.[93]

Rhee's threat was far from mere rhetoric—his forces had in fact killed and buried suspected communists and dissenters and their families, including children, in their tens of thousands in mass graves in South Korea, exactly as he described, during peacetime.[94] These killings escalated immediately after the outbreak of the war, with a Reuters' dispatch reporting shortly after the war began: "Twelve hundred Communists and suspected Communists have been executed by South Korean police since the outbreak of the hostilities, Kim Tai Sun, chief of National South Korean police, said today."[95]

The Rhee government's frequent practice of burying suspected communists and their families in mass graves was widely attested to by both government and allied American sources. The U.S. 3rd Engineers Company witnessed one such an incident, with private Donald Lloyd recalling the actions of ROKAF personnel: "We heard the machine-gun fire and saw them burying them in this big pit. There were women in that pit holding babies. I'd say one hundred people."[96] CIA Operative Colonel Donald Nichols detailed in his book the systematic slaughter of political prisoners in South Korea near Suwon in the first week of July 1950 by much the same means. He wrote:

> I stood by helplessly, witnessing the entire affair. Two big bulldozers worked constantly. One made the ditch-type grave. Trucks loaded with the condemned arrived. Their hands were already tied behind them. They were hastily pushed into a big line along the edge of the newly opened grave. They were quickly shot in the head and pushed into the grave.[97]

The South Korean government's Truth and Reconciliation Commission conducted a thorough investigation into these incidents after the establishment of democratic rule in the country, several decades after Rhee's overthrow. The commission proved using declassified records that the Rhee government, with full American compliance, was responsible for extermination programs targeting suspected dissidents and their families, uncovering mass burial sites containing thousands of bodies, including many children.[98] Although the United States had knowingly falsely attributed many of the mass graves and massacres to the North Koreans, publicising footage of the remains as evidence of its enemy's war crimes most prominently in the Humphrey Bogart narrated film, *The Crime of Korea*,[99] South Korean government investigations proved that the Rhee government was in fact the perpetrator. The victims among South Korea's civilian population numbered in the hundreds of thousands in the weeks following the outbreak of the Korean War alone.[100]

Even Britain and France expressed major doubts as to whether the Rhee government was a suitable administrator for Korea should the peninsula be unified by military force—opposing his imposition on northern Korea. They claimed the ROK government had shown itself to be weak, corrupt and highly repressive and would in all likelihood "provoke a widespread terror." They questioned not only whether the Rhee government should be given control over the north, but whether it should even be allowed to retain control over the south after the war's end.[101]

Rhee's government did not recognize the DPRK, much as it had wholly dismissed the Korean People's Republic in southern Korea and the people's committees on Cheju island, so would the communist forces be treated honourably as a defeated enemy or as treasonous seditionists attempting to overthrow the "one true government of Korea?" Almost certainly the latter. Considering that an unconditional surrender would leave North Koreans at the mercy of such a leader, who had demonstrated even according to his allies gross and inhumane mistreatment of suspected dissidents and their families, it seemed that there was little if nothing to lose in fighting on—not merely out of pride but due to a basic need to survive. It was clear that General MacArthur's surrender terms could never be accepted, and that they therefore guaranteed the war would continue. The North Koreans would fight to the bitter end.

Regarding the course the Korean state would take should it be forcefully unified, the CIA had strongly advised the White House against an invasion of North Korea and particularly against imposing the Rhee government on the North Korean people. The agency noted, however, that if instead of imposing Rhee, free elections were to be held to unify the country then it would very likely bring about a communist government for the whole of Korea.[102] The *New York Times* similarly reported that free elections in Korea "would produce a communist majority, thus bringing about the same result as if the United Nations had not intervened."[103] While the United States had anointed itself the world's champion of democratic values, it was more than willing to subvert the democratic process overseas should an outcome contrary to Western interests be expected. Lawmakers from across the American political spectrum, alongside South Korean officials and others, all spoke of reunification following the forced dismantling of the DPRK, but all seemed aware that a genuine democratic process which allowed the communists to contend for power could not be allowed.[104] Warren Austin, U.S. ambassador to the UN, thus made a speech on August 17 which "revealed that the United States wants them [elections] to be held on the basis that the Republic of Korea's jurisdiction would be extended over North Korea automatically." With the Rhee government imposed as the overseer of the electoral process, a favourable outcome could be engineered—likely after the execution of the hundreds of thousands of members of the Korean Workers' Party and further executions and intimidation of their extended families.[105]

In the eyes of the North Korean leadership unconditional surrender could mean absolutely anything—including the sexual enslavement of the Korean women,[106] organized mass politicide of hundreds of thousands or more,[107] and an indefinite Western military occupation[108]—exactly what happened under the Rhee government in the south. It would mean an industrialized and fast modernizing country falling under the administration of a government which had left its people destitute and was so inept it would never draft an economic policy in its 12 years in office.[109] The North Koreans would thereby lose all say in determining their future.

Such harsh surrender terms may well have been put forward by MacArthur with the expectation that they would not be accepted. The General's desire for an expanded campaign which took the fight to China's borders, in line with his support for a "rollback" of communism and designs to return the Guomindang to power, was a significant incentive for him to seek to ensure the war would continue. MacArthur spoke openly of plans to reverse the outcome of the Chinese Civil War by force, for which control of Korea was key.[110] The General was on record, alongside many in the Pentagon and State Department, as advocating using the momentum from the Korean conflict to take offensive action against the newly formed Chinese People's Republic.[111] He maintained close ties with Taipei and would repeatedly advocate deploying sizeable Guomindang forces to the Korean front to participate in an American-led offensive[112]—something also called for by other American military leaders.[113] These factors combined with a demonstrated eagerness to advance northwards right up to the Chinese border where the risk of clashes with Chinese forces was known to be high, have been highlighted by a several analysts as indicators of MacArthur's final goal.[114]

American historian Alan Levine, who made no secret of his hard-line anti-communist position in his works, noted regarding the widespread support in the West for an invasion: "Even those who cared nothing about Korea found handing the Communists a beating emotionally satisfying."[115] With the North Koreans having caused the wholly unexpected and humiliating months-long routing of the U.S. Military, the need for vengeance against the North Korean state and people was a motivating factor. This would find often horrific expressions in the conduct of American forces towards the DPRK's population (see Chapter 7). A statement by MacArthur, though addressing the ROK rather than the DPRK, is remarkably true when applied to the latter considering the surrender terms offered: "They have chosen to risk death rather than slavery."[116]

NOTES

1 Congressional Record: Proceedings and Debates of the 82nd Congress, First Session, Appendix, vol. 97, part 15, September 18, 1951, to. October 20, 1951 (p. A6817).
2 Boggs, Carl, *Masters of War: Militarism and Blowback in the Era of American Empire,* Abingdon, Routledge, 2003 (p.205).
3 Harden, Blaine, 'The U.S. war crime North Korea won't forget,' *Washington Post*, March 24, 2015.
4 Lindqvist, Sven, *A History of Bombing*, New York, The New Press, 2001 (p. 131).
Chossudovsky, Michel, 'Know the Facts: North Korea Lost Close to 30% of its Population as a result of the U.S. Bombings in the 1950s,' *Centre for Research on Globalization*, November 27, 2010.
Deane, Hugh, *The Korean War, 1945–1953*, San Francisco, CA, China Books and Periodicals, 1999 (p. 191).
5 Garner, Dwight, 'Carpet-Bombing Falsehoods About a War That's Little Understood,' *New York Times*, July 21, 2010.
Young, Marilyn, Bom*bing Civilians from the Twentieth to the Twenty-First Centuries*, in Bombing *Civilians: A Twentieth Century History*, Tanaka, Yuki and Young, Marilyn, New York, New Press, 2009 (p. 157).
6 Cumings, Bruce, *The Korean War: A History*, New York, Modern Library, 2010 (p. 152).
7 Malik, John S., *The yields of the Hiroshima and Nagasaki nuclear explosions,* Los Alamos National Laboratory report number LA-8819, 1985.
8 Talmadge, Eric, '64 years after Korean War, North Korea still digging up bombs,' *Associated Press*, July 24, 2017.
'Legacy of Terror: Dozens of Unexploded American Bombs Found at Construction Site of Pyongyang General Hospital,' *Military Watch Magazine,* May 19, 2020.
9 Russell, Edmund, *War and Nature: Fighting Humans and Insects with Chemicals from World War I to Silent Spring*, Cambridge, Cambridge University Press, 2001 (pp. 187–188).
10 Stone, I. F., *Hidden History of the Korean War*, Amazon Media, 2014 (Chapter 7: The Stage Was Set).
11 Lie, Trygve, *In the cause of peace: seven years with the United Nations*, New York, The MacMillan Company, 1954 (Chapters 18 and 19).
12 Hazzard, Shirley, *Countenance of Truth: The United Nations and the Waldheim Case*, New York, Viking Penguin, 1990 (pp. 13–22).
Lie, Trygve, *In the cause of peace: seven years with the United Nations*, New York, The MacMillan Company, 1954 (p. 389).
13 Stone, I. F., *Hidden History of the Korean War*, Amazon Media, 2014 (Chapter 24: The China Lobby Responds).
14 Stone, I. F., *Hidden History of the Korean War*, Amazon Media, 2014 (p. 50).
15 Cotton, James and Neary, Ian, *The Korean War in History,* Manchester, Manchester University Press, 1989 (pp. 49–50).
Kim, Han Gil, *Modern History of Korea,* Pyongyang, Foreign Languages Publishing House, 1979 (pp. 306–307).
16 Blum, William, *Killing Hope: U.S. Military and C.I.A. Interventions Since World War II*, London, Zed Books, 2003 (p. 48).
17 Blum, William, *Killing Hope: U.S. Military and C.I.A. Interventions Since World War II*, London, Zed Books, 2003 (pp. 46–48).
New York Times, June 25, 1950 (page 1 for South Korean Announcement, page 3 for North Korean Announcement).
18 National Records Center, USFIK 11071 file, box 62/96, G-2 'Staff Study,' February 1949, signed by Lieutenant Colonel B. W. Heckemeyer of Army G-2.

19 Stone, I. F., *Hidden History of the Korean War*, Amazon Media, 2014 (Chapter 7: The Stage Was Set).
20 Stone, I. F., *Hidden History of the Korean War*, Amazon Media, 2014 (Chapter 7: The Stage Was Set).
21 Barnes, Robert, 'Between the Blocs: India, the United Nations, and Ending the Korean War,' *Journal of Korean Studies*, vol. 18, no. 2, 2016 (pp. 266–267).
22 *New York Times*, June 26, 1950.
23 *New York Times*, October 1, 1950 (p. 4).
24 Stone, I. F., *Hidden History of the Korean War*, Amazon Media, 2014 (Chapter 7: The Stage Was Set).
25 UN Security Council Resolution 84, July 7, 1950.
26 Eisenhower, Dwight, *The White House Years: Mandate for Change, 1953–1956*, New York, Doubleday, 1963 (p. 340).
27 Halliday, Jon, *The United Nations in Korea*, in: Baldwin, Frank, *Without Parallel: The American-Korean Relationship Since 1945*, New York, Pantheon, 1974 (pp. 130–33).
28 Stokesbury, James L., *A Short History of the Korean War*, New York, William Morrow and Company, 1988 (pp. 39, 42–43).
29 Interview with John M. Allison, New York, April 20, 1969, conducted by Richard D. Challenger, John Foster Dulles Oral History, Seely G. Mudd Manuscript Library, Princeton University Archives.
30 Cumings, Bruce, *The Korean War: A History*, New York, Modern Library, 2010 (p. 24).
31 Abrams, A. B., *Power and Primacy: The History of Western Intervention in the Asia-Pacific*, Oxford, Peter Lang, 2019 (Chapter 3: Emergence of a People's Republic in China: Efforts to Undermine the Rise of an Independent Asian Power).
32 Hearing Before the Subcommitteee on International Organisations of the Committee on International Relations, House of Representatives, Ninety-Fifth Congress, First Session, Part 1, June 22, 1977 (pp. 13–14).
33 Cumings, Bruce, *The Korean War: A History*, New York, Modern Library, 2010 (p. 14).
34 Hearing Before the Subcommitteee on International Organisations of the Committee on International Relations, House of Representatives, Ninety-Fifth Congress, First Session, Part 1, June 22, 1977 (pp. 13–14).
35 Cumings, Bruce, *Korea's Place in the Sun: A Modern History*, New York, W. W. Norton & Company, 2005 (p. 212).
36 Lowe, Peter, *The Frustrations of Alliance: Britain, The United States, and the Korean War, 1950–1951*, in Cotton, James, and Neary, Ian, *The Korean War in History*, Manchester, Manchester University Press, 1989.
37 Kwang, Sung Song, *The Impact of U.S. Military Occupation (1945–1949) on Korean Liberation, Democratization and Unification* (Ph.D Dissertation), Los Angeles, University of California, 1989 (pp. 155–160).
MacDonald, Callum, '"So terrible a liberation"—The UN occupation of North Korea,' *Bulletin of Concerned Asian Scholars*, no. 23, vol. 2 (pp. 3–19).
38 Halberstam, David, *The Fifties*, New York, Ballantine Books, 2012 (p. 71).
39 Cumings, Bruce, *The Korean War: A History*, New York, Modern Library, 2010 (p. 27).
40 Fehrenbach, T.R., *This Kind of War: The Classic Korean War History—Fiftieth Anniversary Edition*, Lincoln, Potomac Books Inc., 2001 (p.71)
41 Gugeler, Russell A, *Combat Actions in Korea*. University Press of the Pacific, 2005 (p.16).
Fehrenbach, T.R., *This Kind of War: The Classic Korean War History—Fiftieth Anniversary Edition*, Lincoln, Potomac Books Inc., 2001 (p.78)

42 Alexander, Bevin, *Korea: The First War We Lost*, New York City, Hippocrene Books, 2003 (p.66).
43 Alexander, Bevin, *Korea: The First War We Lost*, New York City, Hippocrene Books, 2003 (p.67).
44 '"Kill 'Em All": American War Crimes in Korea,' *Timewatch*, February 1, 2002.
45 Ecker, Richard E., *Battles of the Korean War: A Chronology, with Unit-by-Unit United States Casualty Figures & Medal of Honor Citations*, Jefferson, NC, McFarland & Company, 2004 (p.6)
46 Zaloga, Steven J., *T-34-85 vs M26 Pershing; Korea 1950*, Oxford, Osprey, 2010 (p. 56)
47 '"Kill 'Em All": American War Crimes in Korea,' *Timewatch*, February 1, 2002.
48 Princeton University, Dulles Papers, John Allison oral history, April 20, 1969.
Cumings, Bruce, *The Korean War: A History*, New York, Modern Library, 2010 (pp. 14–15).
49 Hastings, Max, *Korean War*, London, Michael Joseph, 1988 (p. 103).
50 Cumings, Bruce, *The Korean War: A History*, New York City, Modern Library, 2010 (p. 29).
51 'USS New Jersey (BB 62) History' in *Dictionary of American Naval Fighting Ships*, United States Navy.
52 Fehrenbach, T.R., *This Kind of War: The Classic Korean War History—Fiftieth Anniversary Edition*, Lincoln, Potomac Books Inc., 2001 (p.139).
Appleman, Roy E., *South to the Naktong, North to the Yalu: United States Army in the Korean War*, Washington, D.C., Department of the Army, 1998 (p. 416)
53 Cumings, Bruce, *The Korean War: A History*, New York, Modern Library, 2010 (p. 31).
54 Cumings, Bruce, *Korea's Place in the Sun: A Modern History*, New York, W. W. Norton & Company, 1997 (p. 275).
55 Cumings, Bruce, *Korea's Place in the Sun: A Modern History*, New York, W. W. Norton & Company, 1997 (p. 275).
56 *The Truman-MacArthur Wake Island Conference*, October 15, 1950.
Hopkins, William B., *One Bugle, No Drums: The Marines at Chosin Reservoir*, Chapel Hill, Algonquin Books, 1986 (p. 46).
57 *Time Magazine*, October 6, 1950.
Stone, I. F., *Hidden History of the Korean War*, Amazon Media, 2014, Chapter 13, 'MacArthur's Blank Check.'
58 Schobell, Andrew and Sanford, John M., *North Korea's Military Threat: Pyongyang's Conventional Forces, Weapons of Mass Destruction, and Ballistic Missiles*, U.S. Army War College Strategic Studies Institute, April 2007 (p. 62).
59 Cumings, Bruce, *The Korean War: A History*, New York, Modern Library, 2010 (p. 30).
60 Levine, Alan J., *Stalin's Last War; Korea and the Approach to World War III*, Jefferson, McFarland & Company, 2005 (p. 71)
61 Stone, I. F., *Hidden History of the Korean War*, Amazon Media, 2014 (Chapter 13: MacArthur's Blank Check).
62 *United States Army in the Korean War: Volume 4*, Washington, DC, Government Printing Office, 1961 (p. 84).
63 Hastings, Max, *Korean War* London, Michael Joseph, 1988 (p. 22).
64 Cumings, Bruce, *Origins of the Korean War: The Roaring of the Cataract, 1947–1950, Volume 2*, Princeton, NJ, Princeton University Press, 2004 (p. 693).
65 Cumings, Bruce, *Origins of the Korean War: The Roaring of the Cataract, 1947–1950, Volume 2*, Princeton, NJ, Princeton University Press, 2004 (p. 693).
Schnabel, James F., and Watson, Robert J., *The Korean War*, part I, History of the Joint Chiefs of Staff (pp. 178–181).

66 Appleman, Roy E., *South to the Naktong, North to the Yalu: United States Army in the Korean War*. Washington, D.C.: Department of the Army, 1998,(p. 393)

67 Choe, Sang Hun, 'South Korea Says U.S. Killed Hundreds of Civilians,' *New York Times,* August 3, 2008.
Rozman, Gilbert, *U.S. Leadership, History, and Bilateral Relations in Northeast Asia*, Cambridge, Cambridge University Press, 2011 (p.61).

68 Utz, Curtis, *Assault from the Sea: The Amphibious Landing at Inchon*, Washington D.C., Naval Historical Center, 1994 (p. 25).

69 Spurr, Russel, *Enter the Dragon: China's Undeclared War Against the U.S. in Korea, 1950–1951*, New York, William Morrow and Company, 2011 (p. 284).

70 Deane, Hugh, *The Korean War, 1945–1953*, San Francisco, CA, China Books and Periodicals, 1999 (pp. 112, 118).

71 Cumings, Bruce, *The Korean War: A History*, New York, Modern Library, 2010 (p. 32).

72 Ibid. (p. 32).

73 Thompson, Reginald, *Cry Korea*, London, Macdonald & Company, 1951 (pp. 39, 72).

74 Schram Stuart, *Mao's Road to Power: Revolutionary Writings, 1912–1949, Volume 4: The Rise and Fall of the Chinese Soviet Republic*, Abingdon, Routledge, 1997 (p. 374).

75 Stone, I. F., *Hidden History of the Korean War*, Amazon Media, 2014 (Chapter 16: Reversal on the Parallel).

76 Ibid. (Chapter 16: Reversal on the Parallel).

77 Cotton, James and Neary, Ian, *The Korean War in History*, Manchester, Manchester University Press, 1989 (p.67).

78 Stone, I. F., *Hidden History of the Korean War*, Amazon Media, 2014 (Chapter 16: Reversal on the Parallel).

79 Citino, Robert and Byers, Samuel, 'Why Did the German Army Fight to the End?,' Talk for the *Project of Military and Diplomatic History* at the *Centre for Strategic International Studies*, Headquarters, Washington D.C., March. 6, 2018.

80 Matray, James I., 'Truman's Plan for Victory: National Self-Determination and the Thirty-Eighth Parallel Decision in Korea,' *The Journal of American History*, vol. 66, no. 2, 1979 (p. 332).

81 *New York Times*, August 18, 1948

82 MacArthur to Joint Chiefs of Staff, July 7, 1950, Korea File 1, Box 2, RG 6, MacArthur Papers.
Truman, Harry S., *Memoirs, Vol. II: Years of Trial and Hope*, Garden City, Doubleday, 1956 (p. 347).
MacArthur, Douglas, *Reminiscences*, New York, McGraw, 1964 (p. 337).
Collins, J. Lawton, *War in Peacetime: The History and Lessons of Korea*, Boston, Houghton Mifflin, 1969 (pp. 82–83).
Schnabel, James F., *Policy and Direction: The First Year*, Washington, Office of the Chief of Military History, United States Army, 1972 (pp. 106–7).

83 Matray, James I., 'Truman's Plan for Victory: National Self-Determination and the Thirty-Eighth Parallel Decision in Korea,' *The Journal of American History*, vol. 66, no. 2, 1979 (p. 332).

84 Ibid. (p. 331).

85 John M. Allison to Dean Rusk, July 1, 1950, Washington, Department of State, Foreign Relations of the United States: 1950, vol. VII: Korea, 1976 (p. 272).

86 Hamby, Alonzo L., *Beyond the New Deal: Harry S. Truman and American Liberalism*, New York, Colombia University Press, 1973 (p. 407).

87 Bodenheimer, Thomas and Gould, Robert, *Rollback!: Right-wing Power in U.S. Foreign Policy,* Boston, South End, 1989 (p. 18).

88 Matray, James I., 'Truman's Plan for Victory: National Self-Determination and the Thirty-Eighth Parallel Decision in Korea,' *The Journal of American History*, vol. 66, no. 2, 1979 (p. 331).

89 'The Background of the Present War in Korea,' *Far Eastern Economic Review*, August 31, 1950.
Cumings, Bruce, *The Korean War: A History*, New York, Modern Library, 2010 (p. 189).

90 Ibid. (p. 189).
Hanley, Charles J., and Change, Jae-Soon, 'Summer of Terror: At least 100,000 said executed by Korean ally of U.S. in 1950,' *The Asia-Pacific Journal*, Volume 7, Issue 7, July 2, 2008.

91 '최소 60만명, 최대 120만명!,' ['More than 600,000, less than 1,200,000!,'] *Hankyoreh,* June 20, 2001.

92 Kim, Monica, *The Interrogation Rooms of the Korean War; The Untold History,* Princeton, NJ, Princeton University Press, 2019 (pp. 231–232, 236).
Kim, Seong Nae, "The Cheju April Third Incident and Women: Trauma and Solidarity of Pain," paper presented at the Cheju 4.3 Conference, Harvard University, April 24–26, 2003.
Nichols, Donald, *How Many Times Can I Die?,* Brooksville, FL, Brooksville Printing, 1981 (pp. 119–120).

93 Rhee quoted by president of United Press International Hugh Baillie in: Baillie, Hugh, *High Tension: the Recollections of Hugh Baillies*, London, Thomas Werner Laurie, 1960.
MacDonald, Callum, '"So terrible a liberation"—The UN occupation of North Korea,' *Bulletin of Concerned Asian Scholars,* no. 23, vol. 2 (pp. 3–19).

94 *The Times* (UK), December 18, 21 and 22, 1950.
Cumings, Bruce, *The Korean War: A History*, Modern Library Edition, 2010 (pp. 168, 181).

95 Stone, I. F., *The Hidden History of the Korean War* (Chapter 16: Reversal on the Parallel).

96 Hanley, Charles J. and Choe, Sang Hun, and Mendoza, Martha, *The Bridge at No Gun Ri: A Hidden Nightmare from the Korean War*, New York, Henry Holt and Company, 2001 (p. 169).

97 Nichols, Donald, *How Many Times Can I Die?* Brooksville, FL, Brownsville Printing Co., 1981.

98 Spencer, Richard, 'More than 100,000 massacred by allies during Korean War,' *The Telegraph*, December 29, 2008.

99 Cumings, Bruce, *The Korean War: A History*, Modern Library Edition, 2010 (p. 177).

100 Shaines, Robert A., *Command Influence: A story of Korea and the politics of injustice*, Denver, CO, Outskirts Press, 2010 (p. 54).

101 Cumings, Bruce, *The Korean War: A History*, 2010 Modern Library Edition (p. 179).

102 Hanley, Charles J. and Choe, Sang Hun, and Mendoza, Martha, *The Bridge at No Gun Ri: A Hidden Nightmare from the Korean War*, New York, Henry Holt and Company, 2001 (p. 170).

103 Stone, I. F., *Hidden History of the Korean War*, Amazon Media, 2014 (Chapter 17, 'Free Elections?').

104 Matray, James I., 'Truman's Plan for Victory: National Self-Determination and the Thirty-Eighth Parallel Decision in Korea,' *The Journal of American History*, vol. 66, no. 2, 1979 (pp. 331–332).

105 Stone, I. F., *Hidden History of the Korean War*, Amazon Media, 2014 (Chapter 17: Free Elections?).

106 Moon, Katherine H. S., *Sex Among Allies*, New York, Colombia University Press, 1997.

107 Cumings, Bruce, *The Korean War: A History*, New York, Modern Library, 2010 (p. 189).

108 Bandow, Doug, 'Why Are U. S. Troops Still in Korea?' *Forbes*, May 3, 2011.
Rebuilding America's Defenses, Strategy, Forces and Resources For a New Century, A report of the Project for the New American Century, September 2000 (p. 18) (see for U.S. intention to maintain forces on the Korean Peninsula even after reunification to project power on the Asian mainland).

109 Heo, Uk, and Roehrig, Terence, *South Korea Since 1980*, Cambridge, Cambridge University Press, 2010 (p. 18).
Henderson, Gregory, *The Politics of the Vortex*, Cambridge, MA, Harvard University Press, 1968 (pp. 348–349).

110 Philips, Steve, *The Cold War: Conflict in Europe and Asia,* Oxford, Heinemann, 2001 (pp. 71–72).

111 Epstein, Israel, *My China Eye: Memoirs of a Jew and a Journalist,* San Francisco, Long River Press, 2005 (p. 251).
Bodenheimer, Thomas and Gould, Robert, *Rollback!: Right-wing Power in U.S. Foreign Policy,* Boston, South End, 1989 (p. 18).

112 Levine, Alan J., *Stalin's Last War; Korea and the Approach to World War III,* Jefferson, McFarland & Company, 2005 (p. 193)

113 BBC Summary, Far East, No. 221, January 23, 1953.

114 Scott, Daniel, 'An Old Soldier's View Of The Early Cold War, 1949–1953,' Theses and Dissertations, Illinois State University, 2015.

115 Levine, Alan J., *Stalin's Last War; Korea and the Approach to World War III,* Jefferson, McFarland & Company, 2005 (p. 93)

116 Douglas MacArthur's Farewell Address to Congress, April 19, 1951.

Chapter 4
THE BATTLEFIELD MOVES TO NORTH KOREA—AND CHINA

A Note on Naming of Warring Parties

While more commonly used terminologies in Western scholarship to refer to the two warring parties are "the Communists" and the "UN Forces," an assessment of these terms reveals them to be somewhat misleading regarding the true nature of the belligerents and the conflict itself. The fundamental cause for the revolutions in North Korea and China, and the primary reason why the Koreans and the Chinese were fighting, was not to preserve a certain social or economic system—but rather to assert their right to national dignity, sovereignty and independence which had long been denied to Asian states under the Western dominated order. They will therefore be identified by their national identities rather than their ideological affiliations, as is more fitting given the nature of their struggle.

The "forces of the United Nations" meanwhile would indicate some form of international consensus and a united cause of world powers—but the true nature of the force was nothing of the kind. As previously mentioned, the organisation was founded as an initiative of the U.S. State Department and there was little doubt that it was a heavily Western dominated body. The four permanent Security Council members in attendance included three Western states and the losing side of the Chinese civil war—now an effective Western protectorate controlling under 0.5% of Chinese territory. States with greater independence from Western influence such as Yugoslavia and India notably did not support the UN force—although they too were heavily reliant on U.S. aid. The UN force was itself placed under the direct command of the U.S. Military which answered to Washington rather than the UN.

To refer to the war as one fought by the United Nations, therefore, is to mask its true nature—as a war fought by the Western Bloc alongside a number of its client states to suppress East Asian resistance to Western domination. The terms "East Asian Allies" and "U.S.-led coalition" are thus used in their stead to give a more accurate picture of the nature of the belligerent parties. These refer respectively to the Chinese and North Korean allied force and the predominantly Western coalition operating under American command.

Invading North Korea and Provoking China: How the U.S. Turned a Prospective Victory into a Second Routing

The first U.S. troops crossed into North Korean territory on September 26, with paratroopers dropped from the air by the 21st Airlift Squadron operating from Tachikawa Airbase in Japan. The Joint Chiefs of Staff and President Truman would only authorize the invasion the following day.[1] U.S.-led coalition forces subsequently advanced across northern Korea rapidly, with the KPA providing little resistance and continuing its strategic withdrawal. The advance was met with much apprehension in neighbouring China. On October 1st, in an address at the first anniversary of the founding of the People's Republic of China, Premier Zhou Enlai warned that his country would not "supinely tolerate" an invasion of North Korea. Despite strong rhetoric however, Beijing appeared eager to avoid war and would intervene only when its own territorial integrity was directly threatened.

Regarding China's propensity to intervene in the defence of its neighbour, the CIA provided President Truman with a top-secret report on October 12th titled: *Threat of Full Chinese Intervention in Korea* (ORE 58-50). The document stated: "Despite statements by Chou [Zhou] Enlai [and] troop movements to Manchuria…there are no convincing indications of an actual Chinese Communist intention to resort to full scale intervention in Korea." The agency report further noted: "such action is not probable in 1950…the most favorable time for intervention in Korea has passed." The CIA observed, as many did at the time, that had China sought to support the DPRK, the provision of even limited material assistance could have turned the tide at the Pusan perimeter in August—let alone a large manpower contribution.

With the approach of U.S.-led forces openly hostile to the new Chinese republic, and its leaders pledging to "roll back" communism, Beijing feared for the security of its Manchurian industrial centres on the Korean border, which included key power plants the two countries used jointly. Having spent 13 years under the Japanese Empire, which had prioritized industrial development in its Northeast Asian territories with impressive results, Manchuria was by far the most industrialized and developed area of China and a vital part of the nation's economy. A *New York Times* correspondent at the time pointed out that the Yalu River power plant on the border with Korea "has been supplying electrical power for the Manchurian industrialization program," which the Chinese regarded as their "pilot zone" for nationwide industrialization. This industrial zone was thus of great importance to Beijing. A detachment of Chinese infantry was deployed to form a thin buffer on the Korean border to protect Beijing's vital industrial interests. To avoid risks of a direct conflict with the U.S., these forces were deployed under the Chinese People's Volunteer Army (PVA)—the thirteenth corps under General Peng Dehuai—rather than from the main armed force of the PRC, the People's Liberation Army.

U.S.-led coalition forces for their part, fully aware of the presence of Chinese ground troops, continued to advance rapidly towards them ignoring Chinese concerns regarding the security of its industrial zone. On October 16, General Peng reinforced border units by dispatching the 42nd Army of the PVA, followed by troops from the 370th Regiment. This too failed to deter the coalition advance, with U.S. forces simultaneously spearheading an assault on the North Korean capital Pyongyang which was captured on October 20. Subjected to an intensive bombing campaign by the U.S. Air Force, population centres in the DPRK from the capital to small hamlets had been thoroughly ravaged, with the KPA making little effort to defend them in order to avoid direct confrontation with the overwhelming capabilities of its enemy and instead continuing its ordered withdrawal north. The fall of Pyongyang thus came quickly and with relatively few losses for the invading force.

What is perhaps most notable about China's early deployment of PVA forces to form a buffer south of the border to protect its power plants was that reports of this deployment were censored from American media. As a result, when reports emerged that Chinese forces had been engaged in Korea, they made it seem as if an act of Chinese aggression had taken place and the PVA had assaulted coalition forces from their side of the border. It was in fact U.S.-led coalition forces on October 25 which had approached Chinese lines, where the PVA had been known to be operating for over a week, close to the Sino-Korean border. The resulting battle ended in a Chinese victory, the complete disintegration of the South Korean 2nd Infantry Regiment, and the capture of two U.S. Army officers.[2] The defeat of these forward deployed units was insufficient to stall the advance of coalition forces, with a joint U.S., British and Australian force encountering minor KPA resistance at Chongju just 80km from the Chinese border on October 29 and continuing to press their advance northwards.

As U.S.-led coalition forces continued to advance towards Chinese lines, chances of further direct clashes continued to increase. October 25 saw the beginning of the Battle of Unsan, a ten-day clash between the PVA and two elite U.S. Cavalry regiments, the 5th and 8th, with South Korean support. The result was a routing of the U.S. Army and their ally, with heavy casualties estimated at between 1680 and 2000—the vast majority of them American. [3] Chinese forces were estimated by UN Command to have taken over 600 casualties.[4] The battle ended on November 4, with the PVA advancing from the Chinese border and beginning to capture ground from retreating coalition forces. In a show of strength, Chinese forces began to fly MiG-15 jet fighters over the border regions from November 1st. Chinese forces sought to avoid escalation, and while they had proved effective in repelling hostile advances on their positions they still avoided actively engaging U.S. forces with their aircraft.

Seeking to negotiate peace in the aftermath of their overwhelming victory at Unsan, the PVA abruptly broke contact with coalition forces on November 5 rather than pressing their advantage with a pursuit. General MacArthur for his part, apparently aware of the importance of industrial assets on the Sino-Korean border to Beijing, recommended the following day that the large Yalu River hydroelectric dam vital to the Manchurian economy should be bombed if Chinese forces refused to withdraw from Korea unconditionally.[5] The Sui Ho dam represented one of the largest economic assets in Japanese Manchuria, and had the third largest power station in the world and the largest outside the United States. China's moves to deescalate were met with a positive response from the United Nations, with the UN Interim Committee on Korea issuing a statement on November 7 "to reassure the Chinese Communists regarding their interests on the Korean-Manchurian border." China quickly responded, and on the same day Tokyo HQ released that: "Chinese and North Korean troops in a surprise manoeuvre broke contact with United Nations forces on the defence line north of Anju this morning."[6] These Chinese moves were widely interpreted by American analysts as intended to reduce tensions at the expense of the PVA's own advantageous position in order to facilitate the opening of peace talks with the United Nations.[7]

MacArthur's headquarters did not seem to welcome the ending of hostilities and asserted that a withdrawal must be taking place with the intention to "regroup large concentrations of…communist troops for a new onslaught rather than retreat." The withdrawal from combat had to be depicted as having aggressive intent.[8] This narrative was quickly undermined, however, with the People's Volunteer Army maintaining a defensive line which within two weeks had persuaded most of the American command that China's intentions were not aggressive. Staff members of the U.S. Eighth Army increasingly ascribed China's motive for intervention as nothing more than the protection of its industrial infrastructure, including its vital hydropower plants, located on the Yalu River.[9] Over two weeks after the PVA broke contact with U.S. forces, the U.S. Army X Corps intelligence reported on November 22 that Chinese forces were "apparently preparing to make a defensive stand in his present positions," and that there was "no evidence to indicate any considerable number of [PVA] units have crossed the border since the initial reinforcement."[10]

With the PVA having sacrificed the opportunity to press an offensive southward using the considerable momentum from their prior victories, or to reinforce their forces in Korea with additional units, Beijing had engineered a lull in the fighting from which peace may well have emerged through direct negotiations. By November 8, a Chinese delegation was set to arrive at peace talks with the United Nations, which would begin a week later on the 15th. For MacArthur, now close to the Chinese border and with what were widely perceived to be sufficient assets not only to expel the PVA from Korea, but to bring about the total capitulation of the Chinese People's Republic, the prospects for a negotiated peace threatened prospects for a rollback of communism that he desired. This was particularly true given the likelihood that at least a partial withdrawal of the U.S. military presence in northern Korea would be a likely outcome of negotiations. Thus, on November 8, just hours before the first round of UN peace talks were set to begin, a new and very significant provocation was announced.

A U.S. Air Force spokesman in Washington announced on November 8: "an earlier ban against flights within three miles of Manchuria" put in place to avoid provocation of China had been lifted and that "United States pilots in Korea are operating right up to the Chinese border along the Yalu River." A devastating attack soon made it clear why the words "are operating," rather than "may operate" as would normally be the case when lifting regulations, were used. The target was Sinuiju, a Korean city which lay right on the Chinese border, over which 79 B-29 Superfortress bombers and three fighter planes flew that day. This massive formation carried several hundred tons of ordinance and indiscriminately obliterated the city. The American attack was "said to have destroyed ninety percent of the city" using "rockets, demolition bombs, and 85,000 incendiaries."[11] The scenes were reminiscent of the firebombing of Tokyo five years prior, with the very same weapons again being used to ravage a densely populated East Asian city.

It later emerged that MacArthur had personally ordered the bombing of "every means of communication, every installation, factory, city and village" in North Korea on November 5—which was agreed to by the Joint Chiefs of Staff.[12] That day eight North Korean Yak-9 fighters attacked an American bomber unit—with Soviet accounts claiming five B-26 and one B-29 bomber downed and the Americans claiming damage to just two bombers. The Koreans suffered no losses.[13] Unlike the Chinese the KPA had far fewer reservations about employing its air power, which appeared to have now been replenished but was still extremely limited, against the adversary. MacArthur's directive for indiscriminate attacks on population centers and infrastructure across northern Korea was announced three days later on November 8 and christened with the ravaging of Sinuiju. The result was a renewed bombing campaign against the population of North Korea.

The destruction wrought by large scale firebombing raids was comparable to and often exceeded that of nuclear attack—depending on the warhead, weather conditions and the building materials used in the target population centre. The *New York Times* reported regarding the firebombing of Sinuiju on November 8: "the attack came almost simultaneously with an announcement by an Air Force spokesman in Washington that United States fliers had received permission to bomb right up to the Manchurian border instead of remaining three miles south in an attempt to avoid possible frontier violations."[14] Considering the preparation such a large strike force would need and the timing and circumstances of the bombing, it is highly likely that the attack had been planned and prepared long before authorization was been given—if not that the bombers had already been dispatched by that time. It was another *fait accompli* by MacArthur's HQ, a provocation staged just when there was a chance for peace and the Chinese evidently sought de-escalation and a negotiated settlement. A massive attack on a civilian population centre in a particularly sensitive area was the best way disrupt the peace process.

American journalist I. F. Stone, assessing the policy of MacArthur's headquarters, the effect on the civilian population, and what he concluded were attempts by the supreme commander to quash prospects for a negotiated peace with China, reported:

> Just when there was a lull in the fighting and it looked as if peace were possible, MacArthur staged a gigantic and murderous raid directly across from the Chinese frontier, destroying most of a city in an area where bombings had been forbidden to prevent border violations. He had gotten the Air Force to lift the bombing restriction—how, when or why nobody knows. Perhaps he did it by starting the raid first and asking permission afterwards…this is what he is reported to have done the very first week of the war, in forcing the President to "allow" him to bomb north of the 38th parallel. "There were reports," the *New York Times* said, "that General MacArthur had ordered the first bombings of North Korean cities without authorization from Washington."
>
> The pretext for the raid was "to eliminate Sinuiju as a future stronghold for supplies and communications." This was stated in the announcement later issued by Lieutenant General George E. Stratemeyer, commander of the Far East Air Forces. The description based on the briefing in Tokyo is not pleasant reading. The attack began in the morning "when fighter planes swept the area with machine guns, rockets and jellied gasoline bombs." They were followed by "ten of the superforts" which "dropped 1000-pound high-explosive bombs on railroad and highway bridges across the Yalu River and on the bridge approaches" (if dropped on the bridges as well as the approaches, the bombers were obviously operating right up to the boundary line on the river itself). After this, "the remaining planes used incendiaries exclusively on a two and one-half mile built-up area along the southeast bank of the Yalu." General Stratemeyer maintained that all targets were of a military nature and bomb runs "had kept away from the city's hospital areas." At the same time the Air Force claimed ninety percent of the city had been destroyed. How

> these statements can be reconciled I do not know. There is an indifference to human suffering to be read between those lines which makes me as an American deeply ashamed of what was done that day at Sinuiju.
>
> Tokyo Headquarters, with or without connivance by Washington, ravaged a city when a truce was in prospect. It deliberately took action which might have provoked a third world war—when the Chinese, of whose intervention it complained, were withdrawing. That the military knew what they were doing is indicated by a short Associated Press dispatch from Seoul which was printed the same day as the news of the mass raid on Sinuiju. A United States Eighth Army spokesman said that "Chinese Communist troops might be avoiding fighting in North Korea pending high level diplomatic moves that would affect the course of the Korean War." This spokesman stated that the withdrawal of the Chinese in the northwest "has been gradual over a four-day period" while in the northeast "a Tenth Corps spokesman said the Chinese 184th Division was 'in retreat' from the giant Changjin hydroelectric complex." If the Chinese were even abandoning their dams, they must have wanted peace badly. Was the mass raid intended to goad them to war?
>
> The mass bombing raid on Sinuiju November 8 was the beginning of a race between peace and provocation. A terrible retribution threatened the peoples of the Western world who so feebly permitted such acts to be done in their name. For it was by such means that the pyromaniacs hoped to set the world afire.[15]

While the beneficiaries of continued hostilities may have hoped that, in response to the massacre of Sinuiju's population on November 8, Beijing would withdraw from peace talks or order the PVA under General Peng to launch a renewed assault, the Chinese and North Koreans appeared to endure the obliteration of the city without significant response. With prospects for peace nevertheless diminished by the bombing raid, America's most powerful coalition partner, Great Britain, moved quickly to draft a peace plan to bring the conflict to a swift conclusion. This was presented by Prime Minister Clement Attlee and Foreign Secretary Ernest Bevin, and proposed the establishment of a buffer zone through

North Korean territory between Chinese People's Volunteer Army and U.S.-led coalition forces—which would extend 60 to 100 miles south of the Yalu River which divided Korea and China.[16] The peace proposal was widely criticized in the United States—with the notion of a basic concession to the Western Bloc's new adversaries drawing comparisons to the Munich Agreement of 1938 which had acknowledged the Nazi German annexation of Czechoslovakia.[17] General MacArthur in particular was highly vocal in his outrage at the peace plan, relaying that "to yield to so immoral a proposition would bankrupt our leadership and influence in Asia and render untenable our position both politically and militarily."[18]

Ultimately MacArthur, much like Rhee, appeared to seek only a military solution which would end in the United States asserting its authority over both East Asian states and dictating terms. The possibility for compromise which could save lives was consistently dismissed out of hand. As Chairman of the Joint Chiefs of Staff General Omar Bradley observed: "the only possible means left to MacArthur to regain his lost pride and military reputation was now to inflict an overwhelming defeat on those Red Chinese generals who had made a fool of him. In order to do this, he was perfectly willing to propel us into an all-out war with Red China and possibly the Soviet Union."[19] MacArthur thus chose to press the offensive through provocation of the inoffensive adversary, continuing to target PVA with bombs and incendiaries[20] and attempting to dispatch troops to the Chinese border—which the U.S. Army X Corps 7th Division briefly achieved on November 21st.[21] General Peng continued to respond with restraint, with the PVA conducting basic defensive manoeuvres when necessary but refraining from major counter-offensives. While Tokyo HQ was going to great lengths to avoid a truce, the Chinese appeared to be doing everything they could to facilitate a quick and peaceful solution. On November 22, in a gesture of goodwill, Chinese forces released 27 wounded American prisoners of war—delivering them to the care of the U.S. Army.[22] The American response was further escalation.

On November 22, General MacArthur announced that he expected that the Korean War would be over by the end of the year, which given his rejection of peace proposals provided some indication that a major new offensive was being prepared to force the East Asian Allies to yield to his terms. He further announced plans for the formal integration of northern Korea into the Republic of Korea—which was expected to commence as soon as the peninsula could be placed under his complete control.[23] The offensive materialized on November 24 in an all-out assault on Chinese positions—again escalating hostilities after the PVA had gone to great lengths to engineer a de-escalation seventeen days prior. The "Home By Christmas Offensive" saw hundreds of thousands of coalition forces, primarily U.S. Army I Corps and IX Corps divisions with limited British, Turkish and ROK support, press northwards with massive air support provided by the U.S. Fifth Air Force.

The American military leadership, despite its forces' previous three-month routing by the KPA and subsequent losses to the PVA, had again made the mistake of grossly underestimating their Northeast Asian adversaries. Despite its immense material advantages, the "Home By Christmas Offensive" ended in disaster for the coalition. What the offensive did achieve, however, was a wearing out of the patience of the Chinese—bringing a final end to prospects for an early negotiated solution without a full-scale confrontation between the PVA and the U.S. Military on the peninsula. The Chinese military leadership from that stage onwards committed their forces to the full recovery of northern Korea and restoration of the DPRK up to the 38th parallel.

The Second Routing of the U.S. Military

The fate of the "Home By Christmas Offensive," as massive as it was ambitious, was effectively decided in the Battle of Ch'ongch'on River—a week long confrontation with the Chinese PVA starting on November 25. The battle pitted over 254,000 coalition forces against 230,000 Chinese troops,[24] and saw the outnumbered and outgunned People's Volunteer Army attempt a counteroffensive against their enemy—which if successful would blunt the U.S.-led attack and turn the momentum of the wider campaign against them. With no substantial air units of their own capable of contesting air superiority or launching airstrikes, Chinese units were forced to rely heavily on the cover of night. The destruction of the U.S. Eighth Army's right flank and effective collapse of the South Korean II Corps allowed Chinese troops outflank their enemy, and by December 2, eight days, later they had won a decisive victory and routed coalition forces.

While U.S.-led coalition forces benefitted from superior numbers, it was hardly their only major advantage. Again the massive capacity of the American defence sector, which uniquely for a major industrial power was wholly unscathed by war, provided a vast superiority in weaponry which was thought to guarantee an American victory. The Chinese, by contrast, had seen their country devastated by a war with Japan, by a civil war, and by preceding decades of conflict both among warlords and with Western powers. The country's manufacturing and military industrial bases were thus negligible, failing to provide not only heavy weapons, aircraft or naval vessels, but even small arms matching the calibre of the Americans. The PVA was forced to rely either on weapons captured from Japanese imperial forces or those American weapons which had been sent as aid to the Guomindang forces during the Civil War.[25] Even basic equipment such as armoured vests gave U.S. forces a distinct advantage, reducing casualties by 30 percent. The Chinese had no such luxury.[26] The PVA victory, despite a significant numerical disadvantage and without armour, artillery or air support which the Americans had in abundance, thus came as a surprise at Ch'ongch'on—the first major victory by a Chinese force over a Western army in over a century and the first large battle waged by the forces of the new Chinese People's Republic.

Losses at Ch'ongch'on had taken the coalition's Turkish Brigade, four South Korean divisions and most of the U.S. Eighth Army out of action—leaving just two Army corps combat ready.[27] The U.S. Eighth Army alone was estimated to have suffered over 11,000 casualties against the Chinese,[28] with Turkish and South Korean forces also losing several hundred men. Major General Laurence B. Keiser, a veteran of both world wars, was relieved of his command following the battle's conclusion.[29] Defeat at Ch'ongch'on ended prospects for U.S.-led coalition forces to hold on to territory so far north of the 38th parallel and so near the Chinese border, and U.S. Eighth Army Commander General Walton Walker ordered the retreating forces to stage a complete withdrawal from North Korean territory the day after the battle concluded on December 3.[30]

Simultaneously to the Battle of Ch'ongch'on, a smaller engagement pitting two forces of over 100,000 troops against one another occurred at Chosin Reservoir. The battle began two days after Ch'ongch'on and ended sixteen days later in an overwhelming victory for the Chinese PVA and the Korean People's Army—again against overwhelming odds. Chinese and Korean forces' lack of any significant air or air defence assets had allowed the U.S. air units to take a particularly high toll on their numbers, and bombardment from the sky was very heavy. There were never less than 24 F4U Corsair aircraft pounding their positions with guns and napalm—sometimes as many as sixty—and these were not the only Western aircraft operating.[31] The sub-freezing temperatures meanwhile took a serious toll on the Chinese and Korean forces—which were scantily clad and supplied relative to their adversaries. Up to 90 percent of the People's Volunteers involved suffered some form of frostbite, with the 27th Army taking thousands of non-combat casualties as a result, which supplemented the overwhelming material advantages of the U.S. and its allies.[32] A document from the PVA 27th Army from November 1950, which U.S. forces claimed to have captured, stated regarding the difficulties faced at Chosin: "a shortage of transportation and escort personnel makes it impossible to accomplish the mission of supplying the troops. As a result, our soldiers frequently starve…they ate cold food and some had only a few potatoes in two days. They were unable to maintain their physical strength for combat; the wounded could not be evacuated. The firepower of our entire army was basically inadequate." Tinnitus and a wholly deficient signal communication network further undermined the Chinese war effort, according to PVA reports.[33]

British Military Historian Max Hastings reported regarding the crippling disadvantage faced by the PVA in the winter months:

> The men of the UN complained of the difficulty of fighting the ferocious cold as well as the enemy. But the winter was neutral. The Chinese were far less well-equipped to face the conditions than their opponents, possessing only canvas shoes and lacking such indulgences as sleeping bags. General Peng's casualties from frostbite dwarfed those of the Americans. And the Chinese could expect no ready evacuation or medical care.[34]

Where a swift and absolute coalition victory had been expected, the "Home By Christmas Offensive" resulted in decisive defeat and heavy casualties at its two most major battles, Ch'ongch'on and Chosin, and further losses in smaller engagements such as the three day Battle of Wawon. The U.S. and its allies were forced into a full retreat which came to be known as The Big Bugout.

Hastings compared the collapse of the divisions of the U.S. Eighth Army to that of the French in 1940 and the British in Singapore in 1942—both large forces which despite considerable material advantages had ceased to function as fighting forces in the face of adversity. He wrote regarding the surprise of PVA and KPA victories:

> Most Americans expected Chinamen to be dwarves, but they found themselves assaulted by units which included men six feet and over. Yet the enemy wreaking such havoc with the Eighth Army was still, essentially, fighting a large-scale guerrilla war [in that it was] devoid of all the heavy firepower every Western army considered essential. It was a triumph not merely for the prestige of Communism, but for that of an Asian army… From [General Walton] Walker's headquarters to Tokyo [command centre] and on to the Joint Chiefs' offices in the Pentagon, there was bewilderment and deep dismay about the collapse of the Eighth Army. For public consumption, the sheer surprise and weight of the Chinese offensive were emphasized. But professional soldiers knew that these were not enough to explain the headlong rout of an army that still possessed absolute command of sea and air, and firepower on a scale the communists could not dream of. The Chinese victories were being gained by infantry bearing small arms and regimental support weapons—above all mortars. The Americans had been subjected to very little artillery fire, and no air attack whatsoever.[35]

American Lieutenant Colonel Roy E. Appleman wrote regarding the ability of Chinese forces to engage U.S. and other allied troops in a climate more brutal than the Battle of Stalingrad despite significant material disadvantages:

> Looking at the other side of the hill…one cannot withhold some admiration, and humanitarian sympathy, for the Chinese peasants who made such great effort and sacrifice in trying to carry out their orders. One must say of them that Sung's IX Army Group did some spectacular things. It fought without air support, it had no tanks or artillery and almost no heavy mortars, it had poor and almost nonexistent ammunition after the first day or two of battle and no food or ammunition resupply once it crossed the Yalu River…and it possessed no adequate footgear for the feet or mitten for the hands of its soldiers in an arctic clime… In fact, the operations were a mismatch of a fine modern, mechanized body of soldiery against a peasant army of light infantry—but one that was

> highly mobile and expert at night fighting. The best weapons the Chinese possessed were the American Thompson submachine guns, 81mm mortars, grenades, and rifles they had captured from Chiang Kaishek's armies… Yet they did drive the X Corps completely out of northeast Korea and occupied and held henceforth that part of the country. No American troops ever returned there.[36]

The decisive defeat of coalition forces shifted the calculus of the U.S. Military leadership dramatically, leading to their not only abandoning ambitious goals for absolute victory in northern Korea but even drafting contingency plans for the a complete withdrawal from the peninsula.[37] President Truman, seeking to reassure the indignant General MacArthur, sent him a letter on January 12th to restore some heart. He assured the Supreme Commander that even if the Korean Peninsula was lost, the campaign would be continued from offshore islands.[38] Such a strategy closely resembled the case in China a year prior, where U.S. and Guomindang forces would continue serious harassment and at times offensives against the mainland for over two decades using a network of bases on outlying islands centred around Taiwan.[39] A second option was the use of nuclear arms against Chinese and North Korean assets, which Truman confirmed on November 30 was under active consideration.[40]

The performance of Chinese forces and their victories despite every material disadvantage stunned the West, much as the victories of the KPA had before them.[41] Such overwhelming Asian victories against Western armies in turn undermined theories of Western supremacy which had been the basis for regional and global order for centuries. Max Hastings observed regarding the way Chinese used their tactical and combat skills to compensate for their vast material disadvantages:

> The undoubted Chinese skills as tacticians, night-fighters, navigators, masters of fieldcraft and camouflage, caused even many senior [UN] officers to forget the enemy's huge disadvantages in resources and firepower. Worse, the leaders of the UN forces in Korea found themselves facing the stark fact that, man for man, most of their troops were proving nowhere near as hardy, skilful, and determined upon the battlefield as their communist opponents. It is difficult to overestimate the

psychological effects of this conclusion upon strategic and tactical decision-making.[42]

The U.S. Army Second Division published the following regarding the strengths of the Chinese soldier, and his ability to operate with far less firepower and supplies:

> He is well and courageously led at the small unit level and the results of actions at this level offer definite proof that he is thoroughly disciplined. His conduct of the defense is accomplished in spite of UN air superiority, UN liaison aircraft and inferior communications equipment. He is operating on a shoestring basis as is evidenced by the hodge-podge of equipment piled up on the battlefield after every encounter.[43]

This bore a stark contrast to perceptions of East Asian military potential before the war. By contrast to the Chinese forces' ability to make do with very little, General Matthew Ridgway, who would succeed MacArthur as Supreme Commander, referred to American personnel as "pampered troops."[44] He noted "the unwillingness of the army to forgo certain creature comforts, its timidity about getting off the scanty roads, its reluctance to move without radio and telephone contact, and its lack of imagination in dealing with a foe whom they so outmatched in firepower and dominated in the air and on the surrounding seas."[45]

With the PVA for the first time taking to a prolonged offensive, coalition forces were forced to make the longest retreat in United States military history.[46] While Chinese forces advanced, seeking to evict coalition forces from northern Korea while themselves under intensive bombardment from the air, Beijing continued diplomatic efforts to end hostilities. On December 3, the same day as the U.S. Marines reported that the Korean town Huksu had been "wiped off the map" by air attack due to a suspected PVA presence,[47] the Chinese made a major release of wounded American prisoners. Also that day, four soldiers of the British Army saw their weapons carrier stall north of Pyongyang—forcing them to drop out of a retreating convoy. Expecting capture or death, the soldiers were found by the PVA who helped the British push their truck and restart their engine. An English-speaking Chinese soldier reassured them: "we don't want to hurt you guys. We just want you to get off the peninsula."[48] Assessment of reports from both sides indicates such actions were not reciprocated.

The coalition retreat continued through the first four weeks of December, with the British 29th Independent Infantry Brigade the last to leave Pyongyang on December 5, which was subsequently recaptured by PVA and KPA forces. Civilian infrastructure in the North Korean capital was destroyed entirely as part of the American scorched earth policy. Before the war Pyongyang had a large number of factories manufacturing primarily textiles, shoes, food products, tobacco, wine, beer and fertilizers—with an opera house, nine theatres, 20 cinemas, seven universities and over 100 schools. Little of this remained when the city was retaken, not due to collateral damage from fighting which had been minimal—but rather as part of systematic program to deny the DPRK the benefits of its prior economic development. Many of the buildings were themselves of little military value but could have been used to rehouse the millions the bombing campaign had left homeless. All Pyongyang's tram cars, bridges, schools and its water system were intentionally destroyed beyond repair, and the city was scattered with hidden time-bombs.[49] A large airstrike on its eastern airport was carried out on December 10,[50] and further bombings of Pyongyang would continue throughout the war to undermine rebuilding efforts.

The Hungnam evacuation, which commenced on December 11, named after the North Korean port city where the withdrawal took place, saw 105,000 coalition personnel and considerable war materials evacuated from northern Korea. These included the elite 1st Marine Division which had spearheaded the assault on Inchon, two of the Army X Corps' infantry divisions, the 1st Marine Air Wing and two South Korean divisions. The PVA and KPA made no serious efforts to interfere with the withdrawal, which continued over a period of 15 days and saw 350,000 tons of cargo and 18,422 military vehicles redeployed.[51] Again facilitated by its vast military industrial base, America's massive superiority in logistical assets was key to facilitating this successful withdrawal by air and sea. On December 17, U.S. forces evacuated Yonpo Airfield, a captured North Korean airbase near the 38th parallel and one of the final coalition strongholds in northern Korea. Somewhat ironically, given the deadline of Christmas Day set by the U.S. Military leadership for a final victory, by December 25, PVA and KPA forces had reached the 38th parallel and began to mass their forces there. The second stage of the Korean War, the battle to protect the DPRK's sovereignty, was over. The coalition, with the exception of Syngman Rhee's hard-line government, had effectively conceded at least a temporary defeat of their ambitions in the northern half of Korean in the wake of the devastating Chinese-led counteroffensive.

While the momentum for a further offensive south was on their side, and the PVA and KPA had consistently demonstrated battlefield superiority over their adversaries, the limitations of their logistics and strain on their supply lines would make any further offensives southwards difficult against the more numerous and better armed and supplied coalition forces. The flow of food, fuel, munitions and other vital war materials was further impeded by American air superiority, which saw supply routes intensively bombarded. Logistical difficulties for the PVA resulting primarily from the deindustrialised and war-ravaged state of China's economy was arguably the most critical factor which prevented it, with Korean support, from going on to force a full withdrawal of U.S. and coalition forces from the peninsula. According to General MacArthur, Chinese supply lines could support 1 million troops at the Sino-Korean border where initial engagements had taken place. At Pyongyang this fell to 600,000; at the 38th parallel it fell to 300,000; by the time they reached 40 miles south of Seoul this fell to just 200,000, leaving Chinese and Korean forces impossibly outnumbered.[52] The Supreme Commander's assertions were supported by statements from the Chinese military leadership. Hu Seng, a member of General Peng Dehuai's staff, stated to similar effect: "while we wished to continue to push the enemy, we could not open our mouth too wide… China was unprepared for the new military situation created by the deep advance. We were now in a position where we could not continue to reinforce our army in Korea."[53]

The martial power of Chinese soldiers sharply contrasted with the PVA's material weakness, with the former heavily compensating for the latter and allowing them to operate with a small fraction of the supplies and armaments of the Western powers.[54] Where PVA supply lines were strained, the devastation of North Korea under an intensive American firebombing campaign and subsequent scorched earth policy on retreat made supplying its forces near impossible for the North Koreans without external assistance. Pyongyang had not anticipated or prepared for a full-scale war with the United States and lacked adequate reserve supplies of food or of war materials. Nevertheless, the quick routing of U.S.-led coalition forces may have imbued the PVA and KPA with a degree of overconfidence, which led them to briefly attempt an offensive southwards.

Chinese Prime Minister Zhou Enlai had implied to Indian ambassador K. M. Panikkar, who served as a conduit for messages between Beijing and Washington, that while China was "eager to know the whole opinion of the USA and the UN regarding conditions for an armistice," it would continue its offensive until the U.S. was willing to begin peace talks. "As to the 38th parallel issue, it has long since been violated by the American invading armies and MacArthur, and is no longer in existence," he had said. Beijing's patience had been thoroughly tested the month before, and with the U.S. refusing repeated overtures for peace proposed by China, Great Britain and the UN, a further offensive was perhaps the only means by which to force the Americans to reach an accommodation.[55]

On December 26, a joint PVA-KPA contingent crossed the 38th parallel, and two days later engaged the U.S. Military at Kaesong. The battle ended quickly in an overwhelming Chinese and Korean victory. Seoul was put to siege soon afterwards on December 31st, and U.S. forces operating with British, Australian, South Korean and Thai support were successfully routed within eight days by the PVA's 13th Army and KPA's I Corps. The U.S.-led coalition again had considerable numerical superiority to back up their material advantage, with 136,500 personnel from the U.S. Army backed by tens of thousands of allied forces, including three whole South Korean divisions, facing an army of approximately 170,000 Chinese and North Koreans.[56] They were nevertheless routed from the city and again forced to retreat southwards. A day after the third Battle of Seoul began, a three-day battle for the city of Uijeongbu saw a joint British and Australian force withdraw with light casualties—conceding further ground to the PVA-KPA offensive. Morale among coalition forces reportedly sank to its lowest point in early January.[57]

Facing considerable criticism over its failures, Tokyo HQ on January 9 "replied by suddenly imposing censorship regulations far more severe than any known in World War II," with even speculation as to the reasons for censorship strictly forbidden. The purpose appeared to be to boost flagging morale both domestically and on the front, and to allow the military to downplay future defeats.[58] State Secretary Dean Acheson had called for reports on the devastating impacts of the American bombing campaign on Korean civilians to be censored since November, and the need to cover up the ongoing mass killings of civilians also likely motivated the unprecedentedly harsh new restrictions put in place.[59]

Advancing so far south of the Yalu River, the unmechanised Chinese and Korean force operating under American controlled skies and without an airlift capacity of its own saw its already strained supply lines further stretched. Casualties among KPA and PVA forces were considered light, but their frontline capabilities weakened the further south they pressed due to the strain on logistics.[60] This was further exacerbated by the initiation of "Interdiction Campaign No. 4" by the U.S., which aimed to use its air superiority to attack supplies in transit over northern Korea.[61]

The tide began to turn against the East Asian allies just two weeks after their victory in Seoul. On January 8, the U.S. 2nd Infantry was ordered to mount a counteroffensive against KPA and PVA forces in Wonju, with 80,000 U.S. troops backed by three European battalions and two ROKAF Army Corps engaging a smaller predominantly Korean force of around 61,500 personnel.[62] The outnumbered Korean and Chinese units were forced to retreat on January 20—taking the vast majority of casualties from air and artillery strikes to which they were unable to respond. The coalition's capture of Wonju secured the eastern flank of the retreating U.S. Eighth Army, which logistical constraints had prevented KPA and PVA from pursuing. Under new and more competent leadership from General Matthew Ridgway, the Eighth Army was thus able to regroup for a counteroffensive and launch a renewed assault on Chinese and Korean positions under Operation Thunderbolt.

Thunderbolt was launched on January 25 and saw the beginning of three weeks of clashes between U.S.-led coalition and East Asian allied forces in which both sides suffered heavy casualties. The U.S.-led offensive was comprised of American, Turkish and South Korean units and saw a force of almost 100,000 push back PVA and KPA forces northwards over the Han River—establishing a more defensible perimeter.[63] The operation's success was limited by staunch resistance and a number of Chinese counterattacks which were often highly costly for the Americans, with coalition forces gaining ground at a slow pace. Alongside the advances made under Thunderbolt, the U.S. Army X Corps spearheaded a similar offensive northwards with South Korean and French support under Operation Roundup, winning a decisive victory at the Battle of Twin Tunnels on February 1st and making promising initial advances.

The situation on the frontline quickly developed into a rapid series of offensives and counteroffensives with few major changes in the lines of battle. The KPA and PVA leadership responded to the loss of ground in early February with counteroffensives (counter-counter-counteroffensives to the "Home By Christmas Offensive"), engaging the X Corps and routing them at the Battle of Hoengsong from February 11 to 13 in which coalition forces suffered heavy casualties of approximately 12,000 men. Casualties for this battle were approximately one third this number for the East Asian Allies, which lost a little over 4,100 men according to American sources.[64] Momentum from this victory, however, was soon lost with coalition victories at the Third Battle of Wonju and the Battle of Chipyong Ri—both of which began on February 13.

The two-day Battle of Chipyong Ri concluded on February 15, and saw a small Chinese force inflict heavy casualties in close quarter fighting before being shattered by napalm bombardment. American control of the air and to a lesser extent its access to battle tanks proved decisive here. For the PVA, which had reportedly expected coalition forces to retreat in the wake of their losses at Hoengsong, the defeat at Chipyong Ri came as a surprise.[65] The simultaneous battle at Wonju saw a KPA-led offensive achieve initial successes against the U.S. Army X Corps and supporting South Korean assets, but eventually lose momentum largely due to a scarcity of supplies. General Ridgway, who commanded the coalition, took measures to increase oversight of the ROKAF due to South Korea units' prior tendency to abandon their positions and compromise coalition actions.[66] U.S. forces heavily fortified the town in preparation for an expected assault. The East Asian allies never made any serious attempt to capture Wonju however, engaging in skirmishes in the surrounding countryside before withdrawing on February 18. The nature of their objective remains unclear. The battles at Chipyong Ri and Wonju marked the height of Chinese and North Korean joint penetration below the 38th parallel.

Defeats at the hands of his East Asian adversaries led Supreme Commander MacArthur to propose more extreme escalatory solutions—including the contamination of Chinese and Korean territory with radioactive waste to stop PVA and KPA troop movements.[67] On February 22, he urged the Joint Chiefs of Staff to support anti-government insurgents in China and to make preparations for an eventual landing of Guomindang forces with American support near Shanghai.[68] Radioactive contamination was deemed overly provocative and impractical—particularly now that the United States had lost its monopoly on nuclear arms to the USSR, while the Guomindang were deemed in no shape to fight China even with America's backing. They had repeatedly proven wholly incompetent despite vast material advantages and massive American support during the Chinese Civil War, and an invasion of China risked provoking Soviet intervention. Support for anti-government forces within China, however, would become a staple of U.S. policy towards the country for the next two decades.[69]

The U.S. Military leadership responded to the slowdown of the PVA-KPA offensive with an offensive of their own, initiating "Operation Killer" under General Ridgway's command on February 20 with the intention of destroying all enemy forces east of the Han River up to the artificial "Arizona Line" established between Yanpyeong and Hoengsong. The Arizona Line lay 90km under the 38th parallel and pressing PVA and KPA forces in this sector back towards the inter-Korean border was seen as a vital first step towards a larger and more ambitious pushback. The Chinese and Koreans for their part withdrew northwards, allowing Ridgway's forces spearheaded by the X Corps and IX Corps to establish themselves on the Arizona Line by March 6 with relatively few casualties on either side.

Operation Killer was immediately followed by the initiation of "Operation Ripper" on March 7, which saw more intensive fighting as coalition forces again pressed northwards and attempted to recapture the South Korean capital, Seoul. Although the ROKAF failed in many of their key objectives, the U.S. Eighth Army succeeded in recapturing the city, which changed hands for the fourth time during the war. KPA and PVA forces appeared increasingly willing to fall back northwards given the difficulty of sustaining an offensive so far south, using terrain to their advantage to delay coalition forces. Before the operation's conclusion in early April, coalition forces had already initiated "Operation Courageous" which involved parachuting the U.S. Army I Corps from over 100 C-119 and C-46 transports to positions 30km north of the frontlines—making use of airlift capabilities and air superiority to strategically redeploy assets to encircle the KPA and PVA. The East Asian allies' almost complete lack of air cover or air defense capabilities meant that none of the slow and bulky American aircraft were lost. U.S. forces then spearheaded an offensive northwards, which saw the KPA and PVA quickly withdraw from most of their positions and reestablish their frontline near the 38th parallel. Losses among the East Asian allies were very light compared to the initial expectations of the U.S. and their coalition partners, and KPA and PVA units evaded encirclement multiple times and succeeded in withdrawing with their forces largely intact.[70] The successive American offensives had gained them approximately 80km of ground, which the KPA and PVA became increasingly aware it would be near impossible to hold given the state of their supply lines, the vulnerability of both ground forces and supply convoys to air attacks and the overwhelming advantages in both manpower and firepower of the U.S.-led coalition.

The Chinese and North Koreans attempted one final offensive to recapture Seoul, known as the "Chinese Spring Offensive," which saw far larger forces massed at the 38th parallel and, from April 22, launch a 30-day assault. This was PVA Commander in Chief Peng Dehuai's final attempt to rout the U.S. and their coalition forces, amassing an estimated 700,000 men of which 270,000 were dispatched to attack Seoul—the III, IX and XIX Army Groups. Although they had amassed a considerable force in terms of manpower, the East Asian allies' newfound frontline numerical advantage was only slight—with 200,000 men serving as a strategic reserve and the remaining 500,000 facing approximately 420,000 coalition troops on the front. The immediate objective was to force a major American retreat as the PVA and KPA had done in November, although logistical issues and the new leadership of the coalition made this extremely difficult. Supreme Commander MacArthur, for his failure to respect the authority of the president and repeated military provocations of both China and the Soviet Union on his own authority, had been dismissed on April 11 with General Ridgway taking his place effective immediately.

While the KPA and PVA made gains during the Spring Offensive, they were ultimately turned back due to the coalition's effective use of air power and unprecedentedly intensive artillery bombardments which caused unsustainable casualties. The disproportionately high quantities of artillery U.S. forces deployed during this period of the conflict—five times the standard numbers—combined with the ever present strain on KPA and PVA supply lines exacerbated by Western air attacks, ended prospects for a routing of the U.S.-led force south of the 38th parallel.[71] Again, however, the U.S.-led coalition's hopes of eliminating KPA and PVA forces were frustrated by the quick and orderly nature of the Asian allies' withdrawal once their offensive had proven unsuccessful. What followed was an effective stalemate approximately along the 38th parallel, with each side holding some territory on the enemy's half of the dividing line.

NOTES

1 Cotton, James and Neary, Ian, *The Korean War in History*, Manchester, Manchester University Press, 1989 (p.67).

2 Appleman, Roy E., *South to the Naktong, North to the Yalu: United States Army in the Korean War*, Washington D.C., Department of the Army, 1998 (p. 674, 691)

3 Ecker, Richard E., *Korean Battle Chronology: Unit-by-Unit United States Casualty Figures and Medal of Honor Citations*, Jefferson, McFarland, 2005 (p. 47).
Chae, Han Kook and Chung, Suk Kyun and Yang, Yong Cho and Yang, Hee Wan and Lim, Won Hyok and Sims, Thomas Lee and Sims, Laura Marie and Kim, Chong Gu and Millett, Allan R., *The Korean War, Volume II*, Lincoln, NE, University of Nebraska Press, 2001 (p.124).
Chinese Military Science Academy 抗美援朝战争史 [*History of War to Resist America and Aid Korea], Volume II*, Beijing, Chinese Military Science Academy Publishing House, 2000 (p.35).

4 McMichael, Scott R., *A Historical Perspective on Light Infantry*, Fort Leavenworth, KS, US Army Combined Arms Centre, 1987 (Chapter 2: The Chinese Communist Forces in Korea)

5 'China Crisis Appealed to U. N. Council,' *Chicago Daily Tribune*, November 7, 1950 (p.1)

6 Stone, I. F., *Hidden History of the Korean War*, Amazon Media, 2014 (Chapter 24: The China Lobby Responds).

7 Ibid. (Chapter 24: The China Lobby Responds).

8 Ibid. (Chapter 24: The China Lobby Responds).

9 Appleman, Roy E., *South to the Naktong, North to the Yalu: United States Army in the Korean War*, Washington D.C., Department of the Army, 1998 (p. 755)

10 Ibid. (p. 756)

11 Stone, I. F., *Hidden History of the Korean War*, Amazon Media, 2014 (Chapter 24: The China Lobby Responds).
Merrill, Frank J., *A Study of the Aerial Interdiction of Railways During the Korean War*, Normanby Press, 2015 (Chapter V).

12 Acheson, Dean G, *Present at the Creation: My Years in the State Department*, London, W. W. Norton, 1969 (pp. 463, 464).
Far Eastern Air Forces HQ to MacArthur, 8 November 1950, RG 6 FECOM Box 1, General Files 10, Correspondence Nov-Dec 1950, MACL.

13 Seidov, Igor and Britton, Stuart, *Red Devils over the Yalu: A Chronicle of Soviet Aerial Operations in the Korean War 1950–53*, Warwick, Helion and Company, 2014 (p.63).

14 Stone, I. F., *Hidden History of the Korean War*, Amazon Media, 2014 (Chapter 24: The China Lobby Responds).

15 Ibid. (Chapter 24: The China Lobby Responds).

16 Farrar, Peter N., 'Britain's Proposal for a Buffer Zone South of the Yalu in November 1950: Was It a Neglected Opportunity to End the Fighting in Korea?,' *Journal of Contemporary History*, April 18, 1983 (p.66).
White, Brian, *Britain, Detente and Changing East-West Relations*, Abingdon, Routledge, 2002 (pp. 40–41).

17 'Britain Seeks a Munich with Chinese Reds,' *Chicago Daily Tribune*, November 22, 1950 (p.1).

18 Edwards, Paul M., *United Nations Participants in the Korean War: The Contributions of 45 Member Countries*, Jefferson, NC, McFarland, 2013 (p.32).

19 Halberstam, David, *The Fifties*, New York, Ballantine Books, 2012 (p. 113).
Ward, Greg, *The Rough Guide History of the USA*, London, Rough Guides, 2003 (p.287).

20 Latham, Jr., William C., *Cold Days in Hell: American POWs in Korea*, College Station, A&M University Press, 2012 (pp. 82, 118–119)
21 Kleiner, Jürgen, *Korea, a Century of Change*, Singapore, World Scientific, 2001 (p.78)
22 'Peace Rumors in Tokyo,' *Chicago Daily Tribune*, November 23, 1950 (p.1)
23 'End of War by January Seen by MacArthur,' *Chicago Daily Tribune*, November 23, 1950 (p.1).
24 Appleman, Roy, *Disaster in Korea: The Chinese Confront MacArthur*, College Station, Texas A and M University Military History Series, 1989 (p. 40).
Roe, Patrick C., *The Dragon Strikes*, Novato, Presidio, 2000 (p. 223).
25 Deane, Hugh, *The Korean War, 1945–1953*, San Francisco, CA, China Books and Periodicals, 1999 (p. 128).
26 Did You Know, Land of the Morning Calm, The Korean War, Veterans Affairs Canada, Government of Canada. (http://www.veterans.gc.ca/eng/remembrance/history/korean-war/land-morning-calm/didyouknow).
27 Mossman, Billy C., *Ebb and Flow: November 1950—July 1951, United States Army in the Korean War*, Washington D.C., Center of Military History, United States Army, 1990 (p.150).
28 Chae, Han Kook and Chung, Suk Kyun and Yang, Yong Cho and Yang, Hee Wan and Lim, Won Hyok and Sims, Thomas Lee and Sims, Laura Marie and Kim, Chong Gu and Millett, Allan R., *The Korean War*, Volume II, Lincoln, NE, University of Nebraska Press, 2001 (p.283).
29 Appleman, Roy E., *South to the Naktong, North to the Yalu: United States Army in the Korean War*, Washington D.C., Department of the Army, 1998 (p. 290–291)
30 Mossman, Billy C., *Ebb and Flow: November 1950—July 1951, United States Army in the Korean War*, Washington D.C., Center of Military History, United States Army, 1990 (p.150).
Appleman, Roy E., *South to the Naktong, North to the Yalu: United States Army in the Korean War*, Washington D.C., Department of the Army, 1998 (p. 312).
31 Levine, Alan J., *Stalin's Last War; Korea and the Approach to World War III*, Jefferson, McFarland & Company, 2005 (p. 134)
32 Hastings, Max, *Korean War*, London, Michael Joseph, 1988 (pp. 170–171).
33 McKelvey Cleaver, Thomas, *The Frozen Chosen: The 1St Marine Division and the Battle of Chosin Reservoir*, London, Bloomsbury, 2016 (p.257–258).
34 Hastings, Max, *Korean War*, London, Michael Joseph, 1988 (p. 171).
35 Ibid. (p. 170).
36 Appleman, Roy E., *Escaping the Trap: The U.S. Army X Corps in Northeast Korea, 1950*, College Station, TX, A&M University Press, 1990 (pp. 367–368).
37 Brown, Ronald J., *Counteroffensive: U.S. Marines from Pohang to No Name Line*, Quantico, Virginia, History and Museums Division, Headquarters, U.S. Marine Corps, 2001 (p.1–2).
38 Hastings, Max, *Korean War*, London, Michael Joseph, 1988 (p. 280).
39 *Two CIA Prisoners in China, 1952–1973*, Central Intelligence Agency, April 5, 2007.
Washington Post, August 20, 1958.
McGhee, Ralph W., *Deadly Deceits: My 25 Years in the CIA*, New York, Sheridan Square Press, 1983.
40 Truman, Margaret, *Harry S. Truman*, New York, William Morrow & Company, 1973 (pp. 495–496).
'USE OF A-BOMB IN KOREA STUDIED BY U.S.—TRUMAN,' *Pittsburgh Press*, November 30, 1950 (p. 1).
The President's New Conference, November 30, 1950, The American Presidency Project, University of California at Santa Barbara.
41 Hastings, Max, *Korean War* London, Michael Joseph, 1988 (p. 22).
42 Ibid. (p. 171).

43 Hermes, Walter G., *Truce Tent and the Fighting Front*, Washington D.C., Center of Military History, 1992 (p. 511).
44 PRO London WO216/63 836.
45 Malkasian, Carter, *The Korean War*, New York, Rosen, 2009 (p. 36).
46 Edwards, Paul M., *The Korean War*, Santa Barbara, Greenwood Publishing Group, 2006 (p. 25).
47 'Missing: One Korean Town, after Marine Flyers Go to Work,' *Chicago Daily Tribune*, December 4, 1950 (p. 2)
48 'Chinese Reds Help 4 Tommies Start up Truck,' *Chicago Daily Tribune*, December 4, 1950 (p. 2).
49 *We Accuse: Report of the Committee of the Women's International Democratic Federation in Korea, May 16–27, 1951*, Berlin, Women's International Democratic Forum, 1951 (pp. 5–6).
50 Futrell, Frank, *The United States Air Force in Korea, 1950–1953*, Office of Air Force History, 1983 (p. 263).
51 Mossman, Billy, *Ebb and Flow, November 1950–July 1951*, Washington D.C., United States Army Center of Military History, 1990 (p. 167).
X Corps Command Report Summary, December 1950.
Field Jr., James A., *History of U.S. Naval Operations: Korea*, Washington D.C., Government Printing Office, 1962 (pp. 289–290).
52 Hastings, Max, *Korean War*, London, Michael Joseph, 1988 (p. 190).
53 Ibid. (pp. 190–191).
54 Hermes, Walter G., *Truce Tent and the Fighting Front*, Washington D.C., Center of Military History, 1992 (p. 511).
55 Wilson Center Digital Archive, *December 13 1950, Telegram from Zhou Enlai to Wu Xiuquan and Qiao Guanhua* (Accessed May 28, 2019).
56 Appleman, Roy E., *Ridgway Duels for Korea*, College Station, Texas A & M University Press, 1990 (pp. 40–42).
57 Appleman, Roy E., *South to the Naktong, North to the Yalu: United States Army in the Korean War*, Washington D.C., Department of the Army, 1998 (p. 83)
58 Stone, I. F., *Hidden History of the Korean War*, Amazon Media, 2014 (Chapter 32: Seoul Abandoned Again).
59 Cumings, Bruce, *North Korea: Another Country,* New York, New Press, 2003 (pp. 17–18).
60 Zhang, Shu Guang, *Mao's Military Romanticism: China and the Korean War, 1950–1953*, Lawrence, Kansas, University Press of Kansas, 1995 (p.131).
61 Shrader, Charles R., *Communist Logistics in the Korean War*, Westport, Greenwood Press, 1995 (pp. 175–176).
62 Appleman, Roy E., *Ridgway Duels for Korea*, College Station, Texas A & M University Press, 1990 (pp. 42, 99).
63 Appleman, Roy E., *South to the Naktong, North to the Yalu: United States Army in the Korean War*, Washington D.C., Department of the Army, 1998 (Chapter Seven: Transition: Eighth Army in the West).
64 'Ambush at Hoengsong,' *Time,* March 12, 1951.
65 Hooker Jr., Richard, *Essays on Command in Battle,* Combat Studies Institute Press, U.S. Army Combined Arms Center, Fort Leavenworth, Kansas (p. 142).
Chinese Communist Forces, Headquarters XIX Army Group, 'A Collection of Combat Experiences,' (29 March 1951 Critique of Tactics Employed in the First Encounter with the Enemy at Chipyong-ni, Annex Number 1 to Periodic Intelligence Report Number 271, 2nd Infantry Division, translated by ATIS, 29 June 1951) (pp. 2–4).
66 Ltr, Eighth Army IG to CG Eighth Army, 12 Mar 51, sub: Report of Investigation Concerning the Loss of Equipment by X Corps.

S ROKA, 15 Feb 51., Eighth Army SS Rpt., Office of the CG, Feb 51, Incl 14; Rad, GX-2-1551 KGOO, CG Eighth Army to C/S ROKA, 15 Feb 51; Eighth Army G3 Jnl, Sum, 15 Feb 51; Eighth Army G3 Briefing for CG, 16 Feb 51; Hq, FEC, History of the North Korean Army, 31 Jul 52.

67 Tucker, Spencer C., *The Encyclopaedia of the Korean War: A Political, Social, and Military History Volume I*, Santa Barbara, ABC-CLIO, 2010 (p. 645).

68 Levine, Alan J., *Stalin's Last War; Korea and the Approach to World War III*, Jefferson, McFarland & Company, 2005 (p. 193)

69 Abrams, A. B., 'Power and Primacy: The History of Western Intervention in the Asia-Pacific,' Oxford, Peter Lang, 2019 (Chapter 3: Emergence of a People's Republic in China: Efforts to Undermine the Rise of an Independent Asian Power).
Blum, William, *Killing Hope: U.S. Military and C.I.A. Interventions Since World War II*, London, Zed Books, 2003 (Chapter 1: China 1945 to 1960s: Was Mao Tse-tung just paranoid?).

70 Levine, Alan J., *Stalin's Last War; Korea and the Approach to World War III*, Jefferson, McFarland & Company, 2005 (pp. 185–186)

71 Ibid. (pp. 200–201)

Chapter 5

ABSOLUTE DESTRUCTION: THE RAVAGING OF NORTH KOREA

Firebombing as a Weapon of Mass Destruction

One aspect of the conduct of the United States during the Korean War which would leave a particularly profound impression on the North Korean nation was the intensive and indiscriminate targeting of population centres from the air. Modelled on the campaign which had brought ruin to 67 Japanese cities in a matter of months, the firebombing of Korea would be a continuous aspect of the war over three years. The aforementioned details of the bombing of Sinuiju on November 8, 1950 thus represented part of a much wider phenomenon, with population centres across the country similarly targeted.

Taking Sinuiju as an example, the town had 126,000 inhabitants and 14,000 buildings, and housed light industries producing civilian goods such as soya, tofu, shoes, matches, salt and chopsticks.[1] None of its industries contributed to production of war materials. According to data published by an international commission present in North Korea at the time, a single American firebombing raid in November destroyed 2,100 of the 3,017 state and municipal buildings, 6,800 of 11,000 houses, 16 of 17 primary schools, and 15 of 17 places of worship. Eighty percent of deaths caused by the bombing were women and children,[2] as thousands of men had been conscripted into the Korean People's Army after the Inchon landings. In hospitals patients were burned to death in their beds by incendiary bombs. The attack appeared intended to maximize casualties, beginning with incendiaries, followed by explosives, followed by a combination of incendiaries and time bombs. This specific combination and series of bombings was designed to prevent inhabitants from doing any rescue work, thereby maximizing casualties among the targeted population. As a result, many of those who were buried alive could not be reached and died of suffocation.[3] Hospitals which were properly marked to be visible from 6,000–8,000 meters were found to have been intentionally targeted.[4]

Incendiary attacks in Sinuiju were followed by strafing attacks, with low flying American aircraft gunning down civilians who went outdoors either to escape or to put out the fires. Young children were also targeted in this way.[5] The town was hardly the first or the last targeted in this way, and a three year long firebombing campaign against the civilian population would exact a terrible death toll and destroy 85 percent of buildings in the country.[6] By late 1950 the U.S. Air Force alone was dropping 800 tons of munitions on North Korea daily, much of it pure napalm,[7] with considerable further sorties flown by the Navy and by British, Australian and South African air units. Attesting to the bombing campaign's wholly indiscriminate nature, Assistant State Secretary Dean Rusk stated that it would target "everything that moved in North Korea, every brick standing on top of another."[8] There was little pretence that bombs and napalm were only intended for soldiers and munitions factories—the entire population from rice farmers in the countryside to Sinuiju's shoemakers were all condemned to death by fire.

The bombing campaign's intensity had within weeks caused a shortage of targets, threatening to leave the Air Force idle.[9] Head of the Bomber Command in Asia General Emmett O'Donnell, who formerly oversaw the firebombing of Tokyo, testified that within three months of the war's outbreak: "almost all the Korean peninsula" was "just a terrible mess." As a result of the air campaign "everything is destroyed. There is nothing standing worthy of the name… There were no more targets in Korea."[10]

Award winning journalist I. F. Stone reported on the bombings of civilian targets, including those in northern Korea and those in the south suspected of harbouring a KPA presence:

> September, 1950, Far East Air Forces Headquarters announced that the first stage of its bombing program, aimed at industrial installations, was complete, and that there was now a "paucity" of industrial targets for bombers. One of the problems which began to trouble the Air Force in Korea, judging by the communiqués, was that there was nothing left to destroy. These communiqués must be read by anyone who wants a complete history of the Korean War. They are literally horrifying.
>
> "Crews on the B-26 light bombers of the 452nd Bomb Wing," said the Fifth Air Force operational summary at 5

> P.M. Tokyo time, January 31, "reported a scarcity of targets at Hamhung today." According to Staff Sergeant Clark V. Watson of Hutchinson, Kansas, "It's hard to find good targets, for we have burned out almost everything."
>
> Other Air Force units were still managing. "The Eighth Fighter Bomber Wing F-80 jets," said the same communiqué, "reported large fires in the villages in the western sector following attacks with rockets, napalm, and machine guns. A village was hard hit south of Chorwon." Why was not explained. Whether the village represented some military objective was not stated. Sometimes a possible military objective seemed to have been hit by accident. In the same communiqué it was announced that the navigator of one of the light bombers that attacked Pongung near Hamhung reported: "One of our napalms must have hit a gas or oil dump. It landed and there was a big belch of orange flame and black smoke." Peasants do not detonate so colourfully.
>
> Sometimes the reason offered for bombing a defenceless village was that it was "enemy-occupied." The same communiqué said, "One flight dive-bombed the enemy occupied village of Takchong and then rocketed and strafed the area, reporting several buildings destroyed and large fires started." Were all villages in enemy territory regarded as enemy-occupied? The ratio of civilian to soldier dead in these raids must have been very large. This same communiqué said the "largest claim of troops casualties inflicted" in the day's raids were 100 enemy troops killed or wounded by one group of planes. Even in a small village more civilians than that could be killed in one raid. A complete indifference to the noncombatants was reflected in the way villages were given "saturation treatment" with napalm to dislodge a few soldiers.[11]

Napalm was a leading weapon in the American arsenal, and 32,557 tons of it were dropped on North Korea—the largest use in history.[12] The effects of these attacks were far more devastating than they would be when used in Vietnam in later years, not only due to the quantities employed but also due to the DPRK's greater vulnerability as a result of its far more developed and industrialised economy and the resulting greater numbers of densely populated targets.[13] The U.S. Air Force saw napalm as a "wonder weapon" for the massive casualties it inflicted,[14] although British Prime Minister Winston Churchill was among the vocal foreign opponents of its use against civilian targets on moral grounds. Churchill stated in reference to American napalm attacks against Korean civilians: "I do not like this napalm bombing at all. A fearful lot of people must be burned, not by ordinary fire, but by the contents of the bomb... Napalm in the war was devised by us and used by fighting men in action... No one ever thought of splashing it all over the civilian population. I will take no share in the responsibility for this."[15] The British Prime Minister had himself shown no qualms about bombing population centres,[16] had declared himself "strongly in favour"[17] of and personally ordered the use of chemical weapons, and had personally approved the development of biological weapons for use against enemy population centres.[18] The fact that he protested the use of napalm as morally reprehensible bore testament to the severity of the Korean people's suffering under it.

A report on the effects of napalm surfaced when American Private James Ransome Jr.'s unit suffered an accidental "friendly" hit by the substance. This "wonder weapon" fired by their own forces had the same impact on these American personnel as it did on countless thousands of Korean civilians. The American soldiers rolled in the snow in agony and begged to be shot, as their skin burned to a crisp and peeled back "like fried potato chips." These hits were only partial, and reporters in Korea saw countless cases of civilians drenched in napalm—their whole bodies "covered with a hard, black crust sprinkled with yellow pus."[19] One napalm survivor interviewed stated regarding its effects: "Napalm is the most terrible pain you can imagine. Water boils at 100 degrees Celsius. Napalm generates temperatures of 800 to 1,200 degrees Celsius."[20] The incendiary sticks to human skin and cannot be removed. Burns are severe and can be subdermal. When the *New York Times* had described the effects of napalm on Korean civilian population centres, State Secretary Acheson had called for such "sensational reporting" to be censored.[21]

Physician Richard Perry, having spent years treating its victims, would write years later regarding napalm's horrific effects on civilian targets:

> I have been an orthopaedic surgeon for a good number of years, with a rather wide range of medical experience. But nothing could have prepared me for my encounters with... women and children burned by napalm. It was shocking and

> sickening, even for a physician, to see and smell the blackened flesh. One continues for days afterward getting sick when he looks at a piece of meat on his plate because the odour of burning flesh lingers so long in the memory. And one never forgets the bewildered eyes of the silent, suffering, napalm-burned child. What could anyone possibly say to such a child?[22]

The firebombing campaign targeting Korean civilians itself represented part of a wider trend in the U.S.-led order in East Asia, with states across the region which resisted Washington's hegemonic ambitions seeing their population centres similarly targeted. This ranged from relatively minor bombing raids by CIA pilots against Indonesian cities later in the 1950s[23] to massive firebombing raids against Japanese cities the previous decade and similar raids on Vietnamese and Laotian cities the following decade. Indeed, firebombing of Korean population centres had such high tolls largely because the U.S. had refined its technique over Japan to achieve an optimal combination of munition types.

The U.S. Military's propensity to target Asian population centres of little strategic value was demonstrated in all cases. In November 1968, for example, American bombers would target population centres in Laos after they were prevented from reaching targets in North Vietnam. Although there was no strategic value in doing so, the U.S. Deputy Chief of Mission Monteagle Stearns testified to the U.S. Senate Committee on Foreign Relations the following year regarding the Air Force's reason for doing so: "Well, we had all those planes sitting around and couldn't just let them stay there with nothing to do."[24] During the Korean War, American pilots were similarly ordered to target South Korean population centres suspected of harbouring a KPA presence with rockets not for any strategic benefit—but because it was better to use the rockets on a target "rather than carry them home."[25] It was forces commanded under such a mindset with the same value for the lives of Asian peoples, both allied and enemy, to which the Korean population was subjected.

The entry of Chinese forces into the war saw the bombing campaign against population centres further escalate. Journalist Robert Jackson stated that following the PVA's entry into the war: "there was to be no attempt at ultra-precise bombing to avoid high civilian casualties. The B-29s were to carry full loads of incendiaries and their task was to burn the selected cities from end to end."[26] General Ridgway, for one, demanded bigger napalm bombs be quickly developed for use against Korean targets, 1,000-pound versions which could "wipe out all life in the tactical locality."[27] There was little doubt that the vast majority of casualties would be Korean civilians. The U.S. claimed that firebombing population centres would erode morale and thus end the war sooner. This notably failed in Japan,[28] and would fail in Korea, but was repeated again to fail in Vietnam. Repetition of a demonstrably unsuccessful strategy over several decades with such a high cost for East Asia's civilian populations indicates a possible ulterior motive. The bombings didn't win any wars, but they did erase economic progress and impose a terrible punishment against previously successful and modernizing East Asian nations which had defied the designs of the Western-led order.

Eyewitness testimonies in Korea widely attest to the extreme devastation wrought by the American bombing campaign. U.S. Army Major General William F. Dean, following his capture at Taejon, wrote of the destruction he witnessed during his time in North Korea: "The town of Huichon amazed me. The city I'd seen before—two storied buildings, a prominent main street—wasn't there anymore." The General encountered only "unoccupied shells" of town after town. Villages were reduced to rubble or "snowy open spaces"—nothing more remained.[29] Hungarian writer Tibor Meray, an anti-communist who later defected to the Western Bloc, had been a correspondent in the DPRK during the war. Despite his strong anti-communist views, what he witnessed in Korea made him far more sympathetic towards the DPRK, saying afterwards when interviewed in Paris: "I saw destruction and horrible things committed by the American forces… Everything which moved in North Korea was a military target, peasants in the fields were machine gunned by pilots who, this was my impression, amused themselves to shoot the targets which moved." He said he had witnessed "a complete devastation between the Yalu River [Chinese border] and the capital [Pyongyang]." There were simply "no more cities in North Korea…my impression was that I am travelling on the moon, because there was only devastation."[30]

Air Force General Curtis LeMay stated regarding the bombing campaign: "we went over there and fought the war and eventually burned down every town in North Korea anyway, some way or another, and some in South Korea too."[31] The General recalled separately: "we burned down just about every city in North Korea and South Korea both…we killed off over a million civilian Koreans and drove several million more from their homes."[32] The North Korean government instructed the population to build dugouts and mud huts and dig underground tunnels to solve the homelessness problem that had ensued. They had little other choice. As the bombings escalated, the state newspaper *Rodong Sinmun* came to refer to 1951 as "the year of unbearable trials" for the Korean people. According to North Korean figures, the war destroyed 8,700 factories, 5,000 schools, 1,000 hospitals and 600,000 homes.[33] Entire factories, schools and hospitals were moved underground, and farmers were often forced to hide underground during the daytime and tend their crops only under cover of night—with farms made frequent targets for strafing attacks. Agricultural output was reduced to bare subsistence levels as livestock was destroyed and shortages of everything from farm tools to fertilizers ensued. Industry and agriculture essentially ceased to function, bringing the people near famine.[34] To place a further strain on the country's food supplies, elite U.S. Navy SEAL units were tasked with destruction of North Korean fishing nets,[35] and fishing boats were also targeted by American aircraft.[36]

Describing the nature and impacts of the renewed U.S. bombing campaign against Korean population centres, based on his own extensive study of reports from the U.S. Air Force, I.F. Stone wrote:

> in Fifth Air Force operational summary February 4: "Other F-80s from the Eighth reported excellent results in attacks on villages near Chorwon, Kumchon, Chunchon, and Chunchon-ni. The villages were hit with bombs as well as rockets and napalm." The results were "excellent." Not all the reports were so brisk. There were some passages about these raids on villages which reflected, not the pity which human feeling called for, but a kind of gay moral imbecility, utterly devoid of imagination—as if the fliers were playing in a bowling alley, with villages for pins. An example was the Fifth Air Force operational summary 5 P.M. Tokyo time Friday, February 2. This told how the two man crew of a downed Mosquito patrol plane was rescued by helicopter "from the midst of an enemy troop concentration near Hongchon." Some fifty enemy troops had been sighted and between 300 and 400 foxholes reported so it was decided to give the whole area "saturation" treatment.
>
> A mass flight of twenty-four F-51 mustangs poured 5000 gallons of napalm over the area. The flight leader, Lieutenant

> Colonel James Kirkendall, of Duluth, Minnesota—the Air Force communiqués gave names, as if to foster individual pride in such handiwork—reported that "his flight hit every village and building in the area." Perhaps it was some uneasy qualm which led him to add, "There was plenty of evidence of troops living in the houses there." The evidence itself was not disclosed. It might have been hard to find, for Colonel Kirkendall added that "smoke blanketed the area, rising to over 4000 feet when they left." His subordinates were cheerful. Captain Everett L. Hundley of Kansas City, Kansas, who led one group of four planes, as quoted by the communiqué as saying, "You can kiss that group of villages good-bye." Captain Hugh Boniford of Montgomery, Alabama, said he saw "tracks and other evidence of enemy activity in the area." He added, "That place can really be called devastated now." Captain Boniford's remark applies to all Korea.[37]

Following the emergence of a stalemate around the 38th parallel in mid-1951 the bombing of cities, villages and hydroelectric plants allowed the U.S. to inflict devastation on the North Korean population without needing to engage its well-entrenched forces on the ground. This, it was hoped, would force Pyongyang to more urgently accept armistice terms which strongly favoured the Western powers. Every day the DPRK delayed negotiations to push for better terms the slaughter and devastation would continue at the hands of Western aircraft.[38] Defence Secretary Robert Lovett was a leading advocate of this strategy. "If we can stay firm [in our terms for negotiation] we can tear them up by air," he said. "We are hurting them badly…If we keep on tearing the place apart, we can make it a most unpopular affair for the North Koreans. We ought to go right ahead."[39]

In an effort to starve the population and increase pressure on Korean and Chinese negotiators, the U.S would target crucial Yalu River irrigation dams in 1953—flooding whole towns and destroying the DPRK's rice crop which the already malnourished population needed to subsist. Five reservoirs were hit, flooding thousands of acres of farmland.[40] Irrigation damming provided for 75 percent of the country's rice crop,[41] and the U.S. Air Force envisioned destroying 250,000 tons of rice by targeting this infrastructure. This included attacks on the Sui Ho dam—the second largest in the world.[42] U.S. military reports appeared almost gleeful when reporting on the huge floods wiping out rice crops and the desperate response observed from the air of the farmers on the ground. The result was mass starvation, as expected.[43] One report stated regarding the consequents of destroying Korean rice crops by targeting dams: "The Westerner can little conceive the awesome meaning which the loss of this staple commodity has for the Asian—starvation and slow death."[44] Targeting dams to starve an enemy population was a severe war crime, one for which somewhat ironically an U.S.-led tribunal at Nuremburg had recently hung Nazi German military leaders.[i] American perpetrators inevitably escaped such recriminations.[45]

Mass deaths by famine in the DPRK were only prevented by China and the USSR increasing food aid. Interdiction of supplies coming into Korea by American aircraft, however, worked to undermine such efforts. Fittingly named Operation Strangle, the U.S. intentionally targeted relief supplies crossing Korea at night.[46] Despite claims to have destroyed many trucks, the operation ultimately failed to cause mass hunger on the scale intended or to seriously disrupt supplies to the frontlines. Although the number of North Koreans who died of hunger during the war as a direct result of the intentional targeting of their food supplies was high, the U.S. Air Force had sought to make it considerably higher to further exacerbate famine and would have done so had their interdiction operation succeeded.[47] Air Force officers for their part were forced to grudgingly admit admiration for their adversaries' ability to operate supply lines under heavy bombardment and repair damage in short order—described as "little short of phenomenal."[48]

The North Koreans showed much ingenuity in avoiding Western air attacks, proving remarkably effective at repairing bridges, building artificial fords, and on occasion even laying train tracks on log caissons in place of destroyed bridges. Other measures included constructing special "night-only" pontoon bridges over the Han River—assembled after dusk and taken apart before dawn with parts carefully concealed from Western aircraft. Railroad tracks were camouflaged, and at times tracks which had been repaired were disguised to appear destroyed. The trains themselves were concealed by day, and the KPA succeeded in getting trains as far south as Chonui, 100km south of Seoul—a highly impressive feat given the conditions.

---

i Article 6 Clause B of the regulations set forth by the Nuremburg trials stated that the destruction of dams and dikes was considered a war crime, building on Article 23 of the Hague convention which, while not specifying dams, had outlawed unnecessary targeting of civilian infrastructure.

U.S. bombings succeeded in wiping out a significant percentage of the Korean population on a scale without precedent or equal in recent history to this day, with the air campaign killing the majority of the 3–4 million North Koreans estimated to have died in the war.[49] Some estimates by Western scholars have put North Korea's wartime casualties at near 30 percent of the population.[50] Air Force General Curtis LeMay said of the bombing of North Korea: "Over a period of three years or so we killed off—what—twenty percent of the population."[51] This figure does not account for the inevitable hundreds of thousands if not millions more wounded or maimed in the bombings and the fighting, or the tremendous economic losses the country suffered.[ii] Even General LeMay's more conservative estimate would make the losses North Korea suffered relative to the size of its population greater than that suffered by any nation during the Second World War. This death toll is extraordinarily high, not only as a percentage of the population, but as an absolute figure.[iii]

Nuclear War Against North Korea in the 1950s

The U.S. Military's repeated failure to force the East Asian allies to capitulate unilaterally, and its own high losses suffered on the battlefield despite massive material superiority, caused a growing sense of frustration among the American leadership. This led commanders, congressmen and other prominent figures to voice their strong support for escalation through the employment of nuclear arms to subdue Korean and Chinese resistance. Such calls were common following battlefield defeats throughout the war, and at times were responded to, bringing America very close to launching nuclear attacks.

In the aftermath of the battles of Osan, Pyeongtaek and Cheonan, the first U.S.-KPA engagements which saw the Americans decisively routed on the 5th, 6th and 8th of July 1950 respectively, Joint Chiefs of Staff Chairman Omar Bradley raised the possibility of using nuclear

---

ii While there are no available statistics for the number of Koreans wounded, that the death toll was in the millions and statistics from other conflicts where modern weapons such as incendiaries were used, injuries have consistently significantly outnumbered the number of deaths. Hundreds of thousands injured in a war where several million were killed is therefore an extremely conservative estimate; with the number of wounded exceeding the numbers killed, several million is statistically more likely.

iii Pyongyang was forced to file a complaint to the United Nations over the air attacks on civilians, although inevitably this had no impact.

weapons at a Joint Chiefs meeting on July 9.[52] Major General Charles L. Bolte four days later made a similar proposition.[53] Supreme Commander MacArthur also suggested tactical nuclear strikes to destroy bridges and tunnels used by the KPA at this time, although these options were all considered impractical. [54] President Truman at the time denied that nuclear attacks were being considered,[55] but later backtracked in a press conference and stated that nuclear attacks had always been under consideration.[56] He authorised the deployment of ten nuclear capable B-29 bombers to Guam on the recommendation of the JCS on July 28.

As American defeats continued to mount in the first three months of the war, with casualties running high and no meaningful gains made against the Korean People's Army, calls among the civilian, political and religious leadership for nuclear attacks grew. After the nuclear attacks on Japan it was widely believed that nuclear weapons would allow the Western powers to avoid fighting major wars, guaranteeing unchallenged military supremacy for years to come. Many had therefore expected nuclear weapons would be used to "resolve" the Korean War quickly. A notable example was Reverend Kenneth Eyler of the Wesleyan Methodist Church, who stated when addressing President Truman:

> Your excellency... As a minister of the Gospel and a Bible-believing Christian...there is much that has been bothering me lately. This war in Korea. Why is it we fuss around at the fringe instead of getting at the heart of the matter?... You know as well as I do where this whole matter lies. That is in MOSCOW. I would rather see Moscow destroyed than our boys die in Korea at the hands of the Chinese Red... You can use the Atom bomb.[57]

Senator Albert Gore advised to President Truman after the Korean War's outbreak:

> Dehumanize a belt across the Korean Peninsula by surface radiological contamination...broadcast the fact to the enemy...that entrance into the belt would mean certain death or slow deformity to all foot soldiers... And further, that the belt would be regularly re-contaminated until such time as a satisfactory solution to the whole Korean problem shall have been reached.[58]

This was a creative idea for the use of nuclear weapons, a new way for the United States to turn a failing conventional war effort around through employment of unconventional means—in this case by contaminating and regularly re-contaminating an East Asian country with nuclear waste. The implications of this proposal on the Korean peninsula would have been devastating as once contaminated, even if not "re-contaminated," the environmental effects of the repeated use of nuclear weapons would have remained. The effects of such contamination can be seen on Bikini Island and in the Algerian desert today.[59] Similar "solutions" to the conflict based on the use of nuclear weapons were popular with much of the American public, and the majority in the U.S. supported nuclear strikes against North Korea[60] just as they had supported them against Hiroshima and Nagasaki.[61] Gore's son would become vice president from 1993 to 2001 and a leading presidential candidate in 2000 running on a similarly hawkish platform.

The United States came close to using nuclear weapons in November 1950, shortly after the Chinese entry into the war. On the 4th U.S. State Department Director of Policy Planning Paul Nitze met General Herbert Loper, in charge of the Army's nuclear weapons, and members of the U.S. Army Logistics Staff, to discuss the viability of nuclear attacks in Korea. This would represent a tactical role for the nuclear bomb, rather than a strategic role as had been the case when targeting Japanese cities. General Loper informed Nitze that deployment of the bomb would be of little use in such a role given the rarity of large and unmoving concentrations of Chinese and Korean troops.[62]

On November 28, amid the failure of MacArthur's "Home by Christmas" offensive, Representative Lucius Mendel Rivers of South Carolina led several members of Congress in urging that MacArthur be given authority to conduct nuclear strikes. "If there ever was a time to use the A-bomb, it is now," River said. The representatives received considerable support, and sent a telegram to President Truman recommending an ultimatum be issued to Beijing—withdraw all assets from northern Korea or face "relentless atomic warfare."[63] The American lawmakers were unaware of the secret meeting which had occurred earlier in the month or of the intelligence available to the military and the president, obtained through extensive study of the fallout from attacks on Japan,[64] which strongly indicated that nuclear strikes would have a very limited effect in the theatre. This appears to have served as the primary deterrent against the U.S. employing nuclear strikes on the battlefield, as had the use of its most powerful weapon failed to yield decisive results, as was projected, it would have worldwide repercussions for the United States. President Truman nevertheless stated at a press conference two days later that deployment of nuclear weapons was actively being considered.[65]

Regarding the limited viability of nuclear weapons as a game changing weapon to neutralize Chinese and Korean military assets, U.S. Army Chief of Staff General Joseph Lawton Collins stated: "Personally, I am very sceptical about the value of using atomic weapons tactically in Korea. The Communists are dug into positions in depth over a front of 150 miles." He believed that nuclear weapons would not be effective in targeting fortified positions based on the findings of American nuclear tests, stating that these tests "proved that men can be very close to the explosion and not be hurt if they are well dug in." Many other U.S. military leaders similarly perceived nuclear attacks to be of limited use as a tactical weapon in the Korean theatre.[66]

Despite their limited viability as tactical assets, Supreme Commander MacArthur continued to advocate tactical nuclear attacks. On December 9, following a string of major Chinese victories, he requested the president grant him authority to employ nuclear weapons against Chinese and Korean targets, and fifteen days later he submitted a list of targets across China and northern Korea for nuclear attack. These included troop concentrations and airbases in China itself.[67] The general's plan called for 26 nuclear strikes on "retaliation targets" in China and the DPRK—eight on enemy troop concentrations and airbases and 18 on industrial centres.[68] Described by British military historian Max Hastings as "instilled with a yearning for crude revenge upon the people who had brought all his hopes and triumphs in Korea to nothing," this attitude towards the Chinese likely had an impact on MacArthur's willingness to employ nuclear weapons.[69] A JCS committee had previously recommended the use of nuclear arms against Chinese forces, although the plan submitted by MacArthur was not approved by Washington.[70]

MacArthur reportedly also considered contaminating northern Korea and Manchuria with radioactive waste—an extreme form of scorched earth intended to render it unusable to the East Asian allies. He referred to this as a "radioactive by-product cordon." This would have rendered large parts of northeast China and North Korea an uninhabitable wasteland for generations—possibly indefinitely[iv] depending on the method used.[71] On March 10, 1951, the general asked for "D-Day atomic capability" in the Korean theatre after PVA forces began to mass assets near the Korean border. He later demanded that up to 50 nuclear weapons be dropped on Manchuria to thwart the massing "Chinese hordes." At the end of March atomic bomb loading pits at Kadena Air Base on Okinawa were operational. The bombs were moved to the base and assembled there. Only the nuclear cores were missing from these bombs.[72]

The following week, on April 5, the United States came very close to launching nuclear attacks—an incident comparable to the Cuban Missile Crisis in its significance. While nuclear strikes on Chinese ground forces in Korea were considered impractical, the Joint Chiefs of Staff for the first time gave MacArthur authority to use nuclear weapons. The U.S. Atomic Energy Commission (AEC) and JCS had both previously refrained from giving the Supreme Commander this authority, with a good chance that MacArthur would use them prematurely or provocatively based on his previous rhetoric and prior actions.[73] Granting the hawkish General a degree of control over nuclear weapons thus marked a considerably greater willingness to risk nuclear war.

The nuclear warheads transferred were intended to target military facilities and industrial centres on the Chinese mainland itself.[74] The JCS ordered immediate nuclear attacks against bases in northeast China if large numbers of new PVA troops entered the theatre or if bombers were launched against American assets from the area. On the same day AEC Chairman Gordon Dean began arrangements to transfer nine Mk. 4 nuclear capsules to the Air Force's 9th Bomb Group, the group designated to carry nuclear weapons. JCS Chairman Omar Bradley meanwhile gained President Truman's approval for the transfer of Mk. 4 bombs "from AEC to military custody" on April 6. The president then signed an order authorising nuclear attacks against Chinese and North Korean targets, after which nuclear-armed 9th Bomb Group deployed to Guam.[75]

Considering the low threshold required for the U.S. to conduct a nuclear attack, the possibility of nuclear war remained extremely high. That Chinese forces might have reinforced their frontlines for attacks on U.S. and coalition forces from bases in China's northeast remained a significant possibility, and while it had no significant bomber assets at the time China had begun to deploy limited numbers of fighters to the

iv Some forms of nuclear contamination such as that from depleted uranium (uranium-234 or uranium-235) can last for hundreds of thousands or even hundreds of millions of years due to the long half live of these elements.

theatre. There was no guarantee that Chinese forces would not have deployed more troops to the front when pressed onto the defensive as they were in March—the sole precondition for a nuclear attack. A nuclear holocaust in northeast China could well have taken place had the PVA leadership only adopted a different line of tactical decision making.

The PVA's caution to avoid escalation and its limited ability to support more battalions on the frontline due to logistical constraints were key to ensuring that conditions for nuclear attack were not met—as were active measures taken by the Soviet Union to protect its new ally. The Soviet Air Force had introduced its own analogue to the B-29, the Tu-4, two years prior, which was capable of delivering nuclear strikes to U.S. bases across Japan and Korea.

With large numbers of Soviet assets including bombers stationed in China from 1950, the Chinese mainland was to some extent considered under Soviet protection which significantly deterred the U.S. from launching nuclear attacks against its territory. This Soviet presence reportedly grew in early 1951 when the U.S. began to more seriously consider nuclear attacks on China. While direct Soviet intervention was not assured in the case of a limited nuclear strike, Moscow retained other means of escalation, including increasing material support for the PVA and KPA, providing logistical support with trucks and personnel carriers and the latest hardware such as such as the Tu-4 and Il-28 bombers, T-44 and T-54 battle tanks and Whiskey Class submarines. These systems were at the cutting edge of their time, and most were provided to Chinese and Korean forces shortly after the war's conclusion in 1953. They were never provided during the Korean War, likely in an attempt to avoid such escalation.

Although MacArthur, the leading advocate of nuclear attacks, was dismissed as Supreme Commander on April 11, this hardly spelt an end to American nuclear threats. Seventeen days later President Truman increased deployments of nuclear configured bombers to East Asia and authorised reconnaissance flights over airfields in northeast China to obtain targeting data for potential strikes.[76] Using channels in Hong Kong to contact the Chinese leadership, U.S. envoys conveyed that MacArthur's dismissal did not mean that Washington had ruled out expanding the war into China or employing nuclear weapons. They emphasized America's ability to set Chinese economic development back many decades through use of weapons of mass destruction.[77] MacArthur's replacement, the Supreme Commander Matthew Ridgway, himself requested 38 nuclear warheads provided in May, although these were not approved. Two months later the JCS again considered the use of nuclear weapons in a tactical role and would do so again repeatedly before the war's conclusion. Leading nuclear scientists were dispatched to Korea to gauge the feasibility of tactical nuclear attacks.[78]

In October, with effective means of deploying nuclear bombs tactically in Korea still elusive, the U.S. initiated Operation Hudson Harbor. The operation was intended to establish the capability to use nuclear weapons on the battlefield—in the hopes that newer warheads would be able to accomplish what their more cumbersome predecessors could not. To test this lone B-29 bombers were flown over northern Korea on simulated atomic bombing runs, dropping "dummy" bombs or heavy conventional bombs. The project called for "actual functioning of all activities which would be involved in an atomic strike, including weapons assembly and testing and more." Findings confirmed that bombs were not technically useful in Korea. "Timely identification of large masses of enemy troops was extremely rare," military reports from the operation concluded. With KPA and PVA forces operating in fluid and constantly changing formations, they were unsuitable targets for a weapon conceptualised to level enemy cities.[79]

For the North Korean and Chinese leadership to see nuclear bombings simulated over their territory, never knowing which "simulation" was a dud and which may be the weapon that had so recently irradiated Hiroshima and Nagasaki, must have caused considerable trepidation. In Japan the United States Army Air Force had also flown lone B-29 bombers over potential targets for nuclear strikes in the weeks leading up to the actual nuclear attacks, and two of these seemingly routine overflights had destroyed two cities taking around 230,000 lives.[80] In the eyes of the North Koreans and Chinese, why would these simulated flights over Korea necessarily be any different?[81]

Following the inauguration of President Dwight D. Eisenhower in 1953 U.S. nuclear policy in Korea was put under review. At the outset of the war Eisenhower, then a Major General, had advised that employment of nuclear weapons should be considered, warning that a ground war would otherwise require general mobilisation of the U.S. population.[82] Two months into his administration, on March 27, the president and State Secretary John Foster Dulles agreed "that somehow or other the taboo which surrounds the use of atomic weapons would have to be destroyed." Dulles stated that "in the present state of world opinion, we could not use an A-bomb, we should make every effort now to dissipate this feeling." If public perceptions towards nuclear weapons were to soften, the United States could employ them to force a capitulation on American terms. The following year the administration would consider employing nuclear weapons in Vietnam to aid French colonial forces besieged there.[83]

Eisenhower stated in May that he "thought it might be cheaper, dollar-wise, to use atomic weapons in Korea than to continue to use conventional weapons against the dugouts which honey-combed the hills along which the enemy forces were presently deployed." He hoped to thereby break the stalemate that had emerged around the 38th parallel which had prevented U.S.-led coalition forces from further advancing into northern Korea. This would press the East Asian allies to make further unilateral concessions in the negotiating process. Nuclear threats were later extended under the Eisenhower administration to China and Chinese population centres. The president "expressed with great emphasis the opinion that if the Chinese Communists attacked us again, we should certainly respond by hitting them hard and wherever it would hurt most, including Peiping [an earlier romanization of Peking—today Beijing] itself." The implication was that nuclear strikes were a possibility, and a key part of plans for what Eisenhower referred to as "all-out war against Communist China."[84]

While the U.S. was effectively deterred from initiating an all-out war against China, the viability of tactical nuclear strikes was repeatedly assessed and reassessed. The idea that the "wonder weapon" credited with ending the Second World War could not bring a theatre victory in Korea was difficult to comprehend but, based on multiple military reports concluding it had only limited tactical viability, this proved to be the case.[85] While the advent of "bunker buster" tactical nuclear bombs heavily modified to penetrate deep underground would decades later make these nuclear warheads America's weapon of choice to neutralise fortifications, nuclear weapons of the Korean War era were ill suited to such a role or to neutralising troops on the open battlefield.[86]

Biological Warfare

As the U.S.-led coalition saw its position deteriorate from November 1950, despite the concentration of what was nearly America's entire active conventional force to the Korean front,[87] evidence began to emerge that biological weapons were being deployed against Chinese and North Korean targets. This was at a time when the intensity of an already brutal firebombing campaign was escalating, dousing population centres across North Korea with napalm, and when deployment of nuclear weapons against the two non-nuclear East Asian states was being actively prepared for.[88] While weapons of mass destruction were well beyond the capabilities of China and North Korea to deploy at the time, with these states lacking even sufficient tanks or artillery, the United States in its desperation to reverse its defeats seemingly saw fit to target their populations with any practical means at its disposal.

During the Sino-Japanese War Japanese Imperial forces had pursued an ambitious bacteriological warfare program, which included experimentation on live human subjects to gain valuable data for the weaponization of plague.[89] Following Tokyo's surrender several prominent Japanese scientists involved in this program were given full immunity from prosecution by the United States, thwarting Soviet efforts to try them for war crimes. Soviet trials of those found to have experimented on live human subjects were dismissed as propaganda and ignored in the West, and it was only years later that the nature of the Japanese biological weapons program was revealed.[90] According to a British report the U.S. military found the information provided by Japanese biological warfare scientists "absolutely invaluable." It "could never have been obtained in the United States because of scruples attached to experiments on humans," and "the information was obtained fairly cheaply."[91] The scientists, many from the notorious biological weapons Unit 731, provided extensive technical information on biological warfare to American scientists from the Army biological research centre at Fort Detrick. Much of this information had been obtained through human experimentation. The U.S. used this as a basis to advance its own biological warfare program, and the details of this agreement with Japanese biological warfare scientists would only emerge in the 1980s as a result of the extensive research of journalist John W. Powell.[92]

The use of biological weapons was among the most severe of the war crimes carried out by U.S. forces in Korea, with American aircraft dropping insects and feathers carrying anthrax, cholera, encephalitis and bubonic plague over the country and parts of north-eastern China. Such operations were kept secret at the time, in part to avoid affecting public opinion both domestically and abroad due to the impact this particular form of warfare would have on the war effort's public image. The Chinese and North Koreans devoted much effort to publicizing their claim that the United States was conducting germ warfare against them, issuing statements asserting that quantities of bacteria and bacteria-laden insects were being dropped by U.S. aircraft.[93] They presented the testimonies of 38 captured American airmen who they claimed had flown the planes carrying these weapons. Many of these men went into precise and substantial details of the types of insects being carried, the types of containers dropped and the diseases used. The Chinese government published photographs of the germ bombs and the insects.[94]

Amid Korean and Chinese allegations of biological weapons being used against their population centres, the World Peace Council established the International Scientific Commission for the Facts Concerning Bacterial Warfare in China and Korea in Oslo, Norway, on March 29, 1952. It was comprised of scientists from Sweden, France, Great Britain, Italy, Brazil and the Soviet Union. After over two months of investigation in China, the commission produced a report comprising some 600 pages and many photos that concluded: "The peoples of Korea and China have indeed been the objectives of bacteriological weapons. These have been employed by units of the U.S.A. armed forces, using a great variety of different methods for the purpose, some which seem to be developments of those applied by the Japanese during the Second World War."[95]

Conclusions reached by the World Peace Council's international commission were based on highly rigorous methodology, interrogation of Chinese and Korean witnesses, testing of material evidence, careful checks on the collected specimens, and elaborate statistical calculations. Four of the investigators were renowned scientists at world leading universities, two were laboratory directors and the other was Dr Joseph Needham. Dr Needham, a professor at Cambridge University, represented one of the most esteemed British scientists of his time—a fellow of the Royal Society who would become a much renowned fellow of the British Academy and personally conferred the Companionship of Honour by Queen Elizabeth II and the only living person to hold all three titles. Except for a single professor from the Soviet Academy of Medicine, Dr N. N. Zukov-Verzhnikov, all members of the commission were Westerners unlikely to hold biases supporting North Korea or China. No Chinese or Koreans were involved. Despite this, as the findings implicated the United States in severe crimes, the commission was vilified and its conclusions were dismissed by the U.S. and Britain. Those organizations and commissions which collected evidence of biological weapons use were dismissed as "communist" in order to discredit their investigations, allegations based on little more than that their findings implicated the U.S. in waging germ warfare.[96] Those who were not "with us" or who were considered remotely critical of the American intervention were widely labeled "with the communists," and international commissions carrying out scientific research, no matter how impartial, were no exception.

Among the commission's findings, it reported: Evidence of a swarm of voles being dropped on several villages in Kan Nan, Northeast China, on April 4, 1952, following the flight overhead of an American F-82 Twin Mustang fighter. 717 rodents, many evidently sick, were found. Most of the rodents were buried deep underground by the frightened villagers. Plague bacilli were found on the few rodents which were not buried. Kan Nan had never known plague in its recent history, and its appearance on the rodents was spontaneous and extremely difficult to explain unless introduced artificially. A telling detail was that all the voles without exception were adults of similar age, not a natural distribution of ages. The commission concluded: "there remains no doubt that a large number of voles suffering from plague were delivered to the district of Kan-Nan during the night of 4–5 April, 1952 by…an American F-82 double-fuselage night-fighter."[97] Imperial Japan's Unit 731 had themselves devised means of landing plague rats from planes in much the same way.

In Liaotung and Liaoshi, northeast China, the commission found beetles, houseflies and feathers contaminated with anthrax had been artificially introduced after overflights by American aircraft.[98] Five people, four of whom had been hunting for the insects, died of respiratory anthrax and haemorrhagic anthrax—exceedingly rare diseases in the area. Near Pyongyang the commission found evidence of cholera vibrio being artificially introduced, appearing in food dropped from the air on May 16, 1952, by a plane circling overhead.[99]

The International Association of Democratic Lawyers sent an observer mission of experts to Korea in 1952 to investigate claims that the United States was guilty of genocide based on the framework of the Genocide Convention of 1948, and their commission released its own report that year based on its findings. The association is an international NGO which researches legal issues affecting human, political and economic rights worldwide. It works as a consultative organization with the UN, UNESCO, UNICEF and ECOSOC, and has headquarters in Brussels and Tokyo. Observers found overwhelming evidence implicating the United States in conducting biological warfare against North

Korea and China. They carefully documented the types of insects which were being dropped from American planes and referred these to experts. The commission made many notable discoveries, reporting:

> In many cases special kinds of flies, fleas, spiders, beetles, bugs, crickets, mosquitoes and other insects were found, many of which were hitherto unknown in Korea. Insects were found in different cases far from human habitation, on snow, on the ice of rivers, on grass and among stones. Considering the very low temperatures prevailing at the time [on average far below freezing] which normally prevent the appearance of insects, and also considering that the insects were often found in great quantities and even in mixed groups of clusters consisting of different varieties of insects which would normally never be found together, like flies and spiders, the appearance of these insects roused suspicion. The results of expert examination showed that great quantities of insects were infected. In many cases it was also found that the insects were carrying eggs [not a natural occurrence in such weather and at such a time of year]. In the opinion of experts it could be safely assumed that these insects were bred artificially.[100]

The observers detailed finding half rotten fish infected with cholera in large quantities near mountain settlements far from where such species would naturally be found. The report listed the bacteria found: "Vibrio cholera, pasteurella pestis, Eberthella typhosa, Bacillus paratyphi A and B, Rickettsia prowazeki and shigella dysenteriae." The commission's findings were published in a 1952 report concluding that the United States was employing biological warfare in Korea and China, and that it had committed war crimes and well as crimes against humanity. The report stated: "taking into account that the employment of bacteriological and chemical weapons over extensive areas of the country must constitute an attempt to destroy a whole people or part of a people, the commission is of the opinion that the American forces are guilty of the crime of Genocide as defined by the Genocide Convention of 1948."[101]

While the United States denied charges of biological attacks, it was clear that the Chinese and North Koreans themselves believed that they had been targeted by biological weapons due to the great effort and expense they undertook to carry out a counteracting public health campaign despite the extreme scarcity of resources at the time. In March 1952 they had established 129 teams, over 20,000 people, and 66 quarantine zones. Nearly 5 million people in China's north-eastern regions specifically were inoculated against plague.[102] Chinese authorities requested Soviet assistance for disease prevention and four anti-bacteriological warfare research centres were set up quickly on the Korean front. 5.8 million doses of vaccine and 200,000 gas masks were delivered, and the Chinese government initiated the Patriotic Health and Epidemic Prevention Campaign which directed citizens to kill flies, mosquitoes and fleas.[103] Journalist Tibor Méray attested to seeing the North Koreans carrying out "an unprecedented campaign of public health" in response to the reported biological attacks.[104] These measures are thought to have succeeded in preventing the outbreak of a large-scale epidemic, which had been the intention of the biological attacks.[105]

Many Western experts who investigated claims of biological warfare against Chinese and Korean civilians went on to verify them, despite the often significant pressure from both state and non-state entities in their home countries not to do so. Dr Gene Weltfish, an anthropologist at Colombia University, was fired for reaching the scientific but unpopular conclusion that the U.S. was engaged in biological warfare against the North Korans and Chinese populations.[106] Dr Joseph Needham stated he remained "95–97 percent convinced" that the Chinese and North Korean charges that the United States was waging germ warfare against them were true. James Endicott, a Canadian peace activist, launched his own investigation and verified the Chinese and Korean charges of American biological attacks in his conclusion. He faced harassment from his government, as Canada was heavily involved in the war alongside the U.S., and had his papers seized at the airport. He was tailed by the Canadian Mounted Police and strongly criticized by his church, but despite this pressure stood by his claims.[107]

Findings by impartial international scientists and investigators implicating the U.S. in biological warfare efforts have been supported by a number of other sources. U.S. personnel taken prisoner during the war confessed to participating in biological attacks. While testimonies given in custody were dismissed in the West, the assumption being that they had been extracted under coercion, after returning to the United States former prisoners persisted in making their claims publicly. These confessions could never be disproved and were backed up by independent scientific reviews.[108] The military's response to their soldiers' confessions was to claim that they had been "brainwashed" by the communists, an entirely unfounded theory intended to save the government and military's image. The term "brainwashing" was in fact coined in 1950 by Edward Hunter, an outspoken anti-communist and CIA agent who was working undercover as a journalist to discredit the testimonies of returning or captured U.S. personnel whose accounts contradicted Washington's narrative on the war.[109] The military personnel who detailed the use of biological weapons were notably associated with Fort Detrick in Maryland, a major biological warfare facility. The fact that those U.S. personnel accused of waging biological warfare later turned out to have come from a biological weapons facility would, if it were a coincidence as those who sought to refute China's claims asserted, be a remarkable and highly improbable one.[110]

North Korea continues to display what it alleges are biological warfare agents including preserved carrier rodents at Korean War related museums such as the Sinchon Museum of American War Atrocities. The descriptions of the means by which the United States waged biological warfare against them are fully consistent with the reports of the international commissions. Based on other uses of biological and other unconventional weapons by the United States, including extensive evidence that such weapons were employed multiple times against Cuba in the 1960s,[111] Chinese and North Korean claims to have been subjected to biological warfare cannot be easily dismissed. Allegations of biological weapons use were supported by professor Jacob G. Hornberger, founder and president of the Future of Freedom Foundation who concluded:

> Given that the U.S. military had just a few years before dropped atomic bombs on Hiroshima and Nagasaki, why would they have any compunctions about bombing North Koreans with napalm and fleas with bubonic plague? Don't forget, after all, the mindset of the U.S. national-security state … A commie is a commie and a gook is gook; no big deal to send any and all of them to the hereafter.[112]

Hugh Deane, reporter and former Coordinator of Information and naval intelligence officer on General MacArthur's staff, extensively researched his country's waging of biological warfare in Korea, as well as its incorporation of Japanese war criminals into its own biological weapons program, and concluded on the matter:

> The charge that the U.S. was indeed guilty of germ warfare can hardly be dismissed on the grounds that Americans would not consider such criminality. That persuaded great numbers at the time, but since then evidence of ongoing American development of bacteriological warfare capabilities and the actual use of chemical weapons in Vietnam have come to light. Several American military high-ups, including General Charles E. Loucks of the Army Chemical Corps, on January 22, 1951, made statements unequivocally giving their support to resorting to germ warfare.[113]

One notable more recent case of censorship of evidence regarding American use of biological weapons in Korea was the publishing of the book *Unit 731: Japan's Secret Biological Warfare in World War II* by British and American professors Peter Williams and David Wallace. The book was published in Britain in 1989, but American publishers refused to publish the book unless the 17th chapter was removed.[114] This chapter covered the legacy of Unit 731 in relation to the Korean War, giving substantial evidence of U.S. involvement in biological warfare against the Korean and Chinese populations. Prominent among the evidence was that collected by the International Scientific Commission for the Facts Concerning Bacterial Warfare in China and Korea, the evidence of which Wallace and Williams claimed was "generally accepted today as being of high quality."[115]

Canadian and American professors Stephen Endicott and Edward Hagerman conducted an exhaustive 20 year study into the issue of biological weapons attacks, and concluded with a high degree of certainty that the U.S. both experimented with and deployed biological weapons during the Korean War, and that the administration lied to both Congress and the public claiming that the American biological warfare program was purely defensive. The two were prominent experts in East Asian history and military affairs respectively, with the latter contributing to textbooks for the U.S. Military Academy at West Point, the U.S. Army Command and General Staff college, the U.S. Air Force Academy, and the Air War College of the U.S. Air Force. Their work was published by Indiana University Press in 1998.[116]

The details of American biological warfare operations were given, and Chinese allegations thoroughly analysed, by researcher Dave Chaddock in his book *This Must Be the Place: How the U.S. Waged*

Germ Warfare in the Korean War and Denied It Ever Since. It built on the earlier Endicott and Hagerman investigation, and provided evidence that former members of Japan's Unit 731 were deployed with their equipment to South Korea in 1951 to support biological warfare operations. Dr Shiro Ishii and Dr Masaji Kitano, 2nd Commander of Unit 731, were among those reportedly involved in these operations in Korea.[117]

The fact that the world's leading superpower could be involved in deploying biological weapons against population centres was difficult for many to accept, and denial came naturally. Indeed, the tone used to refute Chinese claims was the same as that used to flatly deny the operations of CIA agents on Chinese territory in the same period—despite the CIA later declassifying information which fully verified Chinese claims.[118] Only an analysis of hard evidence could overcome inclinations to deny the uncomfortable truth of U.S. intentions towards China and North Korea and the means they were willing to employ against them. As George Wald, an expert from the Harvard Biological Laboratories and Nobel Prize Winner concluded after studying the evidence: "As for the allegation that the U.S. used germ warfare in the Korean War, I can only say with some shame that what I dismissed as incredible then seems altogether credible to me now."[119] America's position as the world's dominant power and its formidable soft power made it extremely difficult to accuse it of committing such actions despite strong evidence from a wide range of impartial and predominantly Western sources near unanimously supporting the allegations.

NOTES

1 *We Accuse: Report of the Committee of the Women's International Democratic Federation in Korea, May 16–27, 1951*, Berlin, Women's International Democratic Forum, 1951 (pp. 4–5).

2 Ibid. (pp. 4–5).

3 Ibid. (pp. 5–6).

4 Ibid. (p. 6).

5 Ibid. (pp. 4–5).

6 Harden, Blaine, *King of Spies: The Dark Reign of America's Spymaster in Korea*, New York, Viking, 2017 (p. 9).

7 Cumings, Bruce, 'Nuclear Threats Against North Korea: Consequences of the "forgotten" war,' *The Asia-Pacific Journal*, vol. 3, issue 1, no. 0, January 13, 2005 (p. 2).

8 Harden, Blaine, 'The U.S. war crime North Korea won't forget,' *Washington Post*, March 24, 2015.

9 Grosscup, Beau, *Strategic Terror: The Politics and Ethics of Aerial Bombardment,* London, Zed Books, 2003 (Chapter 5: Cold War Strategic Bombing: From Korea to Vietnam, Part 4: The Bombing of Korea).
Futrell, Robert F., *United States Air Force Operations in the Korean Conflict,* 1 July 1952–27 July 1953, USAF Historical Study no. 127, Maxwell Air Force Base, Ala, USAF Historical Division, Research Studies Institute, Air University, 1956 (pp. 183–207).
10 Deane, Hugh, *The Korean War, 1945–1953*, San Francisco, CA, China Books and Periodicals, 1999 (p. 145).
11 Stone, I. F., *Hidden History of the Korean War*, Amazon Media, 2014 (Chapter 34: Lost and Found).
12 Cumings, Bruce, *The Korean War: A History*, New York, Modern Library, 2010 (p. 152).
13 Williams, Christopher, *Leadership Accountability in a Globalizing World*, London, Palgrave Macmillan, 2006 (p. 185).
14 Bullene, E. F., 'Wonder Weapon: Napalm,' *Army Combat Forces Journal*, November 1952.
'Napalm Jelly Bombs Prove a Blazing Success in Korea,' *All Hands*, April 1951.
Townsend, Earle J., 'They Don't Like Hell Bombs,' *Armed Forces Chemical Journal*, January 1951.
15 Deane, Hugh, *The Korean War, 1945–1953*, San Francisco, CA, China Books and Periodicals, 1999 (p. 144).
MacDonald, Callum A, 'Korea: The War Before Vietnam,' London, Macmillan, 1986 (pp. 234–235).
McCormack, Gavan, 'Cold War Hot War: An Australian Perspective on the Korean War,' Sydney, Hale and Iremonger, 1983 (p. 132).
16 Grey, Tobias, 'Hitler didn't start indiscriminate bombings—Churchill did,' *Spectator,* October 26, 2013.
17 Milton, Giles, 'Winston Churchill's shocking use of chemical weapons,' *The Guardian*, September 1, 2013.
18 Lewis, Julian, *Changing Direction: British Military Planning for Post-war Strategic Defence, 1942–1947*, Abingdon, Routledge, 2008 (Appendix 8).
19 Cumings, Bruce, *The Korean War: A History*, New York, Modern Library, 2010 (p. 146).
20 Omara-Otunnu, Elizabeth, 'Napalm Survivor Tells of Healing After Vietnam War,' *University of Connecticut Advance*, November 8, 2004.
21 Williams, Christopher, *Leadership Accountability in a Globalizing World*, London, Palgrave Macmillan, 2006 (p. 185).
22 Perry, Richard E., and Levin, Rebert J., 'Where the Innocent Die,' *Redbook*, January 1967 (p. 103).
23 Kahin, Audrey, and Kahin, George McT., *Subversion as Foreign Policy*, New York, New Press, 1995 (pp. 179–184).
Blum, William, *Killing Hope: U.S. Military and C.I.A. Interventions Since World War II*, London, Zed Books, 2003 (p. 103).
Burkholder Smith, Joseph, *Portrait of a Cold Warrior*, New York, Putnam, 1976 (pp. 220–221).
24 Chomsky, Noam, *Who Rules the World?*, London, Hamish Hamilton, 2017 (p. 215).
25 Hanley, Charles J. and Choe, Sang Hun and Mendoza, Martha, *The Bridge at No Gun Ri: A Hidden Nightmare from the Korean War*, New York, Henry Holt and Company, 2001 (p. 163).
26 Jackson, Robert, *Air War Over Korea*, London, Ian Allen, 1973 (p. 61).
27 Cumings, Bruce, *The Korean War: A History*, New York, Modern Library, 2010 (p. 146).

28 Wilson, Ward, 'The Bomb Didn't Beat Japan…Stalin Did,' *Foreign Policy*, May 30, 2017.
Wilson, Ward, 'Did Nuclear Weapons Cause Japan to Surrender?,' *Carnegie Council*, January 16, 2013.
Carney, Matthew, 'Hiroshima atomic bombing did not lead to Japanese surrender, historians argue nearing 70th anniversary,' *ABC News*, August 5, 2015.

29 Dean, William F., *General Dean's Story, as told to William L. Worden*, New York, Viking Press, 1954 (p. 274).

30 Thames Television, transcript for the fifth seminar for *Korea: The Unknown War*, November 1986.

31 Kohn, Richard H., and Harahan, Joseph P., *Strategic air warfare: an interview with generals Curtis E. LeMay, Leon W. Johnson, David A. Burchinal, and Jack J. Catton*, Washington D.C., Office of Air Force History, 1988 (p. 88).

32 LeMay, Curtis, and Cantor, MacKinley, *Mission with LeMay*, New York, Doubleday, 1965, (p.382).

33 'The Three Year Plan,' *Kyŏngjekŏnsŏl* [EconomicConstruction],September, 1956 (pp. 5–6).
Koh, B. C., 'The War's Impact on the Korean Peninsula,' *The Journal of American-East Asian Relations*, vol. 2, no. 1, Spring 1993 (p. 59).

34 Kim, Monica, *The Interrogation Rooms of the Korean War: The Untold History*, Princeton, NJ, Princeton University Press, 2019 (p. 320).
Armstrong, Charles, 'The Destruction and Reconstruction of North Korea, 1950–1960,' *Asia-Pacific Journal,* vol. 8, no. 51, 2010.

35 'Navy SEAL History,' *navyseals.com* (accessed November 28, 2019).

36 Hanley, Charles J. and Choe, Sang Hun and Mendoza, Martha, *The Bridge at No Gun Ri: A Hidden Nightmare from the Korean War*, New York, Henry Holt and Company, 2001 (pp. 177, 163, 195, 183).

37 Stone, I. F., *Hidden History of the Korean War*, Amazon Media, 2014 (Chapter 34: Lost and Found).

38 Bernstein, Barton J., *The Struggle over the Korean Armistice: Prisoners of Repatriation*, in: *Child of Conflict: The Korean-American Relationship, 1943–1953*, Seattle, University of Washington Press, 1983 (pp. 274–283).
Lacey, Michael James, *The Truman Presidency,* Cambridge, Cambridge University Press, 1991 (p. 440).

39 Connelly, Matthew, 'Notes on Cabinet Meeting,' September 12, 1952, Connelly Papers, HSTL.

40 Callum MacDonald, *Korea: The War Before Vietnam*, London, Macmillan, 1986 (pp. 241–242).

41 *SSSR i Korea* [*The USSR and Korea*], Moscow, USSR Academy of Sciences, 1988 (p. 256).

42 Cumings, Bruce, *The Korean War: A History*, New York, Modern Library, 2010 (p. 147).

43 Chomsky, Noam, *Who Rules the World?*, London, Hamish Hamilton, 2016 (pp. 132–133).

44 Williams, Christopher, *Leadership Accountability in a Globalizing World,* London, Palgrave Macmillan, 2006 (p. 185).

45 Kolko, Gabriel, 'Report on the Destruction of Dikes: Holland, 1944–1945 and Korea, 1953' in: Duffett, John, *Against the Crimes of Silence: Proceedings of the Russell International War Crimes Tribunal, Stockholm and Copenhagen*, New York, O'Hare Books, 1968 (pp. 224–226).

46 Merrill, Frank J., *A Study of the Aerial Interdiction of Railways during the Korean War*, Fort Leavenworth, Kansas, U.S. Army Command and General Staff College, 1965 (pp. 91–93).

Futrell, Robert F., *United States Air Force Operations in the Korean Conflict,* 1 July 1952–27 July 1953, USAF Historical Study no. 127, Maxwell Air Force Base, Ala, USAF Historical Division, Research Studies Institute, Air University, 1956 (p. 473).

47 Armstrong, Charles K., 'The Destruction and Reconstruction of North Korea, 1950–1960,' *The Asia-Pacific Journal*, vol. 7, issue 0, March 16, 2009.
Balázs Szalontai, *The Four Horsemen of the Apocalypse in North Korea: The Forgotten Side of a Not-So-Forgotten War* in: Springer, Chris, and Szalontai, Balázs, *North Korea Caught in Time: Images of War and Reconstruction*, Reading, Garnet Publishing, 2010 (pp. xiv-xv).

48 Far Eastern Air Forces Intelligence Roundup, 11 August 1952, No. 101, K 720.607A, Air Historical Section, Bolling AFB. Futrell (pp. 408–416).

49 Deane, Hugh, *The Korean War, 1945–1953*, San Francisco, CA, China Books and Periodicals, 1999 (p. 191).

50 Chossudovsky, Michel, *Know the Facts: North Korea Lost Close to 30% of its Population as a result of the U.S. Bombings in the 1950s*, Centre for Research on Globalization, November 27, 2010.
Lindqvist, Sven, *A History of Bombing*, New York, The New Press, 2001 (p. 131).

51 Harden, Blaine, 'The U.S. war crime North Korea won't forget,' *Washington Post*, March 24, 2015.

52 Crane, Conrad C, *American Airpower Strategy in Korea, 1950–1953*, Lawrence, Kansas, University Press of Kansas, 2000 (pp. 37–39).

53 Weintraub, Stanley, *MacArthur's War: Korea and the Undoing of an American Hero*, New York, Free Press, 2000 (p. 252).

54 Crane, Conrad C., *American Airpower Strategy in Korea, 1950–1953*, Lawrence, Kansas, University Press of Kansas, 2000 (pp. 37–39).
Cumings, Bruce, *Origins of the Korean War: The Roaring of the Cataract, 1947–1950, Volume 2*, Princeton, NJ, Princeton University Press, 2004 (pp. 749–750).

55 Dingman, Roger, *Atomic Diplomacy during the Korean War*, Cambridge, Massachusetts, The MIT Press, 1988 (pp. 62–63).

56 The President's News Conference, November 30, 1950, The American Presidency Project, University of California at Santa Barbara.

57 Giangreco, Dennis M., and Moore, Kathryn, *Dear Harry: Truman's Mailroom, 1945–1953*, Mechanicsburg, PA, Stackpole Books, 1999 (p. 320).

58 Ham, Paul, *Hiroshima Nagasaki: The Real Story of the Atomic Bombings and their Aftermath*, New York, Doubleday, 2012 (p. 503).

59 Magdaleno, Johnny, 'Algerians suffering from French atomic legacy, 55 years after nuke tests,' *Al Jazeera*, March 1, 2015.

60 'The Gallup Brain: Americans and the Korean War,' Gallup (http://www.gallup.com/poll/7741/Gallup-Brain-Americans-Korean-War.aspx).
Haynes, Richard F., *The Awesome Power: Harry S. Truman as Commander-in-Chief*, Baton Rouge, Louisiana State University Press, 1999 (p. 95).

61 'Majority Supports Use of Atomic Bomb on Japan in WWII,' Gallup, (http://www.gallup.com/poll/17677/Majority-Supports-Use-Atomic-Bomb-Japan—WWII.aspx).
Tannenwald, Nina, *Nuclear Taboo: The United States and the Non-Use of Nuclear Weapons Since 1945*, Cambridge, Cambridge Studies in International Relations, 2008 (pp. 129–130).
Ryan, Mark, *Chinese Attitudes Toward Nuclear Weapons: China and the United States During the Korean War*, New York, Routledge, 1990.

62 MacDonald, Callum, 'The atomic bomb and the Korean War, 1950–53,' in: Richardson, Dick, *Decisions and Diplomacy: Studies in Twentieth Century International History*, Abingdon, Routledge, 2005 (p. 185)

63 'Jittery Capital Hears Demands for Use of Atom Bomb,' *Chicago Daily Tribune*,

November 29, 1950 (p. 1).

64 Ham, Paul, *Hiroshima Nagasaki: The Real Story of the Atomic Bombings and their Aftermath*, New York, Doubleday, 2012 (pp. 435–427).

65 Truman, Margaret, *Harry S. Truman*, New York, William Morrow & Company, 1973 (pp. 495–496).
'USE OF A-BOMB IN KOREA STUDIED BY U.S.—TRUMAN,' *Pittsburgh Press*, November 30, 1950, (p. 1).
The President's News Conference, November 30, 1950, The American Presidency Project, University of California at Santa Barbara.

66 Gwertzman, Bernard, 'U.S. Papers Tell of '53 Policy to Use A-Bomb in Korea,' *New York Times*, June 8, 1984.
Levine, Alan J., *Stalin's Last War; Korea and the Approach to World War III*, Jefferson, McFarland & Company, 2005 (p. 279).

67 'Thaw in the Koreas?,' *Bulletin of Atomic Scientists*, vol. 48, no. 3, April 1992 (p.18).
Weintraub, Stanley, *MacArthur's War: Korea and the Undoing of an American Hero*, New York, Free Press, 2000 (p. 263).

68 U.S. National Archive, FR7: 1326.

69 Hastings, Max, *Korean War*, London, Michael Joseph, 1988 (p. 192).

70 Grosscup, Beau, *Strategic Terror: The Politics and Ethics of Aerial Bombardment*, London, Zed Books, 2013 (Chapter 5: Cold War Strategic Bombing: From Korea to Vietnam, Part 4: The Bombing of Korea).

71 Tucker, Spencer C., *The Encyclopaedia of the Korean War: A Political, Social, and Military History Volume I*, Santa Barbara, ABC-CLIO, 2010 (p. 645).
James, D. Clayton, *The Years of MacArthur: Volume 2, 1941–1945*, Boston, Houghton Mifflin, 1975 (pp. 578–579).
Crane, Conrad C, *American Airpower Strategy in Korea, 1950–1953*, Lawrence, Kansas, University Press of Kansas, 2000 (p. 71).
Deane, Hugh, *The Korean War, 1945–1953*, San Francisco, CA, China Books and Periodicals, 1999 (p. 145).

72 'Thaw in the Koreas?,' *Bulletin of Atomic Scientists*, vol. 48, no. 3, April 1992 (pp.18–19).

73 Anders, Roger M, *The Atomic Bomb and the Korean War: Gordon Dean and the Issue of Civilian Control*, Lexington, Society for Military History, 1988, (pp.3–4).
James, D. Clayton, *The Years of MacArthur: Volume 2, 1941–1945*, Boston, Houghton Mifflin, 1975 (p. 591).

74 Ibid. (p. 591).

75 Cumings, Bruce, *Korea's Place in the Sun: A Modern History*, New York, W. W. Norton & Company, 1997 (p. 149).

76 Pape, Robert A., *Bombing to Win; Air Power and Coercion in War*, Ithaca, NY, Cornell University Press, 1996 (p. 146).

77 Dingman, Roger, *Atomic Diplomacy during the Korean War*, Cambridge, MA, The MIT Press, 1988 (pp.75–76).

78 Elliot, David C., 'Project Vista and Nuclear Weapons in Europe,' *International Security*, vol. 2, issue, 1, Summer 1986 (pp.163–183).

79 Hasbrouck, S. V, 'memo to file (November 7, 1951), G-3 Operations file, box 38-A,' Library of Congress, 1951.
Army Chief of Staff, 'memo to file (November 20, 1951), G-3 Operations file, box 38-A,' Library of Congress, 1951.
Cumings, Bruce, *Origins of the Korean War: The Roaring of the Cataract, 1947–1950, Volume 2*, Princeton, NJ, Princeton University Press, 2004 (p. 752).
Tucker, Spencer C., *The Encyclopaedia of the Korean War: A Political, Social, and Military*, Santa Barbara, ABC-CLIO, 2010 (p. 645).
'Thaw in the Koreas?,' *Bulletin of Atomic Scientists*, vol. 48, no. 3, April 1992 (p. 19).

80 'Nagasaki remembers atomic bomb victims 73 years on,' *Deutsche Welle*, August 9, 2018.
Pilkington, Ed, 'Would I drop the atomic bomb again? Yes, I would,' *The Guardian*, May 20, 2010.
81 Cumings, Bruce, *Korea's Place in the Sun: A Modern History*, New York, W. W. Norton & Company, 1997 (p. 150).
82 Levine, Alan J., *Stalin's Last War; Korea and the Approach to World War III*, Jefferson, McFarland & Company, 2005 (p. 57)
83 Gwertzman, Bernard, 'U.S. Papers Tell of '53 Policy to Use A-Bomb in Korea,' *New York Times*, June 8, 1984.
J. Whitfield, Stephen, *The Culture of the Cold War*, Baltimore, MD, Johns Hopkins University Press, 1996 (pp. 6–7).
84 Winnington, Alan, and Burchett, Wilfred, *Plain Perfidy, The Plot to Wreck the Korea Peace*, Britain-China Friendship Association, 1954 (p. 12).
Gwertzman, Bernard, 'U.S. Papers Tell of '53 Policy to Use A-Bomb in Korea,' *New York Times*, June 8, 1984.
85 Ibid.
Levine, Alan J., *Stalin's Last War; Korea and the Approach to World War III*, Jefferson, McFarland & Company, 2005 (p. 279).
86 Bennett, Bruce W., 'A surgical strike against North Korea? Not a viable option,' *Fox News*, July 14, 2017.
87 Cumings, Bruce, *The Korean War: A History*, New York, Modern Library, 2010 (p. 30).
88 Cumings, Bruce, *Korea's Place in the Sun: A Modern History*, New York, W. W. Norton & Company, 1997 (p. 149).
89 Williams, Peter, and Wallace, David, *Unit 731; Japan's Secret Biological Warfare in World War II*, The Free Press, 1989.
90 Nie, Jing Bao, 'The West's Dismissal of the Khabarovsk trial as "Communist Propaganda": Ideology, evidence and international bioethics,' *Journal of Bioethical Inquiry*, vol. 1, issue 1, April 2004 (pp. 32–42).
91 Taylor, Jeremy, 'Biology at War: A Plague in the Wind,' *BBC Horizon*, (Documentary), October 29, 1984.
92 Powell, John W., 'A Hidden Chapter in History,' *Bulletin of Atomic Scientists*, vol. 37, no. 8, December 1989 (pp. 44–52).
93 Blum, William, *Killing Hope: U.S. Military and C.I.A. Interventions Since World War II*, London, Zed Books, 2003 (p. 26).
94 Ibid. (p. 26).
95 Hearings, United States Congress House Committee on Un-American Activities (p. 1652).
96 Knightley, Philipp, *The First Casualty: The War Correspondent as Hero and Myth-Maker from the Crimea to Kosovo* (revised edition), London, Prion, 2000 (p. 388).
97 Report of the International Scientific Commission for the Investigation of the Facts Concerning Bacterial Warfare in Korea and China, 1952.
98 Williams, Peter, and Wallace, David, *Unit 731; Japan's Secret Biological Warfare in World War II*, The Free Press (British ed.), 1989 (Chapter 17: 'Korean War').
99 Ibid. (Chapter 17: Korean War).
100 *Report on U.S. Crimes in Korea*, Commission of International Association of Democratic Lawyers, March 31, 1952.
101 Ibid. (pp. 7–8).
102 Deane, Hugh, *The Korean War, 1945–1953*, San Francisco, CA, China Books and Periodicals, 1999 (p. 158).
103 Zhang, Shu Guang, *Mao's Military Romanticism: China and the Korean War, 1950–1953*, Lawrence, University Press of Kansas, 1995 (p. 185).

104 Méray, Tibor, *On Burchett*, Kallista, Victoria, Callistemon Publications, 2008 (pp. 261–262).
105 Zhang, Shu Guang, *Mao's Military Romanticism: China and the Korean War, 1950–1953*, Lawrence, University Press of Kansas, 1995 (p. 185).
106 Caute, David, *The Great Fear: The Anti-Communist Purge Under Truman and Eisenhower*, New York, Touchstone, 1979 (p. 415).
107 Deane, Hugh, *The Korean War, 1945–1953*, San Francisco, CA, China Books and Periodicals, 1999 (p. 155).
108 Chaddock, Dave, *This Must Be the Place: How the U.S. Waged Germ Warfare in the Korean War and Denied It Ever Since,* Seattle, Bennett & Hastings, 2013.
109 Marks, John, *The Search for the Manchurian Candidate: The CIA and Mind Control*, New York, Times Books, 1979 (p. 8). In September 1950, the *Miami News* published an article by Edward Hunter titled *'Brain-Washing' Tactics Force Chinese into Ranks of Communist Party*. It was the first ever printed use in any language of the term 'brainwashing.' Hunter, a CIA propaganda operative who worked undercover as a journalist, turned out a steady stream of books and articles on the subject for the purpose of delegitimising the claims of returned American veterans.
110 McCormack, Gavan, 'Korea: Wilfred Burchett's Thirty Year's War,' in: Kiernan, Ben, *Burchett: Reporting the Other Side of the World, 1939–1983*, Quartet Books, London, 1986 (p. 204).
111 Blum, William, *Killing Hope: U.S. Military and C.I.A. Interventions Since World War II*, London, Zed Books, 2003 (Chapter 30: Cuba 1959 to 1980s: The Unforgivable Revolution).
112 Hornberger, Jacob C., 'The Pentagon's B-52 Message to North Koreans,' *The Future of Freedom Foundation*, January 15, 2016.
113 Deane, Hugh, *The Korean War, 1945–1953*, San Francisco, CA, China Books and Periodicals, 1999 (p. 155).
114 Ibid. (p. 156).
115 Ibid. (p. 155).
116 Endicott, Stephen and Hagerman, Edward, *The United States and Biological Warfare: Secrets from the Early Cold War and Korea,* Bloomington, Indiana University Press, 1998.
117 Harris, Sheldon H., *Factories of Death: Japanese Biological Warfare, 1932–1945, and the American Coverup*, Abingdon, Taylor & Francis, 2002 (p. 230).
118 Wise, David, and Ross, Thomas, *The Invisible Government*, New York, Random House, 1965 (p. 114).
'The People of the CIA…John Downey & Richard Fecteau,' Website of the Central Intelligence Agency, News & Information, November 14, 2007.
119 Lockwood, Jeffrey A., *Six-Legged Soldiers: Using Insects as Weapons of War*, Oxford, Oxford University Press, 2010 (p. 189).

Chapter 6

AS IF ALL KOREANS WERE THE ENEMY:

AMERICAN WARTIME CONDUCT TOWARDS SOUTH KOREAN CIVILIANS

Although North Korea's population bore the brunt of the killings by the U.S.-led coalition, perpetrated through firebombings, massacres on the ground and the destruction of food supplies among other means, the nature of U.S. perceptions towards the Korean people as an Asiatic race and suspicions of widespread pro-DPRK and anti-Western sentiments among the ROK's population led to South Koreans being intentionally targeted on several of occasions. While its remarkable tolerance for collateral damage to South Korean civilians had devastating results, the U.S. Military also adopted an official policy of targeting and killing ROK civilians shortly after the outbreak of hostilities.

From the war's outset, while carrying out a constant retreat southwards, the U.S. Army carried out a brutal scorched earth policy against South Korean populations centres, destroying the homes, crops, livestock and other properties in which many families had lived for generations to deny them to the advancing North Koreans. This left millions destitute. Upon taking command of the 8th Army in December 1950 General Matthew Ridgway referred to this strategy, which by then had ravaged settlements across almost all of southern Korea over the past six months, as "destruction for destruction's sake."[1] As later affirmed by General Curtis LeMay: "we burned down just about every city in North Korea and South Korea *both*."[2] Ralph Bernotas, an American serviceman from F Company, recalled of the application of scorched in Korea: "Food—whatever the hell—they left nothing… I used to sit over at the farm at my fireplace, and I'd think, boy, in our country nothing like that could happen—somebody come in here and tell me to move out, they're going to burn my house!" These policies continued into the winter, and Koreans were left without food or shelter to face the country's harsh subfreezing climate.[3] The *National Interest* thus described American scorched earth tactics as having "inflicted a tremendous death toll" on the local population.[4]

The South Korean city of Yongdong exemplified the application of the scorched earth policy. An Associated Press reporter observed, following the departure of the U.S. military, that what had for millennia been a major population centre "no longer exists as a city. It looks like Nagasaki after the atom bomb… Yongdong has probably been here for 4,000 years—and never known such silence."[5] The United Press similarly reported from Wonju, a South Korean city destroyed by the retreating U.S. Army 2nd Division: "before the retreat, every house in Wonju was set afire, every bridge demolished, every morsel of food destroyed. Patrols were sent into the countryside to set fire to huts and haystacks… Then the artillery and aviation entered the picture." The London *Times* reported on the same incident that on January 15 alone, 22 villages and 300 haystacks were burned.[6]

The American scorched earth policy bore a strong contrast to the conduct of the Korean People's Army and later the Chinese People's Volunteer Army, gaining the East Asian allies a far higher standing in the eyes of the Korean population including those south of the 38th parallel. On November 16, 1950, the London *Times* published an article showing that the DPRK leadership rejected a scorched earth program, refraining on principle from burning or destroying the local population's housing, crops or food supplies while retreating. Although it would have denied U.S.-led coalition forces valuable supplies, the North Koreans left the countryside almost untouched. A *New York Times* correspondent noted regarding the stark contrast that emerged:

> when the Koreans saw that the Communists had left their homes and schools standing in retreat while the United Nations troops, fighting with much more destructive tools, left only blackened spots where towns once stood, the Communists even in retreat chalked up moral victories.[7]

The London *Times* report came to much the same conclusion.[8] This proved one of multiple cases where sharply contrasting conduct towards civilians indicated which of the warring parties had the best interests of the Korean people at heart.

The devastation caused by the scorched earth campaign was very far from the full extent of American misconduct towards the South

Korean population. The U.S. Military was heavily complicit in the killings of over 200,000 South Korean political prisoners and their families by the Rhee government in the early days of the war, often observing and photographing the massacres.[9] American personnel on the ground also received direct orders to target fleeing civilians leading to massacres of South Koreans across the country. While the nature of the Syngman Rhee government meant that no official investigation was permitted, and claims of massacres thus received negligible coverage until the Cold War's end, reports from the U.S. Military itself and interviews with U.S. servicemen, South Korean survivors and other eyewitnesses provide key insight into the killings perpetrated. These eyewitness sources provide valuable accounts of the events which took place, giving insight into the mindsets of the perpetrators and impressions of the victims as only first-hand sources can.

The view that Koreans as a people could not be trusted was highly prevalent throughout the U.S. Military. This was partly due to the large number of South Korean soldiers who had either abandoned their positions or defected to the KPA in the war's early stages, the warm welcome the KPA received in many population centres[10] and the known unpopularity of the Rhee government.[11] CIA intelligence reports showed that even in the South Korean capital, the stronghold of the Rhee government, most of the student population actively worked with the North Koreans and welcomed the arrival of the Korean People's Army.[12] The KPA was equally popular in the countryside if not more so, with the rural population having endured great hardship under USAMGIK and later under Rhee. The North Koreans by contrast, according to the conservative London *Times*, were viewed "as the leaders of agricultural and other reforms" which had long been demanded.[13] Indeed, even those hard-line anti-communist South Koreans who described the government in Pyongyang and its leader Kim Il Sung as "detestable" often saw DPRK rule as the lesser evil next to the "criminality" of the Rhee government.[14] Thus there was strong pretext on which to doubt the people's loyalty or affinity to the United States, Rhee and the order they represented.

Award-winning Special Correspondent for the Associated Press Charles Hanley noted regarding the reasons for widespread South Korean support of the KPA: "Many [South] Koreans were simply disgusted with the corrupt, autocratic Rhee years. That opposition deepened with the bloodbath of executions carried out by the retreating government through the summer, when military police and other agents shot thousands of leftist political prisoners and dumped their bodies in mass graves outside Taejon and Taegu and elsewhere in the South." He noted that the restoring of people's committees, which had enjoyed widespread support until their forcible abolishment under U.S. military rule, as well as the promotion of women's organizations and redistribution of land, all served to make the KPA highly popular.[15] The contrasting brutality of the U.S. and ROK forces only exacerbated this. According to the accounts of South Korean villagers given years later, the KPA were highly respectful towards the southern population. Villagers interviewed particularly emphasized the North Koreans' respect for local women, which bore a stark contrast to Western soldiers who had committed widespread rapes.[16]

The Rhee government, like the Americans, was well aware of the alienation of its own population, and after regaining control of South Korean territory it quickly arranged mass executions of suspected KPA sympathisers. According to the former U.S. diplomat Gregory Henderson, by November 1950: "16,115 suspects had been arrested and over 500 condemned to death, often after summary trial: "Additional tens of thousands—probably over 100,000—were killed without any trial whatsoever when ROK soldiers and the Counter-intelligence Corps re-captured…areas of leftist repute."[17] In towns and villages known to hold pro-North Korean sympathies, brutal massacres by Rhee's forces were the norm.

An assessment of military records sheds light on the orders given to American units to massacre South Korean civilians from the earliest days of the war, although not all reports from this time have been made available. Groups of Korean refugees displaced by the scorched earth campaign, and at times by American bombing raids on their homes, were particularly prominent targets. An example of such orders to kill refugees came on July 25, 1950, when the U.S. 5th Air Force Advanced Headquarters reported: "The army has requested that we strafe all civilian parties that are approaching our positions. To date we have complied with the army request."[18] The following day the 25th Infantry Division reported: "General [William B.] Kean directed that all civilians moving around in the combat zone will be considered as unfriendly and shot." It later became increasingly clear that what was considered the combat zone was far from limited to the frontlines of conflict.[19]

One of the most notorious massacres of South Korean civilians was that at the village of No Gun Ri. Survivor Suh Jong Gap recalled in an interview: "The Americans forced us out of our village. We didn't know anything, so we just followed them because they said they would take us to safety." The civilians were forced onto a railway line overlooked by the 7th Cavalry's main positions. Suh Jong Gap recalled: "I was at the head of a long line of people. I could see the American soldiers standing with rifles, trying to keep us on the tracks. They seemed to make sure that we couldn't move at all." Troops then withdrew and left the refugees on the railway line. "Just after 1 o'clock I could see a reconnaissance plane circling above us. Then the Americans seemed to talk to each other on the radio." Planes from the U.S. Air Force appeared overhead, "and then they dropped bombs on the contained group of people." Survivor Cho Soo Jaoc recalled of the same event: "I crawled out from under my mother and climbed on top of her. I shouted "mum, mum" but she was dead. When I stroked her head with my hand, I found my hand sliding inside. I didn't know what hit my mother, but the back of her head was blown off."[20]

One South Korean survivor, Yang Hae Chan, recalled when interviewed: "American soldiers broke into our house with rifles and bayonets. They didn't even take off their boots. They searched inside the house with a torch, found us and ordered us out. I was young and scared. I hid behind my mother and father clinging to them. My father said the Americans had come to evacuate us, and we should pack up and leave our home." He and his family too, along with those of Suh and Cho, were intentionally targeted by American soldiers and aircraft. Chan then recalled: "After the strafing and bombing everything went quiet. Then I saw the American soldiers reappear. They started checking through the dead and the living, poking the bodies lying on the railway line with their bayonets. Those who were still alive were forced to get up at gunpoint. The Americans herded us further down the railroad tracks, so those of us who survived the bombing were made to move on again." Many of the survivors of the bombing were badly wounded, but they were all herded on towards the village of No Gun Ri, directly beneath the guns of the 2nd Battalion of the 7th Cavalry. They were then exterminated by small arms fire.[21]

Joe Jackman from the U.S. Army's 7th Cavalry 2nd Battalion recalled of the targeting of civilians near No Gun Ri that, in regard to the Korean civilians, he and his unit were ordered to:

> "kill them all." Then of course there was a lieutenant who was screaming like a mad man "fire on everything, kill them

> all"... There was a hell of a lot of fire going. Hell of a lot of shooting. A hell of a lot of shooting. Because I know the infantrymen, the infantrymen, we used to carry 10–15 bandoliers of ammunition, and even help machine gunners carrying ammunition. There was a hell of a lot of expenditure of ammunition.

Regarding the nature of the targets, Jackman recalled: "Kids, there was kids out there. It didn't matter what it was. 8 to 80, blind, crippled or crazy they [U.S. personnel] shot them. It just seemed like all Koreans were the enemy."[22]

George Early of the 7th Cavalry's heavy mortar company recalled being given the order to massacre Korean refugees:

> A lot of refugees came down the road in a group. It was 50–60–70 people. So I ran up the road there by the railroad tracks to Captain Johnson and told him. He said go down, take the machine gun, shoot those people and we'll pull out. I said we can't kill all these people, and he pulled out his handgun, a 45, and pointed it at my head and he said, he said "I said kill them," said "you're disobeying a direct order in combat." He says "I will kill you myself." He said "go back there and kill those people." I said "yes sir."[23]

Hundreds of survivors of the first round of shooting at No Gun Ri ran into railway tunnels seeking shelter. They remained there under fire for the next three days. Survivor Yang Hae Chan recalled: "The floor inside the tunnel was a mix of gravel of sand. People clawed with their bare hands to make holes to hide in. Other people piled up the dead like a barricade and hid behind the bodies as a shield against the bullets." George Early of the 7th Cavalry's heavy mortar company recalled the situation as follows: "Everybody just ceased moving. No one was moving over there. They either were dead, or so seriously wounded they couldn't move, or if there were alive they weren't moving. Because if they move they know they're gonna be fired at some more."[24] Early later recalled: "I remember seeing this woman on her hands and knees. She was crawling. You could just see the bullets bouncing...bouncing around her. She kept crawling, crawling. And finally I guess she was just hit. And that was it. And she just stopped, just, just like that. Just like she was hanging on the side of this hill with her fingers." Buddy Wenzel, another serviceman from the 7th Cavalry, also testified to his role in the No Gun Ri massacre. Wenzel, recalling the orders he received, stated: "Word came through the line, open fire on them. They were running toward us and we opened fire… We understood that we were fighting for these people, but we had orders to fire on them and we did."[25]

A Korean survivor at No Gun Ri recalled the desperation of the victims:

> A baby boy's mother was killed during the strafing on the rail track. The father managed to get the baby to the tunnels, but the boy was hungry and frightened. He cried and cried. And the American troops fired their guns into the tunnels whenever the boy cried. The bullets fired in the direction of the crying. People screamed that more would be shot if the baby kept crying. The father didn't know what to do. He might have thought the baby would die anyway, but he decided to silence it in order to save the others. He took to boy to the back of the tunnel and pushed him face down into a pool of water. I watched him doing that and thought, what could be more tragic than this.

Yang Hae Chan recalled of the incident: "I clung to my mother and, despite her pain and injuries, she hugged me tightly. I cried like mad. I was so scared of the dead bodies piled up inside the tunnels. I still have vivid memories of people crying and moaning because of the shooting. There were so many cries in the tunnel. I can still see bodies writhing in agony."[26] Koreans who strayed outside the tunnel to collect food or drink stream water were shot. One survivor, Koo Hun, recalled: "It looked like the Americans were shooting us out of boredom."[27]

While many of the Korean survivors presented their cases against the United States Military, the Pentagon dismissed all such allegations as impossible and claimed the U.S. Army 7th Cavalry was not in the area where the massacre took place. It was only after a private investigation was launched into the allegations 49 years later that they could be proven. The investigators, an Associated Press reporting team, mapped the movements of U.S. forces and analysed documents from high ranking officers which elaborated on the policy of engaging Korean civilians as enemy targets. The final report was difficult for many Americans and

South Koreans to comprehend, as such conduct was wholly at odds with common portrayals of the Americans intervening as benevolent protectors of Korean freedom. The Pentagon amended its position in response to the evidence presented, reporting the deaths as unfortunate tragedies inherent to war, but did not take responsibility for the actions of U.S. forces. They claimed no orders were given to target Korean civilians, despite substantial evidence to the contrary, including claims made by soldiers who participated in the massacre. The Pentagon declined to be interviewed on the matter when presented with evidence by investigators.[28]

According to the investigators there were orders for American aircraft to strafe refugees, but this evidence was omitted from the Pentagon's report, which claimed that the strafing of civilians by the Air Force was not deliberate. Other evidence however, such as a memo written the day before the events at No Gun Ri by Fifth Air Force operations chief Colonel Turner Rogers, strongly indicates that the Air Force had orders to target civilians and supports the claims of investigators against those of the Pentagon. The memo states: "The Army has requested we strafe all civilian refugee parties that are noted approaching our positions. To date, we have complied with the army request in this respect."[29] American and South Korean eyewitness reports strongly support the investigators' claim that organised strafing took place.

Korean War Veteran, former U.S. Congressman and Pentagon advisor Pete McCloskey confirmed that the U.S. pilots had orders to target South Korean civilians. He stated that American fighters:

> did have orders to strafe "people in white" [a term for Korean civilians, who traditionally wore white] approaching their position. At the Valley Forge [aircraft] carrier they unearthed a log that the Navy pilots were told to shoot any group of eight or ten civilians approaching the army position. I don't think there is any question that the strafing occurred—under orders. There was no question that that was the order the Air Force was obeying from the army—strafe the refugees.[30]

Associated Press correspondent Charles Hanley, who was heavily involved in the No Gun Ri investigation, indicated that there was a cover-up by the U.S. military during the investigation to prevent the orders to target civilians from being publicized. The log for the 7th Cavalry which contained a record of the orders they were given, including any orders to target civilians, inexplicably disappeared from the Pentagon's archives during the investigation. The military had, according to Hanley, "suppressed vital documents and testimony, as it strove to exonerate itself of culpability and liability"—highlighting "glaring irregularities" in the official narrative the Pentagon put forward.[31] He stated regarding this:

> What is extremely important to realize is that the single critical document that would have carried the orders to shoot the refugees at No Gun Ri, the 7th Cavalry regiment log, is missing inexplicably. And not only is it missing, but the Pentagon report does not disclose the fact that it is missing. And yet this report declared that there were no orders at No Gun Ri, declared that flatly although it does not have the document that would prove that one way or the other.[32]

If the Pentagon admitted to having ordered its soldiers to kill hundreds of South Korean civilians at No Gun Ri, or many thousands more across the country in similar incidents, it would seriously challenge the image of the United States as a protector of the Korean people. America's primary pretext for retaining a sizeable and indefinite military presence on the peninsula would thus be undermined. While orders were recorded in the communications logs of each division and the log of the 8th Cavalry and others were all available, only the 7th Cavalry communications log, which based on the testimonies of witnesses from both sides would have been the most incriminating source of evidence, had disappeared.[33] Based on these highly suspicious circumstances, it is likely that the information logged in the 7th Cavalry communications record held evidence the Pentagon preferred to keep away from the public and the investigators. George Preece, a career soldier who was present during the massacre, concluded regarding the disappearance of the log: "it must have been covered up."[34]

Charles Hanley commented on the threat information on the widespread massacres posed to the image of the U.S. Military: "This is a Pandora's Box for the U.S. government. It does seem that a decision was made that they had to close the door on No Gun Ri in order to close the door on God knows how many other cases." Despite the orders tying directly to No Gun Ri being absent, at least 14 other documents from high ranking officers in the first months of the war point to a widespread policy of treating South Korean refugees as enemy targets. These include orders such as: "shoot all refugees coming across the river," "refugees will be considered 'enemy' and dispersed by all available fire including artillery" and "all refugees are fair game" among others.[35] In the mid-2000s, six years after the Associated Press investigation, a letter from U.S. ambassador John Muccio to the U.S. State Department emerged from archives and further confirmed that killing refugees was official U.S. policy, leading survivors to demand the investigation be reopened but to no avail.[36]

Pete McCloskey commented on the U.S. approach to allegations of war crimes: "The American government, the Pentagon, don't want the truth to come out if it will embarrass the government. I think it is almost a rule of political science. It is a law. The government will always lie about embarrassing matters. I think the army just chose to try to downplay the terrible character of army leadership in 1950."[37] On the day the first Associated Press report of the No Gun Ri massacre was published, it was discovered that the South Korean government had recently plastered over the bullet holes where refugees had hidden from the U.S. 7th Cavalry over 40 years before. This fuelled allegations by survivors of a coverup.[38] The U.S. government for its part announced that it would not investigate any more reported incidents of attacks on civilians, despite many similar cases being brought forward by South Korean survivors.

The No Gun Ri massacre was hardly a unique incident, but it gained unique publicity because of the professional and well-publicized investigation which addressed it. Much like My Lai in the Vietnam War, the single most well-known massacre was remarkable only because it happened to be investigated and its details publicized—not because such occurrences were not commonplace.[39] The targeting of civilians at No Gun Ri did not take place on the initiative of American soldiers themselves, but rather was ordered by the military's command with similar orders being given to ground and air units operating across the country as part of a general policy. The investigators who covered No Gun Ri did not attempt to prove any other incidents of the massacre of civilians, although similar claims by survivors of other massacres have been extremely common.

The consistency of the accounts of the American perpetrators with those of the Korean survivors diminishes considerably the possibility of fabrication at No Gun Ri and other massacre sites. The lack of any incentive to fabricate atrocities, and the pressure not to testify at all due to the serous risks involved on the Korean side,[40] mean survivor-reported massacres are generally likely to be true. Criticism of the U.S. Military was strictly forbidden by ROK governments for decades, as Seoul gained much of its legitimacy from supposedly defending the Korean people from the "evils of communism" with American backing. This narrative rested heavily on covering up the reality of U.S. conduct towards the population and on demonising North Korea to make America appear the lesser evil. As one No Gun Ri survivor, Eun Yong, recalled: "We couldn't say publicly that the Americans committed such things during the war. The United States was such a powerful country. Speaking against the Americans was tantamount to calling yourself a communist."[41] Suspected communists were known to be disappeared, shot and buried in mass graves—a fate which awaited suspected dissenters. With testifying against the U.S. Military itself extremely dangerous, atrocity fabrication by survivors remains highly unlikely.

Further supporting the claims of both the survivors and the U.S. soldiers, journalists accompanying North Korean forces, who arrived at No Gun Ri in the wake of the American retreat, reported finding "indescribably gruesome scenes" there. North Korean journalist Chun Wook reported: "Shrubs and weeds in the area and a creek running through the tunnels were drenched in blood and the area was covered with two or three layers of bodies. About 400 bodies of old and young people and children covered the scene so that it was difficult to walk around without stepping on corpses."[42] With chances of co-ordination between the North Korean journalists, South Korean refugees and American soldiers in their testimonies negligible to non-existent, it is highly likely that the stories of all three match one another because all were reporting the truth as they saw it.

The Pentagon elected not to pay compensation to the victims of No Gun Ri, nor to issue an apology or co-operate with any further investigations.[43] The emergence of further evidence of orders to kill refugees in the early 2000s led then-Secretary of State Condoleezza Rice to cable the U.S. embassy in Seoul, outlining that South Koreans would not be offered an explanation—allowing for further obfuscation in accordance with American interests.[44] The U.S. faced the prospect of setting a precedent which would allow the victims of numerous massacres throughout the country to similarly make claims against the U.S. Military. Worse still, victims of hundreds of alleged massacres in North Korea, former

South Vietnam and other countries could begin to openly testify as well. David Straub, the political chief at the U.S. Embassy in Seoul during the No Gun Ri investigation, noted that meeting survivors' demands would have set an undesirable precedent for similar cases.[45]

Given the considerable quantities of firepower brought to bear and the scarcity of survivors, it is highly likely that many other incidents of massacres were never reported because they left no survivors. The South Korean authorities have logged reports of 61 separate massacres of civilians carried out by U.S. forces, including the naval shelling of refugees at the port of Pohang in September 1950 and killings of families sheltering in a shrine at Kokkan Ri.[46] These did not include the massive and indiscriminate air attacks and saturation napalm attacks on southern population centres with a suspected North Korean presence which were extremely common. South Korean survivors, in interviews with foreign investigators many decades later, recalled multiple grotesque scenes of carnage.[47] Oh Won Rok, president of a South Korean association of 80 groups of massacre survivors, indicated in 2010 that the investigations had so far revealed very little of the full extent of the massacres—further noting that the ROK government had gone to considerable lengths to bury information on the massacres.[48]

A week after the No Gun Ri massacre the U.S. 1st Cavalry is reported to have carried out a massacre at the Naktong River. The unit had just retreated across the river via the bridge, and thousands of refugees were massed on the other side eager to cross. General Hobart Gay ordered the demolition of the bridge which, according to his own memoirs, went down with hundreds of refugees still on it. The advancing North Korean forces, which had forced the U.S. 1st Cavalry's retreat, would not reach the river for another four days, and the decision to kill the refugees was thus in no way prompted by urgency. A second bridge elsewhere on the front was also blown up on the same day by the 14th Combat Engineers as refugees were running across it. The Engineers only noted: "results excellent," failing to mention the civilians they had just killed.[49]

Cut off with the bridges blown, South Korean civilians waded across the river. A survivor, Kim Jin Suk, recalled: "when we were half way across the river, what looked like American soldiers began shooting at us. First my father, who was in front, was shot. Then my brother was hit. I hid behind our cow, holding its tail. As the shooting became heavier, I saw piles of dead bodies floating down the river like straw."[50] Kim later identified that they were American soldiers which had fired on him, and he recalled that his father and many others died soon afterwards. Private Leon L. Denis reported of the Korean civilians targeted: "They were average folks, ladies, children and old men, carrying their baggage on their heads."[51] Cho Koon Ja, another refugee, similarly reported U.S. troops firing on refugees crossing the river and the resulting carnage. Cho survived and fled to her hometown, No Gun Ri, where a more terrible sight awaited her.[52]

Melvin Durham, a U.S. Army serviceman of F Company, recalled the orders to fire on civilians to prevent them from crossing the river:

> We was holding that railroad bridge to keep them from coming across that. But those people—there was women, children, old people—we had to eliminate them... Our orders was to start opening fire and when we did, there wasn't nothing standing but a couple of cows. We fired for about an hour, an hour and a half.[53]

The 8th Cavalry too were ordered by their commander, Colonel Raymond D. Palmer, on August 9, to "shoot all refugees coming across the river." These stranded Koreans carried with them a sign stating "Americans, We Are Not Communists," unaware that U.S. commanders were under no such impressions and knowingly gave the orders to target ordinary civilians. Whether they were communist or not was irrelevant—all Korean people in the area were targets. U.S. Air Force P-51 fighters proceeded to strafe the Korean refugees on the far side of the river—even those who did not attempt to cross.[54]

It seemed that nowhere in their own country were South Koreans safe from American attacks, and after the Americans burned down their homes, refugees were targeted even in their places of hiding. On August 11, 1950, refugees sheltering in a Confucian shrine were massacred by U.S. forces of the 25th Infantry Division. Survivors recall that 80 were killed. A few days later thousands of South Korean civilians took refuge from a battle on a sheltered beach, where they remained for days in apparent safety. While they seemed to have escaped the U.S. Army, they were in full view of U.S. Navy warships stationed off the coast. In the morning hours of September 1, 1950, the warships suddenly opened fire on the civilians. This was done completely without warning, and there were no North Korean units nearby. The U.S. Navy was found in an investigation conducted by the ROK's Truth and Reconciliation Commission decades later to have knowingly targeted refugees sheltering on the shoreline at Pohang.[55] Pak Ke San, a survivor, recalled:

> Of all the terrible images I remember the most, it is the moment my sister's head was blown off and my mother lost one of her breasts. These two images have haunted me for my entire life. A little baby from our family was also killed. But how could I possibly forget seeing my sister's head being blown off in front of my own eyes.[56]

As the U.S. military was pressed into a second major retreat following China's entry into the war, ending prospects of a conclusive "Home By Christmas Offensive," resentment towards Koreans as an East Asian race grew. This had significant repercussions for treatment of South Korean civilians. Professor Callum MacDonald, a British Korea expert, noted that following the routing of the U.S. Eighth Army, American soldiers engaged in "looting, rape and assaults on civilians. The 'gooks' were resented and blamed for the rout beyond the Chongchon." This combined with the policy of burning houses, killing livestock and destroying rice supplies as part of the American scorched earth policy imposed on Korea provoked a reign of terror which left South Korean civilians in the Army's path desperate and often destitute. [57]

U.S. forces had also closely collaborated with South Korean military units in carrying out mass killings among the civilian population. After the ROK's capital was handed over to Rhee government forces, *Time* magazine reported: "since the liberation of Seoul last December, South Korean firing squads have been busy liquidating 'enemies of the state'… With savage indifference, the military executioners shoot men, women, and children."[58] Similar massacres were reported across the country. Americans too gathered several hundred politically suspect Korean women and held them by force in a warehouse. There they were forced to satisfy the sexual needs of the American personnel—sexual slavery.[59]

Orders for American units to target South Korean civilians were not exclusively given in the opening stages of the war. On January 3, 1951, the 8th Army Headquarters instructed: "You have complete authority in your zone to stop all civilian traffic. Responsibility to place fire on them to include bombing rests with you."[60] Strafing of South Korean civilians continued to be a widespread practice of the U.S. Air Force.

Although strict censorship prevented him from reporting it, Associated Press correspondent Stan Swinton wrote in a letter to his parents on January 30, 1951:

> the most horrifying part of this last advance has been the hundreds of refugees killed by our strafing. The children weren't hit; they just tumbled off their mothers' back and froze to death on the roadside… Do not the enemies we make among the civilian population counterbalance and more than counterbalance the damage we do to the Reds?[61]

Other reports of the strafing of civilians were common. A four-plane mission flying near Taejon, for example, reported strafing fishing boats when military targets could not be found. Much like the North Koreans, South Korean civilians in areas occupied by northern soldiers adapted to hiding in the daytime and cultivating their rice fields only at night to avoid being targeted by American planes, who regularly gunned civilians down in their fields on both sides of the 38th parallel. South Korean civilians recalled after the war ended that North Korean soldiers had warned them not to go out in the daytime and advised them how best to avoid being targeted by American aircraft.[62]

In January 1951 South Korean refugees were still being targeted by the U.S. Air Force, even those as far from the battlefront as several miles south of Seoul. Air Force planes were known to target refugees with incendiaries without provocation, killing hundreds at a time. Fifth Air Force operations chief Colonel Turner Rogers had previously recommended that the Army should shoot the refugees themselves rather than rely on the Air Force to do it for them. This recommendation was not heeded, and even years after the war when the U.S. Army War College conducted a study on the lessons learned in Korea on handling refugees they concluded: "strafing fire from low-flying aircraft is very effective in clearing a road."[63]

The extensive study by the International Association of Democratic Lawyers, previously mentioned in chapter 5, found that massacres of refugees by the U.S. Military occurred across both North and South Korea. They noted that these massacres occurred primarily in two periods as follows:

a) When the American troops were advancing Northwards in September and October 1950, large number of refugees fleeing northwards were cut off by the advancing troops particularly in the areas of Sinchon and Anak. These refugees were clearly distinguishable as refugees, whole families including women and children. The men wearing traditional Korean white clothes, and the women long skirts in colour who were not at the time intermingled with troops of the Korean People's Army. It was these groups which were systematically exterminated.

b) When the American troops retreated in November–December 1950, it is established that large numbers of the inhabitants of the major cities were induced by leaflets and threats to believe that the atom bombs would be dropped and that they should move south with the American troops. These refugees were deliberately exterminated in their thousands by American forces.[64]

Although North Korean and Chinese sources witnessed several similar massacres their accounts were inevitably dismissed. Western and international reports did tell very similar stories, however. *New York Times* correspondent Charles Grutzner, citing U.S. Military sources, reported "the slaughter of hundreds of South Korean civilians, women as well as men, by some U.S. troops and police of the Republic [ROK]."[65] An article in the American Newark *Star-Ledger* in July 1950 stated: "It's not the time to be a Korean, for the Yankees are shooting them all." This corroborated several other Western sources which reported indiscriminate killings of Koreans, northern and southern, by U.S. forces. Pak Chan Hyun, a South Korean lawmaker, found during an investigation in the 1960s that an estimated 10,000 had been executed in Pusan. American Air Force intelligence officer Donald Nichols attested in his 1981 memoir to witnessing an "unforgettable massacre" of "approximately 1,800" at Suwon during the war.[66]

British author Elizabeth Comber had accompanied American forces in the early stages of the war and observed their conduct towards the South Korean population—which included indiscriminate targeting of civilians on a massive scale. She wrote in her diary on July 14, 1950, regarding U.S. forces in Korea: "they think every Korean is an enemy, firing at, and sometimes killing refugees." Two weeks later she described a more serious situation, writing of the U.S. military: "Day after day with their aircraft the Americans are laying waste towns and cities, killing fifty civilians for every one soldier."[67]

Alongside orders to directly target South Korean civilians, the U.S. Military's tolerance of extreme collateral damage to achieve highly limited military objectives proved devastating. A prominent example was the bombing of Seoul's Yongsan district on July 16, 1950, targeted indiscriminately by U.S. bombers when under North Korean control. The attack killed 1,587 South Korean civilians, but was considered a military necessity to slow down the KPA.[68] This attack differed from massacres such as No Gun Ri, as the bombing of Yongsan represented a willingness to kill South Koreans to achieve military objectives against the north—whereas the massacres targeted civilians for no tactical or strategic benefit. While the attack on Yongsan, much like the scorched earth campaign, showed a willingness to impose terrible death and destruction on the South Korean population in order to achieve limited objectives against the north, the massacres took this further, indicating a prevailing sense of enmity towards the Koreans as a race. As the U.S. serviceman Joe Jackman said, "It just seemed like all Koreans were the enemy."[69] While targeting civilians for strategic benefit, as the U.S. Air Force did at Yongsan, is a severe war crime, even the need for strategic gain could not explain the widespread and extremely brutal massacres of civilians under wholly different circumstances.

American conduct, far from being an inevitable part of the nature of war, bears a strong contrast to that of the Chinese and Koreans they were fighting—"an army of barbarians" and the "most primitive of peoples" in the words of the *New York Times*' esteemed military editor Hanson Baldwin.[70] The prevailing American attitude towards the South Korean people can be effectively summarized by a quote from the lauded fighter pilot Ensign David Tatum: "I figured if we had to kill 10 civilians to kill one soldier who might later shoot at us, we were justified." His statement was published in *Time* magazine on January 1, 1951, the edition which awarded the American Fighting Man with the man of the year award for their conduct in Korea in which stories from such supposedly exemplary personnel were published.

Chinese military personnel by contrast were not only strictly forbidden from any forms of vandalism or destruction of Korean property, they were also given the following instructions by Chairman Mao Zedong upon entering the war:

> The Chinese comrades must consider Korea's cause as their own and the commanders and fighters must be instructed to cherish every hill, every river, every tree and every blade of grass in Korea and take not a single needle or a single thread from the Korean people, just the way we feel about our own country and treat our own people. This is the political basis for winning victory. So long as we act this way, final victory will be assured.[71]

Just as the good conduct of the PLA towards China's rural population had been instrumental in winning the Chinese Civil War and gaining mass public support against the Western-backed Guomindang,[72] so too was this prioritized in the Korean theatre.[73]

New York Times reporter George Barrett noted the stark contrast between the Korean population's perception of Chinese forces compared to those of the United States and other Western nations as a result of their vast discrepancy in their conduct. He wrote that widespread and regular rapes committed by U.S. and Canadian forces "have created a deep animosity among large sections of the Korean populace." The Koreans noted in particular that Western soldiers could commit crimes including brutal rapes and killings against civilians with impunity and without reprimand by their superiors. By contrast, Barrett noted, the Chinese military "have impressed many Koreans with the discipline of their troops. Many residents of Seoul seem to go out of their way to tell about the good Chinese behaviour, and especially about executions of two rapists the Chinese are said to have held."[74]

One critical difference between Chinese and Western forces intervening in Korea was that there was no institutional bigotry towards the Korean people in the Chinese military. Racial contempt towards East Asian peoples, communist or otherwise, was prevalent at the highest levels of the U.S. Military and UN command, allowing its soldiers to conduct themselves as conquerors and brutalize those under their power. The war was consistently portrayed in Western reporting as a struggle for Western civilisation against an Asiatic menace—with wide ranging reports from American missionaries to the *New York Times* to General MacArthur himself all portraying the Koreans as fanatical, drone-like, barbaric and above all as sub-human inferiors.[75] This closely reflected portrayals within the U.S. Military and by American media of the war with Imperial Japan shortly before as "a racial war in all but name" against an adversary "considered racially and irredeemably evil,"[76] which had led to severe and brutal war crimes against both Japanese civilians and soldiers directly resulting from their subhuman status in the eyes of Western personnel. In both cases, the entire population was targeted for demonization on racial and cultural grounds rather singling out the leadership or ideology as had been the case with ethnically European adversaries such as Nazi Germany.[77]

As a joint study published by members of America's National Defense Intelligence College and the Air Force Office of Special Investigations, among others, concluded, American conduct towards Japan had been influenced significantly by their enemy's East Asian ethnicity—seen as a threat to Western values and the West's global primacy in a way European adversaries never were. They wrote: "Conflict in Asia differed greatly from that in Europe, for Japan was considered to be a 'racial menace' as well as a cultural and religious one. If Japan proved victorious in the Pacific, there would be 'perpetual war between the Oriental ideas and the Occidental.' At the time, the conflict was perceived as a clash of civilizations."[78] Beginning less than five years after Tokyo's surrender, the Korean war exhibited many of the same Western perceptions of Asian adversaries, influencing their conduct towards civilians on both sides of the 38th parallel.

In contrast to the Western powers, the Chinese military not only lacked a resentment of the Korean race and people, but also punished any transgressions against them severely. It is notable that Chinese forces left North Korea five years after the end of the war in 1958, after supporting reconstruction efforts, and have never returned to date.[79] Chinese influence over North Korea's internal politics remained negligible to non-existent. The United States military by contrast has maintained tens of thousands of personnel in South Korea to this day and continues to maintain wartime operational command over the South Korean military[80]—as well as an extensive influence over domestic political affairs and foreign policy.[81] The distinction between the way the intervening powers treated the two Koreas, one as a lesser client state and the other as an ally and equal partner, was thus clear both during and after the war.

NOTES

1 Hanley, Charles J. and Choe, Sang Hun and Mendoza, Martha, *The Bridge at No Gun Ri: A Hidden Nightmare from the Korean War*, New York, Henry Holt and Company, 2001 (p. 177).

2 Neer, Robert M., *Napalm: An American Biography*, Cambridge, MA, Belknap Press, 2013 (p. 100).

LeMay, Kurtis and Kantor, MacKinlay, *Mission with LeMay: My Story*, New York, Doubleday, 1965 (p. 382).

3 Hanley, Charles J. and Choe, Sang Hun and Mendoza, Martha, *The Bridge at No Gun Ri: A Hidden Nightmare from the Korean War*, New York, Henry Holt and Company, 2001 (pp. 175, 234).

4 Cavanaugh, David, 'The Korea War: The Most Brutal of All-Time?,' *National Interest,* May 5, 2019.

5 Hanley, Charles J. and Choe, Sang Hun and Mendoza, Martha, *The Bridge at No Gun Ri: A Hidden Nightmare from the Korean War*, New York, Henry Holt and Company, 2001 (p. 121).

6 Stone, I. F., *Hidden History of the Korean War*, Amazon Media, 2014 (p. 256).

7 Deane, Hugh, *The Korean War, 1945–1953*, San Francisco, CA, China Books and Periodicals, 1999 (p. 143).

8 *London Times*, November 16, 1950.

9 *Activities of the Past Three Years*, Republic of Korea Truth and Reconciliation Commission, March 2009.

10 Hanley, Charles J. and Choe, Sang Hun and Mendoza, Martha, *The Bridge at No Gun Ri: A Hidden Nightmare from the Korean War*, New York, Henry Holt and Company, 2001 (pp. 195–196).

11 Stokesbury, James L., *A Short History of the Korean War*, New York, William Morrow and Company, 1988 (pp. 39, 42–43).

Lowe, Peter, *The Frustrations of Alliance: Britain, The United States, and the Korean War, 1950–1951*, in: Cotton, James, and Neary, Ian, *The Korean War in History*, Manchester, Manchester University Press, 1989 (pp. 80–99).

12 Hanley, Charles J. and Choe, Sang Hun and Mendoza, Martha, *The Bridge at No Gun Ri: A Hidden Nightmare from the Korean War*, New York, Henry Holt and Company, 2001 (pp. 195–196).

13 *Times* (London), 15 July 1950.

MacDonald, Callum, '"So terrible a liberation"—The UN occupation of North Korea,' *Bulletin of Concerned Asian Scholars,* vol. 23, no. 2 (pp. 3–19).

14 Kim, Monica, *The Interrogation Rooms of the Korean War: The Untold History*, Princeton, NJ, Princeton University Press, 2019 (p. 265).

15 Hanley, Charles J. and Choe, Sang Hun and Mendoza, Martha, The Bridge at No Gun Ri: A Hidden Nightmare from the Korean War, New York, Henry Holt and Company, 2001 (pp. 195–196).

16 Ibid. (pp. 195–196).

17 Henderson, Gregory, *Korea: The Politics of the Vortex,* Cambridge, MA, Harvard University Press, 1969 (p. 167).

18 Memo to General Timberlake, Fifth Air Force, AFO 970, Unit 1, July 25, 1950, U.S. National Archives.

19 Williams, Jeremy, '"Kill 'Em All": The American Military in Korea,' *BBC*, February 17, 2011.

Hanley, Charles J., 'No Gun Ri: Official Narrative and Inconvenient Truths,' *Critical Asian Studies*, vol. 42, issue 4, 2010 (pp. 589–622).

20 '"Kill 'Em All": American War Crimes in Korea,' *Timewatch*, (Documentary), February 1, 2002.

21 Ibid.
22 Ibid.
23 Ibid.
24 Williams, Jeremny, '"Kill 'Em All": The American Military in Korea,' *BBC*, February 17, 2011.
25 Hanley, Charles J. and Choe, Sang Hun and Mendoza, Martha, *The Bridge at No Gun Ri: A Hidden Nightmare from the Korean War*, New York, Henry Holt and Company, 2001 (p. 126).
26 Williams, Jeremny, '"Kill 'Em All": The American Military in Korea,' *BBC*, February 17, 2011.
27 Hanley, Charles J. and Choe, Sang Hun and Mendoza, Martha, *The Bridge at No Gun Ri: A Hidden Nightmare from the Korean War*, New York, Henry Holt and Company, 2001 (p. 129).
28 *Suh,* Jae-Jung, '*Truth and Reconciliation in South Korea: Between the Present and the Future of the Korean Wars*,' London and New York, Routledge, 2013 (pp. 68–94).
'"Kill 'Em All": American War Crimes in Korea,' *Timewatch*, (Documentary), February 1, 2002.
Hanley, Charles J., 'No Gun Ri: Official Narrative and Inconvenient Truths,' *Critical Asian Studies*, vol. 42, issue 4, 2010 (pp. 589–622).
29 '"Kill 'Em All": American War Crimes in Korea,' *Timewatch*, (Documentary), February 1, 2002.
30 Ibid.
31 Hanley, Charles J., 'In the Face of American Amnesia, The Grim Truths of No Gun Ri Find a Home,' *The Asia-Pacific Journal,* vol. 13, issue 10, no. 4, March 2015.
32 '"Kill 'Em All": American War Crimes in Korea,' *Timewatch*, (Documentary), February 1, 2002.
33 Hanley, Charles J., 'In the Face of American Amnesia, The Grim Truths of No Gun Ri Find a Home,' *The Asia-Pacific Journal,* vol. 13, issue 10, no. 4, March 2015.
34 Hanley, Charles J. and Choe, Sang Hun and Mendoza, Martha, *The Bridge at No Gun Ri: A Hidden Nightmare from the Korean War*, New York, Henry Holt and Company, 2001 (p. 142).
35 '"Kill 'Em All": American War Crimes in Korea,' *Timewatch*, (Documentary), February 1, 2002.
Hanley, Charles J. and Choe, Sang Hun and Mendoza, Martha, *The Bridge at No Gun Ri: A Hidden Nightmare from the Korean War*, New York, Henry Holt and Company, 2001 (pp. 140–141).
36 'Report: Korean War-Era Massacre Was Policy,' *CBS News,* April 14, 2007.
37 Williams, Jeremny, '"Kill 'Em All": The American Military in Korea,' *BBC*, February 17, 2011.
38 '"Kill 'Em All": American War Crimes in Korea,' *Timewatch*, (Documentary), February 1, 2002.
39 Turse, Nick, *Kill Everything That Moves: The Real American War in Vietnam*, London, Picador, 2014 (pp. 229–230).
40 Halloran, Richard, 'Seoul's Vast Intelligence Agency Stirs Wide Fear,' *New York Times*, August 20, 1973.
41 Hanley, Charles J. and Choe, Sang Hun and Mendoza, Martha, *The Bridge at No Gun Ri: A Hidden Nightmare from the Korean War*, New York, Henry Holt and Company, 2001 (p. 246).
42 *Chosun Min Bo*, August 19, 1950.
43 Choe, Sang-Hun, 'Korean War Panel Finds U.S. Attacks on Civilians,' *New York Times*, July 9, 2010.
44 'Response to Demarche: Muccio Letter and Nogun-ri,' U.S. State Department cable from Secretary of State Condoleezza Rice to U.S. Embassy, Seoul, August 31, 2006.

45 Straub, David, *Anti Americanism in Democratizing South Korea*, Stanford, CA, Walter H. Shorenstein Asia-Pacific Research Center Books, 2015 (p. 65).
46 Williams, Jeremny, '"Kill 'Em All": The American Military in Korea,' *BBC*, February 17, 2011.
47 Hanley, Charles J. and Choe, Sang Hun and Mendoza, Martha, *The Bridge at No Gun Ri: A Hidden Nightmare from the Korean War*, New York, Henry Holt and Company, 2001.
48 Choe, Sang-Hun, 'Korean War Panel Finds U.S. Attacks on Civilians,' *New York Times*, July 9, 2010.
49 Williams, Jeremny, '"Kill 'Em All": The American Military in Korea,' *BBC*, February 17, 2011.
Washington Post, September 30, 1999 (p. 1), October 14 (p. 14), December 29 (p. 19).
50 '"Kill 'Em All": American War Crimes in Korea,' *Timewatch*, (Documentary), February 1, 2002.
51 Hanley, Charles J. and Choe, Sang Hun and Mendoza, Martha, *The Bridge at No Gun Ri: A Hidden Nightmare from the Korean War*, New York, Henry Holt and Company, 2001 (p. 151).
52 Ibid. (pp. 188, 189).
53 Ibid. (p. 133).
54 Hanley, Charles J., 'No Gun Ri: Official Narrative and Inconvenient Truths,' *Critical Asian Studies*, vol. 42, issue 4, 2010 (pp. 589–622).
Hanley, Charles J. and Choe, Sang Hun and Mendoza, Martha, *The Bridge at No Gun Ri: A Hidden Nightmare from the Korean War*, New York, Henry Holt and Company, 2001 (pp. 163, 187).
55 Truth and Reconciliation Commission of the Republic of Korea, Comprehensive Report, Volume 1, Part 1, December 2010 (p. 121).
56 '"Kill 'Em All": American War Crimes in Korea,' *Timewatch*, (Documentary), February 1, 2002..
57 Macdonald, Callum, *Korea: The Last War Before Vietnam,* New York, Palgrave Macmillan, 1986 (p.216)
58 Smith, Robert, *MacArthur in Korea*, New York Simon & Schuster, 1982 (p.228)
59 Pollock, Sandra, *Let the Good Times Roll: Prostitution and the U.S. Military in Asia*, New York, New Press, 1992 (pp. 172–173).
Hanley, Charles J. and Choe, Sang Hun and Mendoza, Martha, *The Bridge at No Gun Ri: A Hidden Nightmare from the Korean War*, New York, Henry Holt and Company, 2001 (pp. 195–196).
60 Williams, Jeremy, '"Kill 'Em All": The American Military in Korea,' *BBC*, February 17, 2011.
61 Hanley, Charles J. and Choe, Sang Hun and Mendoza, Martha, *The Bridge at No Gun Ri: A Hidden Nightmare from the Korean War*, New York, Henry Holt and Company, 2001 (p. 177).
62 Ibid. (pp. 177, 163, 195, 183).
63 Ibid. (pp. 176, 181).
64 *Report on U.S. Crimes in Korea*, Commission of International Association of Democratic Lawyers, March 31, 1952 (p. 21).
65 Blakely, Ruth, *State Terrorism and Neoliberalism: The North in the South*, Abingdon, Routledge, 2009 (p. 87).
66 Nichols, Donald, *How Many Times Can I Die? The Life Story of a Special Intelligence Agent,* Pensacola, Brownsville Printing, 1981 (p. 128).
67 Han, Suyin (penname of Elizabeth Comber), *Love is a Many Splendored Thing*, London, Jonathan Cape, 1952 (pp. 342, 349).

68 Gil, Yoon-hyeong, 'U.S.'s Yongsan bombing of 1950 caused 1,587 civilian deaths U.S. air raids accounted for 25 percent of civilian deaths in the first 3 months of the war,' *Hankyoreh*, July 16, 2010.

69 Ibid.

70 Cumings, Bruce, *North Korea: Another Country,* New Press, New York, 2003 (p. 12). Katsiaficas, George N., *Asia's Unknown Uprisings: South Korean Social Movements in the 20th Century*, Oakland, PM Press, 2012 (p. 12).

71 Mao, Zedong, *Directive to the Chinese People's Volunteers: The Chinese People's Volunteers Should Cherish Every Hill, Every River, Every Tree and Every Blade of Grass in Korea, January 19, 1951* in: *Selected Words of Mao Tsetung, Volume V,* Oxford, Pergamon Press, 1977 (p. 44).

72 Abrams, A. B., *Power and Primacy: The History of Western Intervention in the Asia-Pacific*, Oxford, Peter Lang, 2019 (pp. 86–88).

73 Conn, Peter, *Pearl S. Buck: A Cultural Biography*, Cambridge, Cambridge University Press, 2010 (p. 316).
Blum, William, *Killing Hope: U.S. Military and C.I.A. Interventions Since World War II*, London, Zed Books, 2003 (p. 21).
Mitter, Rana, *China's War with Japan 1937–1945; The Struggle for Survival*, London, Allen Lane, 2013 (pp. 331–333).

74 'Koreans Watch U. N. Murder Trial as Test of Curb on Unruly Behavior,' *New York Times*, August 21, 1951.

75 Cumings, Bruce, *North Korea: Another Country,* New Press, New York, 2003 (pp. 12–13).

76 Ham, Paul, *Hiroshima Nagasaki: The Real Story of the Atomic Bombings and their Aftermath*, New York, Doubleday, 2012 (p. 14).

77 Dower, John, *War Without Mercy: Race and Power in the Pacific War*, New York, Panthoen, 1986 (p. 18).

78 Stone, James A. and Shoemaker, David P. and Dotti, Nicholas R., *Interrogation: World War II, Vietnam, and Iraq*, Washington D.C., National Defence Intelligence College, September 2008 (p. 34).

79 Zhang, Shu Guang, *Mao's Military Romanticism: China and the Korean War, 1950–1953*, Lawrence, University Press of Kansas, 1995 (p. 529).

80 'Goodbye to America's 4 Million Man Army? Inter-Korean Summit Risks Compromising U.S.' Most Formidable Pacific Asset,' *Military Watch Magazine,* April 28, 2018.

81 Kim, Bo-eun, 'Trump's remarks infringe national sovereignty,' *Korea Times,* October 11, 2018.
Choe, Sang-Hun, 'South Korea Backtracks on Easing Sanctions After Trump Comment,' *New York Times,* October 11, 2018.

Chapter 7
AN INDELIBLE IMPRESSION: WESTERN CONDUCT TOWARDS NORTH KOREAN CIVILIANS AND PRISONERS OF WAR

War Crimes on the Ground

War crimes perpetrated by the United States in Korea were not restricted to the aforementioned firebombing of population centres, dive-bombing of hospitals or strafing of farmers. While widespread massacres of civilians were carried out in South Korea under orders, conduct towards the population in North Korea was predictably considerably worse. Three months of near continuous American defeats at the hands of a scantly armed "peasant army" a fraction of its size and the heavy casualties which ensued in this period meant that there was a strong element of retribution towards the East Asian nation and its population influencing U.S. conduct towards the North Koreans. What thus ensued in the brief American military occupation of northern Korea were atrocities with few parallels in modern history.

Reports from multiple sources consistently show U.S. personnel on the ground committing widespread rapes and extreme sexual violence against Korean women and girls, brutalisation of the general population, and destruction and deliberate targeting of Korean cultural and religious heritage. The vast majority of primary sources on the events that took place in northern Korea are from the Chinese People's Volunteer Army and the North Koreans themselves. There were, however, non-aligned international commissions sent to observe and investigate claims of war crimes being carried out by U.S. forces, as well as some foreign journalists who reported from the north. It is these international sources which can be better relied on to more impartially give an account of American and coalition conduct in North Korea.

The Women's International Democratic Federation (WIDF) an international women's rights organization founded in Paris in 1945, sent a commission to Korea during the war. The federation was considered the most influential women's organization of the post-war era,[1] and was a consultant to the United Nations Economic and Social Council. The WIDF issued a report after observing Western and ROK conduct towards the DPRK's population in their brief occupation of the country from October 1950. The report stated:

> in the period of occupation, hundreds of thousands of civilians, entire families, from old men to little children, have been tortured, beaten to death, burned and buried alive. Thousands of others have perished from hunger and cold in overcrowded prisons in which they were thrown without charges being levelled against them, without investigation, trial or sentence. These mass tortures and mass murders surpass the crimes committed by Hitler's Nazis in temporarily occupied Europe.[2]

The WIDF commission reported that brutal sexual crimes had been widely committed by U.S. and other coalition forces. It stated regarding Pyongyang: "The Americans made the Opera and the remains of the adjoining house into an Army-brothel. To this brothel they took by force women and young girls caught in the streets. As she [a young girl interviewed] feared a similar fate, she didn't leave her dug-out for 40 days." The report continued:

> The husband of her friend, Ri San Sen, was beaten up by Americans because he hid his wife from them. An inhabitant of Pyongyang…confirmed this statement. Many other residents of Pyongyang recounted the atrocities by Americans. Kim Sun Ok, 37, the mother of four children [who had been] killed by a bomb, stated that she was evacuated in the village by the Americans, among them the secretary of the local women's organization. The Americans led her naked through the streets and later killed her by pushing a red-hot iron bar into her vagina. Her small son was buried alive.

Similar punishments were frequently given to women who resisted rape. In Mih Yen Ri, a small village, three women who defended themselves against rape by American soldiers had their breasts cut off. Hot irons were thrust into their vaginas which killed them. This was reported by the commission, although it was not an exceptional case.[3]

Members of the WIDF commission from Austria, China, Cuba (not then communist), Canada, the USSR and Britain visited the province of Whang Hai. Their investigation found that along with the 120,000 civilians who had been killed by U.S., British and ROK forces, civilian prisoners including children as young as two were beaten with iron bars and kept for 15 days without food in cells so crowded that there was no room to sit. Afterwards the prisoners, including the women and young children, were taken to the hills nearby and buried alive in trenches. A young mother managed to dig herself out, but she was captured and buried again. There was a separate mass grave especially for children. These reports were based on the testimonies of North Korean survivors. One survivor, Kim San Yen, found his son and his son's wife's bodies dead and buried with no wounds—as they had been buried alive. He told the commission that he was a religious Christian man and could not bring himself to believe that Western Christians would conduct themselves in such a way.

These findings have since been corroborated by North Korean government sources, which have since discovered the mass graves of civilians killed by live burial—presenting photographic evidence which affirmed the findings of the WIDF commission and the testimonies of survivors.[4] Such reports are highly consistent with reports verified by the South Korean government's own commission regarding atrocities committed in the southern half of the peninsula, which show almost the exact same conduct—confinement in cramped cells, brutal rapes by American soldiers and burials of women and children including infants in mass graves. This makes reports of similar conduct towards civilians in the north far from implausible. Women and children have been found executed and buried in mass graves on both sides of the 38th parallel by U.S. and ROK forces, so such reports from an international commission in the north are hardly isolated or unusual.[5]

As a result of their reports on American conduct in Korea, at a time when criticism of anti-communist policy was little tolerated in then strongly McCarthyist America, the WIDF was labelled a communist front organization. This label came from the strongly McCarthyist House Un-American Activities Committee, referred to by the BBC as "McCarthy's House Un-American Activities Committee."[6] Ties to communist powers or a communist agenda at the time remain unproven, and indeed it was highly common for any dissenters in to be labelled "communist agents"—or in the case of military personnel who gave accounts of U.S. war crimes "brainwashed" by the communists.[7]

The WIDF commission visited the Pyongyang Museum after U.S. forces had withdrawn and found the Americans had stripped it of many treasures including two famous statues of Buddha which were over 2,000 years old. Priceless frescoes discovered in thirty ancient Korean tombs were also stolen, and six of these tombs were found to have been used for torturing Korean women. Cultural relics such as the shrine of Mo Ran Bon and the Yen Myen Sa temple of Buddha among others were destroyed. This ancient temple of Buddha, Yen Myen Sa, which stood overlooking a hill surrounded by nothing but parkland, was reportedly also deliberately targeted by retreating American forces.

Interviewing survivors of the brief occupation period, the WIDF commission indicated that the majority of massacre and torture victims were farmers and workers without connection to the DPRK's government. It collected the following testimonies from survivors regarding the conduct of the U.S. Military. A woman who survived said that American soldiers who had killed her family had tortured her by shoving hot needles under her fingernails. The commission observed the clear signs of disfigurement, as well as the blood on the walls of the prisons where civilians had been tortured. An 11-year-old girl called Shin Soon Dza said that she and her mother and sister had been captured by American forces. Her mother and sister were shot and she was severely beaten and put in prison. Deep scars in her head as a result of the beatings were observed by members of the commission.[8]

Kim Sen Ai, another 11-year-old girl from the same school as Shin Soon Dza, said that she was in the fourth class in school when American soldiers entered her village and apprehended her and her parents. Her mother was a member of the Korean Workers' Party, and so earned special treatment—her breasts were cut off. Her father was tortured and thrown in a river, and her four-year-old sister was then buried alive. She asked to be able to speak to the commission and gave the mutilation of her family members as evidence for her claims.[9] Ree Sam Sil, a leading member of Kaichen's women's organization, was jailed by American soldiers, tortured by electricity, stripped, raped by two soldiers and dragged naked through the streets. On the day of the withdrawal of U.S. forces she managed to escape and survived the ordeal.[10] The chairman of the Wonsan women's organization, aged 25 and nine months pregnant, was arrested and beaten by American soldiers, exposed publicly in the town square, and killed when a rod was thrust into her womb. Eyewitnesses were forced to be present.

Korean women associated with the Korean Workers' Party or any women's organizations consistently received particularly brutal treatment. Jo Ok Hi, chairman of the Haeju women's organization was imprisoned and submitted to slow torture. Her eyes were pulled out, and after some time her nose and breasts were cut off. Tzen Man Suk, chairman of Ko Ri village's women's organization, was arrested and raped by soldiers repeatedly for two days. A large aspect of these rapes was to assert dominance over the society of the DPRK and over symbols of the independent and fully self-governed East Asian nation. U.S. soldiers appeared to do so by particularly targeting Korean women in leadership positions with sexual violence.

Yan Yen Dek, a 28-year-old woman, said her five children and husband had all been killed during the occupation. She was imprisoned by American soldiers with her two-year-old child who was trampled to death by GIs. Yan was subsequently raped and tortured by two soldiers, but survived the ordeal. In the Song San Ri village in Anak county in October 1950 reports of rapes and torture were also widespread. One woman, Kim Hwa Sil, defended herself against attempted rape and was put naked in the courtyard of a building where much of the population was being interned. The others were forced to watch her torture as a club one meter long was forced into her vagina. She immediately died and her body was hung on a telegraph pole, where it remained for the rest of the occupation period. These scenes were photographed by American soldiers. Ten other women were then raped in succession by two or three soldiers, beaten by clubs, kicked, and had clubs forced between their legs. Children were taken from their mothers and beatings, rapes and murders went on for eight days. On October 26, the survivors were taken to the seashore and shot. One witness escaped the convoy when it was held up on the road and was the only survivor. Atrocities by American soldiers occurred across the province. In nearby Sam Seng Ri a 12-year-old boy who tried to defend his father from a beating by American troops had his eyes gouged out.[11]

One 42-year-old woman was raped by American soldiers in succession (soldiers tended to be from 18 to 22 years old). Unlike many of the Korean women raped by U.S. personnel she survived, although at the time of the commission's investigation she was still very ill and bedridden. Older women were also raped by the young soldiers one third their age, such as in a report of American soldiers gang-raping a 56-year-old woman when they occupied Sariwon, or a 64-year-old woman in Soonchen.[12] These aforementioned cases represent only a small sample of the numerous and widespread cases of war atrocities under occupation that the WIDF commission recorded. The commission collected only a very small sample of reports of what the Korean population suffered under the U.S.-led occupation.

The WIDF Commission's findings were strongly supported by North Korean journalistic and military reports,[13] and North Korean accounts of their experience of the U.S. occupation point to very similar conduct. This is also highly consistent with South Korean reports of U.S. conduct in their own country. Reports from the northern side of the conflict by foreign journalists were relatively few. Two journalists who did gain access to North Korean victims however, Alan Winnington and Wilfred Burchett from Australia and Britain, gave accounts regarding the conduct of U.S. personnel which strongly supported the findings of the WIDF Commission's investigation and the survivors' testimonies. The journalists reported from both sides of the war, and their testimonies were considered invaluable by Western media who otherwise had very restricted access to information due to wartime censorship.[14] Burchett was renowned by many major U.S. media outlets as a reliable source,[15] praised even by hard-line anti-communist papers such as the *U.S. News and World Report* which stated that Burchett "never lied, so far as anyone could discover."[16] In 1971 he would be invited to the White House by National Security Advisor Henry Kissinger who consulted him regarding prospects for peace in Vietnam—a war which Burchett also covered extensively.[17]

Burchett and Winnington interviewed North Korean women captured by the U.S. Military. One woman, Kim Kyong Suk, gave the following account, as several other women who were captured with her sat at the interview and affirmed her story—correcting various dates and details. Kim had been put into a prison for juveniles at Kaesong under the U.S. military occupation, then sent to a large group of around 150 women at Inchon. She recalled:

> The Americans treated us like animals from the day we were captured. On the pretext of searching us, they forced us to strip nude. They hurled insults at us. They paraded us

> naked in the streets with their bayonets prodding us along and almost bursting through our skin. They brought along photographers and took pictures which they later posted on our prison compound notice board. Americans would come with ROK troops and select girls for raping.[18]

Kim recalled having been paraded naked through Seoul along with 50 other women in October 1950. She stated:

> No one was safe from their bestialities. They even violated one 14-year-old girl whom they had rounded up as a "prisoner of war." At the Inchon camp, two mothers with babies on their backs were repeatedly dragged off at bayonet-point. The children had their mouths gagged while the mothers were taken into the American guards' quarters and raped.

Kim reported that at least one young girl who had suffered from rape and torture lost her mind as a result of the psychological trauma.[19]

Winnington and Burchett observed evidence of the North Korean women's testimony. Where they alleged they had suffered from torture, including nails being put under their fingernails, severe beatings or electric torture, they had the physical scars and burn marks to prove it. The two journalists noted that the "sadistic crimes" committed against the Korean population by U.S. forces were due to mentality of extreme racial bigotry akin to that which had caused the Nazi German atrocities shortly beforehand. The frustration of repeated military defeats by "inferior races" only worsened the brutal reprisals against the peoples of these nations.[20] For his coverage of the brutality of U.S. forces, the British cabinet considered charging Winnington with treason.[21]

What was notable about Winnington and Burchett's reporting was its accuracy. While reports on war crimes committed by U.S. forces in South Korea were at the time denied by the U.S. government as "atrocity fabrication," they were proved to be entirely true when American intelligence reports, photographic evidence and other documents were decades later declassified. On example was his description of the massacres of South Korean civilians and their burial in mass graves by ROK forces. This was totally dismissed at the time but later fully verified by U.S. military sources.[22] Based on the accuracy of Winnington and Burchett's reporting on war crimes in South Korea, and of American attempts to deny their involvement, there is little reason to believe that their claims regarding the conduct of the United States Military in North Korea would not be true as well.

The reports by the few non-communist sources present in North Korea during the war on the conduct of U.S. occupying forces reached very similar conclusions and strongly support one another. These were highly consistent with reports and evidence of extreme U.S. and allied misconduct towards the population in South Korea—a population towards which the Americans would be expected to conduct themselves better. A leading member of the South Korean government's Truth and Reconciliation Committee, a government body established in 1993 at the official end of the country's authoritarian rule to investigate incidents in Korean history, reported in 2004 on the conduct of American personnel towards South Korean civilians. The report by renowned Professor Kim Dong Choon stated that atrocities were committed as a direct result of American soldiers' "deep racial prejudices" towards the Korean people. It detailed as follows:

> With total ignorance of Asia, young soldiers regarded Koreans and Chinese as "people without history." They usually called Koreans "gooks," a term used during World War II for Pacific Islanders. The fact that many Korean women in the villages were often raped in front of their husbands and parents has not been a secret among those who experienced the Korean War. It was known that several women were raped before being shot at No Gun Ri. Some eyewitnesses say that U.S. soldiers played with their lives like boys sadistically playing with flies.[23]

The fact that the testimonies of North Korean survivors of massacres carried out by U.S. forces were so similar to those separately collected from South Korean survivors of similar massacres—all committed by the very same perpetrators—strongly indicates the veracity of their claims.

The Commission of the International Association of Democratic Lawyers gave similar accounts regarding the conduct of U.S.-led coalition forces occupying the DPRK. One account details that conduct of American soldiers in Sinchon, which was highly similar to that described by the WIDF. Describing one case it reported:

> Wool Mal Che's daughter-in-law, seeing the American soldiers torturing her father-in-law tried to defend him. The Americans attached her by the hair to a tree, cut off her breasts, put a wooden club in her vagina, poured fuel-oil on it and set fire to it. They then poured oil over her and burned her alive. About 20 American soldiers took part in this murder.[24]

The Lawyers' Association's commission report concluded regarding American conduct in occupied areas:

> The tortures and bestialities committed against individuals again reveal a common pattern of behaviour throughout the area visited, and cannot be passed over as the sadistic excesses of individuals. The whole series of cases cited in this chapter of the report must not be taken as the whole evidence of cases committed but as typical of a vast number of similar cases brought to the attention of the Commission for examination [of which but a small fraction are listed]. [Accounts of] the torturing of people by beating, kicking, electric shocks, pouring water in the nose and throat to excess, cutting off various parts of the body, mutilation and the killing by shooting, bayoneting, suffocation, blowing up, burning alive and burying alive could be repeated again in sickening detail.[25]

The report further elaborated:

> the Commission has confined itself to a statement of those facts which were proved by direct evidence which in the opinion of the Commission was corroborated and established beyond doubt. A considerable volume of written statements was submitted to the Commission, which have been taken into account only by way of corroboration of facts proved by primary evidence. We were invited to investigate many similar cases to those stated above in various parts of the country, and it was time alone that prevented this from being done.[26]

The report concluded: "Taking the view that the extensive murders are not the result of individual excesses, but indicate a pattern of behaviour by the U.S. forces throughout the areas occupied by them…

the Commission is of the opinion that the American forces are guilty of the crime of Genocide as defined by the Genocide Convention of 1948." The United Nations Genocide Convention defines genocide as acts committed "with the intent to destroy, in whole or in part, a national, ethical, racial or religious group." This would include "deliberately inflicting on the group conditions of life calculated to bring about its physical destruction in whole or in part." This definition entered into force in 1951, as the United States carried out massacres of South Korean civilians in tandem with massacres, indiscriminate use of incendiaries and weapons of mass destruction against population centres and the destruction of dams and crops intended to cause starvation in the north. The Korean population itself appeared to be the war's target.

Although American war crimes against the Korean population are a scarcely covered subject outside the DPRK, allegations of genocide have been made by a number of respected sources from several countries. Kim Dong Choon, professor at Song Kong Hoe University in Seoul and a leading member of the ROK's Truth and Reconciliation Commission, published his findings in an article for the *Journal of Genocide Research* in 2004. Professor Kim concluded that the United States Military was guilty of genocide during the Korean War, citing orders to commit indiscriminate and widespread massacres such as at No Gun Ri, as evidence. Regarding the scarcity of investigations into the matter, Kim noted that it was due to the demonization of North Korea which:

> served to justify any methods that the U.S. and South Korean army employed to oppose it. This is why existing books or articles dealing with massacres or genocides have never included the cases of the Korean War. Except for a few Western scholars who dared to mention the misconduct of American soldiers and the brutality of the ROK army, only a small number of scholars or reporters have ever raised the issue of "criminal" actions of the U.S. and ROK army.

Anti-communism was in such fervour in the West, and the value of Asian lives so little regarded, that even genocidal actions against East Asian populations could be somewhat condoned in the war against a communist Asian power.[27]

Michel Chossudovsky, a Canadian Professor at Ottawa University and the Director of the Center for Research on Globalization, similarly concluded that the United States had committed genocide during the Korean War. This was based on the extreme civilian death toll and the indiscriminate and extreme way the American bombing campaign was conducted. Chossudovsky, citing several U.S. military sources, concluded that what was done to the North Korean people would be classified as genocide under international law.[28] American Professor Patricia Hynes similarly concluded when analyzing the conduct of the U.S. air campaign, the orders to "wipe out all life in tactical sites" when targeting population centers, and the intentional targeting of irrigation dams at the onset of rice growing season to starve the North Korean population, that the actions of the United States amounted to genocide.[29]

East Asian Studies Professor Bruce Cumings, an American holding South Korea's honourable Kim Dae Jung Academic Award for Outstanding Achievements and Scholarly Contributions to Democracy, Human Rights and Peace, reached a very similar conclusion regarding U.S. conduct in Korea. Citing the United Nations Genocide Convention signed in 1948 and implemented in 1951, as well as the 1948 Red Cross Convention on the Protection of Civilians in Wartime, Cumings concluded that although both were fully in effect during the Korean War, "neither measure had the slightest impact." Through their actions in Korea, particularly their air campaign, the United States had violated both conventions and was guilty of genocide against the Korean people.[30]

North Korean official histories today attribute the country's wartime suffering overwhelmingly to U.S. war crimes—an attribution largely justified given the leading role the U.S. Military took committing these crimes and the fact that all coalition forces were under direct U.S. command. Other coalition members, however, were also involved in similar conduct during the war. Canadian soldiers were found to have frequently killed and raped Korean civilians despite the country's limited participation in the war. According to a study by University of Victoria Professor John Price, an expert on Canada's role in the Cold War in East Asia, brutalities committed against the Korean population were "substantial and exceeded anything seen during the fighting in Europe and WWII"—alluding to a racialist cause for the discrepancy.[31]

British troops were also widely reported to have committed severe war crimes against civilians in northern Korea. Kim Sun Sek, mother of Kim Chun Dze, stated in a testimony given to the WIDF commission that U.S. and British forces had rounded women to serve as sex slaves after taking control of her village. Extremely brutal treatment meant that 240 of these died while only three survived.[32] Pak On In from Sa Ok Ri said her husband was arrested along with his three brothers. All were peasants and non-combatants, but all were killed in custody. She said she saw a teenage girl raped and killed by both American and British soldiers in front of her, and later found her husband's severely mutilated body. Song Chun Ok, a 42-year-old woman also interviewed by the WIDF commission, said all her family had been killed including her young children. American and British soldiers used axes and knives to do this. "It was not only the American soldiers who did these things. It was the English soldiers too," she recalled. "I will go to the front and do anything until the whole of Korea is free from Americans," was her defiant response to the slaughter of her family.[33]

Yu Tong Dze, a woman from Kwon Chou village, attested in 1951 to the killing of 35,000 non-combatants in her district alone. Her husband and five-month-old child were killed. Massacres were carried out by both British and American soldiers. She said both equally behaved "like beasts," and she witnessed first-hand how they threw innocent people in the river. She said she could identify them only by their different uniforms, but their conduct had been the same. "Do they have no pity in England? Do they believe in killing little children?" she asked.[34] Hwan Ik Su, a fourteen-year-old Korean girl from San Chen village, said several of her family members were killed by American, British and Canadian soldiers. She was arrested and showed injuries as evidence of the beatings the soldiers gave her. These reports were highly consistent with reports of British conduct less than five years prior towards another East Asian population when its troops were deployed against Republican nationalist forces in Indonesia.[35]

Proponents of Western-led order and advocates for continued Western military intervention in Asia or the "liberation" of North Korea by Western military force until today, of which there are many, would likely find it difficult to believe that the self-proclaimed upholders of "rules based order" would conduct themselves in such a way. Others argue that any power would conduct themselves in such a way in war, and that brutalities and atrocities are inherent to the nature of war. This however is far from the case. The conduct of North Korean and Chinese forces, which suffered greater casualties and far greater hardship with poorer equipment, fewer supplies and even a lack of winter clothing in battles at sub-freezing temperatures were found by international reports to have committed no comparable acts. Atrocities in war are often considered by both military experts and psychologists to be at least in part results of the hardships and stresses faced by soldiers, and development of such conditions as post-traumatic stress disorder which increase soldiers' likelihood to commit crimes and violent acts.[36] In the Korean War, however, Chinese and North Korean soldiers, facing far harsher conditions, conducted themselves far better towards both their enemies and the civilian population. The extent of the misconduct of U.S. and other Western forces was thus hardly an inevitable feature of war—and accordingly was much less excusable.

The two critical factors which allowed people to commit atrocities in war were, according to West Point psychologist Dave Grossman, "an intense belief in moral superiority" and racial factors which allowed an enemy to be dehumanized. These factors both strongly applied to the U.S. Military in Korea.[37] Atrocities were not endemic to the nature of war, but rather to how the forces involved perceived the population relative to themselves—as inferiors and conquered subjects or as equals. Western military powers in the Asia-Pacific have consistently shown themselves to perceive local populations, particularly those outside the Western sphere of influence in states such as Imperial Japan, North Korea, China and North Vietnam, in the latter way. The Korean War provides an exemplary case of this which is highly consistent with conduct towards Japanese civilians less than a decade prior and those in Vietnam shortly afterwards. Very similar types of misconduct and behavioural patterns were widely reported in all three conflicts.

Treatment of Prisoners of War on Both Sides

Treatment of prisoners of war has long been considered one of the most critical indicators of the ethicality and general nature of warring parties and reflects both their overall conduct towards and perceptions of their adversaries. Under the Geneva Conventions, the body of the prisoner of war—in terms of how it was clothed, fed, sheltered, marked, administered, transported, guarded, and surveyed—provided a measure of the detaining society's civilization. As renowned Russian writer and philosopher Fyodor Dostoevsky famously observed: "the degree of civilization in a society can be judged by entering its prisons,"[38] and this applies equally if not more so to the treatment of prisoners of war. It is therefore vital to understanding the nature of the parties involved in the Korean War.

Treatment of U.S. military personnel held prisoner by the East Asian allies was significantly worse during the war's early stages, as battle lines were constantly changing, supply lines were strained or non-existent and from September 1950 the KPA was forced to very quickly withdraw northwards. No prisoner of war camps could be established, meaning prisoners could only be kept with troops at the constantly moving front, and food for American captives as well as for the Korean soldiers themselves was scarce. An estimated 90 percent of U.S. prisoners who died thus passed in the first year of the war,[39] with many lost during long and cold marches accompanying Korean troops. As a result of the intensive U.S. bombing campaign Korea had been brought to ruin, and civilians were often eager to take revenge against the U.S. military by attacking prisoners. KPA soldiers often intervened to protect prisoners from civilians. An order of the DPRK's advanced headquarters strictly forbade "the unnecessary killing of enemy personnel when they could be taken prisoners of war… Those who surrender will be taken as prisoners of war."[40]

Reporter Hugh Deane, former Coordinator of Information and naval intelligence officer on General MacArthur's staff, stated regarding the conditions for Americans in custody "during this early chaotic period the plight of the prisoners was often no worse than that of the northern soldiers and people. An unknown number of prisoners were killed along with North Korean civilians when U.S. planes bombed and strafed villages immediately south of the Yalu."[41] North Korean military reports indicate that not all personnel followed orders when it came to sparing prisoners' lives however, particularly after seeing the devastation wrought on their country by the scorched earth policies and bombing campaigns and the massacres of civilians carried out by American units. An order given on August 26, 1950, in the 2nd Division stated: "some of us are still slaughtering enemy troops that come to surrender. Therefore, the responsibility of teaching the soldiers to take prisoners of war and to treat them kindly rests on the Political Section of each unit."[42] The Political Section referred to the KPA's General Political Bureau which was responsible for exercising political authority over the military and ensuring that it complied with state policy.

As North Korean forces withdrew there was at times a risk that prisoners would either substantially slow the retreat or else fall back into enemy hands. In such cases prisoners were often executed out of strategic necessity in the traditional military manner with a bullet in the back of the head. There were no reports of sadistic excesses, unprofessionalism or the causing of unnecessary suffering by KPA personnel but executing prisoners still not only contravened high level orders but was also a war crime committed at the lower levels of the military. The options of KPA personnel who did choose to disobey their orders in such a way were very limited however—the only alternative was slowing down and risking death and the hands of the fast pursuing U.S. Military or else freeing prisoners, risking their giving away valuable intelligence and then seeing these same American soldiers continue the war against them and their people.

Within a year of the war's outbreak fighting was localized around the 38th parallel and secure prison camps were quickly established behind the frontlines. Conditions for American prisoners quickly improved, and these camps were opened to press including Western reporters. Although reports of "communist atrocities" against prisoners were spread by the U.S. Military, particularly by General MacArthur's Tokyo Headquarters, they strongly contradicted the press' findings and the pictures of decently fed smiling prisoners who were allowed exercise—prisoners who had allegedly been slaughtered. This raised serious questions among American reporters, and such rumours were suspected of having been fabricated as support for the war waned. A need to legitimise the struggle by demonising the enemy had arisen, but the claims of massacres proved to have no basis in reality.[43]

Britain's former Chief of Defense Staff, Field Marshal Lord Richard Carver, observed regarding conditions for prisoners: "The UN prisoners in Chinese hands, though subject to 'reeducation processes'… were better off in every way than any held by the Americans, whether the latter's compounds were dominated by the Communists or by the Korean or Chinese Nationalists (Guomindang)." Re-education involved communist propaganda and lessons on the "evils of capitalism" and the history of Western imperialism.[44] Evidence of Chinese and Korean forces slaughtering prisoners at this time was non-existent, and reports from prisoners once released and returned to the United States painted a very different picture to the claims of Tokyo HQ regarding their treatment.[45]

American prisoners reported Chinese guards would invite them to their quarters "for drinking and talking" and liked to play music with them in joint "jam sessions."[46] One American prisoner of war, Shelton Foss, recalled regarding his treatment that he, alongside his North Korean captors, "played chess, sang American songs…and talked generally about the U.S. and Korea."[47] As one U.S. prisoner recounted upon being freed, conditions in Chinese camps were as follows:

> Prisoners rose at 7 a.m. and either took a short walk or performed light calisthenics. They washed their faces and hands, and at 8 a.m. representatives from each squad drew the appropriate number of rations from the kitchen. Food was cooked by the Chinese and the diet was essentially the same as that provided the Communist soldiers consisting of singular items such as sorghum seed, bean curd, soya bean flour, or cracked corn and on certain special occasions such as Christmas or Lunar New Year, the prisoners received small portions of rice, boiled fatty pork, candy and peanuts.[48]

American prisoners recalled being given access to an English language library of "more than a thousand books," with those less literate Americans being given tuition to improve their literacy skills.[49]

American prisoner Howard Adams reported not only the far better treatment of prisoners in Chinese and Korean custody relative to those held by coalition forces, but also of the mishandling of peace talks and extensive coercion of Chinese and Korean prisoners by U.S. forces. He recalled in an interview: "the [American] prisoners' hopes soared when the peace talks began. We thought we'd be free soon. The Chinese thought so too at one point and gave us a feast, but the talks dragged on and on as the U.S. side made ridiculous demands regarding prisoners and other issues." Adams was one of many who strongly opposed the treatment of prisoners by his own side, who he alleged were subjected to immense pressure to defect and as a result in many cases could never see their families again (see Chapter 10).[50]

The Associated Press reported on April 12, 1953, as U.S. prisoners were first being released, that "American soldiers returning from communist prison camps told a story today of generally good treatment." One former prisoner, Kenyon Wagner, had much praise for his medical treatment, saying he had been given "the whole works." Another, Corporal Theodore Jackson, similarly praised the quality of medical treatment he and his fellow prisoners had received. "To my idea" he said, "they did fair, about the best they could do with the medicines they had." Former British prisoner Arthur Hunt said that there was a daily sick call and prisoners' health was well taken care of, with inoculations given against various diseases. Albert Hawkins, another former British prisoner, said that he had reported his feet were feeling slightly numb, and was carefully attended to and fed vitamin pills as a result. Former prisoner Private William R. Brock Jr. stated that conditions in prison camps were agreeable and he had never seen a prisoner ill-treated. He said that there was no barbed wire around the camps and that each man was issued with a quilt and blanket and their houses had floor heating.[51] Upon examination when returning home, the U.S. Military was surprised by the excellent physical health and low number of fatalities among the prisoners—although it was concerned by what was termed the "Oriental brainwashing" of the servicemen.[52] Statements from American prisoners indicated that interrogation rooms in Chinese and Korean camps were devoid of torture.[53]

Despite the severe war crimes committed by the U.S. Military and their partners in Korea, the North Korean and Chinese leaderships made provisions for the humane treatment of prisoners and provided food and sanitation equal to what they provided for their own troops. By contrast to the conduct of Korean and Chinese forces, mistreatment of North Korean and Chinese prisoners by U.S. and coalition forces was widespread and often sadistic. This was, however, motivated far less by military necessity and more by genuine neglect and at times racial contempt for prisoners. Prominent British military author and journalist specializing in military affairs Max Hastings found when interviewing American officers that many

> admitted knowledge of, or participation in, the shooting of communist prisoners when it was inconvenient to keep them alive. It is fair to suggest that many UN soldiers did not regard North Korean soldiers as fellow combatants, entitled to humane treatment, but as near animals, to be treated as such.[54]

Robert William Burr of the U.S. Army second infantry division recalled one such incident in which his platoon sergeant shot a dozen prisoners personally. He stated regarding the prevailing attitude towards killing East Asian soldiers: "At the time I would have felt worse if I had run over someone's dog with my car."[55] A very similar attitude could be observed five years prior in the Pacific War, when U.S. forces frequently gunned down surrendering Japanese soldiers or else killed them after interrogation, meaning very few prisoners were taken. Killing the

Japanese, too, was frequently compared by GIs to killing animals in a way killing European soldiers never could be.[56] This conduct was overwhelmingly influenced by racial factors and perceptions of the enemy as subhuman—leading to multiple studies highlighting the considerable discrepancy in conduct with American treatment of surrendering ethnically European adversaries.[57]

On Koje island Chinese and Korean prisoners were forced to construct a massive compound which would come to hold over 170,000 people.[58] Resistance to Western occupation involved all parts of society, and as such it was not unheard of to see three generations of the same family imprisoned together. Many children were also held in the prisoner camps.[59] The fatality rate among the prisoners was high with many not adequately fed and dying due to malnutrition[60]—and more intentionally killed by soldiers after their capture. Prisoners were shot by soldiers for insulting their guards, hunger striking, and even for singing.[61] An example of one such incident saw around fifty women gathered in the common area of the compound begin to sing folk and political songs—and this behavior quickly spread to other compounds. They were met with gunfire by the guards, causing 29 casualties.[62] Another incident on July 29 saw protesting prisoners shot by soldiers—with three killed and four wounded.[63] This was far from the most brutal case of suppression of prisoner protests. The arrival of Brigadier General Haydon Boatner saw American paratroopers, battle tanks and flamethrowers deployed against protesting prisoners who had not even a rifle among them. The prisoners themselves seemingly expected to be gassed by the Americans and had made makeshift gas masks to protect themselves. The General stated regarding the carnage of the crackdown: "What a gruesome sight it was!... A battlefield in every respect. Entrenchments, wounded, dead, burning buildings and tests [tents] with a few human hands, legs or feet here and there."[64]

One prominent case of prisoner mistreatment was that of Pak Sang Hyong, a KPA officer who was repeatedly interrogated, severely beaten, half-starved and kept in solitary confinement. Pak was subsequently kept in a six-by-three-foot cage with only strands of barbed wire for walls. He was given one blanket and no shoes and left outdoors for three winter months. He recalled after his release: "I lived like an animal. I collected every scrap of refuse. Every bit of dried grass or grain stalk was a treasure to me. I used everything I could find for padding in my clothes. I burrowed into the dirt like a rabbit and wrapped my feet up with bits of grass, straw, paper and old rags." Pak said he did not believe he would be repatriated until an ambulance door opened and he saw Korean People's Army uniforms, and a minute later a North Korean general was hugging him.[65]

Conditions for regular North Korean prisoners were similarly inhuman. A British officer noted that U.S. forces treated prisoners "as cattle" and subjected them to racial abuse. Similarly, "like animals," Korean prisoners were often subjected to medical experimentation at the hands of U.S. forces—a severe war crime. Articles 13 and 19 of the Geneva Conventions forbade the medical or scientific experimentation on prisoners against their will and stressed that detaining powers were "bound to take all sanitary measures necessary to ensure the cleanliness and healthfulness of camps and to prevent epidemics." Chinese and Korean prisoners were often operated on to give young surgeons practice, in line with their status as sub-humans in the eyes of their captors.[66] Hugh Deane noted when reporting this experimentation: "The American doctors, if they had qualms, could always remind themselves that the purpose was to add to medical knowledge, making possible saving of more lives, and that the victims were inferior beings, gooks to many, near animals to others."[67]

Experimentation took place in two large military hospitals, the U.S. 14th Field Hospital near the Pusan prison camp and the U.S. 64th Field Hospital at Koje. Evidence of experimentation was collected and analysed by both China's *Xinhua* agency and by British and Australian journalists Alan Winnington and Wilfred Burchett. One of their sources were North Korean doctors released after the war and subsequently interviewed. It was revealed that three North Korean doctors who had been captured as prisoners had been transferred to different camps for complaining about the widespread unnecessary amputations being carried out on Korean prisoners. A fourth doctor who had raised the issue was arrested and never heard from again. One doctor, Kim Yong Suk, who had been a prisoner at the No. 4 Compound of the 14th field hospital, noted that over a period of just 10 months from October 1950 to August 1951, over 4,000 prisoners had died, most of them due to dysentery. He stated:

> We were living in tents, two patients sharing an army stretcher and one blanket. It was bitterly cold. For the first twenty days after my arrival, there was no medical attention at all.

> Patients were merely ordered to remain on their stretchers… Later the dysentery patients began to get treatment that can only be described as experimental—patients in the same stages of disease receiving widely different treatments. One group would be ordered to take 8 sulfadiazine tablets, another group 16 or 24, 32 or up to 48 tablets daily. The maximum liquid they got with the pills was two cups of cold water daily and patients became seriously ill… Many patients were also suffering from hunger endema… There could be no doubt that it was experimentation to test the effects of very high sulfa intake and many patients died of sulfa poisoning.[68]

Dr Kim continued: "Schistosomiasis [a disease caused by parasitic worms in the intestines] cases were not treated at all, but were examined under the direction of an American, Dr. Berry, who was interested only in determining the distributions and localization of this disease." Another Korean doctor, Pak Chu Bong, was barred from the surgical section at Pusan after protesting the severe misconduct of medical staff towards North Korean prisoners. He recalled that limbs stiff from lack of exercise or from having just been released from plaster casts were amputated.[69]

The former chief of the Korean People's Army 10th Division Hospital, Dr Rhee Tok Ki, was removed for surgery after his capture for protesting malpractices. He recalled:

> This hospital had no floors in the tents. Twenty patients were packed onto stretchers into each tent as close as they could be fitted. Air circulation was very poor. There was no regular medical treatment… Patients went where they wanted for toilet needs. Later they built their own toilet. There was no purified water. If we POW medical assistants asked too often for drugs, or if the American doctor was in a bad mood, or didn't like the patient, we would be taken off and beaten up for "agitation."… Twice daily and nightly patients were forced to strip naked to prove they had no concealed weapons or "propaganda."[70]

Sanitary conditions in the Korean camps were so poor that there were often outbreaks of disease, primarily forms of dysentery. Prisoners were living in compounds at four times the legal density of U.S. federal prisons, itself far from a high standard at the time, in conditions "considered appropriate to Asian peasants." British historian Max Hastings noted that "Western treatment of the Koreans and the Chinese was dictated by a deeply rooted conviction that these were not people like themselves, but near-animals."[71] Prisoners held on Koje Island by U.S. forces described the state of their captivity in a letter they signed in 1952: "Koje Island is a living hell. The shores of this island are no longer washed by sea water, but by our tears and blood. There is no breath of fresh air here, the pungent stench of blood fills our nostrils in every corner of the island."[72]

From January 1951 to August 1952 around 2,700 patients died in captivity, mostly from prolonged starvation and lack of medical treatment.[73] The results of this severe mistreatment became clear when prisoners were exchanged at Panmunjom near the end of the war. Journalist Hugh Deane reported on this:

> The American ambulances and trucks bringing wounded and ill prisoners to the exchange site at Panmunjom were an appalling sight—many were emaciated and so many lacked one or more limbs. The American correspondents heard their angry words at press conferences but knew better than to report them. Accompanying interviews confirmed and added details to the American shame. For some months what passed for hospitals were thin mats in tents. There was little or no organized sanitation, rarely latrines, no water purification. Teams of young surgeons arrived every few months, served several months and were replaced. They operated in surgeries from which other medical personnel were barred and performed many amputations, on occasion as many as five or six on a single prisoner. Repeated amputations were performed on a single limb. Of 170 chest operations on prisoners suffering from bronchitis or pleurisy, between April 1951 and July 1952 only 37 survived.[74]

Reports of the dire conditions faced by the Koreans and Chinese and their widespread mistreatment when in coalition custody also emerged from the American Medical Association. In two articles from the 1953 March and April editions the treatment of 1,408 cases of acute amoebic dysentery at Koje was described. In lieu of treatment, an experiment was carried out. One group of patients was given no treatment, only bed rest, nutritional supplements, sedatives and fluid replacement. They were not expected to recover, only to act as a control group for the experiment. These 66 patients were essentially denied any real treatment. The other five groups were given five different drugs in various dosages, the effects of which were closely monitored. This methodology was clearly one of experimentation rather than treatment.[75]

A report from *The American Journal of Tropical Medicine and Hygiene* similarly showed that the primary concern towards sick Chinese and Korean prisoners was experimentation rather that treatment. One epidemic at Koje resulted in 19,320 hospitalizations and a very high 9 percent fatality rate—1,729 deaths. This was referred to as "150 epidemics in one." It was inexplicably not reported to Washington for four months. Treatments varied greatly, and some 1,600 cases of the same disease followed 18 different treatment and dosage schedules. The article noted: "the Korean outbreak demonstrated again that an epidemic situation provides the opportunity to accumulate valuable scientific data very rapidly." This seemed to be the priority, rather than the wellbeing of the Korean and Chinese patients.[76]

Separate crimes were committed against Korean female prisoners, who had often fought alongside men in the KPA and of whom there were many among the prisoners of war. Women were particularly singled out for abuse by their captors. Pulitzer Prize–winning American historian John Toland, the war's contemporary, described this in his own study. He stated in one case:

> One girl, Kim Kyung Suk, told how they had forced a group of women prisoners into a large room. Here they were stripped. Then nude male North Korean prisoners were shoved in. "We heard you Communists like to dance," an American shouted. "Go on! Dance!" They pointed bayonets and revolvers at the prisoners, who began to dance, while drunken, cigar smoking, guffawing American officers stubbed out cigars on the girls' breasts and committed indecencies. [77]

Alan Winnington and Wilfred Burchett, who were present in Korea during the prisoner exchange, witnessed the stark contrast in the health of prisoners from either side and the quality of treatment they had received. They described the North Korean prisoners being returned to their country as:

> Haggard, with faces dank and moist like corpses, bearing the hideous mutilations of experimental surgery, some vacant eyed, girls driven mad by attempted rapes… Half of the prisoners in many ambulances were lacking legs, often both legs. Even men missing two legs and without artificial ones were not treated by the Americans as stretcher cases, so plentiful were amputees. In a single hour it was possible to see six people delivered who lacked all four limbs—hacked back to mere torsos.[78]

The journalists observed the stark contrast this bore to the treatment of Americans in Chinese and Korean custody. For example they noted that even those U.S. prisoners with minor leg injuries had been given a stretcher.[79] It is revealing that the treatment of Korean and Chinese prisoners in the custody of what was by far the world's wealthiest nation was far poorer and conditions including accommodation, food and above all medication were far worse that those provided by war torn and impoverished East Asian nations to the Americans in their custody.

Despite their harrowing experiences in American camps, General MacArthur had said to President Truman in October 1950 regarding the treatment of prisoners of war: "The prisoners are the happiest Koreans in Korea. They are clean and well-fed for the first time."[80] Ultimately not only was there rampant abuse, murder and scientific experimentation performed on prisoners, but also unnecessary and severe bodily mutilation, sexual abuse of female prisoners and a lack of sanitation or conditions fit for human beings. The extensive coercion used to prevent prisoners from returning home and forced defections from the DPRK and China to Western-aligned East Asian states is covered in the following chapter.

The Consistency of War Crimes in Korea: Reflections on Broader Trends in Western Wartime Conduct Towards East Asian Populations

While the war crimes committed by the United States and its allies are a scarcely known phenomenon outside the DPRK today, they remain a critical factor in shaping the perceptions of the U.S. and its intentions among the North Korean population. An understanding of what several experts and researchers from multiple countries including the United States, Canada and South Korea have termed a genocide is essential to comprehending both the motives behind North Korean foreign policy since 1950 and the potential impacts of American military intervention in the Asia-Pacific in future—for both allied and enemy populations in the region. Not only have findings been corroborated by multiple sources, including those from the U.S., Britain, Australia, South Korea and several predominantly Western international commissions, which have been highly consistent with one another, but an assessment of American conduct in other conflicts in East Asia also demonstrates similar trends. Assessment of the treatment of civilians in Japan five years prior, and in Vietnam throughout the next decade and beyond, indicates that reports on the atrocities carried out against the Korean people on both sides of the 38th parallel are far from out of line with the general trend of American wartime conduct towards East Asian populations. Indeed, with dehumanisation and similar portrayals of the enemy as a "racial menace" and as sub-humans common to all three major American wars, many of the facilitators of such conduct were common to the three.

During the Pacific War and subsequent U.S. occupation of Japan, conduct towards Japanese soldiers and civilians closely resembled that in the Korean War. Political science professor Eiji Takemae, an expert on the period, wrote regarding the conduct of American soldiers:

> In Yokohama, China and elsewhere, soldiers and sailors broke the law with impunity, and incidents of robbery, rape and occasionally murder were widely reported in the press. When U.S. paratroopers landed in Sapporo an orgy of looting, sexual violence and drunken brawling ensued. Gang rapes and other sex atrocities were not infrequent.[81]

An example of such an incident was in April 1946, when approximately 50 U.S. personnel in three trucks attacked the Nakamura Hospital in the Omori district. The soldiers raped over 40 patients and 37 female staff. One woman who had given birth just two days prior had her child thrown on the floor and killed, and she was then raped as well. Male patients trying to protect the women were also killed.[82] The following week several dozen U.S. military personnel cut the phone lines to a housing block in Nagoya and raped all the women they could capture there—including girls as young as ten years old and women as old as fifty-five.[83] Such behaviour was far from unique to American soldiers. Australian forces conducted themselves in much the same way during their own deployment in Japan. As one Japanese witness testified: "As soon as Australian troops arrived in Kure in early 1946, they dragged young women into their jeeps, took them to the mountains, and then raped them. I heard them screaming for help nearly every night." These were hardly isolated incidents, but news of the rapacious behaviour of Western occupation forces was quickly suppressed through strict censorship—much as it would be in Korea.[84] Sexual slavery and trafficking of Japanese women were also widespread,[85] and these cases exemplified a wider phenomenon of the way Western soldiers treated East Asian populations under their power.

Orders issued to American scientists and doctors operating in Hiroshima and Nagasaki led to widespread allusions among both historians and military officials[86] to medical experimentation. Victims of the nuclear attacks were closely studied, but doctors were forbidden from providing any information on the cures for the effects of radiation sickness or of providing any form of treatment.[87] As Australian historian Paul Ham concluded: "in short, irradiated Japanese civilians were to serve as American laboratory rats."[88] Again, the perception of East Asian civilians as sub-humans was key to facilitating such conduct. Where U.S. conduct in the Pacific War notably differed from that in Korea was that the U.S. Military was more reluctant to take prisoners, and of those Japanese soldiers taken into custody many were killed in a variety of ways including being thrown off airplanes after interrogation—meaning there were no large prison camps.[89] It is notable, however, that not only were American[90] and Canadian[91] citizens of Japanese origin forced into in concentration camps during the war, but they were treated considerably worse than the ethnically European Nazi German prisoners of war held in the U.S.[92]

Further lending credibility to reports of gross misconduct towards the Korean population, an assessment of the conduct of the U.S. Military in the subsequent war in Vietnam shows extremely similar patterns of behaviour towards East Asian civilians. U.S. reports show that brutal torture and killings of civilian prisoners were far from uncommon, which was done using fists, sticks, bats, water and electric shocks.[93] Rape of Vietnamese women and children was highly common, and was carried out sadistically—symbolizing the assertion of dominance over the Vietnamese race where military victory remained elusive. Women were often raped using bottles and rifles.[94] An example of such conduct and of the prevalent attitudes among U.S. personnel was recalled by former GI John Ketwig, who witnessed a "ceremony," what he referred to as a "revenge type of thing : hate against the Vietnamese, the 'gooks.'" When three young Vietnamese women were captured, he recalled: "everybody circled around and they tortured these women with lit cigarettes…the one girl, they held her down and put the hose from the fire truck between her legs and turned on the water and exploded her. And the explosion of body fluids splashed across our faces."[95]

Rape was such a common occurrence that it was considered standard procedure in Vietnam. Many U.S. personnel recalled being told by instructors from the Marine Corps: "we could rape the women," "spread them open" and "drive pointed sticks or bayonets into their vaginas." As a squad leader in the 34d platoon attested: "That's an everyday affair…you can nail just about everybody on that—at least once." While the military officially disapproved of such practices, in practice they turned a blind eye to it—accepting it as necessary for morale and effective performance in combat. Rape and threat of rape were widely used recreationally. as well as strategically—an effective way of "enforcing submission" as well as obtaining information from both prisoners and civilians.[96] American investigative journalist and historian Nick Turse reported regarding the extent of U.S. sexual crimes against Vietnamese civilians: "I felt I didn't have the language to describe exactly what I found in the cases, because rape or even gang rape didn't seem to convey the level of sexual sadism."[97]

Treatment of prisoners in Vietnam was similar to and in some cases more brutal than that in Korea. In 1968 and 1969 the International Committee of the Red Cross toured sixty U.S. administered detention facilities and found evidence of beatings, burnings, electrical torture and other abuses of prisoners of war and civilian detainees alike in every one of those camps.[98] Some prisoners were kept in tiny barbed wire "cow cages," similar to that of KPA officer Pak Sang Hyong, and others were subjected to "stress positions" as a means of both physical and psychological torture. Other examples of mistreatment included purposefully confining prisoners with others suffering from contagious diseases, chaining prisoners with their hands over their heads, arms fully extended, so that their feet could barely touch the ground—known as strappado, and placing prisoners in large drums filled with water. The containers were then struck with great force, which caused internal injuries but left no physical scars. The "water cure," a common torture technique from the U.S. invasion of the Philippines, was also widely used.[99] Historian Nick Turse noted regarding U.S. treatment of Vietnamese prisoners: "Some had their fingernails torn out or pins or bamboo slivers stuck beneath them, or their fingertips crushed, or whole fingers cut off. Others were cut, suffocated, burned by cigarettes, or beaten with truncheons, clubs, sticks, bamboo flails, baseball bats, and other objects. Many were threatened with death or even subjected to mock executions. Daily torture was just part of a larger system of mass detention in prisons designed to break the spirit."[100]

These examples complement the consistency among the various sources reporting on the Korean War regarding U.S. and Western conduct. They do so by showing a wider trend towards very similar conduct by Western soldiers towards East Asian civilians when attempting to project power into the region over several decades. Accounts from all three conflicts are highly consistent. While U.S. conduct in Vietnam and Japan are shown as examples here, other examples pointing to a similar trend include British and Dutch conduct in Indonesia,[101] U.S. conduct in the Philippines[102] and perhaps worst of all, French conduct in Vietnam.[103] The brutalities in these conflicts equalled and in many cases far exceeded those later committed against the Korean people, and again demonstrate a longstanding and highly consistent trend towards extreme wartime misconduct by Western militaries towards East Asian populations.

Perhaps due to the lack of assessments of Western war crimes in Asia as a consistent part of a wider trend, supporters of the Western-led order have repeatedly insisted that atrocities against Korean civilians are "Kim regime fabrications"—on the basis that no allegations coming out of the "enemy" state could be trusted and that Western interventionism is ultimately a positive and benevolent force. The fact that such a wide variety of reports from all sides in Korea, from multiple international commissions to the South Korean government commission, Western journalists, and multiple studies by Western and South Korean scholars, alongside reports from the North Koreans themselves, paint the same picture, makes such allegations far more difficult to dismiss.

NOTES

1 De Haan, Francisca, *The Women's International Democratic Federation (WIDF): History, Main Agenda, and Contributions, 1945–1991*, Women and Social Movements, International-1840 to Present, Central European University, 2012.
2 *We Accuse: Report of the Committee of the Women's International Democratic Federation in Korea, May 16–27, 1951*, Berlin, Women's International Democratic Forum, 1951.
3 Ibid.
4 'Sinchon Accuses the U.S. Barbarians,' 2002, Pyongyang Cultural Preservation Center. Also see records at Sinchon's Museum of American War Atrocities.
5 Hanley, Charles J. and Choe, Sang Hun, and Mendoza, Martha, *The Bridge at No Gun Ri: A Hidden Nightmare from the Korean War*, New York, Henry Holt and Company, 2001 (pp. 195–196).
Cumings, Bruce, *The Korean War: A History*, New York, Modern Library, 2010 (pp. 168, 181).
The Times (UK), December 18, 21 and 22, 1950.
6 Brown, Sarah, 'Pleading the Fifth,' *BBC News*, February 5, 2002.
7 Kim, Monica, 'Brainwashed,' *Foreign Policy*, February 18, 2019.
8 *We Accuse: Report of the Committee of the Women's International Democratic Federation in Korea, May 16–27, 1951*, Berlin, Women's International Democratic Forum, 1951.
9 Ibid..
10 *Report on U.S. Crimes in Korea*, Commission of International Association of Democratic Lawyers, March 31, 1952 (p. 20).
11 Ibid. (p. 18).
12 Ibid. (pp. 19, 20).
13 'Sinchon Accuses the U.S. Barbarians,' 2002, Pyongyang Cultural Preservation Center. Also see records at Sinchon's Museum of American War Atrocities.
14 Winnington, Alan, *Breakfast with Mao: Memoirs of a Foreign Correspondent*, London, Lawrence and Wishart, 1986 (p. 128).
Cumings, Bruce, *The Korean War: A History*, New York, Modern Library, 2010 (p. 84).
Parrott, Lindesay, 'Peiking Radio is Busy,' *New York Times*, October 12, 1951.
15 Fromson, Murray, 'Parallels in Crisis,' *Saturday Review*, June 1, 1968 (p. 29).
16 'Mouthpiece for the Reds: The Strange Role of Wilfred Burchett,' *U.S. News and World Report*, February 27, 1967 (pp. 19–20).
17 Burchett, Wilfred, *At the Barricades*, London, Quartet Books, 1971 (pp. 274–79). (In the introduction to the book, Harrison Salisbury described Burchett as a 'well-informed, useful source and a warm and decent friend.')
18 Winnington, Alan, and Burchett, Wilfred, *Plain Perfidy, The Plot to Wreck the Korea Peace*, Britain-China Friendship Association, 1954 (pp. 69, 71).
19 Ibid. (pp. 69, 71).
20 Ibid. (pp. 71, 72).
21 Jenks, John, 'The Enemy Within: Journalism, the State and the Limits of Dissent in Cold War Britain, 1950–1951,' *American Journalism*, vol. 18, no. 1, winter, 2001.
22 Carter, Dave, and Clifton, Robin, *War and Cold War in American Foreign Policy, 1942–1962*, London, Palgrave Macmillan, 2002 (pp. 159–160).
23 Kim, Dong-Choon, 'Forgotten war, forgotten massacres—the Korean War (1950–1953) as licensed mass killings,' *Journal of Genocide Research*, vol. 6, issue 4, December 2004 (pp. 523–544).
24 *Report on U.S. Crimes in Korea*, Commission of International Association of Democratic Lawyers, March 31, 1952 (p. 18).

25 Ibid. (p. 21).
26 Ibid. (p. 21).
27 Kim, Dong-Choon, 'Forgotten war, forgotten massacres—the Korean War (1950–1953) as licensed mass killings,' *Journal of Genocide Research*, vol. 6, issue 4, December 2004 (pp. 523–544).
28 Chossudovsky, Michael, Presentation to the Japanese Foreign Correspondents Club on U.S. Aggression against the People of Korea, Tokyo, August 1, 2013 (https:// off-guardian.org/2017/05/08/video-u-s-crimes-of-genocide-against-korea/).
29 Hynes, Patricia, 'The Korean War: Forgotten, Unknown and Unfinished,' *Truthout*, July 12, 2013.
30 Cumings, Bruce, *The Korean War: A History*, New York, Modern Library, 2010 (p. 154).
31 Denney, Steven, 'Speaking the Truth to Power: Canadian War Crimes in Korea,' *The Diplomat*, November 3, 2014.
32 *We Accuse: Report of the Committee of the Women's International Democratic Federation in Korea, May 16–27, 1951*, Berlin, Women's International Democratic Forum, 1951.
33 Ibid.
34 Ibid.
35 McMillan, Richard, *The British Occupation of Indonesia: 1945–1946: Britain, The Netherlands and the Indonesian Revolution*, London, Royal Asiatic Society Books, 2005 (pp. 73–75).
36 Morris, David J., 'War Is Hell, and the Hell Rubs Off,' *Slate*, April 17, 2014. Green, Bonnie L., *Trauma Interventions in War and Peace: Prevention, Practice, and Policy*, New York, Springer, 2003 (pp. 274–275).
37 Alvarez, Alex, *Governments, Citizens, and Genocide: A Comparative and Interdisciplinary Approach*, Bloomington, Indiana University Press, 2001 (p. 15).
38 Pahomov, Larissa, 'Building a Collective Understanding of Prisons,' *The English Journal*, vol. 102, no. 4, March 2013 (pp. 38–44).
39 Hastings, Max, *The Korean War*, New York, Simon and Schuster, 1987 (p. 298).
40 Ibid. (p. 298).
41 Ibid. (p. 298).
42 Cumings, Bruce, *Origins of the Korean War: Liberation and the Emergence of Separate Regimes, 1945–1947, Vol. 1*, Yeogsabipyeongsa Publishing, 2004 (pp. 702–703).
43 Stone, I. F., *Hidden History of the Korean War*, Amazon Media, 2014 (Chapter 45: Atrocities to the Rescue) and (Chapter 46: Weird Statistics).
44 Deane, Hugh, *The Korean War, 1945–1953*, San Francisco, CA, China Books and Periodicals, 1999 (p. 164).
45 Stone, I. F., *Hidden History of the Korean War*, Amazon Media, 2014 (Chapter 45: Atrocities to the Rescue) and (Chapter 46: Weird Statistics).
46 Sayre, George, 950774-RECAP-K, Intelligence Document File, Assistant Chief of Staff, G-2, Intelligence, Box 1025, RG 0319 Army Staff, NARA, College Park, Maryland.
47 Kim, Monica, *The Interrogation Rooms of the Korean War; The Untold History*, Princeton, NJ, Princeton University Press, 2019. (p. 330).
48 Paschall, Rod, *Witness to War: Korea*, New York, Perigee Trade, 1995 (p. 173).
49 Adams, Clarence, *An American Dream: The Life of an African American Soldier and POW Who Spent Twelve Years in Communist China*, Amherst, University of Massachusetts Press, 2007, (p. 56).
50 Deane, Hugh, *Good Deeds & Gunboats*, San Francisco, CA, China Books & Periodicals, 1990 (Chapter 22).
51 Winnington, Alan, and Burchett, Wilfred, *Plain Perfidy, The Plot to Wreck the Korea Peace*, Britain-China Friendship Association, 1954 (p. 19).

52 Mayer, William E., *Beyond the Call: Memoirs of a Medical Visionary, Volume 1*, Albuquerque, Mayer Publishing Group International, 2009 (p. 350).
53 Kim, Monica, *The Interrogation Rooms of the Korean War; The Untold History*, Princeton, NJ, Princeton University Press, 2019. (p. 338).
54 Deane, Hugh, *The Korean War, 1945–1953*, San Francisco, CA, China Books and Periodicals, 1999 (p. 166).
55 Burr, Robert William, [2nd Inf div. 38th inf. Reg, 2nd battalion, Company E], Korean War Veterans' Survey Questionnaire, Military History Institute Archives, Carlisle, Pennsylvania.
56 Glenn Gray, Jesse, *The Warriors, Reflections of Men in Battle*, Winnipeg, Bison Books, 1998 (p. 150).
Munro, Victoria, *Hate Crime in the Media, A History*, Santa Barbara, CA, Praeger, 2014 (pp. 42–43).
57 Fenton, Ben, 'American Troops Murdered Japanese Pows,' *The Telegraph* August 6, 2005.
Munro, Victoria, *Hate Crime in the Media, A History*, Santa Barbara, CA, Praeger, 2014 (p. 44).
Krammer, Arnold, 'Japanese Prisoners of War in America,' *Pacific Historical Review*, vol. 52, no. 1, 1983 (p. 70).
Hastings, Max, *Nemesis: The Battle for Japan*, New York, Harper Perennial, 2008 (pp. 173–174).
58 Reports by Bieri May 29 to June 9, 1951, Transmission des rapports de visites de camps aux Nations Unies, aux Etats-Unis et a la Coree-du-Nord, 16/01/1951—12/05/1952, B AG 210056-21, Archive of the International Committee of the Red Cross.
59 Kim, Monica, *The Interrogation Rooms of the Korean War; The Untold History*, Princeton, NJ, Princeton University Press, 2019 (p. 93).
60 Ibid. (p. 87).
61 Ibid. (pp. 112–115).
Case file #104, Box 5, POW Incident Investigation Case Files, 1950–53, Office of the Provost Marshal, Office of the Assistant Chief of Staff, G-1, Headquarter, U.S. Army Forces, Far East, 1952–57, Record Group 554, NARA, College Park, Maryland.
62 Kim, Monica, *The Interrogation Rooms of the Korean War; The Untold History*, Princeton, NJ, Princeton University Press, 2019. (pp. 83–84).
63 Case File #40, Box 2, POW Incident Investigation Case Files, 1950–53, Office of the Provost Marshal, Office of the Assistant Chief of Staff, G-1, Headquarter, U.S. Army Forces, Far East, 1952–57, Record Group 554, NARA, College Park, Maryland.
64 Typed unpublished manuscript, Box 7, Haydon Boatner Collection, Hoover Institution Archives.
Kim, Monica, *The Interrogation Rooms of the Korean War; The Untold History*, Princeton, NJ, Princeton University Press, 2019 (pp. 204–205).
65 Deane, Hugh, *The Korean War, 1945–1953*, San Francisco, CA, China Books and Periodicals, 1999 (p. 166).
66 Williams, Peter, and Wallace, David, *Unit 731; Japan's Secret Biological Warfare in World War II*, The Free Press (British edn.), 1989 (pp. 385–387).
Winnington, Alan, and Burchett, Wilfred, *Plain Perfidy, The Plot to Wreck the Korea Peace*, Britain-China Friendship Association, 1954 (Chapter 10).
67 Deane, Hugh, *The Korean War, 1945–1953*, San Francisco, CA, China Books and Periodicals, 1999 (p. 176).
68 Ibid. (p. 177).
69 Ibid. (p. 177).
70 Ibid. (p. 178).
71 Hastings, Max, *The Korean War*, New York, Simon and Schuster, 1987 (Chapter 17: The Pursuit of Peace, Part 1, Koje-do).

72 Deane, Hugh, *The Korean War, 1945–1953*, San Francisco, CA, China Books and Periodicals, 1999 (p. 166).
73 Ibid. (p. 178).
74 Ibid. (p. 178).
75 Ibid. (p. 176).
76 Ibid. (p. 176).
77 Toland, John, *In Mortal Combat: Korea, 1950–1953*, New York, William Morrow & Co., 1991.
78 Winnington, Alan, and Burchett, Wilfred, *Plain Perfidy, The Plot to Wreck the Korea Peace*, Britain-China Friendship Association, 1954 (p. 9).
79 Ibid. (p. 19).
80 Substance of Statements Made at Wake Island Conference on 15 October 1950, compiled by General of the Army Omar N. Bradley, Chairman of the Joint Chiefs of Staff.
81 Takemae, Eiji, *Allied Occupation of Japan*, New York, Continuum International Publishing Group Ltd., 2002 (p. 67).
82 Tanaka, Yuki and Tanaka, Toshiyuki, *Japan's Comfort Women: Sexual Slavery and Prostitution During World War II*, Abingdon, Routledge, 2003 (p. 163).
83 Ibid. (p. 163).
84 Takemae, Eiji and Ricketts, Robert *Inside GHQ: The Allied Occupation of Japan and Its Legacy*, New York, Continuum International, 2003 (p. 67).
85 Tanaka, Yuki, *Japan's Comfort Women: Sexual Slavery and Prostitution During World War II and the U.S. Occupation*, London, Routledge, 2002 (pp. 138–147).
86 Alperovitz, Gar, 'The War Was Won Before Hiroshima—And the Generals Who Dropped the Bomb Knew It,' *The Nation*, August 6, 2015.
87 Ham, Paul, *Hiroshima Nagasaki: The Real Story of the Atomic Bombings and their Aftermath*, New York, Doubleday, 2012 (pp. 436, 447).
88 Ibid. (p. 436).
89 Munro, Victoria, *Hate Crime in the Media, A History*, Santa Barbara, CA, Praeger, 2014 (p. 44).
Hastings, Max, *Nemesis: The Battle for Japan*, New York, Harper Perennial, 2008 (pp. 173–174).
Krammer, Arnold, 'Japanese Prisoners of War in America,' *Pacific Historical Review*, vol. 52, no. 1, 1983 (p. 70).
90 'The Trauma of Internment,' *Washington Post,* June 25, 2018.
Leigh-Brown, Patricia, 'Life in a Japanese Internment Camp, Via the Diary of a Young Man,' *New York Times,* December 1, 2015.
91 James, Kevin, *Seeking specificity in the universal: a memorial for the Japanese Canadians interned during the Second World War*, Nova Scotia, Dalhousie University, 2008 (p. 22).
92 Gilligan, Heather, 'Even Nazi prisoners of war in Texas were shocked at how black people were treated in the South,' *Timeline,* October 26, 2017.
Svan, Jennnifer H. and Kloeckner, Marcus, 'German POW asks: "Why did America give their young men for us?,"' *Stars and Stripes*, May 26, 2019.
93 Turse, Nick, and Nelson, Deborah, 'Civilian Killings Went Unpunished,' *Los Angeles Times,* August 6, 2006.
94 Denvir, Daniel, 'The Secret History of the Vietnam War,' Interview with Nick Turse, *Vice News*, April 17, 2015.
95 Kendall, Bridget, *The Cold War; A New Oral History of Life Between East and West*, London, BBC Books, 2017 (p. 305).
96 Meger, Sarah, *Rape Loot Pillage: The Political Economy of Sexual Violence in Armed Conflict*, Oxford, Oxford University Press, 2016 (pp. 60–61).
Askin, Kelley Dawn, *War Crimes Against Women: Prosecution in International War Crimes Tribunals*, The Hague, Kluwer Law International, 1997 (p. 50).

97 Denvir, Daniel, 'The Secret History of the Vietnam War,' Interview with Nick Turse, *Vice News*, April 17, 2015.

98 Greiner, Bernd, *War Without Fronts: The USA in Vietnam,* London, Bodley Head, 2009 (p.78).
Leslie, Jacques, *The Mark*, New York, Four Walls Eight Windows, 1995, (pp. 166–167, 174).

99 Valentine, Douglas, *The Phoenix Program,* New York, Morrow, 1990 (p. 310).
Civilian Casualty, Social Welfare and Refugee Problems in South Vietnam, Part 1, Hearings before the Subcommittee on Refugees and Escapees, Senate Judiciary Committee, June 24–25, 1969 (pp. 102–103).
Kelly, James, *Casting Alpha: Amtracs in Vietnam*, Bloomington, 1st Book, 2002 (p. 71).
Indochina Peace Campaign, Women Under Torture, Santa Monica, The Campaign, 1973 (p.19).
Schanberg, Sydney, 'Saigon Torture in Jails Reported,' *New York Times*, August 12, 1972.

100 Turse, Nick, *Kill Everything That Moves: The Real American War in Vietnam*, London, Picador, 2014 (p. 178).

101 McMillan, Richard, *The British Occupation of Indonesia: 1945–1946: Britain, The Netherlands and the Indonesian Revolution*, London, Royal Asiatic Society Books, 2005 (pp. 73–75).
Pisani, Elizabeth, *Indonesia Etc.: Exploring the Improbable Nation*, London, Granta Books, 2014 (p. 17).
Hanna, Willard A., *Indonesian Banda: Colonialism and its Aftermath in the Nutmeg Islands*, Philadelphia, PA, Institute for the Study of Human Issues, 1991 (p. 55).

102 Simons, Geoff, *The Vietnam Syndrome: Impact on U.S. Foreign Policy*, Abingdon, Palgrave Macmillan, 1998 (p. 125).
Ash, Chris, *Kruger, Kommandos & Kak: Debunking the Myths of The Boer War*, Pinetown, 30 Degrees South Publishers, 2014 (p. 321).
Welman, Frans, *Face of the New Peoples Army of the Philippines: Volume Two*, Bangkok, Booksmango, 2012 (pp. 137, 139).

103 Rydstrom, Helle, 'Politics of colonial violence: Gendered atrocities in French occupied Vietnam,' *European Journal of Women's Studies*, vol. 22 (pp. 191–207).

Chapter 8

ENDING THE WAR: MAXIMUM PRESSURE AND A HARD LESSON ON AMERICAN POWER

The Negotiating Process: Abnormal Terms and Violation of International Law

The process by and circumstances under which open hostilities in the Korean War came to an end would have lasting impacts on U.S.-DPRK relations—and continue to have a profound influence on Pyongyang's strategic planning in the 21st Century. The U.S. benefitted from a number of advantages during the negotiating process, foremost among which were its superior capability to carry out strikes on its adversaries' infrastructure and population centers, its better economic position which allowed it to more easily sustain a war effort, and its wider range of options for escalation to inflict further pain on the Chinese and Korean populations. This last advantage came from America's greater power projection assets and its access to both overseas military bases and weapons of mass destruction. The Korean and Chinese economies by contrast were both ravaged by war and poorly placed to sustain a war effort, and both militaries lacked the capability to threaten U.S. targets as near as Japan or even Pusan—much less the American mainland itself. The discrepancy in power projection capabilities was thus truly immense with considerable implications for the peace process, allowing the U.S. to exert far greater leverage during negotiations and ensuring that the final terms of the armistice which ended hostilities strongly favored the Western Bloc.

March 1951 saw renewed calls among the U.S. military leadership for an offensive north of the 38th parallel. Its aim would be to establish a new front—a Pyongyang-Wonsan Line—which would place 85% of the Korean population and the majority of North Korea's food supply under Western control.[1] An advance to the less ambitious "Kansas Line" would push the frontline over the 38th parallel, after which further offensives to reach the Wonsan line could be staged. This advance began on April

3, under "Operation Rugged," and coalition forces were successful in reaching their objective after nine days of fighting which placed the new frontline of the conflict over the border and on North Korean soil. The coalition quickly initiated the followup "Operation Dauntless" on April 11 to advance further north to positions 15–30km north of the 38th parallel forming the "Utah Line."

While U.S.-led coalition forces made some initial gains and were able to press an offensive into North Korean territory for little over two weeks, these were quickly reversed by an effective KPA and PVA counteroffensive. Known as the "Spring Offensive," this pushed U.S.-led coalition forces back to the 38th parallel. The cost of victory again demonstrated, however, that a total routing of the coalition forces was not feasible, given the disparity in resources favoring them, the tenacity of their new Supreme Commander Matthew Ridgway, and above all the extremely strained logistics of the KPA and PVA. The East Asian allies' inability to contest air superiority south of Pyongyang was another major disadvantage, which put pressure on their frontlines due to intensive airstrikes on both troops and supply lines. The Spring Offensive was the last major offensive by the East Asian allies for the remainder of the war, and the Chinese and North Koreans would come to again press hard for a diplomatic solution while heavily fortifying their positions roughly in line with the 38th parallel to force a stalemate on the U.S-led coalition. Coalition efforts to breach these defenses and again push into northern Korea repeatedly ended in failure, and even nuclear attacks were deemed insufficient to penetrate the new PVA and KPA emplacements built along the parallel.[2]

The emergence of a stalemate roughly along the 38th parallel forced both parties to the negotiating table, and coalition forces were initially receptive to calls for an armistice. In the first week of June State Secretary Acheson and UN General Secretary Lie both declared they favored an armistice approximately along the 38th parallel. The Chinese and Koreans also sought to restore an armistice on the 38th parallel as the boundary between the two Koreas, with a small neutral zone on each side of the line. Seeking to encourage a quick end to the war, Beijing confirmed that it would not tie its demands for UN recognition to the ending of hostilities.[3] The USSR expressed its agreement to the idea of ending a war in armistice on June 23, informing U.S. ambassador Alan Goodrich Kirk in Moscow that the armistice should not involve political or territorial issues and should be a strictly military arrangement.[4]

On June 29, the Joint Chiefs of Staff advised Supreme Commander Ridgway of the requirements for armistice. A demilitarized zone 20 miles wide should be created, no reinforcements or additional war materials were to be brought into Korea except one-for-one replacements, and prisoners would be exchanged on a one-for-one basis—which would advantage U.S. and coalition forces as they were holding far more prisoners than the East Asian allies. The U.S. initially wanted to hold negotiations on a Danish ship, although as Denmark was one of the European participants in the war and a NATO member, this was hardly seen as neutral territory. Thus, it was agreed to hold negotiations in Kaesong—the ancient Korean capital located within ten kilometers of the 38th parallel. Although the U.S. appeared receptive to the opening of talks, offers to cease hostilities for their duration were firmly refuted due to concerns that the lifting of constant aerial bombardment and naval blockade by the Western powers would allow the Chinese and Koreans time to recover and mass supplies.

Delegations met for the first time on July 10, 1951. The U.S. faced a dilemma: how to negotiate with the DPRK and China while continuing to deny both states recognition. It was thus decided to delegate the task of negotiating to the "military commanders in the field" rather than to diplomats or politicians. The tents at Panmunjom accordingly partitioned the military from the political. As Secretary of State Dean Acheson noted: "The case for military talks through commanders in the field was strong for the following reasons: First, because neither the Chinese nor the North Korean authorities were official entities recognized by the United States."[5]

The UN delegates were all Americans. The delegation for the East Asian allies was headed by North Korean Vice Preimer and Chief of Staff General Nam Il, closely backed by Chinese Major General Xie Fang—an officer specializing in political affairs and General Peng's Chief of Staff. Initial proposals by General Nam Il calling for both sides to withdraw to the 38th parallel, a withdrawal of all foreign forces from Korea, and formation of a 20-mile demilitarized zone were flatly rejected by the U.S.

For the coming two years the course of negotiations would above all else be influenced by one key factor—the Western Bloc's ability to cause the Chinese and Korean nations considerable pain and hardship at relatively little cost to themselves. This came primarily in the form of continued and intensive bombing and shelling of Korean territory—with an average daily death toll comparable to that of the September 11th attacks on the U.S. fifty years later,[6] and a massive and unsustainable cost in both material and manpower imposed on the post–civil war Chinese economy. The newly formed Chinese republic was forced to allocate half all government spending to the armed forces in 1951, a huge burden on the economy.[7] Lack of government funding for the civilian economy was particularly critical considering both the extent of wartime damage from previous decades, and the new republic's state-led economic model under which government expenditure was considered vital to stimulate growth. The war-torn country could ill afford a major conflict with a broad alliance of Western powers and had entered into it only when its own borders had been threatened.

Under pressure, the East Asian allied negotiators finally dropped requirements for a withdrawal of foreign forces on July 25. Their demands to restore the 38th parallel as the demarcation line, however, were then also rejected. While the contemporary zigzagged frontline meant this would require both sides to yield territory, after operations Rugged and Dauntless, the Western powers held considerably more territory north of the parallel than the KPA and PVA held south of it. State Secretary Dean Acheson thus suspected that the adversary "could well have been surprised, chagrined, and even given cause to feel tricked" at the American insistence on not accepting the status-quo ante bellum—a restoration of the 38th parallel as the armistice line.[8] This hardline position was adopted despite statements a few weeks prior by Secretary Acheson, JCS Chairman Omar Bradley, Defense Secretary George Marshall and UN Secretary General Trygve Lie that an armistice based on the 38th parallel was the objective. A sudden shift appeared to have taken place to press the East Asian allies for greater concessions.[9]

On August 10, Admiral Charles Turner Joy, who led the U.S. delegation, stated his refusal to discuss restoration of the 38th parallel border any further. General Ridgway further wanted to issue an ultimatum, insisting that the East Asian Allies alter their negotiating position and accept the new borders decided by the Western powers or talks would be broken off—although Washington overruled him on this. Ridgway nevertheless led calls for a hard line on the 38th parallel issue, leading some American accounts to place responsibility for this first impasse in negotiations solely on his shoulders. American historian James I. Matray noted that "his motives for presenting a DMZ proposal certain to infuriate the other side included gaining bargaining leverage, humiliating his

Communist adversary, and placating South Korea…[and] to show his toughness in forcing the Communists to accept an armistice on American terms."[10]

On August 18, the East Asian allies again compromised, considering "adjustments" to accommodate Western interests so the demarcation line did not need to be entirely consistent with the 38th parallel. The U.S. negotiators accepted the following day. Achieving such a major concession, a net loss of territory for the DPRK, was trumpeted as a "phenomenal feat" by Secretary Acheson[11] and perceived by the U.S. military and civilian leadership as a strong sign that both Beijing and Pyongyang wanted a swift end to the war.[12] Their compromise appeared to be met with bad faith however, with the Koreans and Chinese charging that coalition forces had violated the neutral zone around Kaesong where the negotiations were being held multiple times. UN Command admitted to two of the incidents, but claimed they were accidental. On August 23, the East Asian allies claimed Western warplanes had bombed the site of the conference, although the American representatives denied this leading the Chinese and Koreans to suspend talks until October. It remains unclear whether the bombings did occur, but considering that the East Asian powers had been far more accommodating in their positions and had a far more pressing incentive to end the war sooner, it is unlikely that they broke off talks without provocation.

The Chinese and Koreans had little choice but to return to negotiations promptly despite what they viewed as an extremely provocative act. The price of failing to do so and proving overly-defiant to Western terms would be high—not only as an extension of the bombardment of the North Korean population and the crippling and unsustainable cost of war to the small Chinese economy, but also because the U.S. promised harsh retaliation to force the East Asian allies back to the table. Should the Chinese and Koreans refuse to return to negotiations as the coalition forces demanded—without explanation for the bombing incident—the Joint Chiefs of Staff favored lifting restrictions on bombing North Korean power plants, imposing a naval blockade on China, allowing for a "hot pursuit" of Chinese and Korean aircraft across the Sino-Korean border and attempting an advance further northwards. All these measures appeared to have the strong support of the State Department.[13] Permitting "hot pursuits" could be the first step of bringing the air war to the Chinese mainland, which many in the American leadership strongly supported despite the risk it would provoke Soviet intervention.[14]

Commander of the Eighth Army General James Van Fleet sought to apply further pressure to negotiations by advancing in force to push the front northwards to the Pyongyang-Wonsan line. While the East Asian allies appeared to have given up prospects of improving their negotiating positions through offensive actions, the Americans often appeared eager to do so—time was on their side. Prospects for such an ambitious advance were seriously undermined by subsequent battles in August against the Korean People's Army which, unlike previously when it had staged strategic withdrawals, for the first time fought for every inch of land and proved extremely reluctant to fall back. While the battles of Punchbowl, Bloody Ridge and Heartbreak Ridge from late August to mid-October were all won by the Western powers with some South Korean support, the KPA was well dug in, launched multiple small counteroffensives against coalition positions, and caused very heavy casualties. Key to the coalition victory was the U.S. military's ability to "rain fire" on Korean positions with massive air and artillery strikes, in particular using napalm and other incendiaries. Korean forces lacked the means to respond to such attacks in kind. The last of the three battles saw the U.S. Army deploy battle tanks in considerable numbers which proved decisive, with the Koreans already hard pressed in their defense and lacking the firepower needed to neutralize such a large armored offensive.

While the KPA had suffered tactical defeats its effective performance against considerable odds amounted to a strategic victory—with the heavy casualties suffered by the U.S. and its allies ending prospects for further northward offensives and forcing the coalition to return to the negotiating table. The KPA's performance led to far higher estimates for the casualties that coalition forces would incur from a push to the Pyongyang-Wonsan line. These were expected to be in the hundreds of thousands—200,000 at a conservative estimate.[15] The frontline moved little after this. The East Asian allies sought to end the war quickly and to this end avoided provoking the Western Bloc with further offensives, while the Western powers saw the manpower costs of further offensives as unacceptable. The U.S. would later reconsider new offensives in 1953, however, when contemplating using tactical nuclear strikes to neutralize fortified KPA positions.

The Chinese government remained strongly incentivized by its economic circumstances to avoid further offensives and conclude the war quickly. Beijing hoped that by keeping the PVA on the defensive in 1952, military expenditures could be cut by 20%. Both the leadership of the Chinese Communist Party and the PLA's General Staff Department were eager to reduce the military presence in Korea even before the war was over, and to end it as quickly as possible even if additional concessions were necessary. So desperate was Beijing to reduce military expenditures, that in October 1951 the General Staff Department planned to send 260,000–300,000 troops back to China to "substantially reduce the burden of supplying" them.[16]

While the Chinese were planning to wind down their military involvement the Western powers were only increasing their firepower—while also furnishing the South Koreans with tanks, heavy 155mm artillery guns and other advanced equipment which the East Asian allies could not match. The expansion of the ROKAF to 14 divisions was decided on by Washington and the U.S. Far East Command in May 1952, and additional divisions were furnished with considerable American supplies.[17] The gross imbalance between the war-torn economies of China and the DPRK, neither of which could sustain the war effort or furnish its troops with even a fraction of the equipment of their Western counterparts, compared to the vast American war economy supplemented by its allies, gave the Western powers further room to play for time while losing relatively little in the process. Their uncompromising line in the negotiations thus only became worse when talks resumed in late October.

Talks resumed on October 25 at Kaesong, although little was discussed in the first two weeks. On November 6, the East Asian allies sought to fix a demarcation line, which would mean a de facto ceasefire. The Western powers opposed this—seeking to continue the air and naval bombardment of northern Korea to maintain pressure until they gained more favorable terms in all aspects of the negotiations. On November 8, Soviet Foreign Minister Andrey Vyshinsky attended the United Nations and urged an end to the fighting in 10 days and withdrawal of all foreign forces within three months—terms the East Asian allies had initially proposed but been forced to abandon under Western pressure.[18] Soviet General Secretary Joseph Stalin later explained, on November 20, that this statement had been made to demonstrate the injustice of the American position and that the Chinese and Koreans had been willing to make considerable compromises for peace already—while the Western powers had not.[19] The U.S. intended to enlarge the territory of the ROK and also ensure its ability to maintain a sizeable military presence in the strategically located South Korean state indefinitely. A return to the original inter-Korean border and withdrawal of foreign forces was thus rejected, and the U.S. would continue to press for further concessions and had the leverage needed to dictate a hard line.

Ending prospects for a quick ceasefire, the American delegation on November 17 made clear that military operations would continue until the armistice was signed. A few days later the East Asian allies agreed, and on November 26 conceded that the inter-Korean border would not be restored to the 38th parallel to the advantage of the Western Bloc.[20] On November 27, the American negotiators put forward further terms—an armistice commission with unlimited access to all of Korea, rights to air observation over all of Korea, and guarantees that the Chinese and North Koreans would not rehabilitate airfields destroyed by Western bombing after the war's end—the third being a particularly unusual requirement. There were to be no reciprocal restrictions on the construction or maintaining of airfields by Western or ROK forces south of the 38th parallel. The East Asian allies accepted the formation of an armistice commission so long as it was formed by representatives from both sides but rejected "free access" by a supervisory organ to their territory. They also opposed limitations on post-war reconstruction. The allies proposed an early evacuation of military forces from the demilitarized zone and coastal islands, although this was not accepted by the coalition which were in control of the majority of the islands.

On the first day of the following week, December 3, the East Asian allies agreed to a further concession. They offered to accept restrictions on the introduction of new weapons into Korea after the armistice but proposed that a supervisory organ of neutral nations inspect ports and ensure compliance by both sides. This turned out to be a well thought out move and appeared to catch the Western powers off guard. While the American negotiators were expected to refuse any free inspections by the North Koreans or Chinese of their ports, non-aligned nations such as India had repeatedly demonstrated neutrality at the United Nations and could not be denied as easily.

While the U.S. and its allies discussed prospects for neutral observers, the East Asian allies moved to speed up negotiations by moving to the next item on the agenda on December 11—prisoner exchanges. They began exchanging data on prisoners with coalition forces, a prelude to negotiating the exchanges. The following day the American negotiators agreed to concede control of offshore islands, their first major concession, if the allies agreed to a free rotation of foreign forces into and out of Korea. The Chinese and Koreans, with their demand for a complete withdrawal of foreign forces rebuffed, put forward a compromise—an allowance for the rotation of 5000 foreign troops per month. This was not accepted by the U.S. negotiators, who envisaged a lasting presence of tens if not hundreds of thousands of Western troops in southern Korea.[i]

The East Asian allies sought to accommodate American demands without overly compromising their own security, and indicated that they would be willing to agree to looser limitations on the circulation of foreign forces if the Western Bloc loosened restrictions on postwar reconstruction—namely on the reconstruction of Korean airfields. This was a reasonable compromise between the interests of both parties, although still strongly favoring Western interests which would retain full access to airfields in South Korea and planned for a far larger troop deployment to Korean territory after the armistice. The Western negotiators, however, did not accept this compromise—and would seek to force the Chinese and Koreans to make concessions unilaterally.[21]

The East Asian allies made further concessions early in 1952, agreeing to a rotation of 35,000 men a month—enough for the Western powers to keep a very substantial force in the ROK. They further allowed for foreign inspectors to enter North Korean territory, but only at limited sites. Both sides agreed to allow the other five ports of entry, although the five largest ports in North Korea were off the list. The Western powers refused to compromise on the issue of a unilateral ban on repairs to North Korean airfields, however, so negotiations continued to stall.

Prisoner exchanges would emerge as a major sticking point in negotiations. When the issue began to be discussed in December 1951 the East Asian allies proposed an "all for all" exchange under which each side would repatriate all enemy prisoners in their custody—in line with international law and the Geneva Conventions. The U.S. negotiators initially did not make their position on the prisoner of war issue clear, and the American position was revealed only on January 2 of the following year when negotiators proposed terms for an exchange. These were, according to many in the U.S. military leadership themselves, predictably wholly unacceptable to the Chinese and North Koreans. Firstly, they stipulated that prisoners returned would be paroled and would be forbidden from fighting again. While this first term was harsh and highly irregular, they believed that the East Asian allies would be forced to

i The post-armistice Western military presence was primarily American, but not exclusively.

concede on it. The second point, however, was in direct violation of the Geneva Conventions—which the Chinese and Koreans repeatedly protested—and saw the Americans introduce an entirely unheard-of concept of "voluntary repatriation." According to the U.S.-proposed plan, at the end of the conflict, a soldier would be able to "exercise his individual option as to whether he will return to his own side or join the other side." In his argument, Admiral Ruthven Libby, the U.S. delegate, used phrases such as "principle of freedom of choice" and "the right of individual self-determination."[22] Or in the words Libby put forth—the voluntary repatriation proposal was essentially "a bill of rights" for the prisoner of war. "As regards repatriation, it permits freedom of choice on the part of the individual, thus ensuring that there will be no forced repatriation against the will of the individual."[23]

In response to the new terms put forward, the Chinese and Korean delegates immediately pointed out that the 1949 Geneva Conventions on the Treatment of Prisoners of War stipulated mandatory repatriation at the end of the war and refused the proposal. These protests and the requirements of international law were brushed aside by the American negotiators and in Washington itself. A mass defection of the nature the United States and their allies envisioned engineering would be unprecedented and was intended to affirm the West's position of moral superiority in the eyes of the world and of history. The U.S.-led coalition would prove willing to go to great lengths, including extreme means of coercion, to ensure that prisoners would consent to "defect" and refuse repatriation—thus providing the Western world with the public relations coup it sought.

The Joint Chiefs of Staff had considered using a hard line on prisoner repatriation to gain concessions on the airfield issue—namely by holding prisoners hostage until the East Asian powers agreed to Western terms limiting postwar reconstruction.[24] Insofar as they enjoyed a strongly advantageous position in negotiations, the benefits of proposing "voluntary repatriation" were far greater for the Western Bloc, given their failure to decisively defeat the PVA, destroy the KPA or place North Korea under their control. The Joint Chiefs came to believe that for prisoners from the adversary Asian states to be depicted as refusing a return to their homelands in favor of life in Western client states would be a major propaganda coup for the Western world with implications far more significant than concessions the airfield issue. The American leadership increasingly became fixated on the need for such a victory—in particular the Presidency and the State Department. British Prime Minister Winston Churchill also lent it his full support, although his Foreign Secretary Anthony Eden admitted "our legal grounds were so poor" for pursuing such action.[25]

American policy was effectively settled by February 27 on an insistence on "voluntary repatriation," following a White House cabinet meeting in which President Truman had given his final agreement and issued relevant orders to Supreme Commander Ridgway. Attending the meeting were the secretaries of state, treasury and defense, three staff members from the state and defense departments and two of the Joint Chiefs of Staff. The policy they agreed on would emerge as the main sticking point in negotiations for well over a year.[26] While the East Asian allies had been willing to compromise heavily to meet Western terms previously, they were, as many in the American military leadership had predicted, far from willing to compromise on the return of their prisoners—a basic right afforded to all warring states under international law. The prisoner of war issue became so heated in light of the wholly unexpected and illegal new Western demands that the signing of the ceasefire was effectively delayed for eighteen months—with Western warplanes, artillery and warships all the while continuing to bombard northern Korea. Given the details which would later emerge regarding the conditions for Chinese and Korean prisoners in the Western prison camps, and the brutal means of coercion used to force their defections and provide the West with the propaganda coup it so coveted, the East Asian allies' decision to refuse Western terms despite the cost to their populations of extending the war were arguably vindicated.

Engineering a mass defection of East Asian prisoners was further intended to provide justification for the Western war effort, the ravaging of Korea and the millions of deaths which resulted. Portraying the reluctance of much of the Chinese and Korean populace to live under communist governments—but more importantly their unwillingness to live outside the Western sphere of influence—was intended to vindicate any and all measures taken by the Western powers to retain their client states and their hegemony in northeast Asia.[27] As Monica Kim, professor of history and New York University and a leading expert on the Korean War prisoner repatriation issue, stated: "For the United States, to have prisoners of war choose *not* to repatriate to the northern Democratic People's Republic of Korea would be to validate the U.S. project of liberation through military occupation in the south." Thus the U.S. was seeking to be able to justify not only the deployment of hundreds of thousands of American troops from 1950—but the imposition of American rule from 1945 both directly and later through the Rhee government. Engineering mass defections could at the same time serve to negate if not seriously undermine the DPRK's claim to sovereignty over its people—much as it could for the recently founded People's Republic of China.[28]

Reports from the American negotiators indicate that China was willing to concede to the voluntary repatriation of a small number of prisoners after screening—the latest of many compromises despite the Western Bloc's demands violating international law. The figure of 116,000 prisoners returned quoted by a UN command staff officer to his Chinese counterpart was reportedly tacitly accepted on April 1—confident that the vast majority of prisoners would elect to return to their homes rather than face an uncertain fate at the hands of the Americans, the Europeans and the Guomindang. Thus when the East Asian representatives were informed eighteen days later that only 70,000 prisoners would be returned from the Western camps they were incensed.[29] It appeared as if the Western powers were continuing to push the limits to which the allies would compromise for peace—and they finally met it when these staggering figures were cited. What the Chinese and the North Koreans may themselves have been unaware of, however, were the methods of persuasion used by the U.S. and their partners during screening to coerce prisoners to defect against their will.

Forced Repatriation or Forced Defection? Justifying Western Intervention at Any Cost

From the spring of 1952, as it became increasingly clear that the East Asian allied forces could not be routed, the prisoner defection issue became central to the United States' strategic interests regarding the resolution of the Korean War. CIA Director Allen Dulles was not overstating the importance of the issue when he referred to alleged mass defections as "one of the greatest psychological victories so far achieved by the free world against communism."[30]

The importance of engineering prisoner defections went beyond the need for a propaganda victory for the West however—and would come to form the basis of the American claim to be a benevolent as opposed to an imperial power. Western rhetoric increasingly placed a new emphasis on moral universalism to frame the rationale of its interventionism abroad in a new light. A world order based on the dominance of Western military might ever-present across the globe would remain as it had in the colonial era—but the pretext for this order and for Western interventionism would change. The West's wars were now "humanity's wars" fought on behalf of mankind, and those such as the Chinese and North Koreans who resisted the West were thus portrayed to be acting not only against Western interests—but against the interests of humanity, the "international community" and even their own people. The will of the "free world" and the "international community" and the designs of the West were to be indistinguishable. The first use of this rhetoric, and new justification for Western dominated order and the quashing of independent anti-imperial forces by Western might, came in Korea.

In order to represent humanity, the Western Bloc had to portray the order it presided over as one with universal appeal to all peoples—thus delegitimizing opposition to Western hegemony and legitimizing Western military interventions overseas. The engineering of defections by prisoners from China and North Korea—the two decolonizing states at the forefront of the conflict against the Western-led order at the time—was thus an extremely valuable and vital contributor for these designs.

Monica Kim stated to this effect:

> The choice of the Korean War POW would be further evidence of the fundamental appeal of U.S. mandated projects of democracy on the global stage… The notion of defending humanity came to the fore as the moral impetus for war. Sovereign recognition, decolonizing imperatives, or state interests—including those of the United States—none of these elements were placed on the table regarding how the American public should imagine the U.S. military intervention abroad.

She then concluded: "Desire on the part of the decolonized Korean POW and the Chinese POW would enable the critical disavowal of imperial ambitions on which the United States insisted—if others demonstrated their wish to belong to the U.S.-defined liberal order, then the United States was not imposing an imperial design on the globe. Desire, however, was not a predictable variable in the interrogation room."[31] Thus the need emerged to ensure that prisoners from the East Asian allied powers which resisted Western dominance would act in a way the ideology of the "free world" would presuppose. Brutal coercion was often the only means of achieving this.

Playing a central role in manipulation of the prisoner of war issue to further the designs of American grand strategy, the Psychological Strategy Board (PSB) established in 1951 recognized that the figure of the prisoner of war could be emblematic of a new kind of war—one which was expected to continue long after the official cessation of hostilities in Korea. This was psychological war—or war for world opinion—in which the U.S. president had taken a personal interest. The undermining of the image of unchallenged Western military might—which had provided the East Asian allies with much prestige—could be heavily compensated for by effective psychological operations. This was described as "a new frontier for U.S. ambitions and conquest."[32]

The PSB was heavily responsible for engineering the American effort to depict the war as a struggle between a "Western Good" against an "Asian Communist Evil"—a redefining of the war effort as being in the name of universal values rather than Western interests. PSB thus strongly advocated the abandonment of language of "containment," and instead call for "liberation" of the enemy—to cite one example. Another was to drop the "made in America" labels used in aid programs. Instead use tags stating: "Peace Partnership of Free Humanity."[33] The legacy of what PSB started remains prominent in Western rhetoric to this day—particularly in regard to the justification for military interventionism and the projection of American and European power.[34]

By redefining war as the imposition and protection of universal values under the pretexts of universal moralism, the world was effectively placed in a total struggle between the Western-led order and those such as the DPRK and neutral non-aligned nations which remained outside it. Carl Schmitt, a prominent political theorist and former Nazi German jurist, observed at the time regarding the West's construction of universal moralism that it "would bring into existence—in fact allow only the existence of—wars on behalf of humanity, wars in which enemies would enjoy no protection, wars that would necessarily be total."[35] In the early 1950s, the prisoner repatriation issue lay at the crux of this. Under such a paradigm, the self-righteousness of the West allowed it to justify gross violations of international law.

When in early April 1952 American negotiators had offered to return only 70,000 prisoners—down from a prior offer of approximately 116,000—Chinese and Korean negotiators were stunned as the Americans had predicted. Hugh Deane, American reporter and former Coordinator of Information and naval intelligence officer on General MacArthur's staff, reported on the U.S. strategy which necessitated a high number of defections from the armies of the East Asian allied powers:

> Reduced estimates reflected the results of savage coercion in the compounds. President Truman and an increasing number of others in the leadership had come to envisage a substitute for the victory the U.S. had failed to win on the battlefield—a propaganda triumph in line with the rollback doctrine that was prevailing over mere containment. An impressive number of prisoners were to refuse adamantly and publicly to go home to the communist evils awaiting them.
>
> To do the brunt of the dirty work in selected compounds (there were 32 of them on Koje, all overcrowded) the U.S. secured some 75 persuaders from Taiwan, mostly from Chiang Kaishek's equivalent of the Gestapo, and a larger number of members of terrorist youth groups sent in by the Syngman Rhee government. Some wore neat American uniforms, others were posing as prisoners… Their continuing task was to locate prisoners who wished repatriation and to do whatever was necessary to dissuade them. Control of the food supplies was a powerful means, and that, threats, beatings, slashings and the killing of the most stubborn, led to a gratifying number who muttered "Taiwan, Taiwan, Taiwan" when asked the key question… Thus many Chinese who didn't want to go to Taiwan found themselves there. Of the Chinese prisoners 6,670 were repatriated to China, 14,235 were sent to Taiwan.[36]

The Anti-Communist Youth League, one of the aforementioned far right youth groups which had played a key role in brutally quashing dissent against the USAMGIK and Rhee in southern Korea, maintained a strong presence in the prison camps. They were in several cases given jurisdiction over meal distributions, disciplinary beatings, surveillance and interrogations, and reserved the right to punish and if they saw fit to execute prisoners.[37] Comparisons of prison camps where Chinese and North Korean personnel were held to Nazi concentration camps were common even in internal U.S. reports.[38] John Muccio, U.S. Ambassador to the ROK, himself alleged that the Taiwanese representatives involved in repatriation were "members of Chiang Kai-shek's Gestapo." He passed on reports that Chinese prisoners were being forced to sign petitions in blood and undergo tattooing to prove they were anti-communists and wanted to go to Taiwan. One report from a prison stated, regarding the harsh enforcement of this policy:

> In early 1952, the brigade leader, Li Da'an, wanted to tattoo every prisoner in Compound 72 with an anti-Communist slogan… He ordered the prison guards to beat those who refused the tattoo in front of the five thousand prisoners. Some of those who couldn't stand the beatings gave up and agreed to the tattoo. One prisoner, however, Lin Xuepu, continued to refuse the tattoo. Li Da'an finally dragged Lin up to the stage, and in a loud voice asked Lin: "Do you want it or not?" Bleeding and barely able to stand up, Lin, a nineteen-year-old college freshman, replied with a loud "No!" Li Da'an responded by cutting off one of Lin's arms with his big dagger. Lin screamed but still shook his head when Li repeated the question. Humiliated and angry, Li followed by stabbing Lin with his dagger… Li yelled to all the prisoners in the field: "whoever dares to refuse the tattoo will be like him."[39]

The State Department were under no illusion as to the nature of the voluntary repatriation process, with Ambassador Muccio reporting to State Secretary Acheson as early as May 1952 that Guomindang within the compounds "dominated proceedings through violent systematic terrorism and physical punishment of those choosing against going Taiwan throughout both orientation and screening phases. Severe beatings, torture, some killings."[40] He had reported four months prior in January to Secretary Acheson's aide, Ural Alexis Johnson, that "beatings, torture and threats of punishment are frequently unitized to intimidate the majority of Chinese POWs" as part of "an attempt at forced coerced removal to Formosa [Taiwan] in direct contradiction of the UNC [United Nations Commission] stand at Panmunjom on voluntary repatriation of internees."[41] He later again emphasized in a report to Secretary Acheson the use of "physical terror including organized murders, beatings, threats, before and even during the polling process" to ensure a favourable outcome on the repatriation issue. His findings were confirmed by others in the State Department.[42] Muccio would later refer to news on the treatment and coercion of Chinese and Korean prisoners as "very disturbing reports of horrors being perpetuated in the prisoners camps," for which he said the United States was responsible.[43]

A report from the Department Office of Intelligence research similarly observed: "During the months preceding the screening, KMT [Guomindang] POW trusties, with Chinese Nationalist and American encouragement and aid, had built up a police-state type of rule over the main Chinese POW compounds, which provided the foundation and means for powerfully influencing the screening against repatriation." This included "enforced tattooing of the POWs" and "violent and terroristic coercion of the POWs by the KMT trusties during the screening" which the report concluded has seriously inflated the numbers of prisoners who "chose" to defect.[44]

U.S. State Department officers A. Sabin Chase and Philip Mansard were sent to Korea to ascertain why such large numbers of prisoners refused repatriation. They concluded in their report that the main reason was "violent tactics of the PW [POW] trustees before and during the screening process." They reported a "police state type of rule" over the prisoner compounds and that prisoners were not only subjected to an "information blockade," but also that physical terror including organized threats, beatings and murders before and during the polling process were all widespread. While the investigators found substantial evidence of coercion, they did not find any significant lack of support for the Chinese communist government or the People's Army among Chinese prisoners.[45] North Korean doctor Rhee Tok Ki concurrently reported that ill patients were harassed to the detriment of their recovery to ensure that they would refuse repatriation. He stated: "TB patients especially need rest, but they were hounded day and night as a sort of specially refined torture to get them to renounce repatriation."[46]

The Red Cross similarly reported "some very grave incidents" regarding the treatment of Chinese and North Korean prisoners—particularly surrounding the issue of prisoner repatriation and related coercion. Although reporters were not allowed near prison camps, one reporter for the *Toronto Star* managed to enter with a British delegation. His report affirmed that the prisoners were choosing not to be repatriated due to "physical threats, often carried out." In some cases prisoners were instead given the option either to remain imprisoned indefinitely or to go to Taiwan, and so elected to go to Taiwan based on false information.[47] The final report by the Neutral Nations Repatriation Commission gave the same conclusion, that "any prisoner who desired repatriation had to do so clandestinely and in fear for his life."[48]

The extreme and often brutal means of coercion employed to force Chinese and Korean prisoners to defect often left them desperate. An example was prisoner Ju Yeong Bok, who threw himself at the barbed wire fence of his compound seeking to escape the constant interrogation and torture he was forced to endure in relation to the repatriation issue. According to the prisoner's memoir, those suspected of choosing not to defect to the Western aligned East Asian states were closely scrutinised, often treated violently and subject to routine interrogation.[49] Indian General Kodandera Subayya Thimayya, sent to represent the neutral nations, noted regarding the perceptions of many prisoners towards the coalition forces holding them: "These men were terrified of the UN in general." He observed the immense pressure placed on the prisoners regarding the repatriation issue. Prisoners were terrified of the brutalities of the Western dominated United Nations command, the American sponsored extremist youth groups running many of the camps, and the Republic of Korea itself—to the extent that they tried to place their lives in the hands of an entirely foreign party, the Indian observers, in hope of better treatment. Prisoners on one occasion were reported to have broken out of line and "thrown themselves" at the Indian forces—perhaps the only source of humanity they could hope to find in the prison camps.[50]

Even reports from hard line anti-communist sources admitted that the compounds housing prisoners were run by "fanatically anti-communist" officers—with observers widely reporting that their use of violence and intimidation succeeded in inflating the number of non-repatriate "defectors" as intended. American officers reported to chief negotiator Admiral Joy that the screening process was not indicative of real choice by the prisoners.[51] Admiral Joy himself wrote of the Guomindang controlled compounds that "the results of the screening were by no means indicative of the POWs' real choice," and that, should Guomindang leaders be removed, the numbers wishing to be repatriated would rise "from 15% to 85%." He further noted reports that "a mock screening which had taken place in compound 92 prior to the regular screening. The [Guomindang] leaders had asked those who wished to return to step forward. Those doing so were either beaten black & blue or killed." Regarding his Army interpreters who witnessed the repatriation process, Joy reported they had "said their experience watching Chinese POWs at the polls convinced them that the majority of the POWs were too terrified to frankly express their real choice. All they could say in answer to the questions was 'Taiwan' repeated over & over again."[52] Thus the moral victory of the Western-led "free world" over the independent Chinese and Korean republics, referred to in most Western histories of the Korean War as a key affirmation of the superiority of Western values and the Western-led order, was truly a hollow one. It reflected not moral superiority, but rather the true depravity of the U.S.-led alliance and the hollowness of their claims to represent any sort of "free world."

The Triumph of Coercion

On October 8, 1952 negotiations entered an indefinite recess, with the American negotiators unwilling to compromise on their new and illegal demands regarding prisoner repatriation, and the East Asian allies for their part, while willing to compromise on this vital issue, not willing to do so to the extreme extent their adversaries were demanding. To do so would have been a betrayal of their armed forces and of tens of thousands of soldiers who had risked their lives on the front—in a way that would have significantly lowered their standings in the eyes of their populations and seriously undermined their mandates to rule. The U.S.-led coalition responded by applying maximum pressure to force the Chinese and Koreans to accept their terms.

Key to the pressure campaign on the East Asian allies was not only the Western Bloc's ability to continue the war—unaffordable for the allies in the long term both financially and in human lives—but also their ability to intensify and possibly even expand their aerial and naval bombardments. Such threats had been issued previously to force concessions in negotiations, but they escalated considerably over the prisoner issue on which the Chinese and Koreans were less willing to accede to Western demands. Indeed, as early as June 1951, Secretary of Defense George Marshall had considered recommending that Premier Zhou Enlai be told that unless the Chinese agreed to Western armistice terms "we are going to give them a taste of the atom."[53] As the repatriation issue emerged as a major sticking point the Joint Chiefs of Staff recommended lifting some bombing restrictions and blockading China if the armistice talks continued to stall. The State Department and the British supported this—although Britain opposed the imposition of a blockade. Intensification of bombing during the armistice negotiations was popular among the American public.[54]

Stalling negotiations over the repatriation issue in mid-1952 saw the bombardment of North Korea's civilian infrastructure intensify, with Operation Pressure Pump initiated in July seeing raids on vital infrastructure targets in Pyongyang. Bombardments were continuous and were carried out 24 hours a day for several weeks, causing significant casualties. The attacks were directly linked by the newly appointed Supreme Commander of United Nations forces, General Mark W. Clark, who had succeeded Ridgway in May, to force the East Asian allies to alter their negotiating position.[55] The Chinese and North Koreans for their part could not retaliate in kind with pressure of their own—which seriously undermined their ability to negotiate on equal terms.

As negotiations stalled over the prisoner repatriation disagreement the Joint Chiefs of Staff again proposed imposition of a naval blockade if the allies did not agree to U.S. terms for armistice. Chair and founder of the State Department's Policy Planning Staff George Kennan advocated that selective bombing of targets in south and central China could be necessary to force Beijing to agree to American terms.[56] In May 1952 the American military leadership threatened to send Guomindang forces to the Korean front. Involvement of the Guomindang had long been associated with a continuation of the Chinese Civil War to determine the fate of the Chinese mainland—rather than the fate of Korea—and implied an extension of the war to Chinese territory which was Taipei's final goal. On the 19th of that month the Joint Chiefs recommended that if armistice talks continued to stall, a new offensive should be launched using nuclear weapons against targets in both China and Korea—although the effectiveness of these against KPA and PVA positions remained in doubt. Pressure escalated considerably in the final months of 1952 when more serious attempts were made to intimidate the East Asian allies into submission to the Western terms. The CIA was tasked with spreading rumors that the Americans planned to expand their bombing campaign to China and begin a total war with the new republic if their demands were not met. The Joint Chiefs meanwhile asked Supreme Commander Clark, to consider plans for future operations against the Chinese mainland without restriction.[57]

In October 1952 Clark advocated an offensive towards the Pyongyang-Wonsan line, an addition of seven divisions to the coalition force including three Guomindang divisions and 12 artillery and 20 anti-aircraft battalions, and expansion of the bombing campaign across China. He further advocated for the use of nuclear weapons in a tactical role to support this campaign.[58] The inauguration of the new Dwight D. Eisenhower administration three months later saw the pressure mount further. China's state newspaper, the *People's Daily,* had announced shortly beforehand on January 23, 1953 that the new president was considering further expanding the South Korean military, blockading Chinese coasts, supporting a Guomindang offensive and carrying out nuclear strikes against northeast China.[59] On February 2, two weeks after assuming office, the new president announced that the neutralization of the Taiwan Strait was over, meaning the Guomindang were free to attack the Chinese mainland.[60] The announcement was accompanied by a massive increase in American military aid to Taipei.[61] This was a particularly critical threat considering that Chinese forces were already so overstrained, and the fact that Guomindang forces would be protected from retaliation by the vast U.S. military presence which remained in and around Taiwan. The Guomindang had begun raids on the Chinese coast in 1951 with extensive American assistance, which could be construed as a prelude to a wider invasion which would press Chinese forces on three fronts. The U.S. was also arming Guomindang forces to conduct raids into Chinese territory from Myanmar, which were carried out with the aid of CIA advisors—the third front.[62]

The death of Soviet General Secretary Joseph Stalin in March 1953 marked a turning point in the armistice negotiations and played well into the Western Bloc's hands. The Soviet commitment to defending China in the event of a Western attack—the primary factor holding the U.S. and its allies back from expanding their military campaign beyond the Korean Peninsula—was now in serious doubt. Moscow quickly withdrew its pilots from the Korean theatre where they had been carrying out limited operations. At Stalin's funeral on March 15 a notable shift in the rhetoric of the Soviet leadership was evident—emphasizing peace and reconciliation with the Western Bloc at a time when their East Asian allies were under maximum pressure. The new Soviet government's support for the East Asian allies would come to decline significantly. The U.S. proved far more willing to explore more provocative actions after the Soviet leader's death, most notably the bombing of the irrigation dams in northern Korea, and there was a very real chance that they would be willing to follow through on threats to attack China, should the East Asian allies fail to accommodate Western terms. The bombing of the dams and escalation of the conventional air campaign thus raised the credibility of American nuclear threats.

Ending the War

Armistice talks would resume in 1953, after Supreme Commander Clark wrote to Chinese and Korean commanders on February 22 proposing an exchange of sick and wounded prisoners. They replied favorably, and the exchange took place from April 20 to May 3. Seizing on the momentum of Clark's letter, Zhou Enlai in March proposed a further compromise with the Western demand for voluntary repatriation which would be more palatable to the East Asian allies—that prisoners whom the Western Bloc alleged were refusing repatriation should first be handed over to a third party, a neutral state.[63] There, it was presumed, efforts to coerce prisoners to defect , often extremely brutally, would be reduced and the number of defectors would drop significantly—with prisoners given a far more genuine and free choice when out of the captivity of Rhee, the Guomindang and the Western powers. Beijing and Pyongyang were accommodating the illegal demands of the U.S.-led coalition regarding prisoner repatriation, but they were attempting to do so in a way less compromising to the rights of their captured soldiers so as to bring a faster end to the war.

Predictably, propositions for the transfers of prisoners to a neutral state were opposed by the U.S. and their allies, as allowing them a more genuine say in whether they wanted to repatriate seriously undermined prospects for the propaganda coup the self-proclaimed "free world" so desired. On May 7, the East Asian allies made further concessions. The prisoners would not leave Korea—but would be placed in the custody of neutral nations for six months. The American negotiators, however, continued to press their demands and sought an early release for Korean defectors—who would not be allowed the luxury of time in the custody of neutral states and would transfer directly from prison to the Rhee government's jurisdiction. They further demanded that time in the custody of the neutral states be confined to 60 days—where the East Asian allies had previously proposed a period of six months.[64] Unwilling to compromise, the coalition moved to apply further pressure to force the East Asian allies to accede to their terms.

On May 13, 1953 the U.S. began the aforementioned attacks on irrigation dams deep in northern Korean territory, a war crime they were likely willing to commit only in light of the recent developments in Moscow which reduced the commitment of the allies' primary protector. The official U.S. Air Force history claimed that two of the larger attacks on irrigation dams were the most devastating air operations of the entire war, and "portended the devastation of the most important segment of the North Korean agricultural economy."[65] The DPRK's ability to sustain the war effort or feed its population were now in serious doubt.[66] A week later, on May 20, the Joint Chiefs of Staff recommended a large scale attack involving "air and naval operations directly against China and Manchuria" and "a coordinated offensive to seize a position generally at the waist of Korea"—making clear that nuclear strikes would need to be employed "on a sufficiently large scale to ensure success."[67] On May 22, State Secretary John Foster Dulles told Indian Prime Minister Jawaharlal Nehru, increasingly seen as a conduit for messages between the Western Bloc and the East Asian allies, that the war would be expanded to China unless Western terms for armistice were acceded to in short order.[68] U.S. ambassador to the USSR Charles Bohlen conveyed a similar message through the Soviets on May 28.[69]

Even with an apparent shift in Soviet policy, the U.S. was inclined to avoid further offensives due to a number of factors. These included the large Soviet military presence in China, which made attacks on the mainland unfavorable, the heavily fortified nature of KPA and PVA positions, which limited the applicability of bombing including nuclear bombing, and the massive casualties which were expected should an all-out assault be carried out based on the precedents set by North Korean resistance at Punchbowl, Bloody Ridge and Heartbreak Ridge. The positions of the East Asian allies had only grown more fortified since. The U.S. military warned that attacks on targets in China would require use of nuclear weapons which, even with Stalin dead, risked provoking a Soviet response. The new government forming in Moscow, though apparently less committed to the defense of its allies, remained in transition. Western use of nuclear weapons against its neighbors seriously risked provoking the Soviets to again adopt more hardline position.[70]

While American willingness to follow through on its threats and escalate the war remained ambiguous, the threat appeared all the more imminent after the U.S. and its allies launched an unprecedented escalation in May with the bombing of the irrigation dams. In the final week of May Supreme Commander Clark warned the Korean and Chinese negotiators that the Western terms for an armistice were "final" and compromises to these would not be accepted. He further warned that if the new Western terms were not accepted, the negotiations would not be recessed but permanently terminated.[71] This hardline ultimatum was further conveyed to the Soviet Union through ambassador Bohlen on June 3.[72] Threat and maximum pressure appeared to work, and the Chinese and Korean parties both acceded to the General's terms with the signing of the armistice on that basis scheduled to come into effect on July 27. The final agreement saw almost no compromise made on the Western hard line on the return of prisoners, with time in the custody of neutral nations limited and, in the case of many Korean prisoners, non-existent.

UN Command representatives at the signing of the armistice, much like the UN negotiators and the high command of UN forces on the field, were all Americans. The armistice was signed by U.S. Army Lieutenant General William K. Harrison Jr. and Korean People's Army Lieutenant General Nam Il. Both representatives sat at separate tables and wordlessly signed nine copies of the armistice—which was to take effect twelve hours later. The Generals signed at 10:10 and 10:11 A.M. respectively. While General Nam left promptly, his American counterpart exited more leisurely—pausing to smile, greet UN representatives and pose for photographs.

Alongside an end to hostilities, the armistice stipulated under Article IV Paragraph 60 that a conference be held within three months to settle the question of Korea's division. A late conference was held in Geneva in April 1954 attended by the U.S., China, the USSR, Britain, the two Koreas and thirteen other members of the U.S.-led coalition force, at which the ROK representative took a characteristically hard line insisting Seoul could be the only legitimate representative of Korea. It called for U.S. and other Western personnel to remain in Korea indefinitely, imposition of a unilateral withdrawal of Chinese forces, and elections to be held under its own jurisdiction to reunify the peninsula under it. The DPRK suggested that all foreign forces leave Korea, and that unifying elections be held under the jurisdiction of neither Korean state but instead under a joint all-Korean commission agreed upon by both states to ensure fairness. This more equitable proposition was rejected outright, even after China proposed an amendment which would see a group of neutral nations supervise unifying elections—to which the DPRK consented. Again, the knowledge that free and fair elections would almost certainly yield a result strongly favoring the north, as attested to by the CIA among other prominent sources,[73] had a tangible influence on U.S. and ROK decision making. Unification under anything less than their own complete authority had to be rejected outright. Seoul and Rhee himself in particular had, according to U.S. sources, favored forceful reunification and been highly reluctant to enter into any kind of negotiation requiring compromise, which partly explains why such an intransigent set of terms was put forward.[74] Although the U.S. supported South Korea's proposal, Britain and other allies were skeptical that such terms were ever a viable negotiating position.[75] While even America and South Korea's allies did not voice support for these terms, which due to their one-sidedness and uncompromising nature had effectively ended the possibility of a negotiated settlement, the Belgian and British representatives notably said that they did not reject the ideas of the Chinese proposal.[76] The conference ended with participants failing to agree on any declaration.

It is important to note that had the Western Bloc sought to end the Korean War quickly at any time from November 1951, it could have simply dropped the demand for voluntary repatriation and commenced negotiations as law abiding nations in accordance with the Geneva Conventions. Indeed, a peace agreement could have been reached over a year earlier even with voluntary repartition at the original quoted figure of 116,000 prisoners to be returned, which had been accepted to by the Chinese in April 1952.[77] Additional demands made after multiple rounds of Chinese and Korean concessions served to prolong the conflict by almost two years.[78] While the East Asian allies appeared tolerant of small Western deviations from their treaty obligations under the convention, including the illegal transfer of small numbers of prisoners to Taiwan and South Korea, they were unwilling to accept what can only be described as gross violations of the law and serious war crimes. These pertained to the brutal mistreatment of prisoners including killings, medical experimentation, torture and coercion of the most extreme kind to force them to remain indefinitely behind enemy lines after the war's end. The U.S. and their allies were effectively able to play for time and exert pressure in a way the Chinese and North Koreans were not, and what little leverage the East Asian allies had was further diminished by the death of General Secretary Stalin and resulting shift in Moscow's position.

Overhanging the entire negotiating process was a threat to intensify the conflict, up to and including initiating nuclear strikes against Chinese population centres. This threat escalated in 1953 and is widely credited by both scholars and policymakers with breaking the deadlock in the armistice negotiations.[79] State Secretary John Foster Dulles, for one, told his British and French counterparts at the Bermuda Conference five months after the armistice signing that "it was the [Beijing and Pyongyang's] knowledge of the U.S. willingness to use force that broke hostilities," referring to the fact that America was "prepared for a much more intensive scale of warfare."[80] In April 1954, at the Geneva Conference, Dulles more publicly stated that American position was advanced due to the enemy's realisation that if it failed to comply with the terms set, "the battle area would be enlarged so as to endanger the source of aggression in Manchuria."[81] President Eisenhower himself asserted without hesitation, when asked how the war had ended, that it had been due to: "Danger of an atomic war… We told them we could not hold it to a limited war any longer if the communists welched on a treaty of truce. They didn't want a full-scale atomic attack. That kept them under some control."[82] The President came to the same conclusion in his memoirs.[83] The fact that the armistice was concluded so shortly after an escalation of nuclear threats convinced the Eisenhower administration that this approach had played a significant role in furthering American designs, and that the ability to issue such threats at times and in ways of their own choosing could be key to bringing about favourable resolutions to future crises.[84] This strategy was implemented by many of the administration's successors, and American attempts to coerce the DPRK through threats of nuclear force were frequent as long as there was total nuclear asymmetry on the Korean Peninsula.

Use of nuclear threats to press Pyongyang to accept American demands would continue after the signing of the armistice during a number of disputes and would increase considerably in the 1990s following the Soviet collapse. This would eventually lead the DPRK to seek to correct the asymmetry with its adversary by pursuing its own nuclear arms. This same phenomenon was also responsible for sparking Chinese interest in a nuclear deterrent capability—which appears to have emerged during the negotiating process as a direct result of America's use of nuclear threats to force unilateral concessions. A spokesman for a prominent Chinese Scientific Association stated to this effect regarding the nature of negotiations with the United States: "only when we ourselves have the atomic weapon, and are fully prepared, is it possible for the frenzied warmongers to listen to our just and reasonable proposals [for ending the war]."[85] The state newspaper *People's Daily* similarly emphasized the importance of a nuclear weapons capability to contain America's "atomic militarism."[86]

Alongside threats of nuclear escalation, the ability of the U.S. and its Western allies to heavily bombard North Korean population centres, supply lines, military positions and vital infrastructure until an agreement favouring their interests was accepted was hardly lost on the country's leadership. It remains contested which means of coercion was the predominant one in forcing the East Asian allies to make concessions, with both bombardments and nuclear threats escalating considerably in the lead up to the war's end, but it is clear that both of these played a significant role in ensuring concessions remained one-sided due to the East Asian allies' lack of similar capabilities. Many decades later, Pyongyang would come to heavily prize the ability to bombard U.S. military facilities in South Korea, in the wider Asia-Pacific region, and eventually the population centres in the United States itself [87]—ensuring a more equal position which had long been denied to it. Without military bases on America's doorstep, as the Americans themselves had in Japan, South Korea, Guam and elsewhere, and without comparable conventional capabilities suited to overseas power projection such as carrier strike groups, the ballistic missile would emerge as the only viable tool for this.

NOTES

1 Levine, Alan J., *Stalin's Last War; Korea and the Approach to World War III*, Jefferson, McFarland & Company, 2005 (pp. 188–189).

2 Gwertzman, Bernard, 'U.S. Papers Tell of '53 Policy to Use A-Bomb in Korea,' *New York Times*, June 8, 1984.

3 Levine, Alan J., *Stalin's Last War; Korea and the Approach to World War III*, Jefferson, McFarland & Company, 2005 (p. 214).
Pak, Chi Young, *Korea and the United Nations*, The Hague, Kluwer Law International, 2000 (p. 83).

4 U.S. Department of State, *Foreign Relations of the United States*, VII, Washington, D.C., Government Printing Office, 1976 (p. 561).

5 Acheson, Dean, *Present at the Creation: My Years in the State Department*, New York, Norton, 1969 (p. 533).

6 Lindqvist, Sven, *A History of Bombing*, New York, The New Press, 2001 (p. 131).
Grosscup, Beau, *Strategic Terror: The Politics and Ethics of Aerial Bombardment*, London, Zed Books, 2003 (Chapter 5: Cold War Strategic Bombing: From Korea to Vietnam, Part 4: The Bombing of Korea).

7 Garthoff, Raymond L., *Sino-Soviet Military Relations*, New York, Praeger, 1966 (p. 8).

8 Acheson, Dean G., *Present at the Creation: My Years in the State Department*, New York, W. W. Norton, 1969 (pp. 535–536).

9 Matray, James I., 'Mixed Message: The Korean Armistice Negotiations at Kaesong,' *Pacific Historical Review*, vol. 81, no. 2, May 2012 (p. 230).

10 Ibid. (pp. 223–224, 231).

11 Acheson, Dean, *Present at the Creation: My Years in the State Department*, New York, Norton, 1969 (p. 535).

12 Matray, James I., 'Mixed Message: The Korean Armistice Negotiations at Kaesong,' *Pacific Historical Review*, vol. 81, no. 2, May 2012 (p. 230).

13 Foreign Relations of the United States 1951, Vo. VII (pp. 610, 667–668, 771–774,838–842).
Hermes, Walter, *Truce Tent and Fighting Front*, Washington, Department of the Army, 1966 (p. 19).

14 Dockrill, M. L., 'The Foreign Office, Anglo-American Relations and the Korean War, June 1950–June 1951,' *Royal Institute of International Affairs 1944–*, vol. 62, no. 3, Summer, 1986 (p. 465).
15 Hermes, Walter G., *Truce Tent and Fighting Front*, Washington D.C., Center of Military History, 1992 (p. 181).
16 Telegrams, Nie Rongzhen to Mao and Zhou Enlai, October 9, 1951, *Nie Rongzhen Junshi Wenxuan* [Selected military writings of Nie Rongzhen], Beijing, CCP Central Archives, 1992 (pp. 359–361).
17 Tucker, Spencer T., *The Encyclopaedia of the Korean War,* Santa Barbara, ABC-CLIO, 2010 (p. 469).
Levine, Alan J., *Stalin's Last War; Korea and the Approach to World War III,* Jefferson, McFarland & Company, 2005 (pp. 221, 278).
18 Vyshinsky, Andrey, *On Measures Against the Threat of Another War and for Strengthening Peace and Friendship Among Nations*, Sixth Session of the United Nations General Assembly, November. 8, 1951.
19 'The Cold War in Asia,' *Cold War International History Project Bulletin*, issues 6–7, Winter 1996–1996 (p. 73).
20 Pape, Robert A., *Bombing to Win: Air Power and Coercion in War,* Ithaca, NY, Cornell University Press, 1996 (pp. 138–139).
21 Hermes, Walter, *Truce Tent and Fighting Front,* Washington, Department of the Army, 1966 (pp. 121–130, 152–153).
Vatcher, William H., *Panmunjom*, New York, Praeger, 1958 (pp. 88–89).
Foreign Relations of the United States 1951, Vol. VII (pp. 1177, 1206–1208, 1212–1239, 1250–1252, 1321–1331, 1345, 1366, 1377–1382, 1401–1402, 1420–1421, 1427–1428).
22 Meeting dated January 2, 1952. Minutes of Meetings of Subdelegates for Agenda Item 4 on Prisoners of War, 12/11/1951—02/06–1952; Korean Armistice Negotiation Records; Secretary, General Staff; Headquarters, United Nations Command (Advance); Record Group 333; National Archives at College Park, College Park, MD.
23 Kim, Monica, *The Interrogation Rooms of the Korean War; The Untold History,* Princeton, NJ, Princeton University Press, 2019 (p. 8).
24 Levine, Alan J., *Stalin's Last War; Korea and the Approach to World War III,* Jefferson, McFarland & Company, 2005 (p. 252)
25 Jager, Shella Miyoshi, *Brothers at War: The Unending Conflict in Korea*, London, Profile Books, 2013 (p. 205).
26 Memorandum of Conversation by the Deputy Assistant Secretary of State for Far Eastern Affairs, 'U.S. Position on Forcible Repatriation of Prisoners of War,' February 27, 1952, Top Secret, Top Secret, *Foreign Relations of the United States*, 1952–1954, vol. 15, part 1 (p. 69).
27 Kim, Monica, *The Interrogation Rooms of the Korean War; The Untold History,* Princeton, NJ, Princeton University Press, 2019 (p. 13).
28 Kim, Monica, *The Interrogation Rooms of the Korean War; The Untold History,* Princeton, NJ, Princeton University Press, 2019 (pp. 9, 207).
29 Bernstein, Barton J., *The Struggle Over the Korean Armistice: Prisoners of Repatriation* in: Cumings, Bruce, *Child of Conflict: The Korean-American Relationship, 1943–1953,* Seattle, University of Washington Press, 1983 (pp. 281–284).
Negotiating While Fighting: The Diary of Admiral C. Turner Joy at the Korean Armistice Conference, Stanford, Hoover Institution Press, 1978 (p. 368).
Rose, Gideon, *How Wars End: Why We Always Fight the Last Battle,* New York, Simon and Schuster, 2010 (p. 132).
30 Memorandum of discussion at the 181st meeting of the NSC, January 21, 1954; Eisenhower Library, Eisenhower papers, Whitman file.

31 Kim, Monica, *The Interrogation Rooms of the Korean War; The Untold History,* Princeton, NJ, Princeton University Press, 2019 (pp. 107, 128).
32 Ibid. (p. 99).
33 Document: Overall Strategic Concept for our Psychological Operations, May 7, 1952, Folder: 091.412, File #2, 'The Field and Role of Psychological Strategy in Cold War Planning,' Box 15, SMOF: Psychological Strategy Board files, Papers of Harry S. Truman, Harry S. Truman Presidential Library Archives.
34 Roberts, Adam, 'NATO's "Humanitarian War" on Kosovo,' *Survival*, vol. 41, no. 3, Autumn 1999 (pp. 102–123).
'Bush Renews Vow to "Free" Iraqi People,' *New York Times,* April 1, 2003.
Hong, Adrian, 'How to Free the North Korean People,' *Foreign Policy,* Dec. 19, 2011.
Zenko, Micah, 'The Big Lie About the Libyan War,' *Foreign Policy*, March 22, 2016.
Marks, Jesse and Pauley, Logan, 'America Must Find New Ways to Protect Syrian Civilians,' *National Interest,* November 20, 2018.
35 Schmitt, Carl, *The Nomos of the Earth in the International Law of the Jus Publicum Europaeum,* New York, Telos Press, 2003 (p. 419).
36 Deane, Hugh, *The Korean War, 1945–1953*, San Francisco, CA, China Books and Periodicals, 1999 (p. 167).
37 Thimayya, Kodendera Subayya, *Experiment in Neutrality,* New Delhi, Vision Books, 1981 (p.113).
Kim, Monica, *The Interrogation Rooms of the Korean War; The Untold History,* Princeton, NJ, Princeton University Press, 2019 (pp. 278, 281).
38 Carruthers, Susan Lisa, *Cold War Captives: Imprisonment, Escape and Brainwashing*, Oakland, University of California Press, 2009 (p. 125).
39 Westad, Odd Arne, *The Cold War; A World History*, London, Allen Lane, 2017 (p. 180).
Peters, Richard, and Li, Xiaobing, *Voices from the Korean War: Personal Stories of American, Korean and Chinese soldiers*, Lexington, University Press of Kentucky, 2005 (pp. 244–245).
40 Muccio to Secretary of State, May 12, 1952, Top Secret, *Foreign Relations of the United States*, 1952–1954, vol. 15, part 1 (p. 192).
41 Memorandum by P. W. Manhard of the Political Section of the Embassy to the Ambassador in Korea, Secret, March 14, 1952, *Foreign Relations of the United States*, 1952–1954, vol. 15, part 1 (pp. 98–99).
42 The Ambassador in Korea to the Department of State, Top Secret, June 29, 1952, *Foreign Relations of the United States*, 1952–1954, vol. 15, part 1 (p. 360).
Muccio to Secretary of State, July 2, 1952, Top Secret, *Foreign Relations of the United States*, 1952–1954, vol. 15, part 1 (pp. 369–370, 379).
Rose, Gideon, *How Wars End: Why We Always Fight the Last Battle,* New York, Simon and Schuster, 2010 (pp. 146–147).
43 Muccio, John J., *Oral History Interview*, Harry S. Truman Library, February 10 and 18, 1971 (pp. 100–101).
44 Chase, A. Sabine, *Estimate of Action Needed and Problems Involved in Negotiating and Implementing an Operation for Re-Classification and Exchange of POWs,'* July 7, 1952, Top Secret, National Archives, 693.95A24/7-752 (pp. 3–4, 7).
45 Foot, Rosemary, *A Substitute for Victory: Politics of Peacemaking at the Korean Armistice talks*, Ithaca, NY, Cornell University Press, 1990 (pp. 120–121).
46 Deane, Hugh, *The Korean War, 1945–1953*, San Francisco, CA, China Books and Periodicals, 1999 (p. 178).
47 Ibid. (pp. 178, 169).
48 Young, Charles S., *Name, Rank, and Serial Number: Exploiting Korean War POWs at Home and Abroad,* Oxford, Oxford University Press, 2014 (p. 89).
49 Ju, Yeong Bok, *76 P'orodul [The 76 Prisoners of War],* Seoul, Daegwan Publishing, 1993 (p. 47).

Kim, Monica, *The Interrogation Rooms of the Korean War; The Untold History,* Princeton, NJ, Princeton University Press, 2019 (p. 291).

50 Thimayya, Kodendera Subayya, *Experiment in Neutrality,* New Delhi, Vision Books, 1981 (p.79).
Kim, Monica, *The Interrogation Rooms of the Korean War; The Untold History,* Princeton, NJ, Princeton University Press, 2019 (p. 291).

51 Levine, Alan J., *Stalin's Last War; Korea and the Approach to World War III,* Jefferson, McFarland & Company, 2005 (pp. 253–254)

52 *Negotiating While Fighting: The Diary of Admiral C. Turner Joy at the Korean Armistice Conference,* Stanford, Hoover Institution Press, 1978 (p. 355).

53 Brower, Charles F., *George C. Marshall: Servant of the American Nation,* New York, Palgrave Macmillan, 2011 (Chapter 6: Fighting the Force Problem: George C. Marshal and Korea).
Levine, Alan J., *Stalin's Last War; Korea and the Approach to World War III,* Jefferson, McFarland & Company, 2005 (p. 208).

54 Ibid. (p. 277)

55 Edwards, Paul M., *Historical Dictionary of the Korean War,* Lanham, Scarecrow Press, 2010 (p. 212)

56 Foreign Relations of the United States 1951, Vol. VII (pp. 667–668, 881–882, 1106–1109).
Foot, Rosemary, *The Wrong War*, Ithaca, Cornell University Press, 1985 (pp. 148–153, 176).
Hermes, Walter, *Truce Tent and Fighting Front,* Washington, Department of the Army, 1966 (pp. 56, 107).
Pogue, Forrest C., *George C. Marshall, Volume 4: Statesman, 1945–1959,* New York, Viking, 1987 (p. 488).

57 Levine, Alan J., *Stalin's Last War; Korea and the Approach to World War III,* Jefferson, McFarland & Company, 2005 (pp. 278, 280)

58 G-3 381 Pacific, G-3 Staff Study, 'Capability of U.S. Army to Implement CINCUNC Operations Plan,' ca. 21, Jan 53.
Levine, Alan J., *Stalin's Last War; Korea and the Approach to World War III,* Jefferson, McFarland & Company, 2005 (pp. 277–278).

59 BBC Summary, Far East, No. 221, January 23, 1953.

60 Chang, Su-Ya, *Unleashing Chiang Kai-shek? Eisenhower and the Policy of Indecision toward Taiwan, 1953*, Taipei, Institute of Modern History, Academia Sinica, 1991.

61 Kuo, Fang Pu and Shih, Cheng Chu, *The Working Record of the U.S. Military Assistance Advisory Group: The Headquarters*, Taipei, Historic Office, Republic of China Ministry of National Defense, 1981 (pp. 10–12).
Chang, Su-Ya, *Unleashing Chiang Kai-shek? Eisenhower and the Policy of Indecision toward Taiwan, 1953*, Taipei, Institute of Modern History, Academia Sinica, 1991.

62 Levine, Alan J., *Stalin's Last War; Korea and the Approach to World War III,* Jefferson, McFarland & Company, 2005 (p. 278).
Blum, William, *Killing Hope: U.S. Military and C.I.A. Interventions Since World War II*, London, Zed Books, 2003 (pp. 24–25).
Washington Post, August 20, 1958.
Mitchell, Arthur H., *Understanding the Korean War: The Participants, the Tactics, and the Course of Conflict*, Jefferson, NC, McFarland, 2013 (p. 177).

63 *Survey of the China Mainland Press*,, Hong Kong, U.S. Consulate General, No. 541 (March 28, 1953); and No. 542 (March 30, 1953).

64 Hermes, Walter, *Truce Tent and Fighting Front,* Washington, Department of the Army, 1966 (pp. 409–425).

65 Futrell, Robert F., *United States Air Force Operations in the Korean Conflict,* 1 July 1952–27 July 1953, USAF Historical Study no. 127, Maxwell Air Force Base, Ala, USAF Historical Division, Research Studies Institute, Air University, 1956 (pp. 93, 126).

66 Levine, Alan J., *Stalin's Last War; Korea and the Approach to World War III,* Jefferson, McFarland & Company, 2005 (p. 283)
67 Foreign Relations of the United States 1952–1954, vol. 15, *Korea*, May 19, 1953 (pp. 1061–1062).
68 *Congressional Record: Proceedings and Debates of the 86th Congress*, vol. 105, part 7, May 20–June 4, 1959 (p. 8703).
Futrell, Robert Frank, *The United States Air Force in Korea, 1950–1953,* Washington D.C., Office of Air Force History, 1983 (p. 667).
69 Foreign Relations of the United States 1952–1954, vol. 15, *Korea*, May 19, 1953 (p. 1068).
Levine, Alan J., *Stalin's Last War; Korea and the Approach to World War III,* Jefferson, McFarland & Company, 2005 (pp. 283–284).
70 Foreign Relations of the United States 1952–1954, vol. 15, *Korea*, May 19, 1953 (p. 1065).
71 Ibid. (pp. 1082–1086).
72 Record Group (RG) 59, 795.00 Korea, Box 4268, May 28, 1953, NA.
73 Hanley, Charles J. and Choe, Sang Hun, and Mendoza, Martha, *The Bridge at No Gun Ri: A Hidden Nightmare from the Korean War*, New York, Henry Holt and Company, 2001 (p. 170).
Foreign Relations of the United States, 1950, vol. VII, Korea, Washington D.C., Government Printing Office, 1976 (p. 602).
Stone, I. F., *Hidden History of the Korean War*, Amazon Media, 2014 (Chapter 17: Free Elections?).
74 U.S. Department of State, Foreign Relations of the United States, 1952–1954, The Geneva Conference, Volume XVI, 795.00/2-1954: Telegram from Seoul to Washington, February 19, 1954.
75 Bailey, Sydney D., *The Korean Armistice*, New York, Palgrave MacMillan, 1992 (p. 163).
76 Ibid. (pp. 167–168).
77 Sandler, Stanley, *The Korean War: An Encyclopedia*, New York, Routledge, 2005 (p. 29).
78 Pape, Robert A., *Bombing to Win: Air Power and Coercion in War,* Ithaca, NY, Cornell University Press, 1996 (pp. 137, 139).
79 Brodie, Bernard, *War and Politics,* London, Macmillan, 1973 (p. 105).
George, Alexander L., and Smoke, Richard, *Deterrence in American Foreign Policy: Theory and Practice,* New York, Colombia University Press, 1974 (p. 239).
Rees, David, *Korea: The Limited War,* New York, St. Martin's Press, 1964 (pp. 419–420).
80 Foreign Relations of the United States, 1952-54, vol. 5, *Western European Security*, Washington D.C., U.S. Government Printing Office, 1979 (pp. 1811–1813).
81 Freedman, Lawrence, *The Evolution of Nuclear Strategy*, London, Macmillan, 1983 (p. 85).
82 Adams, Sherman, *Firsthand Report: The Inside Story of the Eisenhower Administration,* London, Hutchinson, 1962 (p. 102).
83 Eisenhower, Dwight D., *The White House Years: Mandate for Change, 1953–1956*, New York, Doubleday, 1963 (pp. 179–180).
84 Foot, Rosemary, *Nuclear Coercion and the Ending of the Korean Conflict,* International Security, vol. 13, no. 3, MIT Press, Winter 1988–1989 (p. 93).
85 Harris, William R., 'Chinese Nuclear Doctrine: The Decade Prior to Weapons Development (1945–1955),' *The China Quarterly,* no. 21, January-March 1965 (p. 94).
86 Ibid. (p. 94).
87 Warrick, Joby and Nakashima, Ellen and Fifield, Anna, 'North Korea now making missile-ready nuclear weapons, U.S. analysts say,' *Washington Post,* August 8, 2017.
Baker, Peter and Choe, Sang-Hun, 'Trump Threatens "Fire and Fury" Against North Korea if It Endangers U.S.,' *New York Times,* August 8, 2017.
' Pompeo calls Iran more destabilizing than N. Korea,' *France 24*, February 14, 2019.

Part Two

THE COLD WAR YEARS

Chapter 9

WAR IN PEACETIME:
ONGOING CONFLICT AFTER THE KOREAN WAR ARMISTICE

Legacy of the Korean War

Before the military intervention of the United States and its Western allies the Korean War had been expected to last little over two weeks and end relatively swiftly and bloodlessly. Neither of the Korean belligerents had made extensive use of air power, deployed weapons of mass destruction or carried out intensive scorched earth campaigns. South Korea had been crippled by low morale and widespread public support for the North Koreans among its own population,[1] and its military had all but collapsed within days due to mass defections and general disorder.[2] The status quo on the peninsula would thus have resembled that in early September 1945 before the forceful abolition of the People's Republic of Korea by the United States Military, with the Korean People's Army gaining much popularity in South Korea for its reestablishment of the people's committees and effective restoration of the participatory democratic system which had existed beforehand.[3] It would have also brought an end to the bloodshed which had been ongoing in South Korea for five years under American rule and later under the U.S.-imposed Rhee government, which had seen hundreds of thousands killed and brutal atrocities committed by ROK forces and the militant groups they and the U.S. had sponsored.

Western military intervention brought terrible consequences to the severe detriment of the interests of all Koreans other than Rhee and the small minority which benefitted from his rule. As former CIA Operations Officer and intelligence expert Robert R. Simmons observed of the results of this heavy handed external intervention Korea's civil war: "a potentially swift and relatively bloodless reunification was converted into a carnage."[4] South Korea's population was left destitute, and their newfound poverty and desperation would be taken advantage of in full (see Chapter 11). The ROK lost approximately 1 million of its population, many of them from the military,[5] with tens of thousands killed by the U.S. and allied Western forces in numerous incidents ranging from careless laying down of fire to direct orders to massacre civilians. The country remained under the U.S. client government of Sygman Rhee and would see little improvement to its quality of life, among the very lowest in the world, until his overthrow. As Associate Research Fellow at South Korea's Center for Strategic Foresight at the Science and Technology Policy Institute Park Seong Won noted: "The Korean War…destroyed Korean society. In the 1960s, South Korea was one of the poorest countries in the world." In 1965, 85 percent of its population were still in abject poverty,[6] and economic dependence on the U.S. was extreme. Alongside considerable American aid, prostitution serving U.S. military personnel was strongly encouraged by the Rhee government and relied on to provide a source of foreign currency.[7] It was only after the toppling of the American-installed Rhee regime by popular protest that living conditions for South Korea's population finally began to improve under a new, more patriotic and independent military government, with president and former general Park Chung Hee proving a highly competent developmentalist.

Insofar as South Korea's territory only endured a brief period of Western bombing when under KPA control, with no significant air attacks carried out by Chinese or North Korean forces, damage was considerably lighter and the country was able to begin some reconstruction more than two years before the war had ended. This was far from the case for the north, which remained under constant Western bombardment from air, land and sea for over three years until twelve hours after the signing of the armistice on July 27, 1953. The extent of the destruction was thus far greater north of the 38th parallel, with the firebombing campaign, scorched earth policies, targeting of irrigation dams and the loss of up to 30 percent of the workforce forcing the DPRK to rely almost entirely on food from abroad. American estimates of the numbers of Koreans killed range up to 5 million,[8] and 20–30 percent of North Koreans are estimated to have died with many more left homeless, wounded or otherwise unable to work.[9] The level of wartime destruction surpassed that done to any country during the Second World War, or any at all in modern military history.

Which party, if any, "won" the Korean War remains open to interpretation. The U.S. and the Rhee government had failed to destroy the People's Republic in the north and forcefully reunify the peninsula under a Western client regime. They had however succeeded in preventing the imminent peaceful reunification and the expected unifying elections which, according to sources on all sides, from the CIA[10] to the Kremlin,[11] would have brought about a democratic victory for the DPRK government due to its considerable popularity among the southern population. The gains made towards this by the election of a parliament strongly supporting such a peaceful unification process and the marginalisation of Rhee, less than a month before the war's outbreak, were thus lost. Despite his extreme unpopularity, which had made a loss of power appear imminent before the war began, Syngman Rhee and his administration were able to remain in power. The alleged "communist invasion" gave further pretext to strengthen the suppression of opposition, including mass executions of the politically suspect who were previously held in concentration camps.[12]

The DPRK for its part may have won by virtue of its very survival, although even without considering the loss of life and wartime damage, its position had deteriorated significantly. Before the outbreak of hostilities, southern Korea had appeared poised to be peacefully integrated into the new republic and the Rhee government faced prospects for a loss of power from within. The DPRK nevertheless succeeded in surprising its adversaries both during the war with its effective battlefield performance and afterwards with its rapid and efficient reconstruction program. The Korean People's Army's months long string of early victories in particular, against overwhelming odds, undermined Western perceptions of their own superiority and of the impotence of Asian armies which had previously led Western sources to predict their own victory within hours or days.[13] The British *National Air Review* predicted the KPA's defeat within 72 hours of the U.S. Air Force's entry into the war—and such expectations were hardly unique or outstanding.[14] General MacArthur had himself stated within a few weeks of engaging the KPA, in stark contrast to his previous assessments: "The North Korean solider must not be underestimated. He is a tough opponent, well led," with this assessment echoed throughout the U.S. military leadership.[15] The United States has remained highly wary of the KPA's capabilities ever since.

Receiving significant support from China and the Soviet Bloc, the DPRK succeeded in achieving annual economic growth rates of over 20 percent in the war's aftermath with living standards restored to pre-war levels relatively quickly, given the extent of the damage done. Mass mobilization of its population allowed the country to economically outpace the ROK despite having suffered the vast majority of wartime destruction. While industries, dams and homes could be rebuilt and crops resown, the scars of the war would remain for many years to come. Unexploded munitions continue to be dug up 70 years later, endangering civilians and continuing to cause serious injuries. The clean-up operation is expected to take at least 100 years.[16] Figures are not available for the maiming and scarring, both physically and psychologically, of the surviving population, but given the scale of destruction and the substantial death toll it is expected to be very considerable. North Koreans today consider the Korean War, or in their parlance the Great Fatherland Liberation War, a victory. Considering the thwarting of Western designs and those of Rhee to subjugate the Korean nation this remains partially true. It was, however, a victory for which a very high price was paid.

A New North Korea

The beginning of American involvement in the Korean War marked the end of North Korea as it had once been, and the devastation of the nation resulted in a second revolution in national identity. While previously the Korean revolution's defining struggle was that against Japanese rule, its victory marked by the establishment of people's committees through which the population could determine their own future, the destruction subsequently wrought on such a scale by the U.S.-led Western powers over three years traumatised and shattered the population and redefined their national struggle as one for survival against Western subjugation. The national security state was born, power was increasingly centralised, and a strong defence and large standing army were increasingly prioritised. These measures did not face significant public opposition due to the population's newfound experience and understanding of the realities of war, the intentions and conduct of the Western adversaries, and the imperative of preparation.

The wartime experience would become a central aspect of life in the new Korea, as would apprehensions towards and preparations for its possible recurrence. In particular, there was a fear of a second wave of Western firebombing attacks against both civilian and industrial targets, which would again douse the country with hundreds of thousands of tons of explosives, napalm and other incendiaries threatening millions of lives. The government's responses to address this threat were manifold. One was the decentralisation of industry to reduce vulnerability to air attacks, with entire factories built and operated underground at considerable cost and inconvenience due to the imminent nature of the American threat. Across the country underground retreats for the population were also constructed for the same purpose.[17]

The influences of the wartime experience and particularly of the American-led bombing raids on both state and military planning were far from short lived and persist to this day. The Korean People's Army would focus heavily on strengthening its aerial warfare capabilities through the deployment of more interceptor aircraft and air defence systems. Shortly after the signing of the armistice Pyongyang became the only city in the world other than Moscow to deploy a Soviet S-25 (NATO Reporting SA-1) long range surface to air missile network, a heavy platform with multichannel guidance capabilities unique for its time, which was relied on heavily to defend the Soviet capital until the early 1980s. These were supported by other lighter and more common systems such as the S-75 (NATO Reporting SA-2) and by large numbers of MiG-15, MiG-17 and MiG-19 fighter jets. The primary purpose of all of these assets was to deny Western aircraft access to North Korean airspace and deter them from considering future incursions.

The already high perception of threat by the DPRK would grow considerably from 1958, when the fear of new firebombing attacks was supplemented by a heightened danger of American nuclear strikes. The DPRK had been aware of U.S. plans to use nuclear weapons in the Korean War, their deployment to Okinawa and preparation for use, the implementation of Operation Hudson Harbor to determine their effectiveness, and the role of American nuclear blackmail in gaining more favourable terms for an armistice. Widespread calls by prominent figures in the U.S. military and civilian leadership for nuclear strikes during the war were hardly kept secret. Nuclear weapons overshadowed and played a considerable role in the American war effort despite never having been dropped—hence why the conflict is referred to even today in North Korea as "a confrontation between the rifle and the atomic bomb."[18]

Perceptions of an imminent American nuclear threat grew when the United States unilaterally abrogated article 13 (d) of the Korean War armistice agreement on June 21, 1957. Aware that the cessation of hostilities remained far more important to the Chinese and North Koreans than to its own interests, with American cities and the vast majority of its regional bases still well out of harm's way, the U.S. was able to risk illegally violating the armistice. Although State Secretary John Foster Dulles had initially intended to portray the abrogation as a response to a

Korean or Chinese violation, both were found to be fully in accordance with the agreement meaning no such pretext could be used.[19] American violations were made in the knowledge that a response by either Beijing or Pyongyang which risked jeopardising the armistice would harm the East Asian allies far more than it would the United States—their leverage remained minimal as a result of their still limited military capabilities. The Rhee government for its part had opposed a cessation of hostiles from the outset, at a time when the Chinese, Americans and North Koreans all supported it, taking measures to sabotage the armistice negotiations and insisting the war be continued until all Korea was placed under its control regardless of the cost to the population.[20] Measures which risked new hostilities were thus hardly against its interests either. The United States thus became the first party to nuclearize the Korean Peninsula, and unilaterally deployed nuclear weapons to South Korea from January 1958.[21] Approximately 950 warheads were deployed,[22] an excessive amount of force by any measure and enough to erase North Korea and much of China from the map.

America's nuclearization of the Korean Peninsula was seen as a particularly dire threat due not only to the scale of the deployment, but also to how the U.S. Military intended to use the new weapons. The Joint Chiefs of Staff had recommended even before the deployment of warheads to Korea that any renewal of hostilities should immediately be followed by a "massive atomic air strike" against North Korean forces, and directives were given to employ nuclear arms in short order.[23] With President Rhee still in power until 1960, State Secretary Dulles repeatedly expressed his concern regarding the high risk that Seoul would itself initiate a new round of hostilities. The secretary informed the National Security Council to this effect: "if war were to start in Korea…it was going to be very hard indeed to determine which side had begun the war."[24]

U.S. intelligence reports indicated that Rhee's government was actively contemplating launching an attack in the mid-1950s. In a 1954 address to the U.S. Congress Rhee had shocked even his more hawkish American supporters by calling for use of the hydrogen bomb against the DPRK.[25] The Eisenhower administration's new Korea policy under NSC 5702/2, dated August 9, 1957, further allowed U.S. forces including their nuclear warheads to provide "support for a unilateral ROK military initiative" against the DPRK.[26] Rhee's previously demonstrated tendency to provoke the DPRK with his own forces,[27] his insistence on nothing less than forced reunification under his rule, and the knowledge that any new war would be aided by American nuclear force, meant there was a considerable risk he could seek to restart hostilities if not properly held in check by the Americans themselves.

The deployment of American nuclear arms within close artillery range of its territory had severe implications for North Korean security. While the USSR previously may have been expected to provide its ally with proportional protection in the form of a Soviet nuclear arsenal deployed to North Korean territory, even if a token force a small fraction of the size of the American one in the ROK, such support was not forthcoming. This was but one example of the unequal support the Koreas received from their superpower backers. The U.S. would also conduct multiple surveillance flights over North Korean territory and gain detailed and extremely valuable intelligence on KPA defences, which was subsequently shared with the ROKAF. While the Soviets had comparable surveillance aircraft of their own, these were not used to provide the KPA with similar intelligence.[28] With the new post-Stalinist government in Moscow not only drastically revising its ideological position, but also seeking détente with the West at the expense of several of its old allies,[29] there was a growing rift in relations with Pyongyang from the mid-late 1950s. Faith in Soviet protection was further shaken in 1962 when the USSR was seen to have effectively capitulated under Western pressure and withdrawn its nuclear deterrent from Cuba—despite an imminent threat of American attack against the small allied state. [30] This not only strengthened arguments within the DPRK for pursuit of an independent deterrent capability, which included both conventional arms and longer ranged strike capabilities, but it also forced Pyongyang to take additional precautions against an American nuclear attack.

By the end of January 1958, the first month of deployments of nuclear weapons to Korea, the United States had stationed approximately 150 nuclear warheads across four different weapons platforms in the ROK. These included the MGR-1 Honest John rocket artillery system, 280mm gun and 203mm nuclear howitzers and the Atomic Demolition Munition nuclear landmine. In March American strike fighters were equipped with nuclear warheads of their own, and this deployment was closely followed by further delivery systems for tactical nuclear weapons, including the MGM-18 Lacrosse and MGM-29 Sergeant nuclear tipped ballistic missiles and the M-28 Davy Crockett smooth sabre guns. By the mid 1960s over eight different types of American nuclear warhead were deployed to South Korea, including Hercules nuclear armed surface to air missiles designed to neutralise formations of Korean aircraft.[31] The deployment of nuclear warheads near the border on low level systems such as howitzers and rocket artillery allowed the U.S. to launch strikes against targets in the DPRK at any moment with only a few seconds warning.

American helicopters regularly flew nuclear weapons up to the inter-Korean border, and nuclear artillery systems were later complemented with 20 kiloton atomic demolition mines designed to contaminate large areas of South Korea for up to two weeks to deny it to KPA forces. This was a new and more extreme form of "scorched earth." These mines were forward deployed by special teams who carried the nuclear warheads in their backpacks and moved around in jeeps. Forward deployment of nuclear weapons necessitated a very low threshold for use, or a policy of "use 'em or lose 'em," as all nuclear warheads would need to be expended within hours of a war's outbreak to avoid the risk of their capture by the KPA.[32]

The North Koreans themselves had no means of responding to a potential nuclear attack other than the shelling of heavily fortified American military positions with their own conventional artillery assets—hardly a credible deterrent. The DPRK thus was forced to undertake considerable investments to fortify potential targets against American nuclear attacks in response. While it had already invested heavily in a vast network of underground tunnels and bomb shelters for protection against Western firebombing attacks, deeper and stronger fortifications were needed to withstand nuclear strikes, particularly as tactical nuclear warheads quickly grew more sophisticated. Attacks on high value targets such as the capital Pyongyang using multiple nuclear bombs were expected, and the U.S. was developing increasingly sophisticated penetrative nuclear warheads to ensure it could reach even the best defended targets.

The DPRK's considerable investments in fortifying its positions with underground defences would make the country the most tunnelled in the world, and provide the KPA with a rare skillset which it would later pass on to many of its allies (see Chapter 10). Indeed, President Kim Il Sung would offer both China and North Vietnam technical expertise in building fortified underground airfields which could accommodate regiments of 32 fighter jets—a skill developed in response to the Western powers' prioritisation of targeting airfields in the Korean War.[33] Perhaps the most prolific such tunnelling effort was the construction of the Pyongyang Metro, which began planning as the U.S. began to deploy nuclear warheads to the Korean Peninsula, with construction beginning in 1965. The metro was designed from the outset as a shelter from American bombing raids and nuclear strikes, with transportation arguably only a secondary function. For this purpose, the state went to considerable extra expense to construct the deepest and best fortified underground public railway system in the world—which at over 110 meters below the surface is today the deepest in the world. Protection for civilians sheltering underground was further improved with reinforced steel blast doors.

The ability not only to shelter its people and assets underground, but eventually to wage war from underground as the network of tunnels and bunkers grew more sophisticated, itself seriously complicated American and allied war plans and served as something of a deterrent in its own right. Several decades later, when the U.S. considered a new attack on the DPRK in the early 2000s, Defence Secretary Donald Rumsfeld stated regarding the sophistication of the underground network of fortifications: "They have gone underground across that country in a way that few nations have done… They have underground emplacements of enormous numbers of weapons." This was part of an argument against military action made at Rumsfeld's confirmation hearing, in which he referred to the KPA as "world class tunnelers."[34] This network would continue to be expanded with techniques for fortification refined over several decades.

A Small War in the Demilitarised Zone: 1966–1969

Amid high tensions in the post–Korean War years multiple direct U.S.-KPA clashes took place on the inter-Korean border. Although the Chinese People's Volunteer Army was withdrawn from Korea in 1958, after having provided not only protection but also a considerable labour contribution to reconstruction efforts,[35] the U.S. intended to maintain a large presence in South Korea indefinitely. In all future clashes with the United States and its allies, the rebuilt and now better armed Korean People's Army faced them alone. The first major series of clashes, known in the U.S. as the Korean DMZ Conflict, was a series of small skirmishes at the demilitarised zone from October 1966 to December 1969. These saw South Korean military and police units take the bulk of casualties at over 1,000 personnel, and the U.S. Military take over 300 casualties. Of these, 374 U.S. and ROK troops were killed. KPA casualties were considerably lower, although a far higher proportion of these were deaths due to the nature of their missions—infiltration behind enemy lines. 397 North Koreans were killed in the conflict.[36]

Theories on the causes of the Korean DMZ Conflict differ, with some placing the blame on the United States for provoking KPA units on the border while others have indicated that conflicts were part of a broader North Korean grand strategy. This supposedly entailed supporting an insurgency in South Korea while wearing out the U.S. military with low intensity conflict, with the intent to exhaust American forces and force them to split their resources between two fronts—the second being the then-escalating war in Vietnam.

The South Korean state had by this time grown considerably more resilient that it had been in the 1950s, with the new nationalist President Park Chung Hee's governance providing a strong contrast to that of the corrupt and regressive Rhee years. The new president was a former officer in the Imperial Japanese Army who was later jailed and sentenced to death under Rhee on charges that he led a communist cell. Evading this sentence with support from other officers, Park returned to active service after the outbreak of the Korean War and rose to the rank of Brigadier General. As acting president from 1962, Park did much to increase the legitimacy of the South Korean state in the eyes of the population and is widely credited today with having set the ROK on course for its economic rise—the result of which was a considerable improvement in general living standards. While Park was still constrained in his powers by the nature of the alliance with the United States he had come to power through his own machinations, rather than being hand-picked by the Americans and flown in from Washington as Rhee had been. This, combined with a strong nationalism and vision for a modern Korea,[37] made him considerably more independent.

Changes in governance in South Korea itself following Rhee's popular overthrow, combined with an extremely tight security state and an ongoing state of fear inspired by the brutal treatment of leftist sympathisers, were likely themselves largely responsible for the failure of the KPA to ignite a major insurgency in the ROK. Where the Korean People's Army could rely on widespread support among the rural population in South Korea during the Rhee years, impoverished and brutalised as the peasants were by his policies, genuine efforts to raise rural living standards and a decline in the indiscriminate violence towards the population by the authorities and affiliated youth groups under President Park meant this vital segment of the population was far less alienated from Seoul. A root cause for sympathies with North Korea was thus undermined.

With a new more charismatic leader and a government seen as far more legitimate than its predecessor, morale in South Korea was considerably higher. The military had also evolved into a far more formidable force under new leadership, and U.S. reports showed South Korean soldiers to be considerably better trained and better disciplined than their American counterparts.[38] Indeed, by contrast to the South Koreans, U.S. commanders lamented the quality of their own soldiers during the DMZ conflict, resulting in multiple casualties from what could only be described as careless actions from during minelaying, piloting, weapons maintenance and other routine activities. Rumours of drug abuse among U.S. personnel were rampant.[39]

High tensions during the DMZ Conflict saw the Korean People's Army Air Force shoot down a number of combat jets from the U.S. Air Force which Pyongyang claimed infringed on DPRK airspace. These included the downing of an RF-4C Phantom on August 31, 1967, an F-105D five months later on January 14, 1958 and an F-4B Phantom the following month on February 12. The aircraft lost, specifically the Phantoms, were the most capable in the Western Bloc at the time and were downed by Korean operated MiG-21 fighters. These jets had been acquired from the Soviet Union from 1963, possibly earlier, and were the most advanced fighters deployed by the Soviet Bloc at the time.

Perhaps the most significant incident during the DMZ conflict was the capture of the U.S. Navy surveillance warship *USS Pueblo* by the Korean People's Army Navy on January 23, 1968, and the imprisonment of 82 of its crew. With the KPA at that time involved in the Vietnam War (see Chapter 10), the seizure is speculated to have been coordinated with the Viet Minh who just seven days later launched the large-scale Tet Offensive against American forces in South Vietnam to further stretch the U.S. military presence in the region. The seizure also came six days after President Lyndon B. Johnson's State of the Union address which focused heavily on the state of conflict in Southeast Asia, but was widely considered a complete failure in America indicative of the fragile morale and questionable unity on the home front.[40]

The DPRK claimed that the American warship entered its territorial waters multiple times near Wonsan on the country's eastern coast—citing the ship's logbook as evidence. The U.S. denied that their warship had done so. The *Pueblo* was carrying out surveillance operations but had been intercepted by a submarine chaser and three torpedo boats with cover from a pair of MiG-21 fighters. These were followed by further Korean light warships. KPA forces eventually boarded and commandeered the *Pueblo,* killing one crewmember who they claimed resisted detention. The remaining 82 crew reportedly succeeded in destroying some classified information, but the majority was captured. While the *Pueblo* was armed, the size of the Korean force deployed against it left little chance of mounting an effective defence.

Following the *Pueblo's* capture CIA-operated Lockheed A-12 surveillance jets flew sorties over Korean territory, locating the ship near Wonsan and photographing potential targets for attack.[41] The use of the A-12 demonstrated the importance of the incident to the United States with only 13 of the extremely costly aircraft ever built and the platforms reserved for only the most vital surveillance missions. The CIA jets were tracked but not fired on, and succeeded in locating the *Pueblo* which had been escorted to Wonsan Harbour.[42] A previously unknown site for high altitude surface to air missiles was observed in Wonsan, possibly deployed in anticipation of or to deter an American intervention.[43]

Cables since declassified show that the Pentagon was ready to use nuclear weapons to force Pyongyang to comply with American demands over the *Pueblo* incident—much as threats to use them had helped facilitate favourable terms to the Korean War armistice.[44] As American historian Peter Hayes noted: "the initial reaction of American decisionmakers was to drop a nuclear weapon on Pyongyang… The fact that all the U.S. F-4 fighter planes held on constant alert on [South] Korean airfields were loaded only with nuclear weapons did not help the leaders to think clearly."[45] President Johnson was reportedly advised by a number of officials to respond to the ship's capture with an act of war, with attack plans presented involving nuclear strikes against the Korean leadership and KPA airbases.[46] The new geopolitical situation limited the feasibility of an escalatory response, however, with prevention of an outbreak of wider hostilities vital to the American interest at the time. Seeking to avoid opening a second front alongside Vietnam, Washington was forced to take a measured and proportional response. The administration considered a blockade of the DPRK and conventional airstrikes on Korean targets, but ultimately did not pursue these options for similar reasons.[47]

The U.S. response was restricted to the aforementioned reconnaissance flights, increased deployments of air, naval and ground forces, official protests through the United Nations and cabling of the Soviet Union.

A massive show of force under Operation Combat Fox and Operation Formation Star, the latter which involved six American aircraft carriers, was conducted to send a strong signal to Pyongyang. Six fighter squadrons, between them comprised of over 200 fighters, were deployed to bases across South Korea alongside reconnaissance and electronic warfare units—primarily to airbases in Kunsan and Osan.

Pyongyang's actions indicated awareness of the weak position America was in, and the KPA did not carry out a retaliatory mobilisation of its own forces as the U.S. had expected.[48] With public opinion in America fast turning against the war in Vietnam, where the U.S. Military was increasingly hard pressed with no end in sight, the opening of a second front in Korea even in response to perceived provocations was not a politically viable option. Although their displays of force and new deployments attempted to demonstrate otherwise, the U.S. was extremely limited in the military options it had available.

The KPA demonstrated a greater level of hostility towards the United States during the *Pueblo* incident than it had previously during the Korean War, and testimonies of captured American sailors show their treatment bore stark contrast to that of U.S. prisoners fifteen years prior. While a far cry from the excessive amputations, medical experimentation, rapes, killings and squalor of the U.S. run camps holding Korean and Chinese prisoners during the Korean War, American captives from the *Pueblo* still reportedly received beatings and threats. It is possible that the North Koreans lowered the standards of care offered to American prisoners after seeing the state of their own prisoners returned from American hands—many of whom were terribly damaged and returned with missing limbs and severe trauma due to their gruesome experiences in custody.[49]

The DPRK appeared to have no intention of holding the American prisoners indefinitely, and they were released on December 23, eleven months after their capture. In return the United States provided assurances that it would not conduct similar spying missions in future, while the senior American representative at the Military Armistice Commission of Korea, Major General Gilbert H. Woodward, officially admitted that the *Pueblo* had been carrying out espionage operations in North Korean waters when captured.[50] This confession and similar confessions by American sailors appear to have been coerced, and the crew themselves all quickly refuted their stories upon returning home. This again bore stark contrast to the confessions of war crimes made by American prisoners in the Korean War, who reported no such coercion, had their statements supported by considerable evidence and in a significant number of cases maintained their stories even after release.[51] It thus remains uncertain whether the *Pueblo* was in fact violating Korean waters, or whether the seizure of the vessel occurred in international waters and was an intended KPA provocation coordinated with and supporting the Tet Offensive in Vietnam.

The *USS Pueblo* itself would remain in KPA hands, and today rests on the Botong river in Pyongyang where it is displayed as a symbol of triumph over American aggression. Communications equipment from the warship was reportedly studied and information shared with the Soviet Union, with both nations replicating these to access U.S. Navy communications. American encryption devices onboard proved particularly useful for the USSR for future espionage operations. A number of U.S. reports, including a prominent thesis presented at the U.S. Army Command and General Staff College, indicate that the Soviet Union was itself heavily involved in the *Pueblo* incident, as it required access to the warship's equipment to make full use of its valuable new spy ring in the U.S. Navy. This spy ring was led by U.S. Navy Chief Warrant Officer and communications specialist John Walker who had shortly beforehand volunteered his services to Moscow in 1968. While U.S analysts and the Johnson administration itself seriously underestimated Pyongyang's level of independence from the Soviets,[52] this remains a plausible theory given the situation in the USSR at the time and considering that a seizure was in the interests of both countries, albeit for different reasons.[53] The Soviet Union notably provided increased economic and military support to the DPRK following the incident.[54]

The second major incident in the period of the DMZ Conflict occurred on April 5, 1969 when a U.S. Navy EC-121 Warning Star reconnaissance aircraft was shot down over the Sea of Japan by North Korean MiG-21 fighters.[i] Pyongyang claimed that the aircraft had penetrated its airspace and was conducting espionage operations, while the U.S. Navy claimed it had been over international waters. Thirty-one American personnel were killed—the largest single loss of an American air crew during the Cold War. While the incident itself represented a major loss, the American response and its implications were perhaps even more important in their impact on relations between the two states.

---

i The MiG-21 by this time served as the KPA's primary fighter with around 60 in service and would be relied on more heavily than its growing ground-based air defence network to intercept potential threats during the DMZ conflict.

The new Richard Nixon administration was initially at a loss in forming a response to the shootdown which, if American reports on the location of the interception are to be believed, represented a considerable escalation of hostilities. With the U.S. planning an imminent drawing down of its military presence in the Asia-Pacific, escalation against the DPRK remained against its interests at the time. President Nixon did however authorise plans to be drawn up for a massive counterattack—one which was intended to destroy the DPRK's capacity to wage war within hours and thereby avoid involving the U.S. in a long and drawn out campaign. Operation plan Freedom Drop envisaged the U.S. Military using its massive nuclear arsenal to "conduct strikes against military targets in North Korea employing one nuclear weapon on each target."[55] Over a dozen tactical nuclear weapons would be used to destroy Korean command centres and airfields across the country, although it is unclear whether this would be followed by a ground invasion by U.S. forces. Attack plans were supported by Nixon's National Security Advisor Henry Kissinger, but those more experienced regarding the Korean situation including the American ambassador in Seoul, the JCS chairman, the CIA director and the commander of U.S. forces in Korea all strongly warned of the dangers of escalation such an attack would incur.[56] [ii]

CIA officer George Carver, the Agency's top Vietnam specialist, reported that President Nixon went so far as to authorise a nuclear attack on the non-nuclear East Asian country. The American leader was at the time inebriated, but this did not stop the military leadership from taking his orders seriously. Carver stated: "Nixon became incensed and ordered a tactical nuclear strike… The Joint Chiefs [of Staff] were alerted and asked to recommend targets, but [National Security Advisor Henry] Kissinger got on the phone to them. They agreed not to do anything until Nixon sobered up in the morning."[57] Recently published testimonies from U.S. Air Force pilots stationed in South Korea indicate that units were placed on high alert and ordered to prepare for a nuclear strike on North Korean targets. F-4 pilot Bruce Charles recalled that his fighter was to deploy a B61 thermonuclear gravity bomb with a 330-kiloton yield—22 times that of the 15 kiloton "Little Boy" bomb dropped on

ii Even when the KPA had been ill prepared for a conflict in 1950, American and allied projections that North Korea's ability to wage war could be neutralised within hours or days were decisively disproven. Initiating a new war with the country, now far better armed and fortified, on the basis that such an early 'knockout blow' could be dealt, thus hardly appeared a sound strategy, particularly for those who had served during the previous war.

Hiroshima. According to American sources, "Little Boy" had killed an estimated 192,000 residents—the vast majority of them Japanese civilians. The death toll from even a single B61 was expected to be several times greater.[58] The nature of Charles' target remains uncertain, but given the size and strategic nature of the bomb it is highly likely that the target was a population centre—with a nuclear attack on Pyongyang a near certainty in the event of a major war. Airmen were on high alert for nuclear attack for several hours, with Charles recalling: "The order to stand down was just about dusk, and it was not a certainty. The colonel said, 'It looks like from the messages I'm getting, we will not do this today. I do not know about tomorrow.'"[59]

It is notable that, according to Henry Kissinger, the president was unwilling to launch nuclear retaliation against the Soviet Union even in the event of a Soviet conventional attack on NATO—fearing that escalating to a nuclear war would devastate America.[60] He appeared to have far less qualms regarding authorisation of a nuclear attack on the non-nuclear East Asian state, however. Thus, the DPRK's lack of even basic retaliatory capabilities against American targets beyond the Korean Peninsula again served to place it at serious risk in its conflict with the United States—including the risk of nuclear annihilation.

Ultimately a combination of factors including the situation in Vietnam, the heavily fortified nature of Korean targets which undermined the effectiveness of planned nuclear attacks, the strength of Korean air defences and the presence of a sizeable KPA force near the DMZ—too close to American forces for nuclear attack—all likely influenced Washington's final decision. While the Soviet Union showed no signs of support for the DPRK, it remained bound by Article I Paragraph 2 of the 1961 Treaty of Friendship Cooperation and Mutual Assistance to support its East Asian neighbour in the event it was attacked. The Soviet commitment to fully honour this treaty, particularly after the deterioration of relations with North Korea in the 1960s, was questionable—more so in light of Pyongyang's neutral position and unwillingness to adopt the Moscow's hard line against neighbouring China following the Sino-Soviet split.[61] Despite this, action as provocative as an American thermonuclear attack on the DPRK would likely warrant at least some measure of Soviet response. U.S. efforts to improve relations with the People's Republic of China, on which the Nixon administration's entire Cold War strategy in the Asia-Pacific depended, also made alienating a major treaty ally of the DPRK through disproportionate nuclear attacks an unfavourable policy. Ultimately the U.S. relegated its response to working to bring a faster end to the DMZ Conflict, staging major naval exercises in the Sea of Japan and providing fighter escorts for future surveillance missions. This proportionate if underwhelming response reflected the fragility of the American position at the time.[62]

Conflict in Korea deescalated significantly after July 1969 following the announcement of the Nixon Doctrine, which called for a reduced commitment to the defence of allied states and heralded the beginning of America's disengagement from Vietnam. With U.S. forces bogged down in Southeast Asia and overstretched and overcommitted globally, with negative implications for both its finances and morale, the adoption of such a radically different new doctrine was seen as indicative of a failure of the prevailing policies and a victory for the Viet Minh and their allies. From that time not only did the number of U.S. troops in Vietnam drastically decline, but the number of skirmishes in Korea appeared to decrease—the only major incident being the shooting down of an American OH-23 Raven helicopter which by all accounts was operating in North Korean airspace. The conflict is considered to have come to a final close in December 1969 when commander of United States Forces in Korea General John H. Michaelis, newly appointed two months prior, negotiated the release of the three American servicemen captured from the helicopter.[63]

While the Korean DMZ Conflict continued for over three years, longer than the period of open hostilities in the Korean War itself, its low intensity and the very different geopolitical context under which it took place made it inconsequential relative to the other conflicts of the time, even for DPRK-U.S. relations. The death toll of the three-year conflict was just a fraction of that of an average day in the Korean War. The conflict did illustrate to both sides, but particularly to the United States which was increasingly on the defensive and contemplating withdrawing from the region at the time, the considerable risks of a new war. Washington needed to avoid the compromising of relations with China and to a lesser extent the USSR, and moreover was eager under both the Johnson and Nixon administrations to avoid a new quagmire amid considerable public pressure to withdraw forces from the Asia-Pacific. President Nixon stated to this effect regarding his rationale for avoiding escalation over the EC-121 shootdown: "I still agreed that we had to act boldly. I just wasn't convinced that this was the time to do it… As long as we were involved in Vietnam, we simply did not have the resources or public support for another war in another place."[64]

For the DPRK, its perception of an American nuclear threat was reinforced by the speed with which the U.S. proposed to escalate to nuclear war and its reliance on nuclear assets in the event of war. Had clashes occurred under a different geopolitical context, it is likely that nuclear attacks would have been employed very quickly on multiple occasions. The vast asymmetry between the nuclear armed superpower with long range strike assets and the small East Asian state which could not threaten any American targets beyond Korea was thus emphasized. The KPA's failure to ignite a significant popular insurgency in South Korea also persuaded Pyongyang that a strategy for unification based on that of the Viet Minh was no longer viable,[65] as the new leadership in Seoul had proven considerably more competent and popular than the American-installed regimes of Diem in South Vietnam or of Rhee, which had both proven far more vulnerable in this regard.

The end of the DMZ Conflict coincided with the beginning of the end of the Vietnam War, with U.S. forces beginning to make serious reductions in their military presence from 1969. The low intensity conflict in Korea, which like that in Vietnam appeared set to continue indefinitely and necessitated a large and costly American presence in South Korea, is likely to have contributed to the Nixon administration's decision to deescalate and withdraw assets from overseas. The intensification of the conflict in Korea in its final year presented the very real risk of opening a second front, which could have influenced the outcome of the Vietnam War by contributing to an overall shift in U.S. policy towards the Asia-Pacific.

Enemies at Cold War

The end of the Korean DMZ Conflict hardly spelt an end to tensions between Washington and Pyongyang, although it did mark the beginning of a new phase of hostilities which would see the U.S. regather its forces and again assume a position of strength. Despite suffering from high inflation rates, a fast weakening dollar and considerable economic uncertainty, the successful exploitation of the Sino-Soviet split and a growing defence partnership with China, withdrawal from Vietnam and the reorganisation of the U.S. Military improved the American geopolitical position in the Pacific considerably from the mid 1970s. Western dominance in Southeast Asia was consolidated by Indonesia's emergence as a major ally, with a Western backed coup killing up to 3 million communists, suspected communists and their families.[66] Emergence of Indonesia as a major Western client, and the collapse of the region's leading communist party and non-aligned government, was seen to more than compensate for the loss of South Vietnam.[67] Beyond the Pacific the collapse of the Arab Nationalist Bloc and assertion of Western dominance in the Middle East furthered the trend towards a recovery of the Western advantage in the Cold War.[68] While the U.S. was in a strong position to increase pressure against the DPRK, Pyongyang itself increasingly suffered from the unfavourable balance of power. The American defence commitment to South Korea remained strong, and while the ROK's economy and military were negligible in the Rhee years the country was beginning to emerge as a major power its own right.

In South Korea GDP had grown from just $2.7 billion in 1962 to $10.8 billion in 1972 under the military rule of Park Chung Hee,[69] while growth in the DRPK began to stagnate. This can largely be attributed to the overall performances of the alliance systems each was participating in, with South Korean products gaining favourable access to markets in most of the world, including all of the Americas (except Cuba), Oceania, most of Southeast Asia and the Middle East as well as Japan and Western Europe. Trade and labour exports to oil rich Western aligned Middle Eastern states alone brought billions to the South Korean economy,[70] while access to the U.S. market was also highly prized.

In 1965, Japan provided the ROK with "economic cooperation" grants and loans totalling $800 million, over $6 billion in the currency of 2020,[71] and Seoul subsequently began to receive "massive injections of Japanese economic aid" alongside the benefits of trade with the world's third largest economy.[72] While South Korea could trade with America, Japan and Western Europe among others, which between them invested billions in capital and absorbed billions in exports, the only major economy which was not prohibited from maintaining close economic ties to North Korea was the Soviet Union. Even this relationship from the 1960s to the mid-1980s was fragile at best due to political tensions.

The Soviet sphere of the world economy was considerably smaller, and the Soviet Union and Warsaw Pact nations at its centre were themselves beginning to stagnate with no comparable network of economically interconnected allied states to match that of the Western Bloc. From the outset of the Cold War the disparity between the Soviet-led and the Western-led worlds in population, resources and economic capacity was considerable—largely a result of the colonial legacy of the Western Bloc which provided a dominant influence across four continents, which was only seriously disputed in Europe and Asia. Sanctions such as those under the Trading With the Enemy Act, which targeted the DPRK directly, ensured that Western aligned states and many neutral states were limited in their ability to trade with North Korea. Thus, regardless of how efficient or sophisticated North Korean industry was, the vast majority of the world economy had been locked into a system which prevented states from buying its goods or financially supporting its research and development efforts. The ROK faced no similar constraints.

North Korea's successes in forming major trading relationships outside the Soviet Bloc were few, the only significant gain being the opening of Iran to trade the 1980s, with threats of Western economic sanctions and political pressure forcing most of the world to keep its distance. This was key to the West's containment strategy against the Soviet Union,[73] and when applied to a state as small as the DPRK, the effects were devastating for its growth potential. Thus, while both the DPRK and the ROK pursued state-led growth models, Pyongyang increasingly appeared to be locked into the wrong alliance system from the economic perspective which seriously restricted its opportunities for growth and modernisation.

In spite of its isolation from the majority of the world economy, North Korea was still a strong economic performer relative to Soviet Bloc and communist nations and by far the most developed of these in Asia. In terms of registered industrial designs, according to data from the Geneva-based World Intellectual Property Organization, by the mid 1980s the DPRK was second only to the Soviet Union among communist nations and far ahead of all other socialist states. Major sustained investment in this field would place it in fourth place in the world after the Cold War's end in 1990, behind Japan, South Korea and the United States but well ahead of China or the Soviet Bloc nations.[74] High levels of technical education among the workforce, even in rural areas, were repeatedly reported by external observers, and domestic industrial works such as hydroelectric dams were, according to experts from companies such as the Swiss-Swedish ABB Group, considered nothing less than "engineering masterpieces."[75] Despite a highly educated workforce and considerable investments in high end technologies, however, the DPRK was unable to compete at the level of South Korea or others which were better integrated into the global economy and were not sanctioned by the dominant economic powers in the West.

Pyongyang's actions demonstrated an awareness that in an increasingly globalised world, the outcome of its conflict with America was as much contingent on the success of the global struggle against the Western Bloc as it was on the events on the Korean Peninsula itself.[76] The direct consequences of the Sino-Soviet split in undermining Pyongyang's position, much as it had seriously undermined that of the Viet Minh,[77] and the very considerable aforementioned effects of America's position in Southeast Asia on its policy towards Korea in the late 1960s, had all effectively demonstrated the importance of the global struggle. The end of the DMZ Conflict and beginning of a new phase of conflict between the Western superpower and the small East Asian state thus also marked the beginning of greater efforts by North Korea to bolster forces beyond the Korean Peninsula which challenged the Western dominated order. The strengthening of these forces, including both state and non-state actors, could potentially benefit the Korean struggle, much as the success of the Viet Minh had benefitted Pyongyang and the Sino-Soviet split had undermined it. Korean efforts to undermine the Western-led order and strengthen independent actors were thus linked to the increasingly unfavourable power trajectories in Northeast Asia. (North Korean efforts to engage the United States by proxy and bolster its adversaries across the third world are elaborated in Chapter 10.)

The post-DMZ conflict years not only saw the economic balance turn sharply against North Korea, but also saw a growth in the American military advantage. The balance of forces in the air epitomised this. From 1974 the U.S. Navy began to deploy its first fourth generation fighter jets, the F-14 Tomcats, which were followed by the Air Force's deployment of the F-15 Eagle two years later. These aircraft were two generations ahead of the MiG-21 in the Korean fleet and outperformed it in all parameters—with over three times the take-off weight, twice the missile carriage, considerably heavier and more powerful radars and much longer ranged missiles. These aircraft were both deployed to the Asia-Pacific in large numbers and left the KPA fleet effectively obsolete. South Korea too was increasingly well equipped for aerial warfare, acquiring F-5A and F-4C fighters of which six squadrons were in service by 1975, and receiving more advanced third generation F-5E and F-4E platforms soon afterwards.[78] With the KPA lacking access to the latest Soviet arms due to Pyongyang's neutral position in the Sino-Soviet split, it was increasingly at risk of losing control of the skies in a war's early stages with no major new classes of fighter or surface to air missile system deployed.[79]

While continuing to expand its already vast nuclear-proof underground tunnel and bunker network, the DPRK expanded its conventional forces in the late 1970s and redeployed ground assets from the KPA Army close to the DMZ. The purpose of this was to shield personnel and armoured units from nuclear attack by ensuring they would operate in close proximity to American and ROK forces from the war's outset. This strategy became less viable when smaller and more precise tactical nuclear weapons were later developed.[80] While a number of Western sources claimed that these forward deployed KPA units were stationed near the border in preparation for an offensive southwards, they remained heavily outnumbered more than 3:2 (344, 000: 535,000) by ROK units at the border—even without counting the sizeable American presence.[81] The claim that the redeployment was carried out with the intent of invasion were refuted by later declassified CIA documents and other official sources.[82]

Even the largest border clashes between KPA and U.S. forces which occurred during the 1970s were relatively minor compared to those in prior years. The DPRK's strategy of opening low level hostilities had been abandoned after the U.S. began its withdrawal from Vietnam, and Pyongyang overall appeared to be intending to reduce rather than raise tensions. Washington meanwhile increasingly focused its attentions away from the Asia-Pacific, with the rift between China and the USSR, China's new partnership with the Western Bloc, and the Western-backed coup in Indonesia together ending imminent threats to Western dominance in the region. As the Chinese and Cambodian conflicts with Soviet backed Vietnamese forces demonstrated, forces which had opposed Western hegemony were now effectively divided against one another. While the balance of power increasingly favoured the U.S. and its allies, the importance of close ties with China to America's new Cold War strategy served as a major deterrent to its antagonising the DPRK, which remained Beijing's treaty ally. Pyongyang and Washington thus both sought to avoid provoking the other.

The only major military incident in Korea during the decade occurred on August 18, 1976, when officers from the U.S. Army attempted to cut down a tree in the Joint Security Area (JSA) in the Demilitarised Zone. The tree was not in South Korean territory and the area was jointly administered by both the DPRK and the American-led UN Command, but the Americans nevertheless ignored repeated calls from Korean personnel to cease their activities. Calling on reinforcements, KPA Lieutenant Park Chul indicated that the Koreans would use force if their warnings were not heeded. U.S. reports indicate that when these warnings were ignored, two American officers were attacked and killed in hand to hand combat. North Korean reports claimed that the U.S. personnel had themselves initiated attacks on KPA forces.

The U.S. Military responded by raising readiness levels for its units in Korea the following day and considered retaliatory artillery attacks. The presence of KPA artillery units which were bound to respond, and the considerable risk of escalation, led to a decision against an attack. If U.S. reports are taken at face value and the Koreans initiated hostilities, it is unclear whether the attack was premediated or the soldiers present were simply incensed at the sight of American personnel cutting down a tree without consulting them in the neutral zone. The latter appears more likely to be the case, considering that the KPA could not have known that the American officers would ignore repeated requests to stop cutting down the tree.

It is important to take in consideration that although Pyongyang did not see any benefit in antagonising the United States at this time, public sentiment towards America remained extremely hostile. The aforementioned experience of the Korean War and its continuing impact on the daily lives of the population were very significant, with up to 30% of the population killed and many more wounded.[83] The vast majority of the population had lost their homes and livelihoods, and the brutal atrocities committed remained within living memory for the majority. The possibility of sporadic attacks on Americans initiated by lower level officers, or even soldiers themselves, can be better understood in this context.

In response to the killing of two of its soldiers, the U.S. launched Operation Paul Bunyan with ROK support. The operation was quickly approved by newly inaugurated President Gerald Ford and was intended to demonstrate American strength and resolve. It entailed making a point of cutting down the tree in the neutral zone the KPA soldiers had sought to protect, backed by overwhelming force. In the early hours of August 21st, a task force comprised of 813 U.S. and ROK military personnel entered the Joint Security Area without warning the North Koreans. This included 64 South Korean special forces and two eight-man teams of

U.S. Army engineers with chainsaws. Soldiers secured the entrances to the JSA while others watched over the engineers to prevent intervention by the heavily outnumbered North Korean garrison. Soldiers were armed with M79 grenade launchers, claymore mines and other heavy equipment and set charges on the bridges to cut off potential KPA reinforcements.

Operation Paul Bunyan entailed an effective armed takeover of the Joint Security Area by the U.S. and its ally using overwhelming force. It would ensure that even over a matter as trivial as the cutting down of a tree, which appeared to hold much meaning for the North Korean soldiers, the Americans would have their way. While the armistice had not given one party superior rights over the governing of the neutral zone, these rights had been assumed. The U.S. deployed rather spectacular and wholly disproportionate force to support its units tasked with cutting down the tree—a tree which had come to symbolise North Korea's resistance to American demands over the demilitarised zone. Assets deployed included nuclear capable B-52 Stratofortress heavy bombers flown from Guam, escorted by American F-4 and South Korean F-5 fighters. The site was circled by 27 American military helicopters, and the aircraft carrier battle group led by the warship *USS Midway* was moved into position offshore. A U.S. intelligence analyst following North Korean communications noted that the massive and wholly disproportionate deployment of force "blew their f***ing minds."[84]

The KPA deployed 200 lightly armed personnel near the JSA but otherwise did not intervene. The massive demonstration of American power, which included nuclear assets, emphasized Pyongyang's position of weakness at the time, a message the U.S. Military would press home. Some analysts have concluded that it was as a direct result of this particular event that led the North Korean leadership to begin to more seriously invest in higher-end and more capable deterrence capabilities including weapons of mass destruction.[85]

As the balance of power had shifted from the previous decade, the U.S. used its position of strength to press for an apology—much as the Koreans had themselves done a decade prior over the *Pueblo* incident. Pyongyang did not issue an official apology and maintained that the incident had been provoked by the Americans themselves. Korean President Kim Il Sung did however issue the following conciliatory expression of regret to the senior member of the Military Armistice Commission on the American side, stating:

> It was a good thing that no big incident occurred at Panmunjom [JSA] for a long period. However, it is regretful that an incident occurred in the Joint Security Area, Panmunjom, this time. An effort must be made so that such incidents may not recur in the future. For this purpose both sides should make efforts. We urge your side to prevent the provocation. Our side will never provoke first, but take self-defensive measures only when provocation occurs. This is our consistent stand.[86]

This was the first and only time Kim Il Sung personally answered a protest made by a commander of the U.S.-led UN command.

While the U.S. made further demands for an apology, an admission of guilt on the Korean side and the punishment of KPA personnel responsible for the killings on August 18, an effective endorsement of the American narrative of how the killings took place, these were not met by the DPRK. The joint Military Armistice Commission held six sessions from August 31st under which a new means of administering the JSA were laid out, which obliged the North Koreans to construct a new road and agree to a joint observer team to survey the military demarcation line. While these were relatively minor concessions, particularly given the scale of the American threats and the relative weakness of the Korean position, they demonstrated the imbalance in the positions of the Western superpower and the small Northeast Asian state which had emerged in the early 1970s. This imbalance had grown considerably since then as a result of the geopolitical trends in the wider world.

The 1980s: A Cold Arms Race

Power trajectories would continue to strongly favour the position of the United States relative to the DPRK throughout the early 1980s. With the inauguration of President Ronald Reagan in 1981, who favoured maximum pressure against the Soviet Union and its allies particularly through expanding military force, the DPRK was increasingly placed in the crosshairs of the American nuclear arsenal. At the turn of the decade Pyongyang's relations with both the Soviet Union and China were far from close due to its continued neutrality in the Sino-Soviet split, and increasingly in China's case, due to Pyongyang's own uneasiness regarding Beijing's rapprochement with the Western Bloc. This meant that in the early 1980s, while still economically closely integrated through trade into the Soviet Bloc's economy, the DPRK lacked the political and military support from its neighbours needed to counter emerging threats.

A major escalation of the nuclear threat during the early 1980s resulted from the application of the AirLand Battle warfighting doctrine to the Korean Peninsula. This new doctrine called specifically for extensive use of specialised nuclear weapons to penetrate hardened facilities across enemy territory, supported by massive airstrikes and followed by an American ground invasion, the capture of Pyongyang, and the destruction of the DPRK. The annual Team Spirit exercises held by the U.S. Military and ROKAF were expanded from little over 100,000 to approximately 200,000 troops.[87] These exercises, the largest in the world, played out an offensive under AirLand Battle near North Korea's borders on a regular basis.[88]

The U.S. also altered its doctrine for employing nuclear weapons on the Korean Peninsula to further lower the threshold for nuclear attacks on North Korea. The nuclear arsenal was to be deployed within an hour of the outbreak of hostilities (H+1)—even if the ROK or the Americans themselves initiated hostilities. A report from the *Bulletin of Atomic Scientists* noted that American plans for nuclear strikes immediately after outbreak of a potential conflict in Asia starkly differed from doctrine for nuclear use in the European theatre against the nuclear armed Warsaw Pact: "The logic was that we dared not use nuclear weapons in Europe, because the other side had them, except in the greatest extremity, but we could use them in Korea because the other side didn't have such weapons. South Korean commanders…had gotten used to the idea that the United States would use nuclear weapons at an early point in a war with North Korea."[89]

The nuclear threat further increased when the U.S. Military strategy began to incorporate employment of neutron bombs against Korean population centres. These miniaturised thermonuclear bombs—also known as "enhanced radiation weapons"—have a relatively small yield but are designed to maximise emissions of lethal neutron radiation. The effect of this radiation is to cause a process of neutron activation, which for those caught in its vicinity turns body tissues radioactive leading to painful death. These bombs were notably also intended to be deployed against South Korean cities if captured by the Korean People's Army, in particular Seoul which had a civilian population of 9 million people at the time. Use of these particularly lethal weapons of mass destruction was expected to kill millions—indiscriminately targeting both allied and adversary populations on the Korean Peninsula.[90]

The neutron bomb as a weapon of war in the arsenal of the Western Bloc traced its origins to the Korean War. American nuclear scientist Samuel Cohen had developed the idea in 1951 after he had been sent to Korea to gauge the feasibility of tactical use of atomic weapons under Operation Hudson Harbor. He imagined them as a means of deploying weapons of mass destruction against enemy population centres without damaging property or infrastructure—which could then be captured intact and used by advancing U.S. forces. *Washington Post* reporter Walter Pincus, one of the first to cover the bomb's development in the 1970s, referred to the new weapons as: "specifically designed to kill people through the release of neutrons rather than to destroy military installations through heat and blast."[91] The new weapon was considered to have a lower threshold for use than other nuclear weapons, thus further increasing the threat of a nuclear war against the non-nuclear DPRK.[92]

The new nuclear threat further reinforced North Korea's perception of its own vulnerability, which was particularly difficult to address given that more advanced Soviet aerial warfare systems capable of intercepting American air attacks, both conventional and nuclear, remained unobtainable. This, combined with the growing economic disparity favouring its adversaries and the growing disparity in conventional forces, led the DPRK to seek a deterrent capability of its own. While the country had shown some early interest in acquiring a greater retaliatory strike capability with the purpose of more effectively deterring America by asymmetric means, efforts to acquire such capabilities appear to have escalated at this time.

Early efforts by the KPA to extend its strike range were aided considerably by the acquisition of the Scud-B, a Soviet short-range ballistic missile which had been sold to the DPRK by Egypt. Although the Scud-B had been in Soviet service since 1964 and was far from state of the art when received between 1979 and 1980, the missiles were never deployed by the KPA. They were intended solely for the purpose of reverse engineering, providing technologies which kickstarted an auspicious indigenous ballistic missile program.[93] The Koksan artillery system was a smaller but still ambitious project to develop the world's longest ranged artillery gun—which it succeeded in doing by a considerable margin with a very long 60km range. This was over triple the range of its most capable Western analogue at the time, the M109, and allowed the KPA to threaten targets far deeper behind enemy lines and fire on them from more secure rear positions. The M1985 240mm rocket artillery system[iii] was also a notable development with an estimated range of 60km, which would be significantly improved on in later years.

The Korean People's Army's Guided Missile Division, the 4th Machine Industry Bureau and the Engineering Research Institute of the Academy of Defence Sciences were reportedly all involved in reverse engineering of the Scud-B,[94] which they succeeded in doing in a remarkably short period. The first North Korean ballistic missile, the Hwasong-5, entered service in 1984 and marginally improved on the specifications of the Scud-B with a 320km range. New guidance systems were also developed for the missile, alongside unique warheads with specialised submunitions. The costs of mass producing the system were heavily subsidised by considerable exports, with Iran alone known to have purchased at least 100 and Egypt also acquiring large numbers to build on its Scud-B arsenal. The munitions were manufactured at a rate of around 10 per month, and their deployment to the Korean Peninsula provided an asymmetric asset which seriously undermined the growing superiority of the U.S.-led alliance.

Although North Korea had increasingly struggled to counter the growing conventional power of its adversaries from the early 1970s, the development of tactical ballistic missiles would increasingly come to be relied on for its defence. An enhanced longer ranged missile, the Hwasong-6, began production in 1989 and retained a 500km range, allowing it to strike U.S. military bases across all of South Korea from launch sites safely behind KPA lines near Pyongyang. Like its predecessor, the missile gained considerable foreign interest and was exported to Iran, Egypt, Syria, Yemen, Libya and Vietnam which helped cover the program's costs and future research and development efforts.

Although North Korea appeared to have the beginnings of a highly promising missile program, it still sought to update the KPA's conventional capabilities by acquiring more advanced foreign hardware. As relations with Beijing grew more distant, Pyongyang attempted to restore its relationship with Moscow as a means of improving its economic and military situation. The latter had particularly suffered over the past two decades due the KPA's restricted access to Soviet arms. In May 1984 President Kim Il Sung paid a five day visit to Moscow in which the

iii The rocket artillery system's Korean name is unknown, and it is thus referred to in the West as M1985 based on the first year it was observed.

terms of a new economic and military partnership were laid out. The Korean leader made specific requests for a number of advanced weapons systems required to counter growing American power, and his Soviet counterpart, General Secretary Konstantin Chernenko, pledged to provide all the supplies needed.[95] As the DPRK was by this time increasingly self-sufficient in many fields of its military industries, manufacturing its own advanced Chonma Ho battle tanks which were heavily specialised for its mountainous terrain[96] and Najin Class frigates for its Navy[97] among other systems, requests for Soviet assistance focused heavily on improving the country's aerial warfare capabilities. President Kim would pay a second visit to Moscow in October 1986 where further deals for more advanced arms were made and economic and military cooperation was further improved.

With South Korea having placed its first order for American fourth generation fighters, lightweight F-16 Fighting Falcons, in December 1981, and with the U.S. by this time stationing a vast fleet of more advanced fourth generation jets to the region, the acquisition of new air defence systems and new combat jets was seen as a priority for the DPRK's security. The mass destruction of the Korean War had taught a lasting lesson regarding the consequences of allowing U.S. aircraft access to North Korean airspace. At the time of President Kim's first visit, only the United States and Soviet Union had developed fourth generation combat aircraft which were fully active, which combined with the USSR's place as a world leader in air defence technologies made access to Soviet systems particularly vital. A first bloc of Soviet arms shipments included 60 MiG-23 third generation fighters, which were equipped with new R-23 missiles that provided the KPA with the ability to engage targets beyond visual range for the first time. These were supplemented by S-125 (NATO reporting SA-3) low altitude missile systems to complement both the existing medium range S-75 platforms and indigenous shorter ranged handheld systems such as the Hwasung-Chong. While these were not the latest Soviet systems available and had been in service for some time, U.S. reports reflected on their deliveries with considerable apprehension.[98]

The second bloc of Soviet arms delivered to the DPRK from October 1986 consisted of a number of newer and less widely used systems. These included MiG-29 fourth generation fighters, Su-25 attack jets, a Tin Shield early warning target acquisition radar, and S-200 (NATO reporting SA-5) long range surface to air missile systems.[99]

According to a number of reports including the South Korean Ministry of National Defence's 1997 White Paper, MiG-25 Foxbat interceptors were also delivered to the KPA "to improve tactical air combat capability." Evidence of this reported delivery remains elusive, but if true it would have provided North Korea with the fastest combat jets in the world. The KPA Air Force also acquired more advanced air to air missiles, namely the R-27, which not only closed the capability gap but also provided it with a capability advantage over its U.S. analogue, the AIM-7 Sparrow, relied on by the Americans and South Koreans. The impact of these systems was to restore the KPA Air Force as a near-peer fighting force, at least qualitatively speaking, and to strengthen the country's air defence network so as to seriously complicate plans for a potential air attack. While the KPA was still outnumbered and outgunned, and an offensive remained unfeasible even if this had been Pyongyang's intention, its modernisation could contribute significantly to deterring an American attack.

Two primary factors prompted the change in Soviet policy towards the DPRK. The strengthening of U.S. forces in East Asia was seen as a common threat to both states—particularly as China's position remained ambiguous as it continued to improve ties to the Western Bloc. Providing the KPA with modern arms, which it would itself man and maintain, was considerably cheaper than expanding the Soviet air and air defence forces in the Far Eastern regions and plugged a gaping hole in the defences of the two allies. A second related factor was the increasingly skewed balance of power on the Korean Peninsula from the mid 1970s, which Moscow perceived as raising the risk of the stronger party initiating a war. By helping the DPRK to strengthen its defences, the KPA would be better able to deter potential aggression which in turn made war less likely, and thereby reduced the chances that the Soviet Red Army would be called into action under its treaty obligations.

North Korea's support from the Soviet Union against an increasingly assertive adversary would be short lived, with the coming to power of General Secretary Mikhail Gorbachev in March 1985 marking the beginning of the end for the superpower which had been the DPRK's primary sponsor since its independence. The new Westphilian leader for the first time recognised the Republic of Korea in September 1990 and downgraded diplomatic relations with the DPRK while seeking rapprochement with the Western Bloc. The new neutral stance of the USSR in the Korean conflict, while the United States itself refused the DPRK recognition and maintained the goal of the state's destruction and its territory's absorption into the ROK, prompted Pyongyang to question the feasibility of continued reliance on Soviet support or military protection.

While a boosting of ties to the Soviet Union and the benefits of newfound alliances in the Middle East, namely with the newly declared Islamic Republic of Iran, did provide some respite for the DPRK from the overall decline in its economic and military positions, negative trends would accelerate towards the late 1980s. The coming decade would see tensions between the United States and the DPRK escalate further, the risks of war increase considerably and the very survival of the Korean republic brought into serious question as a tumultuous shift in world order occurred.

NOTES

1 Hanley, Charles J. and Choe, Sang Hun and Mendoza, Martha, *The Bridge at No Gun Ri: A Hidden Nightmare from the Korean War*, New York, Henry Holt and Company, 2001 (pp. 195–196).
2 Lowe, Peter, *The Frustrations of Alliance: Britain, The United States, and the Korean War, 1950–1951*, in: Cotton, James, and Neary, Ian, *The Korean War in History*, Manchester, Manchester University Press, 1989.
3 Hanley, Charles J. and Choe, Sang Hun and Mendoza, Martha, *The Bridge at No Gun Ri: A Hidden Nightmare from the Korean War*, New York, Henry Holt and Company, 2001 (pp. 195–196).
4 Deane, Hugh, *The Korean War, 1945–1953*, San Francisco, CA, China Books and Periodicals, 1999 (p. 191).
5 'Casualties of Korean War,' Ministry of National Defence of Republic of Korea.
6 Park, Seong Won, 'The Present and Future of Americanization in South Korea,' *Journal of Futures Studies*, vol. 14, no. 1, August 2009 (pp. 51–66).
7 Moon, Katherine H. S., *Sex Among Allies*, New York, Colombia University Press, 1997.
8 Lindqvist, Sven, *A History of Bombing*, New York, Thè New Press, 2001 (p. 131).
9 Deane, Hugh, *The Korean War, 1945–1953*, San Francisco, CA, China Books and Periodicals, 1999 (p. 191).
10 Hanley, Charles J. and Choe, Sang Hun and Mendoza, Martha, *The Bridge at No Gun Ri: A Hidden Nightmare from the Korean War*, New York, Henry Holt and Company, 2001 (p. 170).
11 Stone, I. F., *Hidden History of the Korean War*, Amazon Media, 2014 (Chapter 17: Free Elections?).
12 Republic of Korea Truth and Reconciliation Commission, Report Activities of the Past Three Years, March 2009.
13 Cumings, Bruce, *The Korean War: A History*, New York, Modern Library, 2010 (p. 27).
14 Stone, I. F., *Hidden History of the Korean War*, Amazon Media, 2014 (Chapter 47: Six Months of Futile Slaughter).
15 Cumings, Bruce, *Origins of the Korean War: The Roaring of the Cataract, 1947–1950, Volume 2*, Princeton, NJ, Princeton University Press, 2004 (p. 693).

United States Army in the Korean War: Volume 4, Washington, DC, Government Printing Office, 1961 (p. 84).
Hastings, Max, *Korean War* London, Michael Joseph, 1988 (p. 22).

16 Talmadge, Eric, '64 years after Korean War, North Korea still digging up bombs,' *Yahoo News*, July 24, 2017.

17 Lê Thanh Nghị, 'Report on Meetings with Party Leaders of Eight Socialist Countries,' 1965.
Kim, Il Sung, *Chojak Sonjip* (The Selected Works of Kim Il Sung), Pyongyang, Choson Rodong Dang Chulpansa, 1967 (pp. 401–402).

18 Kim, Jong Un, *War Veterans Are Our Precious Revolutionary Forerunners Who Created the Indomitable Spirit of Defending the Country*, Congratulatory Speech Delivered at the Fourth National Conference of War Veterans, July 25, 2015.

19 MacDonald, Donald Stone, *U.S.-Korean Relations from Liberation to Self-Reliance: The Twenty-Year Record: An Interpretive Summary of Archives of the U.S. Departmetn of State for the Period 1945 to 1965,* Boulder, Westview Press, 1992 (pp. 23, 78–79).

20 Leonard, Thomas M., *Encyclopaedia of the Developing World, Volume 3,* London, Routledge, 2006 (p. 1365).
Matray, James I., 'Mixed Message: The Korean Armistice Negotiations at Kaesong,' *Pacific Historical Review,* vol. 81, no. 2, May 2012 (p. 224).

21 Moon, Katherine H. S., *Sex Among Allies*, New York, Colombia University Press, 1997.

22 Mizokami, Kyle, 'Everything You Need to Know: The History of U.S. Nuclear Weapons in South Korea,' *The National Interest*, September 10, 2017.
Kristensen, Hans M. and Norris, Robert S., 'A history of U.S. nuclear weapons in South Korea,' *Bulletin of the Atomic Scientists*, vol. 73, no. 6, 2017 (pp. 349–357).

23 Memorandum of Discussion at the 173d Meeting of the National Security Council, Thursday, December 3, 1953, Office of the Historian, Foreign Relations of the United States, 195201954, Korea, Volume XV, Part 2.

24 'Thaw in the Koreas?,' *Bulletin of Atomic Scientists*, vol. 48, no. 3, April 1992 (p. 19).

25 Cumings, Bruce, *Korea's Place in the Sun: A Modern History*, New York, W. W. Norton & Company, 1997 (pp. 478–479).

26 Macdonald, Donald Stone, *U.S.-Korean Relations from Liberation to Self-Reliance: The Twenty-Year. Record: An Interpretive Summary of the Archives of the U.S. Department of State for the Period 1945 to 1965,* Boulder, CO, Westview Press, 1992 (pp. 23–24, 80).

27 National Records Center, USFIK 11071 file, box 62/96, G-2 'Staff Study,' February 1949, signed by Lieutenant Colonel B. W. Heckemeyer of Army G-2.

28 *Preliminary Assessment of Black Shield Mission 6847 Over North Korea*, Central Intelligence Agency, Document Number: 0001474986, January 29, 1968.

29 Woodward, Jude, *The U.S. vs China: Asia's New Cold War?* Manchester, Manchester University Press, 2017 (p. 86).

30 Buzo, Adrian, *The Guerilla Dynasty: Politics and Leadership in North Korea,* Boulder, CO, Westview Press, 1999 (p. 67).
Minnich, James, *North Korea's People's Army: Origins and Current Tactics*, Annapolis, MD, Naval Institute Press, 2005 (p. 67).
Schobell, Andrew and Sanford, John M., *North Korea's Military Threat: Pyongyang's Conventional Forces, Weapons of Mass Destruction, and Ballistic Missiles*, Carlisle, PA, U.S. Army War College Strategic Studies Institute, April 2007 (p. 31).
North Korean Intentions and Capabilities with Respect to South Korea, Special National Intelligence Estimate, Number 14.2-67, Central Intelligence Agency, September 21, 1967 (p. 6).

31 Kristensen, Hans M. and Norris, Robert S., 'A history of U.S. nuclear weapons in South Korea,' *Bulletin of the Atomic Scientists*, vol. 73, no. 6, 2017 (pp. 349–357).

32 Hayes, Peter, *Pacific Powderkeg: American Nuclear Dilemmas in Korea,* Lanham, MD, Lexington Books, 1991 (p. 49).
Cumings, Bruce, *Korea's Place in the Sun: A Modern History*, New York, W. W. Norton & Company, 1997 (p. 480).

33 Lê, Thanh Nghị, 'Report on Meetings with Party Leaders of Eight Socialist Countries,' 1965.

34 Afternoon Session of a Hearing of the Senate Armed Services Committee; The Nomination of Donald Rumsfeld to be Secretary of Defense, Chaired by Senator Carl Levin, January 11, 2010.
Bowman, Tom, 'As North Korea Tensions Rise, U.S. Army Trains Soldiers To Fight In Tunnels,' *NPR*, January 9, 2018.

35 Shen, Zhihua and Xia, Yafeng, *China and the Post-War Reconstruction of North Korea, 1953–1961*, Woodrow Wilson Center for Scholars, May 2012.

36 Bolger, Daniel, *Scenes From a Unfinished War: Low-Intensity Conflict in Korea, 1966–1969,* Fort Leavenworth, Kansas, Combat Studies Institute, Leavonworth Papers no.19, June 1991 (pp. 111–113).

37 Chung Hee, Park, *To Build a Nation,* Washington, D.C., Acropolis Books, 1971.
Breen, Michael, 'Park Chung-hee: the man who transformed Korea,' *Korea Times,* August 10, 2011.
Kim, Byung-Kook, The Park Chung Hee Era: The Transformation of South Korea, Cambridge, MA, Harvard University Press, 2013.

38 Bolger, Daniel, *Scenes From a Unfinished War: Low-Intensity Conflict in Korea, 1966–1969,* Fort Leavenworth, Kansas, Combat Studies Institute, Leavonworth Papers no.19, June 1991 (pp. 49, 95, 108).

39 Ibid. (pp. 107, 108).

40 Longley, Kyle, 'Lyndon Johnson's 1968 State of the Union was a disaster. Can President Trump avoid his fate?,' *Washington Post*, January 30, 2018.

41 *Black Shield Reconnaissance Missions, 1 January—31 March 1968,* Central Intelligence Agency Document Number 0001472531 (p. 14).

42 McIninch, Thomas, 'The Oxcart Story,' *CIA Historical Review Program*, Central Intelligence Agency, 2 July 1996.
Preliminary Assessment of Black Shield Mission 6847 Over North Korea, Central Intelligence Agency, Document Number: 0001474986, January 29, 1968.

43 *Black Shield Reconnaissance Missions,' 1 January.—31 March 1968*, Directorate of Science & Technology, Central Intelligence Agency, April 30, 1968 (p. 11).

44 'Inquiry Into the U.S.S. Pueblo and EC-121 Plane Incidents, Report of the Special Subcommittee on the U.S.S. Pueblo of the Committee on Armed Services House of Representatives,' Ninety-first Congress, First Session, July 28, 1969.

45 Hayes, Peter, *Pacific Powderkeg: American Nuclear Dilemmas in Korea,* Lanham, MD, Lexington Books, 1991 (pp. 47–48).

46 Prados, John and Cheevers, Jack, 'USS Pueblo: LBJ Considered Nuclear Weapons, Naval Blockade, Ground Attacks in Response to 1968 North Korean Seizure of Navy Vessel, Documents Show,' National Security Archive Electronic Briefing Book no. 453, January 23, 2014.

47 Ibid.

48 Jacobsen, Annie, *Area 51*, London, Orion Publishing, 2011 (p. 274).

49 Deane, Hugh, *The Korean War, 1945–1953*, San Francisco, CA, China Books and Periodicals, 1999 (pp. 177–178).
Winnington, Alan, and Burchett, Wilfred, *Plain Perfidy, The Plot to Wreck the Korea Peace*, Britain-China Friendship Association, 1954 (p. 9).

50 'Pueblo Officer Says He Tricked Captors with False Charts,' *New York Times*, December 27, 1968 (p. 1).

51 Mayer, William E., *Beyond the Call: Memoirs of a Medical Visionary, Volume 1*, Albuquerque, Mayer Publishing Group International, 2009 (p. 350).
Kim, Monica, *The Interrogation Rooms of the Korean War; The Untold History*, Princeton, NJ, Princeton University Press, 2019 (p. 338).
52 Herring, George C., *The American Century and Beyond: U.S. Foreign Relations, 1893–2015*, Oxford, Oxford University Press, 2008 (p. 453).
53 Heath, Laura J., *An Analysis of the Systematic Security Weaknesses of the U.S. Navy Fleet Broadcasting System, 1967–1974, As Exploited by CWO John Walker*, Faculty of the U.S. Army Command and General Staff College, Fort Leavenworth, Kansas, 2005.
Roblin, Sebastien, 'North Korea Almost Started a Nuclear War When It Captured a U.S. Spy Ship,' *National Interest*, January 21, 2018.
54 Radchenko, Sergey S., *The Soviet Union and the North Korean Seizure of the USS Pueblo: Evidence from Russian Archives*, Washington D.C., Woodrow Wilson International Center for Scholars. (pp. 2, 5).
55 McGreal, Chris, 'Papers reveal Nixon plan for North Korea nuclear strike,' *The Guardian*, July 7, 2010.
Foster, Peter, 'Richard Nixon planned nuclear strike on North Korea,' *Telegraph*, July 8, 2010.
56 Bolger, Daniel, *Scenes From a Unfinished War: Low-Intensity Conflict in Korea, 1966–1969,* Fort Leavenworth, Kansas, Combat Studies Institute, Leavonworth Papers no.19, June 1991 (102).
57 'Drunk in charge (part two),' *The Guardian,* September 2, 2000.
58 Hall, Michelle, 'By the Numbers: World War II's atomic bombs,' *CNN,* August 6, 2013.
59 Shuster, Mike, 'Nixon Considered Nuclear Option Against N. Korea,' *NPR,* July 6, 2010.
60 Graff, Garrett M., 'The Madman and the Bomb: The nuclear launch process once haunted Nixon's aides. 43 years later, is it finally time to reform the system?,' *Politico*, August 11, 2017.
61 Radchenko, Sergey S., *The Soviet Union and the North Korean Seizure of the USS Pueblo: Evidence from Russian Archives*, Washington D.C., Woodrow Wilson International Center for Scholars. (p. 15).
62 Bolger, Daniel, *Scenes From a Unfinished War: Low-Intensity Conflict in Korea, 1966–1969,* Fort Leavenworth, Kansas, Combat Studies Institute, Leavonworth Papers no.19, June 1991 (pp. 105–106).
63 Ibid (Chapter 4).
64 Nixon, Richard M., *RN: The Memoirs of Richard Nixon,* New York, Warner Books, 1978 (pp. 473–475).
65 Bolger, Daniel, *Scenes From a Unfinished War: Low-Intensity Conflict in Korea, 1966–1969,* Fort Leavenworth, Kansas, Combat Studies Institute, Leavonworth Papers no.19, June 1991 (p. 113).
66 'Indonesia's killing fields,' *Al Jazeera*, December 21, 2012.
'Looking into the massacres of Indonesia's past,' *BBC*, June 2, 2016.
67 Burkholder Smith, Joseph, *Portrait of a Cold Warrior*, New York, Putnam, 1976 (pp. 246–247).
68 Heikal, Mohamed, 'Arab Nationalism: Alive or Dead?,' Interview with David Swift, 2002 (p. 21).
69 World Bank national accounts data, and OECD National Accounts data files.
70 Levkowitz, Alon, 'The Republic of Korea in the Middle East: Economics, Diplomacy, and Security,' *Korea Economic Institute*, vol. 5, no. 6, August 2010.
71 Harrison, Selig S., 'Promoting a Soft Landing in North Korea,' *Foreign Policy,* no. 106, Spring 1997 (p. 65).

72 *North Korean Intentions and Capabilities with Respect to South Korea*, Special National Intelligence Estimate, Number 14.2-67, Central Intelligence Agency, September 21, 1967 (p. 5).

73 Walt, Stephen M., 'Yesterday's Cold War Shows How to Beat China Today,' *Foreign Policy,* July 29, 2019.

74 *The first twenty-five years of the World Intellectual Property Organization, from 1967 to 1992,* Geneva, International Bureau of Intellectual Property, 1992 (pp. 294–295 for DPRK statistics).

75 Abt, Felix, 'A Capitalist in North Korea: My Seven Years in the Hermit Kingdom,' North Clarendon, VT, Tuttle, 2014 (Chapter 2: Malaise into Opportunity, Part 3: Will North Korea Strike Gold?).

76 Haggard, M. T., 'North Korea's International Position,' *Asian Survey*, vol. 5, no. 8, August 1965 (pp. 375–388).

77 *The Sino-Soviet Dispute on Aid to North Vietnam (1965–1968)*, Central Intelligence Agency, United States of America, Directorate of Intelligence, Intelligence Report, Reference Title ESAU XXXIX.
Heikal, Mohamed, *Sphinx and Commissar, The Rise and Fall of Soviet Influence in the Arab World*, New York, HarperCollins, 1979 (pp. 150–151).

78 International Institute for Strategic Studies, *The Military Balance*, Volume 75, 1975, Part V: Asia and Australasia (p. 56).

79 Ibid. (p. 56).
Bermudez, Jr., Joseph S., *A History of Ballistic Missile Development in the DPRK*, Occasional Paper No. 2, Monterey, Monterey Institute for International Studies Center for Nonproliferation Studies, 1999 (p. 2).

80 'Thaw in the Koreas?,' *Bulletin of Atomic Scientists*, vol. 48, no. 3, April 1992 (p. 20).

81 North Korean Intentions and Capabilities With Respect to South Korea, CIA, Director of Central Intelligence, Special National Intelligence Estimate, no. 14.2-67, September 21, 1967 (p. 11).

82 Ibid. (pp. 7, 9).
'Thaw in the Koreas?,' *Bulletin of Atomic Scientists*, vol. 48, no. 3, April 1992 (p. 20).
Hayes, Peter, *Pacific Powderkeg: American Nuclear Dilemmas in Korea,* Lanham, MD, Lexington Books, 1991 (pp. 148–149).

83 Lindqvist, Sven, *A History of Bombing*, New York, The New Press, 2001 (p. 131).

84 Oberdorfer, Don, *The Two Koreas: a contemporary history*, New York, Perseus Books, 1997 (p. 74–83).

85 Jackson, Van, *On the Brink,* Cambridge, Cambridge University Press, 2018 (p. 24).

86 Michishita, Narushige, *North Korea's Military-Diplomatic Campaigns, 1966–2008*, Abingdon, Routledge, 2010 (p. 80).
Folder: 'Korea—North Korean Tree Incident,' 8/18/76 (3), Box 10, Presidential Country Files for East Asia and the Pacific, 1974–77, Gerald R. Ford Presidential Library.

87 Farrell, John, 'Team Spirit: A Case Study on the Value of Military Exercises as a Show of Force in the Aftermath of Combat Operations,' *Air and Space Power Journal*, Fall 2009.
Cumings, Bruce, *Korea's Place in the Sun: A Modern History*, New York, W. W. Norton & Company, 1997 (p. 482).

88 'Thaw in the Koreas?,' *Bulletin of Atomic Scientists*, vol. 48, no. 3, April 1992 (p. 20).

89 Ibid. (p.19–20).

90 Ibid. (p. 20).

91 Pincus, Walter, 'Neutron Killer Warhead Buried in ERDA Budget,' *Washington Post,* June 6, 1977.

92 Biddle, Wayne, 'Neutron Bomb: An Explosive Issue,' *New York Times*, November 15, 1981.

93 Bermudez, Jr., Joseph S., *A History of Ballistic Missile Development in the DPRK*, Occasional Paper No. 2, Monterey, Monterey Institute for International Studies Center for Nonproliferation Studies, 1999 (pp. 10–12).
Lee, Chung-min, 'North Korean Missiles: Strategic Implications and Policy Responses,' *Pacific Review*, vol. 14, no. 1, 2001.

94 Bermudez Jr, Joseph S., *The Armed Forces of North Korea,* London, I. B. Tauris & Co. Ltd, 2001 (p. 249)

95 Volkognov, Dmitri, *Autopsy for an Empire: The Seven Leaders Who Built the Soviet Regime,* New York, The Free Press, 1998 (p. 418).

96 'Chonma Ho; How North Korea Developed and Has Extensively Modernised its First Indigenous Battle Tank,' *Military Watch Magazine,* June 14, 2019.

97 Oliemans, Joost. And Mitzer, Stijn, 'KPA Navy flag ship undergoing radical modernization,' *NK News,* December 15, 2014.

98 'North Korea's Air Force: Impact of Soviet Deliveries, An Intelligence Assessment,' *Central Intelligence Agency Office of East Asian Analysis*, December 1985. Approved for Release on January 22, 2010.

99 Joo, Sung Ho and Kwak, Tae Hwan, 'Military Relations Between Russia and North Korea,' *Journal of East Asian Affairs*, vol. 15, no. 2, Fall/Winter 2001 (p. 299).

Chapter 10

PROXY WARS:

HOW NORTH KOREA AND AMERICA WAGE WAR THROUGH THIRD PARTIES

Global Conflict

Conflict between the United States and North Korea has taken many forms over 70 years, and since the stalemate and armistice of 1953 it has continued to evolve and expand to theatres well beyond the Korean Peninsula. A part of what can be considered a minor Cold War between the small East Asian state and the Western superpower has come in the form of personnel deployments to support third parties fighting the other—either through the provision of armaments and training or through a direct combat role. There have also been multiple incidents of both sides providing considerable expertise, arms and other material support to opposing parties in various conflicts without directly participating themselves.

Provision of advanced armaments and training to a number of the West's adversaries emerged particularly from the early 1980s as a means for Pyongyang to shift the balance of power in various conflicts against the Western Bloc and its allies. Its ability to do so increased from this time as the country developed a significant technological base and production capacity for asymmetric weapons systems such as ballistic missiles. Such arms transfers have seriously impeded Western designs for unrestricted power projection. With America relying on its global network of military bases to project power overseas, the proliferation of ballistic missile technologies capable of targeting these military bases and potentially vulnerable allied targets such as oil fields and airports has caused major difficulties.

Leading American expert on North Korean arms sales Professor Bruce Bechtol observed that the DPRK was "not just a threat to American interests in East Asia because of its advancing weapons systems.... North Korea is in fact an equally menacing threat to American interests and the interests of the international community because of its military proliferation…" Regarding the nature of the threat to U.S. and Western interests, he noted: "The WMD and related platforms (ballistic missiles) that North Korea continues to proliferate in the Middle East present a threat that could directly challenge the United States or nations in Europe."[1] The expert thus referred to the DPRK's development of new and more capable weapons systems as "two headed threats," which not only shifted the balance of power in northeast Asia against the Western Bloc—but did the same in other regions such as the Persian Gulf.[2] Korean arms have undermined freedom of action for Western militaries on multiple fronts by providing potential targets with a deterrent capability and when needed a battlefield capability. A comprehensive understanding of the nature of the U.S.-DPRK conflict thus requires an assessment of the wars by proxy between the two states.

Fighting in Vietnam: 1960s

Information regarding North Korea's participation in the Vietnam War remains limited, but Korean People's Army pilots, air defence crews and other personnel were involved in supporting the Viet Minh against the United States and its allies during the protracted conflict. Premier Kim Il Sung had referred to the war as "the focal point" in global struggle, and expressed the belief that the war presented an opportunity to destroy illusions of American strength with potential global implications.[3] In August 1965 the Korean leader reportedly stressed the importance of assisting the Vietnamese struggle in a meeting with a visiting Chinese delegation, stating: "If the American imperialists fail in Vietnam, then they will collapse in Asia… We are supporting Vietnam as if it were our own war. When Vietnam has a request, we will disrupt our own plans in order to try to meet their demands."[4] As North Korea began to provide large scale assistance to the Southeast Asian state, the French Foreign Ministry concluded "Pyongyang is not content to just verbally support the opponents of the U.S. in Vietnam… Marshal Kim Il Sung himself repeatedly recommended the sending of volunteers to Vietnam by all socialist countries." The Korean leader declared in December 1966 that North Korea was going to bring "even more diverse forms of active aid to the Vietnamese people."[5]

Perhaps the best-known Korean contribution to the Viet Minh's war effort was the dispatching of pilots to fly air defence missions for the Vietnam People's Air Force. An official Vietnamese military history published in 2001 stated regarding this assistance: "Under the terms of an agreement between Korea and Vietnam, in 1967 a number of pilots from the Korean People's Army were sent to Vietnam to provide us training and the benefit of their experience and to participate in combat operations alongside the pilots of the People's Army of Vietnam. On a number of flights Korean pilots scored victories by shooting down American aircraft."[6] The exact size of the North Korean air contingent in the country remains uncertain—with neither party having revealed details. A 2007 report from a retired Major General from the North Vietnamese Air Force who had worked closely with the KPA indicates that 87 Korean pilots had served in the country between 1967 and 1969—losing 14 men and downing 26 American aircraft.[7] Vietnamese military sources placed the figure at 384 KPA Air Force personnel including 96 pilots.[8] *Reuters* reported the number of North Korean airmen in the Vietnam war was in the hundreds.[9]

Documents from the Vietnamese armed forces indicated that Pyongyang made an official request on September 21,1966 for permission to send aircraft to protect North Vietnamese population centres from American air attacks, which was subsequently approved by the Vietnamese Communist Party's Central Military Party Committee. Subsequent discussions held from the 24th to the 30th of that month saw Vietnamese and KPA military delegations headed by the respective chief of general staff of each arrange for the dispatch of a Korean People's Army Air Force contingent to North Vietnam. The agreement stipulated that the KPA would provide pilots for one regiment consisting of two companies of MiG-17 and one company of MiG-21 fighter jets—classes of aircraft operated in large numbers by both services. Vietnam would meanwhile provide the aircraft and all necessary technical equipment, maintenance, and logistics support for the Korean pilots. Korean air units would operate under the command and control of the North Vietnamese Air Defence Command. The arrival of KPA airmen was a very considerable asset to the Viet Minh's war effort, with the units providing a 50% increase to North Vietnam's fighter strength at a time when air defence was becoming particularly critical.[10] Capable fighter pilots took several years and a great deal of material investment to train, leaving them in far shorter supply than fighter jets themselves, and this had seriously restricted the Viet Minh's ability to upgrade its air defences before the arrival of Korean pilots. According to allied sources, KPA frontline pilots around the year 1970 were highly experienced, many with over 2000 flight hours, which was a level it would have taken Vietnamese pilots at least a decade to reach.[11]

Given the timing of the first deployment of North Korean air units, it was likely initiated in response to Operation Rolling Thunder—under which the United States intensively bombarded North Vietnamese population centres from mid-1965, losing over 900 aircraft in the process.[12] The intensive bombing of Hanoi saw direct American attacks on North Korean airfields nearby and more direct clashes between KPA and U.S. air units. Increasingly effective American electronic warfare systems at this time left North Vietnam's S-75 anti-aircraft batteries effectively useless, meaning combat jets had to be relied on more heavily for defence against mounting U.S. air attacks. The value of a large contingent of experienced Korean pilots, who comprised half of the Vietnamese fighter fleet, was thus very significant.[13] Former Vietnamese deputy defence minister and a former Vietnam War pilot, Tran Hanh, stated regarding the performance of Korean pilots deployed to counter the Americans in Vietnam: "We found them to be very brave. Their national pride was so high… They feared nothing, even death."[14] At Pyongyang's Victorious Fatherland Liberation War Museum, North Korean leader Kim Il Sung is quoted as having told KPA units to "defend the skies of Vietnam as if they were the skies of Korea."[15]

The KPA for its part gained valuable experience for its pilots in engaging the latest American combat aircraft such as B-52 Stratofortress bombers and F-4E Phantom fighters, which were very different from and two generations ahead of those which had participated in the Korean War. These new jets were expected to spearhead any future American offensive on the Korean Peninsula. A number of reports also indicate that KPA forces participated in ground battles alongside Viet Cong insurgents in South Vietnam, although this has not been officially confirmed. A delegate of the Vietnamese National Liberation Front, Nguyen Long, reportedly told a Romanian diplomat in Pyongyang that "the North Koreans had plenty of people active in South Vietnam," and had sought to send a larger contingent. Language barriers and communication difficulties made larger operations alongside the Viet Cong guerrillas difficult, however.[16] South Korean reports indicate that KPA psychological warfare specialists were also sent to aid the Viet Minh, and that guerrilla forces were trained in North Korea for operations against South Vietnamese and U.S. forces. These reports were supported by the research of U.S. Army intelligence officer Kim Jiyul, citing North Vietnamese military and Romanian diplomatic sources among others.[17]

Alongside personnel contributions, the DPRK dispatched large quantities of construction materials, tools, and automobiles as aid to the Viet Minh.[18] Technical assistance in a field of particular Korean specialty, the construction of fortifications for civilians and for military and industrial assets against American bombing, was also provided. As the war began to escalate in 1965 President Kim Il Sung stressed the importance of fortifications in his discussions with the Viet Minh leadership, stating:

> Based on Korea's experience, you should build your important factories in the mountain jungle areas, half of the factories inside the mountains and half outside—dig caves and place the factories half inside the caves and half outside.... Building a factory in a cave, such as a machinery factory, will require a cave with an area of almost 10,000 square meters. It took Korea from 1951 to 1955–1956 to finish building its factories in man-made caves, but today we can do the work faster.

He offered 500 Korean experts and workers to assist the Viet Minh in constructing the necessary fortifications, stating that the KPA had learned how to build larger cave fortifications to house entire regiments of fighter aircraft underground and had overseen such construction to assist the Chinese PLA.[19]

North Vietnamese Deputy Prime Minister and Politburo member Le Thanh Nghi concluded in his confidential report following his discussions with the Korean leadership and President Kim's offer for assistance in fortifying North Vietnam: "The North Korean leaders were very honest and open; they expressed total agreement with us; and their support was very straightforward, honest, and selfless."[20] Korean state media made multiple calls for volunteers to fight in Vietnam, a cause which reportedly had widespread public support. An ideological solidarity with a second East Asian nation which, following its liberation from colonial rule was placed under intensive bombardment by the United States and its allies, may have struck a chord with the Korean experience. An example of such a call for support was that by the first vice chairman of the Korean Democratic Women's Union, Kim Ok Sun, who wrote a column in *Rodong Sinmun* on April 7, 1965, stating: "Korean women will send their husbands, sons, and daughters, as volunteer forces to support the Vietnamese people," urging the nation to send its "beloved husbands, sons, and daughters...in order to support the South Vietnamese people and women who are fighting the U.S. imperialists."[21] This report and others like it lent credence to reports of KPA forces assisting the Viet Cong in South Vietnam. Many Korean workers and students reportedly volunteered to assist the Vietnamese cause as a volunteer force.[22]

The U.S. embassy in Moscow at the time described the stance of the Korean leadership towards the war as follows: "one's position on Vietnam is [a] touchstone for judgment on whether one is resolutely combatting imperialism and actively supporting [the] liberation struggle."[23] While China and the Soviet Union, then embroiled in the Sino-Soviet split, repeatedly blocked one another's assistance to the Viet Minh, denied North Vietnam access to the latest weapons systems and attempted to force Hanoi to choose a side between them,[24] the DPRK appeared the most resolute supporter of the Viet Minh's cause. The contribution of KPA pilots to the Vietnamese war effort is commemorated in Vietnam today, with a memorial to the fourteen fallen pilots standing at Bac Giang just outside Hanoi. Duong Van Dau, a Vietnam War veteran and caretaker of the memorial, stated regarding its meaning: "it commemorates the fight against America with our North Korean brothers who fought alongside us and sacrificed themselves for our country."[25]

Fighting in Egypt: 1970s

The involvement of the Korean People's Army in the Middle East and North Africa region (MENA) began in the early 1970s and has grown considerably since then. Egypt in particular emerged as the DPRK's first major strategic partner in the region following a military coup against the country's Western aligned monarchy in 1952. Pyongyang formed a strong basis for positive ties with Egypt shortly afterwards as Cairo's relations with the Western Bloc rapidly deteriorated, providing 60,000 won in financial aid following a joint British, French and Israeli invasion attempt in 1956. Pyongyang proceeded to provide 5,000 tons of food aid after Egypt's overwhelming defeat by the Western backed Israeli Defence Force (IDF) in 1967.[26] The first deployment of Korean units to MENA came shortly afterwards during the War of Attrition, which saw Egyptian and Soviet forces engage the IDF in several skirmishes across the Suez Canal. Shortly following the inauguration of a new Egyptian President, Anwar Sadat, an unexpected decree was issued to remove Soviet forces from Egyptian territory. Soviet personnel had played a key role operating Egypt's fighter jets and air defences, which the Egyptians themselves had proven less competent at doing, and these assets were vital to denying IDF total control of the skies. With Egypt's defences compromised, and suffering a shortage of trained pilots, the North Korean leadership offered assistance including the dispatching of a KPA contingent.

Egyptian Chief of Staff Saad Al Shazly noted in his report on the war effort that KPA assistance proved critical at a time of great need. Recalling that Soviet personnel had been flying approximately 30% of Egypt's MiG-21, he noted that following their departure, the Egyptian Air Force had struggled with a significant shortage of trained fighter pilots. Regarding North Korea's role in solving this issue, the general stated in his memoirs:

> The solution occurred to me in March 1973, during the visit to Egypt of the Vice President of the Democratic [People's] Republic of Korea. On March 6, while escorting their Vice Minister of War, General Zang Song, on a tour of the Suez front, I asked if they could support us—and give their pilots useful combat training—by sending even a squadron of men. I knew at that time that his country flew MiG-21s. After much political discussion, in April I went on an official visit to president Kim Il Sung to finalise the plan. My fascinating ten-day tour of that extraordinary republic, an inspiring an example of what a small nation of the so called Third World can achieve with its own resources is, alas, rather outside the scope of this memoir, as is my stopover in Peking.
>
> Korean pilots—all highly experienced, many with more than 2,000 hours, arrived in Egypt in June and were operating by July. Israel or her ally [the United States] soon monitored their communications, of course, and on August 15 announced their presence. To my regret, our leadership would never confirm it. The Koreans were probably the smallest international military reinforcement in history: only 20 pilots, eight controllers, five interpreters, three administrative men, a political advisor, a doctor and a cook. But their effect was disproportionate. They had two or three encounters with the Israelis in August and September and about the same number in the war. Their arrival was a heartwarming gesture. I mention the story here mainly to pay tribute to them and to apologise for the churlishness of our leadership in not also doing so.[27]

According to Western and Israeli reports, KPA pilots fared considerably better than their Arab counterparts in the air—with one incident seeing a single Korean MiG-21 hold its own against two heavier Israeli F-4E Phantoms and evade multiple rounds of missiles before the Israeli jets returned to base. Korean piloted MiGs reportedly took losses to Egyptian surface to air missile crews, which due to rushed training and a poor command structure were prone to shooting down their own aircraft.[28]

The participation of the KPA in the Yom Kippur War represented the first of many conflicts in which North Korea undermined U.S. and allied interests in MENA by bolstering the capabilities of Western adversaries. While the KPA flew Egyptian MiG-21s, pilot shortages which emerged among the Israelis soon after the outbreak of the Yom Kippur War resulted in American airmen reportedly flying Israeli Air Force combat jets. U.S. Air Force SR-71 strategic reconnaissance aircraft were also flown to assist the Israeli war effort—providing intelligence vital to turning the tide of the war.[29] Thus the KPA represented the only non-Arab participant in the air war against Israel, and the United States provided the only foreign pilots for the Israeli air campaign. With Pyongyang and Washington each actively supporting one Middle Eastern party against the other, North Korea's participation in the Yom Kippur War can be interpreted as a conflict by proxy with America and its interests in MENA. Korean units are not known to have directly clashed with American airmen but, given that it was not announced which Israeli jets were flown by Americans, it remains a possibility.

Egypt's government came to rely increasingly heavily on North Korean assistance after the war, seeking to ensure mutual vulnerability with a nuclear armed Israel through the development of an advanced ballistic missile capability. North Korea seriously undermined the Western favoured balance of power by providing Egypt with assistance in upgrading its military capabilities and in particular its ballistic missile arsenal. Multiple visits by President Hosni Mubarak to Pyongyang in the 1980s following the death of his more Westphilian predecessor saw the agenda of cooperation in missile development repeatedly raised, and as a result Egypt's ballistic missile forces came to be comprised almost entirely of North Korean platforms. In 1996 CIA sources indicated that Pyongyang was delivering manufacturing facilities to Egypt which "could allow Egypt to begin Scud-C [Hwasong-6] series production."[30] Washington considered applying sanctions to prevent this proliferation, but ultimately refrained to avoid the risk of alienating Cairo. Subsequent acquisition of the longer ranged Rodong-1 missile allowed Egypt to threaten targets across the Middle East and U.S. bases in Greece, Turkey, Italy and Romania. The Korean missile remains Egypt's most capable ballistic platform to date, and deliveries of missile components reportedly continued throughout the 2010s.[31]

Fighting in Syria: 1980s and 2010s

Of all America's adversaries, it is the Syrian Arab Republic which has relied most heavily on North Korean support in the face of Western and allied military and economic pressure. The effective collapse of the Egyptian-led Arab Nationalist Bloc in the 1970s following Cairo's defection to the West left Syria increasingly isolated in the face of considerable security threats, both internally from Islamist elements receiving foreign support and externally from neighbouring western allies, Turkey and Israel. Although the Soviet Union was Syria's primary external supporter, arming it with some of the most capable weapons in its inventory in the 1980s from MiG-25 interceptors to T-72 tanks, North Korea also played a significant role in training and arming the Syrian Arab Army. Syria remained on the frontlines against U.S. and allied designs in MENA throughout the 1980s, and was described by Egypt's Chief of Staff Saad Al Shazly as "the rock stemming the tide of Israeli hegemony in the Middle East."[32] Prominent British defence specialist Jonathan Marcus observed in 1989: "Syria alone remains in the front line of the anti-Israeli struggle," noting that the other members of the former Arab Nationalist alliance had been taken out of the picture.[33]

The KPA bolstered Syria's defences with a permanent stationing of forces including pilots, tank operators, missile technicians and officers who trained much of the country's military. North Korean operators of M1977 rocket artillery batteries were, according to Israeli reports, killed and one of the Korean made launchers captured during the Lebanon War in 1982.[34] The KPA was an active participant in the Lebanon War, a conflict which saw Syrian forces directly clash with both American and Western-backed Israeli forces—in one incident shooting down three American naval fighters on December 4, 1983.[35] The Korean People's Army and the United States Military were thus again providing material and manpower support to opposite sides of a Middle Eastern conflict against the other.

While Syria's reliance on North Korean support grew from the late 1970s when diplomatic ties with Egypt were severed, Pyongyang had provided support to Damascus before then. U.S. and Israeli sources reported that KPA pilots also flew fighters for the Syrian Arab Air Force in the Six Day War and Yom Kippur War, although this remains unconfirmed.[36] In 1970 the KPA was reported to have dispatched 200 tank crewmen, 53 pilots and 140 missile technicians to Syria and provided extensive training for Syrian pilots in preparation for conflict with Israel. In 1975, amid ongoing skirmishes with the Israeli Air Force, the KPA provided 75 air force instructors which were followed by 40 trained fighter pilots in 1976.[37]

The Soviet collapse in 1991 served to strengthen the unofficial Korean-Syrian alliance, with both countries losing access to Soviet military aid, protection and advanced new weapons systems. This weakened both considerably relative to their respective Western-aligned neighbours, South Korea and Israel. Syria remained Pyongyang's only partner other than Cuba which continued to deny recognition to South Korea, and Pyongyang reciprocated by refusing to recognise Israel. Trade with Syria was particularly prized following North Korea's loss of the vast majority of its trading partners with the collapse of the Soviet Bloc, and while there are no verifiable statistics on trade between the two, a visit to any of Pyongyang's trade expos shows the presence of Syrian products in large numbers and prominent positions wholly disproportionate to the small size of its economy.

By 2000, Tel Aviv University's Jaffee Center of Strategic Studies concluded regarding Syria's security situation: "that the strategic balance between Israel and Syria has never been so tilted in Israel's favor, and that Damascus has no real military option."[38] Syria's growing inability to mount a symmetric defence against potential American or allied attacks led it to invest more heavily in asymmetric systems from the early 1990s[39]—for which North Korean assistance was vital. Syria began to acquire Korean Hwasong-6 ballistic missiles from 1991 to 1995, allowing Syria's armed forces to retain a viable deterrent capability as its conventional forces deteriorated. The Koreans provided Syria with Hwasong-6 construction facilities near Aleppo and Hamah, and the Syrian military carried out its first test of the missile in July 1992 in the presence of Korean observers. Russian An-124 aircraft were also leased to Syria and used to lift missiles from Sunan airfield near Pyongyang. Syria's armed forces also received Korean cluster warheads for the missiles, and Syrian weapons technicians were simultaneously sent to the DPRK in large numbers for training.[40]

Supplementing the capabilities of the Hwasong-6, Syria became the only foreign operator of the Korean KN-02 Toksa—a derivative of the Soviet 9K79 Tochka with an extended range. First tested in May 2005, initial production beginning the following year and the Toksa was officially unveiled during a military parade in April 2007. Syria was thought to have received the missile at around this time and is speculated to have jointly funded the program. The Tochka variant on which the Korean platform is based, the Scarab C, entered service in 1989, and represented technology decades ahead of the Scud and Hwasong-6 designs. The missile seriously improved on the Scud's precision, with Western analysts reporting integration of "an advanced GPS system for near pinpoint guidance."[41] The compact solid fuelled missile's short launch time and high mobility were also highly advantageous, guaranteeing a higher degree of survivability. The missile's firing cycle of just 16 minutes, launch time of 2 minutes, and 20 minutes reload time meant it could fire approximately three times as quickly as its liquid fuelled predecessors.[42]

North Korea reportedly developed a specialised class of missile specifically for Syria's defence needs, known as the Scud-ER. The missile has the same payload and launch time as the basic Scud-B and Hwasong-6 but has an estimated range of 1000km—more than three times as long as that of the former and twice the latter. The missile is manufactured in Syria under licence with Korean assistance and is the longest-range ballistic missile in the country's arsenal. A sizeable arsenal of Korean missiles and the setting up of manufacturing facilities in Syria has allowed the country to threaten U.S. military bases in the Middle East as well as U.S. allies Israel and Turkey, ensuring mutual vulnerability in the case of hostilities and a highly survivable deterrent. As the U.S. provided considerable assistance to Israel to upgrade its missile defences, seeking to undermine the Syrian deterrent by provision of the PAC-2 Patriot[43] and later with joint development of the David's Sling system,[44] the DPRK provided Syria with technologies for a manoeuvring re-entry vehicle (MaRV) for its own missiles—making them extremely difficult to intercept and thereby countering the effects of the U.S. arms transfer to Israel. According to the British information group IHS Jane's, assistance was provided by engineers from North Korea's Tangun Trading Corporation. "The upgrade, which incorporates a bespoke canard system, will enable the MaRV of the Scud to alter its original planned trajectory when it re-enters the atmosphere, significantly improving its accuracy and increasing warhead survivability by making its flight path problematical to assess for missile-defence interceptors."[45]

Without continued Korean assistance Syria's deterrent capability likely would have eroded into obsolescence in the post-Soviet era, leaving the state highly vulnerable. Korean actions thus served to severely constrain Western and allied freedom of military action against a leading regional adversary. Syrian missile capabilities were highlighted by a number of analysts as an important factor deterring potential U.S. attacks in the aftermath of the invasion of Iraq in 2003 at a time of high tensions between Damascus and Washington.[46] Alongside development of the Syrian missile arsenal, servicing of older Syrian hardware from armoured personnel carriers to air defence systems and MiG-21 fighters also fell to the KPA, with Korean upgrades keeping these systems from falling into complete obsolescence. An example was the equipping of T-54/55 battle tanks with Korean laser rangefinders, upgraded turrets and improved armour—with Syria fielding around 2200 of these ageing platforms.[47] The fact that the two parties operate much of the same hardware had made such cooperation easy to implement, with technologies developed to augment Soviet armaments in the Korean arsenal highly compatible with armaments in the Syrian arsenal.

Western reports also indicate that the DPRK provided Syria with nuclear technologies, with a CIA report stating that a project to construct a gas cooled and graphite moderated nuclear reactor based on the Korean plutonium production graphite reactor at Yongbon began "as early as 1997."[48] An Israeli airstrike neutralised what was reported by Western sources to be an Iranian financed Korean nuclear facility in Syria in September 2007, killing Korean technicians. The veracity of such reports remains uncertain. A number of nuclear experts and intelligence officials, among them the Director General of the International Atomic Energy Agency (IAEA), have asserted that not only was there no evidence of a plutonium reprocessing plant, or of any notable defences which would be expected at such a facility, but also no sign of any facility to produce nuclear fuel in Syria.[49] To fill this hole in the narrative, it was subsequently claimed by Western sources that the reactor was part of a wider plutonium program which Iran had partially outsourced to Syrian territory.[50] Why Tehran would do so given such a reactor's far greater vulnerability and proximity to both Israel and U.S. forces in Iraq is hard to fathom however, as is the construction of an unconcealed reactor for over five years in plain sight and just 50km from the Iraqi border without alerting U.S. intelligence. Other Israeli sources claimed the reactor used uranium fuel which was delivered by ship from the North Korean capital Pyongyang itself. This too seemed very unusual given both the lack of major ports or nuclear facilities there and the low viability of a nuclear program reliant on fuel shipments from so far away.[51] It was noted by a number of reporters that allegations of the development of weapons of mass destruction, often fabricated, were frequently used as a pretext for hostile and illegal actions by the U.S. and its allies in the 2000s.[52] The true nature of the Israeli target and the extent of Korean involvement can only be speculated.

The DPRK's consistently provided considerable support for Syria's armed forces throughout the 1990s and 2000s, with frequent reported shipments of missile components and other military equipment[53] vital to facilitating their much-needed military modernisation. This partnership strengthened following the outbreak of a Western-backed[54] insurgency in Syria in 2011, which pitted the Syrian Arab Army against a number of well-funded militant groups, the vast majority Islamist jihadists,[55] which sought the state's overthrow and imposition of Islamic law. These operated with considerable funding and equipment from external sponsors[56] and represented an imminent threat to the Syrian state. The outbreak of war empowered the country's Ba'ath Party and the security apparatus, which had over the past decade resisted recently appointed British-educated President Bashar Al Assad's Westphilian reform process,[57] and led to revitalised Syrian ties with traditional allies including Pyongyang.

Pyongyang and Damascus have exchanged high level delegations, including a visit by Defence Minister Kim Kyok Sik, a close confidant of former General Secretary Kim Jong Il, in 2013. An artillery officer, fluent Arabic speaker and former deputy military attaché at the Korean embassy in Damascus, his visit at a time of escalating conflict and multiple losses against a number of jihadist groups was seen as a sign of growing Korean support for the Syrian war effort. Korean Foreign Minister Ri Su Yong visited Damascus the following year and met with President Assad. North Korean embassy staff paid several visits to wounded Syrian soldiers as the country provided considerable humanitarian assistance. This has included the construction and full staffing of three hospitals by the DPRK.[58] Syria in turn opened Kim Il Sung park in honour of the DPRK's founding father in 2015, adjacent to Kim Il Sung Street in Damascus—seen as a wartime tribute in thanks for Pyongyang's extensive assistance during the crisis. At the park's opening ceremony, which marked the 70th anniversary of the Korean Workers' Party, Syria's deputy Foreign Minister Faisal Mikdad praised the DPRK's leader and its current government for "standing with Syria against terrorism"[59]—a reference to the ongoing jihadist insurgency.

During the war the Korean People's Army reportedly set up a command and control logistical assistance centre to support the Syrian war effort,[i] with Korean officers deployed to multiple fronts, including the frontlines of engagements against jihadist forces in Aleppo.[60] A number of Western sources have meanwhile claimed regarding the KPA role on a second front in 2013: "Arab-speaking North Korean military advisors were integral to the operational planning of the surprise attack and artillery campaign execution during the battle for Qusair."[61] According to a 2013 statement by the former president of the Syrian National Council Burhan Ghalioun, a Western-backed Islamist opposition group, KPA pilots were operating Syrian aircraft against jihadist forces. Considering the significant shortages of trained pilots Syria has endured since the mid-1990s, this report has some plausibility. Other reports by Western-backed anti-government figures indicate that North Korea dispatched two special forces units named Chalma-1 and Chalma-7 to Syria to engage jihadist forces, and that these units proved "fatally dangerous" on the battlefield.[62]

Deployment of Korean Special Forces overseas could provide the Korean People's Army with valuable experience in modern warfare, including in mountainous terrain and urban areas. Former Chief of Staff for the U.S. Special Operations Command Korea David Maxwell, among others, expressed considerable concern at the benefits such overseas experience would bring the KPA.[63] These elite forces have been described in British reports as "highly motivated, politically well indoctrinated and well trained.... units are expected to seek the initiative continuously, to turn all unforeseen events to their advantage, and advance all to achieve their objectives regardless of cost."[64] Their notoriously rigorous training programs reportedly included "skills, such as abseiling, mountain climbing, swimming, martial arts, airborne, demolition, and rigorous physical

i It is important to note that these reports have emerged from Western-backed anti-government sources which have openly sought a Western-sponsored overthrow of the Syrian government and have not been independently verified. There is an incentive for Damascus and Pyongyang to underplay the extent of their defence cooperation, much as the Western Bloc and their allies have a strong incentive to exaggerate it, and ultimately a more accurate picture of the extent of Korean involvement in the current conflict is likely to remain elusive for many years to come.

fitness, and training designed to produce individual initiative, creativity, flexibility and aggressiveness."[65] The KPA fields the largest special forces in the world with an estimated 180,000–200,000 personnel,[66] which proved highly capable in clashes with South Korean forces during a 1996 infiltration incident. They are likely to be a highly formidable asset in counterinsurgency operations.

The Syrian economy and post-war reconstruction efforts have been seriously impeded by Western economic sanctions—to be lifted only if the government accepts U.S. and European demands to cede power and adopt Western-style political reforms.[67] Korean pledges to provide assistance in post-war reconstruction and strengthen economic ties have thus been highly valued by Damascus.[68]

Bolstering Iran: 1980s to 2020s

North Korean support for Iran dates back to the early 1980s, long before the two were declared part of the "Axis of Evil" and targets for regime change under the George W. Bush administration in 2002. Pyongyang saw the overthrow of Iran's western aligned Pahlavi dynasty in 1979, and the ambiguous alignment of the newly declared Islamic Republic which harshly denounced both the Soviet and Western Blocs, as an opportunity to gain a major new partner. The works of Ayatollah Ruhollah Khomeini, the leader of Iran's revolution, were reportedly translated into Korean in the DPRK for the purpose of forming a better understanding of the republic, and multiple overtures of friendship were made to Tehran. The Iraqi invasion of Iran in 1980 saw both sides move to cement ties, particularly in the field of defence.

The Western Bloc provided Iraq with modern military equipment including F1 fighter jets, Exocet missiles, and even Soviet-style arms acquired from third parties under the "Bear Spares" program.[69] They further shared valuable intelligence on Iranian troop movements,[70] assisted Iraq's nuclear development[71] and chemical weapons program,[72] and later directly intervened to sink much of the Iranian Navy, destroy manufacturing plants and oil rigs[73] and enforce a blockade on Iranian oil exports. Thus, by supporting the Iranian war effort, Pyongyang was waging war by proxy against Western interests. The KPA provided training in fields such as air defence, ballistic missiles use and guerrilla warfare, and the two states concluded their first arms contract in 1980.[74] Alongside several hundred Hwasong-5 ballistic missiles, North Korea supplied Iran with Koksan 170mm howitzers and M1985 240mm rocket artillery systems—the latter later licence produced in Iran as the Fajr-3. The Koksan was the longest range artillery gun in the world at the time, and proved a valuable asset.[75] North Korea was also the only provider of modern battle tanks to Iran during the war, providing Chonma Ho platforms to compensate for the heavy losses Iranian armoured units suffered.[76] Other armaments from Bulsae-2 anti-tank missiles down to the level of small arms were also provided—with the Korean Type 73 light machine gun purchased in large numbers and later passed on to Iranian defence partners in Yemen, Iraq, Lebanon and Syria.[77] Iran has since regularly purchased arms from North Korea to equip a number of its non-state partners, including Hezbollah and various Iraqi government aligned militias.[78]

By bolstering Iran, at a time when the Western Bloc was both strongly supporting Iraq, and on many occasions directly engaging Iranian forces, Pyongyang was again undermining U.S. and Western designs in a strategically critical conflict. Cooperation continued to expand after the war's conclusion, with Iranian President Ali Khamenei visiting Korea in May 1989 and declaring the importance of solidarity between the two states before the Supreme People's Assembly. "You have proved in Korea that you have the power to confront America," he announced, standing beside President Kim Il Sung. Khamenei would assume the office of Supreme Leader less than a month later and repeatedly reiterated the importance of cooperation for both states. Meetings between the Supreme Leader and the DPRK's own leadership have occurred frequently ever since.[79]

The U.S. and its allies have on multiple occasions come close to taking military action against Iran, and with the country's air force, surface fleet and armoured divisions all poorly suited to mounting an effective symmetric defence, Iran's access to Korean missile technologies has served as its most vital deterrent over almost four decades. Iran began to invest in a ballistic missile capability in the 1980s through the acquisition of Korean technologies, with its first platforms, the Hwasong-5 and Hwasong-6, soon supplemented by longer range systems capable of reaching targets across the Middle East, including Saudi Arabia, Israel, Turkey and Western military bases. The most prominent was the Rodong-1, which was manufactured under licence as the Shahab-3 and forms the mainstay of the Iranian strategic arsenal until today. Significant efforts, including American threats and Israeli diplomatic overtures aimed at Pyongyang, were expended to attempt to prevent the sale, but these ultimately failed to prevent an Iranian acquisition of the Rodong-1.[80] The platform has an estimated range of up to 1,500km, and entered North Korean service in 1990 with deliveries to Iran beginning shortly afterwards. Transfers of Korean weapons technologies have been repeatedly cited as a source of major concern by U.S. government and intelligence sources.[81]

The Shahab-3 has since been modernised with Korean assistance, improving its accuracy, lengthening its frame to accommodate larger fuel tanks, using a lighter aluminium fuselage, and integrating new guidance systems, manoeuvring warheads with higher velocities and specialised munition types. The Ghadr-1 and Emad are the best known examples of enhanced Shahab-3 variants, and have extended ranges of 2,500km and 2000km respectively and improved guidance systems for greater precision.[82] The Rodong-1, as Shahab-3, is the only North Korean or Iranian medium range ballistic missile confirmed to have been combat tested. Israeli intelligence sources reported the missile was deployed in June 2017 against Islamic State jihadist insurgents in Syria.[83] Iranian reports indicate the missile proved highly effective and precise—as confirmed by drone footage.[84]

Further building on the capabilities of the Shahab-3, Iran reportedly received complete Musudan missiles from the DPRK in the mid-2000s, with a first batch of 18 shipped as early as 2005 and a first test launch conducted in January the following year.[85] These missiles were in active service by 2010.[86] The Musudan was significantly more sophisticated than its predecessor and reportedly deploys multiple warheads, making it extremely difficult to intercept. The missile entered Iranian service both in its original form, renamed Shahab-4 in Iran, and later in modified form as the Khorramshahr. The modified variant "has become smaller in size and more tactical" at the expense of range—according to the Commander of the Iranian Revolutionary Guard Corps' Aerospace Division.[87] This variant is still reportedly capable of striking targets as far as Western Europe.[88] The two Musudan variants are currently the most capable strategic platforms in the Iranian inventory. Another longer ranged missile in Iranian service, the indigenous solid fuelled Sejil, was, according to multiple reports, developed with North Korean assistance, making extensive use of Korean components.[89]

The DPRK has also provided Iran with the foundation of a second stage deterrent in the form of a cruise missile submarine program. Iran has manufactured approximately two dozen Korean Yono Class attack submarines under licence as the Ghadir Class, and the platforms were later fitted with licence-built Chinese C-704 cruise missiles allowing them to fire on targets while submerged.[90] The first test[91] came two years after the KPA first attempted to launch missiles from its own submarines, and technical knowhow is likely to have been exchanged. Some sources indicate that the Iranian Navy also intends to equip its submarines with Korean cruise missiles—either alongside or in place of the C-704.[92] It has been speculated that Iran could seek to develop a ballistic missile submarine based on the technologies of the Korean Gorae Class ships in future.

Approximately 90% of Iranian submarines are of North Korean origin, including the Yono Class licence-built as the Ghadir and the Yugo Class acquired directly from Korean shipyards. According to U.S. analysts writing for the *National Interest*, Iran's submarine units acquired from North Korea, while much smaller than the fleet in Korean service, represent the "one notable caveat" in American conventional superiority over Iranian forces.[93] Iran's submarine capabilities have been referred to as "by far the most numerous and technically capable arm of its navy and slated to remain so for the foreseeable future," and as the one conventional field where it can challenge the United States.[94] The ships grant Tehran considerable political leverage at times of high tension with the U.S., and are considered central to potential Iranian plans to close the Strait of Hormuz to American shipping as Tehran has often threatened to do.[95] Submarines thus represent yet another critical field of the defence in which Iran has been heavily reliant on Korean assistance. The country's indigenous Fateh Class submarines, first commissioned in February 2019, are speculated to have been developed with Korean support and make use of Korean components and technologies. Modern Air-Independent Propulsion systems in particular are key to a submarine's survivability, and as North Korea is one of only a few countries to have developed them,[96] it is likely these Korean systems have been integrated onto the Fateh Class.

Western sources have also claimed that Iran's military and civilian satellite programs have benefitted from North Korean ICBM technologies—with Iranian satellite launch vehicles reportedly based on the Korean Hwasong-14 missile.[97] These claims remain unverified but are a significant possibility. Reports from America's Missile Technology Control Regime indicate that technologies from Korean intermediate range missiles such as the Musudan could also assist the Iranian space program.[98] U.S. State Department cables indicate that Iran's Safir satellite launcher is heavily based on the Rodong-1, but features steering engines in its second stage derived from Musudan technology.[99]

Other forms of military cooperation have also seriously augmented Iran's defences. North Korea has trained Iranian crews to operate MiG-29 fighters, the most modern jets in Iran's inventory, and sold parts for aircraft. North Korea has manufactured the MiG-29 domestically under licence providing a high degree of familiarity with the design, and is speculated to have assisted Iran in refurbishing and modernising the jets.[100] More directly affecting Iran's deterrence capabilities, Korean expertise was reportedly key to efforts to harden and heavily reinforce Iranian nuclear facilities such as the Fordow uranium enrichment plant, which was built under a mountain in the early 2000s. Such fortifications have been a field of KPA expertise for over half a century. North Korea has constructed over ten thousand meters of nuclear infrastructure and underground facilities for Iran—reportedly with reinforced concrete ceilings, doors and walls intended to withstand strikes from the U.S. Air Force's penetrative bombs. Myong Lyu Do, a leading Korean expert on fortifications and underground construction, was confirmed to have travelled to Iran in 2005 to personally oversee these construction efforts.[101] With the threat of an American or allied attack on Iranian nuclear facilities remaining high, added durability seriously complicates potential offensive operations against Iran.[102]

Although it is thought to be at least a decade behind that of the DPRK, and has progressed at a far slower pace, Iran's nuclear program has benefitted considerably from Korean support. The DPRK's near total self-sufficiency in the production of both nuclear energy and nuclear armaments placed it in a strong position to provide such assistance.[103] Due to the secretive nature of both programs, only limited details have emerged regarding cooperation. In 2011 Pyongyang reportedly supplied Iran with a computer program and complex software to assist its nuclear development, and a delegation travelled from Pyongyang to Tehran that year to train Iranian defence specialists in using the software.[104] The *Washington Post* that year quoted intelligence provided to UN officials, which stated that North Korea had provided Iran with "crucial technology" which "helped propel Iran to the threshold of nuclear capability.... Iran relied on foreign experts to supply mathematical formulas and codes for theoretical design work." These "originated in North Korea," according to "diplomats and weapons experts" cited by the *Post*.[105]

Quoting diplomatic sources, prominent South Korean media outlet *Chosun Ilbo* reported in 2011 that "hundreds of North Korean scientists and engineers are working at about 10 nuclear and missile facilities in Iran, including Natanz."[106] Accelerating Iran's nuclear development at a time when the United States and its allies were going to great lengths to stall it, from massive economic pressure to multiple assassinations of Iranian scientists,[107] seriously undermined U.S. interests in the Middle East. Western experts have also assessed that North Korea assisted Iran in developing a plutonium reactor—potentially a second more efficient path to developing nuclear weapons alongside the uranium program should Tehran decide to pursue such a course.[108]

Korean assistance to Iran's deterrence program has been truly comprehensive. Almost all the Iranian inventory of ballistic missiles in service today could not exist without Korean technology transfers, parts, designs and assistance—neither could Iran's nuclear program have accelerated as it did leading up to 2015. Iranian nuclear sites, too, would have lacked fortification—making them relatively soft targets for preventative strikes much as the Iraqi Osirak reactor was in 1981. As covered below, Iran's most valued military capability other than its ballistic missiles—its cooperation with highly trained and heavily armed militias—also would have been seriously undermined without extensive Korean assistance and training for these groups. Thus it is no exaggeration to say that Iran's aspiration to major power status has been facilitated by North Korean assistance—without which the state would have lacked the deterrence capabilities and resulting confidence in its security needed to pursue its current policies, or the rapid progress in nuclear development needed to drive a hard bargain under the 2015 Joint Comprehensive Plan of Action nuclear agreement. As American expert on North Korean weapons sales Bruce Bechtol noted: "The overwhelming majority of Iranian ballistic missiles tested to date or used in combat have had their genesis in North Korea, were built with North Korean assistance and parts, and remain the key component of Tehran's missile program."[109] As military analysts have widely noted, Iran without its ballistic missile capabilities would not be able to balance the vastly greater conventional strength of its adversaries, and would thus be forced to adopt a much more restrained policy in asserting its interests.[110]

Aside from ideological solidarity, ties to Iran have provided the DPRK with a means to seriously undermine U.S. interests abroad relatively cheaply—if not profitably with the oil rich state's purchases subsidising Korea's own weapons programs and facilitating larger and more efficient production lines for many key platforms. Iran's access to advanced Korean technologies—ballistic missile technologies in particular—in contrast to the generally poor state of most of its military inventory,[111] has caused a major shift in the balance of power in the Middle East against Western and allied interests.

Libya

Libya's defence and economic partnership with North Korea dates back to the 1980s, when the African state emerged as a leading adversary of the Western Bloc. Military clashes between Libyan and U.S. forces were not infrequent at the time, with multiple attempts made on the lives of the Libyan leadership.[112]A year after Libyan and American fighter jets clashed over the Gulf of Sidra, Tripoli signed a treaty of friendship and cooperation with the DPRK in November 1982, which stipulated the exchange of military data, specialists and equipment, providing Libya with considerable quantities of Korean armaments including ZPU-4 anti-aircraft artillery, howitzers, and BM-11 rocket artillery systems among others.[113] Many of these munitions would be put to use against anti-government militias armed and backed by NATO in 2011.[114]

Korean-Libyan defence ties were overshadowed by cooperation in other sectors such as construction and medicine, and the limitations of Libya's heavily rentier-oriented economy made Korean labour a much-appreciated asset. Fuelled by high oil prices, Libya's 1980s construction boom saw North Korean workers contracted for projects from new apartment blocks to military barracks. Where South Korean labour was sending back considerable remittances from Western-aligned Arab Gulf states, Libya proved highly attractive for North Korean workers. The writer previously met with a married couple, both doctors, who worked in Libyan hospitals for over six years until the mid-2000s. The money they earned allowed them to take regular holidays to Egypt and other neighbouring countries and to visit their families once every one-to-two years in Korea. Korean workers in Libya numbered in the tens of thousands, several thousand of them in the medical sector, and such ties proved highly beneficial to both parties.

North Korea played a central role in Libya's ballistic missile program, providing Hwasong-6[115] and Rodong-1 platforms which outperformed its prior arsenal of Soviet Scud-Bs. A number of South Korean and Western reports indicate that the Rodong-1 was first delivered in July

2000, and provided a strategic deterrent for Libya's armed forces with the ability to strike targets in Europe.[116] Despite the country's general neglect of military modernisation in the post–Cold War years, this provided a degree of security following the Soviet collapse. This deterrent capability would be neutered after Libya agreed under U.S. pressure to unilaterally disarm and surrender its missile arsenal in exchange for economic sanctions relief in the mid-2000s. Having ignored direct warnings from both Tehran and Pyongyang[117] not to pursue such a course, Libya's leadership would later admit that disarmament, neglected military modernisation, and trust in Western good will proved to be their greatest mistake—leaving the country near defenceless when the Western powers launched their offensive in 2011.[118] For the U.S. and its allies, Libya's deterrent capabilities acquired from the DPRK had stood in the way of their designs to impose regime change. It was only after these were removed from the equation that Western bombs and cruise missiles could be rained down on the African state without fear of retaliation.[119]

Southern Africa: 1970s and 1980s

North Korea was a leading supporter of several of nationalist groups in southern Africa during the Cold War, directly undermining Western dominance over the region. The People's Movement for the Liberation of Angola (MPLA) was a leading recipient of Korean support during its war against the U.S. and South African-backed National Union for the Total Independence of Angola (UNITA) in the 1980s. After Portuguese colonial rule ended in 1975 the U.S. had sought to promote an anti-Soviet government firmly aligned with the Western Bloc in the resource rich southern African state, and supported UNITA to this end. While the United States provided UNITA with considerable material support, the armed forces of South Africa, then ruled by a European settler elite under the apartheid system, directly intervened in Angola to back their cause.

The MPLA received material aid from the Soviet Union but relied heavily on Cuban and North Korean manpower contributions. Cuba's armed forces reportedly deployed over 35,000 troops to Angola at the height of the conflict,[120] and Cuban-operated MiG-23 fighters fought multiple battles with the South African Air Force's European-made jets over Angolan skies. The KPA did not deploy for a direct combat role, but dispatched 1,500 personnel in 1986 as advisors and trainers for the MPLA's militias.[121] The Koreans reportedly sought to use Angola as a staging ground to support operations by the African National Congress

(ANC) and the South West African People's Organization (SWAPO) against the government of South Africa. Some reports indicate that by 1984 there were 3,000 North Korean regular troops and 1,000 advisors in the country. As these movements opposing apartheid rule were widely portrayed as terrorist movements in the U.S., this support was used as a pretext for accusing the DPRK of sponsoring terrorism overseas.[122] The Zimbabwean African National Liberation Army (ZANLA) also received Korean training and faced Western-backed forces in the Rhodesian Bush War. The Angolan Civil War and the struggle between apartheid rule and the ANC in South Africa represented other instances in which the DPRK and the United States provided considerable support to opposing sides of major conflicts.

The eventual victories of the MPLA, the ANC and ZANLA provided a strong foundation for close ties between the three new African governments and North Korea. The DPRK retains an embassy in Angola, and the two maintain close ties in defence, health, construction and information technology.[123] The DPRK also established an embassy in Pretoria following the end of apartheid rule, and relations between the two states have remained strong with the ANC Youth League in particular expressing continued solidarity with the Korean cause.[124] Relations with Zimbabwe, which was also targeted by Western economic sanctions following its independence, were particularly strong, with the KPA taking a leading role in training the country's armed forces and the two countries establishing a robust barter trading system to evade Western sanctions.

Southern Lebanon and Hezbollah: 1980s to 2020s

Defence ties between the southern Lebanese militia and political party Hezbollah and the DPRK were first established in the early 1980s, and much of Hezbollah's central leadership, including current Secretary General Hassan Nasrallah, Security and Intelligence chief Ibrahim Akil and head of counter-espionage operations Mustapha Badreddine, were trained in Korea. The militia's intelligence sharing, command structures and security apparatus today all closely reflect this influence.

While Hezbollah's defence doctrine, ideology and organization have often simplistically been compared to those of their primary sponsor Iran—an analysis of the close ties the group has had to North Korea since its foundation indicates otherwise. The circumstances under which Hezbollah was formed, as a resistance movement to neighbouring Israel's annexation of southern Lebanon with considerable support from the local Lebanese population, are highly similar to those of the KPA—originating in the guerrilla resistance movement to Japanese occupation and forging its modern identity in later resistance to an attempted American invasion from 1950. While Hezbollah's primary financial sponsor, Iran, has never conducted a revolutionary war as Lebanon and Korea have, the comparable circumstances faced by the latter two—extreme proximity to their adversaries, similar arms and tactics used by their adversaries, and similar terrain—have all led to the evolution of Hezbollah's military wing as effectively a smaller reproduction of the Korean People's Army.

Some indications of the extent of defence cooperation between the two parties were highlighted in the aftermath of the 2006 Israeli-Hezbollah War—a conflict in which the militia's means of waging war indicated a strong Korean influence. Israeli experts described Hezbollah's war effort as "a defensive guerrilla force organized along North Korean lines," concluding: "All the underground facilities [Hezbollah's], including arms dumps, food stocks, dispensaries for the wounded, were put in place primarily in 2003–2004 under the supervision of North Korean instructors."[125] Other intelligence sources indicated that the Korean People's Army had a military presence on the ground, concluding that Hezbollah was "believed to be benefiting from assistance provided by North Korean advisers." [126] A further decisive factor was Hezbollah's high degree of discipline and effective command and control—a strong contrast to the disorderly Arab armies Israel had previously faced. These factors were reportedly strongly focused on by the KPA when training Hezbollah's special forces and officer corps, and allowed the militia to function in a league of its own among Arab forces at a level comparable to the Koreans themselves.[127]

Southern Lebanon has since the 1980s been shaped into a garrison state—largely self-governing under Hezbollah and with a distinct identity from the remainder of the country. Like North Korea, this emphasis on security has come about as a result of the perception of imminent threat from a far larger enemy force at the border seemingly poised to invade. The construction of historical memory in both societies of occupation plays a key role in forging such an identity and maintaining a state of resistance—something which cannot be found in Iran which as a far larger actor which did not know occupation has not seen its society reshaped in the same way. While the southern Lebanese experience of occupation was certainly far less extreme than that in Korea, with the Israeli Defence

Force proving a far more humane occupier than the United States or its Western allies had been north of the 38th parallel, this is partially compensated for by its more recent memory of occupation.

While the KPA had been able to build up considerable quantities of armoured units, air defences, artillery units, attack submarines and combat aircraft since the 1953 Korean War armistice, which it was beginning to complement with ballistic missiles when it first established ties to Hezbollah, the Lebanese militia had little equipment at the time above the level of handheld weapons—with rocket propelled grenades and mortars at the heavier end of its inventory. Hezbollah's strategy thus evolved to closely reflect that of the immediate post-Inchon phases of the Korean War—allowing it to wage an asymmetric resistance to occupation despite overwhelming Israeli air, armoured and naval superiority. There were notable differences however—the Israeli Defence Force never firebombed population centres, brutalised civilians or waged war indiscriminately as America and its allies had and took measures to avoid rather than maximise civilian casualties. As a result, the civilian casualty rate was 2–3 orders of magnitude lower[ii] than it had been in Korea.[128]

The effectiveness of Hezbollah's tight security network in southern Lebanon, its emphasis on using complex and often extremely deep underground tunnel and bunker networks to move troops, store munitions and infiltrate enemy territory safe from detection or air attacks, and more recently its deployment of vast arsenals of rocket artillery and ballistic missiles, all closely reflect not only Korean influences—but active Korean assistance. KPA advisers have reportedly assisted Hezbollah in building the complex tunnel infrastructure deemed key to its success in 2006—and Israel's discoveries since then of infiltration tunnels under its own territory meant for wartime penetration were highly reminiscent of those discovered by South Korea coming from the DPRK.[129] It is notable that layout of the tunnel network in southern Lebanon closely mirrors that on the northern side of the inter-Korean demilitarised zone.[130]

To provide some indication of how extensive and well-fortified the Korean-built tunnel and bunker network in southern Lebanon was, the region south of the Litani river alone was thought to have over 600

ii It is estimated that the number of civilians killed by the IDF in more than 70 years of frequent war are less than the U.S.-led coalition killed in an average week of war in Korea. Israel's war crimes, even when taking the most exaggerated allegations at face value, pale in comparison to the scale and severity of those committed by the powers of the Western Bloc, of which those committed against Korea are but one of the more severe examples.

ammunition and weapons bunkers eight or more meters underground—alongside better fortified command bunkers constructed to a depth of 40 meters using poured concrete.[131] These were not as deep as those in Korea itself, designed to withstand multiple American nuclear strikes, but were still sufficient to weather anything in Israel's arsenal or any known non-nuclear bunker buster in service in the Western Bloc at the time. The network built in southern Lebanon was 25km long—and has reportedly been expanded significantly since the war's end. There were at least ten Korean-built tunnel and bunker networks in southern Lebanon—each with dozens of command bunkers which in turn were each divided into several rooms.[132] The bunker network also served as an effective cover for the launch of missile and artillery strikes against Israeli targets.[133] Much of Hezbollah's rocket artillery and tactical ballistic missile arsenal was comprised of Korean-made systems—according to Israeli reports. Whether these are weapons systems acquired directly from Korea, or Korean systems assembled in Iran under licence using Korean made components, remains uncertain.[134] Rocket artillery systems were often deployed from firing pits five meters deep—with foot thick poured concrete frames reinforced with blast walls and covered with sandbags and thermal blankets. These firing pits minimised the rockets' heat signatures and made firing positions extremely resilient to Israeli air attacks.[135]

Had Hezbollah lacked the tunnel networks, intelligence network, high level training, or missile assets provided by the DPRK, it is highly likely that it would have faced a swift and outright defeat in the summer of 2006 as the Israeli government had initially predicted. The tunnel and bunker network in particular, alongside the communications network and fortified armouries, were all reportedly built by the Korea Mining Development Trading Corporation (KMDTC). These were all assets which Israel was unaware Hezbollah had access to,[136] and are widely credited by U.S. and Israeli sources with having been decisive[137] in thwarting Israeli war aims.[iii] The fact that such a large building operation right on the Israeli border could be kept secret despite the considerable intelligence gathering capabilities of Israel is further credit to Hezbollah's own intelligence and security network—itself also built

---

iii It is notable that the IDF never succeeded in knocking out either Hezbollah's Korean built tunnel and bunker network or in breaking down the command and control network the DPRK set up for the Lebanese militia. The system reportedly remained impervious to the listening efforts of the Israeli Signals Intelligence Unit 8200.

by the Korean-trained specialists, foremost among whom were Ibrahim Akil and Mustapha Badreddine, and run on Korean lines.

Although Korean forces are not known to have directly taken part in hostilities, the 2006 Israeli-Hezbollah war is likely the most significant case of KPA intervention overseas against the interests of the United States. The Korean-Hezbollah partnership represents the only time an allied military organization has been modelled so closely on the KPA—with the Lebanese militia built since its foundation in the 1980s from the ground up as a fighting force based closely on Korean lines. It therefore followed that many of the most prolific systems in Hezbollah's inventory today were provided by the DPRK either directly or through Syria or Iran. Examples include 122mm rocket artillery batteries deployed in very large numbers, the militia's main anti-tank weapon the laser guided Bulsae-3, which replaced supplies of the Russian Kornet,[138,iv] and even Hwasong-9 ballistic missiles manufactured in Syria.[139] Support from the DPRK for Hezbollah played a pivotal role in determining the conflict's outcome against one of the United States' most valued allies—with ripple effects from the militia's military successes affecting the entire region to the detriment of U.S. and Western interests. Considering the vast quantities of American armaments provided to Israel under its aid program and the substantial Western interest in an Israeli victory, Korea's assistance to Hezbollah and very likely turning of the tide of the war can be interpreted as a conflict by proxy against the interests of the United States.[v]

---

iv Israel notably placed considerable pressure on Russia to better monitor exports of the Kornet to the Middle East after its armour took heavy losses in 2006. This would have likely seriously impeded Hezbollah's anti-tank capabilities due to its demonstrated reliance on the missile, had North Korea not manufactured a reverse engineered and allegedly heavily improved variant which was sold to both Syria and Hezbollah.

v Hezbollah's military wing has been designated a terrorist organisation by all Western countries except Switzerland, Norway and Iceland (U.S., EU, Canada, Australia, New Zealand), as well as Israel, Japan and a number of Arab states. Hezbollah is not classified as a terrorist organisation by the United Nations, has considerable public support and several parliamentary seats in Lebanon, and retains close ties to a number of state actors including China, Cuba and Russia.

NOTES

1 Bechtol Jr., Bruce E., *North Korean Military Proliferation in the Middle East and Africa,* Lexington, University Press of Kentucky, 2018 (pp. ix, 1)

2 Ibid. (p. 139)

3 *North Korean Intentions and Capabilities with Respect to South Korea,* Special National Intelligence Estimate, Number 14.2-67, Central Intelligence Agency, September 21, 1967 (p. 6).

4 'Record of Conversation between Premier Kim and the Chinese Friendship Delegation,' August 20, 1965, PRC FMA 106-01479-05, 46–51.

5 Pyongyang's Attitudes Towards The Conflict in Vietnam," 7 June, 1967, Asie-Océanie, Corée du Nord Période 1956–1967, série 11, Politique étrangère, Carton 11-23-1, vol. 4 (3), Politique étrangère: Fichier général-Conflit du Vietnam, French Ministry of Foreign Affairs. Housed at National Institute of Korean History, Gwacheon, South Korea, Box MU0000540.

6 Military History Institute of Vietnam, *Lich su khang chien chong My, cuu nuoc, 1954–1975, Tap V: tong tien cong va noi day 1968* [History of the Resistance War Against the Americans to Save the Nation, 1954–1975, Volume V: The 1968 General Offensive and Uprising], People's Army Publishing House, Hanoi, 2001 (p. 271).

7 Tuoi Tre Weekend Edition, 17 August 2007 (http://tuoitre.vn/Tuoi-tre-cuoi-tuan/273979/14-chien-binh-Trieu-Tien-tren-bau-troi-Viet-Nam.html).
Nguyen, Kham and Park, Ju Min, 'From comrades to assassins, North Korea and Vietnam eye new chapter with Trump-Kim summit,' *Reuters*, February 15, 2019.

8 Kim, Jiyul, 'North Korea in the Vietnam War,' in: Sorley, Lewis and Yarborough, Tom and Celeski, Joseph, *Year of the Cock—1969,* Houston, Radix Press, 2017 (pp. 106–145).
Sổ công tác của Đại tướng Văn Tiến Dũng [General Van Tien Dung's Work Notebook], General Staff Headquarters, Historical Review Section, vol. 20, no. 59.

9 Nguyen, Kham and Park, Ju Min, 'From comrades to assassins, North Korea and Vietnam eye new chapter with Trump-Kim summit,' *Reuters*, February 15, 2019.

10 Toperczer, István, *MiG-17 and MiG-19 Units of the Vietnam War*, Oxford, Osprey, 2001 (pp. 14–19).

11 El-Shazly, Saad, 'The Crossing of the Suez,' *American Mideast Research*, 2003 (p. 83).

12 Schlight, Colonel John, *The War in South Vietnam: The Years of the Offensive, 1965–1968*, Washington D.C., Air Force History and Museums Program, 1999 (p. 53).

13 Kim, Jiyul, 'North Korea in the Vietnam War,' in: Sorley, Lewis and Yarborough, Tom and Celeski, Joseph, *Year of the Cock—1969,* Houston, Radix Press, 2017 (pp. 106–145).

14 Nguyen, Kham and Park, Ju Min, 'From comrades to assassins, North Korea and Vietnam eye new chapter with Trump-Kim summit,' *Reuters*, February 15, 2019.

15 Writer's visit to the Victorious Fatherland Liberation War Museum, May 25, 2016.

16 'Telegram from Pyongyang to Bucharest, no. 76.247,' July 6, 1967, Romanian Foreign Ministry Archive.

17 Kim, Jiyul, 'North Korea in the Vietnam War,' in: Sorley, Lewis and Yarborough, Tom and Celeski, Joseph, *Year of the Cock—1969,* Houston, Radix Press, 2017 (pp. 106–145).

18 'Cable from the Chinese Embassy in North Korea to the Foreign Ministry, "On the Transportation of North Korea's Material Aid for Vietnam,"' November 2, 1965, PRC FMA 109-02845-03, 33.
'Cable from the Chinese Embassy in North Korea, "Supplement to the Cable of 25 September 1965,"' September 26, 1965, PRC FMA 109-02845-01, 4.

19 Lê Thanh Nghị, 'Report on Meetings with Party Leaders of Eight Socialist Countries,' 1965.

20 Ibid.

21 *Rodong Sinmun,* April 6, 1965.
'Call for Resolute Action: Kim Ok Sun,' *The Pyongyang Times*, July 29, 1965.

22 *Rodong Sinmun,* April 6, 1965.

23 Telegram, From AmEmbassy, Moscow to SecState, Subject: North Korea, November 14, 1967. Folder POL 7, KOR N, 1/1/67. Box 2262. RG 59: General Records of the Department of State, Central Foreign Policy Files 1967–1969, Political and Defense, POL 7 KOR N to POL 7 KOR N. NARA II.

24 Central Intelligence Agency, United States of America, Directorate of Intelligence, Intelligence Report, *The Sino-Soviet Dispute on Aid to North Vietnam (1965–1968)*, Reference Title ESAU XXXIX.
Abrams, A. B., 'Power and Primacy: The History of Western Intervention in the Asia-Pacific,' Oxford, Peter Lang, 2019 (pp. 563–564).

25 Nguyen, Kham and Park, Ju Min, 'From comrades to assassins, North Korea and Vietnam eye new chapter with Trump-Kim summit,' *Reuters*, February 15, 2019.

26 Gills, Barry K., *Korea versus Korea: A Case of Contested Legitimacy*, London, Routledge, 1996 (p. 64).

27 El-Shazly, Saad, *The Crossing of the Suez*, American Mideast Research, 2003 (pp. 81–83).

28 Leone, Dario, 'An unknown story from the Yom Kippur war: Israeli F-4s vs North Korean MiG-21s,' *The Aviationist,* June 24, 2013.

29 El Shazly, Saad, *The Arab Military Option,* London, Mansel, 1986 (pp. 84–85, 124).
Cenciotti, David, 'Declassified Top Secret: SR-71 Blackbird Mission Over the Middle East,' *The Aviationist,* September 1, 2013.

30 'Egypt's Missile Efforts Succeed with Help from North Korea,' *Wisconsin Project on Nuclear Arms Control,* September 1, 1996.

31 Bechtol, Bruce and Maxwell, David, 'North Korean Military Proliferation in the Middle East and Africa: A Book Launch' Presentation at the Korea Economic Institute of America, September 25, 2018.

32 El Shazly, Saad, *The Arab Military Option,* London, Mansel, 1986 (pp. 189–190).

33 Marcus, Jonathan, 'The Politics of Israel's Security,' *International Affairs*, vol. 65, no. 2, Spring 1989 (p. 233).

34 Berger, Andrea, *Target Markets, North Korea's Military Customers in the Sanctions Era*, Abingdon, Routledge, 2017 (pp. 64–65).

35 El Shazly, Saad, *The Arab Military Option,* London, Mansel, 1986 (pp. 109, 124).

36 Bechtol, Bruce and Maxwell David, 'North Korean Military Proliferation in the Middle East and Africa: A Book Launch' Presentation at the Korea Economic Institute of America, September 25, 2018.
McCarthy, David, *The Sword of David: The Israeli Air Force at War,* New York, Skyhorse, 2014 (p. 9).

37 Mansourov, Alexandre, 'North Korea: Entering Syria's Civil War,' *38 North,* November 25, 2013.

38 Kaplan, Fred, 'Assad's Situation; Syria's Military Machine May be Hollow—But it Isn't' Harmless,' *Slate,* April 15, 2003.

39 Ibid.

40 Berger, Andrea, *Target Markets, North Korea's Military Customers in the Sanctions Era*, Abingdon, Routledge, 2017 (p. 65).

41 Bechtol Jr., Bruce E., *North Korean Military Proliferation in the Middle East and Africa,* Lexington, University Press of Kentucky, 2018 (p. 20).

42 KN-02 Short Range Ballistic Missile, Missiles, *Military Today* (http://www.military-today.com/missiles/kn_02.htm).

43 Borger, Julian and Arie, Sophie, 'US equips Israel with Patriot missile batteries,' *The Guardian*, January 17, 2003.

44 Nagel, Jacob and Schanzer, Jonathan, 'US-Israeli missile defense cooperation sends

clear message to foes,' *The Hill,* August 5, 2019.

45 'Missile Technology Control Regime (MTCR): North Korea's Submitted Pursuant to Resolution 2050 (2012),' S/2013/337, 11 June 2013.
Hughes, Robin, 'SSRC: Spectre at the Table,' *Jane's Defence Weekly*, 22 January 2014.

46 Kaplan, Fred, 'Assad's Situation; Syria's Military Machine May be Hollow—But it Isn't' Harmless,' *Slate,* April 15, 2003.
Gordon, Philip H., 'After Iraq: Is Syria Next?,' *Brookings Institute,* April 25, 2003.

47 *The Military Balance*, Volume 110, International Institute for Strategic Studies, 2010 (Chapter 5, 'Middle East and North Africa').

48 Crail, Peter, 'U.S. Shares Information on NK-Syrian Nuclear Ties,' *Arms Control Today,* vol. 38, no. 4, May 2008.
'Syria Had Covert Nuclear Scheme,' *BBC News,* 25 April 2008.

49 Reynolds, Paul, 'Will Syrian site mystery be solved?,' *BBC*, June 23, 2008.
Broad, William J. 'Syria Rebuilds on Site Destroyed by Israeli Bombs,' *New York Times*, January 12, 2008.

50 Lovelace Jr., Douglas C., *Terrorism: Commentary on Security Documents, Volume 145, The North Korean Threat,* Oxford, Oxford University Press, 2017 (pp. 129–130).

51 Katz, Yaakov and Hendel, Yoaz, *Israel Vs. Iran: The Shadow War,* Dulles, Potmac Books, 2012 (Chapter Three: Operation Orchard).

52 Marcus, Jonathan, 'US Syria claims raise wider doubts,' *BBC News,* April 25, 2008.

53 Berger, Andrea, *Target Markets, North Korea's Military Customers in the Sanctions Era*, Abingdon, Routledge, 2017 (pp. 67–69).

54 Black, Ian, 'UK: Syrian opposition "sole legitimate representative" of the people,' *The Guardian*, November 20, 2012.
Kalman, Aaron, 'US, France recognize Syrian opposition as "legitimate representative" of the people,' *Times of Israel*, November 13, 2012.

55 'Most Syrian rebels sympathise with Isis, says think tank,' *The Guardian,* December 20, 2015.
Peralta, Eyder, '60 Percent Of Syrian Rebels Are Islamist Extremists, Think Tank Finds,' *NPR*, December 20, 2015.

56 'Arms supplied by U.S., Saudi ended up with Islamic State, researchers say,' *Reuters,* December 14, 2017.
Sanger, David E., 'Rebel Arms Flow Is Said to Benefit Jihadists in Syria,' *New York Times,* October 14, 2012.

57 Schneider, Barry R., and Post, Jerrold M., *Know Thy Enemy: Profiles of Adversary Leaders and Their Strategic Cultures*, Montgomery, United States Air Force Counterproliferation Centre, 2003 (p. 224).
Bensahel, Nora and Byman, Daniel, *The Future Security Environment in the Middle East: Conflict, Stability, and Political Change*, Santa Monica, CA, RAND Corporation, 2004 (pp. 154–155).

58 'DPRK Ambassador affirms his country's readiness to support health sector in Syria,' *Syrian Arab News Agency*, July 25, 2016.

59 'Syria names park in capital after N Korea Founder,' *Al Jazeera*, August 31, 2015.

60 'Bechtol, Bruce E., *Military Proliferation to the Middle East in the Kim Jong-un Era: A National Security and Terrorist Threat*, Presentation at Shurat HaDin Law Center, March 5, 2016.

61 Gady, Franz-Stefan, 'Is North Korea Fighting for Assad in Syria?' *The Diplomat*, March 24, 2016.
Mansourov, Alexandre Y., 'North Korea Coming to Assad's Rescue,' *The Korea Times*, June 13, 2013.

62 Gady, Franz-Stefan, 'Is North Korea Fighting for Assad in Syria?' *The Diplomat*, March 24, 2016.

63 Bechtol, Bruce and Maxwell, David, 'North Korean Military Proliferation in the Middle East and Africa: A Book Launch' Presentation at the Korea Economic Institute of America, September 25, 2018.
64 Bermudez, Joseph S., *North Korean Special Forces,* Coulsdon, Jane's Publishing, 1988 (p. 2).
65 Ibid. (p. 2).
66 Fitzpatrick, Mark, *North Korean Security Challenges: A Net Assessment*, London, International Institute for Strategic Studies, 2011 (p. 50).
67 McDowall, Angus, 'Long reach of U.S. sanctions hits Syria reconstruction,' *Reuters*, September 2, 2018.
Spyer, Jonathan, 'Trump's Syria Policy Is Working,' *Foreign Policy,* July 1, 2020.
Website of the U.S. Department of State, Under Secretary for Economic Growth, Energy, and the Environment, Bureau of Economic and Business Affairs, Counter Threat Finance and Sanctions, Economic Sanctions Policy and Implementation, Syria Sanctions (https://2009-2017.state.gov/e/eb/tfs/spi/syria/index.htm).
68 'Report: North Korea wants to help Syria rebuild,' *Washington Post*, May 1, 2019.
69 Statement by former NSC official Howard Teicher to the U.S. District Court, Southern District of Florida, January 31, 1995.
70 Galbraith, Peter W. 'The true Iraq appeasers,' *The Boston Globe*. August 31, 2006.
Statement by former NSC official Howard Teicher to the U.S. District Court, Southern District of Florida, January 31, 1995.
71 Dowell, William, 'Iraqi-French nuclear deal worries Israel,' *Christian Science Monitor,* July 31, 1980.
72 Drury, Tom, 'How Iraq built its weapons programs, with a little help from its friends,' *St. Petersburg Times*, March 16, 2003.
73 Friedman, Alan, *Spider's Web: The Secret History of How the White House Illegally Armed Iraq*, New York, Bantam Books, 1993.
Cushman Jr., John H., 'U.S. Strikes 2 Iranian Oil Rigs and Hits 6 Warships in Battles Over Mining Sea Lanes in Gulf,' *New York Times,* April 19, 1988.
74 Armstrong, Charles, *Tyranny of the Weak: North Korea and the World, 1950–1992*, Ithica, NY, Cornell University Press, 2013 (pp. 185–196).
75 'World's Biggest Guns; North Korea's Massive Koksan Howitzers and the Evolution of the Country's Strike Capabilities,' *Military Watch Magazine*, June 15, 2018.
76 Trade Registers, Arms Transfer Database, Stockholm International Peace Research Institute (Retrieved August 13, 2019).
'Chonma Ho; How North Korea Developed and Has Extensively Modernised its First Indigenous Battle Tank,' *Military Watch Magazine,* June 14, 2019.
77 Trevithick, Joseph, 'Why These Really Strange North Korean Guns Are Turning Up Almost Everywhere,' *National Interest*, November 7, 2018.
Mitzer, Stijn, 'N. Korean Arms Found in Vessel Intercepted Off Coast of Oman,' *NK News*, March 16, 2016.
78 Kubota, Yoko, 'Israel Says Seized North Korean Arms Were for Hamas, Hezbollah,' *Reuters*, 12 May 2010.
79 'Leader Meets with Chairman of North Korean Assembly,' *Khamenei.ir,* September 1, 2012.
Shim, Elizabeth, 'North Korea's Kim Yong Nam leaves for 10-day Iran trip,' *UPI,* August 1, 2017.
80 Segal, Udi, *IDF Radio* (Tel Aviv), March 22, 1994.
81 Worldwide Intelligence Review, Hearing Before the Select Committee on Intelligence of the United States Senate, One Hundred Fourth Congress, First Session on Worldwide Intelligence Review, January 10, 1995 (p. 105).
82 Hume, Tim, 'Iran Test-Fires New Generation Long-Range Ballistic Missiles, State Media Report,' *CNN*, October 11, 2015.

Lennox, Duncan, *Jane's Strategic Weapons Systems*, Issue 50, Surrey, Jane's Information Group, 2009 (p. 78).

83 'Iran Launches Missile Strike into Syria in Response to Tehran Attacks,' *Times of Israel*, June 18, 2017.

84 'Iran shows strong hand with strike + impact video,' *Press TV*, June 19, 2017.

85 Bechtol Jr., Bruce E., *North Korean Military Proliferation in the Middle East and Africa,* Lexington, University Press of Kentucky, 2018 (p. 88).
Spencer, Richard, 'N Korea "Tests New Missile in Iran,"' *The Telegraph*, May 17, 2007.

86 Broad, William J. and Glanz, James and Sanger, David E., 'Iran Fortifies its Arsenal with the Aid of North Korea,' *New York Times,* November 28, 2010.

87 Uria, Daniel, 'Iran conducts successful test of Khorramshahr ballistic missile,' *UPI*, September 23, 2017.

88 Broad, William J. and Glanz, James and Sanger, David E., 'Iran Fortifies its Arsenal with the Aid of North Korea,' *New York Times,* November 28, 2010.

89 Berger, Andrea, *Target Markets, North Korea's Military Customers in the Sanctions Era,* Abingdon, Routledge, 2017 (p. 76).
Crail, Peter, 'Iran Lauds Development of Solid Fuel Missile,' *Arms Control Today*, vol. 38, no. 1, January/ February 2008.
'Iran-Bound Rocket Fuel Component Seized in Singapore,' *Iran Watch*, September 1, 2010.

90 Binnie, Jeremy, 'Iran shows submarine-launched missile,' *Janes*, February 27, 2019.

91 'Iran attempts submarine cruise missile launch—US officials,' *RT*, May 3, 2017.

92 Bechtol Jr., Bruce E., *North Korean Military Proliferation in the Middle East and Africa,* Lexington, University Press of Kentucky, 2018 (p. 95).

93 Episkopos, Mark, 'Iran's Islamic Revolutionary Guard Corps Are Some of the Toughest Fighters in the World,' *National Interest,* August 15, 2019.

94 Episkopos, Mark, 'Behold: Iran's Mini-Submarine Force Is Dangerous (Partly Thanks to North Korea),' *National Interest,* May 26, 2019.

95 Shahla, Arsalan and Nasseri, Ladane, 'Iran Raises Stakes in U.S. Showdown with Threat to Close Hormuz,' April 22, 2019.

96 Gao, Charlie, 'China Will Be Mad: Did North Korea Offer to Help Taiwan Build Submarines?,' *National Interest,* April 20, 2019.

97 Nagasawa, Tsuyoshi and Tanaka, Takayuki, 'Could Iran be behind North Korea's nuclear, missile advances?,' *Nikkei Asian Review*, September 26, 2017.

98 'Missile Technology Control Regime (MTCR): Iran's Ballistic Missile Program,' cable #08STATE105013, October 1, 2008 (accessed via Wikileaks on June 10, 2019).

99 'Update concerning Conversion of Space Launch Vehicles to Ballistic Missiles,' *US State Department*, February 24, 2010 (published on Wikileaks).

100 Berger, Andrea, *Target Markets, North Korea's Military Customers in the Sanctions Era,* Abingdon, Routledge, 2017 (p. 72).
Ait, Abraham, 'Is North Korea's MiG-29 Fleet Growing?,' *The Diplomat*, November 29, 2018.
Joo, Sung Ho and Kwak, Tae Hwan, 'Military Relations Between Russia and North Korea,' *The Journal of East Asian Affairs*, vol. 15, no. 2, Fall/Winter 2001 (pp. 287–323).

101 Hughes, Robin, 'Tehran Takes Steps to Protect Nuclear Facilities,' *Jane's Defence Weekly*, January 25, 2006 (pp. 4–5).
Niksch, Larry A., *North Korea's Nuclear Weapons Development and Diplomacy*, Congressional Research Service, 2010 (p. 25).

102 Katz, Yaakov, 'It's up to Israelis to stop Iran's nuclear program. Here's how they did it before,' *Washington Post,* May 14, 2019.
Keck, Zachary, 'US Tests Iran "Bunker Buster" Bomb…So What?,' *The. Diplomat,* June 12, 2013.

'Iran nuclear sites may be beyond reach of "bunker busters,"' *Reuters,* January 12, 2012.

103 Pearson, James, and Park, Ju-min, 'North Korea overcomes poverty, sanctions with cut-price nukes,' *Reuters*, January 11, 2016

104 'North Korea Supplied Nuclear Software to Iran: German Report,' *Reuters*, August 4, 2011.

105 Warrick, Joby, 'IAEA Says Foreign Expertise Has Brought Iran to the Threshold of Nuclear Capability,' *Washington Post*, November 6, 2011.

106 'Hundreds of N. Koreans Working at Iran Nuke Facilities,' *Chosun Ilbo*, November 14, 2011.

107 Bergman, Ronen, 'When Israel hatched a secret plan to assassinate Iranian scientists,' *Politico*, March 6, 2018.

108 Solomon, Jay, 'Iran Seen Trying New Path to a Bomb,' *Wall Street Journal,* August 5, 2013.
Asculai, Ephraim, 'The Plutonium Track: Implications for the Completion of Iran's Heavy Water Reactor at Arak,' Discussion Meeting, International Institute for Strategic Studies, London, Arundel House, September 11, 2013.

109 Bechtol Jr., Bruce E., *North Korean Military Proliferation in the Middle East and Africa,* Lexington, University Press of Kentucky, 2018 (p. 93).

110 'France's Intervention in the Persian Gulf—Why Restricting Iran's Missile Program is Critical for the West to Maintain a Favourable Balance of Power in the Region,' *Military Watch Magazine,* November 13, 2017.

111 'Poor Deterrent? Of Iran's Seventeen Fighter Squadrons, Only Two Retain Long Range Air to Air Capabilities,' *Military Watch Magazine,* May 14, 2019.
Cordesman, Anthony H., *Iran's Military Forces in Transition: Conventional Threats and Weapons of Mass Destruction*, London, Praeger, 1999 (pp. 70–71).
Childs, Nick, 'Iran sanctions cripple ageing military,' *BBC News,* July 28, 2010.

112 Hersh, Seymour M., 'Target Qaddafi,' *New York Times,* February 22, 1987.

113 Oliemans, Joost and Mitzer, Stijn, 'North Korea and Libya: friendship through artillery,' *NK News*, January 5, 2015.

114 Risen, James and Mazzetti, Mark and Schmidt, Michael S., 'U.S. Approved Arms for Libya Rebels Fell Into Jihadis' Hands,' *New York Times,* December 5, 2012.
'MPs attack Cameron over Libya "collapse,"' *BBC*, September 14, 2016.

115 Missile Defense Project, "Hwasong-6 ('Scud C' Variant)," Missile Threat, *Center for Strategic and International Studies*, August 8, 2016, last modified June 15, 2018 (https://missilethreat.csis.org/missile/hwasong-6/).

116 'N, Korea sells missiles to Libya,' *Dong-A Ilbo*, September 25, 2000.
Seth, Michael, J., *North Korea: A History,* London, Red Globe Press, 2018 (p. 211).
Ramsey, Syed, *Tools of War: History of Weapons in Modern Times,* New Delhi, Alpha Editions, 2016 (Chapter 4: Ballistic Missile).

117 'Gaddafi's son: Libya like McDonald's for NATO—fast war as fast food,' *RT,* Interview with Saif Al Islam Published on July 1, 2011.

118 Ibid.

119 Ibid.

120 Trainor, Bernard E., 'South Africa's Strategy on Angola Falls Short, Enhancing Cubans' Role,' *New York Times,* July 12, 1988.

121 James III, W. Martin, *A Political History of the Civil War in Angola: 1974–1990,* New Brunswick, Transaction Publishers, 2011 (p. 207–214, 239–245).

122 Bechtol, Bruce E., 'North Korea and Support to Terrorism: An Evolving History,' *Journal of Strategic Security,* vol. 3, no. 2, Summer 2010 (p. 47).

123 'Angola/North Korea relations considered excellent,' *Agencia Angola Press*, November 18, 2013.

124 Young, Benjamin R., 'North Korea: Opponents of Apartheid,' *NK News,* December 16, 2013.

125 'Hezbollah a North Korea-Type Guerilla Force,' *Intelligence Online*, no. 529, August 25–September 7, 2006.
'Hezbollah As A Strategic Arm of Iran,' *Intelligence and Terrorism Information Centre at the Centre for Special Studies,* September 8, 2006.
126 'North Koreans Assisted Hezbollah with Tunnel Construction,' *Terrorism Focus, The Jamestown Foundation*, vol. III, issue 30, August 1, 2006.
127 Dilegge, Dave and Bunker Robert J. and Keshavarz, Alma, *Iranian and Hezbollah Hybrid Warfare Activities: A Small Wars Journal Anthology*, Amazon Media, 2016 (p. 258).
128 Gabriel, Richard A., *Operation Peace for Galilee, The Israeli-PLO War in Lebanon*, New York, Hill & Wang, 1984 (pp. 164, 165).
129 'North Koreans Assisted Hezbollah with Tunnel Construction,' *Terrorism Focus, The Jamestown Foundation*, vol. III, issue 30, August 1, 2006.
Staff, Toi and Ari Cross, Judah, 'IDF reveals "longest most significant" Hezbollah tunnel on northern border,' *Times of Israel*, May 30, 2019.
Hancocks, Paula, 'Is North Korea still digging tunnels to the South?,' *CNN*, November 2, 2014.
130 Spyer, Jonathan, 'Behind the Axis: The North Korean Connection,' *Jerusalem Post,* May 22, 2010.
131 Dilegge, Dave and Bunker Robert J. and Keshavarz, Alma, *Iranian and Hezbollah Hybrid Warfare Activities: A Small Wars Journal Anthology*, Amazon Media, 2016 (p. 261).
'Iranian officer: Hezbollah has commando naval unit,' *Sharq al-Awsat*, July 29, 2006.
132 Dilegge, Dave, Bunker, Robert J. and Keshavarz, Alma, *Iranian and Hezbollah Hybrid Warfare Activities: A Small Wars Journal Anthology*, Amazon Media, 2016 (pp. 260–261).
133 'The Hezbollah Challenge . . . An Alternate Paradigm?' Assistant Deputy Chief of Staff for Intelligence (DCSINT), U.S. Army Training and Doctrine Command, Fort Monroe, VA, No Date.
Tira, Ron, interview by Matt M. Matthews, 23 September 2007.
134 Mohammed, Arshad, 'North Korea may have aided Hezbollah, LTTE—U.S. report,' *Reuters*, December 13, 2007.
Moon, Chung-in, 'The Syrian Nuke Connection,' *Joongang Ilbo*, November 26, 2007.
135 Blanford, Nicholas and Shaab, Alma, 'Inside Hizballah's Hidden Bunkers,' *Time*, March 29, 2007.
Dilegge, Dave, Bunker, Robert J. and Keshavarz, Alma, *Iranian and Hezbollah Hybrid Warfare Activities: A Small Wars Journal Anthology*, Amazon Media, 2016 (pp. 260–261).
136 Lenny Ben-David, 'Mining for Trouble in Lebanon,' *Jerusalem Post*, October 29, 2007,
137 Blanford, Nicholas and Shaab, Alma, 'Inside Hizballah's Hidden Bunkers,' *Time*, March 29, 2007.
138 'Bulsae-3 in South Lebanon: How Hezbollah Upgraded its Anti-Armour Capabilities with North Korean Assistance,' *Military Watch Magazine*, September 3, 2019.
139 Binnie, Jeremy, 'IDF corroborates Hizbullah "Scud-D" claims,' *IHS Jane's 360*, March 2, 2015.
Harel, Amos and Issacharoff, Avi, 'Syria Is Shipping Scud Missiles to Hezbollah,' *Haaretz,* April 12, 2010.
Badran, Tom, *Hezbollah's Growing Threat Against U.S. National Security Interests in the Middle East,* Hearing before House Foreign Affairs Committee Subcommittee on Middle East and North Africa, Washington D. C., March 22, 2016.

Chapter 11

THE U.S. MILITARY IN SOUTH KOREA

"Liberation": Imposing American Military Rule and Abolishing the People's Republic

Critical to understanding the nature of the relationship between North Korea and the United States—the resistance state and the imperial hegemon—is an understanding of the parallel but opposite relationship which exists between South Korea and the United States—the client state and its former ruler. An assessment of the history and nature of the U.S.-ROK relationship reveals much regarding both American intentions towards the Korean nation as a whole, and the fate Pyongyang has ardently sought to avoid for three quarters of a century.

Paving the way for the first landing of U.S. forces in Korea, American military aircraft dropped three thousand leaflets over southern Korea for four consecutive days starting on September 1, 1945 by order of General Douglas MacArthur. Addressed "To the People of Korea," they announced:

> The armed forces of the United States will soon arrive in Korea for the purpose of receiving the surrender of the Japanese forces, enforcing the terms of surrender, and insuring the orderly administration and rehabilitation of the country. These missions will be carried out with a firm hand, but with a hand that will be guided by a nation whose long heritage of democracy has fostered kindly feeling for peoples less fortunate. How well and how rapidly these tasks are carried out will depend on the Koreans themselves.[1]

A more threatening second proclamation was issued in the same way on September 7, carrying a personal address from General MacArthur, who identified himself as "Commander-in-Chief, United States Army Forces, Pacific." It proclaimed:

> Any Person Who:
>
> Violates the provision of the Instrument of Surrender, or any proclamation, order or directive given under the authority of the Commander-in-Chief, United States Army Forces, Pacific, or does any act to the prejudice of good order or the life, safety or security of the persons or property of the United States or its Allies, or does any act calculated to disturb public peace and order, or prevent the administration of justice, or wilfully does any act hostile to the Allied forces, shall upon conviction by a military Occupation Court, suffer death or such other punishment as the Court may determine.[2]

Whether the Koreans would be killed or punished depended on how well they abided by the will of their new master. In imposing its military rule, the United States expected total obedience. At this time, however, the Korean population was already governing itself through elected officials and committees under the People's Republic of Korea, which made the imposition of foreign military rule without consultation of the Koreans themselves appear more like an invasion to assert foreign interests than an attempt to restore order. The way this was imposed raised a number of questions regarding the consistency of the military's rhetoric—with the persona of the benevolent liberator expressed in the first set of leaflets contrasting with that of an invader imposing its will indicated in the second. Could America claim to "liberate" southern Korea while at the same time occupying it, forcefully dismantling its existing government and threatening those Koreans who did not abide by its will with death? Ernst Fraenkel, an influential jurist and leading advisor for the U.S. Military Government in Korea, summarised his observations of the nature of American military rule over the country: "Military occupation of a 'liberated country' is basically self-contradictory."[3] "Liberation" during the Cold War increasingly became a euphemism for bringing a country into the Western sphere of influence—or what soon began to be called the "Free World" to conceal its Western-dominated nature. This new definition of "liberation" would become commonplace and remains so today.[4]

Protests against American rule, described by Western observers as "absolutely ordered and peaceful," were widespread and made it clear that the imposition of foreign authority and undermining of self-governance was not welcome. Korean independence groups slammed bans by the U.S. Military Government on public protest and public assembly, and the position of the general populace was well known to the Americans.[5] As the governor Lieutenant General John R. Hodge observed: "The Koreans want their independence more than any one thing and want it now."[6]

The accounts of Ernst Fraenkel, who arrived in Korea as the occupation was being established, are insightful as to the state of affairs at this time. Korea was one of the few places on Earth which Western militaries had yet to occupy, and as such Western cultural influences remained relatively few. Fraenkel thus described the lives of the Korean populace as a "completely separate world" from that of the Western occupiers, for whom the prospect of eating Korean food was "phantastic"—something beyond consideration. Based on the vast differences between the American military governance and those upon whom American rule was being imposed, Fraenkel questioned:

> whether it is possible to have any contacts with them, except a very small crust of intellectuals who have been educated in U.S., Europe and Japan… And now we try to do the job to govern these people of whom we know so little and whom we will probably never understand. We enact statutes and even a constitution, establish institutions which are wholly based on occidental thinking and apply ideas to the government of this country which are meaningful only in the framework of our tradition and civilisation.[7]

According to the German jurist, the goal of the American military government he was serving was to remake southern Korea in America's image—into a "virulently anti-Communist" state indefinitely intertwined with American material and political interests.[8]

The treatment of the Korean population by U.S. military personnel was particularly poor, contrasting strongly with conduct towards allied European populations at the time. This served as another demonstration of the true nature of the two nations' relationship—far from that of liberator and liberated which the Americans claimed as pretext for imposing their rule. As the office of General Hodge itself observed: "Americans act as though Koreans were a conquered nation rather than a liberated people."[9] Widespread portrayals in American state media of the Pacific War with Imperial Japan as a race war, as part of the "perpetual wars between Oriental ideas and Occidental" and a crusade for Western civilisation, likely influenced Americans to perceive Koreans as part of the East Asian resistance to Western rule under the Japanese Empire—rather than as an involuntary colony of Japan.[10] It was notable that during the war, Korean comfort women forced to serve the Japanese Imperial Army overseas had been targeted for rape by American soldiers just as Japanese women were—there was no distinction made between them.[11] Perceptions of the Japanese Empire as one which would "combine most of the Asiatic peoples against the whites"[12] had a key influence on perceptions of Asian populations, stimulating greater animosity towards them.[13] This only grew as Korean resistance and the Korean People's Republic were depicted as affiliates of global communism—which even before Japan's subjugation had begun to replace the Empire of the Sun in Western propaganda as the new great adversary of both America and the wider Western world.[14]

The office of General Hodge had observed regarding the occupation period: "Americans are ignorant of Korean customs, show no appreciation of Korean art or culture, and openly ridicule the idea that there can be any good in anything Korean."[15] Staff sergeant Robert H. Moyer, who served in southern Korea, stated: "Before the war, Koreans considered us as another occupier of their county. And after the elections in 1948, we were only permitted off post in groups of 3 or more, for safety reasons. They disliked us."[16] Indeed, even many of those South Koreans considered Americanized before the war, those who "went to school in the USA, smoked USA cigarettes, spoke American," appeared to loathe the U.S. occupation and would go on to side with the Korean People's Army in the Korean War.[17]

South Koreans' ill feeling towards Americans came not only from the forceful abolition of their republic, sustainment of the Japanese imperial system and protection of collaborators from what was widely seen to be the people's justice, but also from American soldiers' abusive treatment of Korean civilians. Perceptions and treatment of Koreans remained relatively consistent both during the occupation period and in the following decades. The U.S. Eighth Army reported in 1951 regarding the apparently sadistic pleasure personnel took in tormenting the Korean people that soldiers: "take a perverse delight in frightening civilians" and using force to "drive the Koreans off roads and into ditches."[18] U.S. personnel were known to regularly commit violent, humiliating and abusive acts against regular South Korean civilians who had worked for them.[19]

As one U.S. Marine stated, effectively summarising what appeared to be the predominant attitude among Americans in Korea: "They're just a bunch of gooks. Who cares about the feelings of people like that?"[20] Historian Lloyd Lewis wrote regarding the indoctrination American personnel received before being sent to war in East Asia: "soldiers in all branches of the armed services recount receiving the same indoctrination, that the enemy is Oriental and inferior."[21] The population in southern Korea and those in other East Asian states hosting American forces were forced to bear the brunt of this.

An American survey carried out in the 1960s in South Korea and West Germany showed how the attitudes of U.S. personnel towards populations in countries where they were deployed influenced how they were perceived. Of South Koreans questioned, only 13 percent thought Americans "liked them" while 70 percent of West Germans assumed Americans not only liked them but viewed them "as friends."[22] While Americans had greater historical reasons to mistreat the German population as an enemy, cultural and racial factors meant that treatment of a Western population was always far more respectful than that towards an East Asian nation. The U.S. Military itself appeared to make the difference official through its publications. While the opportunity to explore cultural sites such as castles and learn about a new country were used to promote deployments to Germany, by contrast easy access to servile comfort women was used to attract soldiers to Korea—there was not considered to be any culture to speak of worth promoting.[23] The nature of the relationship between the United States and South Korea was demonstrated by the former's extensive use of comfort women from the latter. The comfort women system was established under direct American military rule but would continue long afterwards. U.S. Army Colonel Donald Portway had thus concluded regarding the prime function of the U.S. Military Government in southern Korea: "The American Military government had as its basic purpose the provision of banquets, gifts and feminine company"—a conclusion he was far from alone in reaching.[24]

Serving the U.S. Military: Comfort Women in South Korea

Describing the perks of deployment to Korea, the American military newspaper *Stars and Stripes* specifically highlighted the attraction of access to servile Korean women—strongly objectifying them, and in doing so, encouraging similar perceptions from readers. It wrote: "Picture having three or four of the loveliest creatures God ever created hovering around you, singing, dancing, feeding you, washing what they feed you down with rice wine and beer, all saying at once: 'you are the greatest.' This is the Orient you heard about and came to find." The paper encouraged American soldiers to take part in Korea's "night-time action," calling it "the ultimate experience"—which was thought to allude to the experience at camptowns near U.S. bases where soliciting prostitutes, many coerced into the trade, was extremely common.[25]

Approximately 84 percent of Americans deployed in the Korea surveyed admitted to having been with comfort women. A U.S. captain deployed in Korea said there was an overwhelming cultural pressure among enlisted men to seek out prostitutes, and even those initially against the idea would end up participating.[26] When U.S. Navy ships were set to dock in the Philippines or Korea, officers "threw the men condoms as if they were Hallmark cards." Officers were known to tell their men that prostitution was a way of life for East Asians, and that Asians like prostitution, which they "enthusiastically promoted."[27] Although this was used to justify the exploitation of Korean women, the extent to which chastity was valued in Korean society, and extra-marital sex or prostitution was abhorred, had few equals in the world. In her comprehensive study of the evolving Korean perceptions of chastity, Professor Katrina Maynes repeatedly emphasized how chastity was vital for a woman to be respected and considered of value. She wrote:

> Respectable women…were expected to uphold their chastity at all times. Their virginity was their greatest asset and their key to an honourable marriage. They were instructed to guard their chastity with their life, and in the case of rape, women were taught that suicide was preferable. Respectable women could prove their honour through demonstrating chastity and upholding their husbands in life and death.[28]

Nevertheless, it suited the American agenda to depict Koreans as a population which "liked prostitution" to dispel any moral qualms soldiers may have had against making full use of the opportunities provided to them.

U.S. military personnel's use of comfort women reportedly began as soon as the first American soldiers landed in Korea, with the comfort women held to serve Japanese imperial forces raped by the Americans.[29] Again the contrast between the depiction of the U.S. as a liberator and actual American conduct, that of a particularly brutal conqueror, was evident. Japan's system of comfort stations was later vastly expanded under American rule and women were provided with modest salaries. Many of the first generation of prostitutes working for the U.S. were in fact former comfort women for the Japanese Imperial Army, working under a remarkably similar system.[30] In the centre of downtown Seoul the U.S. Army occupied the 640-Acre Yongsan garrison that had been built for the Japanese Army. The neighbourhood quickly filled with brothels servicing U.S. troops, and GIs came to call the area "Hooker Hill." American expert Professor Arissa Oh noted on the comfort system's origins: "During the period of U.S. occupation (1945–1948) camptowns, or *kijich'on* quickly sprang up around American military bases throughout South Korea. The system of US-oriented prostitution was built on the foundation established by the Japanese colonial government."[31]

Scholars Maria Hohn and Seungsook Moon, who carried out a detailed investigation into the comfort women system, noted regarding its establishment to service the U.S. Military:

> The demise of [Japanese] colonial rule did not end the use of women's sexual labour for foreign soldiers in Korea. Projecting its image as a "benevolent liberator" to teach democracy to Koreans, the U.S. military was deeply implicated in various forms of prostitution from the dawn of its occupation of Korea… The so-called decolonizing process led by the U.S. military continued to provide fertile soil for the rapid growth of private and unregulated prostitution (sach'ang) in Seoul, Ascom, Taejon, Kwangju, and Pusan… Well-paid American soldiers aggressively sought out local women for sexual services. American GIs chased after Korean women in the context of racialized cultural difference, coupled with racism against the Koreans by GIs… Military authorities had to deal with the pervasive problems of the deterioration of military courtesy, discipline, appearance, and training. Under the category of courtesy, the authorities addressed widespread racism against the Koreans, ranging from the use of the racial slur "gooks," physical assaults, reckless driving, and undue arrests of Koreans to making aggressive passes at Korean women…. GIs viewed sexual access to Korean women outside the respectability of marriage as their entitlement,

> as agents of European colonialism did towards colonized women of colour.[32]

Much like in Japan at the time, where Western occupation was also imposed,[33] from the early days of the U.S. Military Government in early September 1945 there were widespread reports of rapes by American military personnel outside the comfort women system. While there are scant records of the individual cases of rape, as it was in the interest of neither the military government nor the subsequent Syngman Rhee government to keep them, there is substantial evidence from both Korean and American sources that widespread rapes did take place, including testimonies from South Korean victims. According to the U.S. National Archives and Records Administration, the Korean population, though forced to tolerate the GIs' relations with prostitutes, complained of the widespread rapes of women outside this system.[34] A South Korean soldier interviewed stated to similar effect: "I was conscripted into the ROK army and had to do sentry duty at the house of a big-shot American. Each night they took our Korean girls in there to be defiled. I don't want your sort of 'Free World.'"[35] Professor Arissa Oh, an expert on the occupation period, noted regarding these incidents: "Rape of local women was largely undocumented but widespread enough to prompt complaints from South Korean officials." It was highly in keeping with their conduct elsewhere for U.S. troops deployed across the region to commit rapes *en-masse* against women—a practice also extremely common from 1945 in Japan[36] and later in Vietnam.[37]

Franziska Donner, the Austrian wife of President Syngman Rhee, claimed that establishment of comfort stations where Korean women would serve American personnel had been necessary, as GIs had previously kept "taking" any woman they wanted—a reference to widespread rapes.[38] From a woman who strongly supported the occupation, whose husband had been hand-picked by the U.S. military to assume power, this admission was a powerful indicator as to the extent of the sexual crimes being perpetrated. Reports by victims and their families of mass rapes were so widespread and pervasive that they prompted complaints by South Korean officials to U.S. commanders.[39] Comfort stations were seen as a way to prevent this by providing American personnel with controlled access to Korean women. While it was an essential part of the American occupation to try to be seen as benevolent democratizing saviours, rather than as rapacious conquerors, accounts from the time strongly indicate the latter was much closer to the truth.

Comfort Women After American Military Rule

The end of formal U.S. military rule over southern Korea in 1948 and the establishment of the Republic of Korea under Syngman Rhee's rule saw the country continue to provide comfort women to service American personnel. The government put in place by the U.S. Military was instrumental in encouraging the continuation of the comfort women system, both directly and indirectly. Professors Seungsook Moon and Maria Hohn concluded in their study of the comfort women system that the Rhee government relied heavily on prostitution to provide foreign currency as a result of its ineptitude in economic management, stating: "In the face of dire wartime poverty, the way the Korean government viewed prostitution as an inevitable means to feed its people."[40] Ms. Kim, a former prostitute, recalled when interviewed regarding government policies: "They urged us to sell as much as possible to the GI.s, praising us as 'dollar earning patriots.'"[41] By the early 1960s the South Korean government relied on the comfort women system to provide 24 percent of the country's Gross National Product (GNP), far more than the system serving the Japanese Imperial Army ever had.[42] As Kim Ae Ran, a 58-year-old former prostitute interviewed in 2009, said: "Our government was one big pimp for the U.S. military."[43]

During 12 years in office Rhee's administration never instituted a national economic policy and the ROK made almost no economic or social progress. As professors Uk Heo and Terrence Roehrig noted in their study of South Korean political history, alongside rampant corruption "Rhee also had little expertise or interest in economic development, and his economic ministers were similarly inexperienced and untrained in economic policy making."[44] Supporting the comfort women system provided the Rhee government with a means of earning foreign currency, compensating for its own economic ineptitude.

Few investigations were made into government involvement in the comfort women system in South Korea, although the *New York Times* was several decades later able to conduct an investigation and interview former prostitutes. Those interviewed claimed their government had been heavily involved in human trafficking in relation to the sex trade and provision for the U.S. Military for many decades. The investigators reviewed South Korean and American documents, which they concluded "do provide some support for many of the women's claims." Although the South Korean government remained silent on the issue, in 2006 Kim Kee Joe, a government official and former high level liaison to the U.S.

Military, admitted in a televised interview: "Although we did not actively urge them to engage in prostitution, we, especially those from the county offices, did often tell them that it was not something bad for the country either."[45]

The state's active encouragement of the comfort women system servicing the U.S. Military was confirmed in a ruling by the Seoul High Court on February 8, 2018. This policy had been adopted for the sake of both strengthening the military alliance and earning foreign currency. The court concluded: "In regarding the right to sexual self-determination of the women in the camptown and the very character of the plaintiffs as represented through their sexuality as means of achieving state goals, the state violated its obligation to respect human rights." It further reported: "according to official Ministry of Health and Welfare documents, [the state] actively encouraged women in the military camptowns to engage in prostitution to allow foreign troops to 'relax' and 'enjoy sexual services' with them."[46]

A number of means were used to coerce women into entering the comfort women system and providing sexual services to American personnel. One very significant, though indirect, means of coercion was the destitution which had resulted from the policies of both the U.S. Military and Rhee government. The wartime scorched earth policy, destroying entire towns and villages across Korea and burning the crops and livelihoods which people had relied on for generations, left a large segment of the population with few possessions and no means of providing for themselves. At a conservative estimate, the war created two million refugees in South Korea—and between 20 and 25 percent of the population at the end of the war could not support themselves. Little was done to compensate these families or help them restart their livelihoods.[47] This combined with Rhee's economic ineptitude, his focus on militarisation, the low wages available to conscripts and the poor social welfare available meant many Korean families faced very serious destitution. Thus, both during the war, and afterwards when a presence of hundreds of thousands of Americans remained, many women, particularly mothers with dependants, had no choice but to enter the comfort women system. The claim that the comfort women system was based on consent thus strongly contradicts the available evidence from both South Korean and U.S. sources.

Professor Arissa Oh concluded in her own study: "Many women had few options other than questionable employment in tearooms, restaurants, and bars, where a thin line separated the hostess and the sex worker. Other women were seduced through false promises, or raped. Widows often resorted to sex work to support their children."[48] It was often the reality that women had to either sell their bodies to Western soldiers or see their children starve. In 1952, the final year of the Korean War, the U.S. State Department reported that of the "UN Aunties," a term for the prostitutes servicing the Western soldiers, half were widows. This statistic alone is highly indicative as to the true nature of prostitution in wartime and post-war South Korea and the desperation of those who entered the trade.[49]

Seungsook Moon and Maria Hohn publicized the findings of their investigation on the methods of coercion used to obtain comfort women for American forces after the Korean War, stating:

> It appears that, while some women would have been trafficked through force and deception, the masses of impoverished Korean women, single and married, were mainly recruited by private businesses that secured approval from authorities. The majority of women working in UN comfort stations were married, which suggests that sexual labour was a desperate attempt to feed children and families. The force of abject poverty and the death, disability, and displacement of men during the Korean War further multiplied the number of women who had to prostitute themselves for survival.[50]

Based on an analysis of the circumstances, it is clear that what was called consensual was actually very far from consensual work, with a primary workforce of widows and married women being a strong indicator of this. The conditions which forced women into prostitution were caused by the very same external actors who benefited from having access to large numbers of desperate Korean women.

A number of other studies of the comfort women system reached similar conclusions regarding the supposed "consent" of the women who were forced to sexually service Western solders. Referring to the continuity between this system and that which had preceded it on a smaller scale under the Japanese Empire, associate professor at American University in Washington D.C. and expert on foreign and military policy David Vine concluded in his research: "With the assistance of Korean officials,

U.S. authorities continued the system absent formal slavery, but under conditions of exceedingly limited choice for the women involved."[51]

Professor Lee Jin Kyung, an expert on labour migration in South Korea, noted regarding the nature of the "consent" of South Korean women to serve American soldiers that it was hardly worthy of the term. It was in fact very similar to the system of "comfort women" Japan operated, but on a far greater scale. She concluded regarding the nature of prostitution in South Korea:

> Prostitution is an occupation "choice" that is largely forced on them as a matter of bare subsistence and survival… prostitution is an institutionalization of sexual violence via commercialization, for the ways in which the "consent" is forcibly manufactured out of unequal social and economic relations among sex workers, their employers and their clients. In other words, considering this inherent coerciveness and structural violence built into prostitution, I would like to conceptualize prostitution as another kind of necropolitical labour.

"Necropolitical labour" is a term she coined for forced labour, in which there are significant risks of violence and death, evidenced by the number of prostitutes killed or otherwise seriously harmed in their work by GIs, but the alternative to which is death.[52]

In her "Research for the Reform of Law and the Prevention of Prostitution," Elaine Kim concluded that the Korean War and the U.S.–Republic of Korea Mutual Defense Treaty had between them laid the basis for the comfort women system, with wartime destruction separating families and creating orphans and widows. This system "mass produced" women who had no choice but to enter the comfort women system or else starve—leaving women and young girls without homes or livelihoods.[53] Was not the intentional destruction of Korea and the livelihoods of millions with an intensive bombing and scorched earth policy, and with the forceful imposition of leadership as corrupt and inept as that of Rhee, not an indirect way of forcing women into sexual slavery? By destroying a people's lives and their ability to provide for themselves, they were left helpless—after which a reliance on American resources could be fostered. These resources came at the price of comfort women for sexual service. American sociologist Kathleen Barry was one of a number of scholars who observed the similarities between the "industrialization of sex" and the scale of sexual exploitation in South Korea with the sexual exploitation of conquered women by traditional imperial conquerors.[54] Professor Lee Jin Kyung at the University of California also noted that the approach of the United States to guaranteeing access to Korean women was merely a "shift from the Japanese Imperial System of Comfort Women" to a new system with the same ends.[55]

Regarding the means by which South Korean women entered prostitution, coercion and fraud were also extremely common means of recruitment. Flesh-traffickers and pimps would often wait by train and bus stations to greet young girls coming from the countryside, promising them employment and a place to stay. These girls, who often left the countryside to seek work, would then be "initiated" through rape.[56] They would then be employed in sex work or sold to brothels in the camptowns. Advertisements offering jobs as waitresses, shopkeepers and singers were very frequently used to lure women to their "initiation ceremonies," after which they were psychologically broken by the shock and social shame of rape and could be sold into prostitution. Once a girl or woman was in the power of such a system, it was extremely difficult for her to get out. Cultural and psychological reasons were significant factors as these women were now considered fallen and would face significant social stigma and isolation. Pimps and brothel owners who coerced women into prostitution also made extensive use of a debt-bond system, confiscating women's incomes, getting them into debt and punishing any transgressions with violence.[57] It was not unusual for Korean women to have to hand over 80 percent of their earnings to brothel owners, making it nearly impossible for them to pay off their debts.[58]

The South Korean police, notoriously corrupt in the Rhee years, were themselves reported to be involved not only in trading drugs, but also in trafficking women for the comfort women system. According to a prominent study by Professor Lukasz Kamienski: "the police were… actively involved in trafficking in women and smuggling them to brothels, thus providing cover and protection for the entire underground sex and drug trade economy." With police themselves heavily involved in trafficking women, it is difficult to claim that the comfort women system was based on consent. Kamienski was far from the only one to comment on these reports.[59]

Katherine H. S. Moon's research described the reluctance of women to service foreign soldiers and how women were forcefully broken down to be able to provide sexual services to the American soldiers. She stated:

> Most women do not come into the clubs equipped with the "hostessing skills" and the willingness to share flesh with the GIs. For women who are new to the club scene, an initiation process often takes place. Some women attest to having been raped by their pimp/manager; others have been ordered by the club owner to sleep with a particular soldier; yet others stumble into bed with GIs on their own; some receive advice on the type of man to avoid (e.g. violent types) from more experienced prostitutes.[60]

Interviews with a number of comfort women indicated the true nature of "consent" in the system they worked in. Jeon, a former sex worker aged 71, was interviewed by the *New York Times* in 2009. Orphaned in the war at 18 years old she had been forced to begin work in the comfort women system in Dongducheon camptown near the frontlines to service American soldiers. "The more I think about my life, the more I think women like me were the biggest sacrifice for my country's alliance with the Americans. Looking back I think my body was not mine, but the government's and the U.S. Military's," she had said. Jeon had a son in the 1960s but gave him up when he was 13. Selling mixed-race children to families in the United States was common practice for comfort women at the time, many of whom could not afford to raise the children themselves. At the time she was interviewed, Jeon was subsisting by selling items she picked up from trash for a living.[61]

"Johnston's Mom," a pseudonym used by another woman in the comfort woman system, was in her late twenties when interviewed in Songsan, Uijongbu, north of Seoul. Her interviewer described where she lived as "a run-down cement building-front off an alley…a small dark room with gray cement walls and a few pots and pans-the kitchen." Her sons were the children of two different American servicemen, and an American soldier, the father of neither of the boys, had shortly beforehand been living with them. He had provided food in return for sexual services, a "contract cohabitation" which was common in camptowns. She could not bear to sell her sons (European-looking children sold for $50–200) and was forced to resume working as a prostitute to feed them. The interviewer discovered that as per their "contract," "Johnston's

Mom" would have regular sex with the U.S. soldier in the same room as the young boys, as there was nowhere else to go. This case was not particularly outstanding among the millions of relations that a million comfort women had with U.S. soldiers. Such poverty, depravity and exploitation were commonplace.[62]

Comfort Women and U.S.-Korean Relations

The significance and symbolism of the comfort women system as a central part of U.S.-ROK relations sheds considerable light on the nature of American conduct and intentions towards the Korean nation, presenting strong evidence of the fate the DPRK has managed to spare its population by continuing a policy of resistance to forceful integration into the U.S.-led order. Indeed, this issue alone arguably vindicates the DPRK decision to fight for its sovereignty at all costs, and awareness of American intentions based on U.S. relations with South Korea may well contribute to fuelling the north's staunch defiance against America's hegemonic ambitions. As Professor Katherine H. S. Moon wrote: "The sexual domination of tens of thousands of Korean women by 'Yangk'I foreigners' [she later puts the total figure at around 1 million women] is a social disgrace,"[63] one which given the importance of chastity and ethnic pride in Korean culture is something any self-respecting and fully sovereign Korean state would do its utmost to avoid.

Renowned American professor and historian of East Asia Bruce Cumings, a specialist in Korea, holder of South Korea's honourable Kim Dae Jung Academic Award for Outstanding Achievements and Scholarly Contributions to Democracy, Human Rights and Peace and former member of the U.S. Peace Corps stationed in Korea, observed in his assessment of the centrality of the comfort women system to U.S.-ROK relations and its symbolism regarding the overall nature of the relationship:

> One element in the Korean-American relationship has been constant: the continuous subordination of one female generation after another to the sexual servicing of American males, to the requirements of a trade in female flesh that simply cannot be exaggerated. It's the most common form of Korean-American interaction, whether you're a private in the Army, a visiting Congressman (for who special stables are maintained), or a Peace Corps teacher... It's also the

> most silent exchange, as if the trade were chaperoned by the deaf, dumb and blind... It is the aspect that most struck me when I first lived in Korea, creating indelible impressions of a relationship that, because of the use made of Korean women, could not be what it was said to be: a free compact between two independent nations dedicated to democracy and anticommunism.[64]

As a member of the Peace Corps stationed in Korea, who witnessed first-hand what took place in camptowns and the prevalent attitudes among Americans towards Korean society and its women, Cumings' accounts are particularly useful. He observed:

> If someone called attention to the ceaseless orgy, all the usual bromine pour forth to drown out the faint cries of peasant girls yanked off a train in Seoul and thrown into a brothel, a thousand little justifications for the abasement of a thousand little girls at American hands...the social construction of every Korea female as a potential object of pleasure for Americans. It is the most important aspect of the whole relationship and the primary memory of Korea for generations of young American men who have served there... When I told an older "Korea hand" that I was going to Seoul with spouse, he remarked, "why take a sandwich to a banquet?"[65]

In his description of the "whoring district" near an American military base Cumings described what he saw: "ridiculous-looking painted Korean girls—often very young—peer from the doors...a middle -aged woman with two kids hanging on to her who, in the middle of the street, asked me to come and 'hop on' in the chimdeh [bed]." He further observed: "Goofy-looking, stupid soldiers walk arm-in-arm with whores who are often only young girls—*very, very* young girls. How do these men justify this to themselves... [Koreans] simply hate them [the Americans] and exist by pandering to their ever-base desires...the adults avert their eyes when you look at them, and if they don't, they glare at you with a hatred that can be measured—an American who speaks Korean is the only things that shocks them."[66]

According to Cumings, Korean prostitutes of all ages including children were sold under the comfort system. He recalled: "In Seoul women were available on almost every block—in a bathhouse, massage room, restaurant, or in the ubiquitous tea houses all over the city. You could get them very young, probably around twelve; kids were shanghaied into a kind of slavery as they got off the train from the countryside, looking for work to support their peasant families. Kidnapped, gang-raped and beaten by pimps while learning their few necessary words of English, they were ready for the street in a week."[67] His use of the term "slavery," undermines the image of a consensual sex trade which is used to partially justify its existence and deflect criticism from the United States and the Rhee government.

In the 1950s the South Korean population was just 19 million. Of these just over half were females (96.1 males to 100 females as of 1956)[68] and around half again were young women. American soldiers deployed to the country, technically a battle zone due to the armistice, had short rotations of around one year, and those with wives were discouraged from bringing them. The short rotations and significant number of soldiers deployed meant that between 1950 and 1971 around 6 million American soldiers served in Korea. In this time it is estimated that around 1 million Korean women worked in the comfort women system.[69] This was at least five times the number that worked for the Japanese army, the highest estimate for which was "up to 200,000 women, mostly from Korea, but also from other parts of Asia" (meaning well under 200,000 from Korea itself and even less for Korea below the 38th parallel).[70] The figure of 1 million also excludes the significant number of women who were raped by GIs and other foreign personnel outside the comfort women system from 1945 onwards, as the number of rapes committed were not recorded by the government or police. There is only evidence from testimonies, as previously mentioned, that they did take place and on a very wide scale—but there are no exact figures.

It is notable when observing Korean-American and Korean-Japanese relations in the twenty-first century that Japan's taking of under 200,000 Korean comfort women (the majority of its 200,000 comfort women from all Asia, as a highest estimate) is frequently made an issue by politicians and activists, and is a well-publicized crime. At the same time, however, the more recent American use of 1,000,000 South Korean comfort women under terrible conditions and with often highly questionable consent, as well as the rapes of many more, is not mentioned or addressed. South Korea demands apologies from the Japanese government, builds statues in the honour of the comfort women, and is paid reparations by Tokyo. On the other hand, Seoul makes almost no mention of similar crimes committed by the United States, which occurred both more recently and on a larger scale.

The trafficking of comfort women to serve the U.S. forces in the ROK has meanwhile continued on a considerable scale, although many are now trafficked from abroad particularly from the Philippines and sold at auction.[71] Women from overseas continue to be offered jobs in Korea and subsequently forced to service American personnel, with the number of women effectively enslaved in this way numbering in the thousands.[72] A U.S. State Department report found that trafficked Filipina women working in the ROK in the 2000s were so desperate and hungry as to beg U.S. soldiers to bring them bread.[73] A study carried out in 2007 by three professional researchers similarly concluded that U.S. bases in the ROK were "a hub for the transnational trafficking of women from the Asia-Pacific and Eurasia to South Korea and the United States."[74] This raises serious questions regarding the consistency of South Korean condemnations.

The purpose of comparing the coercion of Korean women into military sex work by the Japanese Empire with the far larger scale on which this took place under the U.S. military is not to exempt the former or lessen the rapaciousness or degrading nature of its crime against the Korean people, but rather to bring to light the inherent double standards present in South Korean claims against Japan when considering more recent American crimes. One explanation for these double standards is that the United States exerts very considerable influence over the ROK and has left Seoul dependent on American good will for military and economic support. Just as the Japanese collaborators in Korea did not raise the issue of the Japanese Empire's use of comfort women, publicize their suffering, or demand compensation for their countrywomen, it is similarly unlikely for closely U.S.-aligned South Korean governments to make a case against the United States. A second reason is that the comfort women in Korea were in most cases unpaid by the Japanese, and were essentially slaves.[i] The women serving the United States on the

---

i The United States Office of War Information reported based on interviews with 20 Korean comfort women servicing Japanese forces in Myanmar that they were induced by the offer of plenty of money, an opportunity to help provide their families and pay off family debts, easy work, and for some a new life in Singapore. Many Korean women enlisted for overseas duty based on these promises and were even rewarded with an advance payment of a few hundred yen. The women were forced to remain abroad until they paid their debts, after which many returned to Korea. While this was not how all Korean women who served the Japanese forces were recruited,

other hand are more often depicted as having chosen sex work consensually for financial benefits. While the first is a plausible explanation, the common notion that Korean women consented to sell themselves to the American soldiers, and that the means the U.S. Military used to obtain comfort women were therefore fundamentally different from those used by the Japanese Empire, proves to be largely untrue.

Methods used to recruit comfort women to serve American soldiers involved rape and violence to disorient and break women in. They would afterwards have little choice but to "consent" to sex work for the U.S. Military. The Japanese in Korea had often employed middlemen using similar methods. Pimps recruiting women for the U.S. forces would often advertise jobs as nurses or factory workers and would then force the respondents into sexual slavery. One major difference was that the Japanese saw comfort women as a temporary wartime measure to satisfy soldiers and began recruiting them in large numbers in wartime when they believed men risking their lives for the empire required special rest and recreation. The recruitment of comfort women was not however ever meant to be a permanent state of affairs which would continue into peacetime. By contrast, although there was no open war in Korea for over two decades after 1953, the U.S. Military recruited hundreds of thousands of comfort women during this period. In fact the prostitution industry in South Korea expanded significantly after the war had ended and after the signing of the Korea-U.S. Mutual Defense Treaty that year.[75] While access to comfort women has been considered by a number of militaries throughout history as a means to redress men for risking their lives and enduring the stresses and exhaustion of combat, even this somewhat feeble pretext used by Imperial Japan could not be put forward as an excuse by the United States Military for their conduct in South Korea.[76] In contrast to the Japanese case, the American military's access to comfort women could not be considered a necessary evil of wartime. It was in fact a permanent and indefinite state of affairs, continuing even in peacetime.

Due to the poor state of the ROK's economy under the Rhee government, worsened further by the bombings and scorched earth tactics of the U.S. Military, South Korean women had hunger, even in peacetime, as an incentive to sell themselves. The Japanese Empire had not left the

---

it draws a revealing comparison with how women were similarly recruited women to serve U.S. forces (<http://www.exordio.com/1939-1945/codex/Documentos/report-49-USA-orig.html>).

Asian peoples they conquered starving in peacetime, and to the contrary had made efforts to increase agricultural[77] and industrial[78] outputs of their overseas territories which were highly successful. Due to massive investments in damming and other key infrastructure, Korean agricultural output increased manifold under Japanese rule.[79]

Had the Japanese colonial administration instead left Koreans starving as the American imposed Rhee government had, and as American wartime policies such as scorched earth had exacerbated, perhaps the Imperial Army would have not needed to forcibly recruit comfort women. Directly causing the population's destitution and starvation, and imposing inept administrators—then paying a bare subsistence wage for sexual services was the American way, not that of the Japanese. Did this really make the American comfort women system more "consensual" and "voluntary?" Had the Japan firebombed Korea and enacted scorched earth policies to destroy the people's means of providing for themselves, rather than investing in infrastructure and raising living standards as they did, perhaps more Korean women would have been drawn to "consensual" sex work out of desperation as they were under the American comfort women system. How genuine was the "consent" of Korean women servicing American personnel, who outnumbered those serving the Japanese many times over, and was America's conduct really more moral than that of the Japanese Empire—or could it be considered even more immoral and depraved?

As for the treatment of Korean women when under the power of foreign soldiers—sources almost unanimously indicate similar if not greater levels of brutalisation by American soldiers as was the case under the Japanese. An independent survey of 243 South Korean comfort women servicing American personnel found well over two thirds experienced "beating, sexual violence, theft and robbery, in declining order of frequency" at the hands of American soldiers.[80] As one said anonymously when interviewed, "some GIs are mean and nasty, especially when they are drunk…at worst a woman encounters a GI who beats her and murders her." American conduct towards Korean women, as in many other Asia-Pacific nations, was strongly influenced by perceptions that they were dealing with an inferior people. A U.S. military chaplain quoted by *Time* magazine noted that personnel tended to view Korean women as property, much as Westerners serving at imperial postings across the world once "owned" sex slaves of conquered nations in Africa,[81] the Americas[82] and elsewhere. He stated: "Some of them *own* their girls…

before leaving Korea, they sell the package to a man who is just coming in."[83] Another noted regarding prevailing attitudes among American servicemen to East Asian women: "They were property, things, slaves… Racism, sexism—it's all there. The men don't see the women as human beings—they're disgusting, things to be thrown away… They speak of the women in the diminutive."[84] Koreans were perceived as a culture and people with whom Americans were entitled to do as they pleased, including inflicting abuse and demanding sexual favours. According to one comfort woman interviewed, GIs would tell Korean women that they would never beat women in America but as they were in Korea they were free to do so to Korean women—supposedly to justify their behaviour. It was common for Korean women to be harshly beaten by drunk soldiers, and other women interviewed consistently painted a very similar picture.[85]

South Korea today remains profoundly influenced by the comfort women system put in place under U.S. military rule—arguably far more so than that which took place under the Japanese Empire. As Katherine H. S. Moon noted regarding the social changes which occurred in South Korea as a result: "Increasingly Koreans view the history of prostitution and the contemporary forms of sex tourism in Korea as manifestations of foreign domination over the country."[86] She further noted that many in South Korea saw the comfort women system "as representative of U.S. domination over Korean politics and the continued presence of U.S. military bases as perpetuation of South Korea's neo-colonial status vis-à-vis the United States."[87]

The comfort women system began to decline only with South Korea's economic rise, which forced American servicemen in the country to increasingly rely on trafficked women from Southeast Asia from the late 1970s.[88] The system would leave behind a considerable cultural legacy—including a normalisation of the sex trade. By 1989 the country's nightclubs, bars and entertainment sector made up 5 percent of the Gross National Product, with 400,000 establishments offering sexual services and between 1.2 and 1.5 million South Korean women selling sex. This was one fifth of the total number of women aged 15 to 29. A range of services were offered at a variety of locations, from seedy inns to luxury hotels, to cater for the very large numbers of clients.[89] In the early 2010s the sex trade in South Korea made up 4 percent of GDP, as much as fishing and agriculture combined.[90] Up to one fifth of South Korean women between 15 and 29 have at some point worked in the sex industry—over 1 million women.[91] A report by the U.S. State Department released in 2008 indicated that young girls and women from South Korea are very often made victims of human trafficking to Western nations in significant numbers. These include Western Europe, Canada, Australia, New Zealand and the United States as well as to Japan.[92]

The comfort women system which was continued and expanded in South Korea, and the experiences of those whom through various circumstances were forced into it, provides key context to the ongoing conflict between the DPRK and the United States. Pyongyang not only abolished the comfort women system from 1945, but also strictly enforced the outlawing of prostitution entirely and establishing formal legal equality for women. The country remains highly sexually conservative until today, with adultery remaining a serious crime by law and even divorce being rare and strongly discouraged.

Had Pyongyang yielded to Western pressure, or accepted the American Supreme Commander's demand for unconditional surrender during the war, it is almost certain its women and young girls would have been subjected to very similar if not worse treatment including sexual violence on a massive scale at the hands of the U.S. Military. While the country would pay a price for its defiance of the Western-led order, from firebombing and demonization to seven long decades of harsh economic sanctions, the nation's dignity, pride and right to self-determination were never violated—neither were its women. The fate of South Korea as a U.S. client state, including not only comfort women issues and widespread rapes but also factors such as the imposition of intense Western cultural influences, the indefinite and costly American military presence, and continued American influence over state policy, arguably vindicate North Korea's choice of resistance to intense external pressure over the harsh alternative. As a statement from the DPRK's Foreign Ministry read, amid talk of American military intervention in 2017: "Three million people have volunteered to join the war if necessary…in terms of dignity we are the most powerful in the world. We will die in order to protect that dignity and sovereignty."[93]

Americanisation in South Korea

In parallel to the comfort women system, another major phenomenon that emerged during the U.S. military occupation and would come to shape South Korean society and its relationship with the United States was the deep Americanisation and westernisation of South Korean society. This again led to a sharp contrast between U.S. relations with the two Koreas and provides context key to comprehending the nature of conflict between North Korea and the United States.

American efforts to westernize South Korean society and develop a soft power base were considerable from the beginning of the military occupation period, with the U.S. Information Service reporting it had: "one of the most extensive country programs that we are operating anywhere"—a very large investment considering the underdeveloped state of the country compared to other American client states. The service had nine centers in Korea which offered American cultural items including films, publications and other such services.[94] The early stages of the American appropriation of soft power were described by British Minister Vyvyan Holt in his visit to the ROK in 1950, shortly before the outbreak of the war, when he observed: "Radiating from the huge ten-storied Banto Hotel, 'American influence' penetrates into every branch of administration and is fortified by an immense outpouring of money." Cultural influence was spread by scholarships to study in the United States, missionary denominations, travelling cinemas and theatres playing American films, the Voice of America and sports such as baseball. This cultural influence was described by the minister as "exceedingly strong" and as a result "American is the dream land" to fast growing numbers of Koreans—an allusion to the growing idolization of the U.S.[95]

Korea expert Professor Robert Jervis noted in a paper for the *Journal of American-East Asian Relations* that an

> intangible effect of the war is the penetration of American ideas and values into South Korean society. While the three-year American military occupation (1945–1948) has already laid the ground-work for the Americanisation of South Korean society, the war, by bringing hundreds of thousands of American soldiers to Korea, by inundating South Korea with American goods, books, and films, and by multiplying South Korea's links with the United States manifold, helped to quicken its pace and broaden its scope. Whether this is good or bad is open to debate.[96]

American soft influence in South Korea, as in its other East Asian client states, would only grow as these states further modernised. In his research paper "The Present and Future of Americanization in South Korea," appearing in the *Journal of Future Studies,* Professor Pak Seong Won noted: "South Korea has done nothing to curb Americanization since the 1950s, and in an era of globalization, Korean society is becoming more influenced by the United States in terms of economic, political, and psychological realms." Pak indicated that South Korea was influenced by the United States through three main means:

> 1) the number of U.S.-educated Ph.D.s in universities and government, 2) the propensity to adopt American lifestyles, and 3) the high market shares of American movies and television programming. These categories represent knowledge, life, and playfulness—in short culture. Results of the examination in the three categories are astounding, because South Korea is deeply influenced by Americans. Even though Korea was decolonized from Japan in 1945, Korea now seems to be colonized by the U.S. in economic, political, and cultural realms.[97]

Arguably one of the most conspicuous impacts on South Korean society, and on those of many East Asian nations in the Western Bloc's sphere of influence, has been that on aesthetics—namely towards an idealisation of Western physical features. In his paper published by University of Hawaii, titled "Dynamic Beauty: Cultural influences and Changing Perceptions—Becoming Prettier or Erasing One's Own Culture," American researcher Christopher Frazier observed: "A culture's ideals of physical appearance are dynamic. Change can be induced by external cultural contact and, particularly, domination. Do these affected standards of beauty imply a kind of reversed ethnocentrism?" Frazier went on to write, referring to the extensive growth of plastic surgeries and other emerging methods among East Asian populations of "Europeanising" their appearances: "All the above trends seem to illustrate the growing influence of Western cultural domination. From actual imperialism to modern cultural colonialism via mass media."[98]

Lisa Takeuchi Cullen's article "Changing Faces" in *Time* magazine assessed the growing popularity and rising trend towards altering one's features to appear more Western in Western-aligned East Asian countries. Regarding the influences which caused East Asians to favour Western features, she noted:

> The culturally loaded issue today is the number of Asians looking to remake themselves to look more Caucasian. It's a charge many deny, although few would argue that under the relentless bombardment of Hollywood, satellite TV, and Madison Avenue, Asia's aesthetic ideal has changed drastically.[99]

Harvard psychology Professor Nancy Etcoff, author of *Survival of the Prettiest: The Science of Beauty*, noted to much the same effect: "Beauty, after all, is evolutionary… Asians are increasingly asking their surgeons for wider eyes, longer noses and fuller breasts, features not typical of the race." Concepts of beauty evolve over time and reflect what is seen as desirable—the traits of the dominant people or caste. Under the Western sphere of influence, "under the relentless bombardment of Hollywood, satellite TV, and Madison Avenue" among other mediums through which an idealisation of the West is promoted, concepts of beauty have shifted to idealise the aesthetics of the dominating power.[100]

As *Time* magazine reported, common surgeries to "Europeanise" appearances in South Korea went beyond facial features:

> Just as Asian faces require unique procedures, their bodies demand innovative operations to achieve the leggy, skinny, busty Western ideal that has become increasingly universal. Dr. Suh In Seock, a surgeon in Seoul, has struggled to find the best way to fix an affliction the Koreans call muu-dari and the Japanese call daikon-ashi: radish-shaped calves. Liposuction, so effective on the legs of plump Westerners, doesn't work on Asians since muscle, not fat, accounts for the bulk. Suh says earlier attempts to carve the muscle were painful and made walking difficult. "Finally, I discovered that by severing a nerve behind the knee, the muscle would atrophy," says Suh, "thereby reducing its size up to 40%." Suh has performed over 600 of the operations since 1996. He disappears for a minute and returns with a bottle of fluid containing what looks like chopped up bits of ramen noodles. He has preserved his patients' excised nerves in alcohol. "And that's just since November," he says proudly.[101]

Professor Pak Seong Won concluded regarding the extent of westernization, as demonstrated by the aforementioned surgeries and idealization of western aesthetics: "we can see how Koreans internalize U.S. values and how they undervalue Korean uniqueness in terms of beauty and body."[102] The origins of "Europeanisation" surgeries in Korea notably has close connections to the early U.S. Military presence in the country—which is indicative of their nature as a manifestation of Western dominance over and consequences of westernisation of South Korean modern culture. Prominent American plastic surgeon David Ralph Millard worked with the U.S. Military in post-war South Korea from 1954 and explored the possibility of surgically altering the appearance of the human eye from "Oriental to Occidental." A Korean translator approached him, seeking to be "made into a round-eye," as he felt that his Asian appearance was leading the Americans he worked with to mistrust him. Millard agreed, writing: "As this was partly true, I consented to do what I could."[103]

The status of westerners as a superior class in Korea, and the idealisation of the West which followed, led the popularity of "Europeanisation" surgeries to surge. Millard sought to devise further procedures not only to alter eyelids, but also to raise nasal bridges and widen eyes. The interpreter was very happy with the results, noting that he was often thought to be an Italian or Mexican as a result—an improvement in his eyes from the status of a Korean. "Asianness" and Korean features were increasingly associated with inferiority as western influence grew.[104]

Millard went on to train local doctors to apply his methods and published two papers on the subject, titled "Oriental Peregrinations" and "The Oriental Eyelid and its Surgical Revision." Both of these works had highly racialist tones. By the 1990s "Europeanisation" surgeries had become a widespread and normalized part of modern South Korean culture. This not only revealed but also cemented Koreans' sense of racial inferiority. As Professor Nadia Y. Kim noted: "the U.S. military and [Millard] were crystallizing Koreans' sense of inferiority to their White racial bodies."[105] The most popular plastic surgeries to date, with the exception of hair transplants, are all "Europeanisation" surgeries, including double eyelid and eye widening surgeries, rhino-plasticity used to give the nose a high bridge—and so make them protrude further from the face as European noses do, and forehead augmentation—which makes the forehead protrude from the face as European foreheads do. Others include chin augmentations—using implants or fillers do make the face look more angular in the western style, and V-line jaw reduction surgeries which have much the same effect. The popularity of these surgeries in South Korea remains very high.[106]

While the Korean translator who approached Dr. Millard had wanted to Europeanise his features to prevent discrimination from his American bosses, South Korean society appears to have internalised these Western values and paradigms to the extent that Korean features are widely looked down on by Koreans themselves. As South Korean writer Carol Eugene Pak noted in the Canadian magazine *The Varsity*: "Many South Koreans envy and idolize 'Western' facial features, whether they are conscious of it or not. Perhaps it is because of a Western-dominated media or the pedestal South Korean society places the United States upon. Whatever the reason, contemporary South Korean society has deeply internalized its bias towards Western beauty, so that Koreans who do not possess 'Western' features often face prejudice in the workplace and in daily life." She was one of many to attribute the prominence of plastic surgery in the country, with the world's highest rates of plastic surgery per capita,[107] not to a high beauty standard, but to a deep idolisation of the West—one which dates back to the time of American military rule.[108]

The importance of inferiority complexes among a target population and pressing the idea of Western racial prestige was frequently alluded to by European leaders during the colonial era as key to sustaining Western leadership.[109] Such trends could be observed in the post-colonial era beyond South Korea. In her paper titled "Retto-kan: Japan's Inferiority Complex with the West in Contemporary Media and Culture," Dr. Erika Engstrom noted that under U.S. occupation, much of the Japanese population had started to believe "that Japan was inferior, not only as an economic power, but also as a race." This developed into "retto-kan," which could be translated as "inferior class feeling." According to Engstrom's study it would prevail even after Japanese living standards and its economy had left most of the Western world behind.[110]

While aesthetics provides a more conspicuous example of the effects of American and Western influence on South Korea, it is an indicator of a much wider phenomenon of idealisation and adulation of the West and one of many examples. South Korean Congressman Choi Soon Young, for one, presented data in 2007 indicating United States' considerable influence on the country through education. He pointed out that Korean society valued U.S. educational ties more than any others—with the majority of professors at leading universities holding degrees from the U.S., which accounted for over 80% of foreign doctoral degrees.[111] Similar trends can be observed among the country's political elite. From 1948–1968 much of the Korean leadership boasted higher education in Japan which, as the previous imperial power occupying Korea, had heavily influenced the Korean elite through education. This Japanese influence would gradually recede to be replaced by an American one, and from 1968 to 2001 71% of ministers in the ROK held degrees from the United States.[112] This fosters not only positive views towards and close ties with the new hegemon, as it was intended to do towards Japan beforehand, but also ensures that American thought will continue to have a major influence over scholarship and political discourse in the country. This influence has, according to the aforementioned study conducted by Pak Seong Won, been very profound, and placed U.S. educated professionals in a superior class leading to discrimination against those lacking an American education.[113]

An understanding of these trends is critical to comprehending not only the nature of the American relationship with South Korea and its other East Asian client states, but also of its conflict with North Korea to which these relationships provide a stark contrast. As one of very few states to have never been subjugated and occupied by a Western power, North Korea lacks the colonial-era foundations for Western soft influence and an idealisation of the West common to many countries formerly under American or European rule. North Koreans were never second class citizens in their own country, which combined with a lack of Western soft influence and a strongly nationalist "Korea-first" identity[114] perpetuated through media and education, means its population are not moved to remake themselves in the image of or to idolise the West—aesthetically or otherwise. The extent of Western influence in South Korea and other Asian client states, and the depths to which it has permeated, shows the alternative fate for the Korean population to that of resistance under the DPRK—namely life under a system which attributes the greatest value not to one's own nation, culture and thought, but instead under one which is heavily influenced by and idolises the Western hegemon. The implications of this have played a central role in the conflict between North Korea and the Western Bloc—led by the United States—throughout its seventy-year duration.

NOTES

1 Mi Kunjongch'ong kwanbo: Official Gazette, United States Army Military Government in Korea, Seoul, Wonju Munhwasa, Proclamation No. 1.
2 Mi Kunjongch'ong kwanbo: Official Gazette, United States Army Military Government in Korea, Seoul, Wonju Munhwasa, Proclamation No. 2.
3 Fraenkel, Ernst, '*Entry 24 January 1946: Augzeichungen vsm 15. Vis 30. Januar 1946 uber Fraenkels Ankunftzeit in Korea,*' in: Franker, Ernst, *Gesammelte Schriften,* Baden Baden, Nomos Verlagsgesellschaft, 1999.
4 One prominent example in East Asia is Singapore's National Museum—which similarly and somewhat ironically refers to the restoration of British colonial rule in 1945 as 'liberation' (National Museum of Singapore, *Surviving Syonan Gallery,* Level 2, accessed March 8, 2018).
5 'Message to U.S.A. Citizens,' *G-2 Weekly*, October 30, 1945.
6 Letter from Commander in Chief, U.S. Army Forces, Pacific to Joint Chiefs of Staff, December 16, 1945. Folder: Papers of Harry S. Truman, SMOF: Selected Records on Korean War, Pertinent Papers on Korea Situation; Box 11, SMOF, National Security Files, Papers of Harry S. Truman, Harry S. Truman Library.
7 Fraenkel, Ernst, '*Entry 24 January 1946: Augzeichungen vsm 15. Vis 30. Januar 1946 uber Fraenkels Ankunftzeit in Korea,*' in: Franker, Ernst, *Gesammelte Schriften,* Baden Baden, Nomos Verlagsgesellschaft, 1999.
8 Kim, Monica, *The Interrogation Rooms of the Korean War; The Untold History,* Princeton, NJ, Princeton University Press, 2019 (pp. 47, 49–51).
9 'Report on Standards of Living Conditions, Military Courtesy Discipline, and Training,' April 29, 1946; 'Deterioration of Standards,' May 3, 1946; 'Courtesy Drive,' November 6, 1946; 'Message from the Commanding General, USAFIK,' January 17, 1947; 'Instructions to Courtesy Patrol Officers,' July 21, 1948; 'Personal Conduct,' August 27, 1948, all in NARA, RG 554, box 50.
Hohn, Maria, and Moon, Seungsook, eds., *Over There: Living with the U.S. Military Empire from World War Two to the Present*, Chapel Hill, NC, Duke University Press, 2010 (p. 43).
10 Dower, John, *War Without Mercy: Race and Power in the Pacific War*, New York, Pantheon, 1986 (p. 7).
11 Schrijvers, Peter, *The GI War Against Japan: American Soldiers in Asia and the Pacific During World War II*, New York, New York University Press, 2005 (p. 212).
12 Diary of Admiral William Leahy, October 20, 1942 (quoted in Thorne, Christopher, *Allies of a Kind: The United States, Britain and the War Against Japan, 1941–1945*, Oxford, Oxford University Press, 1978 (p. 157)).
13 Stueck, William and Yi, Boram, '"An Alliance Forged in Blood": The American Occupation of Korea, the Korean War, and the US–South Korean Alliance,' *The Journal of Strategic Studies*, vol. 33, no. 2, April 2010 (pp. 177–209).
14 Defty, Andew, *Britain, America and Anti-Communism: The Information Research Department*, Abingdon, Routledge, 2007.
15 Schrijvers, Peter, *Bloody Pacific: American Soldiers at War with Japan*, London, Palgrave Macmillan, 2010 (p. 211).
16 Moyer, Robert H., enlisted on August 13, 1947, Korean War Veterans' Survey Questionnaire, Military History Institute Archives, Carlisle, Pennsylvania.
17 Lisiewski, Joseph Vincent, [Sgt, 7th Div. 32nd Inf Rgt.], enlisted in anticipation of the draft on 3-4-51: Korean War Veterans' Survey Questionnaire, Military History Institute Archives, Carlisle, Pennsylvania.
18 Voorhees, Melvin B., *Korean Tales*, Franklin Classics, 2011 (p. 150).
19 Steinberg, David I., *Korean Attitudes Toward the United States: Changing Dynamics*, Abingdon, Routledge, 2015 (p. 234).

20 Hastings, Max, *Korean War*, London, Pan Books, 2012 (Chapter 12: The Stony Road, Part 3: The Cause).
21 Lewis, Lloyd B., *The Tainted War: Culture and Identity in Vietnam Narratives*, Santa Barbara, CA, Praeger, 1985 (p. 55).
22 Moon, Katherine H. S., *Sex Among Allies*, New York, Colombia University Press, 1997 (p. 119).
23 Ibid. (pp. 33, 36).
24 Portway, Donald, *Korea: Land of the Morning Calm*, London, George G. Harrap, 1953 (p. 291).
25 Moon, Katherine H. S., *Sex Among Allies*, New York, Colombia University Press, 1997 (p. 33).
26 Ibid. (p. 37).
27 Nyen Chan, Emily, 'Engagement Abroad: Enlisted Man, U.S. Military Policy and the Sex Industry,' *Notre Dame Journal of Law, Ethics and Public Policy*, vol. 15, issue 2 'Symposium on International Security,' Article 7, 2012 (pp. 631–632).
Moon, Katherine H. S., *Sex Among Allies*, New York, Colombia University Press, 1997 (pp. 33, 37).
28 Maynes, Katrin, 'Korean Perceptions of Chastity, Gender Roles, and Libido; From Kisaengs to the Twenty First Century,' *Grand Valley Journal of History*, vol. 1, issue 1, article 2, February 2012.
29 Schrijvers, Peter, *The GI War Against Japan: American Soldiers in Asia and the Pacific During World War II*, New York, New York University Press, 2005 (p. 212).
30 Moon, Katherine H. S., *Sex Among Allies*, New York, Colombia University Press, 1997 (p. 46).
31 Oh, Arissa, *To Save the Children of Korea: The Cold War Origins of International Adoption*, Stanford, CA, Stanford University Press, 2015.
32 Hohn, Maria, and Moon, Seungsook, eds., *Over There: Living with the U.S. Military Empire from World War Two to the Present*, Chapel Hill, NC, Duke University Press, 2010 (p. 43).
33 Dower, John, *Embracing Defeat, Japan in the Wake of World War II*, New York, W. W. Norton & Company, 2000 (p. 579).
Sims, Calvin, '3 Dead Marines and a Secret of Wartime Okinawa,' *New York Times*, June 1, 2000.
Takemae, Eiji, *Allied Occupation of Japan*, New York, Continuum International Publishing Group, 2002 (p. 67).
Tanaka, Yuki and Tanaka, Toshiyuki, *Japan's Comfort Women: Sexual Slavery and Prostitution During World War II*, Abingdon, Routledge, 2003 (p. 163).
34 Association with Korean Women, January 25, 1947, National Archives and Records Administration, RG 554, box 50.
35 Winnington, Alan, and Burchett, Wilfred, *Plain Perfidy, The Plot to Wreck the Korea Peace*, Britain-China Friendship Association, 1954 (p. 129).
36 Abrams, A. B., *Power and Primacy: The History of Western Intervention in the Asia-Pacific*, Oxford, Peter Lang, 2019 (Chapter 6: Vietnam's Thirty Years of War).
37 Ibid. (Chapter 2: The War Against a Defeated Japan: Elimination of a Threat to Western Hegemony in Asia).
38 Moon, Katherine H. S., *Sex Among Allies*, New York, Colombia University Press, 1997.
39 Hanley, Charles J. and Choe, Sang Hun and Mendoza, Martha, *The Bridge at No Gun Ri: A Hidden Nightmare from the Korean War*, New York, Henry Holt and Company, 2001 (p. 189).
40 Lee, Na Young, 'The Construction of U.S. Camptown Prostitution in South Korea: Trans/Formation and Resistance,' (Thesis, Ph.D.), University of Maryland, Department of Women's Studies, 2006.

41 Choe, Sang-Hun, 'After Korean War, brothels and an alliance,' *New York Times*, January 8, 2009.
42 Moon, Katherine H. S., *Sex Among Allies*, New York, Colombia University Press, 1997 (p. 44).
43 Choe, Sang-Hun, 'After Korean War, brothels and an alliance,' *New York Times*, January 8, 2009.
44 Heo, Uk, and Roehrig, Terence, *South Korea Since 1980*, Cambridge, Cambridge University Press, 2010 (p. 18).
Henderson, Gregory, *Korea: The Politics of Vortex*, Cambridge, MA, Harvard University Press, 1968 (pp. 348–349).
45 Choe, Sang-Hun, 'After Korean War, brothels and an alliance,' *New York Times*, January 8, 2009.
46 Kim, Min-Kyung, 'Court Finds that South Korean Government Encouraged Prostitution Near U.S. Military Bases,' *Hankyoreh*, February 9, 2018.
47 Koh, B. C., 'The War's Impact on the Korean Peninsula,' *The Journal of American-East Asian Relations*, vol. 2, no. 1, Spring 1993 (p. 58).
Nathan, Robert R., *An Economic Programme for Korean Construction,* Washington D.C., United Nations Korean Reconstruction Agency, 1954 (p. 22).
48 Oh, Arissa, *To Save the Children of Korea: The Cold War Origins of International Adoption*, Stanford, CA, Stanford University Press, 2015 (p. 49).
49 Ibid. (p. 49).
50 Hohn, Maria, and Moon, Seungsook, eds., *Over There: Living with the U.S. Military Empire from World War Two to the Present*, Chapel Hill, NC, Duke University Press, 2010 (p. 52).
51 Vine, David, *Base Nation, How U.S. Military Bases Abroad Harm America and the World*, New York, Henry Holt and Company, 2015 (p. 164).
52 Lee, Jin-Kyung, *Service Economies: Militarism, Sex Work, and Migrant Labor in South Korea*, Minneapolis, University of Minnesota Press, 2010 (p. 82).
53 Kim, Elaine, 'Research for the Reform of Law and the Prevention of Prostitution,' *The Women's Studies Quarterly*, vol. 8, issue 1, Spring 1990 (p. 89).
54 Barry, Kathleen, *The Prostitution of Sexuality*, New York, New York University Press, 1996.
55 Lee, Jin-Kyung, *Service Economies: Militarism, Sex Work, and Migrant Labor in South Korea*, Minneapolis, University of Minnesota Press, 2010 (p. 79).
56 Moon, Katherine H. S., 'South Korean Movements against Militarized Sexual Labor,' *Asian Survey*, vol. 39, no. 2, March–April 1999 (pp. 310–327).
57 Hye Seung Chung, *Kim Ki-duk*, Champaign, University of Illinois Press, 2012 (p. 34).
Moon, Katherine H. S., 'South Korean Movements against Militarized Sexual Labor,' *Asian Survey*, vol. 39, no. 2, March–April 1999 (pp. 310–327).
Mal Magazine, vol. 26, August 1988 (p. 108).
Lee, Diana S. and Lee, Grace Yoonkyung, 'Camp Arirang,' *Third World Newsreel*, (Documentary), 1995.
Moon, Katherine H. S., *Sex Among Allies*, New York, Colombia University Press, 1997 (pp. 19–20, 23, 24, 132).
58 Ibid. (p. 131).
Moon, Katherine H. S., 'South Korean Movements against Militarized Sexual Labor,' *Asian Survey*, vol. 39, no. 2, March–April 1999 (pp. 310–327).
59 Kamienski, Lukasz, *Shooting Up; A History of Drugs in Warfare*, London, C. Hurst & Co. Publishers, 2016 (p. 148).
60 Moon, Katherine H. S., *Sex Among Allies*, New York, Colombia University Press, 1997.
61 Choe Sang Hun, 'After Korean War, brothels and an alliance,' *New York Times*, January 8, 2009.

62 Moon, Katherine H. S., *Sex Among Allies*, New York, Colombia University Press, 1997.
Hye Seung Chung, *Kim Ki-duk*, Champaign, University of Illinois Press, 2012 (p. 34).

63 Moon, Katherine H. S., *Sex Among Allies*, New York, Colombia University Press, 1997.

64 Pollock, Sandra, *Let the Good Times Roll: Prostitution and the U.S. Military in Asia*, New York, New Press, 1992.

65 Ibid. (p. 170).

66 Ibid. (p. 171).

67 Ibid. (p. 173).

68 Hohn, Maria, and Moon, Seungsook, eds. *Over There: Living with the U.S. Military Empire from World War Two to the Present*, Chapel Hill, NC, Duke University Press 2010 (p. 351).

69 Moon, Katherine H. S., *Sex Among Allies*, New York, Colombia University Press, 1997.

70 'Japan PM urges S. Korea to remove "comfort woman" statue,' *The Korea Herald*, January 8, 2017.

71 Enriquez, J., 'Filipinas in prostitution around U.S. Military Bases in Korea: A recurring nightmare,' *Coalition Against Trafficking in Women,* 1996.
Vine, David, *Base Nation, How U.S. Military Bases Abroad Harm America and the World*, New York, Henry Holt and Company, 2015 (pp. 167–169).
Irvine, Reed, and Kincaid, Cliff, 'The Pentagon's Dirty Secret,' *Media Monitor*, August 7, 2002.

72 Lee, June, *A Review of Data on Trafficking in the Republic of Korea*, International Organisation for Migration, 2002.
Mary Jacoby, 'Does U.S. Abet Korean Sex Trade?,' *St Petersburg Times*, December 9, 2002.
'Human trafficking severe in Korea :US,' *Korea Times,* June 17, 2010

73 Demick, Barbara, 'Off-Base Behavior in Korea,' *Los Angeles Times*, September 26, 2002.

74 Hughes, Donna M. and Chon, Katherine Y. and Ellerman, Derek P., 'Modern-Day Comfort Women: The U.S. Military, Transnational Crime, and the Trafficking of Women,' *Violence Against Women,* vol. 13, no. 9, 2007 (p. 918).

75 Seungsook Moon, *Regulating Desire, Managing the Empire: U.S. Military Prostitution in South Korea, 1945–1970*, Durham, Duke University Press, 2010.

76 Mikaberidze, Alexander, *Atrocities, Massacres, and War Crimes: An Encyclopedia*, Santa Barbara, CA, ABC-CLIO, 2013 (p. 7).

77 Hsiao, Mei-Chu W. and Hsiao, Frank S. T., *Taiwan in the Global Economy—Past, Present and Future* in: Chow, Peter C., *Taiwan in the Global Economy: From an Agrarian Economy to an Exporter of High-Tech Products*, Westport, Praeger, 2002 (Section V: 'Taiwan in the Global Economy During the Japanese Period').

78 '朝鮮総督府統計年報 昭和17年 [Governor-General of Korea Statistical Yearbook 1942],' Governor-General of Korea, March 1944.

79 Williams, Christopher, *Leadership Accountability in a Globalizing World*, London, Palgrave Macmillan, 2006 (p. 185).

80 Hohn, Maria, and Moon, Seungsook, eds., *Over There: Living with the U.S. Military Empire from World War Two to the Present*, Chapel Hill, NC, Duke University Press, 2010 (p. 351).

81 Klotz, Marcia, *White women and the dark continent: gender and sexuality in German colonial discourse from the sentimental novel to the fascist film*, Thesis (Ph.D.), Stanford University, 2010 (p. 72).
Grobler, John, 'The tribe Germany wants to forget,' *Mail & Guardian*, March 13, 1998.

82 Rankin, John, *Letters on American slavery, addressed to Mr. Thomas Rankin, merchant at Middlebrook, Augusta County, Va*, Boston, Garrison and Knapp, 1833 (pp. 38–39).
83 'South Korea: A Hooch is Not a Home,' *Time*, October 9, 1964 (p. 48).
84 D'Amico, Francine J. and Weinstein, Laurie L., *Gender Camouflage: Women and the U.S. Military*, New York, New York University Press, 1999 (p. 212).
85 Hanley, Charles J. and Choe, Sang Hun and Mendoza, Martha, *The Bridge at No Gun Ri: A Hidden Nightmare from the Korean War*, New York, Henry Holt and Company, 2001 (p. 214).
86 Moon, Katherine H. S., *Sex Among Allies*, New York, Colombia University Press, 1997 (pp. 46–47).
87 Ibid. (p. 9).
88 Hughes, Donna M. and Chon, Katherine Y. and Ellerman, Derek P., 'Modern-Day Comfort Women: The U.S. Military, Transnational Crime, and the Trafficking of Women,' *Violence Against Women* vol. 13, no. 9, 2007 (p. 918).
89 Shin, Hei Soo, 'Women's Sexual Services and Economic Development: The Political Economy of the Entertainment Industry and South Korean Dependent Development,' Thesis (Ph.D.), Rutgers University, New Brunswick, NJ, 1991 (p. 58).
Moon, Katherine H. S., *Sex Among Allies*, New York, Colombia University Press, 1997.
90 Ghosh, Palash, 'South Korea: A Thriving Sex Industry In A Powerful, Wealthy Super-State,' *International Business Times*, April 29, 2013.
91 Moon, Katherine H. S., *Sex Among Allies*, New York, Colombia University Press, 1997.
Ghosh, Palash, 'South Korea: A Thriving Sex Industry In A Powerful, Wealthy Super-State,' *International Business Times*, April 29, 2013.
92 U.S. Department of State, Under Secretary for Civilian Security, Democracy and Human Rights, Trafficking Persons Report 2008.
93 Osnos, Evan, 'The Risk of Nuclear War with North Korea,' *The New Yorker*, September 18, 2017.
94 Cumings, Bruce, *Korea's Place in the Sun*, New York, W. W. Norton and Company, 1997 (p.255).
95 British Foreign Office, FO317, piece no. 84053, Holt to FO, May 1, 1950.
96 Jervis, Robert, 'The Impact of the Korean War,' *The Journal of American-East Asian Relations*, vol. 2, no. 1, Spring 1993 (pp. 57–76).
97 Park, Seong Won, 'The Present and Future of Americanisation in South Korea,' *Journal of Future Studies,* vol. 14, no. 1, August 2009 (pp. 51–66).
98 Fraizer, Christopher, 'Dynamic Beauty: Cultural influences and Changing Perceptions—Becoming Prettier or Erasing One's Own Culture,' *Hohonu Journal of Academic Writing,* vol. 4, 2006 (pp. 5–7).
99 Cullen, Lise Takeuchi, 'Changing Faces,' *Time,* August 5, 2002.
100 *Time,* July 29, 2002.
101 Cullen, Lise Takeuchi, 'Changing Faces,' *Time,* August 5, 2002.
102 Park, Seong Won, 'The Present and Future of Americanisation in South Korea,' *Journal of Future Studies,* vol. 14, no. 1, August 2009 (pp. 51–66).
103 'Eyes Wide Cut: The American Origins of Korea's Plastic Surgery Craze,' *The Wilson Quarterly*, September 2015.
104 Ibid.
105 Ibid.
106 Park, Kyungmee, 'Addiction to Cosmetic Surgery,' *Bokjinews*, March 2007.
Scanion, Charles, 'The price of beauty in South Korea,' *BBC News*, February 3, 2005.
107 Hu, Elise, 'In Seoul, A Plastic Surgery Capital, Residents Frown On Ads For Cosmetic Procedure,' *NPR*, February 5, 2018.
Marx, Patricia, 'About Face,' *The New Yorker,* March 16, 2015.

108 Park, Carol Eugene, 'For many South Koreans, beauty standards represent a cultural struggle,' *The Varsity,* March 5, 2017.
109 Hotta, Eri., *Pan Asianism and Japan's War 1931–1945*, New York, Palgrave Macmillan, 2007 (pp. 217–218).
110 Engstrom, Erika, 'Retto-kan: Japan's Inferiority Complex with the West in Contemporary Media and Culture,' *Human Communication: a Journal of the Pacific and Asian Communication Association,* vol. 1, no. 1, 1997 (pp. 17–23).
111 '서울대 교수 50.5%가 "미국 박사,"' (50.5% of Seoul National University Professors Have American Doctorates), 미디어 오늘 (*Media Today*), January 17, 2005.
112 Park, Seong Won, 'The Present and Future of Americanisation in South Korea,' *Journal of Future Studies,* vol. 14, no. 1, August 2009 (pp. 51–66).
113 Ibid. (pp. 51–66).
114 'Interview: Ashton Carter,' *Frontline*, March 3, 2003.

Part Three

STATE SURVIVAL IN THE UNIPOLAR ERA

Chapter 12

THE 1990s: AN ARDUOUS MARCH AND A NEW WORLD ORDER

One Superpower, No Restrictions

While North Korea had found itself increasingly isolated as part of the Soviet Bloc from the early 1970s, with a sizeable majority of the global economy and majority of states falling under the Western Bloc's sphere of influence, this isolation worsened considerably following the collapse of the Soviet Union and Warsaw Pact and the integration of most of their successor states into the Western-led order. The result was disastrous both for the DPRK's ability to defend its territory and deter potential U.S. military action and for the state's continued economic wellbeing. Although the collapse of the USSR had come as a major shock to Pyongyang and much of the Soviet aligned and non-aligned world, Pyongyang had come to perceive a growing danger from the late 1980s as the Soviet Union increasingly ceased to function as a superpower capable of holding the Western Bloc in check. Moscow's extensive concessions to the United States over a number of issues, including unilateral constraints on its space program,[1] missile defence,[2] deployments of its troops in Eastern Europe and the defence of its allies,[3] all heralded what was to come.

The end of the Cold War, the collapse of the Warsaw Pact in 1990, and Moscow's apparent acquiescence to a new unipolar Western-led order, had led U.S. President George H. W. Bush to declare a "New World Order"—which he did for the first time on September 11 of that year. Under this order the United States was to exercise "world leadership"[4] and the dominance of the U.S.-led Western world would reign unchallenged. While some welcomed an end to bipolar conflict between the two superpower blocs, critics in America referred to the concept of a new order as "rationalization for imperial ambitions" of the United States.[5] The nature of the New World Order as a unipolar moment for America and the Western world following the removal of the primary check on their freedom to shape global affairs, and its implications for the international community of nations, would become clearer six months later in the aftermath of the Persian Gulf War and Operation Desert Storm. As the American *Foreign Affairs* journal would conclude shortly afterwards: "It has been assumed that the old bipolar world would beget a multipolar world… The immediate post–Cold War world is not multipolar. It is unipolar. The centre of world power is an unchallenged superpower, the United States, attended by its Western allies."[6]

The defining moment of the New World Order was the Western military intervention in the Persian Gulf targeting the Ba'athist Iraqi Republic, a close Soviet defence partner, which continued to conduct its foreign policy apparently unaware of its new vulnerability following Moscow's capitulation. Iraq's Western-aligned neighbour, Kuwait, was found to have drilled for oil horizontally and illegally profited from the extraction under Iraqi soil, which alongside the small Gulf State's other oil policies was costing Iraq $7 billion annually.[7] Kuwait refused multiple diplomatic overtures from Baghdad over several months and ignored repeated threats of forceful retaliation to end what Iraq perceived to be theft of its resources.[8] Iraq's response however came not in the form of limited military action, but with a full scale invasion and annexation of its neighbour and absorption of its entire territory in August 1990—citing their historical unity as a single state prior to 1913 as justification for reunification.

Iraq's failure to comprehend its vulnerability now that its superpower patronage was effectively lost cost the country dearly. Baghdad was ordered by the U.S. not only to withdraw its forces from Kuwait, but to comply with several further demands including ending its missile programs and curbing military research—or else face a Western attack. Receiving no Soviet diplomatic support or a rebuffing of Western threats by Moscow which would previously have been expected, Iraq accepted the condition of withdrawal. The country refused these more extensive terms however, which were seen as a violation of its right to self-defence and an attempt to manipulate the regional balance of power further in favour of Western and allied interests.[9] Iraq's lack of a viable deterrent capability due to its inability to threaten Western targets far from its borders, combined with its loss of Soviet patronage, both ensured that the United States was in a strong position to press for more extensive demands and back them with threats.

The United States initiated Operation Desert Shield on August 2. 1990 which saw over half a million troops deployed to the Gulf region alongside vast quantities of equipment, from battle tanks and carrier battle groups to new F-117 stealth fighters. On November 29, Washington gained support from the United Nations Security Council through Resolution 678 to use all necessary means to evict Iraqi forces from Kuwait. Having recently capitulated in the Cold War, the USSR was increasingly dependent on Western aid[10] and voted in favour, and with China seeking to avoid confrontation with the West at a time of high instability and abstaining, the Security Council had for the first time since 1950 authorised Western military action against a third world state. The U.S. would refuse Soviet offers for a joint command, and the campaign would be waged overwhelmingly by the Western powers. The Western Bloc had built up a vast force with the primary purpose of fighting the Warsaw Pact, and with the Cold War's end this considerable war machine could now be directed against those parties which resisted the demands of the Western-led order. Redeployment to the gulf region was followed by Operation Desert Storm, which began on January 16, 1991 with an American-led attack on Iraqi positions. The attack saw Iraq subjected to intensive aerial bombardment with U.S. and allied aircraft flying over 100,000 sorties and dropping 88,500 tons of munitions. Iraq's armed forces, demoralised and poorly organized as they were, were quickly neutralized by America's military might,[11] while the country itself was devastated and its key civilian and military infrastructure was destroyed.

According to a report by the *Washington Post* in 1991, the purpose of the U.S. bombardment was to target Iraqi living standards by destroying key infrastructure such as oil refineries, electrical plants and transportation networks with precision guided weapons. Examples included the destruction of 80 percent of Iraq's power generation capabilities and the crippling of its sewage treatment system.[12] The population was forced to subsist on a starvation calorie intake at half the calories per person of the minimum standard for healthy living,[13] with malnutrition rising steeply across the country.[14] From an upper-middle income country with living standards surpassing many Western nations, Iraq was reduced to the level of an impoverished third world country by the Western Bloc's bombing campaign which was followed by 12 years of harsh economic sanctions. Living standards never recovered to pre-war levels and over 1 million of its population died as a result of war and subsequent sanctions.[15] According to statistics from American sources, by 1996 half a million Iraqi children had died as a result.[16] As Iraq's Foreign Minister and Prime Minister Tariq Aziz then lamented upon witnessing the devastation of his country: "If we still had the Soviets as our patron, none of this would have happened."[17]

The desolation of Iraq was watched closely around the world, particularly by those states such as North Korea, China and Iran which perceived themselves to be potential future targets. The future survival of all states independent of the Western dominated order was in serious jeopardy, and the American leadership, from the president to leading strategists, was calling for a unilateral role in world affairs. The primary focus was the preservation of American and Western dominance, which necessitated the quashing of both remaining outliers and potential challengers.[18] This came in the form of economic warfare, from which Russia[19] and the rising economies of the Asia-Pacific[20] would bear the brunt, as well as through overt military assault. In the 25 years between 1992 and 2017 the U.S. launched 188 military interventions abroad, while during the entire Cold War from 1948 to 1991 they had launched just 46 such interventions—an increase of over 600 percent in the number of interventions per year.[21]

With little to hold the power of the Western Bloc in check, neutral and former Soviet-aligned states across the world could be unilaterally targeted. Iraq was hardly an isolated case in this regard, although its destruction was the most dramatic and spectacular. Western military intervention against Yugoslavia demonstrated that even middle-sized powers could be attacked and ruthlessly bombarded unilaterally, with the attacks taking place without provocation and without a mandate from the United Nations Security Council. Aside from the illegality of the campaign many aspects of the war demonstrated a level of brutality by the attackers which reinforced the conviction of potential future target states to defend themselves. This included the use of cluster bombs[22] and depleted uranium shells[23] in populated areas with devastating and long-lasting impacts for the civilian population, the bombardment of civilian infrastructure[24] and purposeful targeting of media outlets[25] to break morale, and the conduct of Western forces during their subsequent occupation. American soldiers were found to have taken girls as young as 12 as sex slaves in Yugoslavia in the 1990s with multiple cases of rape and child rape.[26] North Korea and China both strongly condemned the Western attacks, and the perception of an imminent threat appeared to bridge the differences between the two East Asian states leading to closer bilateral cooperation. Pyongyang saw U.S. led attacks in 1999 against the Yugoslavia in the Kosovo War, just four years after the signing of the Dayton Peace Agreement with Belgrade, as confirmation of the nature of the new international order which placed its sovereignty at serious risk.[27]

Changes in world order and an increasing number of overseas military interventions by the Western Bloc taking advantage of its new freedom of action were followed by changes in the American rationale for waging war. According to Scott Silverstone, Associate Professor of International Relations at the West Point Military Academy, preventative war, which had been rejected throughout the Cold War as a sole pretext for military intervention, was increasingly considered an acceptable pretext by American governments from the early 1990s. This form of warfare involved initiating conflict to prevent a certain actor from attaining military capabilities the U.S. deemed undesirable. While legal grounds for pre-emptive war—launching an attack preceding the expected initiation of conflict to gain an advantage—were already somewhat fragile, preventive war had little if any justification in international law and was considerably more aggressive and provocative. Conceptually the United States' grounds for waging wars had changed dramatically, enabling those termed "rogue states," even if not directly threatening the U.S. or its allies, to be targeted without legal justification.[28]

The threat to North Korea from Ameriica's adoption of preventative war was considerable. While development of ballistic missiles was entirely legal, the Western Bloc had demonstrated that it could take upon itself the authority to demand, using threats of force, that other states disarm of such weapons. The Hwasong-5 and Hwasong-6 already in service seriously undermined American freedom of action on the peninsula, and Korean efforts to develop more capable asymmetric deterrents were bound to draw Washington's attention. The threat to North Korea and other potential target states worsened when the Pentagon announced a shift in its nuclear deterrence strategy emphasizing its rejection of the no first use policy. The U.S. meanwhile rejected the Non-Proliferation Treaty-linked negative security assurances banning the use of nuclear weapons against non-nuclear states which were parties to the treaty, thus claiming the right to target non-nuclear states with nuclear weapons.[29] A cornerstone of this new strategy relied on unpredictability regarding when and under what pretexts force, including nuclear force, may be used. U.S. planners avidly sought to avoid "portray[ing] ourselves as too rational or cool-headed," according to a critical 1990s report from the United States Strategic Command which emphasized the benefits of appearing an irrational superpower able to strike its enemies at will at any time including with nuclear weapons.[30] While Pyongyang had perceived a serious nuclear threat from the United States before, which had grown considerably during the 1980s, the new and far more imminent nature of this threat was reemphasized by the Americans themselves in the immediate aftermath of the Cold War's end.

Responding to the New World

The spectacle of the Gulf War baptised a new world order in fire and Iraqi blood, followed by the outright collapse of the Soviet Union ten months later, ushered in a new era of hardship for the DPRK which forced the state to adopt a new strategy to survive. With the military and economic balances now overwhelmingly favouring its adversaries, and with its primary defence partner lost, Pyongyang faced crisis and a level of external pressure unprecedented since the Korean War. The loss of the vast majority of its major trading partners placed tremendous downward pressure on the size of the economy and maintaining living standards at their previous levels itself became a difficult task. Coupled with this was an urgent need to strengthen the country's defences, as without Soviet protection or military assistance, and with the United States adopting a new more interventionist policy, there appeared an imminent threat to national security.

To compensate for the loss of Soviet protection the budget of the Korean People's Army was increased considerably and wholly disproportionately to economic growth. The imminence of the American threat was seen to require such measures despite the trying economic situation of the time. Defence expenditure rose from $4.42 billion in 1988[31] to $5.45 billion in 1991[32]—peaking at $5.5 billion in 1992, before economic contraction forced considerable cuts.[33] The nature of the investments made by the KPA appear to have been heavily influenced by its observation of U.S. military strengths in the Gulf War[34] and the later Western campaign in Yugoslavia.[35] While the KPA placed considerable emphasis on underground fortifications based on its experience in the Korean War, the impressive recent performance of American precision weapons reemphasised their importance and led to a redoubling of KPA efforts to fortify key facilities underground. This included increased investment in protection against strikes with non-nuclear tactical weapons—where fortifications built in the 1960s had emphasised defence against nuclear and incendiary strikes. Some of the types of sites fortified underground included command and control centres, storage facilities for food and munitions, artillery emplacements near the demilitarised zone and even military housing. These fortifications allowed the KPA to preserve its equipment and its manpower under bombardment and assemble weaponry underground.[36]

A later U.S. Army War College Strategic Studies Institute study noted regarding the effects of campaigns in Iraq and Yugoslavia on the Korean military and the causes of the KPA's new emphasis of fortifications as a means of protection against American air attacks:

> From the end of the Korean War through Operation IRAQI FREEDOM [2003], North Korea has understood the operational and tactical implications that its underground facilities provide from countering adversarial intelligence surveillance and reconnaissance (ISR) to countering the danger of precision munitions. The 1999 Kosovo War provided North Korea with another opportunity to evaluate U.S. military operations in an area with terrain and weather similar to that of the Korean Peninsula, which included studying the adverse effects that this terrain and weather had upon America's high-tech arsenal.[37]

For modernisation of the KPA's tactical weaponry air defence systems remained a priority, while acquisition of an asymmetric deterrent through development of longer ranged ballistic missiles became increasingly central to its defence plans. North Korea's missile program made strides at this time, successfully testing the Taepodong-1 and Rodong-1 intermediate range platforms which for the first time extended the KPA's retaliatory reach beyond the Korean Peninsula. While the former was intended as a technology demonstrator,[38] the latter began large scale production as a ballistic missile in the mid 1990s and retained a formidable 1,500km range—placing U.S. military facilities across Japan within its range. Considering Japan's importance as a staging ground for American power projection onto Korea, as it had been in the Korean War and remained in U.S. war plans, the fact that targets there were no longer out of KPA reach was a major achievement which seriously complicated any prospective American offensive. The costs of developing the Rodong-1 were largely subsidized by its considerable export successes, with

Pakistan, Iran, Egypt and Libya all purchasing the platform and all but Libya acquiring rights for domestic manufacturing. The Rodong-1 was the first medium range ballistic missile not only for the KPA, but also in the service of all of its export clients.

Complementing the development of a missile deterrent, the Korean People's Army invested heavily in strengthening its air defences—modernising its air fleet and forming one of the densest ground based anti-aircraft missile and artillery networks in the world.[39] With the Western Bloc relying overwhelmingly on air attacks in the Korean War and all major wars since, the value of contesting control of one's airspace was not lost on the KPA leadership. One key measure was the fortification of air defence sites, which the Gulf War had demonstrated would be priority targets for Western attacks following a conflict's outbreak.[40] Unlike Iraq, Iran, Libya, Syria, Yugoslavia and other states in the Western Bloc's sights, the KPA managed to fortify its control centres, surface to air missiles and radar systems by deploying them from hardened underground shelters. Hardened doors in the ground would open and these systems could be raised on lifts to engage targets before being again withdrawn to safety—a resourceful and highly efficient means of seriously complicating potential enemy efforts to suppress its air defences.[41]

Although North Korea's relations with the USSR had deteriorated in the superpower's final years, the Soviet military establishment retained a considerable degree of independence and had largely resisted General Secretary Gorbachev's Westphilian line. Their influence was key to ensuring close cooperation was maintained with the KPA until the Soviet Union's final dissolution in December 1991,[42] and the Russian military retained a degree of cooperation beyond this date despite the firmly Western aligned position of the government in Moscow in the 1990s.[43] As such, the DPRK was able not only to acquire a licence and equipment to manufacture MiG-29 Fulcrum fighters domestically, but was able to produce these aircraft throughout the 1990s with input of Russian components. The first Korean-built MiG-29s flew on April 15, 1993, with a performance comparable to those built in Russia—more sophisticated than the export variants marketed to third world clients such as Iraq and Iran. In 1997 North Korea signed a contract with Russian state-run arms dealer Rosvooruzhenye for military cooperation, which included continuing assistance for the manufacture of MiG-29 jets in the DPRK. The country's Fulcrum fleet is estimated to have numbered around 35–40 jets at the time, and extending indigenous production would see it grow considerably larger.[44] This somewhat lessened the blow of losing Soviet military aid, and with the fighters integrating sophisticated radars and modern munitions supplied by Russia it ensured that the KPA fleet would remain a viable force. Production lines in Korea allowed the KPA to expand its MiG-29 fleet by 2–3 fighters per year.

The KPA acquired hardware at low cost from other cash strapped Soviet successor states, including 40 MiG-21bis fighters from Kazakhstan and sample T-80 tanks from Belarus[45] which were reverse engineered to improve indigenous Korean tank deigns. The MiG-21bis integrated relatively modern avionics, sensors and missiles and remained in production in the USSR until 1985—a considerable improvement of 1–2 generations on the older MiG-21 fighters which previously formed the mainstay of the Korean fleet.[46] Weapons transfers were made through secret channels to avoid detection by the Western Bloc, which sought to prevent North Korea, China[47] and a number of other parties from acquiring modern arms from the former Soviet Union, and often succeeded in blocking major arms deals.[48]

The continuing importance of a strong and stable Korean state in the eyes of Russia's military leadership was demonstrated by their continuing, albeit much reduced, defence cooperation. While Russia had under Western pressure acquiesced to demands to cease major arms exports to Iran, another potential target state,[49] sales to the DPRK quietly continued. The nature of the two most significant foreign acquisitions by the KPA during this period remains somewhat ambiguous, and included S-300 surface to air missile systems and lightweight ballistic missile submarines. Sales of an S-300 missile system, reportedly of the PMU-1 or PMU-2 variant, were rumoured from the mid-late 1990s but remained unconfirmed. Russian state media reported in passing in 2017 that North Korea had such a system in its inventory—although the variant and year of delivery remained unclear.[50] This very new system provided a very high degree of protection for North Korean airspace, complementing other acquisitions of air defence systems and fighter aircraft.

The second acquisition was that of 10 decommissioned Golf II Class diesel-electric submarines. The ships were designed to deploy R-21 ballistic missiles with a 1,650km range, and it has been speculated that missile technologies may have also been provided.[51] Given the Boris Yeltsin administration's directive to Russian arms manufacturers and the time of economic crisis to "sell anything to anyone,"[52] the benefits to Russian security of a more balanced correlation of forces in Korea, and

Pyongyang's willingness to pay in hard currency for valuable technologies, such sales to strengthen the KPA's deterrent capability are far from unthinkable. Indeed, corruption in the post-Soviet states was so severe at the time that the USSR's most capable interceptor jets integrating highly sensitive technologies were being sold for around $2 each when the right officials were adequately bribed.[53] There is no telling how much hardware North Korea was able to obtain, but there are significant indicators that technologies previously well beyond its reach were made accessible due to the Soviet collapse. Some reports also indicate that, despite considerable Western reprimand, the Russian military transferred technologies for more advanced submarine launched missiles and a complete missile for study to the KPA.[54] The state of the submarines, the number and classes of missiles delivered, if any, and whether any were put into active service, all remain uncertain. The technologies acquired, however, almost certainly benefitted Korea's domestic development of ballistic missile submarines which would be deployed from the mid 2010s with more advanced indigenous missiles.

Beginnings of a Nuclear Program

The extent to which the DPRK came to prize long range strike capabilities, and later the potential for a nuclear retaliatory capability, can be attributed to its experience during the Korean War. The discrepancy between the global reach of the Western Bloc's air and naval forces and the extremely limited retaliatory range of Chinese and Korean forces was a predominant if not *the* most predominant factor influencing the course of the war on a strategic level in the final stages. One key example was the ability of the U.S.-led coalition to target Chinese and KPA supply lines while its own logistical assets were effectively immune to retaliation, an imbalance which seriously advantaged the Western powers. The U.S. dreaded the potentially disastrous impacts of an attack on its own supply hubs at Pusan, or worse still on its facilities in Japan, which were key to sustaining the war effort, but because only the Soviet Union retained such a strike range these targets remained effectively invulnerable so long as Moscow was not provoked.

It was evident that the United States feared a conflict with the USSR because of both its long-range strike capabilities—with its Tu-4 bombers placing U.S. military facilities across the world and even the U.S. mainland within range[55]—as well as nuclear warheads. The latter served as a highly effective force multiplier for these assets, allowing a single bomber to carry the firepower of an entire fleet and eradicate a whole city or large military base. The presence of these assets so near the Korean theatre was key to constraining the ambitions of the Western Bloc's military campaign, with the presence of Soviet bombers in China even deterring even many of the more hawkish officials from unconditionally supporting an expansion of the war.

The imbalance in strike capabilities was also reflected in the tangible imbalance between the East Asian Allies and the U.S. coalition during the armistice negotiations, with North Korea intensively bombarded for three years and forced to make repeated concessions from a disadvantaged position while the Western Bloc faced no similar pressure due to its cities' effective invulnerability to attack. Considerable Chinese losses of supplies and equipment under bombardment also significantly increased the cost of the war and thereby placed further pressure on Beijing to bring the war to an end quickly. Not only was the U.S. mainland completely safe from bombardment, which could have been used to exert similar leverage on the negotiation process, but an attack on bases in Japan and Pusan was effectively unthinkable. Had the KPA or their Chinese allies retained a comparable strike capability, it is likely that armistice negotiations would have ended much earlier and without such a one-sided outcome. There is little doubt that the Western powers would have shown considerably more restraint in bombing North Korea—from the destruction of irrigation dams to the incineration of its cities in firebombing raids—if it too was at least somewhat vulnerable to attacks against its own population centres.

Pyongyang recognised that beyond grit and tenacity of its own soldiers and those in the PVA, two primary factors had constrained Western freedom of action during the Korean War. These were the threat of Soviet long ranged strike capabilities and the threat of Soviet nuclear weapons—without which nuclear attacks on both the DPRK and on China would very likely have been attempted. With the USSR no longer present as a constraint on Western designs, it was necessary to at least partially replicate these capabilities domestically for the Korean state to ensure its security. A third constraining factor during the Korean War, the impracticality of nuclear attacks on heavily fortified Korean positions, had largely been negated as technologies for nuclear delivery had advanced—with thermonuclear weapons, neutron bombs, precision guided tactical nuclear bombs and bunker buster nuclear bombs now all fielded in large numbers in the U.S. arsenal and capable of doing what the primitive bombs such as Mark 4 "Fat Man" of the early 1950s could not.

It is unclear whether the DPRK had been committed to developing a nuclear deterrent before 1991, but if there was such a program the U.S.-led air campaign against Iraq appeared to have accelerated it and the accompanying development of a ballistic missile deterrent.[56] The DPRK had sent 30 students to study nuclear science in the USSR in 1956, the first of many, and obtained a small Soviet research reactor of around 4 megawatts in 1964. The Yongbyon Nuclear Scientific Research Center, a 30-wegawatt uranium fueled facility, went into operation in 1986, and in 1989 satellite imagery reportedly showed evidence of a larger reactor with a 50–200 megawatt capacity which was expected to begin operating around 1992. While these facilities would have provided a strong foundation for developing nuclear arms, North Korea had signed the Nuclear Non-proliferation Treaty in December 1985 and could derive considerable benefits from the peaceful development of nuclear energy. In line with its Juche ideology of self-reliance, nuclear power and parallel investments in hydroelectric power had the potential to seriously reduce Pyongyang's considerable dependence on imported fossil fuels.[57]

That there was a strong connection between the demonstration of Western might against Iraq and expected changes to the ongoing conflict on the Korean Peninsula, which was alluded to directly by prominent American sources. The Carnegie Endowment's Leonard Spector and Jacqueline Smith published an article in *Arms Control Today* in March 1991, a month after Desert Storm, which alerted readers that the DPRK posed a threat to the new world order similar if not greater than that of Iraq. Fittingly titled "North Korea: The Next Nuclear Nightmare"—it implied that immediate action of a similar nature had to be taken on the Korean Peninsula. Former director of the Bureau of Politico-Military Affairs and Assistant Secretary of State, Leslie Gelb, who would two years later become president of the highly influential Council on Foreign Relations, published an article in the *New York Times* on April 10 targeting the DPRK with rhetoric closely mirroring that directed against Iraq a month prior. North Korea was, according to the new line increasingly adopted by Western media, "the next renegade state" and "run by a vicious dictator" with "a million men under arms," a ballistic missile arsenal and very likely a nuclear weapon "in a few years." The size and firepower of the KPA were depicted not as precautions for self-defense, but as signs of aggressive intent with the context of U.S. threats to the

East Asian state omitted from the vast majority of reports. While Western portrayals of the DPRK had never been particularly positive, the end of the Gulf War marked the beginning of a three decades-long campaign of propaganda and intense demonization which critically impacted public opinion across much of the world.

A week after the publication of Gelb's article, South Korea's Defense Minister Lee Jong Kuo threatened an attack on the Yongbyon facility—a level of hostility not seen in decades which resulted from the newfound position of strength of the U.S.-ROK alliance relative to the increasingly isolated North Korean state. Rhetoric against the DPRK continued to escalate that year, and in November the chairman of the Joint Chiefs of Staff, General Colin Powell, directly threatened the East Asian state with the same fate as Iraq, stating that if North Korea "missed Desert Storm, this is a chance to catch a rerun."[58] A South Korean defense white paper published at the time stated that the DPRK's nuclear program "must be stopped at any cost"—implying that initiation of hostilities was on the table and the alliance was increasingly countenancing preventative warfare.[59] Media in America and the wider Western world demonstrated a considerable degree of hostility, and an article from the *Bulletin of Atomic Scientists* noted in April 1992: "Alarmist press reports have meanwhile reduced the projections on a North Korean bomb from five years to one year, to this year, to within 'a matter of months,' to the claim that the requisite plutonium is already in hand." The article noted regarding the shift in portrayals of the country and the imminent threat it allegedly posed: "North Korea was, in short, another Iraq."[60] The *Chicago Tribune* twice called for an American attack on the DPRK to destroy the Yongbyon facility in 1991, and similar calls were made by a number of U.S. media outlets.[61]

While North Korea was threatened by the United States, a number of factors meant that it was not immediately targeted with military force in the way Iraq, among others, had been. Foremost among these was the Western Bloc's failure since 1945 to understand the nature of the DPRK—and its predecessor the Korean People's Republic—as independent forces on the world stage representing the aspirations for sovereignty and national dignity of the Korean nation. While a number of U.S. officials had come to this conclusion in their encounters with the Korean People's Republic and its constituent People's Committees in southern Korea during the 1940s,[62] this was not the prevailing view. The need to delegitimize this movement and thereby legitimize the imposition of

Syngman Rhee and American military rule had required portraying the People's Republic and its successor the DPRK as agents of an "international communist conspiracy" run by Moscow, and the U.S. then seemed to fall victim to its own propaganda. A U.S. Army colonel had on this basis described the relationship between Soviet leader Joseph Stalin and his Korean counterpart Kim Il Sung as similar to that between Walt Disney and Donald Duck—discounting the Korean leader's decades long struggle against Japanese occupation or the considerable prestige he enjoyed across the Korean Peninsula including in the ROK for many years.[63] Western portrayals of the nature of the Korean state north of the 38th parallel and the resulting paradigm through which the state was viewed meant its collapse shortly after that of its supposed creator the Soviet Union, much as communist Mongolia and Soviet client states in Eastern Europe had collapsed, was seen as inevitable. As such, forcefully bringing about the end of North Korea was not seen as a matter of urgency—with the application of economic pressure the state was expected to quietly extinguish itself within a relatively short time much as the Warsaw Pact had.

A secondary factor was the DPRK's already formidable military strength, which other than China made it by far the most challenging military target of the states outside the Western-led order. Yugoslavia, Haiti, Cuba, Iran, Iraq, Sudan, Libya, Syria and others were all much softer targets. The KPA boasted the most sophisticated defense industry, densest air defense network, best trained soldiers, hardest fortifications and largest submarine forces and special forces of these states. Of America's potential targets, Korean air, artillery, tank and ballistic missile forces were second only to those of China. North Korea was thus the second highest apple on the tree, which contributed to granting it a temporary reprieve as the U.S. moved to knock other states off its target list in Eastern Europe, the Caribbean and the Islamic World.

The freeing up of assets from the European theater, which were subsequently deployed temporarily to the Middle East to counter Iraq, could be diverted to strengthen America's military presence in Northeast Asia. An array of lethal new weapons from precision guided cruise missiles to radar-evading F-117 strike fighters all turned the military balance further in its favor. Ambiguity regarding American intentions and the deployment of such assets to the theatre complemented mounting economic pressure by forcing Pyongyang to divert more resources to defense, and provided options for preventative military strikes as concerns regarding the Korean nuclear program pervaded. Tensions between the United States and the DPRK would escalate almost immediately after the inauguration of the Bill Clinton administration on January 20, 1993. Fears that North Korea would develop a viable nuclear deterrent, which would provide Pyongyang with an effective means of checking American military power, led to a new hard line against the country involving considerable military pressure. On February 9, 1993 the International Atomic Energy Agency requested unexpected and highly intrusive inspections of North Korean sites outside its nuclear facilities, which the DPRK stated were military facilities and refused the inspectors access to. Such a request from the agency had never been made of any other country in the past and was highly suspicious. Considering later revelations that U.S. used United Nations inspectors to collect intelligence on potential target states, and accessed highly sensitive intelligence gathered by the United Nations Special Commission's teams in Iraq to plan attacks on the country, the Korean response proved to be justified given the considerable national security threat it faced.[64] UN inspection teams, it later emerged, had been heavily infiltrated by U.S. and British intelligence to attempt to engineer a coup in Iraq, organize the assassination of its leader and gather otherwise inaccessible high-value intelligence.[65] Granting them free reign in Korea would have posed a similar threat.

Pyongyang denied the IAEA access to the additional sites for two reasons. The first was that the IAEA's impartiality had been compromised by its cooperation with the CIA and reliance on information provided by American intelligence—a belligerent party in the ongoing Korean War.[66] The second was that the IAEA passed results of its inspections of those Korean facilities to which it was granted access on to the United States—including plutonium samples. Should the DPRK accept these demands it would not only see its security compromised, but its acceptance would also potentially lead to further similar demands by the U.S. aligned agency as a means of exposing the country's entire defense system to U.S. intelligence. Indeed, many officials in the United States had advocated for precisely such a course of action.[67] Bush administration officials had told the *New York Times* a year prior in January 1992 that the U.S. required "a mandate to roam North Korea's heavily guarded military sites at will."[68] The DPRK further noted that the IAEA had not sought to examine former U.S. nuclear sites in South Korea—which it suspected still housed nuclear weapons despite their reported removal in 1991. Later reports from U.S. military sources would give much credence to these suspicions.[69] By its actions the IAEA was acting as an effective proxy for Western intelligence gathering in Korea.

This incident with the IAEA was shortly followed by the announcement of General Lee Butler, head of the U.S. Strategic Command, that part of the American strategic nuclear arsenal previously aimed at the Soviet Union would now be directed at North Korea.[70] Thus the DPRK had not only lost Soviet protection, but American assets both conventional and nuclear formerly tied up against the USSR were now being diverted to the Korean front. 43 years after the KPA and the U.S. Military first clashed, was the Western superpower hoping to crush the Korean resistance to its dominion over Northeast Asia once and for all?

In late February CIA director R. James Woolsey Jr. testified that North Korea was "our most grave current concern"—indicating that, like Iraq before it, the DPRK was likely next to fall into America's crosshairs.[71] This was closely followed by the resumption of the Team Spirit military exercises on March 8, 1993 after their cancellation under the Bush administration the previous year. These were the first such exercises to take place since the Soviet dissolution, and involved around 200,000 troops, new M1 and K1 heavy battle tanks, B-52H and B-1B heavy bombers, and an armada deploying several hundred precision guided cruise missiles, among other new assets. With the Soviet Union gone, this show of force appeared all the more daunting. As the Korean Peninsula was still under a fragile armistice, and America increasingly perceived itself as invulnerable following Desert Storm, there was a very real possibility from Pyongyang's perspective that massive new exercises practicing an assault on the DPRK could be a cover for a genuine attack. Indeed, such a massive presence forced the KPA to divert considerable resources to maintaining a high level of combat readiness throughout the exercises—putting great strain on the state's already struggling finances. According to U.S. Congressman Gary Ackerman, who visited the DPRK in 1993, President Kim Il Sung's voice "quivered and his hands shook with anger" at the mention of the U.S. war drills.[72]

Five days after the beginning of the Team Spirit exercises on March 13, citing its rights under Article X of the Nuclear Non-Proliferation Treaty, Pyongyang gave the required three-month notice for withdrawal from the agreement. While the use of nuclear weapons in previous Team Spirit exercises were deployed under the pretext of engaging both the DPRK and the Soviet Union, it was abundantly clear that the small non-nuclear East Asian state was now being threatened with nuclear weapons. This amounted to a violation of a key principle of the non-proliferation treaty and an imminent threat—a valid reason for withdrawal under the treaty's tenth article.[73] It is possible that this marked the official beginning of the country's pursuit of nuclear weapons, although some sources have also speculated that withdrawal from the NPT in this instance was intended to provide a bargaining chip to reduce American military pressure.[74] The withdrawal, although entirely legal, strengthened calls in the U.S. for military action against the DPRK—an illegal act of aggression which was becoming increasingly normalised in the post-Cold War world when perpetrated by the Western powers. Calls for an attack were widespread, from media to government to influential policy think tanks. Chairman of the Appropriations Subcommittee, on Defence John Murtha called the DPRK "America's greatest security threat" and called for use of "smart weapons" to neutralise its facilities.[75] Leslie Gelb, now head of the Council on Foreign Relations, made a similar argument again comparing the DPRK to Saddam Hussein's Iraq—giving strong indications of aggressive intent on America's part.[76]

With nuclear strikes against the DPRK and other non-nuclear states increasingly legitimized under newly adopted doctrines, and with Washington reported by well-placed sources in 1993 to be planning a strategic nuclear expeditionary force aimed at third world nations such as North Korea, China and Iran,[77] the DPRK moved to accelerate its acquisition of a deterrent capability. The East Asian state achieved considerable results in this regard, and staged a formidable show of force on May 29, 1993 with the launch of a Rodong-1 medium range ballistic missile. What was particularly notable about the test was its precision—successfully targeting a small buoy in the Sea of Japan hundreds of kilometers away. While some Western sources attributed this test to fluke, others saw it as a warning of the country's considerable technological prowess.[78] At the time a ground based medium range missile capability was far from a common asset, and with the Rodong-1 entering service and mass production in 1994, the DPRK became the fourth state in the world which deployed such a system.

Able to negotiate from a position of greater strength with the Rodong-1 augmenting its existing deterrence capabilities, the DPRK could propose terms for discussion with the United States. Major meetings were held from June 2 to June 11, and in a subsequent joint statement both pledged not to attack or ever use nuclear weapons against the other, to respect one another's sovereignty, not to interfere in one another's internal affairs and to continue dialogue.[79] Five months later in November the Korean side proposed a "package deal" which required further assurances from the United States that it would not attack the DPRK, would suspend the Team Spirit Exercises, and most importantly, would end nuclear threats against it. In return the DPRK would remain in the NPT and would renounce its entire system of graphite nuclear reactors in exchange for a supply of light water reactors. These would provide peaceful nuclear energy but could not be used to develop nuclear weapons. The Korean terms allowed IAEA inspections of nuclear sites to continue but would not allow inspections of its military facilities. It also called for a general improvement and normalization of relations between the two states. A number of U.S. sources familiar with the negotiations reported that the Korean proposal in fact went further and called for an end to the Korean War armistice and signing of a conclusive peace treaty, establishment of full diplomatic relations, mutual force reductions and removal of trade restrictions.[80]

Emphasizing that it would remain party to the NPT only in return for security guarantees and a normalization of ties, and not due to American pressure, Pyongyang stated in late November: "When we declared our decision to withdraw from the NPT, we had taken into account all possible consequences, and we are fully prepared to safeguard the sovereignty of our country even if the worst such as 'sanctions' or war is imposed on us."[81] The United States for its part appeared to seek an assertion of its own dominance through the toppling of the Korean state and removal of the Korean Workers' Party from power, rather than a mutually beneficial agreement which did not entail one party acquiescing to the other. Indeed, Western scholarly and journalistic publications increasingly reflected perceptions that an end to the Cold War gave America the chance to set the record straight in Korea and impose a vengeance long since due on "the same evil Kim Il Sung, still all powerful in the half-country he has tortured so much" who had thwarted the Western Bloc's designs for over 40 years.[82] Thus negotiations reached a deadlock, with the U.S. seeking to apply maximum pressure to force the its adversary to yield to unequal terms and the DPRK settling for nothing less than a deal with equitable mutual concessions.

Washington was inclined to defer from resorting to military options due to three primary factors. The strength of the KPA, increasingly well-armed and able to hold its own against an American conventional attack, meant that a war would exert unacceptable costs. In several American wargames simulating a conflict in Korea, the result was a North Korean victory so long as nuclear weapons were not used.[83] Secondly, as previously mentioned, it was widely perceived in the West that a Soviet "puppet state" could not long outlive its master, and that imposition of economic sanctions both unilaterally by the Western world and if possible through the United Nations would speed up this process and guarantee the DPRK's implosion. Thirdly, America and its allies were well aware that a new Korean War would be unprecedented in its scale and destruction at least since 1953—but most likely since 1945—and would require the use of nuclear weapons to neutralize KPA fortifications as AirLand Battle projected. A nuclear war in Northeast Asia could destabilize the post–Cold War world order and prompt dramatic responses from third parties. The position of Russia's military establishment, while diminished, remained distinct from that of Moscow itself. Dropping American nuclear weapons so near Russia's border could prompt a drastic response. This could materialize in political change within Russia itself, or internationally in the form of proliferation of advanced weapons to other U.S. targets such as Iran, Syria and possibly even Iraq. A Chinese response was also a significant factor, with Beijing likely to at the very least to cool relations in response to an attack on its treaty ally, which could jeopardize considerable U.S. economic interests there. These factors were far from a credible deterrent, but nonetheless inclined the United States, which was increasingly preoccupied with conflicts elsewhere, to look to means other than war to force Pyongyang's capitulation.

Tensions continued to escalate in 1994, with the DPRK Foreign Ministry stating: "The United States has created a momentous crisis that is likely to develop into a catastrophe, at this crucial juncture when prospects are in sight for saving the DPRK-USA talks from the current deadlock and striking a package solution to the nuclear issue." The "package solution" referred to Pyongyang's goal of ending the Korean War and fully normalizing relations alongside an end to the nuclear issue. Washington had little pretext not to improve relations, and while propagandized claims regarding the "psychotic" nature of the Korean leadership were widespread in Western media, they did not permeate into the rhetoric of American policymakers at the time. The DPRK had joined the United Nations alongside South Korea on September 17,1991, and with the Cold War's end South Korea had been recognized by both Russia and China and even by Vietnam—putting the onus on America to reciprocate by recognizing the north. The two Koreas themselves were at the time fast improving relations and moving closer to mutual recognition.

In May 1994 Pyongyang moved to force the U.S. to the negotiating table, shutting down a single reactor and withdrawing 8000 plutonium fuel rods. These were subsequently placed in cooling ponds and could provide the material needed to manufacture the country's first nuclear warheads. This was taken as a clear sign of Pyongyang's intent to weaponize plutonium to develop a nuclear deterrent, with heavy water plutonium reactors providing the fastest and most efficient way of doing so. Other than military action, this left negotiations as the only means for Washington to prevent the DPRK from manufacturing nuclear warheads. In response the Clinton administration seriously considered initiating Operations Plan 5027 on June 15, which would see cruise missiles and F-117 stealth fighters attack the Yongbyon facility.[i] Other options included pushing for further economic sanctions through the United Nations and deploying more forces to the Korean Peninsula including 50,000 more troops—neither of which would have prevented the DPRK's nuclearization which U.S. officials deemed unacceptable.[84] Prospects of war with such a heavily armed state, one widely predicted as almost certain to collapse within a decade, made a diplomatic option far more favorable however. Thus when former U.S. President Jimmy Carter visited the DPRK in June and proposed a freeze on activities at Yongbyon and a commitment not to withdraw plutonium fuel rods from the cooling ponds in exchange for delivery of light water reactors, which the Korean leadership accepted, the Clinton administration was more than willing to resume high level talks and shelve options for an attack.[85]

The U.S. and the DPRK eventually reached an agreement in late 1994, known as the Agreed Framework, which was signed on October 21st of that year. It stipulated that the U.S. would provide North Korea with light water reactors in return for DPRK's freezing of its graphite reactors and placing of the cooling ponds storing the plutonium fuel rods from Yongbyon under IAEA inspection. The new reactors would be able to provide for the country's energy needs but could not easily be used to develop nuclear weapons. Oil would be delivered by the U.S. until

i An attack on Yongbyon without a UN Security Council Resolution, and with the DPRK in full compliance with international law, would have amounted to a wholly illegal preventative attack and act of aggression by the United States. That such action was so nearly carried out was a direct result of the U.S. adoption of preventative warfare as a viable means of opening hostilities—to deny independent parties capabilities which challenged the Western Bloc's military freedom of action.

the new reactors were received to meet the DPRK's energy needs in the interim. The framework further stipulated that Washington would simultaneously begin to improve diplomatic ties with Pyongyang with the intention of forming full diplomatic relations and a lifting of economic sanctions, which continued to cut the DPRK off from the vast majority of the world economy.[86] This agreement was largely unprecedented in that it was the first time that the United States had made significant concessions.

It was widely reported in the Western press, and privately admitted by Clinton administration officials, that Washington had signed on to the terms of the Agreed Framework only because it had anticipated that the DPRK would collapse before the program was complete and the reactors would be delivered.[87] The death of President Kim Il Sung in early July, three months before the framework's signing, likely increased Washington's optimism that its oldest adversary would imminently implode—adding to the momentum from the Soviet collapse. North Korean officials also suspected that the American side's anticipation of a swift collapse had influenced their decision making, and that freezing the Korean nuclear program by promising to provide light water reactors, sanctions relief and fuel were intended as means to buy time against the DPRK's nuclear development until this supposed inevitability occurred.[88]

Against the overwhelming predictions of the United States and the wider Western world, North Korea remained stable long past the Agreed Framework, which obliged Washington to fulfill its side of the contract. In 1998 U.S. officials testified to Congress that there had been no fundamental violations of any aspect of the framework agreement by the Korean side.[89] U.S. intelligence confirmed that the fuel rods were under international supervision, that both the Yongbyon reactor and reprocessing plant were not being operated, and that construction of two larger reactors had ceased—placing Pyongyang's actions fully in accordance with its obligations.[90] From 1996, however, promised oil deliveries by the United States began to be delayed, and by 1998 the U.S. had still not even begun to fund the light water reactors. Thus while the DPRK was holding up its end of the deal the Americans, while not directly withdrawing, were falling far short on their commitments.

America's failure to live up to its side of the Agreed Framework was repeatedly reiterated in a U.S. Senate Hearing in 1998, but little action was taken to correct this.[91] Pyongyang's response was to warn that it would restart the Yongbyon reactor if the U.S. did not fulfill its obligations,[92] and chief American negotiator Robert Gallucci warned that the framework could collapse if the U.S. did not do so.[93] The U.S. had, furthermore, failed to meet its commitment to normalize political and economic relations and had kept economic sanctions in place. With the DPRK facing an economic crisis and an unprecedented natural disaster from flooding that took place in 1995, the government appeared closer to collapse than ever in its history. It was hoped that maintaining sanctions could push the country over the brink—thus rendering the entire agreement obsolete and extending Western influence and ROK rule north of the 38th parallel. Delaying agreed upon fuel and reactor deliveries while also denying the DPRK access to nuclear energy from Yongbyon would only further exacerbate its ongoing crisis.

Economic Crisis

The mid 1990s would come to be known in the DPRK as the second "Arduous March"—the harshest trial the nation had faced surpassed only by the Korean War. This was a result not only of escalating military threats and Western-led efforts to bring about its political isolation, but also of economic disaster, which could be attributed to two primary factors. The first was the country's state of newfound economic isolation. The collapse of the Soviet Bloc meant the loss of the DPRK's leading trading partners, the loss of Soviet economic aid and the end of the Soviet-led Council for Mutual Economic Assistance (COMCON), which had been vital to the country's energy security. Taking the USSR and its successor state Russia as an example, trade volume had been $2.5 billion in 1990, but fell to just $38.5 million in 2000—although illicit cross border trade and unannounced arms transfers likely increased this figure.[94] The collapse of trade with eastern European states was, if anything, more dramatic. Pyongyang's isolation was cemented by American actions, including harsh unilateral economic sanctions and imposition of further restrictions on its access to the vast majority of the world economy under the Trading with The Enemy Act and through the Coordinating Committee for Export Control to Communist Areas. The second factor was natural disaster on a scale unprecedented since the 19th century, which perfectly coincided with mounting Western economic pressure with the effects of each complementing the other.

While economic downturn and severe food shortages did not bring about the DPRK's collapse its adversaries had hoped, the crisis was spun in Western reports to accuse Pyongyang of "starving its citizens" and purposefully collapsing food production to cause its people suffering. In doing so, the intention was both to demonise and delegitimise the Korean government internationally. U.S. President George W. Bush would characterize the country in the aftermath of the crisis in 2002 as: "a regime arming with missiles and weapons of mass destruction; while starving its citizens." Similar statements were made by a number of officials, including Under Secretary of State for Arms Control and International Security Affairs John Bolton in 2002[95] and Ambassador to the United Nations Samantha Power in March 2016[96] and have been widely published by Western press since. An assessment of the history of food production in the country, the reasons for its collapse in the 1990s, and the means by which it was restored afterwards, seriously undermine the Western claim that the conditions of the Arduous March delegitimized the Korean government and were engineered by Pyongyang.

Before the division of the Korean peninsula, the southern half had been the breadbasket of the country, with its land and resources far better suited to agriculture. Following the partition the DPRK sought to develop sustainable agriculture without extensive reliance on food imports—a difficult task given its generally poor soil quality and high mountain coverage.[97] In order to attain high enough crop yields to feed the population it invested heavily in both the mechanization of agriculture and the development of a considerable fertilizer and chemical industry. A *London Times* reporter motoring through the country in early 1950 described "a countryside as trim and carefully husbanded as any in Asia,"[98] with crop yields rising considerably in later years as more advanced technologies were applied. According to the CIA, the DPRK attained food self-sufficiency in 1970 with a growth in grain production rates far ahead of population growth rates.[99] CIA reports from 1978 comparing these successes to the ROK stated that grain production was growing faster in the North, and that living standards in rural areas "have probably improved faster than in the South." The agency further reported: "North Korean agriculture is quite highly mechanised, fertilizer application is probably among the highest in the world, and irrigation projects are extensive."[100]

Prominent American Korea expert Professor Bruce Cumings noted, regarding his own findings on Korean agriculture: "When I visited [DPRK] in 1981 and 1987, flying over from China in a propjet, I could see that the fields were a deep green and, when I visited villages, that every inch of land was carefully tended… In the 1980s the DPRK claimed to have the highest per hectare rice output in the world; although that claim cannot be proved, experts who visited the country's did not question the North's general agricultural success."[101] The American Institute for Food and Development Policy published a research report on the DPRK's efforts to attain food self-sufficiency in 1986, which stated:

> The North Koreans started to reorganize agriculture immediately after the 1953 Korean armistice to respond to the productive demands created by their policy of self-reliance.... They sought to produce those foods which could be efficiently produced given their climate, resource endowment, and socio-cultural requirements. Throughout the period since the end of the Korean War they have engaged in international trade in foodstuffs, but have never eased up on their commitment to maintain a balance or a surplus on their foreign account in food and to be able to feed themselves entirely from national supplies. It appears that they have been generally successful in this regard for the past decade.[102]

The DPRK's energy-intensive food production was seriously threatened by the Soviet collapse and the resulting closure of fuel and fertilizer imports from the USSR. Blacklisted as a "rogue state" by the Western Bloc and placed under harsh economic sanctions, the DPRK struggled to import necessary inputs for its agriculture sector from other sources. International organizations such as the World Food Programme responsible for preventing famine remained widely inactive at this time, allowing the crisis to worsen. Although the DPRK was not facing famine, its agriculture was struggling due to the unforeseen political events of the early 1990s.

Food shortages in North Korea only reached critical levels when the situation was exacerbated by natural disaster, with independent observers reporting floods of "biblical proportions" and devastated crops, arable land and economic infrastructure. The United Nations Department of Humanitarian Affairs reported: "between 30 July and 18 August 1995, torrential rains caused devastating floods in the Democratic People's Republic of Korea. In one area, in Pyongsan county in North Hwanghae province, 877mm of rain were recorded to have fallen in just seven hours, an intensity of precipitation unheard of in this area...water flow in the engorged Amnoc River, which runs along the Korea/China border, was estimated at 4.8 billion tons over a 72 hour period. Flooding of this magnitude had not been recorded in at least 70 years."[103]

Senior fellow at the Center for International Policy, senior scholar of the Woodrow Wilson International Center for Scholars and expert on U.S. foreign policy in Asia Selig S. Harrison, a figure who played a central role in negotiations between the U.S. and the DPRK under the Clinton administration, noted regarding the sudden environmental crisis: "The areas most severely damaged in the 1995 and 1996 floods were the 'breadbasket provinces' in the south and west that produce most of North Korea's grain. Moreover, even before the floods struck, North Korean agriculture had been paralyzed by the loss of the Soviet oil that had fuelled its tractors and fertiliser factories." Referring to North Korea as "a mountainous country with only 18 per cent of its land arable," he noted "despite this ambitious irrigation, reclamation, and mechanization programs that have brought impressive increases in food production." Harrison stated that the crisis was further exacerbated by a cut in food imports from China in 1995, a drastic fall from the 600,000 tons imported the previous year, due to growing demand in China itself and the new blanket ban on food exports by Beijing. This "left Pyongyang in the lurch just when the floods struck," exacerbating the setbacks from a loss of Soviet trade, Western economic sanctions, natural disaster and the already poor suitability of the terrain for agriculture.[104]

U.S. reporter Hugh Deane, former Coordinator of Information and naval intelligence officer on General MacArthur's staff, wrote regarding the causes of the Korean agricultural crisis:

> In 1995 the Yalu River, along the northern border, flooded south as torrential rains fell, causing mountain avalanches and rock slides as well as inundated villages. The Korean People's Army evacuated many people in peril, dropping down in helicopters when necessary. The 1996 flood came when the earlier flood had not entirely receded and the damage was even more extensive. Close to a million acres of paddy and dry field were covered with mud or otherwise taken out of cultivation. A million tons of stored grain were washed away. Railroads, roads, bridges, dams and irrigation systems suffered, coal mines were flooded, some to such an extent that they have been abandoned. More industries were lost, some soon torn down for scrap. Then this year the usual rainy season was rainless. Nearly all the maize crop, normally a million tons, was lost. The rice crop was reduced, both

> because of the drought and because there was no fertilizer to apply to it. Such are the circumstances that brought hunger and starvation to a great many.[105]

As the DPRK's extensive grain reserves were largely stored underground, a precaution against American air attacks taken since the Korean War, they were destroyed by flooding. According to the UN, the floods in 1994 and 1995 destroyed 1.5 million tons of the country's grain reserves.[106] According to the UN Development Program's 1998 report, reserves of rice and corn fell from 3–4 and 4–5 million tons respectively in 1989 to significantly less than 1 million tons each in 1996, and the loss of reserves at a crucial time spelt disaster for Korea. The impact on infrastructure was also catastrophic, with 85% of the country's power generating capacity lost and around 5.4 million people losing their homes. Mudflows blocked transportation and communication networks while coal mines were flooded—further exacerbating the country's energy crisis.[107] Though the flooding of 1995 could be considered the largest, most severe of the 20th century, 1996 brought equally heavy flooding followed by a severe drought in 1997.[108]

Dr. Konstantin Asmolov, a leading Korea expert and researcher at the Russian Academy of Sciences and the Institute of Asian and African Studies at Moscow State University, was one of many scholars who noted that the causes of the Korean economic disaster and resulting famine were often intentionally misrepresented by Western sources to demonize and delegitimize North Korea's government. He wrote regarding the second Arduous March:

> Several misconceptions cropped up around the disaster. The most common was that the incompetent policies of the North Korean leadership deliberately lead the country to starvation and millions died… One gets the impression that if just one of the above problems [poor agricultural potential, loss of Soviet partnership, extreme weather, economic sanctions] had been removed from the scales, the situation could have tipped towards a far less tragic outcome.[109]

Dr. Asmolov further detailed how the actions of external powers exacerbated Korea's hardships, stating:

> Under normal circumstances, the international community would intervene in such humanitarian catastrophes, but in the case of North Korea, ideology again played a role.... Many believed that North Korea would collapse very soon on its own accord. So, it was thought that it wasn't necessary to try very hard to help them. That's at least how South Korea acted. First they smugly announced an assistance program (a small amount of aid raised by NGOs). They demanded, however, unacceptable conditions that would have been de facto interference in the internal politics of the country. So when Pyongyang refused to accept, they began to lobby for economic sanctions against North Korea to stop all deliveries of food. It seems they calculated "the worse, the better." A representative of the conservatives who later held a respectable diplomatic post openly told the author that, in seeking to restrict the flow of food aid to Pyongyang, they were pursuing a specific policy goal. In a crisis, the North Korean masses would begin to speak out against the regime, which would leave them to fend for themselves, and if the boat was correctly shaken, the communist state in the north would collapse. Then the nation, in his opinion, would have united before the end of the term of Kim Young Sam, who would have gone down in history not only as the first civilian president, but also as the "destroyer of the DPRK."[110]

This policy was pursued regardless of hardships imposed on the Korean population and the cost in Korean lives.

A number of reports indicate that the United States and its allies took more direct measures, alongside their economic sanctions policy, to exacerbate crisis in the DPRK during the Arduous March. Kim Ryeon Hui, a North Korean citizen living in Seoul who previously resided in China and witnessed the effects of the Arduous March first hand, stated regarding U.S. actions against the DPRK at this time:

> During the Arduous March when food reserves were empty and farming was impossible, the U.S. blocked oil from coming in so 70% of our factories were shut down. We couldn't produce anything. The state needed produce to distribute to the people but we had nothing. All of a sudden [from 1995]

> our collective food source was devastated. We simply had no choice but to starve. South Korea doesn't share borders with other countries, but the north and China and Russia do, and with China there is no concept of a border so people come and go as they please. Back then, we crossed back and forth from China even more and our government let it be because the government knew it couldn't provide, so we traded goods in China and brought food back home constantly. And the damn Americans from the CIA operated in this border and did this: They would approach DPRK citizens and say "go cut off a cow's tail and bring it to me. I will give you a bag of rice for a cow's tail. Go cut down and bring me electric wires. I will match you the weight of the wire with rice." Why do you think the Americans wanted cow tails? We didn't have oil or electricity but we still had to manually farm to produce what little we can. But tractors don't work because gasoline imports are sanctioned by the U.S.. So we had to use cows instead to plough the fields, but when cows lose their tail they lose their balance and power. In order to ruin agriculture even more and to starve out the people, the Americans wanted cow tails so North Korea can starve to death.[111]

Against the near unanimous expectations of U.S. intelligence,[112] the DPRK did not collapse and would begin a slow recovery from crisis in the late 1990s. The conditions of the Arduous March did, however, provide its adversaries with a pretext to delegitimize the government in Pyongyang for failing to provide for its population—with some Western sources blaming the state for an astonishing 3 million deaths[113] in a population of little over 20 million. However, as data from a number of sources showed, while birth rates did not rise during the Arduous March period and remained modest, the population continued to grow at a stable rate. If deaths from starvation or starvation related illness did occur they remained relatively few in number. The World Bank estimated the North Korean population at 21.58 million in 1994 and 22.3 million in 1997, with growth rates remaining consistent with prior and later years. Its sources included the United Nations Population Division, Eurostat, the United Nations Statistical Division and the Secretariat of the Pacific Community, among others.[114] The International Institute for Strategic Studies cited the population at 23,112,000 in 1994,[115] the year before the

Arduous March, and at 24,681,000 on the year it ended in 1997.[116] While there is little doubt that the general health of the population did decline, and the standard of living plummeted during this period, Pyongyang's adversaries spread exaggerated and often entirely fabricated stories—the more horrific the better—to further smear and delegitimize its leadership in order to justify their further pressure for regime change.

While the crisis began to abate in the late 1990s and the Agreed Framework remained firmly in place, U.S. sanctions on North Korea which Washington had pledged to lift under the agreement remained fully in place. The aforementioned expert Selig S. Harrison had played a prominent role in initiating negotiations between Washington and Pyongyang and was reportedly the first to gain President Kim Il Sung's approval for a freeze on the DPRK's nuclear program in June 1994. Despite his often harsh criticisms of the Korean state, Harrison asserted in 1997 that, if assessed impartially, it was the United States which failed to adhere to its commitments under the Agreed Framework, while the DPRK remained fully in compliance with the deal. He stated:

> The removal of U.S. economic sanctions is a prerequisite for the overall liberalisation of economic relations with the West and Japan that the North seeks as the key to solving its economic problems, especially its food shortage. It was primarily because the United States promised to remove these sanctions that Pyongyang decided to conclude the nuclear freeze agreement. Article II, Section One of the agreement stated that "within three months of the date of this document, both sides will reduce barriers to trade and investment." This provision was unconditional and was not linked to performance on other issues.
>
> North Korean leaders express growing impatience with the United States for its failure to honour Article II. When I visited Pyongyang in September 1995, Vice Premier and Foreign Minister Kim Yong Nam said bluntly that the United States has cheated Pyongyang out of the most important benefits promised under the freeze agreement. In December 1996, high-ranking officials who came to New York for negotiations with U.S. diplomats told me in both formal and informal meetings that hardliners in Pyongyang were pushing aggressively for revocation of the agreement. What

> these officials say, in effect, is, "We're living up to our side of the deal. We have frozen our nuclear program, and this has been verified by the International Atomic Energy Agency inspectors and by U.S. government experts. We've given up our nuclear independence, and we've done it for one reason: Because we thought this would lead to friendly relations with the United States, particularly economic relations. But you have made only token reductions in trade and investment barriers. You are not living up to your part of the deal."
>
> An objective evaluation of the sanctions issue indicates that the North Korea grievance is justified. By January 1997, all that the United States had done to implement Article II was to lift sanctions on the export of one commodity (magnesite) and to grant permission to AT&T to open up telephone and fax communications. The few U.S. companies that have shown an interest in investing cannot get Treasury Department licences. General Motors, which looked into building an auto parts plant, is the prime example."[117]

Harrison further noted: "Cargill has received a licence for a barter deal—North Korean minerals for grain—but sanctions prevent U.S. agencies from providing the collateral needed to get grain shipments started."[118] North Korea would ultimately continue to adhere strictly to the terms of Agreed Framework unilaterally, a testament to the importance attributed to the lifting of sanctions at the time, even if only as a distant possibility. Such hopes would ultimately turn out to be misplaced, and relations would take a turn for the worse soon after the turn of the century.

NOTES

1 Tsukanov, Ilya, 'How Gorbachev Destroyed the USSR's Military Space Program, & What It Cost Russia,' *Sputnik*, May 14, 2017.
2 'Plugging the Air Defense "Gorbachev Gap": Russia's Voronezh Radar in Action,' *Sputnik*, June 7, 2017.
3 Friedman, Thomas and Tyler, Patrick E., 'From the First, U.S. Resolve to Fight,' *New York Times*, March 3, 1991.
4 Bush, George H. W., Address Before a Joint Session of the Congress on the Persian Gulf Crisis and the Federal Budget Deficit, September 11, 1990.
5 'George Bush Meet Woodrow Wilson,' *New York Times*, November 20, 1990.
6 *Foreign Affairs*, vol. 69. Issue 5, Winter 1990/91 (p. 23).
7 Heikal, Mohamed, *Illusions of Triumph: An Arab View of the Gulf War*, New York, HarperCollins, 1993 (pp. 175–177).

Nixon, John, *Debriefing the President; The Interrogation of Saddam Hussein*, London, Bantam Press, 2016 (p. 112).
8 Heikal, Mohamed, *Illusions of Triumph: An Arab View of the Gulf War*, New York, HarperCollins, 1993 (pp. 176, 178, 218).
9 Ibid. (p. 365).
10 Kramer, Mark, 'Food Aid to Russia: The Fallacies of US Policy,' PONARS Policy Memo 86, Harvard University, October 1999.
11 *The Military Balance*, Volume 89, International Institute for Strategic Studies, 1989 (pp. 101–102).
12 Gellman, Barton, 'Allied Air War Struck Broadly in Iraq,' *Washington Post*, June 23, 1991.
13 Joy, Gordon, *Invisible War: The United States and the Iraq Sanctions,* Cambridge, MA, Harvard University Press, 2010 (p. 25).
14 Woertz, Eckart, 'Iraq under UN Embargo, 1990–2003, Food Security, Agriculture, and Regime Survival,' in: *The Middle East Journal,* vol. 73, no. 1, Spring 2019 (p. 101).
Blaydes, Lisa, *State of Repression: Iraq under Saddam Hussein,* Princeton, NJ, Princeton University Press, 2018 (pp. 122–124).
15 'Iraq conflict has killed a million Iraqis,' *Reuters*, January 30, 2008.
16 'Sanctions Blamed for Deaths of Children,' *Lewiston Morning Tribune*, December 2, 1995.
Stahl, Lesley, 'Interview with Madeline Albright,' *60 Minutes*, May 12, 1996.
17 Friedman, Thomas and Tyler, Patrick E., 'From the First, U.S. Resolve to Fight,' *New York Times*, March 3, 1991.
18 Miller, Eric A., and Yetiv, Steve A., 'The New World Order in Theory and Practice: The Bush Administration's Worldview in Transition,' *Presidential Studies Quarterly*, vol. 31, no. 1, March 2001 (pp. 56–68).
19 Abrams, A. B., *Power and Primacy: The History of Western Intervention in the Asia-Pacific*, Oxford, Peter Lang, 2019 (Chapter 16: The Russian Factor in the Asia-Pacific).
20 Ibid. (Chapter 14: Economic War on Asia: South Korea and the Asian Tigers).
21 Duffy Toft, Monica, 'Why is America Addicted to Foreign Interventions?,' *The National Interest*, December 10, 2017.
22 Brady, Brian, 'NATO comes clean on cluster bombs,' *Independent,* September 16, 2007.
23 '"Up to 15 tons of depleted uranium used in 1999 Serbia bombing"—lead lawyer in suit against NATO,' *RT*, June 13, 2017.
Simons, Marlise, 'Radiation From Balkan Bombing Alarms Europe,' *New York Times,* January 7, 2001.
24 Williams, Daniel, 'NATO Bombs Serbia Into Darkness,' *Washington Post,* May 3, 1999.
25 McCormack, Timothy, *Yearbook of International Humanitarian Law—2003*, Cambridge, Cambridge University Press, 2006 (p. 381).
26 Vine, David, *Base Nation, How U.S. Military Bases Abroad Harm America and the World,* New York, Henry Holt and Company, 2015 (Chapter 9: 'Sex for Sale,' Section 5: 'Sold Hourly, Nightly or Permanently').
O'Meara, Kelly Patricia, 'US: DynCorp Disgrace,' *Insight Magazine*, January 14, 2002.
27 Ramani, Samuel, 'What North Korea Learned From the Kosovo War,' *The Diplomat,* October 16, 2017.
28 Beinart, Peter, 'How America Shed the Taboo Against Preventative War,' *The Atlantic*, April 21, 2017.
Silverstone, Scott, *Preventative War and American Democracy*, Abingdon, Routledge, 2007.

Smith, Derek D., *Deterring America: Rogue States and the Proliferation of Weapons of Mass Destruction*, Cambridge, Cambridge University Press, 2006 (pp. 116–120).

29 Chomsky, Noam, *The New Military Humanism; Lessons From Kosovo*, London, Pluto Press, 1999 (Chapter 6: Why Force?).

Defense Monitor, Washington, D.C., Center for Defense Information, XXIX.3, 2000.

30 *Essentials of Post–Cold War Deterrence*, Policy Subcommittee of the Strategic Advisory Group (SAG) of the United States Strategic Command, 1995.

Chomsky, Noam, *The New Military Humanism; Lessons From Kosovo*, London, Pluto Press, 1999 (pp. 145–146).

31 International Institute for Strategic Studies, *The Military Balance*, Volume 91, 1991, Part VIII: Asia and Australasia (p. 167).

32 International Institute for Strategic Studies, *The Military Balance*, Volume 92, 1992, Part VIII: Asia and Australasia (p. 167).

33 International Institute for Strategic Studies, *The Military Balance*, Volume 94, 1994, Part VIII: East Asia and Australasia (p. 152).

34 International Institute for Strategic Studies, *The Military Balance*, Volume 111, 2011, Part VI: Asia (p. 206).

35 Schobell, Andrew and Sanford, John M., *North Korea's Military Threat: Pyongyang's Conventional Forces, Weapons of Mass Destruction, and Ballistic Missiles*, Carlisle, PA, U.S. Army War College Strategic Studies Institute, April 2007 (p. 30).

36 Ibid. (pp. 35–36).

Minnich, James, *North Korea's People's Army: Origins and Current Tactics*, Annapolis, MD, Naval Institute Press, 2005 (p. 68).

37 Schobell, Andrew and Sanford, John M., *North Korea's Military Threat: Pyongyang's Conventional Forces, Weapons of Mass Destruction, and Ballistic Missiles*, Carlisle, PA, U.S. Army War College Strategic Studies Institute, April 2007 (p. 36).

38 U.S. Senate Select Committee on Intelligence, World Wide Threat Hearing, February 11, 2003.

Ballistic and Cruise Missile Threat, *National Air and Space Intelligence Centre*, Air Force Intelligence, Surveillance and Reconnaissance Agency, April 2009.

39 Schobell, Andrew and Sanford, John M., *North Korea's Military Threat: Pyongyang's Conventional Forces, Weapons of Mass Destruction, and Ballistic Missiles*, Carlisle, PA, U.S. Army War College Strategic Studies Institute, April 2007 (p. 57).

40 Westermeyer, Paul C., *U. S. Marines in the Gulf War 1990–1991: Liberating Kuwait*, Quantico, VA, United States Marine Corps History Division, 2014 (pp. 77–78).

41 Kopp, Carlo, 'Operation Odyssey Dawn—the collapse of Libya's relic air defense system,' *Defence Today,* vol. 9, no. 1, 2011

42 Joo, Sung Ho and Kwak, Tae Hwan, 'Military Relations Between Russia and North Korea,' *Journal of East Asian Affairs*, vol. 15, no. 2, Fall/Winter 2001 (p. 301).

KCNA, June 3, 1991.

Jencks, Harlan W., *Some Political and Military Implications of Soviet Warplane Sales to the PRC*, Sun Yat Sen Centre for Policy Studies, National Sun Yat Sen University, Paper no. 6, April 1991 (p. 21).

43 *Izvestiya,* March 6, 1992.

44 Ait, Abraham, 'Is North Korea's MiG-29 Fleet Growing?,' *The Diplomat*, November 29, 2018.

45 International Institute for Strategic Studies, *The Military Balance*, Volume 94, 1994, Part IX: Asia and Australasia (p. 166).

46 Farley, Robert, 'The MiG-21 Is Still a Great. Fighter Jet,' *War is Boring,* August 20, 2016.

Bryen, Stephen, 'It's MiG-21 versus the F-16 over Kashmir,' *Asia Times,* March 5, 2019.

47 'Did China Almost Field the World's Strongest Bomber Fleet? How Western Intervention Prevented Beijing from Acquiring the Lethal Soviet Tu-160 from Ukraine in the 1990s,' *Military Watch Magazine,* June 2, 2018.

48 Gordon, Michael R., 'Azerbaijan Detains Russian MIG Shipment,' *New York Times,* March 23, 1999.
Joo, Sung Ho and Kwak, Tae Hwan, 'Military Relations Between Russia and North Korea,' *Journal of East Asian Affairs*, vol. 15, no. 2, Fall/Winter 2001 (pp. 303–304).

49 Ibrahim, Youssef M., 'Iran Said to Commit $7 Billion to Secret Arms Plan,' *New York Times,* August 8, 1992.
'Iran Is Too Much of a Mess to Acquire Russian Weaponry,' *War is Boring,* October 20, 2017.

50 'NATO Will "Drag Serbia Into Major Fight" Over Possible S-300 Deliveries,' *Sputnik*, August 26, 2017 (Russian State Media Confirms Long Suspected Presence of S-300 Missile Batteries in North Korea).

51 Polmar, Norman, *The Naval Institute Guide to the Soviet Navy*, Annapolis, Naval Institute Press, 1991 (p. 387).
Yonhap, 18 January 1994.
JPRS-TND-94-003, 31 January 1994 (p.45–46).

52 Lukin, Alexander, *China and Russia: The New Rapprochement*, Cambridge, Polity Press, 2018 (p. 154).

53 'Think you can't afford a fighter jet? This Russian official sold 4 MiG-31s at $2 each & avoided prison for years,' *RT,* July 4, 2020.

54 Bechtol Jr., Bruce E., *North Korean Military Proliferation in the Middle East and Africa,* Lexington, University Press of Kentucky, 2018 (p. 88).

55 Haslam, Jonathan, *The Soviet Union and the Politics of Nuclear Weapons in Europe, 1969–87: The Problem of the SS-20*, London, Palgrave MacMillan, 1989 (p. 8).

56 Funabashi, Yoichi, 'The Peninsula Question: A Chronicle of the Second Korean Nuclear Crisis,' Washington D.C., Brookings Institution Press, 2007 (p. 126).

57 'Thaw in the Koreas?,' *Bulletin of Atomic Scientists*, vol. 48, no. 3, April 1992 (p. 16).

58 Drezner, Daniel W., *The Sanctions Paradox: Economic Statecraft and International Relations*, Cambridge, Cambridge University Press, 1999 (p. 286).

59 Cumings, Bruce, *Korea's Place in the Sun: A Modern History*, New York, W. W. Norton & Company, 1997 (p. 483).
'Time to End the Korean War,' *The Atlantic,* February 1997.

60 'Thaw in the Koreas?,' *Bulletin of Atomic Scientists*, vol. 48, no. 3, April 1992 (p. 16).

61 'Time to End the Korean War,' *The Atlantic,* February 1997.

62 Meade, Edward Grant, *American Military Government in Korea,* New York, King's Crown Press, 1952 (pp. 56, 72, 188).

63 Lowe, Peter, *The Origins of the Korean War*, London, Routledge, 1997 (p. 180).

64 Weiner, Tim, 'U.S. Spied on Iraq Under U.N. Cover, Officials Now Say,' *New York Times*, January 7, 1999.

65 Ritter, Scott, 'The coup that wasn't,' *Guardian,* September 28, 2005.
Edwards, David and Cromwell, David, *Propaganda Blitz: How the Corporate Media Distort Reality,* London, Pluto Press, 2018 (Chapter 5: Libya: 'It's All. About Oil').
'Scott Ritter and Seymour Hersh: Iraq Confidential,' *The Nation*, October 26, 2005.

66 Thomas, Raju G. C., *The Nuclear Non-Proliferation Regime: Prospects for the 21st Century*, London, MacMillan, 1998 (p. 227).

67 Cumings, Bruce, *Korea's Place in the Sun: A Modern History*, New York, W. W. Norton & Company, 1997 (pp. 489–490).
KCNA, February 22, 1993.

68 'Thaw in the Koreas?,' *Bulletin of Atomic Scientists*, vol. 48, no. 3, April 1992 (p. 16).

69 'US military stokes N Korea flames with "secret nuclear silos" claim,' *RT,* November 16, 2017.

70 Cumings, Bruce, *Korea's Place in the Sun: A Modern History*, New York, W. W. Norton & Company, 1997 (p. 489).
71 *New York Times*, February 25, 1993.
72 Farrell, John, 'Team Spirit: A Case Study on the Value of Military Exercises as a Show of Force in the Aftermath of Combat Operations,' *Air and Space Power Journal*, vol. 23, no. 3, Fall 2009.
73 Hayes, Peter, *Pacific Powderkeg: American Nuclear Dilemmas in Korea,* Lexington, Mass, Lexington Books, 1991.
Cumings, Bruce, *Korea's Place in the Sun*, New York, W. W. Norton and Company, 1997 (p. 475).
74 Mathews, Jessicia, 'Biggest Bargaining Chip,' *Washington Post*, February 20, 1994.
75 *Chicago Tribune*, March 18, 1993.
76 *New York Times*, March 21, 1993 (op-ed page).
Cumings, Bruce, *Korea's Place in the Sun: A Modern History*, New York, W. W. Norton & Company, 1997 (p. 488).
77 Blair, Bruce D., 'Russia's Doomsday Machine,' *New York Times,* October 8, 1993.
78 Cumings, Bruce, *Korea's Place in the Sun: A Modern History*, New York, W. W. Norton & Company, 1997 (p. 490).
79 Joint Statement of the Democratic People's Republic of Korea and the United States of America, New York, June 11, 1993.
80 Thomas, Raju G. C., *The Nuclear Non-Proliferation Regime: Prospects for the 21st Century*, London, MacMillan, 1998 (p. 232).
81 Ibid. (p. 232).
82 *The National Interest,* no. 34, Winter 1993/94 (pp. 38–39).
83 Thomas, Raju G. C., *The Nuclear Non-Proliferation Regime: Prospects for the 21st Century*, London, MacMillan, 1998 (pp. 232–233).
Cumings, Bruce, *Parallax Visions: Making Sense of American-East Asian Relations*, Chapel Hill, NC, Duke University Press, 2002 (p. 146).
84 Erickson, Amanda, 'The last time the U.S. was on "the brink of war" with North Korea,' *Washington Post,* August 9, 2017.
85 Cumings, Bruce, *Korea's Place in the Sun*, New York, W. W. Norton and Company, 1997 (p. 428).
86 Harrison, Selig S., 'Time To Leave Korea?,' *Foreign Affairs*, March–April 2001.
87 Kessler, Glenn, 'South Korea Offers To Supply Energy if North Gives Up Arms,' *Washington Post*, July 13, 2005.
88 Kim, Ji Yong, 'DPRK Will Re-Operate Nuclear Facilities Within A Few Weeks to Produce Electricity,' *The People's Korea*, January 27, 2003.
89 Ryan, Maria, 'Why the US's 1994 deal with North Korea failed—and what Trump can learn from it,' *The Conversation,* July 19, 2017.
90 Worldwide Intelligence Review, Hearing Before the Select Committee on Intelligence of the United States Senate, One Hundred Fourth Congress, First Session on Worldwide Intelligence Review, January 10, 1995 (pp. 103–104).
91 KEDO and the Korean Agreed Nuclear Framework: Problems and Prospects, Hearing Before the Subcommittee on East Asian and Pacific Affairs of the Committee on Foreign Relations, United States Senate, One Hundred Fifth Congress, Second Session, July 14, 1998.
92 'LWR Provision is U.S. Obligation: DPRK FM Spokesman,' *KCNA,* March 6, 1998.
93 Ryan, Maria, 'Why the US's 1994 deal with North Korea failed—and what Trump can learn from it,' *The Conversation,* July 19, 2017.
94 Asmolov, Konstantin, 'Famine in North Korea: Causes and Myths. Part 1,' *New Eastern Outlook,* October 30, 2013.
95 Bolton, John, 'North Korea: A Shared Challenge to the U.S. and ROK,' Speech Before the Korean-American Association, Seoul, August 29, 2002.

96 Explanation of Vote at the Adoption of UN Security Council Resolution 2270 on DPRK Sanctions, United States Mission to the United Nations.
97 Food and Agriculture Organisation/ World Food Programme Crop and Food Security Assessment Mision to the Democratic People's Republic of Korea, November 28, 2013.
98 *London Times*, November 16, 1950.
99 Armstrong, Charles K., *The Koreas*, Abingdon, Routledge, 2007 (p. 71).
100 *Korea: The Economic Race between North and South*, National Foreign Assessment Center, Central Intelligence Agency, 1978.
101 Cumings, Bruce, *Korea's Place in the Sun*, New York, W. W. Norton and Company, 1997 (p. 428).
102 Barkin, David, *Food Self Sufficiency in North Korea,* Research Report No. 4, San Francisco, Institute for Food and Development Policy, January 1, 1986.
103 UN Department of Humanitarian Affairs, 'United Nations Consolidated UN Inter-Agency Appeal for Flood-Related Emergency Humanitarian Assistance to the Democratic People's Republic of Korea (DPRK), 1 July 1996–31 March 1997.'
104 Harrison, Selig S., 'Promoting a Soft Landing in North Korea,' *Foreign Policy,* no. 106, Spring 1997 (p. 66).
105 Deane, Hugh, *The Korean War, 1945–1953,* San Francisco, CA, China Books & Periodicals, 1999 (p. 208).
106 UN Department of Humanitarian Affairs, 'Consolidated UN Inter Agency-Appeal,' 1 July 1996–21 March 1997.
107 Asmolov, Konstantin, 'Famine in North Korea: Causes and Myths. Part 1,' *New Eastern Outlook,* October 31, 2013.
108 Ibid.
109 Ibid.
110 Asmolov, Konstantin, 'Famine in North Korea: Causes and Myths. Part 2,' *New Eastern Outlook,* October 31, 2013.
111 Interview with Kim, Ryeon Hui in: Yun, David, *Loyal Citizens of Pyongyang in Seoul*, October 16, 2018.
112 'Exploring the Implications of Alternative North Korean Endgames: Results From a Discussion Panel on Continuing Coexistence Between North and South Korea,' Central Intelligence Agency, January 21, 1998.
113 'North Korea "loses 3 million to famine,"' *BBC,* February 17, 1999.
114 World Bank Group, Data for Korea, Dm. People's Rep. (https://data.worldbank.org/indicator/SP.POP.TOTL?locations=KP)
115 International Institute for Strategic Studies, *The Military Balance*, Volume 94, 1994, Part IX: Asia and Australasia (p. 178).
116 International Institute for Strategic Studies, *The Military Balance*, Volume 97, 1997, Part VIII: Asia and Australasia (p. 183).
117 Harrison, Selig S., 'Promoting a Soft Landing in North Korea,' *Foreign Policy,* no. 106, Spring 1997 (pp. 62–63).
118 Ibid. (p. 65).

Chapter 13

THE TWENTY-FIRST CENTURY AND RENEWED "MAXIMUM PRESSURE"

After the Agreed Framework: A New Phase in Relations

Following the signing of the Agreed Framework in 1994 U.S. intelligence sources repeatedly reiterated with near complete certainty that the DPRK had adhered to its obligations and would continue to do so. Under the new unipolar order, the framework was perceived by Pyongyang as a means of obtaining both normalization of relations with and relief of economic sanctions and pressure from the world's dominant power—the latter vital to gaining access to the global economy. A report at the Hearing Before the Select Committee on Intelligence in 1995 stated: "we assess that the North Korean leadership under Kim Jong Il will adhere to the Agreed Framework, particularly in the near term, as they perceive their chances for survival best served by strategies that emphasize economic improvement and political-economic opening to the United States and other industrialized nations. Such emphasis, if sustained, would reduce Pyongyang's motivation to resort to reunification by military force."[1]

The DPRK meanwhile moved to strengthen its conventional deterrence capabilities, and while economic crisis had resulted in considerable cuts to defense spending, more asymmetric weapons systems were deployed. These included more sophisticated indigenous long-range artillery and ballistic missile systems which were stationed in forward positions. The British think tank the International Institute for Strategic Studies reported that this included the most capable derivative of the Scud missile ever developed, one with a 600km range and 700kg payload,[2] alongside more capable variants of the Koksan and M1985 artillery systems and the Rodong-1 missile. Analysts repeatedly highlighted the KPA's new emphasis on such "high impact" arms over symmetric systems—which were vital to combatting adversaries with defence expenditures so many times higher.[3] The intelligence committee report noted regarding Korean deployments during the period of the Agreed Framework: "North Korea continues to improve and train its forward deployed forces. This underwrites their desire to maintain current conventional force capabilities and military readiness while maximizing the agreement's political-economic benefits."[4]

The United States benefitted considerably from the Agreed Framework—particularly given the near certainty which pervaded that North Korea would imminently collapse—with the agreement freezing progress on the Korean plutonium based nuclear weapons program for over eight years from 1994. The Clinton administration's Assistant Secretary of Defence for International Security Policy and Senior Advisor on the North Korea policy review Ashton Carter (later Secretary of Defence from 2015) stated in 2003 regarding the framework's benefits: "The Agreed Framework did one thing which was very important to us, which was to freeze North Korea's plutonium program at Yongbyon right up until just a few months ago. Had that not been frozen, by now North Korea would have several tens of nuclear weapons. So by that standard, it certainly did our security a service."[5]

Although it was adhering to the Agreed Framework's restrictions on activities at its plutonium sites, the DPRK was alleged to have sought a second path to develop nuclear weapons from the late 1990s using enriched uranium. Given the failure of the United States to fulfill its side of the Agreed Framework, Pyongyang could have been seeking a means of exerting pressure of its own on the nuclear issue without directly reversing the concessions it had made under the agreement. As noted by Republican Congressman Benjamin A. Gilman and a number of experts, enriching uranium did not technically contravene the Agreed Framework which placed constraints on plutonium-related activities at specific sites.[6] Furthermore, as a number of experts argued, it was highly possible that such uranium enrichment was intended for use in upcoming light water reactors, and such activities could hardly be taken as evidence of plans for weaponization. Indeed, South Korea and other non-nuclear weapons states were carrying out uranium enrichment programs of their own at this time very similar to that the DPRK was allegedly pursuing.[7] Furthermore, the veracity of American allegations regarding an enrichment program remains uncertain, with the Korean side repeatedly pointing out the lack of evidence to substantiate these claims—which remain unproven to this day.[8] *Foreign Affairs* was among the sources which noted the complete lack of evidence provided by the U.S. to support allegations of a DPRK uranium enrichment program.[9] Pyongyang notably granted American inspectors access to a suspected uranium enrichment facility in 1998—where they concluded no evidence of such activities was found.[10] Nevertheless, the unevidenced allegations persisted.

The year 1998 saw the DPRK begin to emerge from the death of its leader, the Arduous March and three years of environmental catastrophe as an increasingly stable state—and according to American reports it was still in full compliance with the Agreed Framework. That year saw American threats escalate and military options reconsidered, with the U.S. Military beginning simulation training exercises for nuclear attacks on the East Asian state.[11] Washington's refusal to hold direct bilateral negotiations and sign an official nonaggression pact, which was at the forefront of Pyongyang's demands,[12] further increased suspicions regarding American intentions. As prospects for an imminent collapse of the DPRK waned and a new U.S. administration came to power from 2001, support grew for a ratcheting up of American economic and military pressure to force a Korean collapse. A termination of the Agreed Framework remained key to achieving American ends in this regard.

Western experts repeatedly noted a lack of any significant evidence for the U.S. claim that North Korea was pursuing a parallel enriched uranium program—a claim which was made from 1998 and increasingly stressed under the subsequent George W. Bush administration.

A paper by the Institute for Science and International Security notably compared the extremely questionable evidence presented for the Korean uranium program to that used by the Bush administration to claim Iraq had weapons of mass destruction—with the latter proving to be entirely false but serving as a valuable pretext for aggressive policies.[13] There was a strong incentive to fabricate such allegations against Pyongyang under the Clinton administration by officials disillusioned with the Agreed Framework, and moreso by the Bush administration which sought pretext to withdraw from the deal almost as soon as it assumed power.[i] As these allegations coincided with the DPRK's emergence from economic crisis, at which point prospects for a state collapse dimmed, there was a significant possibility that the U.S. sought a pretext to exit the deal to avoid meeting its own obligations. The U.S. stalled the

i Bush administration policy was initially dubbed "ABC" (Anything But Clinton), and his party had long called for the dismantling of the Agreed Framework which the new President was under pressure to carry out. Allegations of uranium enrichment, although unproven, provided key pretext for this.

delivery of the lightwater reactors for eight years and did not even obtain funding for them until the Agreed Framework was collapsed.

A U.S. delegation which later visited Pyongyang in October 2002 claimed that the DPRK admitted to the presence of uranium enrichment facilities during meetings.[14] The Korean side denied having made such an admission and chastised the American side for failing to produce any evidence.[15] The DPRK Foreign Ministry later expressed a willingness to respond to any written evidence presented by the United States that it was pursuing a uranium enrichment program, stating that clearing the issue up could open the door to an improvement in relations with Washington.[16] No such evidence was ever presented, but the U.S. continued to maintain its allegations as a basis for hostile actions towards the East Asian state.

U.S. intelligence officials would later come to downplay earlier claims that North Korea was pursuing nuclear weapons through highly enriched uranium and, according to an unnamed intelligence official cited by *USA Today* in 2004, the CIA was not even certain the DPRK had a uranium enrichment plant.[17] Such admissions were not widely publicized, and claims regarding a uranium weapons program have yet to be officially retracted to this day despite no further evidence having been provided.

Considering the entirely discredited nature of the allegations against Iraq regarding its own uranium enrichment program, which could only be definitively proven wrong after the invasion of the country, there are very significant grounds to doubt those made against the DPRK.[18] It is notable that the American intelligence community concluded its assessment on the Korean uranium enrichment program at the same time that it was concluding Iraq too was developing weapons of mass destruction. Much as a falsely alleged WMD program proved useful as a pretext for illegal invasion of Iraq, so too did an alleged but entirely unproven uranium enrichment program at the same time provide the pretext needed for America to collapse the Agreed Framework and place the blame on North Korea. Bearing in mind the DPRK's view of the Agreed Framework's importance its long term economic wellbeing, the demonstrated U.S. use of false allegations of nuclear development to provide pretext for hostile actions,[19] and the complete lack of evidence or of conclusive findings by American inspectors in 1998,[20] claims that Pyongyang had pursued such as program and willingly risked compromising the agreement remain highly questionable.

If one were to assume that U.S. allegations were correct regarding a uranium enrichment program, and that for whatever reason the Western superpower refused to provide evidence either to satisfy the international community or to confront the Koreans, the Agreed Framework still succeeded in forcing the DPRK onto a far slower path to nuclearization by barring the plutonium path. Ending the advanced plutonium program, which was in its advanced stages, proved a major hindrance to the nuclear program and a major asset to the U.S.—one which would have been sufficient to ensure North Korea would have been denuclearized indefinitely if the expected state collapse had occurred in the 1990s. Ashton Carter stated to this effect in 2003 regarding the benefit of barring plutonium development despite an alleged uranium program:

> They [DPRK in 1994] remained a few months away from reprocessing those rods [from Yongbyon], but they didn't reprocess those rods for eight long years. During that time, we could all rest more easily. At the same time the plutonium program was frozen, we now know that they began experimenting with, and then embarking upon a program involving the other metal that you can make nuclear weapons out of—namely, uranium. Now they're not very far along in that. So it doesn't present a clear and present danger in the way that the plutonium program still does. [21]

Plutonium frozen at Yongbyon would, according to a number of sources, provide enough materials to build over 30 nuclear weapons.[22] Had Yongbyon been active, multiple batches could have been produced by the turn of the century.

From the mid-1990s the DPRK adopted a policy of ambiguity regarding its nuclear weapons capabilities similar to that of the Israeli nuclear program. While the bulk of its nuclear materials were still being monitored by international inspectors in cooling ponds, there was still considerable speculation in the American intelligence community that the KPA could develop a small nuclear arsenal from remaining materials—which could have been processed before the Agreed Framework. Indeed, some analysts speculated that the country could have had enough materials for a small arsenal as early as 1989.[23]

According to a report by Colonel William E. Berry, Jr., Head of the Department of Political Science at the U.S. Air Force Academy, as early as 1993 there was a possibility that the DPRK could have had some nuclear capability for deployment in the event of attack. The Colonel wrote: "There was no consensus in the Clinton administration on whether the DPRK already had enough plutonium to build a bomb. For example, former Secretary of State Lawrence Eagleberger testified before a congressional committee that he believed North Korea already had at least one nuclear weapon. R. James Woolsey Jr., the new CIA Director, believed the DPRK already enough plutonium to build a bomb but had not yet done so."[24] The amount of plutonium reprocessed before 1992, if any, remains unknown.

A report from the International Institute for Strategic Studies stated the following year in 1994: "There is still no categorically confirmed information over North Korean possession of nuclear weapons. The Director of the CIA has estimated that, before the reactor closure of April 1994, North Korea had sufficient plutonium to build a nuclear device. U.S. intelligence sources claim to have evidence of high-explosive tests indicative of the development of implosion devices and of the conversion of plutonium nitrate to metal, necessary for bomb manufacture."[25] At a hearing before the Select Committee on Intelligence of the United States Senate in January 1995, in which the DPRK was confirmed to be in full compliance with the Agreed Framework and had placed its fuel rods under IAEA supervision, the possibility was raised that it may have had enough materials to develop a small nuclear arsenal before the agreement. It was stated at the hearing: "The Intelligence Community has concluded that North Korea may have already produced enough plutonium for at least one nuclear weapon, though we cannot be sure of this."[26]

Maintaining such ambiguity and encouraging speculation regarding its nuclear capabilities remained in the DPRK's interest, and likely contributed to the Clinton administration's decision to pull back from the brink of war in 1994 and instead wait out the country's expected collapse. As Professor Derek D. Smith, a lecturer in international relations at Oxford University and expert on nuclear proliferation, stated regarding Korean capabilities at this time "As the bomb on North Korea's bumper became ever more real and menacing, the credibility of the United States to demand disarmament even at the risk of war diminished in kind."[27] When the DPRK announced its intent to pursue nuclear weapons in 2002, Korean officials reportedly warned the Americans they "have more powerful things as well"—leaving their U.S. counterparts uncertain of what capabilities the country had. An unnamed senior official quoted by the *New York Times* at the time said that, given this position of ambiguity, the U.S. had to assume that North Korea may have already built some nuclear weapons.[28]

An incident in 2001, in which the Korean leadership reportedly claimed a small functioning nuclear deterrent, gave an indication of the country's policy of ambiguity at the time. According to a statement by Russian President Vladimir Putin, he had been informed in 2001 in a meeting with Korean Leader Kim Jong Il that the country retained nuclear armaments for use in the event of a U.S. attack. Putin in 2017 stated to this effect: "In 2001, when I was on my way to pay a visit to Japan, I made a stop in North Korea, where I had a meeting with the father of the country's current leader. It was back then when he told me that they had a nuclear bomb. Moreover, Seoul was within the hitting range of their standard artillery systems at that time."[29] Russia could have been seen as a conduit for messages to the West at the time, and under the new Putin administration, which in the early 2000s still maintained close ties to the Western world, it was one of the closest things to a neutral party in the DPRK-U.S. conflict. Alternatively, it is possible Pyongyang had calculated that by warning Russia that a Western attack on the DPRK would likely result in nuclear war on its border, Moscow could be pressed to prevent such an attack with greater urgency—possibly through channels to the U.S. or by helping the DPRK advance its deterrent capabilities more quickly. It is possible that the DPRK had no nuclear weapons at this time, or that its doctrine had already prohibited their use against population centres in East Asia as it later would, but so long as this remained unknown to its adversaries and there was a possibility that the state had an arsenal and a low threshold for use, any military action against it remained extremely risky.

Axis of Evil and Accelerated Nuclearization

While relations between the DPRK and the United States had begun to deteriorate in the final years of the Clinton administration, a more rapid decline began in the second year of the George W. Bush administration when the president labelled North Korea a member of the "Axis of Evil." This was a list of three states in which Washington openly sought to impose a change in government, and included Iran and Iraq alongside Korea. Within a month, in mid-February 2002, President Bush was seen at 38th parallel accompanied by military officials. Looking out over North Korea through military binoculars, he described looking at "evil" and concluded: "we are ready."[30] While the Agreed Framework remained in place, at this stage eight years after its signing the United States had still not begun deliveries of the promised light water reactors—leading to further charges by Pyongyang that Washington was failing to uphold its side of the deal. Criticising the Bush administration's new hardline rhetoric as overtly threatening, the DPRK again pressed for the opening of bilateral negotiations and the security assurances it had long sought—the signing of a peace treaty, mutual recognition and an end to the Korean War.

Where the Clinton administration had adopted negotiations as a means of stalling North Korea's nuclearization, without providing any concrete security assurances in return, the Bush administration appeared perhaps on principle not to want to negotiate with Pyongyang. In doing so, it forced the DPRK to turn from seeking ever elusive American security guarantees to taking full responsibility for its own defence and pursuing a viable deterrent capability. As Korean state newspaper *Rodong Sinmun* would state many years later: "The [George W.] Bush administration's DPRK policy that stemmed from its ignorance of the DPRK resulted in making the DPRK a nuclear weapons state."[31] While Pyongyang was likely to have taken such a course of action even if Clinton's policies had been continued, as the Democratic administration appeared as intent on regime change as its Republican successor and could only stall Korean nuclearization for so long with unfulfilled promises, the Bush administration's policies served to accelerate this process.

Charles Armstrong, Korean Studies professor at Colombia University and prominent expert on U.S.-DPRK relations, observed regarding Washington's approach which had prompted a change in North Korea's policy: "The rhetoric of the Bush administration…seemed to suggest that 'rogue states' with weapons of mass destruction (WMD) were to be eliminated rather than bargained with. During the lead-up to war in Iraq, the general thrust of U.S. policy appeared to be 'regime change' in Pyongyang, not diplomacy."[32] He concluded that American attempts to negotiate with the DPRK were neither genuine nor realistic, stating: "By 'diplomacy' the United States seemed to mean making unilateral demands on the North Koreans rather than anything resembling negotiation."[33] The American administration's hostility was directly cited as the cause for Korea's nuclearization, with a North Korean delegate at the United Nations Disarmament Commission stating to this effect: "The

DPRK's possession of nuclear weapons is a legitimate right to defend its sovereignty today when the Bush administration listed it as part of an 'Axis of Evil' and a 'tyrannical' state and it is getting all the more undisguised in its drive to overthrow it… The DPRK cannot renounce nuclear weapons when the U.S. is intensifying nuclear war rehearsals to make a pre-emptive strike."[34]

In December 2002 oil shipments to the DPRK under the Agreed Framework were halted, a move accompanied by the illegal seizure of a cargo ship carrying Korean missiles to the government of Yemen. The White House later admitted regarding the second incident, a joint operation with the Spanish armed forces: "There is no provision under international law prohibiting Yemen from accepting delivery of missiles from North Korea," later releasing the vessel.[35] A strong enough signal had been sent, however, that the U.S. was willing to take to the offensive against Korean interests even if outside the bounds of international law. Yemen for its part was forced under American pressure to pledge not to make further arms purchases from the DPRK—the implicit assumption being that its shipping would face further illegal interdictions by Western parties if it failed to comply.[36] Already isolated under Western sanctions, North Korea was threatened with further economic isolation through such means.

Interdiction of Korean shipping coupled with maximum military and economic pressure were considered part of American plans to force a capitulation by Pyongyang on the nuclear issue—and if possible, a change in government in line with Western interests. The U.S. Congressional Research Service's East Asia specialist, Larry Niksch, concluded at this time that "regime change in North Korea is indeed the Bush administration's policy objective." Niksch wrote that renewed economic pressure through sanctions and interdiction of Korean shipping were intended to provoke a collapse of government, and if this failed Defence Secretary Donald Rumsfeld was considering "a broader plan of massive strikes against multiple targets."[37] The United States Department of Defence's Nuclear Posture Review was also altered in 2002, and from that year onwards it required the Pentagon to draft contingency plans for the deployment of nuclear weapons against North Korea.[38] U.S. rhetoric meanwhile continued to escalate, and plans for war to "tear this regime down" were strongly supported by such influential figures as Donald Rumsfeld, Paul Wolfowitz, John Bolton and Nicholas Eberstadt.[39]

Pyongyang responded decisively, and in December 2002 it announced an effective withdrawal from the Agreed Framework paving the way for rapid manufacture of nuclear warheads. This occurred almost immediately after the U.S. cut the oil supplies that it was obliged to provide under the Agreed Framework, and included resumption of operations at Yongbyon and two other reactors after eight years frozen.[40] Two weeks later all cameras and seals over the cooling ponds, where the fuel rods were still being stored under surveillance, were removed, preventing the IAEA from monitoring these materials.[41] Defence Secretary Rumsfeld warned on December 23 that North Korea's response was "unacceptable," warning that the United States was able to take military action against the DPRK despite its involvement in Afghanistan and imminent invasion of Iraq.[42]

Pyongyang for its part appeared highly aware of the reality of the U.S. position at the time, which limited Washington's ability to respond to its actions. America's inability to respond to Korea's accelerated nuclear program as a result of overcommitment to other fronts was comparable to the position of weakness which had resulted from overcommitment in the Vietnam War in the late 1960s. Both cases providing Pyongyang with greater freedom of action for similar reasons. Thus on January 10, 2003, the DPRK announced its withdrawal from the Nuclear Non-Proliferation Treaty. The withdrawal was legal under Article X, which guarantees all states the right to withdraw with three months' notice if "extraordinary events, related to the subject matter of this Treaty, have jeopardized the supreme interests of its country." American threats, including nuclear threats,[ii] certainly qualified as such.[43] Withdrawal from the treaty legalised North Korea's the development of nuclear weapons by removing the sole treaty law which had prohibited the country from pursuing such a means of deterrence.

North Korea's withdrawal from the Agreed Framework and the NPT could not have been better timed, with the U.S. Military having deployed tens of thousands of troops to Afghanistan less than two years prior and with momentum in full swing and preparations long underway for an attack on Iraq. The September 11th attacks served as a

---

ii On September 17, 2002 the White House had issued the *National Security Strategy of the United States* announcing the option of using nuclear weapons against rogue states thought to be developing weapons of mass destruction—reaffirming its earlier rejection of the Nuclear Non-proliferation Treaty linked negative security assurances which had previously protected signatories including North Korea from nuclear attack.

valuable pretext for further attacks on targets in the Islamic world, with Afghanistan and Iraq both attacked largely under the pretext of ties to Al Qaeda. (In the case of the latter these were fabricated—but to much of the American public were believable as both were Muslim and Sunni-led.) The wake of 9/11 ensured high approval ratings for military action against Muslim nations—with 70% of Americans believing in 2003 that Saddam Hussein had a role in the attacks and links to Al Qaeda.[44] Even as Pyongyang started up its Yongbyon facilities and retook its fuel rods, it remained far from the top of the American target list giving it sufficient time to complete its deterrent before the United States again turned its attentions eastwards.

Warren Christopher, former Secretary of State under the Clinton administration and Deputy Secretary of State under the Carter administration, was one of the few who warned that American preoccupation in the Islamic world under the Bush administration had given the DPRK far more freedom to strengthen its defences through nuclearization. Referring to threats from the DPRK as "more imminent than those posed by Iraq," he stated:

> In foreign affairs, Washington is chronically unable to deal with more than one crisis at a time... While Defense Secretary Donald Rumsfeld may be right in saying that our military can fight two wars at the same time, my experience tells me that we cannot mount a war against Iraq and still maintain the necessary policy focus on North Korea and international terrorism. Anyone who has worked at the highest levels of our government knows how difficult it is to engage the attention of the White House on anything other than the issue of the day... A United States-led attack on Iraq will overshadow all other foreign-policy issues for at least a year.

Again referring to the DPRK, he concluded: "No doubt the world would be better off without Saddam Hussein reigning in Iraq, but we must recognize that the effort of removing him right now may well distract us from dealing with graver threats."[45]

Cristopher's predictions proved to be almost entirely correct. The spillover from the War on Terror made Iraq, closely followed by Iran, priority targets while the DPRK, with its far more advanced military capabilities, limited nuclear deterrent and lack of casual association with terrorism or Islam, was relatively safe. The U.S. invasion of Iraq, the most harshly criticized member of the "Axis of Evil" and by far the weakest of the three, did however pose potential risks to the DPRK. The American attack demonstrated again that the U.S. was willing to launch large scale invasions illegally and without a UN mandate, and the swiftness with which Baghdad was occupied and its fragile military collapsed threatened to embolden Washington to launch further campaigns in the near future. Ba'athist Iraq was destroyed within two weeks of the first attack on March 20, and the costs to the U.S. Military were negligible. North Korea's leadership appeared to have been aware of this risk, with state newspaper *Rodong Sinmun* stating, just days before the attack on Baghdad was initiated: "It is becoming certain that, in case the U.S. imperialists' invasion of Iraq is successful, they will wage a new war of aggression on the Korean Peninsula."[46]

In late 2003 American officials again spoke of trying to topple the North Korean government, with Bush administration officials repeatedly suggesting that certain "rogue states" could be legitimate targets of pre-emptive nuclear strikes. Following America's initial victories in Iraq, Defence Secretary Rumsfeld stated that the Korean government must draw the "appropriate lesson" from the campaign.[47] He went on to demand revisions in Operations Plan 5030, the American plan for war against North Korea, and sought money from Congress for new bunker-busting nuclear weapons. These were an invaluable asset in a war against dug in and highly fortified KPA assets, which had long been beyond the reach of American conventional strikes.[48] According to American insiders who read the operations plan, the strategy was to "topple Kim [Jong Il]'s regime by destabilizing its military forces." [49] Operations Plan 5030 was pushed "by many of the same administration hard-liners who advocated regime change in Iraq" and were considered by senior administration officials to be extremely aggressive.[50]

In the immediate aftermath of its victory in Iraq the U.S. escalated military deployments and manoeuvres in Northeast Asia specifically targeting the DPRK. Surveillance flights very near North Korean airspace increased, and such operations would commonly precede a military strike by collecting valuable targeting data.[51] The purpose of these flights was reportedly not restricted to intimidation. With the U.S. aware of the country's struggling post-crisis economy, and its lack of vast energy reserves and natural resources as enjoyed by the rentier economies of Iraq and Iran, forcing the KPA Air Force to conduct frequent interceptions of

American warplanes was intended to strain its resources and force it to expend valuable fuel reserves.[52] The U.S. further deployed two dozen nuclear capable heavy bombers to the Asia-Pacific region within range of the DPRK, indicating that it may also send fighter escorts to support reconnaissance flights.[53]

Operations Plan 5030 in particular, which laid out provisions for operations very near North Korea's borders, was said by members of the Bush administration to "blur the lines between war and peace" and was deemed highly provocative. The plan entailed a disruption of Korean financial networks and strategic disinformation activities with the purpose of destabilisation and regime change. It also gave commanders the authority to hold surprise military exercises to force the KPA to maintain a very high level of combat readiness, at great expense, which was also intended to exhaust its personnel and sow confusion among its officer corps.[54] Reports referred to the benefits of "a weeks-long surprise military exercise, designed to force North Koreans to head for bunkers and deplete valuable stores of food, water, and other resources."[55] While American actions appeared to have been carried out primarily for the purposes of intimidation and economic pressure—pressing Pyongyang closer to the internal collapse the West had long expected—the risk of war was raised considerably by the escalatory actions carried out.

Should the United States have proceeded to launch a war against North Korea, the use of bunker busting tactical nuclear weapons would have been almost certain. There was a wide consensus among American defence experts that North Korea's network of tunnels and bunkers was so heavily fortified that it would be all but immune to conventional attack—necessitating employment of bunker-busting nuclear weapons across much of the country to penetrate them. The types of targets fortified ranged from command centres to air defence and ballistic missile sites to armaments factories.[56]

It is unclear to what extent the Bush administration did seriously contemplate opening to a third front against the DPRK, or whether the more hawkish members of the administration may have hoped that repeated provocations and flights into North Korea may provoke a war circumventing the need for Washington's approval. It is possible, much as the DPRK may have been bluffing that it had nuclear weapons, that the United States was bluffing in 2003 about its readiness to launch a third war given the strain this would have placed on its assets.[iii]

A primary factor in Pyongyang's favour, as predicted by Warren Christopher, was that America's preoccupation in the Islamic world and Iraq in particular made Northeast Asia a relatively peripheral issue at least temporarily. Although the Iraqi government had been swiftly toppled, the Iraq War continued as various factions, many formed by former members of the military or by Iranian aligned elements, waged an insurgency against and bogged down U.S. forces causing tens of thousands of casualties. The result was that the U.S. was preoccupied in an increasingly costly quagmire which slaked the American public's taste for further wars in the near future—particularly against far off actors in East Asia with no connection to losses in Iraq or 9/11. Iran, which was accused of developing nuclear arms and presented a much softer target militarily, was a more likely option. As an Islamic Republic, the state could be more easily associated with Al Qaeda and the 9/11 attacks[57] in the eyes of the American public, much as Iraq had been—using the momentum of retaliation against the attacks to topple another Western adversary. Indeed, had Iran not been provided with a powerful missile deterrent capability by the DPRK to compensate for the overall weakness of its conventional forces (see Chapter 10), such a course could well have been taken.[58]

A second factor was the speed at which the DPRK was able to restart the development of nuclear weapons, allowing it to quickly increase its deterrent capability. In December 2002 thousands of fresh fuel rods were moved into Yongbyon,[59] and U.S. satellites soon afterwards detected a movement of the 8,000 stored rods away from the pool sites—leading analysts to predict that the DPRK would be able to produce weapons grade plutonium by the end of March 2003.[60] By June plutonium from the 8,000 spent fuel rods had been fully extracted—enough for 25–30 kilograms worth of weapons to supplement any warheads the KPA may have already fielded. In October of that year Pyongyang publicly announced that the reprocessing had been concluded.[61] Even if the Iraqi campaign had gone ideally as planned and the U.S. was able to quickly

iii America's last major confrontation with the KPA alone from July to October 1950, despite considerable allied support, had required the full might of the U.S. Military other than a single division in Germany. With North Korea considerably better prepared for war in the early 2000s that it had been in 1950, a major war would likely have necessitated a complete withdrawal from Afghanistan, Iraq and other theatres.

prepare for a third campaign, North Korea would have likely already been in a position to assemble new warheads before then.

Win-Win or Kicking Cans Down the Road? Mutual Pressure Yields a Deal Under the Bush Administration

Speculation continued as to whether North Korea possessed nuclear arms, although after 2003 the view of the vast majority of analysts was that the country most likely had some weaponised nuclear capability. While the country's pursuit of a nuclear deterrent was effectively confirmed by its withdrawal from the Nuclear Non-proliferation Treaty, it was only on February 10, 2005 that Pyongyang announced that it possessed such capabilities through a statement by the Foreign Ministry. The United States was caught between its reluctance to accede to Pyongyang's longstanding request for official bilateral talks, and its inability to effectively respond to Korea's nuclearization due in large part to the unexpected and increasingly violent situation on the ground in Iraq. The restarting of Six Party Talks involving the United States, North Korea, South Korea, China, Russia and Japan in July 2005 appears to have been the go-to policy for the Bush administration for the remainder of its first term, with eight more phases of talks held all of which were relatively inconsequential. The impasse between the U.S. and the DPRK—the former unwilling to meet bilaterally or end the Korean War until the latter denuclearised while the latter was unwilling to unilaterally denuclearise until these conditions were met—and even then possibly not—made serious progress beyond unenforced joint declarations extremely difficult. A number of analysts have further contended that the framework for the discussions itself doomed them to failure, with all six parties bringing their own entirely separate agendas to the table which impeded any major gains.[62]

The unfavourable evolution of the Afghan and Iraq wars, Iran's clear place from 2005 as the next target on the American "hit list," and the loss of the post-9/11 momentum for war as approval ratings crashed domestically, between them effectively took the military option against the DPRK off the table for the Bush administration. The wholly unexpected defeat of its ally, Israel, in 2006 by Korean trained and Iranian-funded Hezbollah militants, and the re-emergence of tensions with Russia in 2008 and subsequent defeat of Western aligned Georgia in August that year, further stretched American commitments which served Korean security interests well. By bogging America down in Iraq and

Afghanistan, and allowing other far more powerful adversaries including the DPRK, China, Russia and Iran time to regather their strength, the Bush administration arguably oversaw the beginning of the end for the "New World Order" of unchallenged American power—with very significant consequences for the Korean Peninsula. Economic crisis and recession in the Western world in 2008 would significantly further this trend.

Tensions came to a head in 2006, with U.S. economic pressure on the DPRK mounting and talks under the Six Party forum stalling. The KPA had by this time deployed a new class of ballistic missile, the Musudan, which had been exported to Iran in 2005 and test launched there under Korean supervision in January 2006. The missile had a range of 4000km,[63] was extremely fast and difficult to intercept,[64] and provided the KPA with the potential to strike vital U.S. military facilities as far as Guam. The Musudan was survivable by virtue of its mobility, deploying from a transporter erector launcher, and if conspicuously tested in East Asia it could prove a further major embarrassment for the Bush administration.[65] With the U.S. bogged down elsewhere, Pyongyang recognised that it was unable to respond to Korean escalations in kind.

In order to prevent the DPRK carrying out conspicuous actions it deemed provocative, the United States would be forced to make concessions which would allow it to refocus its attentions to where they were more urgently needed. In an apparent effort to maximise pressure North Korea conducted its largest ballistic missile test yet on July 5, 2006, firing six missiles and one satellite rocket—suspected of also being a demonstrator for ICBM technologies—in sequence. The primary purpose of such a large demonstration was not to evaluate the performances of these platforms—but rather to send a message to the DPRK's adversaries regarding its capabilities. The technologies of the satellite launch vehicle could be used to develop systems to target the U.S. mainland if properly refined, while the four Rodong-1 missiles and two Hwasong-6 missiles demonstrated a capability to strike targets across Japan and South Korea respectively.[66] The demonstration was thus intended for dramatic effect. A secondary purpose of the launch was likely to embarrass the United States into action—namely to restart talks and more seriously consider offering concessions lest Pyongyang initiate further similar tests. The most advanced and dangerous missile in service, the Musudan, was conspicuous by its absence from the first test—the implication being that Pyongyang could escalate by firing it in future tests.

Three months later, on October 9, North Korea conducted its first nuclear test, detonating a warhead in an underground facility with a small yield of between 0.7 and 2 kilotons. This test undermined speculation that North Korea had not mastered technologies needed to sufficiently miniaturise nuclear weapons to deploy them on a ballistic missile. As Defence Secretary Donald Rumsfeld had stated three months earlier in mid-July, it was not clear to Washington "whether or not they [DPRK] have developed the ability to mate a nuclear weapon with a ballistic missile."[67] The test carried out in October 2006, and all subsequent nuclear tests, would be of miniaturised warheads to both demonstrate and further refine this capability.[68] While the test did demonstrate that the DPRK retained a significant deterrent capability, perhaps more importantly given its timing was that it increased pressure on the United States to return to the table and end the standoff promptly—lest it face further embarrassment for its inability to respond.

According to a number of prominent analysts, Pyongyang had expected that its nuclear and missile tests would be followed by greater willingness on the part of the United States to resume negotiations—which proved to be the case with a new phase of Six Party Talks quickly organised and commencing from December 18. While unwilling to end the Korean War, negotiate bilaterally or offer security guarantees, the United States conceded to removing the DPRK from the list of State Sponsors of Terror and suspending application of the Trading with the Enemy Act. Perhaps most importantly the United States ceased targeting or threatening to target third party banks—most notably Banco Delta Asia—which were dealing with North Korean transactions. The U.S. had gone to extreme measures, using the Providing Appropriate Tools Required to Intercept and Obstruct Terrorism (PATRIOT) Act (Section 311) to put pressure on all banks doing business with the DPRK where all other forms of economic warfare seemed to have failed, which placed significant pressure on the East Asian state's economy and further isolated it from global trade. Such actions had begun to be implemented in late 2005, and by mid-2006 had reportedly begun to seriously harm the North Korean economy.[69] A number of analysts speculated that it was such actions that had prompted North Korea to increase pressure on Washington through weapons testing in response.[70] Ending this more extreme form of economic warfare, to which Pyongyang was particularly vulnerable in the aftermath of the Arduous March, was reportedly at the forefront of

North Korean demands during negotiations in 2006, and achieving this significantly reduced pressure on the country's economy.

In return for U.S. concessions North Korea would refrain from carrying out conspicuous weapons tests or other actions deemed similarly provocative, but was tacitly allowed to continue to develop its deterrent capabilities quietly—so as not to embarrass Washington for its inability to respond. The country would also declare its nuclear programs in June 2008, providing information on its plutonium program, but was not required by the agreement to allow free inspections of all sites requested or to allow sampling of soil near its nuclear facilities, meaning its figures could not be fully verified. These terms effectively gave Pyongyang a relatively free hand to continue with development of its nuclear capabilities. There was also reportedly a tacit agreement that North Korea would not proliferate its nuclear weapons to third parties such as Iran—although exports of ballistic missile technologies and cooperation in other military fields remained unaffected.

The scaling back of American economic warfare efforts demonstrated a secondary but still very significant value of the DPRK's nuclear and ballistic missile deterrence programs—their ability to provide leverage with which the state could press for concessions including the loosening of economic pressure. It was previously widely assumed that the Bush administration, through its economic warfare efforts, was "attempting to squeeze the DPRK leadership into submission or into collapse,"[71] but by providing Pyongyang with the ability to itself place pressure on the U.S. through conspicuous testing Washington was forced to relax economic pressure without achieving either of its goals—state collapse or unilateral Korean acquiescence to American terms. Had the DPRK not retained the capability to test such assets, it is likely that the United States would have maintained its economic warfare efforts through the targeting of third parties using the Trading With the Enemy Act and the "State Sponsor of Terror" designation to ensure impoverishment and if possible eventual regime change. Thus, the country's investment in deterrent capabilities was protecting national security in more ways than one—not only as a deterrent against attack but through the leverage their conspicuous testing provided.

After 2006 the DPRK and the Bush administration appear to have reached an unwritten understanding which accommodated the former's nuclearization and the latter's focus on the Middle East and Afghanistan, with both parties offering benefits to the other. This agreement served the short-term interests of the United States very well—and would later be widely referred to as a policy of "kicking the can down the road" in regard to the challenge Korea's nuclearization posed to American foreign policy. The DPRK gained a relaxation of both economic and military pressure, allowing it to accelerate its economic recovery, as well as a chance to further its nuclear and ballistic missile programs with relatively little impediment. Although there were multiple minor disagreements and relations never progressed further, this understanding between the DPRK and the United States remained in effect for the remainder of George W. Bush's tenure as president.

The Barack Obama Administration: America Tries to Look East

The coming to power of the Barack Obama administration saw relations between the DPRK and the United States worsen considerably, with Washington again adopting a much harder line against its old adversary and reversing reductions in tensions made in Bush's second term. While Pyongyang had reportedly seen a change in the U.S. administration as a potential opportunity to further improve relations, and according to some sources even offered to send a representative to the new president's inauguration, these early overtures were rebuffed.[72] The Obama administration set out harsh terms for the normalisation of relations—namely that this could only be pursued if the DPRK fully dismantled its nuclear deterrent as a precondition before which no bilateral talks could be held. This reportedly came as a considerable disappointment to Pyongyang.[73]

The new administration's approach to the DPRK, as with a number of America's adversaries, involved taking a very hard line, often harsher than its predecessor—but going to much greater lengths to frame policies in a way that made the administration appear a reasonable actor which had seemingly exhausted diplomatic options. This policy was observed by a number of prominent experts and was termed by the Bush administration's top advisor for North Korean affairs and Director for Asian Affairs at the White House's National Security Council Victor Cha as "Hawk Engagement."[74]

Three of the new administration's most prominent policies—withdrawal from Iraq and Afghanistan, increased interventionism abroad, and a refocusing of American attentions towards the Asia-Pacific region under the "Pivot to Asia" initiative—all set the stage for renewed conflict. The administration's move to withdraw forces from Iraq was in part due to the Iraqi government's refusal to extend extraterritorial rights for

U.S. personnel in the theatre[75]—but was also prompted by overwhelming public opinion and a need to refocus American efforts away from seemingly endless conflicts in the Middle East and towards the Asia-Pacific. Less American troops in Iraq and Afghanistan did not indicate a less interventionist foreign policy—but to the contrary reduced the wearing down of the military from boots on ground and freed up resources for newer and more efficient attacks primarily focusing on air and missile strikes and in particular unmanned drones. The number of drone strikes under the Obama administration were almost ten times higher than under the Bush administration,[76] and American attacks would come to target forces across seven countries where attacks under Bush had targeted just five—now with much higher intensity.[77] Withdrawing U.S. forces from the Iraqi quagmire in 2009 made the United States appear far more dangerous than it had in at least half a decade—with a refocusing of American assets towards any new theatre now a possibility.

Whereas under the Bush administration North Korea and northeast Asia in general had never been primary foreign policy concerns, for Obama any pretext to increase the American military presence in East Asia—whether the long dormant South China Sea territorial dispute[78] or the Korean War stalemate—was welcome. Accordingly, alongside the South China Sea dispute which emerged as a major hotspot under Obama, handling challenges of "proliferation" was cited as the second key pretext for a greater U.S. involvement in East Asia—a thinly veiled reference to the Korean deterrence program.[79] Thus when North Korea launched the Kwangmyŏngsŏng-2 (Bright Star 2) communications satellite, Washington harshly condemned its actions as a cover for the testing of intercontinental-range ballistic missile technologies. While a number of technologies used by the Unha-2 rocket which launched the satellite were applicable to a ballistic missile, and information from the test could be used to assist the Korean missile program, impeding the state from conducting satellite launches under the pretext that the technologies had dual uses would amount to a serious infringement of Korean sovereignty and its rights under the Outer Space Treaty.

The United States responded by attempting to impose a new round of economic sanctions against the DPRK through the United Nations Security Council, but failing this, moved to tighten enforcement of existing sanctions imposed in 2006. Further threats followed, with Secretary of State Hillary Clinton announcing that the U.S. would increase economic pressure on the DPRK, consider relisting the country as a "State

Sponsor of Terror," and continue to push for UN Security Council resolutions sanctioning North Korea and allowing for interdiction of its international shipping.[80] Secretary Clinton stated regarding North Korean international trade: "We will do everything we can to both interdict it and prevent it and shut off their flow of money."[81] The Obama administration also appeared to be preparing to restart the policy of imposing sanctions on third parties such as banks which had proven so damaging to the Korean economy from 2005 to 2006.[82]

With Washington adopting a new and much harder policy stance under the Obama administration, North Korea responded with a show of force. Pyongyang reportedly threatened further missile tests, accelerated reprocessing of plutonium fuel rods and opening of a uranium enrichment program—which it denied American claims of having previously begun.[83] The state moved to prepare to carry out further nuclear weapons tests, and expelled remaining inspectors from the International Energy Atomic Agency (IAEA). In April 2009 the IAEA confirmed North Korea's claim to be a "fully fledged nuclear power,"[84] and the following month, on May 25, the country conducted its second nuclear weapons test with estimates for its yield ranging widely from 2–20 kilotons.[85] 2009 also saw a major escalation in missile testing. Where after 2006 North Korea had carried out only three ballistic missile tests, all short ranged tactical platforms fired relatively inconspicuously, the year of President Obama's inauguration in 2009 saw testing at record levels with 14 ballistic missiles launched, six with intermediate ranges, supplemented by the launching of the Kwangmyŏngsŏng-2 by long range rocket. Thus, in a period of a few months, North Korea launched as many missiles as it had in the preceding ten years combined.[86]

Pyongyang's response to perceived American hostility, which was itself conducted under the pretext of a response to the Korean satellite launch, was harsh but demonstrated the considerable new confidence and strength that Pyongyang had gained over the past eight years. From 2009, the United States appeared to adopt a multi-faceted strategy to dealing with the DPRK—including tightening the enforcement of sanctions, increasing raids on North Korean shipping and increasing reliance on cyber-attacks. Its policy towards North Korea was otherwise described as being carried out under a doctrine of "strategic patience"—namely that the administration would wait until pressure forced the DPRK to accept American terms or brought about a total state collapse. In this respect, it closely mirrored the strategy of the Clinton administration which had expected an imminent North Korean collapse and took measures to stall its nuclear development in the interim.

Those in the Obama administration awaiting a collapse or destabilising of the Korean state were emboldened in 2009 by claims that General Secretary Kim Jong Il had fallen into ill health. This led to widespread claims among Western sources that the country was increasingly vulnerable[87] and, should the leader die, could face internal conflict or collapse due to resulting political instability. Perhaps the most notable example was a 60-page report published by the highly influential Council on Foreign Relations (CFR) foreign policy think tank in 2009, which predicted political instability and possibly an imminent state collapse on the basis of Kim Jong Il's health issues. It further projected a full-scale U.S.-led invasion of an unstable North Korea and deployment of a "stabilization force" of an expected 460,000 troops to occupy the country. Such an attack was thought to be considerably easier after the leader's expected death—with the country's political system and military expected to effectively fall apart.[88] The influence of the CFR on the U.S. State Department was considerable, particularly under the Obama administration, with Secretary of State Hillary Clinton referring to the relationship as follows: "We get a lot of advice from the council...[the council tells us] what we should be doing and how we should think about the future."[89]

The CFR was far from alone in depicting the DPRK's collapse as an inevitability. Well into his second term in office in 2015, and despite Pyongyang thwarting widespread Western expectations by carrying out a smooth transition of power following Kim Jong Il's death, President Obama expressed his continued belief that a Korean collapse was a historical certainty.[90] It appeared that American policymakers again fell victim to their country's over-simplistic or stereotypical portrayals of the DPRK as a "one man state" similar to Saddam Hussein's Iraq. They thus failed understand the complexities of the party state—or as was the case under Kim Jong Il the "military-party state"—which ensured that strong institutions and a stable political system designed to survive the death of its leadership were in place. These were actively demonstrated when the ill leader took a four month leave of absence in 2008, with the state's institutions continuing to govern the country and advance the deterrence program as normal. The failure of America and the wider Western world to understand the DPRK on the one hand reduced possibilities for dialogue, but on the other bought the country considerable time as its adversaries continued to wait out an internal clash and possibly a state collapse which never came to be.

The Obama administration's efforts to maintain military pressure on American adversaries while avoiding committing ground forces to Iraq-style quagmires materialised in a heavier reliance on offensive cyber warfare.[91] One of the most prominent American cyberattacks was attempted in 2009 using the Stuxnet worm—which American agents attempted to use to infect the DPRK's nuclear infrastructure. Two Stuxnet attacks were carried out in parallel—one against North Korea and the other against Iran. Israel cooperated closely with this American operation, with both parties retaining a mutual interest in setting back the nuclear programs of the two target states. The worm used an unprecedented four "zero-day attacks," and was the largest and costliest development in malware history. The attack proved highly effective against facilities in Iran, inducing excessive vibrations or distortions in the speed of the rotors in Iranian centrifuges causing serious damage. According to the *Washington Post*, Iran was forced to dismantle 900–1000 centrifuges during the time Stuxnet was active.[92] The impact on Korean facilities was intended to be equally damaging, but efforts to insert the worm failed due to "North Korea's utter secrecy, as well as the extreme isolation of its communications systems" which shielded it from the American attack. The fact that the DPRK used a more efficient plutonium enrichment system, where Iran depended on a uranium system with cumbersome cascading centrifuges, also meant that even if the malware had been inserted the damage would have been considerably reduced.[93]

Director of America's National Security Agency (NSA) Keith Alexander was one of many who noted the DPRK's near unique resilience to Western cyberattacks due to its tight security system—which the Stuxnet incident effectively proved.[94] Nevertheless, the Obama administration launched a campaign of cyberattacks against the country throughout its eight year term—a form of warfare against which the DPRK struggled to respond in kind. It is not clear if this was primarily intended to complement the effects of increasing economic pressure in hopes of provoking another crisis, or whether the intention was only to stall the development of the country's nuclear and ballistic missile deterrents.

President Obama reportedly personally called for a stepping up of cyber and electronic attacks on the DPRK a year into in his second term in office in early 2014, which according to intelligence sources cited by the *New York Times* was responsible for a number of failed missile launches for a year from mid-2015. It was hoped that such efforts "delayed by several years the day when North Korea will be able to threaten American cities with nuclear weapons launched atop intercontinental ballistic missiles," although the success rate of Korean missiles appeared to have recovered by the end of 2016. Such attacks were strongly advocated by senior Pentagon officials among others,[95] and targeted Korean missiles either as they left the launchpad or before they even reached their launch sites. It is uncertain to what extent this campaign succeeded, or whether the Obama administration was instead looking for a way to save face in light of its failure to prevent the DPRK from obtaining thermonuclear weapons and extending its arsenal's strike range.

Investments in what came to be known as "left of launch" disruptive technologies appeared to have been considerable and took a significant place in American military planning at the highest levels. Chairman of the Joint Chiefs of Staff General Martin E. Dempsey first announced plans for disruption of enemy missile systems in 2013, referring specifically to a new emphasis on "cyberwarfare, directed energy and electronic attack." While the chairman's policy paper did not mention North Korea by name, an accompanying map showed a Korean missile in flight towards the United States. The program appeared to gain traction from this point, with several officials and defence contractor Raytheon—a specialist in missile defence technologies—all mentioning "left of launch" technologies with increasing frequency. Shortly after JCS Chairman Dempsey's report Ashton Carter, who was now the Obama administration's Defence Secretary, began calling meetings specifically focused on the possibility of disrupting the Korean missile program. Having strongly called for preventative strikes on the DPRK in the 2000s, Carter had notably changed his position to favour a new approach in light of the adversary's new capabilities.[96]

The *New York Times* noted regarding what appeared to be a last ditch effort by the administration to stall the advance of Korea's deterrent capabilities, or at the very least appear to be expending some effort in this direction: "Advocates of the sophisticated effort to remotely manipulate data inside North Korea's missile systems argue the United States has no real alternative because the effort to stop the North from learning the secrets of making nuclear weapons has already failed. The only hope now is stopping the country from developing an intercontinental missile, and demonstrating that destructive threat to the world." It further noted regarding the president's strong personal support for disruptive attacks that "Obama ultimately pressed the Pentagon and intelligence agencies to pull out all the stops, which officials took as encouragement to reach for untested technologies."[97]

The sabotage program reportedly seriously affected testing of new and more capable variants of the Musudan in April and May 2016, although Korean countermeasures appear to have been developed which ensured that subsequent tests were successful. This led several analysts to conclude that the "left of launch" effort may have seriously backfired, as while its effect on North Korea's overall progress towards developing its missile capability was relatively minor it led the KPA to conduct launches under greater duress and secrecy to avoid American interference. This not only further limited intelligence available to the U.S., but also gave the KPA considerable experience in conducting missile launches under strained conditions similar to those which could be expected in wartime.[98]

In 2015 North Korea was accused of launching a small cyber-attack of its own—namely the hacking of Sony Corporation and the publication of company documents in response to its release of the film "The Interview" earlier that year. Pyongyang had requested the production not be shown due to its crude and at times vulgar depictions of the country and gory killing of its leader, with the film widely accused even by North Korea's Western critics of having strong racist and bigoted depictions of East Asian peoples—particularly women.[99] American author and journalist Tim Shorrock, a regular contributor to *Nation* and *The National Interest* and expert on U.S.-Korea relations, observed: "The film used every racist image and trope that [director] Rogen could dream up, from the sing-songy caricatures of Asian speech that were a film staple in the 1940s and '50s, to the concept that Koreans are either robotic slaves (like Kim's security guards) or sex-starved submissives who crave American men."[100] President Obama warned of a proportional response to the alleged Korean hacking, and a large scale cyberattack on Korean internet servers shortly afterwards was speculated to have been carried out by the U.S.[101]

The alleged Korean attack was used as a pretext for additional economic sanctions against the DPRK, although many experts raised serious questions regarding North Korean responsibility. As Kurt Stammburger, senior vice president at the leading American cybersecurity firm Norse Corp, informed law enforcement: "We can't find any indication that

North Korea either ordered, masterminded or even funded this attack... Nobody has been able to find a credible connection to the North Korean government." Data instead pointed to a former Sony employee with insider knowledge of the company. Shlomo Argamon, chief scientist at cybersecurity consulting firm Taia Global, similarly found a complete lack of signs that North Korea was responsible, stating: "there's certainly reason to doubt the total attribution of this to North Korea." A number of other experts, including hackers and security researchers, reached very similar conclusions.[102]

While there was evidence that the DPRK carried out considerable cyber espionage targeting South Korea,[103] there was no evidence of significant retaliatory cyber warfare efforts against the United States and, according to experts, much evidence to the contrary. It is notable that the Obama administration offered a strong contrast to its predecessor in its focus on the weaponization of information and its close work with many media organizations to further its policy objectives.[104] Apparently as a part of this, the Sony hack revealed the extent of the company's close contacts with the Democratic Party and the defense establishment, which had requested production of "The Interview" and directly influenced its content.[105] The film's director, Seth Rogen, himself attested to this, stating: "Throughout this process, we made relationships with certain people who work in the government as consultants, who I'm convinced are in the C.I.A."[106] Chief executive of Sony Entertainment Michael Lynton remained in communication with the State Department during the film's development, and was told that it had the potential of having a real impact on North Korea.[107] Sony was further advised to keep the gory execution of the Korean leader as it was something American defense analysts and Korea experts believed the Korean population "needed to see" that could inspire anti-government activities.[108]

Executive board member of the Korea Policy Institute Professor Christine Hong observed regarding the production and its intentions:

> if you actually look at what the Sony executives did, they consulted very closely with the State Department, which actually gave the executives a green light with regard to the death scene. And they also consulted with a RAND North Korea watcher, a man named Bruce Bennett, who basically has espoused in thesis that the way to bring down the North Korean government is to assassinate the leadership. And he

> actually stated, in consulting with Sony about this film, that this film, in terms of the South Korean market, as well as its infiltration by defector balloon-dropping organizations into North Korea, could possibly get the wheels of a kind of regime change plot into motion. So, in this instance, fiction and reality have a sort of mirroring relationship to each other. [109]

Bennett worked for the Office of the Secretary of Defence, U.S. Forces in Korea (USFK), U.S. Forces in Japan (USFJ) and the U.S. Pacific Command and had made over 100 trips to South Korea as an advisor for senior personnel in the U.S. Army and the ROKAF.

The Obama years saw an escalation in the use of media targeting North Korea, not only internally through increased funding for radio broadcasts and dissemination of propaganda into the country (see Chapter 19), but also through the targeting of the state's external image. North Korea's nature as a threat to the American people was emphasized in a number of productions during this period to an unprecedented extent, from the videogame Homefront to the films Red Dawn and Olympus Has Fallen which all depicted Korean soldiers on American soil attempting to destroy or conquer the United States. Anti-Korean non-government organizations known to have close ties[110] to the CIA and Western intelligence also appeared to step up their efforts in spreading information which demonized the country through publications, social media, guest lectures and other forums. The ability of the U.S. and the wider Western Bloc to use propaganda far more subtly and effectively than their Korean adversaries proved a valuable asset, which was increasingly capitalized on alongside economic pressure and cyber warfare.

In February 2013 North Korea conducted its third nuclear test, reportedly of a lighter warhead with a heavier yield, which at the highest estimate yielded 40 kilotons.[111] That year also saw a resumption of large-scale ballistic missile testing with over half a dozen platforms tested—all short ranged. The foreign policy agenda of the Obama administration at this point appeared increasingly overwhelmed, with growing tensions with Russia, ongoing conflict with Iran, crises resulting from interventionism in Syria and Libya and the ever-present war in Afghanistan drawing attention away from the intended focus of its foreign policy—northeast Asia and more specifically China. This left little room for North Korea, which never appeared to assume an urgency proportional to its importance. A shift in world order and growing challenges to Western leadership elsewhere in the world were increasingly playing strongly in Pyongyang's favour.

The shortage of attention devoted to northeast Asia only worsened in Obama's second term from January 2013. State Secretary Hillary Clinton, Assistant Secretary of State for East Asian and Pacific Affairs Kurt Campbell and National Security Advisor Tom Donilon had all been committed to the "Pivot to Asia" initiative, but these individuals had all left the administration by late 2013. Their replacements appeared to have far less interest in the region and failed to comprehend its growing importance. The new Secretary of State, John Kerry, for example, was advised to make his first trip to the Asia-Pacific as Secretary Clinton had—but gave a disdainful response. "Forget it," he had said, emphasizing his top priority was the Middle East and his first trip was intended to pursue an Israeli-Palestinian peace deal. This repeatedly proved one of many extremely time consuming but unsolvable quagmires for American foreign policy, which appeared to be prioritized due to the personal interests of officials rather than its genuine importance to American interests.

The National Security Council under new National Security Advisor Susan Rice faced similar issues, with its most time-consuming cases almost all taking place in the Middle East far from where the most serious and consequential challenges to American power—those in northeast Asia—were being issued. Priorities were often misplaced, and the Middle East continued to draw attention wholly disproportionate to its actual importance either economically, militarily or geopolitically. Much like Bush's invasion of Iraq beforehand this increasingly tied attentions and resources down away from where they most needed to be, leaving the Obama administration in a poor position to respond to North Korea's new nuclear test and its renewed ballistic missile testing.[112]

The following two years saw very high rates of weapons testing with at least sixteen short range and two medium-range ballistic missiles launched in 2014—more than all the ballistic missiles and satellite launchers tested under the Bush administration, combined.[113] Newer and more capable missiles also began to feature in Korean tests, with 2015 marking the debut of the Pukkuksong-1 solid fuelled submarine launched ballistic missile with an estimated 2000–2500km range. The missile's compactness, reach and use of a solid fuel composite demonstrated the fast technological progress being made, and its launch from an indigenous Gorae Class ballistic missile submarine heralded the attainment of a second stage deterrent. The Gorae was the first Korean warship designed for nuclear delivery, and its presence was intended to complicate any future American plans for a first strike to neutralise the Korean arsenal by providing a retaliatory capability from the sea. Following the Pukkuksong-1's success, a land-based variant known as Pukkuksong-2 would be successfully tested twice in 2017 and would soon afterwards enter mass production.[114]

In January 2016 North Korea carried out its fourth nuclear test, reportedly of its very first thermonuclear warhead. Such warheads seriously strengthened the country's strategic deterrence capabilities with yields several orders of magnitude higher than fission weapons. In response President Obama reiterated that the United States could "obviously destroy North Korea,"[115] while his senior diplomat on Asia, Assistant U.S. Secretary of State Daniel Russel, warned that Leader Kim Jong Un would "immediately die" if he used his nuclear arsenal.[116] North Korea further carried out multiple tests of the Musudan missile, the first from Korean territory, and following failed tests from March, which U.S. media attributed to American cyberattacks and sabotage, a test launch in June demonstrated a number of new features. The design was an upgrade over that previously tested in Iran, and integrated new grid fins and what appeared to be a new engine.[117] The Musudan demonstrated not only the capability to deliver a nuclear warhead to Guam, but to do so at speeds and from altitudes which could comfortably evade American air defence systems. A second test of a thermonuclear warhead was carried out in September that year, and the DPRK afterwards confirmed that it was capable of mounting nuclear warheads on longer ranged ballistic missiles—a capability which had previously been ambiguous. U.S. officials were publicly estimating by 2015 that the DPRK had already developed a miniaturised nuclear warhead,[118] but a thermonuclear capability represented a major step forward for the Korean program.

In response to the DPRK's fourth and fifth nuclear weapons tests the Obama administration reportedly seriously considered attacks on Korean nuclear facilities—preventative strikes intended to destroy the country's deterrence program. The president at this time came far closer to authorising an attack than his predecessor George W. Bush ever had, but was reportedly deterred from doing so by two primary factors. It is notable that none of these were related to the illegality of launching such attacks under international law as crimes of aggression—which were committed elsewhere by the Obama administration, its predecessors and its successor with impunity. The first factor was that North Korea had multiple options for deadly response, from artillery strikes on American forces in South Korea to missile attacks on facilities in Japan and Guam or even nuclear retaliation. With the country's threshold for nuclear use still wholly ambiguous, any major attack thus came at serious risk.

The second factor was that the Pentagon had informed the president that options for a limited preventative strike were effectively non-existent. North Korea by this time was estimated to have dozens of nuclear warheads, which alongside the KPA's highly mobile delivery systems were stored deep underground in facilities which the U.S. could not locate and neutralise from the air. Thus, the Pentagon had concluded, nothing short of a full-scale ground invasion could disarm the DPRK of its nuclear deterrent. This in turn would guarantee, no matter how high the country's nuclear threshold was, that the DPRK would launch retaliatory nuclear attacks. Even in a conventional war, American casualties were expected to reach hundreds of thousands within weeks of the outbreak of hostilities,[119] and use of weapons of mass destruction would only increase these losses. As American journalist Bob Woodward wrote at the time: "The Pentagon reported that the only way 'to locate and destroy—with complete certainty—all components of North Korea's nuclear program' was through a ground invasion… A ground invasion would trigger a North Korean response, likely with a nuclear weapon."[120]

A key facilitator of North Korea's security, and an asset which shifted the White House's calculus regarding a potential attack, was the Korean intelligence and internal security apparatus. As Clinton administration CIA director Robert Gates had noted, North Korea was a unique "black hole" for American intelligence, considered "without parallel the toughest intelligence target in the world"—an assessment widely shared.[121] As a result the locations of the Korean leadership and its nuclear arsenal were unknown to their adversaries—which made arranging an effective first strike against them impossible. Thus, much as with the Stuxnet attacks among several other examples, the DPRK's tight internal security system effectively paid off in shielding the country from potentially devastating American attacks. The *New York Times* reported that in his final year in office President Obama was eager to strike not only North Korean nuclear weapons sites, but also to eliminate the country's leadership. The primary reason why such a course was not taken was that there was a high probability of failure—as gaining timely intelligence on the locations of either was effectively impossible. A failed strike in turn would guarantee massive retaliation.[122]

While North Korea's economy had largely recovered from the Arduous March period by 2009, it had grown considerably throughout the Obama years despite significant economic pressure and successive rounds of economic sanctions passed both unilaterally by Western states and through the United Nations. The new leadership in North Korea from late 2011, which Western analysts had optimistically predicted would either reform the DPRK into a Westphilian state or would oversee its collapse,[123] instead appeared to rejuvenate the economy with a new emphasis on modernisation, high end technologies and the improvement of living standards. This was evident from the new domestically manufactured smartphones under brands such as Arirang, Jinalllae and Phurun Hanul to the considerable investments made in projects for agriculture such as fish farming[124] and floating rice fields,[125] in new facilities for scientific research,[126] and in new modern housing and infrastructure projects. Even entertainment and performing arts appeared to have adopted more modern styles—as did architecture. Thus, the DPRK's economy was in a far stronger position in January 2017 when Obama's administration left office that it had been eight years prior.

Alongside economic growth, North Korea's military capabilities had grown considerably. The reliance on older Soviet-era weaponry, from S-200 air defence systems and Chonma Ho battle tanks to Bulsae-2 anti-tank missiles, was reduced as newer fully indigenous systems entered service—such as the Pyongae-5 (KN-06) for air defence, Pokpung Ho for armoured warfare and Bulsae-3 for tank hunting to name but a few examples. The Pukkuksong-1 had meanwhile provided the beginnings of a second stage deterrent, while new Musudan variants had on multiple occasions proven reliable with a delivery range of 4000km. This alongside testing of a thermonuclear warhead and the further miniaturisation achieved through three nuclear tests gave the DPRK a considerably stronger deterrent capability than it had had eight years prior.

President Obama and his administration would be sharply criticised by his successor, Donald Trump, for failure alongside the preceding Bush and Clinton administrations to stall North Korea's development of thermonuclear weapons and ICBMs.[127] Similar criticisms were levelled across a number of Western media outlets and by several prominent analysts.[128] While the Obama administration's Korea policy was arguably no less competent that those of his predecessors, particularly when considering the far more difficult circumstances it inherited, the development of a Korean thermonuclear bomb and emergence of its first

ICBM prototypes in Obama's final year unnerved many in the West for the limitations it would place on America's ability to take military action in northeast Asia. The successful demonstration of the Musudan's capabilities after multiple tests, which used far more sophisticated engines than its predecessors, opened the possibility for a relatively swift path to ICBM development by addition of more stage separation without the need for designing new engines.[129]

North Korea's progress in developing its deterrent capabilities and strengthening its economy left the new Donald Trump administration with far more limited room to manoeuvre to scale back the country's nuclear and ballistic missile programs. The new president would claim that Obama had advised him shortly before leaving office in 2016 that North Korea would present the toughest foreign policy challenge for the United States.[130] The DPRK's accelerated weapons testing over the two years would come to a head in 2017, when new developments in North Korea's weapons programs would irreversibly change the nature of the relationship between the Western superpower and the small Northeast Asian state.

Sinking of the ROKS *Cheonan:* Crisis at Sea

On March 26, 2010 the ROK Navy Pohang Class corvette ROKS *Cheonan* sank during anti-submarine warfare exercises killing 46 seamen onboard. The incident was initially widely blamed by families of the dead on the incompetence of the Navy itself, but some weeks later South Korean media began to speculate that North Korea may have been to blame. Evidence at the time was extremely questionable—namely citing an unnamed NGO representative who said he received a call from a North Korean officer of high rank boasting that he had orchestrated the entire scheme to target the *Cheonan.*[131] When it was pointed out that there were no traces of North Korean submarines in the area, as verified by its very close monitoring by specialized U.S. and ROK anti-submarine warfare assets, a number of media outlets then claimed that if it was not the KPA Navy, then North Korean saboteur bombers must have been responsible.[132] Some Japanese and Russian outlets meanwhile claimed the corvette was sunk by an American submarine, and the ROK was concealing the truth by blaming the DPRK. Such allegations were supported by notoriously high rates of friendly fire accidents in the U.S. military,[133] and it was confirmed that American submarines had been present. Again, however, no evidence was presented to prove this was the case.[134]

With the new government in Seoul under President Lee Myung Bak under growing American pressure to fall in line with the new maximum pressure strategy, and officially abandoning the previous policy of rapprochement with the DPRK, the spinning of the *Cheonan* incident as a North Korean plot not only shielded Seoul, the ROK Navy and the U.S. from criticism—but also gave a pretext to abandon the previously popular rapprochement with Pyongyang. Experts continued to support the conclusion that the incident was an accident of some sort—rather than a North Korean attack. Indeed, ROK Defense Minister Kim Tae Young suggested that the cause of the explosion which destroyed the corvette was one of the many mines placed by the ROK military in the 1970s, calling reports of a North Korean torpedo attack "unfounded." He cited interviews with surviving crew who had been operating the frigate's sensors as evidence refuting the torpedo theory.[135] A commission of six nations, all but the ROK being Western states, concluded itself concluded on May 7 that the corvette was most likely "destroyed by a torpedo made in Germany"—a weapon widely employed by South Korean submarines which the KPA Navy did not have access to.[136] The commission's report led to speculation that friendly fire may have been to blame.[137] This conclusion, too, was called into question—as the torpedo remains were corroded which led experts to believe they must have been submerged for several years.[138]

The only evidence which could be offered that the torpedo was in fact from North Korea was a "No. 1" inscribed in purple marker on one of the parts. This proved wholly insubstantial and led to widespread satirical responses in the ROK itself. Perhaps the most prominent was the photoshopping of iPhones with the same "No. 1" as supposed "evidence" that they were North Korean.[139] University of Virginia professor Lee Seunghun stated to this effect: "You could put that mark on an iPhone and claim it was manufactured in North Korea. The government is lying when they said this was found underwater. I think this is something that was pulled out of a warehouse of old materials to show to the press."[140]

Dr. Suh Jae Jung, a political analyst at Johns Hopkins University in Washington D.C., was one of many who argued that the evidence cited in no way proved that the KPA had perpetrated the *Cheonan* incident. The biggest inconsistency, he argued, was the white powder found on the *Cheonan*, which could not have resulted from such an explosion. Lab experiments replicating the chemical process showed that the powder was rust from water exposure over time—not the result of an explosion, as the investigation had cited it. He stated instead that the *Cheonan* was most likely sunk by an older South Korean mine—as the defense minister had originally stated.[141] Dr. Konstantin Asmolov, a leading Korea expert and researcher at the Russian Academy of Sciences and at Moscow State University, independently assessed in detail the circumstances of the *Cheonan*'s sinking, which effectively ruled out a North Korean attack. Noting that the warship was "specifically designed to hunt enemy submarines," he stated:

> It is strange that in the close-combat conditions, and low (15–20m) depths in the area of the tragedy, its crew not only did not find an enemy ship, but also could not detect any torpedo firing. In such a case, the enemy boat as described above had to overtake the ASW barrier deployed near the border, make its way unnoticed into the waters off the island of Baengnyeong teeming with enemy ships, submarines and aircraft, then discreetly attack the corvette, sink it with the very first torpedo, and then safely leave, avoiding other anti-submarine ships and helicopters.... The question of how it [alleged KPA submarine] managed to remain undetected during the exercise and sink a vessel intended for combatting enemy submarines remained open, but that no longer bothered anyone.

The likelihood of this seems highly implausible if not impossible. Asmolov called the chances of this happening "miraculous."[142] Asmolov was hardly alone in reaching this conclusion. As a prominent article in the Japanese *Asia-Pacific Journal* noted:

> The *Cheonan* was a patrol boat whose mission was to survey with radar and sonar the enemy's submarines, torpedoes, and aircraft... If North Korean submarines and torpedoes were approaching, the *Cheonan* should have been able to sense it quickly and take measures to counterattack or evade. Moreover, on the day the *Cheonan* sank, U.S. and ROK military exercises were under way, so it could be anticipated that North Korean submarines would move south to conduct surveillance. It is hard to imagine that the *Cheonan* sonar forces were not on alert.[143]

A number of prominent South Korean papers similarly stressed the low likelihood that a submarine could have operated undetected, stressing the advanced anti-submarine warfare capabilities of the *Cheonan*, the state of high combat readiness and the considerable surveillance assets deployed by both U.S. and ROK forces.[144] The Asia Foundation's director for the Center for U.S.-Korea Policy, Scott Snyder, also director of the program on U.S.-Korea policy at the Council on Foreign Relations, cited similar facts and voiced serious doubts regarding the narrative of a North Korean attack.[145]

Further inconsistencies with the new narrative squarely blaming the DPRK were widely reported by South Korean official sources, from Defense Ministry Official Kim Chul Woo and investigative panel member Shin Sang Cheol[146] to lawmaker Lee Jung Hee and former senior presidential secretary Park Seon Won, among others. Many of these figures were openly prosecuted by the state under the pretext of spreading "groundless rumors" which carried with it the charge of undermining national security—deterring others from voicing their own skepticism or carrying out their own independent analysis.[147] Shin had noted regarding his own findings during the investigation: "I couldn't find the slightest sign of an explosion. The sailors drowned to death. Their bodies were clean. We didn't even find dead fish in the sea." He presented considerable evidence for his claim that the ship had run aground and collided with another vessel, concluding that what had occurred was nothing more than "a simple traffic accident at sea." South Korea's Defense Ministry responded by asking the National Assembly to eject Shin from the panel for "creating public mistrust" in the investigation.[148]

Lee Jung Hee was sued for defamation by the ROK's Joint Chiefs of Staff for pointing out, in a speech before the national assembly, that the feed from a thermal observation device showing the moment the warship's stern and bow split apart, which would have indicated how the incident occurred, was being purposefully withheld. Park, meanwhile, was charged with libel for simply requesting greater transparency and expressing doubts about the official narrative, stating regarding the resulting lawsuit: "I asked for the disclosure of information for a transparent and impartial investigation into the cause of the *Cheonan* sinking… the libel suit seeks to silence public suspicion over the incident."[149] As Dr. Asmolov observed: "it started to become clear to experts that what's important is not who actually sank the ill-fated corvette, but who is named responsible for the tragedy."[150] This would hardly have been an isolated occurrence, with Western-led commissions found to have shown strong political biases and manipulated evidence[151] in order to pin blame on adversaries when investigating a number of other attacks since.[152]

The *Cheonan* incident represented the most serious blow to inter-Korean relations since the Cold War, and played well into the hands of the U.S. by driving a wedge between the two states and increasing pressure against the DPRK through furthering its isolation. State Secretary Hillary Clinton visited the ROK soon after the incident and spoke of designs towards "changing the direction of North Korea, making a convincing case to everyone in the region to work together to achieve that outcome, denuclearizing the Korean Peninsula and offering the opportunities for a better life for the people of the North." This was widely interpreted as a thinly veiled call for imposition of regime change, and it was hoped that the *Cheonan* incident would allow the U.S. to rally greater support from other regional actors and support from the South Korean public for the Obama administration to see through its designs.[153]

While it remains uncertain how the *Cheonan* came to be sunk, the narrative which was later pressed by the Western-led investigation team and repeated to the exclusion of all others across Western media—that the KPA had somehow carried out the attack—remains highly implausible. This is particularly true when considering the changing nature of the claims and the nature of the evidence cited. While the *Choenan* sinking would have represented one of the most successful KPA operations since the Korean War, and Pyongyang had historically never shied away from claiming credit for previous strikes, it denied any involvement from the outset with its state media referring to the loss of "fellow countrymen" as a "regrettable accident." The spinning of the incident as a North Korean attack nevertheless proved highly useful for U.S. designs against the DPRK—and was well timed with escalating sanctions to cut North Korea off from its valuable economic relationship with the south. The *Cheonan* sinking was used as a pretext for the new government in Seoul, which had indicated a hardline anti-DPRK position from the outset, to cut almost all trade with North Korea. This was expected to cost the DPRK over $200 million a year in valuable foreign currency. The ROK further moved to increase its participation in American-led military exercises and began to employ psychological warfare using propaganda loudspeakers along the DMZ—leading to a significant further deterioration in relations.[154]

NOTES

1 Worldwide Intelligence Review, Hearing Before the Select Committee on Intelligence of the United States Senate, One Hundred Fourth Congress, First Session on Worldwide Intelligence Review, January 10, 1995 (p. 164).
2 International Institute for Strategic Studies, *The Military Balance*, Volume 94, 1994, Part IX: Asia and Australasia (p. 165).
3 Sokolski, Henry D., 'Planning for a Peaceful Korea', *Strategic Studies Institute,* February 2001 (p. 290).
4 Worldwide Intelligence Review, Hearing Before the Select Committee on Intelligence of the United States Senate, One Hundred Fourth Congress, First Session on Worldwide Intelligence Review, January 10, 1995 (p. 164).
5 'Interview: Ashton Carter,' *Frontline*, March 3, 2003.
6 Gilman, Benjamin A., 'Gilman Releases North Korea Report,' *Press Release*, November 3, 1999.
7 Pollack, Jonathan D., 'The United States, North Korea and the end of the Agreed Framework,' *Naval War College Review*, vol. LVI, no. 3, 2003.
Beal, Tim, *North Korea: The Struggle Against American Power,* London, Pluto Press, 2004 (p. 214).
Harrison, Selig S., 'Did North Korea Cheat?,' *Foreign Affairs*, January/February 2005.
8 'Conclusion of non-aggression treaty between DPRK and U.S. called for,' *KCNA*, October 25, 2002.
9 Harrison, Selig S., 'Did North Korea Cheat?,' *Foreign Affairs*, January/February 2005.
10 Smith, Derek D., *Deterring America: Rogue States and the Proliferation of Weapons of Mass Destruction*, Cambridge, Cambridge University Press, 2006 (p. 75).
11 'North Korea's nuclear program 2003,' *Bulletin of Atomic Scientists,* vol. 59, no. 2 (p. 75)
Kristensen, Hans M., 'Preemptive Posturing,' *Bulletin of Atomic Scientists*, vol. 58, no. 5, September/ October 2002 (pp. 54–59).
12 'Pro-N. Korea Newspaper. Urges U.S. to Open Two-way Talks,' *Yonhap,* May 27, 2009.
13 Albright, David, 'North Korea's Alleged Large-Scale Enrichment Plant: Yet Another Questionable Extrapolation Based on Aluminium Tubes,' *The Institute for Science and International Security*, February 23, 2007.
14 Sanger, David E., 'North Korea Says It Has a Program on Nuclear Arms,' *New York Times,* October 17, 2002.
15 'Conclusion of non-aggression treaty between DPRK and U.S. called for,' *KCNA*, October 25, 2002
16 Von Hein, Matthias, 'The Iraq War: In the beginning was the lie,' *Deutsche Welle,* April 4, 2018.
17 Ibid.
18 Ibid.
19 Ibid.
20 Smith, Derek D., *Deterring America: Rogue States and the Proliferation of Weapons of Mass Destruction*, Cambridge, Cambridge University Press, 2006 (p. 75).
21 'Interview: Ashton Carter,' *Frontline*, March 3, 2003.
22 Struck, Doug, 'Crisis Could Push N. Korea to Expel Nuclear Inspectors,' *Washington Post,* November 14, 2002.
23 Norris, Robert S. and Kristensen, Hans S., 'North Korea's Nuclear Program, 2005,' *Bulletin of Atomic Scientists*, May/June 2005 (pp. 64–67).
Schobell, Andrew and Sanford, John M., *North Korea's Military Threat: Pyongyang's Conventional Forces, Weapons of Mass Destruction, and Ballistic Missiles*, Carlisle, PA, U.S. Army War College Strategic Studies Institute, April 2007 (p. 77).

24 Berry Jr., William E., 'DPRK Briefing Book: North Korea's Nuclear Program: The Clinton Administration's Response,' INSS Occasional Paper 3, *Nautilus Institute*, March 1995.

25 International Institute for Strategic Studies, *The Military Balance*, Volume 94, 1994, Part IX: Asia and Australasia (p. 165).

26 Worldwide Intelligence Review, Hearing Before the Select Committee on Intelligence of the United States Senate, One Hundred Fourth Congress, First Session on Worldwide Intelligence Review, January 10, 1995 (pp. 103–104).

27 Smith, Derek D., *Deterring America: Rogue States and the Proliferation of Weapons of Mass Destruction*, Cambridge, Cambridge University Press, 2006 (p. 74).

28 Sanger, David E., 'North Korea Says It Has a Program on Nuclear Arms,' *New York Times,* October 17, 2002.

29 'Putin says Kim Jong-il told him about North Korea's nukes back in early 2000s,' *TASS*, October 4, 2017.

30 'Bush peers into "evil" North Korea,' *CNN*, February 20, 2002.

31 'To React to Nuclear Weapons in Kind Is DPRK's Mode of Counteraction,' *Rodong Sinmun, KCNA*, January 11, 2016.

32 Armstrong, Charles, *Necessary Enemies: Anti-Americanism, Juche Ideology, and the Torturous Path to Normalization*, Colombia University, Department of History, Korea Studies, Working Paper Series (p. 14).

33 Ibid. (p. 15).

34 'The DPRK delegate made speech at a meeting of the UN Disarmament Commission on April 11,' *KCNA*, April 21, 2006.

35 'Sailing on, the ship with a hold full of Scud missiles,' *The Guardian,* December 12, 2002.

36 Berger, Andrea, 'Target Markets, North Korea's Military Customers in the Sanctions Era,' Abingdon, Routledge, 2017 (pp. 123–124).

37 Park, Kyung Ae, *New Challenges of North Korean Foreign Policy*, London, Palgrave MacMillan, 2010.

38 Arkin, William M., 'Secret Plan Outlines the Unthinkable,' *Los Angeles Times*, March 10, 2002.

39 Park, Kyung Ae, *New Challenges of North Korean Foreign Policy*, London, Palgrave MacMillan, 2010.

40 Gertz, Bill, 'North Korea Can Build Nukes Right Now,' *Washington Times,* November 22, 2002.

41 Sanger, David E. and Dao, James, 'North Korea Says It Regains Access To Its Plutonium,' *New York Times,* December 23, 2002.

42 Stout, David, 'Rumsfeld Says if Necessary, US Can Fight 2 Wars At Once,' *New York Times*, December 23, 2002.

43 Schneider, Barry R. and Post, Jerrold M., *Know Thy Enemy: Profiles of Adversary Leaders and Their Strategic Cultures*, Montgomery, United States Air Force Counterproliferation Centre, 2003 (p. 129).

44 'US public thinks Saddam had role in 9/11,' *The Guardian,* September 7, 2003.

45 Cristopher, Warren, 'Iraq Belongs on the Back Burner,' *New York Times,* December 31, 2002.

46 *Rodong Sinmun,* March 28, 2003.

47 Ramesh, Randeep, 'The two faces of Rumsfeld,' *The Guardian*, May 9, 2003.

48 Pincus, Walter, 'Rumsfeld Seeks to Revive Burrowing Nuclear Bomb,' *Washington Post*, February 1, 2005.

49 Auster, Bruce B. and Whitelaw, Kevin, 'Upping the Ante for Kim Jong Il: Pentagon Plan 5030, A New Blueprint for Facing Down North Korea,' *U.S. News and World Report*, July 21, 2003.
O'Hanion, Machael E., 'North Korea Is No Iraq,' *Brookings Institute*, October 21, 2002.

50 Kim, Suk Hi, *The Survival of North Korea: Essays on Strategy, Economics and International Relations*, Jefferson, NC, McFarland, 2011 (pp. 49–50).
Park, Kyung Ae, *New Challenges of North Korean Foreign Policy*, London, Palgrave MacMillan, 2010.

51 'North Korea: Washington Flew 1,200 Spy Flights Over Country,' *Fox News*, July 25, 2004.
'North Korea Accuses U.S. of Spy Flights,' *Southern Illinoisan*, July 26, 2004.

52 Galen Carpenter, Ted and Bandow, Doug, *The Korean Conundrum: America's Troubled Relations with North and South Korea,* New York, Palgrave Macmillan, 2004 (pp. 64–65).

53 'U.S. Repositioning Bombers Near North Korea,' *USA Today*, March 4, 2003.

54 Galen Carpenter, Ted and Bandow, Doug, *The Korean Conundrum: America's Troubled Relations with North and South Korea,* New York, Palgrave Macmillan, 2004 (pp. 64–65).
Auster, Bruce and Whitelaw, Kevin, 'Upping the Ante for Kim Jong-Il,' *U.S. News & World Report,* July 21, 2003.

55 Park, Kyung Ae, *New Challenges of North Korean Foreign Policy*, London, Palgrave MacMillan, 2010 (p. 218).

56 Bennett, Bruce W., 'A surgical strike against North Korea? Not a viable option,' *Fox News*, July 14, 2017.
Smith, Derek D., *Deterring America: Rogue States and the Proliferation of Weapons of Mass Destruction*, Cambridge, Cambridge University Press, 2006 (pp. 87, 108–109).
Woolf, Christopher, 'The only effective arms against North Korea's missile bunkers are nuclear weapons, says a top war planner,' *PRI*, August 10, 2017.
Sepp, Eric M., *Deeply Buried Facilities: Implications for Military Operations*, Occasional Paper no. 14, Maxwell Air Force Base, AL, Air War College, May 2000 (p. 5).
Levi, Michael A., *Fire in the Hole: Nuclear and Non-Nuclear Options for Counter-proliferation*, Working Paper no. 31, Carnegie Endowment for International Peace, Washington D.C., November 2002 (p. 8).

57 Katersky, Aaron, 'Iran ordered to pay billions to relatives of 9/11 victims,' *ABC News,* May 1, 2018.
'Pompeo says Iran tied to Al-Qaeda, declines to say if war legal,' *France 24,* April 10, 2019.
Gembrell, Jon, 'Bin Laden files back up US claims on Iran ties to al-Qaida,' *Associated Press,* November 2, 2017.

58 Taremi, Kamran, 'Beyond the Axis of Evil: Ballistic Missiles in Iran's Military Thinking,' *Security Dialogue,* vol. 36, no. 1, March 2005 (pp. 93–108).

59 Goodman, Peter S., 'N. Korea Moves to Activate Complex,' *Washington Post*, December 27, 2002.

60 Sanger, David E. and Schmitt, Eric, 'Satellites Said to See Activity at North Korean Nuclear Site,' *New York Times,* January 31, 2003.

61 Schobell, Andrew and Sanford, John M., *North Korea's Military Threat: Pyongyang's Conventional Forces, Weapons of Mass Destruction, and Ballistic Missiles*, Carlisle, PA, U.S. Army War College Strategic Studies Institute, April 2007 (p. 75).
The International Institute for Strategic Studies, *North Korea's Weapons Programmes: A Net Assessment*, London, Palgrave Macmillan, 2004 (p. 42).

62 Lee, Su Hoon, *Nuclear North Korea*, Seoul, Kyungnam University Press, 2012 (p. 88).

63 Secretary of State's Telegram to the Missile Technology Control Regime on North Korea's Missile Program, 13:14, October 6, 2009 (09STATE103755_a).
'North Korea rebuked over missile launches | Financial Times,' *Financial Times,* June 22, 2016.

64 Kang, Jin-Kyu and Jeong, Yong-Soo, 'Musudan's high speed is bad news for defense,' *Korea JoongAng Daily*, June 24, 2016.

65 Bechtol Jr., Bruce E., *North Korean Military Proliferation in the Middle East and Africa,* Lexington, University Press of Kentucky, 2018 (p. 88).
Spencer, Richard, 'N Korea "Tests New Missile in Iran,"' *The Telegraph*, May 17, 2007.

66 Bermudez Jr., Joseph S., *A History of Ballistic Missile Development in the DPRK*, Occasional Paper no. 2, Monterey, Monterey Institute for International Studies Center for Nonproliferation Studies, 1999 (p. 15).

67 Gertz, Bill, 'North Korea Has More Missiles, U.S. Says,' *Washington Times*, July 13, 2006.

68 Lewis, Jeffrey, 'The Game Is Over, and North Korea Has Won,' *Foreign Policy*, August 9, 2017.

69 Greenlees, Donald and Lague, David, 'Squeeze on Banco Delta Asia hit North Korea where it hurt,' *New York Times,* January 18, 2007.

70 Solomon, Jay and King Jr., Neil, 'How U.S. Used a Bank to Punish North Korea,' *Wall Street Journal,* April 12, 2007.

71 Lodgaard, Sverre and Maerli, Vremer, *Nuclear Proliferation and International Security,* Abingdon, Routledge, 2007 (p. 130).

72 Kim, Hong Nack, 'U.S.-North Korea Relations under the Obama Administration: Problems and Prospects,' *North Korean Review,* vol. 6, no. 1, Spring 2010 (p. 21).
JoongAng Ilbo, January 12, 2009.

73 Kim, Hong Nack, 'U.S.-North Korea Relations under the Obama Administration: Problems and Prospects,' *North Korean Review,* vol. 6, no. 1, Spring 2010 (pp. 23–24, 28).

74 Cha, Victor D., 'Hawk Engagement and Preventive Defense on the Korean Peninsula,' *International Security*, vol. 27, no. 1, 2002 (p. 4).
Jackson, Van, *On the Brink,* Cambridge, Cambridge University Press, 2018 (p. 69).

75 Dagher, Sam, 'Maliki Takes Hard Line on American Withdrawal,' *Wall Street Journal*, October 23, 2011.

76 'Obama's Cover. Drone War in Numbers: Ten Times More Strikes Than Bush,' *Bureau of Investigative Journalism,* January 17, 2017.

77 Agerholm, Harriet, 'Map shows where President Barack Obama dropped his 20,000 bombs,' *The Independent,* January 19, 2017.
Bruton, F. Brinley, 'U.S. Bombed Iraq, Syria, Pakistan, Afghanistan, Libya, Yemen, Somalia in 2016,' *NBC News,* January 9, 2017.

78 Abrams, A. B., *Power and Primacy: The History of Western Intervention in the Asia-Pacific*, Oxford, Peter Lang, 2019 (pp. 634–641).

79 'Remarks by President Obama to the Australian Parliament,' *Office of the Press Secretary, The White House*, November 17, 2011.

80 *Boston Globe,* June 8, 2009.

81 Henderson, Nia-Malika, 'Clinton talks tough on N. Korea, Iran,' *Politico,* June 7, 2009.

82 Kim, Hong Nack, 'U.S.-North Korea Relations under the Obama Administration: Problems and Prospects,' *North Korean Review,* vol. 6, no. 1, Spring 2010 (p. 27).

83 *New York Times,* April 30, 2009.

84 Moore, Malcolm, 'North Korea now "fully fledged nuclear power,"' *The Telegraph*, April 24, 2009.

85 Charles, Deborah and Zakaria, Tabassum, 'North Korea's May nuclear test few kilotons: U.S.,' *Reuters,* June 15, 2009.

86 Centre for Strategic International Studies, Missile Defense Project, 'North Korean Missile Launches & Nuclear Tests: 1984–Present' (https://missilethreat.csis.org/north-korea-missile-launches-1984–present/) (Accessed July 20, 2019).

87 International Institute for Strategic Studies, *The Military Balance*, Volume 110, 2010, Part VIII: Asia and Australasia (p. 380).
88 Stares, Paul B. and Wit, Joel S., *Preparing for Sudden Change in North Korea,* Council Special Report No. 42, Council on Foreign Relations Center for Preventative Action, January 2009.
89 'A Conversation with U.S. Secretary of State Hillary Rodham Clinton,' *Council on Foreign Relations*, July 15, 2009.
90 Foster-Carter, Aidan, 'Obama Comes Out as a North Korea Collapsist,' *The Diplomat,* January 20, 2015.
91 Sanger, David E., 'Obama Order Sped Up Wave of Cyberattacks Against Iran,' *New York Times,* June 1, 2012.
92 Warrick, Joby, 'Iran's Natanz nuclear facility recovered quickly from Stuxnet cyberattack,' *Washington Post*, February 16, 2011.
93 Menn, Joseph, 'Exclusive: U.S. tried Stuxnet-style campaign against North Korea but failed—sources,' *Reuters,* May 29, 2015.
94 Ibid.
95 Perry, William J., at: *38 North Press Briefing*, The US-Korea Institute, Washington D.C., January 9, 2017.
Sanger, David E. and Broad, William J., 'Trump Inherits a Secret Cyberwar Against North Korean Missiles,' *New York Times,* March 4, 2017.
96 Carter, Ashton and Perry, William J., 'Back to the Brink,' *Washington Post,* October 20, 2002.
97 Sanger, David E. and Broad, William J., 'Trump Inherits a Secret Cyberwar Against North Korean Missiles,' *New York Times,* March 4, 2017.
98 Jackson, Van, *On the Brink,* Cambridge, Cambridge University Press, 2018 (pp. 77–78).
99 Builder, Maxine, 'The Real Problem With "The Interview" Is Its Racism, Not Its Satire,' *Medium,* December 18, 2014.
Kim, Ji-Sun (Grace), '"The Interview": No Laughing Matter,' *Huffington Post,* January 8, 2015.
100 Shorrock, Tim, 'How Sony, Obama, Seth Rogen and CIA secretly planned to force regime change in North Korea,' *Grey Zone,* September 5, 2017.
101 'North Korean Internet Collapses After Obama's Warning,' *Time,* December 22, 2014.
102 Faughnder, Ryan and Hamedy, Saba, 'Sony insider—not North Korea—likely involved in hack, experts say,' *Los Angeles Times*, December 30, 2015.
'Former Anonymous hacker doubts North Korea behind Sony attack,' *CBS News,* December 18, 2014.
'The Evidence That North Korea Hacked Sony Is Flimsy,' *Wired,* December 17, 2014.
'New evidence Sony hack was "inside" job, not North Korea,' *New York Post,* December 30, 2014.
103 'North Korea "hackers steal US-South Korea war plans,"' *BBC,* October 10, 2017.
Choi, Haejin, 'North Korea hacked Daewoo Shipbuilding, took warship blueprints: South Korea lawmaker,' *Reuters,* October 31, 2017.
104 Assange, Julian, 'Google Is Not What It Seems,' *Wikileaks,* 2016.
Nixon, Ron, 'U.S. Groups Helped Nurture Arab Uprisings,' *New York Times,* April 14, 2011.
105 '"The Interview" Belittles North Korea, But is Film's Backstory and U.S. Policy the Real Farce?,' *Democracy Now,* December 22, 2014.
Thielman, Sam, 'WikiLeaks republishes all Sony hacking scandal documents,' *The Guardian,* April 17, 2015.
'Sony,' *Wikileaks,* April. 16, 2015.

106 Itzkoff, Dave, 'James Franco and Seth Rogen Talk About "The Interview,"' *New York* Times, December 16, 2016.
107 Hornaday, Ann, 'Sony, "The Interview," and the unspoken truth" All movies are political,' *Washington Post,* December 18, 2014.
108 De Moraes, Lisa, '"The Interview" Release Would Have Damaged Kim Jong Un Internally, Says Rand Expert Who Saw Movie at Sony's Request,' *Yahoo News,* December 19, 2014.
109 '"The Interview" Belittles North Korea, But is Film's Backstory and U.S. Policy the Real Farce?,' *Democracy Now,* December 22, 2014.
110 Taylor, Adam and Kim, Min Joo, 'The covert group that carried out a brazen raid on a North Korean embassy now fears exposure,' *Washington Post,* March 28, 2019.
Mount, I. and White, E. and Buseong, K., 'A tale of daring, violence and intrigue from a North Korea embassy,' *Financial Times,* March 29, 2019.
111 'How Powerful Was N. Korea's Nuke Test?' *The Chosunilbo,* February 14, 2013.
112 Rachman, Gideon, *Easternisation, War and Peace in the Asian Century,* New York, Vintage, 2017 (pp. 77–78).
Washington Post, January 18, 2009.
113 Centre for Strategic International Studies, Missile Defense Project, 'North Korean Missile Launches & Nuclear Tests: 1984–Present,' Accessed July 20, 2019 (https://missilethreat.csis.org/north-korea-missile-launches-1984–present/).
114 Cheng, Jonathan, 'North Korea Expands Key Missile-Manufacturing Plant,' *Wall Street Journal,* July 1, 2018.
115 Blair, David, '"We could destroy you," Obama warns "erratic" North Korean leader,' *Telegraph,* April 26, 2016.
116 'N. Korea lambasts Russel for his "immediately die" comment,' *Yonhap,* October 15, 2016.
117 Bechtol Jr., Bruce E., *North Korean Military Proliferation in the Middle East and Africa,* Lexington, University Press of Kentucky, 2018 (p. 21).
118 Jackson, Van, *On the Brink,* Cambridge, Cambridge University Press, 2018 (p. 70).
119 'North Korea: The War Game,' *The Atlantic,* August 15, 2005.
120 Johnson, Jesse, 'Obama weighed pre-emptive strike against North Korea after fifth nuclear blast and missile tests near Japan in 2016, Woodward book claims,' *Japan Times,* September 12, 2018.
'Obama mulled preemptive attack on N. Korea: book,' *Yonhap,* September 12, 2018.
121 Litwak, Roberto, *Rogue States and U.S. Foreign Policy: Containment After the Cold War,* Washington D.C., Woodrow Wilson Center Press, 2000 (p. 223).
122 Sanger, David E. and Broad, William J., 'Trump Inherits a Secret Cyberwar Against North Korean Missiles,' *New York Times,* March 4, 2017.
123 '북, 사회주의 계획경제 포기 선언,' [North Korea Abandons Socialist Planned Economy], *Radio Free Asia,* August 8, 2012.
Cha, Victor D., 'Kim Jong Un Is No Reformer,' *Foreign Policy,* August 21, 2012.
Ascione, Ben, 'Kim Jong-un and the future of North Korean reform,' *East Asian Forum,* October 20, 2012.
124 'North Korea: salmon farming's next superpower?,' *The Fish Site,* February 18, 2019.
125 O'Carroll, Chad, 'Floating rice plants and gardens proliferate in Pyongyang: photos,' *NK News,* June 28, 2017.
126 Williams, Martyn, 'Can Science and Technology Be a Silver Bullet for the North Korean Economy?,' *38 North,* January 8, 2020.
127 Bowden, John, 'Trump hits Obama, Biden over "mess" with China and North Korea,' *The Hill,* July 5, 2019.
128 Fitzpatrick, Mark, 'North Korea: Obama's Prime Nonproliferation Failure,' *Arms Control,* December 2016.

Shaffer, Tony, 'Donald Trump puts past presidents to shame with North Korea policies,' *The Hill,* March 2, 2019.

129 '朝鲜成功研发新型洲际导弹KN-14? 美媒——朝鲜成功研发针对美国本土的新型洲际弹道导弹,' [North Korea Successfully Develops New Intercontinental Ranged Missile KN-14? U.S. Media: North Korea Successfully Develops New Intercontinental Ranged Ballistic Missile Against U.S. Mainland], *People's TV,* (http://tv.people.com.cn/n1/2016/0401/c67816-28245618.html).

130 Baker, Peter, 'The War That Wasn't: Trump Claims Obama Was Ready to Strike North Korea,' *New York Times,* February 16, 2019.

131 Asmolov, Konstantin, 'Has the history of the Cheonan corvette come to an end? P.1,' *New Eastern Outlook,* November 20, 2013.

132 'South Korean ship sunk by crack squad of "human torpedoes,"' *Telegraph,* April 22, 2010.

Asmolov, Konstantin, 'Has the history of the Cheonan corvette come to an end? P.1,' *New Eastern Outlook,* November 20, 2013.

133 Meek, James, 'Iraq war logs: How friendly fire from US troops became routine,' *Guardian*, Octoober 22, 2010.

Ismay, John, 'America's Dark History of Killing Its Own Troops With Cluster Munitions,' *New York Times,* December 4, 2019.

Thompson, Mark, 'The Curse of "Friendly Fire,"' *Time,* June 11, 2014.

Moran, Michael, '"Friendly Fire" is all too common,' *NBC,* March 23, 2003.

Shhuger, Scott, 'The Pentagon's appalling record on "friendly fire,"' *Slate,* April 4, 2002.

134 Asmolov, Konstantin, 'Has the history of the Cheonan corvette come to an end? P.1,' *New Eastern Outlook,* November 20, 2013.

135 'Korean War mine "sunk" South Korean navy ship,' *Telegraph,* March 29, 2003.

136 'Probe concludes torpedo sank South Korea ship: report,' *Reuters,* May 7, 2010.

137 Stein, Jeff, 'Analysts question Korea torpedo incident,' *Washington Post,* May 27, 2010.

138 Asmolov, Konstantin, 'Has the history of the Cheonan corvette come to an end? P.1,' *New Eastern Outlook,* November 20, 2013.

139 Ibid.

140 Demick, Barbara and Glionna, John M., 'Doubts surface on North Korea's role in ship sinking,' *Los Angeles Times,* July 23, 2010.

141 'S. Korean newspaper exonerates North over torpedo,' *RT*, July 29, 2010.

142 Asmolov, Konstantin, 'Has the history of the Cheonan corvette come to an end? P.1,' *New Eastern Outlook,* November 20, 2013.

143 Sakai, Tanaka, 'Who Sank the South Korean Warship Cheonan? A New Stage in the US-Korean War and US-China Relations,' *Asia-Pacific Journal*, vol. 8, issue 21, no. 1, May 24, 2010.

144 'Questions raised following Cheonan announcement,' *Hankyoreh,* May 21, 2010.

145 Stein, Jeff, 'Analysts question Korea torpedo incident,' *Washington Post,* May 27, 2010.

146 Demick, Barbara and Glionna, John M., 'Doubts surface on North Korea's role in ship sinking,' *Los Angeles Times,* July 23, 2010.

147 'Ex-Pres. Secretary Sued for Spreading Cheonan Rumors,' *Dong-A Ilbo,* May 8, 2010.

148 Demick, Barbara and Glionna, John M., 'Doubts surface on North Korea's role in ship sinking,' *Los Angeles Times,* July 23, 2010.

149 'Ex-Pres. Secretary Sued for Spreading Cheonan Rumors,' *Dong-A Ilbo,* May 8, 2010.

150 Asmolov, Konstantin, 'Has the history of the Cheonan corvette come to an end? P.1,' *New Eastern Outlook,* November 20, 2013.

151 OPCW Douma Docs, *Wikileaks,* Released October 23–December 14, 2019.

152 Palansamy, Yiswaree, 'PM: MH17 findings "politically-motivated," no proof Russia to blame,' *Malay Mail*, June 20, 2019.
Bowie, Nile, 'Five years on, no answers to who felled MH17,' *Asia Times,* July 17, 2019.
Helmer, John, 'The Malaysian Airlines MH17 Tragedy, Suppression and Tampering of the Evidence. New Documentary,' *Global Research,* July 27, 2019.
Dorman, Sam, 'Newsweek reporter quits, claiming outlet "suppressed" story on global chemical weapons watchdog,' *Fox News,* December 7, 2019.

153 Choe, Sang-Hun and Landler, Mark, 'U.S. Pledges to Help S. Korea at U.N.,' *New York Times,* May 26, 2010.

154 Carr, Vanessa, 'South Korea says North will "pay a price" for torpedo attack,' *PBS,* May 24, 2010.

Chapter 14

INTRODUCING MUTUAL VULNERABILITY:

IMPLICATIONS OF NORTH KOREA ATTAINING A NUCLEAR-TIPPED ICBM

Race to the Finish Line

The final three years of the Barack Obama administration had seen North Korea's testing of technologies for its missile deterrent escalate significantly, with at least 52 ballistic missile launches[1] taking place demonstrating vastly extended ranges, submarine launch capabilities, and high levels of precision and reliability. The year 2016 also saw the launch of a satellite using an Unha long ranged rocket and two tests of miniaturised nuclear warheads, with a far greater proportion of tests that year being of intermediate-range missiles designed to strike targets far beyond the Korean peninsula. The DPRK appeared poised on the brink of attaining the deterrence capability it had long sought—a weapon capable of threatening the United States mainland with thermonuclear strikes and a complementary arsenal of intermediate and medium-range systems for attacks on American facilities across the Pacific. 2017 would thus mark a pivotal year in the U.S.-DPRK conflict as Pyongyang moved to irrevocably shift the balance of power through its deterrence program.

The inauguration of President Donald Trump in January 2017 closely coincided with North Korea's crossing of Washington's red line for its deterrence program—the attainment of an intercontinental range nuclear delivery capability. The new president quickly came to criticise the policies of his three predecessors, the Barack Obama administration in particular,[2] for having allowed North Korea to come so close to attaining this capability. An assessment of previous presidents' inability to respond to Korea's armaments program or enforce red lines against Korean nuclearization somewhat substantiated such criticism. While the new hard line subsequently taken by President Trump towards North Korea was widely attributed by U.S. and Western media to the brutish style of the new chief of staff, it appears to have more likely been prompted by how close the DPRK had come to attaining an intercontinental-range deterrent which raised concerns across the U.S. establishment. Such concerns were expressed by leading members of both political parties and of the military and intelligence establishments. Indeed, Donald Trump's two leading rivals for the presidency Hillary Clinton[3] and Bernie Sanders[4] both strongly endorsed his more assertive policies targeting the DPRK, and were widely expected to have pursued similarly if not more assertive policies had they themselves come to power.[5] Thus there was a broad consensus towards the need for a change in policy and the importance of placing maximum pressure on North Korea to prevent it from further developing its deterrent, not only across America's political spectrum but also more broadly across the Western world.

While the U.S. moved to increase pressure on Pyongyang in Obama's final years and continuing into Trump's first, calling for successive rounds of economic sanctions, pressing third parties from India to Kuwait to break diplomatic ties and expel Korean diplomats, and deploying large naval fleets off the country's coast, North Korea was far closer to attaining a viable deterrent than almost anyone in the West had predicted. As had been the case in the past, Americans and others fell victim to their own propagandistic depictions of the state as dysfunctional, backward and corrupt, which led them to seriously underestimate not only the unity of its population towards a common goal, but also its technological prowess.[i] It was widely predicted that it would take the DPRK at least five years to develop the technologies needed to strike the U.S. mainland, with technologies for a re-entry vehicle and miniaturised warhead repeatedly stated by American and Western sources to be well beyond North Korea's technological capabilities. The BBC stated in November 2016 regarding the KPA's ability to carry out nuclear attacks on the U.S. mainland: "best expert assessment is that the missiles to deliver them are perhaps five years away."[6]

The year 2017 saw at least 19 ballistic missile launches, an unprecedently high success rate across all launches, and the successful testing of four entirely new missile platforms, all of which subsequently entered

i It is notable that Western sources repeatedly ranked the DPRK as one of the world's most corrupt countries alongside near failed states such as Somalia, Yemen, Sudan and Libya—a conclusion reached consistently despite lack of any data on or access to the country or publication of any methodology. While doing so represented part of a larger trend towards portraying the state negatively, it was indicative of a wider phenomenon which partially explained why U.S. and allied estimates of Korean capabilities were often so far below the reality.

service. The first two new missiles tested were intermediate-range designs, the solid fuelled and extremely compact Pukkuksong-2 with an estimated 2000–2500km range launched on February 11 and May 21, and the Hwasong-12 "Guam Killer" with an estimated range of up to 6000km. The latter missile was tested three times in April, reportedly without success, but was later tested successfully in May, August and September. The Hwasong-12 significantly extended the range of the Korean land-based missile deterrent and allowed for strikes on both Guam and Alaska.[7]

Alongside ballistic missile tests, multiple tests of new long-range anti-ship cruise missile systems and long-range air defence systems were carried out. These were intended to complement a stronger missile deterrent with more modern asymmetric anti-access area denial (A2AD) capabilities at sea and in the air, further complicating a prospective American attack. The Kumsong-3 (KN-19) anti-ship cruise missile demonstrated capabilities wholly unprecedented for the Korean arsenal, with the ability to carry out complex waypoint manoeuvres, follow a low altitude sea skimming trajectory and strike targets up to 250km away. This made the missiles both highly precise and extremely difficult to intercept—seriously complicating any operations by Western surface warships in or near Korean waters. The system's tracked launch vehicle and light weight allowed it to operate in almost any terrain, including mountains and dense forests, making it very difficult to seek and destroy.[8]

The Pyongae-5 (KN-06) air defence system similarly demonstrated capabilities beyond those of previous Korean designs, and is speculated to integrate a number of Russian technologies providing comparable capabilities to the Russian systems such as the S-300PMU-2, which it closely resembles.[9] Both the Pyongae-5 and the Kumsong-3 were intended to compensate for the shortcomings of the KPA Navy's surface fleet and the KPA Air Force's fighter fleet relative to far larger combined forces of the U.S. and its allies by targeting enemy ships with survivable and low-cost asymmetric assets. It mirrors the strategy pursued by Russia following the Soviet collapse, with Russian systems such as the Kh-47M2 anti-ship missile[10] and 40N6E surface to air missile[11] similarly designed for an asymmetric defence against larger Western naval and air forces. Both new Korean systems entered mass production in 2017 and would take centre stage in a military parade marking the country's seventieth anniversary the following year.[12]

Introducing Mutual Vulnerability

While developments for North Korea's A2AD and intermediate-range missile capabilities were nothing short of revolutionary, the most significant development was its successful testing of entirely new intercontinental-range ballistic missile designs demonstrating for the first time the ability to deliver nuclear warheads to the American mainland. The first such test came on July 4 and saw a harsh rhetorical response from Washington and the wider Western world and mass celebrations in Korea itself. The writer was studying in Pyongyang at the time of the launch, and witnessed streets flooded with thousands of men and women, the former in suits and the latter in traditional dresses, dancing and singing. Part of the crowd moved towards Kim Il Sung square in the city centre where a proclamation by party officials regarding the meaning of the weapons test was made. As the writer's knowledge of U.S.-DPRK relations and of general military affairs was known, he was repeatedly questioned regarding what the testing of the Korea's first ICBM—Hwasong-14—meant for the country. While people showed a great deal of pride in their missile program, there was genuine concern that a new U.S. administration would launch a preventative military attack. Initially thinking based on the description that the missile tested was the Hwasong-13, a separate ICBM design with similar capabilities which was previously shown at prototype stage, the writer assured them that the new missile meant mutual vulnerability with the United States mainland, and would be key to taking American military options off the table and guaranteeing Korean security.

While the Hwasong-14 was wholly unknown before the test in July 2017, later research into the design indicated its capabilities were considerably superior to those of the Hwasong-13 prototype which appeared to have been discarded since. The Hwasong-14 is believed to use engines from the Hwasong-12 with the addition of a second stage to further increase its range. The Hwasong-13 is believed to similarly be a derivative of the Musudan with an additional second stage for longer range. Official sources cited by the *Washington Post* in 2016 indicate that the Hwasong-13 was in fact tested as the KPA's first ICBM in October that year, although this remains unconfirmed as does the design's success.[13] The new Hwasong-14 was estimated to have a range of 10,000km, allowing it to strike targets across approximately half of the American mainland with thermonuclear warheads. While the Hwasong-13 and Musudan had introduced a second generation of engine technologies for longer ranged missiles, the Hwasong-14 and Hwasong-12 deployed technologies a generation ahead. This came little over ten years after the first Musudan was first tested in Iran,[14] and little over a year after the first confirmed flight test on the Korean Peninsula itself.

The Hwasong-14 represented a major game changer for the relationship between North Korea and the United States, shifting the balance of power profoundly and irrevocably by introducing genuine mutual vulnerability between the population centres of the two states. While the Soviet Union and China had previously gained such capabilities, the former in 1949 using bombers and ten years later with the R-7 ICBM and the latter in 1981 with the DF-5 ICBM, 2017 represented the first time a medium or small state was able to effectively deter a superpower at such a peer level without need for support from a nuclear umbrella of a superpower sponsor of its own. In this respect North Korea's achievement in 2017 was historically unprecedented, and was referred to by Vice Chairman of the Joint Chiefs of Staff and former Commander of the U.S. Strategic Command John Hyten as having "changed the entire structure of the world."[15] This achievement demonstrated how development of asymmetric technologies was increasingly allowing small states to better safeguard their sovereignty against far larger adversaries with vastly greater populations, economies and military power projection capabilities.

The Hwasong-14 was again tested on July 28, and again demonstrated the capability to strike much of North America. On August 8, the *Washington Post* published part of a leaked Defence Intelligence Agency assessment which confirmed that North Korea had the capability to deliver nuclear strikes against the American mainland. It estimated the KPA retained an arsenal of around 60 warheads, and was capable of miniaturising them for deployment on an ICBM.[16] This capability would later be confirmed by U.S. State Secretary Pompeo.[17] The Hwasong-14 deployed from a transporter-erector-launcher, meaning it could be moved around the country constantly on a sixteen-wheel launch vehicle and required only minutes to set up for launch, making it highly survivable particularly when operating in Korea's mountainous terrain. The missile was later confirmed by U.S. intelligence to deploy a viable re-entry vehicle, one of the most challenging ICBM technologies to develop, allowing its warheads to penetrate the atmosphere intact.[18]

Although North Korea had acquired the capabilities it had long sought with the Hwasong-14 design, continuing threats from Washington and growing calls for military action against the country led the KPA to test a second ICBM design on November 28 of that year. The first and only test of the Hwasong-15 appeared to mark the beginning of the end of the crisis between the DPRK and the U.S. that year, with the missile's demonstrated capabilities ensuring the American military option was conclusively off the table. Like the Hwasong-14, the missile was fired on a lofted trajectory meaning it flew far higher than it would in an actual combat firing, allowing it to demonstrate the extent of its range without actually travelling over U.S. territory. The missile demonstrated a range of 13,000km, enabling it to strike the entire U.S. mainland including Washington D.C. and New York City,[19] and was speculated by some sources to use a multiple re-entry vehicle. This would allow a single missile to deliver multiple thermonuclear warheads in a single strike, and make missile attacks extremely difficult to intercept.[20] The platform's visibly blunter nose on the re-entry vehicle relative to the Hwasong-14 was reportedly intended to accommodate a considerably larger payload. The missile was significantly larger than the Hwasong-14 but retained high mobility and was deployed from a heavier eighteen-wheel transporter-erector-launcher.

The successes of North Korea's defence sector in developing high end missile technologies, and having done so in such a short time, with a very limited budget, totally contradicted predominant Western perceptions of the state as corrupt, inept and backward. This led a number of Western news outlets to speculate on the means by which the DPRK could have obtained such advanced technologies which would put its achievements in a context which fitted with the preconceived nature of the country—namely by claiming these technologies must have been stolen or acquired from abroad. Claims that the Hwasong-12 and Hwasong-14 were using Soviet missile engines were quickly debunked by U.S. intelligence however, forcing North Korea's adversaries to come to terms with the fact that it was a far more capable actor than propagandistic depictions had given it credit for. Similar reports that the advanced hypergolic liquid rocket propellants used by the missiles must have been imported from Russia or China were widespread—how could the failed "Kim Regime" have developed such technologies? This too was debunked by a number of studies by experts as well as by U.S. intelligence. A study by the James Martin Center for Non-proliferation Studies at Middlebury College was particularly detailed in its findings, and showed the extent of the DPRK's self-reliance in its missile development.[21] The study showed that even the fuel used by Korean missiles, known as unsymmetrical dimethylhydrazine (UMDH), was synthesized in a known chemical plant in the country itself using technologies which also had applications in synthetic textile manufacturing.[22] Thus even a complete oil embargo, which Western powers had strongly advocated at the United Nations, could not end Korean missile testing.[23]

Jeffrey Lewis, the director of the centre's East Asia Nonproliferation Program, noted following the publication of findings that dominant Western depictions of North Korea sharply contrasted with its technological achievements, of which the missile program was a prime example, stating: "If you watch them in satellite photos and read their technical publications, it looks like a totally different country... We're in full-scale denial about North Korea's capabilities." [24] *The Diplomat* magazine noted to much the same effect: "With everything we've seen out of North Korea this year, we should both stop being surprised when they demonstrate increasingly more impressive capabilities and also stop underestimating the extent of their knowhow. In the end, *Juche*, the ideology of self-reliance at the core of the North Korean project since the founding of country, is there for more than just show."[25]

The Risk of an American-Initiated Nuclear War

While North Korea demonstrated the capability to deliver thermonuclear warheads to the United States mainland in 2017, the West remained incredulous for some time that the Northeast Asian adversary could have achieved its goal so quickly. Director Jeffrey Lewis, citing uniquely harsh standards being applied to evaluate North Korea's progress towards a nuclear-tipped ICBM, stated: "There is no reason to think that the North Koreans aren't making the same progress after so many successful nuclear explosions...it seems to me a lot of people are insisting on impossible levels of proof because they simply don't want to accept what should be pretty obvious."[26]As late as July 28 of that year the *New York Times* reported that it would take approximately a year for the DPRK to develop a viable ICBM delivery capability—down from four years which had been the consensus before 2017.[27] Less than two weeks later however, the *Washington Post's* publication of a leaked Defence Intelligence Agency assessment confirmed that North Korea would not obtain this deterrence capability in one year or four years—it already possessed it.[28] Further confirmation of this reality, a particularly uncomfortable one for those supporters of a Western-led order in Northeast Asia, was forthcoming from official sources in the coming months.

Introducing Mutual Vulnerability

While North Korea's nuclearization and development of medium range delivery capabilities had been harshly criticised by Western sources in the past, its development of an ICBM capable of striking the American mainland led to widespread calls for a military response, massive Western pressure on states across the world from Mexico to Sudan to India to expel Korean diplomats and break ties, and a redoubling of Western economic warfare efforts against the country. In many respects, the harsh Western response to North Korea's nuclearization was not entirely unique. The acceptability of a country's nuclearization by the Western Bloc, which customarily claimed to speak for the international community in this regard, had long been determined by a consistent standard—the nuclearizing state's geopolitical alignments and how its nuclearization affected Western interests. Thus of ten states which developed nuclear weapons, the nuclearization of Britain, France and the United States were depicted positively as forces for good, those of South Africa, Israel, India and Pakistan ambiguously—they neither upheld nor directly threatened the Western dominated world order, while those of the Soviet Union, China and later North Korea were portrayed as unacceptable.

The nuclear programs of these three powers, in much the same way, were intended primarily as means to end Western attempts at nuclear coercion and to deter potential American nuclear attacks with which all had been threatened. Nuclearization of all three directly impeded the freedom of action of the Western Bloc to shape world order in line with its interests through the projection of military power, and in particular deterred the U.S. from using nuclear force to subjugate these states. Indeed, much like North Korea, both the USSR[29] and China[30] had been directly threatened by massive Western nuclear strikes before their own nuclearization, and preventative military action against both states had been widely advocated in Western political and military circles to ensure a Western favouring balance of power could be perpetuated by denying potential targets access to nuclear arms.

Fears that the Soviet Union would obtain some form of nuclear parity with the United States as early as 1945 led the Pentagon to plan nuclear strikes against 66 Soviet cities using 204 atomic bombs. In this scenario an estimated 10,151,000 people would be killed, wounded or displaced and approximately 600 square kilometres of urban area would be devastated. Ultimately the USSR developed its own nuclear and intercontinental range delivery capability as early as 1949—at least six years earlier than expected—at which time the American nuclear arsenal was still relatively small. [31] A secret memo released decades later from FBI archives revealed that Britain too had persistently lobbied for American nuclear attacks on the USSR to stop it developing its own nuclear deterrent.[32] In the 1960s there were similar calls for nuclear attacks against the People's Republic of China which, following the aforementioned extensive use of nuclear coercion in the Korean War and subsequent deployment of American nuclear arms to the Taiwan Strait, had sought its own deterrent capability.[33] Military action against China to prevent its nuclearization were seriously considered by the John F. Kennedy and Lyndon B. Johnson administrations. "Infiltration, sabotage, invasion by Chinese Nationalists, maritime blockades, South Korean invasion of North Korea, conventional air attacks on nuclear facilities, and the use of tactical nuclear weapons on selected targets" were all seriously considered as means of destabilising the state and setting back its nuclear development—according to U.S. Naval War College Professor Lyle J. Goldstein.[34]

It was little surprise, therefore, that maximum pressure and military action including nuclear attacks were widely advocated in the West and seriously considered by the U.S. leadership in order to prevent North Korea from further undermining of Western dominance through its own nuclear program. The American and wider Western response to Korea's nuclearization and missile program thus fit the trend set by responses to similar developments in China and the Soviet Union. The fact that North Korea was developing a means to hold the Western Bloc and the military might of the United States in check in northeast Asia made its actions unacceptable. As U.S. President Barack Obama stated in 2016 regarding his vision for the future of the Asia-Pacific region: "America should write the rules. America should call the shots. Other countries should play by the rules that America and our partners set, and not the other way around."[35] Through its development of a miniaturised thermonuclear warhead and accompanying ICBM, Pyongyang was setting its own rules and constraining America's ability to shape the future of the region.

Escalating calls for American attacks on the DPRK in 2017 gave a number of insightful indications as to the nature of the U.S.-led order in the Asia-Pacific and the implications for U.S. allies of the DPRK's nuclearization. In particular, the risk-aversion of many figures in America's political and military leadership to collateral damage against U.S. client states in East Asia was highlighted by these calls to action. U.S. Senator Lindsey Graham, for one, stated shortly before the KPA tested its first

ICBM that military action against Korea remained feasible because retaliation and collateral damage would be confined to Northeast Asia—a price worth paying to ensure the U.S. mainland remained beyond the reach of Korean ICBMs. He stated to this effect regarding the consequences of the attack he was advocating: "It would be terrible, but the war would be over there [in Northeast Asia] it wouldn't be here. It would be bad for the Korean peninsula. It would be bad for China. It would be bad for Japan. It would be bad for South Korea. It would be the end of North Korea, but what it would not do is hit America."[36]

In a later interview the senator stated: "There's a military option—to destroy North Korea's program and North Korea itself... If there's going to be a war to stop it [Korean deterrence program] it will be over there. If thousands die, they're going to die over there. They're not going to die here." When asked about his thoughts on the U.S. initiating an attack, the senator responded: "it's inevitable unless North Korea changes because you're making our president pick between regional stability [in Northeast Asia] and homeland security."[37]

Graham was one of many who had lobbied the Trump administration to attack North Korea, with the senator stating in April 2017: "I talked to the president when I had lunch with him about this very topic. I said, 'Do you want on your resume that, during your presidency, the North Koreans developed a missile that could hit the American homeland with a nuclear weapon on top of it?,' and he said, 'Absolutely not,'"[38] Prominent figures in the U.S. military leadership also voiced their strong support for military action, and much like Senator Graham, they repeatedly emphasized that the inevitable damage to allies in Northeast Asia was a price worth paying to prevent the KPA from gaining a deterrent capability. Joint Chiefs of Staff Chairman Joseph Dunford stated that North Korea obtaining a nuclear tipped ICBM was a far more "unthinkable" reality for the United States than a major war in Northeast Asia, and that bringing about the latter to prevent the former was therefore a real option. The chairman stated: "Many people have talked about military options [against North Korea] with words like 'unimaginable'... I would shift that slightly and say it would be horrific. It would be a loss of life unlike any we have experienced in our lifetimes. Anyone who has been alive since World War II has never seen the loss of life that could occur if there's a conflict on the Korean peninsula." He emphasized, however: "It is not unimaginable to have military options to respond to North Korean nuclear capability… What's unimaginable to me is allowing a capability that would allow a nuclear weapon to land in Denver, Colorado."[39]

U.S. Army Lt. Colonel Ralph Peters, in an opinion piece for the *New York Post* titled "The moral answer to North Korea's threats, Take them out!" stated that it was imperative to prioritise the protection of the U.S. mainland and U.S. citizens above all else—regardless of the consequences for allies in Asia. He stated to this effect: "The fundamental reason our government exists is to protect our people and our territory. Everything else is a grace note. And the words we never should hear in regard to North Korea's nuclear threats are, 'We should've done something.'"[40] H. R. McMaster, President Donald Trump's National Security Adviser, remarked in the same vein that the United States could not tolerate a nuclear ICBM in North Korean hands, and should take measures to prevent it even if U.S. military action and a "human catastrophe" in allied South Korea was the price required.[41] McMaster was reportedly one of many in the White House seeking to gain support for such an attack.[42]

Attempts to rationalise and justify an attack on North Korea were made by a number of other Western sources. Edward Luttwak, who served as consultant to the Office of the Secretary of Defense, the State Department, the National Security Council, the defence ministries of a number of European states and separately to the three largest branches of the U.S. Military, was particularly vocal in his calls for an attack. A strong proponent of Western dominated world order, and almost without parallel in the hawkishness of his stances, Luttwak's article titled "It's Time to Bomb North Korea" expressed the belief that the DPRK and states like it should be prevented not only from deploying nuclear weapons—but should also have their access to basic firearms restricted. Luttwak stated that South Korea's vulnerability to KPA retaliation should not hold the U.S. back from carrying out the attack he was advocating, as he blamed South Korea for failing to sufficiently fortify its cities against such an attack and effectively concluded that its population deserved what would be coming to them. Luttwak stated that risks to South Korea "cannot be allowed to paralyse" the U.S. and keep it from launching an attack, and claimed the ROK's vulnerability was "very largely self-inflicted" due to its failure to heed the words of Western advisors to invest billions in bomb shelters and Israeli and U.S. hardware. Thus, according to Luttwak, the KPA's retaliatory capabilities against East Asian allies were not "a good reason to hesitate before ordering an attack on North Korea."[43]

While not specifically mentioning the issue of collateral damage to East Asian allies, Congressman Duncan Hunter made a case for initiating a war which reflected prevalent trends in Western thought regarding the country. This included conflation of pre-emptive and preventative warfare and advocation of the latter on the basis of unsubstantiated assessments of the nature of the North Korean state. He stated: "From my perspective, why would I not hit you first? Why would we not do a pre-emptive strike when you have ICBMs levelled at the U.S. and you're not a logical player in the world scene?" Referring to Chairman Kim Jong Un's alleged "mental issues," corresponding to consistent portrayals of him and the leadership in Pyongyang in general by Western media at the time as deranged and illogical, he highlighted that this gave America cause to launch an attack on the East Asian state.[44] Claims the DPRK's leadership were irrational actors or somehow insane were strongly refuted by both the CIA[45] and the majority of professional analysts in the West including hawks with strongly anti-Korean stances,[46] but were very frequently alluded to by U.S. and European media outlets which helped to build a public consensus for military action.[47]

Defence & Strategy Fellow at the Centre for Strategic Studies and former strategist and policy adviser at the Office of the Secretary of Defense and group chair of the U.S.–ROK Extended Deterrence Policy Committee Van Jackson noted, regarding the double standards of American and Western advocates of preventative war against the DPRK and their gross disregard for the lives of allied citizens in East Asia: "Nuclear war, the very thing preventative war advocates claimed to want to prevent, was almost inevitable if the United States launched a war of choice in Korea. The way war advocates coped with that contradiction was by drawing a false distinction between nuclear weapons used in the Asia-Pacific versus nuclear weapons used against the U.S. homeland…to say nothing of the hundreds of thousands of non-US citizens who would become victims of nuclear conflict in the event of preventive war."[48]

North Korea with a Thermonuclear Armed ICBM: A Force for Stability in Northeast Asia?

To fully understand the implications of North Korea's nuclearization, it is essential to assess the country's nuclear strategic doctrine and the purposes for which nuclear weapons could be deployed. Pyongyang's nuclear doctrine is classified as existential, meaning nuclear weapons are considered distinct from conventional weapons and cannot be used as a means to military victory or material gain—only to deter attack. Existential deterrence is the most defensive doctrine for nuclear use and is currently adhered to only by North Korea and Israel.[49] Korean doctrine differs from that of Israel, however, because the DPRK is also one of three states which adheres to a nuclear no-first-use policy, alongside China and India, meaning it will not use nuclear weapons unless subjected to nuclear attack.[50] While Israel's nuclear deterrent is existential, its doctrine allows for first-use of nuclear weapons in response to non-nuclear attacks to prevent the state's annihilation, whereas North Korea's nuclear threshold requires an enemy nuclear attack. This can be attributed to different historical threats, with the DPRK facing repeated American nuclear threats whereas threats to Israeli sovereignty have been overwhelmingly conventional. North Korea thus has the highest threshold for nuclear use—the only state with both an existential deterrence doctrine and a no-first-use policy.

By contrast to the DPRK, U.S. doctrine is classified as maximum deterrence—under which nuclear weapons can be used to achieve military victory and first strikes are permissible even against non-nuclear states. Nuclear weapons are not considered distinct from conventional weapons, and their use can be limited with the intention of tactical gain as a means to win a war. This is considered the most aggressive nuclear doctrine.[51] Nuclear Weapons expert Susan Turner Haynes described maximum deterrence as "premised on the belief that it is possible to win a nuclear war. This belief derives from the base assumption that nuclear weapons are not qualitatively distinct from conventional weapons. Thus, according to adherents of maximum deterrence, war should be conducted similarly regardless of the weapons employed. Nuclear weapons present more risk but do not shift the entire calculus of war. Such a strategy requires what is known as a 'first strike capability.'"[52]

The United States Military has notably invested heavily in developing low-yield nuclear warheads for limited use—an undertaking widely interpreted as signalling a falling nuclear threshold. Joint Chiefs of Staff Vice Chairman and leading nuclear strategist James Cartwright acknowledged in 2016 that "what going smaller" with lower yield tactical nuclear weapons did was "to make the weapon more thinkable."[53] Air Force Chief of Staff General Norton Schwartz and the U.S. Defence Science Board similarly implied a battlefield role for nuclear weapons in line with America's maximum deterrence strategy.[54] Thus the contrast between the North Korean and the American nuclear doctrines could not be more stark, and can be seen to justify Korean nuclearization. The DPRK's arsenal under an existential and overwhelmingly defensive doctrine can be used to contain a power with an extremely offensive doctrine—one which endangers regional security due to its demonstrated tendency to undertake illegal military interventions overseas, its far lower threshold for nuclear use, its high tolerance of casualties among allied Northeast Asian populations and its operational plans for tactical nuclear strikes.

A broader assessment of North Korean defence planning other than its nuclear doctrine also provides valuable context for evaluating the consequences its nuclearization will have for regional stability. The KPA's most prominent conventional investments have almost all been heavily defensively oriented assets—including well-hardened fortifications,[55] extensive tunnel networks and armaments such as the Pyongae-5, Kumsong-3 and Sang-O Class littoral submarine designed for anti-access area denial to protect Korean waters and airspace.[56] These investments reflect the KPA's strong orientation towards fighting a defensive war. A commonly used means of assessing the orientation of a military organisation, the ratio of logistics to combat assets, indicates that the KPA is among the most defensively oriented in the world, with its power projection capabilities negligible to non-existent[57]—in stark contrast to the U.S. Military which is heavily oriented towards overseas power projection.[58]

The unbalanced orientation of North Korea's military, skewed strongly towards defence and underwhelming in its power projection capabilities, strongly indicates that Pyongyang has no designs, and certainly negligible capability, to deploy forces offensively beyond its borders for material gain. Most other nuclear powers, the United States in particular, have invested in the capability to follow up nuclear strikes with a massive projection of conventional force needed to secure territory and make real material gains. American power projection capabilities are second to none, with substantial logistics, overseas military bases and high endurance assets such as supercarriers, cruisers, amphibious assault ships and aerial tankers all developed for such operations—allowing the U.S. to benefit from taking to the offensive overseas in a way North Korea could never hope to do.

On the basis of the overwhelmingly defensive orientation of both the DPRK's nuclear deterrent and the KPA's conventional forces, it can be concluded that the country's nuclear weapons are only a threat to actors which may intend to attack the country. As prominent Russian nuclear weapons expert Vladimir Khrustalev noted:

> Russia and China are not directly threatened by these [KPA] missiles. Like any other means of nuclear deterrence, they threaten those who would attack the owner of nuclear weapons. It is obvious that it makes no sense for the DPRK to "go crazy" and press the red button for no reason… In this case, any scenario of attack on the DPRK makes no sense because the attacker would pay a price that would scare away anyone considering such attempts. In fact, it is a reproduction of the model, which was between the Soviet Union and the United States and which now exists between India and Pakistan.

The analyst observed that it was precisely for this reason that the Korean nuclear program was naturally strongly opposed by those with offensive designs against the country—a conclusion he was far from alone in reaching.[59]

Considering the rationales widely expressed for American military action against the DPRK, the apparent willingness to bring death and destruction to supposedly allied Northeast Asian states, and the discrepancies in their defence doctrines, there is a strong argument that North Korea's development of a viable nuclear deterrent with an intercontinental range is strongly in the interests not just of its own population—but of peace and stability in the entire region. Had the U.S. and its Western allies been free to initiate a war, South Korea and Japan would have been devastated alongside North Korea and very likely parts of China and Russia as well. By constraining America's ability to start a war in East Asia through introduction of mutual vulnerability, North Korea's deterrence program has ensured that extra-regional actors cannot initiate a regional war by ensuring that they too could be targeted should hostilities break out.

Seoul and Tokyo notably both perceived the possibility of a U.S. attack on the DPRK with much apprehension, and attempted to dissuade Washington from pursuing such a course of action.[60] So long as the U.S. was considering military action against the DPRK, which remained the case until late 2017 or very early 2018, these states remained very much in the firing line—an imminent risk which was only diffused by North Korea's efforts to take the American military option off the table with the thermonuclear warhead and the Hwasong-14 and Hwasong-15 delivery vehicles.

While war against a North Korea without a nuclear ICBM could potentially have brought about an upturn in the American economy, the results for Japan and South Korea and their densely populated and industrialised regions and business districts would have been devastating. A conservative estimate of the death toll in Seoul from a single day of North Korea artillery strikes placed it at 20,000 [61]—although far higher figures have been quoted and overall casualties could very realistically far exceed 100,000 every 24 hours. The Center for the National Interest's Director of Korea Studies, Harry J. Kazianis, referred to KPA artillery aimed at Seoul as able to "start a 9/11-style crisis hundreds of times over in minutes." [62] Bombardment was expected to continue for weeks even if U.S. and allied forces attempted to eliminate KPA artillery units with precision strikes.[63] Death tolls from artillery strikes exclude all types of attack other than artillery, including weapons of mass destruction, air and missile attacks and attacks by special forces units.

Damage to the ROK and to Japan could very likely be significantly increased by the use of weapons of mass destruction by both the KPA and the U.S. Military. Considering that a war with North Korea would be a challenge unprecedented since 1945, with the state named as one of America's four "great power adversaries" and the most formidable other than Russia and China, it is likely that weapons of mass destruction would be deployed extensively in roles for which they were never considered during wars with weaker states. For the U.S., use of chemical weapons has long been advocated as a means to effectively negate the vast numerical strength of the KPA,[64] although with its arsenal having contracted since the Cold War's end from the world's second largest the chances of chemical attack have been reduced. It remains uncertain whether North Korea has a chemical weapons program, although Western and South Korean sources have repeatedly indicated that the KPA possesses a considerable and highly diverse chemical arsenal.

Should North Korea indeed possess such weapons and respond to an American attack by employing them, a prospect made all the more likely should the U.S. itself launch chemical or tactical nuclear attacks, the effects for South Korea and Japan would be devastating. The estimated casualties in South Korea's largest city Seoul from attacks using Sarin nerve agents alone reached approximately 9.5 million people. This was without taking into account possibilities for attacks on other cities, use of more potent chemical weapons such as VX, or casualties from conventional artillery strikes or from other weapons of mass destruction.[65]

While North Korea may well avoid striking civilian population centres with weapons of mass destruction, and KPA conduct towards civilians during the Korean War gives some basis for such predictions, moves by the United States to construct military facilities in or very near Japanese and South Korean cities considerably raises risks to civilians. Yokata Air Base and Tachikawa Air Base in Tokyo and the base of the Navy's 7th Fleet in Yokosuka city among others will all be key to the staging of American attacks on Korean territory, and KPA retaliation to eliminate these forward operating facilities could inadvertently lead to the targeting of these population centres. Proximity of U.S. military facilities to South Korean population centres poses a similar risk to civilians. Attempts by U.S. forces to shoot down Korean missiles approaching their bases, or otherwise redirect them using electronic warfare, further increases this risk to nearby urban areas.[66]

While North Korea remains highly unlikely to use nuclear weapons against targets in South Korea, it remains a possibility, particularly if the U.S itself deploys nuclear assets to ROK territory. There is an especially high risk of this, considering reports that the U.S. may still deploy some warheads in silos in the ROK, which had been alluded to by official U.S. military sources and long suspected by Pyongyang.[67] Declassified documents obtained by the Japanese Kyodo agency in 2004 have supported these suspicions, and showed that the while Washington and Seoul claimed all nuclear weapons had been withdrawn from Korea in December 1991,[68] a post–Cold War gesture to the Soviet Union, they remained on the peninsula until at least 1998.[69] Their removal has never been verified since. According to a RAND Corporation report, even a small 100 kiloton nuclear warhead striking a South Korean city would cause an estimated 1,530,000 casualties.[70] The casualties from multiple nuclear strikes using warheads over ten times power powerful would alone result in casualties measured in the tens of millions.

The U.S. Military would also be almost certain to employ depleted uranium munitions from platforms as small as Abrams tanks—highly toxic weapons the status and legality of which remains contested. These were used extensively by U.S. forces in Yugoslavia,[71] Syria[72] and Iraq[73] and often fired into heavily populated areas.[74] Considering the far greater intensity of a potential war in Korea, use of such munitions would be considerably greater—affecting the populations of both the DPRK and South Korea. Contamination from these weapons lasts for millions of years and has had devastating effects on the Yugoslav and Iraqi populations—including among other things an extreme rise in cancer rates, genetic abnormalities and severe deformities in children at birth.[75] Contamination from these weapons is more dangerous than that from neutron and thermonuclear bombs or chemical weapons. The impacts could be seen on a relatively small scale in Iraq and Yugoslavia in proportion to the weapons' more limited use,[76] and in Korea the very high danger of widespread contamination using depleted uranium alone considerably strengthens the argument that a North Korean nuclear deterrent is in the interests of populations on both sides of the 38th parallel.

Taking into account prevalent attitudes in both the U.S. civilian and military leadership to casualties among the South Korean population when at war with the North Korea—killing tens of thousands of southern civilians at the lowest estimate with its own bombing campaign and actively ordering soldiers and airmen to massacre ROK civilians in the previous war—the American threat to the populations of the ROK and Japan when pursuing its own narrowly defined national interests cannot be taken lightly. If the KPA had neglected to invest in an intercontinental range delivery capability, the possibility of a conflict which would devastate South Korea and Japan to an extent unparalleled in history, with weapons of mass destruction deployed extensively by both sides, would have been far more likely to have taken place at America's initiation in 2017 or 2018. It is perhaps for this reason that North Korea has referred to its nuclear deterrent as protecting "the security of the Korean nation from the U.S. threat of aggression and averting a new war"—an indication that the deterrent protects not only the peninsula north of the 38th parallel but all Korean people from the devastating consequences of a potential U.S.-initiated conflict.[77]

The lull in tensions between the DPRK and the U.S. resulting from a sharp policy shift in the United States in early 2018, and Washington's willingness to finally accept Pyongyang's call for one-to-one dialogue without preconditions, can be directly attributed to the East Asian state's success in developing a viable deterrent capability and demonstrating this with the Hwasong-15 and thermonuclear warhead tests. As prominent Defence & Strategy Fellow at the Centre for Strategic Studies Van Jackson, a former strategist and policy adviser at the Office of the Secretary of Defense and group chair of the U.S.–ROK Extended Deterrence Policy Committee, concluded:

> Everything that helped resolve the crisis in 2018 looked superficially like the decisions of bold leaders taking history in their hands. But their initiatives were only unlocked because North Korea attained its goal of demonstrating a viable nuclear deterrent at the end of 2017. Without North Korea realizing the first principle of its security strategy when it did… Trump would have had little choice but to succumb to the arguments of preventative war advocates.[78]

Thus it can be concluded that, had the DPRK failed to develop such a capability so quickly, the possibility of an American-initiated war in Northeast Asia to the severe detriment of the interests of all regional actors would not have been forestalled.

NOTES

1 Centre for Strategic International Studies, Missile Defense Project, 'North Korean Missile Launches & Nuclear Tests: 1984–Present' (https://missilethreat.csis.org/north-korea-missile-launches-1984–present/) (Accessed July 20, 2019).

2 Jackson, David, 'Trump blames Hillary Clinton for North Korea nuclear weapons program,' *USA Today,* September 20, 2017.

3 Chozick, Amy, 'Hillary Clinton Takes Aim at North Korea, Then at Donald Trump,' *New York Times,* September 9, 2016.

4 Ryan, Josiah, 'Sanders: Trump on right track with North Korea,' *CNN,* April 28, 2017.

5 Flitton, Daniel, 'Yes, Hillary could have led the world to war with Kim Jong-un,' *Lowy Institute,* February 7, 2019.

6 Evans, Stephen, 'How might Donald Trump deal with North Korea's Kim Jong-un?,' *BBC,* November 11, 2016.

7 Bechtol Jr., Bruce E., *North Korean Military Proliferation in the Middle East and Africa,* Lexington, University Press of Kentucky, 2018 (p. 25).
Lee, Chi-dong, 'N. Korea seen closer to ICBM, boosted by new missile engine,' *Yonhap,* May 15, 2017.

8 Panda, Ankit, 'North Korea's New KN19 Coastal Defense Cruise Missile: More Than Meets the Eye,' *The Diplomat,* July 26, 2017.

9 *KN-06 (Pon'gae-5)*, Missile Threat, CSIS Missile Defense Project, June 15, 2018.

10 Ait, Abraham, 'Russia Inducts Its Own 'Carrier Killer' Missile, and It's More Dangerous than China's,' *The Diplomat,* May 12, 2018.

11 'Specs of Russia's new missile capable of hitting hyper-sonic targets "revealed,"' *RT*, August 27, 2018.

12 'North Korean Air Defence Systems Take Centre Stage—Ballistic Missiles Conspicuous by their Absence; What the Latest Military Parade Signifies Regarding Pyongyang's Evolving Strategy,' *Military Watch Magazine,* September 10, 2018.

13 Fifield, Anna, 'Did North Korea just test missiles capable of hitting the U.S.? Maybe,' *Washington Post,* October 26, 2016.

14 Bechtol Jr., Bruce E., *North Korean Military Proliferation in the Middle East and Africa,* Lexington, University Press of Kentucky, 2018 (p. 88).
Spencer, Richard, 'N Korea "Tests New Missile in Iran,"' *The Telegraph,* May 17, 2007.

15 'A Conversation with General John Hyten, Vice Chairman of the Joint Chiefs of Staff,' *CSIS,* January 17, 2020.

16 Warrick, Joby and Nakashima, Ellen and Fifield, Anna, 'North Korea now making missile-ready nuclear weapons, U.S. analysts say,' *Washington Post,* August 8, 2017.

17 'Pompeo calls Iran more destabilizing than N. Korea,' *France 24*, February 14, 2019.

18 Panda, Ankit, 'US Intelligence: North Korea's ICBM Reentry Vehicles Are Likely Good Enough to Hit the Continental US,' *The Diplomat*, August 12, 2017.

19 Dominguez, Gabriel, 'USFK confirms North Korea's Hwaseong-15 ICBM can target all of US mainland,' *Janes,* July 11, 2019.

20 'US missile expert: N. Korean missile larger than thought, could carry decoys,' *Asia Times,* December 2, 2017.

21 Lewis, Jeffrey, 'Domestic UDMH Production in the DPRK,' *Arms Control Wonk,* September 27, 2017.

22 Fisher, Max, 'Remote Textile Plant May Secretly Fuel North Korea's Weapons,' *New York Times,* September 27, 2017.

23 Sanger, David E. and Choe, Sang-Hun, 'U.S. Urges Fuel Cutoff for North Korea, Saying It's "Begging for War,"' *New York Times*, September 4, 2017.
Choe, Sang-Hun, 'Putin Rejects Cutting Off Oil to North Korea,' *New York Times,* September 6, 2017.

24 Fisher, Max, 'Remote Textile Plant May Secretly Fuel North Korea's Weapons,' *New York Times,* September 27, 2017.

25 Panda, Ankit, 'No, North Korea Isn't Dependent on Russia and China for Its Rocket Fuel,' *The Diplomat,* September 28, 2017.

26 Warrick, Joby and Nakashima, Ellen and Fifield, Anna, 'North Korea now making missile-ready nuclear weapons, U.S. analysts say,' *Washington Post,* August 8, 2017.

27 Sanger, David E. and Choe, Sang-Hun, 'North Korea Tests a Ballistic Missile That Experts Say Could Hit California,' *New York Times*, July 28, 2017.

28 Warrick, Joby and Nakashima, Ellen and Fifield, Anna, 'North Korea now making missile-ready nuclear weapons, U.S. analysts say,' *Washington Post,* August 8, 2017.

29 Ham, Paul, *Hiroshima Nagasaki: The Real Story of the Atomic Bombings and their Aftermath*, New York, Doubleday, 2012 (p. 494).

30 Gady, Franz-Stefan, 'How a State Department Study Prevented Nuclear War With China,' *The Diplomat*, October 25, 2017.
Burr, William and Richelson, Jeffrey T., 'Whether to "Strangle the Baby in the Cradle": The United States and the Chinese Nuclear Program, 1960–64,' *International Security*, vol. 25, no. 3, winter 2000–1 (pp. 54–55, 58).

31 Ham, Paul, *Hiroshima Nagasaki: The Real Story of the Atomic Bombings and their Aftermath*, New York, Doubleday, 2012 (pp. 488–490).

32 'Winston Churchill wanted to nuke Kremlin "to win Cold War," FBI memo reveals,'

RT, November 9, 2014.

33 Goldstein, Lyle J., 'When China was a "rogue state": the impact of China's nuclear weapons program on US–China relations during the 1960s,' *Journal of Contemporary China*, vol. 12, issue 37, 2003 (p.740).

34 Ibid. (p. 742).

35 Obama, Barack, 'President Obama: The TPP would let America, not China, lead the way on global trade,' *Washington Post*, May 2, 2016.

36 Friedman, Uri, 'Lindsey Graham Reveals the Dark Calculus of Striking North Korea,' *The Atlantic*, August 1, 2017.

37 Ortiz, Erik and Yamamoto, Arata, 'Senator Lindsey Graham: Trump Says War with North Korean an Option,' *NBC News*, August 2, 2017.

38 McMahon, Patrick, 'Senator calls for "preemptive strike" on North Korea and offers a jaw-dropping justification for war,' *Rare News*, April 20, 2017.

39 Friedman, Uri, 'Lindsey Graham Reveals the Dark Calculus of Striking North Korea,' *The Atlantic*, August 1, 2017.

40 Peters, Ralph, 'The moral answer to North Korea's threats, Take them out!' *New York Post*, September 4, 2017.

41 'Lt. Gen. H. R. McMaster on foreign policy; Sen. Schumer on President Trump's first 100 days,' *Fox News*, April 30, 2017.

42 Dreazen, Yochi, 'Here's what war with North Korea would look like,' *Vox*, February 8, 2018.

43 Luttwak, Edward, 'It's Time to Bomb North Korea,' *Foreign Policy*, January 8, 2018.

44 Brown, Daniel, 'Republican congressman says the US should preemptively strike North Korea,' *Business Insider*, September 22, 2017.

45 Zatat, Narjas, 'Kim Jong-un not mad but a "rational actor," CIA says,' *The Independent*, October 6, 2017.
Youssef, Nancy A., 'Why the U.S. Considers North Korea's Kim a "Rational Actor,"' *Wall Street Journal*, December 5, 2017.

46 Abrahamian, Andray, 'North Korea's Bounded Rationality,' *Survival*, vol. 61, issue 1, January 2019 (pp. 141–160).
Shin, David W., 'Rationality in the North Korean regime: understanding the Kims' strategy of provocation,' *International Affairs*, vol. 95, issue 2, March 2019 (pp. 505–506).
Fisher, Max, 'North Korea, Far From Crazy, All Too Rational,' *New York Times*, September 10, 2016.

47 Thomas, Raju G. C., *The Nuclear Non-Proliferation Regime: Prospects for the 21st Century*, Houndmills, MacMillan, 1998 (p. 228).

48 Jackson, Van, *On the Brink*, Cambridge, Cambridge University Press, 2018 (p. 195).

49 Turner Haynes, Susan, *Chinese Nuclear Proliferation: How Global Politics is Transforming China's Weapons Buildup and Modernization*, Lincoln, NE, Potomac Books, 2016 (pp. 14–15).

50 Talmadge, Eric, 'North Korea will not use its nuclear weapons first, Kim Jong-un tells Congress,' *The Independent*, May 8, 2016.
Yoshihara, Toshi and Holmes, James R., *Strategy in the Second Nuclear Age, Power, Ambition and the Ultimate Weapon*, Washington D.C., Georgetown University Press, 2012 (pp. 92–94).
'DPRK Foreign Ministry Spokesman Totally Refutes UNSC "Resolution,"' *KCNA*, October 17, 2005.

51 Turner Haynes, Susan, *Chinese Nuclear Proliferation: How Global Politics is Transforming China's Weapons Buildup and Modernization*, Lincoln, NE, Potomac Books, 2016 (pp. 14–15)

52 Ibid. (p. 39).

53 Broad, William J. and Sanger, David E., 'As U.S. Modernizes Nuclear Weapons,

"Smaller" Leaves Some Uneasy,' *New York Times*, January 11, 2016.

54 Kristensen, Hans M., 'General Confirms Enhanced Targeting Capabilities of B61–12 Nuclear Bomb,' *Federation of American Scientists*, January 23, 2014.
Coyle, Philip E. and McKeon, James, 'The Huge Risk of Small Nukes,' *Politico*, March 10, 2017.
Feinstein, Dianne, 'There's no such thing as a "limited" nuclear war,' *Washington Post*, March 3, 2017.

55 Kopp, Carlo, 'Operation Odyssey Dawn—the collapse of Libya's relic air defense system,' *Defence Today*, vol. 9, no. 1, 2011 (p. 14).

56 'Orientation of North Korea's Armed Forces: Towards Offence or Defence?,' *Military Watch Magazine,* August 30, 2019.

57 International Institute for Strategic Studies, *The Military Balance*, vol. 119, no. 1, 2019 (pp. 47–62).
Harrison, Selig S., 'The Missiles of North Korea,' *World Policy Journal*, vol. 17, no. 3, Fall 2000 (pp. 13–14).

58 International Institute for Strategic Studies, *The Military Balance*, vol. 119, no. 1, 2019 (pp. 280–283).

59 'North Korea Reached "Point of No Return" in Obtaining Nuclear Technology,' *Sputnik*, September 9, 2016.

60 'Seoul warns Trump: U.S. must not strike North Korea without our consent,' *The Guardian*, November 15, 2017.

61 Daniels, Jeff, 'Pentagon Scenario of a New Korean War Estimates 20,000 Deaths Daily in South Korea, Retired US General Says,' *CNBC*, September 25, 2017.
Demick, Barbara, 'Escalating tension has experts simulating a new Korean War, and the scenarios are sobering,' *Los Angeles Times,* September 25, 2017.

62 Kazianis, Harry J., 'America Must Move Past Its "Sputnik" Moment on North Korea—Or Else,' *National Interest,* March 4, 2019.

63 Peck, Michael, 'Here's Exactly Why War With North Korea Would Be Hell, According To New War Games,' *Task and Purpose*, June 9, 2018.

64 Russell, Edmund, *War and Nature: Fighting Humans and Insects with Chemicals from World War I to Silent Spring*, Cambridge, Cambridge University Press, 2001 (pp. 187–180).

65 Dreazen, Yochi, 'Here's what war with North Korea would look like,' *Vox,* February 8, 2018.

66 'Saudi Arabia's U.S.-made Patriot Missile Defense System "Malfunctions," Crashes in Residential Area,' *Haaretz,* March 27, 2018.

67 'U.S. military stokes N Korea flames with "secret nuclear silos" claim,' *RT*, November 16, 2017.

68 Kristensen, Hans M. and Norris, Robert S., 'A history of US nuclear weapons in South Korea,' *Bulletin of Atomic Scientists,* vol. 73., issue 6, 2017 (pp. 349–357).

69 Staines, Reuben, 'US trained for strikes on NK,' *Korea Times*, November 7, 2004.

70 Baker, Peter, 'The War That Wasn't: Trump Claims Obama Was Ready to Strike North Korea,' *New York Times,* February 16, 2019.

71 '"Up to 15 tons of depleted uranium used in 1999 Serbia bombing"—lead lawyer in suit against NATO,' *RT*, June 13, 2017.

72 Oakford, Samuel, 'The United States Used Depleted Uranium in Syria,' *Foreign Policy*, February 14, 2017.

73 Edwards, Rob, 'U.S. fired depleted uranium at civilian areas in 2003 Iraq war, report finds,' *The Guardian*, June 19, 2014.

74 Ibid.

75 Hindin, Rita and Brugge, Doug and Panikkar, Bindu, 'Teratogenicity of depleted uranium aerosols: A review from an epidemiological perspective,' *Environmental Health,* vol. 4, no. 17, August 26, 2005.

Doyle, P. and MacOnochie, N. and Davies, G. and MacOnochie, I. and Pelerin, M. and Prior, S. and Lewis, S., 'Miscarriage, stillbirth and congenital malformation in the offspring of UK veterans of the first Gulf war,' *International Journal of Epidemiology*, vol. 33, no. 1, 2004 (pp. 74–86).

76 Sen Gupta, Amit, 'Lethal Dust: Effects of Depleted Uranium Ammunition,' *Economic and Political Weekly,* vol. 36, no. 5/6, February 2001 (pp. 454–456).

77 'DPRK Foreign Ministry Clarifies Stand on New Measure to Bolster War Deterrence,' *KCNA*, October 3, 2006.

78 Jackson, Van, *On the Brink,* Cambridge, Cambridge University Press, 2018 (pp. 12–13).

Chapter 15

2017—DONALD TRUMP AND THE BRINK OF CRISIS

Donald Trump—The "Peace Candidate"

The coming to power of the Donald Trump administration in January 2017 coincided with North Korea's approach to completing a viable intercontinental-range deterrent, and after a year of high tensions would see an unprecedented though still limited rapprochement between the two longstanding adversaries. While the shift in American policy towards the DPRK from early 2018 has been attributed primarily to the shift in the balance of power resulting from successful ICBM tests, the character of the new American administration would also heavily influence the relationship.

As a presidential candidate Donald Trump appeared willing to consider a new approach to relations with the DPRK, and in sharp contrast to his contenders both in the Republican Party primaries and in the Democratic Party he expressed a willingness to personally negotiate with and even a degree of praise for the Korean leadership.[1] Regarding Korean leader Kim Jong Un specifically, Trump indicated a willingness to share "a burger on a conference table"[2] and receive him at the White House, further stating: "I would speak to him, I would have no problem speaking to him."[3] This proposal was significant considering that one-on-one official dialogue had been one of Pyongyang's oldest and most consistent demands.[4] Trump's pledges to pull American forces out of Afghanistan and South Korea and end interventionism abroad and his criticisms of the high costs of an overseas military presence,[5] widely slammed as isolationism by allies in Europe[6] and by the Democratic Party establishment,[7] raised the prospects of a change in relations and possible end to the Korean War.

It was notable that Donald Trump's two leading contenders, Hillary Clinton and Bernie Sanders, appeared to take far more hawkish positions. While not singling out North Korea, Clinton had repeatedly taken a hawkish line towards America's traditional enemies both when campaigning and as secretary of state. As a key architect of the Pivot to Asia initiative she had sought to place greater military pressure on and further isolate adversaries in Northeast Asia in particular. Harsher sanctions,[8] a continued refusal to negotiate,[9] and greater state sponsored publicity for alleged Korean human rights abuses, were all expected to be hallmarks of a Clinton presidency, alongside increased military pressure.[10] Former Undersecretary of State Wendy Sherman, set to be one of the most influential figures on Clinton's foreign policy team, openly advocated plans to force regime change in the DPRK[11]—with other figures similarly advocating maximum pressure and a hard line.[12] Retired Admiral James Stavridis, a leading Clinton advisor, also advocated escalating cyber warfare and, if necessary, preventative military strikes.[13]

Candidate Sanders had a similarly long history of supporting offensive military action and regime change overseas as a senator and congressman—including three votes in favour of attacks on Yugoslavia and support for the Iraq Liberation Act of 1998 which enshrined the forced removal of its government as official American policy. He later voted to reaffirm this policy and provide congressional backing to both intensive airstrikes and attempted assassination of Iraq's president. Sanders personally singled out North Korea as the greatest threat to the United States—above Russia or Islamic terrorism—advocating maximum pressure to halt its deterrence program.[14] Sanders was notable for his strong endorsement of measures to economically "get tough" on rising East Asian economies,[15] and increased economic pressure was highly likely, had he won. The contrast in positions on North Korea between the Democratic Party candidates and candidate Trump was thus stark, leading strongly pro-North Korean Singaporean media outlet *DPRK Today* to praise Trump as a "wise politician" and "far sighted candidate" in contrast to "dull Hillary."[16]

It is notable that in the waning months of the Obama administration, a far more hostile policy towards the DPRK appeared to have been adopted, including a strong emphasis on the importance of preventative warfare and imposed regime change. Commander of U.S. Forces in Korea under the Obama administration General Walter Sharp stated on December 1, 2016 that the U.S. should launch an attack if North Korea so much as placed a single ICBM on a launchpad—meaning any tests of long range missiles could be met with an all-out American offensive.[17] Admiral Mike Mullen, Chairman of the Joint Chiefs of Staff under the Obama administration, had advocated much the same policy—proposing attacks which would prevent the KPA from testing an ICBM.[18] Both figures were widely viewed in Washington as respectable mainstream officials—and their statements were highly indicative of the overall nature of discourse on the matter at the time.

The tone of Obama administration officials towards the DPRK was highly reminiscent of that of the George W. Bush administration towards Iraq in 2002 and demonstrated a hostility towards and a resolve to act against the East Asian state arguably unprecedented since the Korean War. In the final week of October 2016, the president of the Centre for Strategic and International Studies and Deputy Secretary of Defence to President Bill Clinton, John Hamre, stated: "I've been at meetings with senior officials who say we need to change policy to formally embrace regime change."[19] Secretary of State John Kerry, in his speech at the U.S. Naval Academy the following month, implied that an approach based on similar lines may be necessary—continued pursuit of a deterrent capability by the DPRK may need to be met by offensive military action to impose a change in government.[20]

Defence & Strategy Fellow at the Centre for Strategic Studies Van Jackson, a former strategist, policy adviser at the Office of the Secretary of Defense and group chair of the U.S.–ROK Extended Deterrence Policy Committee, noted regarding parallel developments in U.S. media at the time:

> national media outlets and commentators started regularly churning out stories with headlines such as "What Would Happen in Minutes and Hours after North Korea Nuked the United States?," "Pre-empting a North Korean ICBM Test," "What the U.S. Would Use to Strike North Korea," and "Should Washington Strike North Korea's Dangerous ICBMs Before It's Too Late?" Commentaries strongly opposed to attacking North Korea were forced to focus primarily on the question of military strikes rather than some non-violent alternative… Not only had the North Korea policy landscape developed a hawkish tilt; the terms of debate about North Korea policy had shifted dramatically into the military realm. This was the prevailing state of mind among Washington policy elites as Trump entered the White House.[21]

Such reporting could be interpreted as a move to prepare the public for a possible strike in the coming year—much as media under the Bush administration had done when reporting on Iraq for over a year before the invasion commenced.[22]

The view that there was a need for a major policy shift, and that initiating an unprovoked war or seeking absolute regime change needed to be seriously considered, were hardly ideas relegated to a minority on the fringes of the Obama administration. Rather, they appeared to reflect a growing consensus which would likely have seen a far more hostile policy towards the DPRK had Obama's term been longer—or had the presidency been passed onto another member of the Democratic Party establishment such as Hillary Clinton. Candidate Clinton was surrounded by many of the same figures and others who similarly, if not more vocally, advocated attacks and the forced overthrow of the Korean government. Had she picked up where her predecessor had left off as had been widely been anticipated, it was likely that Clinton's administration would have acted on this consensus. As it was, the transition between the administrations of Barack Obama and Donald Trump was very far from a smooth one. Even though the new president inherited a foreign policy, military and intelligence establishment which did believe in the need for drastic measures against North Korea, much of the dangerous consensus and momentum towards action which had built up in President Obama's final year was somewhat dissipated.

Standoff in 2017: The Donald Trump Presidency Takes on North Korea

In his annual New Year's address, which in January 2017 focused primarily on economic programs, Chairman Kim Jong Un briefly referred to the country's advancing deterrence capabilities, lauding its first test of a thermonuclear warhead and announcing that it was "entering the final stage of preparation for the test launch of an intercontinental ballistic missile." The chairman further stated that this capability would "remarkably raise the strategic position of the DPRK."[23] The soon-to-be president Trump tweeted in response the following day on January 2: "North Korea just stated that it is in the final stages of developing a nuclear weapon capable of reaching parts of the U.S. It won't happen!"[24] Heralding what would later turn out to be the president's core strategy towards North Korea, Trump's second tweet later that day stated: "China has been taking out massive amounts of money & wealth from the U.S. in totally one-sided trade, but won't help with North Korea. Nice!"[25]

While the first year of the Trump administration saw tensions escalate between Washington and Pyongyang, this would have likely been the case no matter who sat in the Oval Office. If anything the distinctive style of the new president, the importance of his non-interventionist policies to his support base[26] and his separate positions from the majority of the U.S. foreign policy establishment[27] and the increasingly hawkish Democratic Party establishment very likely reduced the potential for conflict. It is notable that, unlike many prominent figures on both sides of the American political establishment, the Trump administration consistently viewed the DPRK as a rational actor.[28] This was something its predecessors appeared to believe but did not emphasize to the same extent, and which prominent figures from both political parties from Bernie Sanders[29] to Lindsey Graham[30] made clear they did not believe.

While President Trump often referred to himself as a "dealmaker" based on his business experience—perhaps the most significant skill he brought to the White House was that of the showman (see Miss Universe, Miss America and The Apprentice), which appeared to give him a taste for the theatrical in a way that resonated strongly with his support base. The result was that when North Korea's arsenal saw a considerable range increase in 2017, which was widely portrayed in Western media as an imminent threat to the American population, the president could talk tough with simple but effective rhetoric, which won people over far better than his predecessors had.

Where the preceding administration's policy appeared to have been to "speak softly and carry a large stick," with Obama's soft spoken demeanour contrasting to the forceful interventionism and bellicosity of his foreign policy, the Trump presidency "spoke very loudly but carried a small stick." While the U.S. Military saw a significant increase in funding in 2017,[31] Trump's often bellicose rhetoric far exceeded his administration's actual tendency for interventionism abroad. Thus harsher rhetoric was repeatedly coupled with a softer hand—at least relative to other post–Cold War American presidencies. While continually slamming China for "raping our country" when on campaign,[32] Trump withdrew from the Trans-Pacific Partnership trade deal in his first week in office, which had been intended to contain China's economic influence in the Asia-Pacific.[33] Referring to the Syrian president as "Animal Assad" and in other harsh terms,[34] Trump still led calls for a withdrawal of U.S.

forces from Syria against strong opposition from his own administration, the foreign policy establishment and other Western states.[35] Although calling for the ouster of the government of Venezuela,[36] President Trump stopped short of military action despite strong indications that such policy was popular in his administration[37]—and despite several precedents set for U.S. invasions and forced regime change in Latin America. It is in this context that the president's policy and harsh rhetoric towards North Korea in his first year in office can be best understood.

It is also important to consider that U.S. foreign policy under the Trump administration quickly came to resemble that of the Soviet Union in its final years under Mikhail Gorbachev in one critical aspect. In both cases the head of state appeared at odds with the military and intelligence establishments and espoused policies which strongly contradicted the status quo, which in turn led these establishments to increasingly conduct foreign policy independently of their presidencies.[38] Clashes with the CIA and the wider intelligence community in particular surfaced repeatedly under the Trump administration,[39] and even at times when the president sought to pursue a policy of rapprochement and reduced tensions, other elements in the American government would not necessarily fall in line. Direct contradictions with the military,[40] the State Department,[41] the intelligence services,[42] and prominent national security advisors[43] were frequent and were widely seen by analysts as indicators of major clashes over foreign policymaking within the government.

Although President Trump had pledged a change in the direction of the state's foreign policy, not only towards North Korea but also towards Syria, Russia and other state actors targeted by his predecessor, the momentum of the foreign policy establishment towards confrontation was considerable and growing, which led to at least a partial revision of Trump's original positions in all three cases. In North Korea's case in particular, with its fast growing deterrence capabilities increasingly portrayed as an imminent threat to America and with much of the general public as well as the political and military leadership supporting a harsh response, the willingness and ability to come down hard on Pyongyang was key to the new president's credibility.

Trump's approach to North Korea appeared closely linked to his parallel plans to take a harder line against China. Statements by administration officials regarding this strategy notably read almost word-for-word like the policy advocated by a task force from the highly influential Council on Foreign Relations (CFR) think tank in a prominent 2016 paper.[i] Titled "A Sharper Choice on North Korea: Engaging China for a Stable Northeast Asia," the paper appeared to shape thinking on U.S. policy towards the DPRK across the political spectrum and profoundly influence the Trump administration. In its opening paragraph, the report directly blamed China for North Korea's growing deterrence capabilities through its failure to more actively support the West's hard line against Pyongyang. It advocated "a major diplomatic effort to elevate the issue to the top of the U.S.-China bilateral relationship"—and raising of a threat of military action against North Korea and a major war on China's border if Beijing failed to comply.[44]

The CFR's members were described by the *Washington Post* as "the nearest thing we have to a ruling establishment in the United States" and includes almost all CIA Directors, National Security Advisors, UN Ambassadors, Federal Reserve Chairs, World Bank Presidents, and Directors of the National Economic Council, several Presidents and Vice Presidents, the majority of state secretaries, several chairs of the Federal Reserve and many high ranking NATO and military commanders. According to the *Post*, the council members were part of a foreign policy establishment with shared values and world views, whose role was not limited to analysing foreign policy but also included taking an active hand in shaping it.[45] Princeton University Professor Stephen F. Cohen, former advisor to President George H. W. Bush and a former member of the CFR, described the council as "America's single most important non-governmental foreign-policy organisation," with the power to "define the accepted, legitimate, orthodox parameters of discussion.... The CFR really is what the Soviets used to call the very top-level of the Nomenklatura."[46] The CFR's publications provide perhaps the best indicator of the position of the U.S. foreign policy establishment, and its policy positions have almost without exception been closely reflected by the policies of their contemporary American administrations.

Placing pressure on China to enforce Western-drafted economic sanctions on North Korea, and a linking of Beijing's compliance in doing so with its future trading relationship with the United States, was seen as a way of pressing Pyongyang to capitulate to Western demands through a third party. Trump administration officials frequently indicated that the terms of future trade agreements would be significantly influenced by the

---

i The paper also indicated a strong preference for regime change in the DPRK, long advocated for by the CFR, and called for giving China a stake in the benefits of a forced reunification under the ROK (pp. 7, 31, 46). The possibility for preventative attacks on the country was also included (p. 11).

extent of Chinese support against the DPRK, which placed Beijing's own economic security under threat.[47] While similar pressure was applied to other North Korean trading partners, as by far North Korea's most important economic partner pressure on China was seen as particularly critical. It is notable that this same strategy was advocated by President Obama to the incumbent Mr. Trump in late 2016—as it was hoped that this new approach of "pressuring China to pressure Korea" could bring crisis to the North Korean economy where Western economic sanctions alone had failed.[48] State Secretary John Kerry has separately strongly recommended the same strategy.[49]

Ultimately the new American approach was doomed to fail from the outset for two reasons. The first was that while the Western Bloc continued to portray North Korea's deterrence program as unacceptable to the international community, the only serious opposition to it came from the Western world and Japan—occasionally from South Korea and Israel[ii] as well. Thus China, like other non-Western parties, was interested not in sanctions enforcement per-se but rather in providing the illusion of enforcement to placate Western demands. With the two East Asian states sharing a porous border, reportedly with extensive tunnel networks for smuggling underground,[50] the West could do little to confirm that external signs of stricter Chinese sanctions enforcement were genuine. Even with limited pressure applied by Beijing, experts assess that trade between Chinese and Korean entities occurs through "remarkably robust networks that can support cross-border trade in adverse conditions"—with traders highly adept at evading restrictions which Chinese authorities alone would struggle to enforce even if this were their objective.[51]

The second reason was that the U.S. and the wider Western Bloc failed to understand the nature of the Chinese relationship with North Korea—seeing that latter as a client state and protectorate of the former and Beijing's role as similar to that of a neo-imperialist power. Western analysts thus appeared to project the nature of the West's own relationship with many of its former colonies, or even that of the Soviet Union with the Warsaw Pact, on the Sino-Korean relationship—which inevitably led to a serious failure to comprehend it.

---

ii North Korea's deterrence program has been cited by some Israeli sources as a national security threat due to the proliferation of advanced Korean missile technologies to its adversaries in the Middle East including Iran, Syria, Hezbollah and the Yemeni Ansarullah Coalition, as well as to potential future adversaries such as Egypt.

Those states which were willingly granted independence from the West have consistently seen extensive and continued Western influence over their policymaking both foreign and domestic. The Philippines,[52] South Korea[53] and Japan[54] are among the leading examples of this trend. In America's case, sovereignty is arguably even more restricted for its small immediate neighbours. It would be unthinkable for a central American state, Honduras for example, to engage in foreign relations with a major power such as China independently—with policies across America's "backyard" very much contingent on Washington's approval. Unbeknownst to the Americans and Europeans, or perhaps incomprehensible to them given the contrast with their own system, China's relations with its neighbours including the DPRK are premised on a wholly different model of mutual respect for sovereignty. While striving for hegemony and imperial dominance has been key to the nature of Western relations with the non-Western world for centuries, since Vasco da Gama first voyaged through the Indian Ocean,[55] Beijing has repeatedly reiterated that it does not seek hegemony or a compromising of the independence of others either near its own borders or further abroad.[56] The fact that North Korea, despite being so heavily dependent on China economically, has remained so fiercely independent in its sovereignty and governance but still on friendly terms with Beijing, bears strong testament to this—as do numerous other examples both historical and current of Chinese relationships with small states.[57]

Western analysts repeatedly failed to understand that the Sino-North Korean relationship was not a neo-colonial one where Beijing dominated Pyongyang—something ideologically abhorrent to both. President Trump himself alluded to the belief that North Korea was some form of Chinese neo-colony on many occasions, stating when on campaign in 2016: "China has control—absolute control—over North Korea. They don't say it, but they do. And they should make that problem disappear.... We have power over China, China should do that. I would force China to do it economically."[58] This was far from the only time he expressed such a sentiment. *Foreign Policy* magazine notably even suggested in 2017 that the Korean crisis could be solved by a permanent presence of tens of thousands of Chinese soldiers in North Korea[59]—something which came naturally to the U.S. and its Western partners which have permanently deployed troops to most of the world's 195 countries[60] and with special forces in many more,[61] but remained an alien concept to the North Koreans and to China.[62] Chinese forces had left North Korea in 1958 after the state's post-war reconstruction was complete—to return only in the event of a new American attack. In the 5000-year histories of both nations, incidences of permanent overseas military presences have been negligible—again drawing a stark contrast to the history of the Western world. A secondary component to the DPRK's maintenance of total sovereignty and independence was its own ideology, which made Chinese "control" over the state a Western fantasy. As Van Jackson observed: "A blanket error of U.S. policymakers since the 1960s has been the incorrect assumption that the Chinese or the Soviets might control North Korea, when the reality was always that no outside power could."[63] Ignorance of the nature of Sino-Korean relations effectively set America and its allies up for repeated failure in seeking to use China against its neighbour.

Tensions Coming to a Head

The first seven months of 2017 saw the United States fast run out of options to deal with the Korean crisis, with Pyongyang seemingly unfazed by military threats and diplomatic pressure. The Korean economy had remained stable[64] despite unprecedented economic pressure which, even when applied far more lightly, had devastated the economies of Iran,[65] Iraq,[66] Venezuela[67] and other Western target states. The window for military action meanwhile appeared to be closing, with the testing of new hardware and particularly the first successful Hwasong-12 and Hwasong-14 tests in May and July respectively demonstrating a significantly increased deterrence capability. On August 8, the day the *Washington Post* published part of a leaked Defence Intelligence Agency assessment concluding that North Korea could deliver nuclear warheads to the American mainland, President Trump warned: "North Korea best not make any more threats to the United States. They will be met with fire and fury like the world has never seen."[68] This was a thinly veiled reference to the very type of attack Pyongyang most feared—intensive firebombing and nuclear strikes against population centres. "Fire and fury" was the term used by U.S. President Harry Truman to describe such attacks on Imperial Japan—with similar firebombings ravaging North Korean population centres during the Korean War.

The DPRK responded to the American threat in kind, within hours issuing a warning that it was considering a strike to create "an enveloping fire" around Guam—which it had recently demonstrated the ability to strike with the Hwasong-12. The territory was home to Andersen Air

Force Base, from where American heavy bombers regularly conducted mock sorties over the Korean Peninsula, as well as to Naval Base Guam, which was a vital staging ground for a war against North Korea. According to a study by the RAND Corporation think tank, such facilities were "seriously threatened" by and extremely vulnerable to such ballistic missile attacks, and even if the missiles deployed conventional warheads "the prospects are grim" for the bases' survival.[69] As KPA General Kim Rak Gyom stated in response to the U.S. President's new threat: "Sound dialogue is not possible with such a guy bereft of reason and only absolute force can work on him."[70]

Pyongyang was aware of its position of strength at this time, and at less than two weeks after its second successful Hwasong-14 test the chances of U.S. military action remained low so long as the DPRK demonstrated a readiness to retaliate forcefully. Referring to the additional level recently added to its deterrent capability beyond the "Guam Killer," the KPA Strategic Force issued a statement, saying:

> Will only the U.S. have the option called "preventive war" as is claimed by it? It is a daydream for the U.S. to think that its mainland is an invulnerable Heavenly Kingdom. The U.S. should clearly face up to the fact that the ballistic rockets of the Strategic Force of the KPA are now on constant standby, facing the Pacific Ocean and pay deep attention to their azimuth angle for launch.[71]

A month later, addressing the United Nations General Assembly on September 19, shortly following the successful Korean testing of a thermonuclear warhead on the 3rd of the month and of another Hwasong-12 missile on the 15th, President Trump stated:

> the United States has great strength and patience, but if it is forced to defend itself or its allies, we will have no choice but to totally destroy North Korea. Rocket Man [Chairman Kim Jong Un] is on a suicide mission for himself and for his regime. The United States is ready, willing and able, but hopefully this will not be necessary.

The president's statement appeared to be intended more as a show of strength and resolve than as a sign the U.S. actually had a plan to roll back Korean nuclear development. Similar statements by the president over the past month, while using extremely bellicose language, were notably all threats of retaliation to a hypothetical Korean attack rather than a threat to initiate any kind of hostilities against the DPRK.[72] Some of Trump's critics even depicted his UN statement as a threat of genocide, which to some extent it was, but it is important to distinguish between professing hostile intent and warning of one's readiness to retaliate.[73] The statement did, however, blunt what several analysts saw as an opening for diplomacy—with some having speculated[74] that U.S. and DPRK delegations could meet informally at the side lines of the United Nations.

To place President Trump's statement in perspective, President Obama previously warned that the U.S. could "destroy North Korea with our arsenals" in April 2016,[75] three months after the state's fourth nuclear test and three days after a successful test of a new submarine-launched ballistic missile. While Trump had warned Pyongyang of the consequences of an attack on the U.S. or its allies—a moot point since the likelihood of Pyongyang itself initiating hostilities was negligible to non-existent—Obama's threat made no mention of a Korean attack as a precondition to "destroy" the country. Rather, his threat appeared to be a reiteration of the option for massive preventative war which, according to a number of reports, was then under consideration in the White House—a far more aggressive intent than anything Trump himself expressed. Thus, while Trump won support at home as the "strong man" with a bombastic style, he spoke loudly but his willingness to attack and his ability to do so remained low.

This was hardly the only time President Trump would use extremely bellicose rhetoric in a purely hypothetical context as a cover for a far more nuanced and at times conciliatory policy. In July 2019 for example, he stated regarding the war in Afghanistan: "if I wanted to win that war, Afghanistan would be wiped off the face of the earth. It would be gone. It would be over in—literally, in 10 days. And I don't want to do—I don't want to go that route." Such rhetoric gave cover to his subsequent moves to draw down the U.S. military presence and deescalate the war in coordination with Pakistan, while pre-empting critics who might claim that he was conceding or "weak on defence."[76] With Washington by September increasingly restricted in its options, and already applying maximum pressure against the DPRK, the bombast of Trump's UN address could effectively cover America's inability to respond effectively.

Following President Trump's speech, Chairman Kim Jong Un derided the American head of state as "mentally deranged" and "a rogue and a gangster fond of playing with fire," vowing to make him "pay dearly for his speech calling for totally destroying the DPRK."[77] North Korea's Foreign Ministry subsequently threatened to shoot down American bombers which were carrying out frequent mock sorties near its airspace—a warning that bombers should not stray too near the country's territory lest the KPA's retaliation provoke an incident which neither side sought. Again, ambiguity regarding how far the North Koreans were willing to go was being used as an effective tool to put pressure on the Americans. In the eyes of the U.S. Military leadership, well aware of the precedent of KPA attacks on its ships and aircraft operating near Korean territory (see chapter 9), could the state's new long-range deterrent capabilities not potentially give it the confidence needed to carry out such attacks?

Director for nonproliferation policy at the Arms Control Association, Kelsey Davenport provided an interesting assessment of North Korea's rhetoric and position at this time, stating: "I think North Korea has typically responded to threats with threats, to provocations with provocations. In part, North Korea is responding to the dangerous and bellicose rhetoric of President Trump." Observing that the DPRK was indirectly expressing a willingness to negotiate should threats from the U.S. cease, Davenport noted: "I read that as keeping the door open for negotiations, if the United States rolls back its more hostile posturing and rhetoric."[78] Through his rhetorical style, President Trump was speaking the same language as the North Korean Foreign Ministry. Neither threatened the other's state directly with the initiation of hostilities, but each threatened massive retaliation should the other dare do so in increasingly bombastic ways.

By September support for a potential military solution appeared to have declined among the American leadership, due largely to the new capabilities the DPRK had demonstrated and the hard line taken by its northern neighbours against a potential U.S. attack. Pyongyang and other regional actors could not be entirely sure of Washington's intentions, however, or which faction or viewpoint in the government would prevail. Some influential figures in the American leadership still doubted the viability of the KPA's intercontinental range deterrent and contemplated a limited "bloody nose" strike, which they believed would not be met with a nuclear response.[79] The overall consensus appeared to be, however, that any military action was too great a risk—North Korea had demonstrated its ability and its readiness to respond to attack and was almost certain to launch some form of counterstrike. This carried the high risk of escalating to a total war in which the U.S. mainland could be targeted.

Although it appeared the U.S. was increasingly forced towards the path of negotiation, it could not be certain at this stage. Rumours of U.S. preparations for war in major American news outlets, many later debunked, still pervaded. These included rumours of an evacuation operation being planned to remove American civilians from South Korea, of U.S. Navy surface ships being given "warning orders" to program North Korean targets into their guidance systems,[80] and of nuclear capable bombers in the Pacific being placed on 24 hour alert—a state of readiness unheard of since the Cold War.[81]

In the immediate aftermath of President Trump's UN address in mid-September, a brief lull in tensions appeared to occur which lasted until late November. North Korea, having miniaturised a thermonuclear warhead and successfully conducted two Hwasong-14 and three Hwasong-12 missile tests capable of threatening the U.S. mainland and Guam respectively, began a self-imposed moratorium on further testing. It was notable that the nature of the KPA's final missile tests before the mortarium—firing Hwasong-12 ballistic missiles—was interpreted by a number of Western analysts as an attempt to avoid provoking the U.S. and a signal of Pyongyang's intent to open dialogue. The KPA did not follow through on its earlier threat to fire missiles into the sea near American bases on Guam but instead tested them far to the north where they landed far from any potential targets.[82]

The beginning of the testing moratorium followed remarks by Chairman Kim Jong Un a month prior on August 14 which were widely seen as conciliatory both by U.S. analysts and by members of the Trump administration—a potential opening for dialogue.[83] The U.S. response, however, was far from reciprocal. On August 28, the United States National Nuclear Security Administration announced a flight test of a new tactical nuclear weapon, the B61-12 gravity bomb, which was widely interpreted as a show of force against North Korea. This was the kind of weapon expected to be used to neutralise KPA troop concentrations, armoured formations and tunnel networks in the event of war—precisely the kind of attack North Korea had developed nuclear weapons to deter.[84] The U.S. Military subsequently redeployed 816,393 bombs (1.5 million pounds of munitions) to Andersen Air Force Base on Guam—the base from which American B-52H, B-1B and B-2 heavy bombers would be deployed to strike North Korea in the event of war and a supply hub for American air units in the Pacific. North Korea was again widely seen as the target of this irregular deployment—although this was not stated explicitly by the U.S. Military.[85]

On November 16, the U.S. Strategic Command published a statement on Twitter with an ominous nuclear threat to North Korea—playing on the country's longstanding fears. It claimed that the U.S. retained "secret silos" of nuclear weapons in South Korea, something Pyongyang had long suspected, since international inspectors had never verified the withdrawal of American nuclear arms from the country. The Strategic Command made a more controversial claim that B-1B Lancer bombers, which were denuclearised after the Cold War, retained the ability to deploy nuclear warheads. The B-1B was the only supersonic bomber in the American inventory, and frequently carried out mock bombings near North Korea's borders.[86] This exacerbated an already dangerously tense situation after a U.S. Ohio Class nuclear submarine carrying over five dozen SEALs—special operations units tasked with infiltrating DPRK territory and assassinating its leadership in the event of war[87]—docked in South Korea.

The U.S. Navy soon afterwards announced unscheduled military exercises in Northeast Asia from November 11–14 involving three Nimitz Class supercarriers and other assets including B-1B bombers. This was the first time since 2007 that three of the 100,000-ton warships, the heaviest in the world, were deployed for joint operations, and could have easily been interpreted as preparation for imminent attack. The carriers between them deployed over 15 squadrons of heavily armed combat aircraft—"loaded to the maximum with magnificent F-35 and F-18 fighter jets" according to President Trump.[88] It was subsequently announced that the Air Force would deploy F-22 Raptor fighter jets to South Korea[89]—the most sophisticated jets in America's inventory designed to penetrate deep into enemy airspace and evade dense air defence networks such as that which protected North Korea.[iii] These highly irregular deployments all occurred shortly after they were announced.

Presenting North Korea with perhaps the most serious threat yet of imminent war, messages to American civilians in South Korea

iii While formidable, the reliability of the Raptor remained questionable. The very public breakdown of a fighter in South Korea in its the first week deployed was cited by analysts a sign of deeper issues with the fleet.

instructing them to evacuate immediately came on the heels of an unusual high-profile inspection of U.S. logistics and evacuation preparations in late September. Such a non-combatant evacuation operation, intended to ensure no collateral damage to U.S. civilians from KPA retaliation, would be standard procedure preceding an attack on the DPRK—and was thus met with considerable apprehension in both Pyongyang and Seoul.[90] This military pressure was supplemented by imposition of yet tighter secondary economic sanctions on the Northeast Asian state by the U.S. Treasury.[91] The U.S. appeared if anything to have taken the North Korean Leader's conciliatory statement as a sign of weakness—or according to President Trump as a sign that Kim Jong Un "is starting to respect us."[92] This was taken as a cue not to negotiate and deescalate, but to double down on military and economic pressure in the hope that it would be met by further conciliatory remarks and the beginnings of a capitulation by the Korean side. Responding to American pressure with anything other than pressure of its own—as it had done on this single occasion—was proving to have been a serious mistake by Pyongyang.

Some analysts speculated that provocations may have been carried out to goad Pyongyang into a military response—which could be used as a pretext for an American attack, further sanctions or other forms of hostile action.[93] If there was a trap, Pyongyang did not fall for it. North Korea maintained its moratorium on weapons testing and did not respond to these developments, apparently seeking to encourage the U.S. to more quickly realise the inevitable—that negotiation was now its only viable path forward with economic sanctions having failed and military action no longer viable after the ICBM tests. The United States Special Representative for North Korea Policy, Joe Yun, had notably previously stated that a Korean moratorium on missile testing would be a signal that Pyongyang was serious about negotiating—although, likely much to Pyongyang's chagrin, when such a moratorium did take place it was subsequently ignored by the administration and dismissed by Yun personally.[94]

The U.S. moved to further escalate tensions in late November, announcing the massive Vigilant Ace joint aerial drills with South Korea scheduled to begin on December 5. High end U.S. weapons systems including B-1B and B-2 bombers and F-15 and F-22 air superiority fighters were deployed for this purpose alongside "decapitation units" tasked with assassinating the North Korean leadership. Such drills trained for offensive action against the DPRK and were seen in Pyongyang as presenting a direct threat of war, which forced it to place its forces on heightened alert. Drills were massive in scale involving tens of thousands of troops, with those scheduled for December being the third that year following drills in March and August. The DPRK had consistently responded to previous "invasion drills" by demonstrating the capabilities of its missile deterrent—and carrying out unscheduled drills in December at a time of high-tension cued Pyongyang to respond with a show of force of its own.

Safeguarding Regional Peace: Korea's Northern Neighbours Step In

North Korea's moratorium on missile testing and calls for negotiation, when brazenly ignored through the announcement of the Vigilant Ace drills, had the effect of winning Pyongyang considerably more international sympathy. Thus the testing of the Hwasong-15 ICBM, which took place five days before Vigilant Ace commenced and demonstrated the capability to retaliate against the entire U.S. mainland, was more widely understood as a response to provocation by a country seeking peace rather than a provocation in itself. Russia and China in particular, through statements from their foreign ministries and the Russian Presidency, showed considerably greater solidarity with Pyongyang as the more responsible party and the one seeking de-escalation. Russia's Foreign Minister slammed the "bloodthirsty tirade" of the U.S. ambassador to the United Nations against North Korea and pledged that Russia would "do our utmost" not to let the United States start a war.[95] These words of indirect support for Pyongyang were soon followed by meaningful actions.

China and Russia had previously drawn a red line at any U.S. military action against the DPRK and had taken steps to enforce it. While both had strongly advocated a "freeze for freeze" agreement at the United Nations, under which North Korea would cease strategic weapons testing if the U.S. ceased military exercises, the U.S. slammed anything other than a unilateral standing down by the DPRK as unacceptable and refused to make any concessions of its own. Indeed, American Ambassador to the UN Nikki Haley had referred to propositions for mutual concessions as "insulting"—on the basis that Pyongyang was a "rogue regime" and could not be held to the same standard.[96] After the U.S. launched large scale military exercises in South Korea in March, Russia had responded in April by deploying its own long range air defence systems near its Korean borders including the S-400 Triumf system. This platform was capable of intercepting targets at high hypersonic speeds up to 400km away and could engage up to 80 targets simultaneously.[97] The Russian Foreign Ministry's acknowledgement that North Korean missile tests were not aimed at or threating Russian security was revealing regarding the motives of these deployments—particularly as the military had stated its readiness to shoot down any missiles fired over North Korean territory. If it was not North Korean missiles which were considered a threat, this indicated that Russia was deploying its air defences to provide cover to North Korea from American attacks. There is no other party against which these systems could have been aimed.

Amid a second round of U.S. drills in August, Senior fellow at the Centre for Korean Studies of the Institute of Far Eastern Studies at the Russian Academy of Sciences Evgeny Kim indicated that Russia could use its air defence coverage over Korean airspace to prevent U.S. attacks against the country—stating with near certainty that if war broke out, it would be America which initiated hostiles. "North Korea's missiles won't fly in the direction of Guam. Most likely if something happens, U.S. missiles will be fired. Of course, our [Russian] air defence systems could intercept them, but it is necessary to conduct a policy which would prevent such a course of events," he said.[98] Russia and North Korea had notably signed an agreement on intelligence and air defence cooperation in 2015,[99] and it was therefore possible that the two could effectively coordinate a defence of North Korean airspace—with Korean Pyongae-5 and other shorter ranged systems serving in a complementary role to longer ranged Russian platforms. Russian air defences were put on high alert in early August 2017 as the U.S. began its second military exercises in South Korea.[100]

Russia was hardly the only party to draw a red line against American attacks on North Korea in August 2017. China's *Global Times*, a state newspaper closely affiliated with the ruling Chinese Communist Party, stated that Beijing would "remain neutral" if North Korea initiated a conflict with the United States. It warned, however, that if America initiated an attack on North Korea, China would intervene to support Pyongyang.[101] That month, in parallel to Russian moves near its own Korean border, China's People's Liberation Army deployed advanced air defence systems near the Korean border. In early September these air defence units held night-time drills intended to prepare for surprise attacks by hostile forces. It remained a possibility for both Russian and Chinese air defence units that plans were in place for them to operate from North Korean territory in the event of war, and the ability to deny U.S. aircraft access to North Korean airspace would seriously undermine American war plans, given the U.S. doctrine's heavy reliance on control of the skies. Deployments of air defence units and warnings that these were ready to respond significantly complemented the deterrent effect of the KPA's own conventional and nuclear assets—a further reason for the United States to avoid war.

Alongside deployment of air defence units, China's Navy in late July and early August held two separate drills in the Yellow Sea off the Korean coast. Both were widely interpreted by analysts as shows of force aimed at the United States—in light of its recent threats to take military action on the Korean Peninsula which Beijing deemed unacceptable. A third round of naval drills next to Korea were held in September, in which Chinese warships particularly emphasized their own formidable air defence capabilities, which could be used to shield Korean airspace from enemy aircraft or missiles in the event of conflict. According to Chinese naval expert Li Jie, the drills showed that "China is prepared and able to stop any power that threatens stability in the region" and were intended to warn the United States against staging an attack on the DPRK.[102] China's latest destroyers deployed sophisticated four-layered anti-air missile networks and could seriously impede hostile aircraft and missiles from reaching Korean territory.[103] While Beijing's adherence to its defence treaty with Pyongyang had been questionable since the 1980s, which was widely cited by proponents of offensive action in the Western world as a reason to consider attacking the DPRK,[104] China's actions emphasizing its commitment to the defence of its neighbour provided a further deterrent to U.S. aggression.

While criticising the announcement of unscheduled U.S.-led military exercises, which took place in early December and ended the DPRK's testing moratorium, Beijing reportedly sent a strong signal to the U.S. and South Korea to back up its threat to intervene in the DPRK's defence. It was reported that China's new J-20 stealth fighters flew into South Korean airspace and near Seoul itself, using advanced stealth capabilities to remain undetected before returning to bases in China's northeast. The J-20 was one of just three fifth generation fighter classes active in the world at the time, and with South Korea neither confirming or denying these reports, the new fighter's presence could have further emphasized the vulnerability of U.S. and allied positions across Northeast Asia.[105] Russia meanwhile conducted a major show of force of its own, deploying large numbers of marines trained in amphibious warfare to carry out sizeable live fire exercises little over 100km from the Korean border.[106] Further live fire exercises involving Russian air units also took place.[107] Combined with the naval exercises, repeated warnings and air defence deployments the signs from Moscow and Beijing could not have been clearer—an American attack would not be tolerated and both parties were willing and well positioned to respond.

While Pyongyang had long pursued a policy of independence in its defence from Beijing or Moscow, it was fortunate that at a time of high tension, when preventative strikes were under serious consideration in Washington, the geopolitical alignment and military capabilities of China and Russia were such that they provided further protection for the DPRK to complement its own deterrence capabilities. Whether this support tipped the balance in Washington against military action, or whether the testing of Hwasong-14, Hwasong-12 and other ballistic missile and modern conventional systems was sufficient to deter an attack, remains uncertain. The fact that the DPRK had not had time to place its new ballistic missiles and miniaturised warheads into mass production, however, meant that a possibility of U.S. attack in late 2017 and even in early 2018—although slim—still remained. Russian and Chinese military support was thus valuable, and its impact was likely very significant.

NOTES

1 Evans, Stephen, 'How might Donald Trump deal with North Korea's Kim Jong-un?,' *BBC,* November 11, 2016.

2 Ko, Dong-hwan, 'Trump up for "hamburger talk" with Kim Jong-un,' *Korea Times,* June 16, 2016.

3 'North Korean media paints Trump as "wise politician," Clinton as "dull,"' *Fox News,* June 1, 2016.

4 Ko, Dong-hwan, 'Trump up for "hamburger talk" with Kim Jong-un,' *Korea Times,* June 16, 2016.

5 Pramuk, Jacob, 'What Trump said about Afghanistan before he became president,' *CNBC,* August 21, 2017.
Herman, Steve, 'Trump Comments on Withdrawing US Forces from Asia Raise Alarm,' *Voice of Asia,* July 21, 2016.

6 Gladstone, Rick, 'In Harvard Speech, Merkel Rebukes Trump's Worldview in All but Name,' *New York Times,* May 30, 2019.
Aleem, Zeeshan, 'Macron just slammed Trump's worldview in a rare address to Congress,' *Vox,* April 25, 2018.
Dathan, Matt, 'An EU army is even MORE necessary with Trump as President, EU chief Jean-Claude Juncker says as he presses ahead with plans to build a European military "superpower,"' *Daily Mail,* November 11, 2016.

7 Gearan, Anne, 'Clinton slams Trump as a dangerous isolationist in American Legion speech,' *Washington Post,* August 31, 2016.
8 Yi, Yong-in, 'Hillary's Campaign Team Signals Hardline Stance on North Korea,' *Hankyoreh*, October 17, 2016.
9 'Clinton's Likely Defense Secretary Says U.S. Should Intensify Sanctions on N.K. Rather Than Negotiate,' *Yonhap*, October 16, 2016.
10 Jackson, Van, *On the Brink,* Cambridge, Cambridge University Press, 2018 (pp. 83–84).
11 Song, Jiwon, 'U.S. Official Encourages Plan for N. Korea Collapse,' *NK News*, May 4, 2016.
12 Yi, Yong-in, 'Hillary's Campaign Team Signals Hardline Stance on North Korea,' *Hankyoreh*, October 17, 2016.
13 Shorrock, Tim, 'Hillary's Hawks Are Threatening Escalation Against North Korea,' *The Nation*, October 28, 2016.
14 'Transcript of the Democratic Presidential Debate,' *New York Times,* February 5, 2016.
15 'Sanders Statement on Trump Tariffs,' *Sanders.Senate.gov,* June 1, 2018.
16 McLaughlin, Elizabeth, 'North Korean Newspaper Endorses "Wise" Donald Trump Over "Dull" Hillary Clinton,' *ABC News,* May 31, 2016.
17 Sisk, Richard, 'Former US General Calls for Pre-emptive Strike on North Korea,' *Defense Tech,* December 1, 2016.
18 Lee, Yon-soo, 'Ex-U.S. Military Chief Suggests Pre-emptive Strike on North Korea,' *Chosun Ilbo*, September 19, 2016.
19 Shorrock, Tim, 'Hillary's Hawks Are Threatening Escalation Against North Korea,' *The Nation,* October 26, 2016.
20 Jackson, Van, *On the Brink,* Cambridge, Cambridge University Press, 2018 (p. 93).
21 Ibid. (p. 93).
22 Hayes, Danny and Guardino, Matt, 'Whose Views Made the News? Media Coverage and the March to War in Iraq,' *Political Commission,* vol. 27, issue 1, 2010 (pp. 59–87).
McSmith, Andy, 'Iraq and the Rupert Murdoch connection: The media mogul's network of pro-war campaigners,' *The Independent,* July 7, 2016.
23 'Kim Jong Un's 2017 New Year's Address,' *KCNA,* January 2, 2017.
24 Haberman, Maggie and Sanger, David, '"It Won't Happen!" Donald Trump Says of North Korean Missile Test,' *New York Times,* January 2, 2017.
25 Ibid.
26 Hemmer, Nicole, 'After the Syria strikes, right-wing non-interventionists are back in the wilderness,' *Vox*, April 15, 2017.
Steinhauer, Jennifer, 'Trump's Opposition to "Endless Wars" Appeals to Those Who Fought Them,' *New York Times,* November 1, 2019.
Thomsen, Jacqueline, 'Trump supporters slam decision to launch strikes against Syria,' *The Hill,* April 14, 2018.
27 Lee, MJ, 'Donald Trump vs. the Republican establishment,' *CNN,* October 26, 2015.
Reilly, Katie, 'Both Former Presidents Bush Won't Endorse Trump,' *Time,* May 4, 2016.
28 Davis, Daniel L., 'It's Time to Face the Truth on North Korea,' *National Interest,* January 2, 2020.
Youssef, Nancy A., 'Why the U.S. Considers North Korea's Kim a "Rational Actor,"' *Wall Street Journal,* December 5, 2017.
29 'Transcript of the Democratic Presidential Debate,' *New York Times,* February 5, 2016.
30 Friedman, Uri, 'Lindsey Graham: There's a 30 Percent Chance Trump Attacks North Korea,' *Atlantic,* December 14, 2017.
31 Crilly, Rob, 'Donald Trump orders £43 billion boost to defence spending,' *The Telegraph,* February 27, 2017.

32 Stracqualursi, Veronica, '10 times Trump attacked China and its trade relations with the US,' *ABC News*, November 9, 2017.

33 'China's Influence Grows in Ashes of Trans-Pacific Trade Pact,' *New York Times,* November 20, 2016.

Perlez, Jane, 'U.S. Allies See Trans-Pacific Partnership as a Check on China,' *New York Times,* October 6, 2015.

34 Nussbaum, Matthew, 'Trump blames Putin for backing "Animal Assad,"' *Politico,* April 4, 2018.

35 Feaver, Peter and Inboden, Will, 'The Realists Are Wrong About Syria,' *Foreign Policy*, November 4, 2019.

Sevastopulo, Demetri and Williams, Aime and Fedor, Lauren, 'House condemns Donald Trump for Syria withdrawal,' *Financial Times,* October 16, 2019.

O'Toole, Gavid, 'Trump's Syria policy dismays Europe as Turkey launches campaign,' *Al Jazeera,* October 10, 2019.

36 Williams, Aime, 'US commitment to regime change in Venezuela tested,' *Financial Times,* May 1, 2019.

37 O'Connor, Tom, 'U.S. Military Must be "Ready To Go" in Venezuela, John Bolton Says,' *News Week,* May 1, 2019.

Shesgree, Deirdre and Jackson, David, '"Military action is possible" in Venezuela, Secretary of State Mike Pompeo says,' *USA Today*, May 2, 2019.

38 Jencks, Harlan W., *Some Political and Military Implications of Soviet Warplane Sales to the PRC*, Sun Yat Sen Centre for Policy Studies, National Sun Yat Sen University, Paper no. 6, April 1991 (p. 21).

Larrabee, F. Stephen, 'Gorbachev and the Soviet Military,' *Foreign Affairs*, Summer 1988.

39 Weiner, Tim, 'When Trump savages his intelligence chiefs, the "deep state" has reason to worry,' *Washington Post,* January 31, 2019.

40 Stewart, Phil, 'As Trump warned North Korea, his "armada" was headed towards Australia,' *Reuters*, April 19, 2017.

'Strategic Confusion,' *The Economist*, April 22, 2017 (pp. 47–48).

41 Caldwell, Leigh Ann, 'Breakdown in North Korea Talks Sounds Alarms on Capitol Hill,' *NBC News*, October 25, 2017.

42 Dionne Jr., Eugene J., 'Trump picked Kim Jong Un over the CIA. Is anyone surprised?,' *Washington Post,* June 12, 2016.

43 Barnes, Tom, 'John Bolton contradicts Trump by saying Syria withdrawal depends on defeating Isis,' *The Independent,* January 6, 2019.

44 Mullen, Mike and Nunn, Sam and Mount, Adam, *A Sharper Choice on North Korea: Engaging China for a Stable Northeast Asia*, Council on Foreign Relations, Independent Task Force Report No. 74, September 2016.

45 Harwood, Richard, 'Ruling Class Journalists,' *Washington Post,* October 30, 1993.

46 Cohen, Stephen F., 'The American Bipartisan Policy Establishment Declares Its "Second Cold War" vs. Russia After Years of Denying It,' *The Nation*, January 24, 2018.

47 *Background Briefing by Senior Administration Officials on the Visit of President Xi Jinping of the People's Republic of China*, Washington D.C., April 4, 2017.

Baker, Gerard and Lee, Carol and Bender, Michael, 'Trump Says He Offered China Better Trade Terms in Exchange for Help on North Korea,' *Wall Street Journal,* April 22, 2017.

48 Lee, Dong Hyuk, 'Analysis: What Trump Inherited from Obama,' *VOA*, June 7, 2018.

49 Kerry John, 'Remarks at the U.S. Navy Academy,' Annapolis, MD, January 10, 2017.

50 'Satellite Spots Cross-border Tunnels,' *CRI News,* August 25, 2014.

51 Hastings, Justin, 'How North Korea keeps its economy humming despite the sanctions,' *South China Morning Post,* September 24, 2017.

52 Abrams, A. B., *Power and Primacy: The History of Western Intervention in the Asia-Pacific,* Oxford, Peter Lang, 2019 (Chapter 5: America in the Philippines: How the United States Established a Colony and Later Neo-Colony in the Pacific).
53 Choe, Sang Hun, 'South Korea Backtracks on Easing Sanctions After Trump Comment,' *New York Times,* October 11, 2018.
54 Abrams, A. B., *Power and Primacy: The History of Western Intervention in the Asia-Pacific,* Oxford, Peter Lang, 2019 (Chapter 13: Modern Japan and Western Policy in Asia).
'Stationing American troops in Japan will lead to bloody tragedy—ex-PM of Japan,' RT, (televised interview), November 6, 2016.
'Ex-Japan FM: I Told Putin We Follow U.S. Policy as We're Surrounded by Nuke States,' Sputnik, May 22, 2018.
55 Gady, Franz-Stefan, 'How Portugal Forged an Empire in Asia,' *The Diplomat,* July 11, 2019.
56 'China will never seek hegemony: white paper,' *Xinhua,* July 24, 2019.
57 Kelly, Robert E., 'A "Confucian Long Peace" in pre-Western East Asia?,' *European Journal of International Relations,* vol. 18, no. 3, 2011 (pp. 407–430).
58 Evans, Stephen, 'How might Donald Trump deal with North Korea's Kim Jong-un?,' *BBC,* November 11, 2016.
59 Frye, Alton, 'China Should Send 30,000 Troops Into North Korea,' *Foreign Policy,* November 28, 2017.
60 Vine, David, 'The United States Probably Has More Foreign Military Bases Than Any Other People, Nation or Empire in History,' *The Nation*, September 14, 2015.
61 Durden, Tyler, 'U.S. Special Forces Deployed To 70 Percent of The World In 2016,' *Ron Paul Institute for Peace and Prosperity*, February 11, 2017.
62 Ibid.
Turse, Nick, 'Special Ops, Shadow Wars, and the Golden Age of the Grey Zone,' *Tom Dispatch*, January 5, 2017.
63 Jackson, Van, *On the Brink,* Cambridge, Cambridge University Press, 2018 (p. 21).
64 Kim, Christine and Chung, Jane, 'North Korea 2016 economic growth at 17-year high despite sanctions: South Korea,' *Reuters*, July 21, 2017.
Lankov, Andrei, 'Sanctions working? Not yet …,' *Korea Times*, May 29, 2016.
Pearson, James and Park, Ju-Min, 'Despite sanctions, North Korea prices steady as Kim leaves markets alone,' *Reuters*, August 8, 2016.
65 'How Sanctions Affect Iran's Economy,' *Council on Foreign Relations*, May 22, 2012.
66 Crossette, Barbara, 'Iraq Sanctions Kill Children, U.N. Reports,' *New York Times*, December 1, 1995.
67 Sachs, Jeffrey and Weisbrot, Mark, 'Economic Sanctions as Collective Punishment: The Case of Venezuela,' *Center for Economic and Policy Research*, April 2019.
Selby-Green, Michael, 'Venezuela crisis: Former UN rapporteur says US sanctions are killing citizens,' *The Independent,* January 26, 2019.
68 Baker, Peter and Choe, Sang-Hun, 'Trump Threatens "Fire and Fury" Against North Korea if It Endangers U.S.,' *New York Times,* August 8, 2017.
69 Heginbotham, Eric and Nixon, Michael and Morgan, Forrest E., *The U.S.-China Military Scorecard,* RAND Corporation, 2015 (Chapter Three, Scorecard 1, Chinese Capability to Attack Air Bases).
70 Serhan, Yasmeen and Gilsinian, Kathy, 'North Korea Answers Trump's Vague Threats. With Specific Ones,' *The Atlantic,* August 10, 2017.
71 Baker, Peter and Choe, Sang-Hun, 'Trump Threatens "Fire and Fury" Against North Korea if It Endangers U.S.,' *New York Times,* August 8, 2017.
72 McCaskill, Nolan D., 'Trump Says "Fire and Fury" Warning to North Korea Maybe Not "Tough Enough,"' *Politico,* August 10, 2017.

73 Kiernan, Ben and Simon, David, 'Donald Trump just threatened to commit genocide,' *Washington Post,* September 26, 2017.
74 Jackson, Van, *On the Brink,* Cambridge, Cambridge University Press, 2018 (p. 146).
75 Blair, David, '"We could destroy you," Obama warns "erratic" North Korean leader,' *Telegraph,* April 26, 2016.
76 Shalizi, Hamid, 'Kabul seeks clarification on Trump talk of wiping out Afghanistan,' *Reuters,* July 23, 2019.
77 'Kim Jong Un calls Trump "deranged," says he will "pay dearly" for comments,' *CBS*, September 21, 2017.
78 Boghani, Priyanka, 'The U.S. and North Korea On The Brink: A Timeline,' *PBS,* February 28, 2019.
79 Luttwak, Edward, 'It's Time to Bomb North Korea,' *Foreign Policy,* January 8, 2018.
80 DeLuce, Dan and McLaughlin, Jenna and Groll, Elias, 'Armageddon by Accident,' *Foreign Policy*, October 18, 2017.
81 Baynes, Chris, 'US "to put nuclear bombers on 24-hour alert" for first time since Cold War,' *The Independent,* October 23, 2017.
82 Jackson, Van, *On the Brink,* Cambridge, Cambridge University Press, 2018 (p. 143).
Choe, Sang-Hun and Sanger, David E., 'North Korea Fires Missiles Over Japan,' *New York Times,* August 28, 2017.
83 Jackson, Van, *On the Brink,* Cambridge, Cambridge University Press, 2018 (pp. 141–142).
84 'USAF completes flight tests of B61-12 gravity bombs from F-15E,' *Air Force Technology,* August 30, 2017.
'The U.S. Military's Development and Testing of the B61-12 Tactical Nuclear Bomb; Why it is Cause for Concern in Russia and North Korea: Part Two,' *Military Watch Magazine,* August 31, 2017.
85 Willis, Gerald, 'Andersen receives 1.5M pounds of munitions during annual in-shipment,' *Defense Visual Information Distribution Service*, October 18, 2017.
86 'U.S. military stokes N Korea flames with "secret nuclear silos" claim,' *RT*, November 16, 2017.
87 Smith, Nicola, 'US Navy Seals tasked with North Korea "decapitation" strike could be part of exercises,' *Telegraph,* October 17, 2017.
88 'American muscle: Three largest aircraft carriers in the world join for sea drills off North Korea,' *National Post,* November 9, 2017.
89 'Six U.S. F-22 stealth fighter jets arrive in S. Korea for joint air drills,' *Yonhap News,* December 10, 2019.
'Raptor has problem after landing during joint war games in South Korea,' *Stars and Stripes,* December 4, 2017.
90 Jackson, Van, *On the Brink,* Cambridge, Cambridge University Press, 2018 (pp. 149–150).
Lee, Yong-soo, 'Top. U.S. Official in Charge of Evacuations Visited S. Korea,' *Chosun Ilbo*, September 20, 2017.
91 'Treasury Targets Chinese and Russian Entities and Individuals Supporting the North Korean Regime,' US Department of Treasury, Press Center, Washington D.C., August 22, 2017.
92 Wadhams, Nick and Epstein, Jennifer, 'Trump Says North Korea's Kim Is "Starting to Respect" America,' *Bloomberg,* August 23, 2017.
93 'US seeks to provoke North Korea by sending F-22 jets to South: Commentator,' *Press TV,* November 25, 2018.
Jackson, Van, *On the Brink,* Cambridge, Cambridge University Press, 2018 (p. 143).
94 Ibid. (p. 156).
95 'Russia calls U.S. threat to destroy North Korea a "bloodthirsty tirade,"' *Reuters,* December 1, 2017.

Gehrke, Joel, 'North Korea ready to negotiate on nukes with Russia's help,' *Washington Examiner,* December 1, 2018.

96 Shinkman, Paul D., 'China's "Freeze for Freeze" Plan for North Korea Gets Chilly Reception in U.S.,' *U.S. News*, September 5, 2017.

97 Bryen, Stephen, 'Russia's S-400 Is Way More Dangerous Than You Think,' *National Interest,* January 18, 2018.

'Hypersonic Weapons on China's S-400 Missile Batteries; A Key Asset for Retaking Taiwan,' *Military Watch Magazine,* January 5, 2019.

98 'Vicious Circle: How to Prevent "Guam Missile Crisis" Between US, N Korea,' *Sputnik,* August 12, 2018.

'Russian East Asian Expert Indicates that Russia's Air Defence Systems Cover North Korea to Deter American Attacks; Could Moscow's Actions Avert War on the Korean Peninsula?,' *Military Watch Magazine,* August 12, 2018.

99 'CNN: Россия «сдружилась» с КНДР назло США,' [CNN: Russia "became friends" with the DPRK in spite of the USA], *RT,* March 15, 2015.

100 'How to Interpret Russia's Growing Surface-to-Air Missile Deployments Near the North Korean Border,' *Military Watch Magazine,* August 11, 2017.

101 Blanchard, Ben and Oliphant, James, 'Chinese State Media Says China Should be Neutral if North Korea Attacks the U.S.,' *Time,* August 11, 2017.

102 Lo, Kinling, 'China "shoots down incoming missiles" during exercise over waters close to North Korea,' *South China Morning Post,* September 5, 2017.

103 'Armed to the Teeth; China Adds Two 7,500 Ton Type 052D Class Destroyers to its Fleet,' *Military Watch Magazine,* May 12, 2019.

104 Luttwak, Edward, 'It's Time to Bomb North Korea,' *Foreign Policy,* January 8, 2018.

Schneider, Jacquelyn, 'Chinese Military Involvement in a Future Korean War,' *Strategic Studies Quarterly*, 2010 (pp. 50–67).

105 'China Allegedly Sends Cutting-Edge Jet to Eye US-S Korea Joint Air Drill,' *Sputnik,* December 10, 2017.

'China's stealth jet may have done flyover of S Korea,' *Asia Times,* December 7, 2017.

106 Nevett, Joshua, 'Vladimir Putin orders 1,000 Russian marines to OPEN FIRE close to North Korea border,' *Daily Star,* December 5, 2017.

107 'Pilots suppress hostile manpower at drills, Primorsky Krai,' *Ministry of Defence of the Russian Federation,* December 21, 2017.

Chapter 16
NORTH KOREA WINS?

Peace Through Strength

Even before the testing of the Hwasong-15 ICBM, which demonstrated beyond reasonable doubt the capability to strike the entire American mainland, it appeared in the final months of 2017 that North Korea had won this major stage in its decades-long standoff with the United States. Shortly after the DPRK's ability to miniaturise nuclear warheads to equip its missiles was confirmed by U.S. intelligence,[1] including Hwasong-12 "Guam Killers" and Hwasong-14 ICBMs, a consensus began to emerge that Pyongyang had a viable means of deterring American military action in Northeast Asia. Indeed, *Foreign Policy* published an article the following day titled: "The Game Is Over, and North Korea Has Won." Its opening lines were indicative of the evolving perceptions in the U.S., stating:

> Donald Trump can whine all he wants, but we're now living in a world where American power is less relevant than ever. The *Washington Post* reported yesterday [citing U.S. intelligence] that North Korea has a large stockpile of compact nuclear weapons that can arm the country's missiles, including its new intercontinental ballistic missiles that are capable of hitting the United States. That's another way of saying: game over.[2]

Pyongyang's effective victory turned out to be one of the few issues on which major media outlets in both the United States and Russia agreed. In a meeting with Russian journalists in early January President Vladimir Putin remarked: "I believe Mr. Kim Jong Un has certainly won this round. He has a nuclear weapon and a missile with a range of up to 13,000 kilometres [Hwasong-15] that can reach almost any place on Earth or at least any territory of his potential adversary. He is already an absolutely shrewd and mature politician."[3]

Complementing Pyongyang's successes in improving its deterrence capabilities, the Korean economy was weathering massive pressure from America and the wider Western world far better than expected. In sharp contrast to Iran, Iraq and Venezuela, living standards in the DPRK had remained stable, as had the prices of key commodities such as rice and corn. The value of the won against the dollar had changed little,[4] and the kind of instability and suffering such economic warfare methods were intended to inflict,[5] and had succeeded in inflicting on other Western target states,[6] were absent north of the 38th parallel (see Chapter 20).[7] The failure of sanctions to have the desired effect, alongside the ruling out of American military options, between them seriously restricted Washington's options to end the crisis other than through negotiations.

Exactly two weeks after the testing of the Hwasong-15, Secretary of State Rex Tillerson heralded changes which had by this point become inevitable—a major shift in Washington's North Korea policy. In a major departure from the American position during the last decade, he stated at the Atlantic Council:

> We're ready to talk any time North Korea would like to talk. We are ready to have the first meeting without precondition. We can talk about the weather if you want. Talk about whether it's going to be a square table or a round table, if that's what you are excited about. But can we at least sit down and see each other face to face, and then we can begin to lay out a map, a road map of what we might be willing to work towards. But can we at least sit down and see each other face to face.

Further clarifying the implications of his statement, in direct contradiction to prior Trump and Obama administration policies, he stated: "It's not realistic to say we're only going to talk if you come to the table ready to give up your program. They have too much invested in it."[8] The Obama administration's failure to acknowledge this by insisting on unilateral Korean disarmament before talks began, perhaps intended to preclude talks under a policy of "Hawk Engagement,"[9] had been a key impediment to negotiations throughout its tenure.

Tillerson's statement was perhaps made in the knowledge that so long as negotiations were underway, military options were unlikely to be taken. Opening the door to a resumption of talks could thus be seen as a response to very real calls by others in the Trump administration to initiate military action against the DPRK[10]—which raised the spectre of nuclear retaliation against U.S. Military forces across the Asia-Pacific and the U.S. mainland itself. Even the limited "Bloody Nose" strike being advocated seriously risked escalation to total war—referred to by lawmakers as "an all out war against the regime" intended "to take the regime completely down."[11] Such actions would guarantee all-out Korean retaliation, including nuclear strikes on the U.S. mainland, and seriously risked war with both China and Russia in light of their recently asserted zero-tolerance line against American attacks on their neighbour.

The rationality of many figures in the Trump administration was questionable at this time, and advocates of an attack which carried a very high risk of nuclear retaliation against American cities were still many. These reportedly included much of the National Security Council as well as CIA Director Mike Pompeo, Defence Secretary James Mattis, Vice President Mike Pence, National Security Advisor H. R. McMaster and Ambassador to South Korea Harry Harris among others. While the consensus among analysts and those officials with some expertise in North Korea was almost unanimously that a strike would be met with significant retaliation, many in the administration appeared to believe otherwise.[12] This may have led Secretary Tillerson, long seen as a voice of reason,[13] to urgently seek to reduce tensions with a new offer of negotiations without precondition. This could at least temporarily delay the initiation of an attack until the hysteria which followed the Hwasong-15 launch had subsided.

The White House, which saw discourse growing increasingly hawkish and beginning to resemble that of the Obama administration in its final months, notably countermanded Tillerson's conciliatory statement within 24 hours. An official statement read: "The administration is united in insisting that any negotiations with North Korea must wait until the regime fundamentally improves its behaviour…clearly right now is not the time."[14] What was meant be "improved behaviour" was not clear, as the DPRK's previous moratorium on nuclear and missile testing and conciliatory statements were notably met only with further pressure and threats just a few months prior. Washington was caught on the back foot by the Hwasong-15's demonstrated capabilities and by new intelligence on miniaturised warheads and viable re-entry vehicles, and a new strategy for dealing with Pyongyang had yet to be devised. Tillerson appeared ahead of the curve among administration officials in recognising that diplomacy was the only option left, and having shown considerable resilience to sanctions and demonstrated a viable deterrent North Korea would force the U.S. to the table sooner or later.

Toning down rhetoric considerably after the previous year, Chairman Kim Jong Un laid out his assessment of the strategic situation during his 2018 new year's address, stating:

> We attained our general orientation and strategic goal with success, and our Republic has at last come to possess a powerful and reliable war deterrent, which no force and nothing can reverse. Our country's nuclear forces are capable of thwarting and countering any nuclear threats from the United States, and they constitute a powerful deterrent that prevents it from starting an adventurous war. In no way would the United States dare to ignite a war against our country. The whole of its mainland is within range of our nuclear strike and the nuclear button is on my office desk all the time; the United States needs to be clearly aware that this is not merely a threat but a reality.[15]

The Korean leader emphasized that he was not making a threat, but by alluding to a "nuclear button" he strongly implied that he had centralised command and control of his country's nuclear arsenal. This optimised reliability, speed and control and would allow Pyongyang to respond rapidly to a potential attack and carry out retaliatory launches with virtually no notice.

Pyongyang appeared to recognise that the new government in South Korea provided a potential channel through which to reduce tensions with the Western Bloc and moved to improve ties with Seoul. Chairman Kim's new year address thus proposed inter-Korean reconciliation, stating:

> This year is significant both for the north and the south as in the north the people will greet the 70th founding anniversary of their Republic as a great, auspicious event and in the south the Winter Olympic Games will take place… The north and the south should desist from doing anything that might aggravate the situation, and they should make concerted efforts to defuse military tension and create a peaceful environment.

> The south Korean authorities should respond positively to our sincere efforts for a détente.... They should discontinue all the nuclear war drills they stage with outside forces, as these drills will engulf this land in flames and lead to bloodshed on our sacred territory. They should also refrain from any acts of bringing in nuclear armaments and aggressive forces from the United States.[16]

As was typical of both political rhetoric and media coverage between states in conflict, the DPRK, ROK and the Western Bloc had come to refer to one another in highly propagandised terms. North Korea, for example, referred to the ROK as the "puppet government" and to the U.S. as the "American imperialists," while Western sources almost unanimously referred to the DPRK's leadership in highly personified terms as the "Kim Regime," "Kim dynasty" and to the state as a "dictatorship" or "monarchy" to the exclusion of all other descriptions. It was easier to demonise an individual head of state than an entire people, and a focus on the persons of the Korean leaders had thus long been adopted. The missiles, for example, were "Kim's missiles" more often than they were "Korean missiles." "Assad regime," "Putin's Russia" and "Ayatollah's regime" were other prominent examples of states which received similar coverage in the West (indeed, leftists in the United States often went so far as to refer to a "Trump regime"—such was the extent of their animosity and of polarisation in the country.[17]) Thus it was rare for any side to refer to the other as a "republic" or to their adversary's "government" or "leadership"—with propagandistic terms being overwhelmingly adopted in their stead. Taking this into consideration, recognition of "their republic" in the speech by Chairman Kim Jong Un, rather than the "puppet regime" or a similar propagandistic terms, was itself a small but very significant signal of recognition and a willingness to work towards reconciliation with South Korea. A similar change in rhetoric would later be adopted by President Donald Trump as part of his efforts to bridge relations with Pyongyang, although Western media coverage generally retained its prior propagandistic terminology, if not in slightly toned-down form.

South Korea, under the new presidency of Moon Jae In, responded with a well-timed diplomatic initiative precisely at a time when Washington desperately needed a way to deescalate the crisis with the DPRK without appearing to have yielded to Pyongyang's newfound power. The timing of the initiative indicates that Seoul was tacitly encouraged if not actively supported by elements in the U.S. leadership. At the very least, the U.S. took no measures to spoil what quickly became a new détente between the two Koreas as it would have been very likely to do before November 2017. Given its extensive influence over the ROK, its ability to derail any negotiations, and the White House's previously derailing of Secretary Tillerson's peace initiative, this indicates that the Moon administration's actions were perceived as being in the American interest. The Trump administration subsequently agreed to a request to delay the massive Key Resolve and Foal Eagle exercises for the sake of the Olympic games. North Korea in turn maintained its self-imposed freeze on nuclear and missile testing, which alongside the delaying of major military exercises appeared to be an informal "freeze for freeze." High level inter-Korean meetings in January subsequently led to conciliatory statements being made by both parties.

In February North Korean Presidium President and Head of State Kim Yong Nam led a high-level delegation to Seoul. With Chairman Kim Jong Un yet to travel abroad or assume full powers in his six years in office, the Presidium President was the highest level official to make foreign visits, and by many accounts, the most powerful man in North Korea. He had been called the "man behind the throne"—the head of the leadership in the DPRK where the younger chairman was its public face. This would remain the case until April 2019, when Kim Yong Nam would retire at 91 years old and Kim Jong Un would three months later be appointed head of state.[18]

President Kim was accompanied by Chairman Kim Jong Un's sister, Kim Yo Jong, who *CNN* reported "Stole the Show" at the Olympic games with her charm and positive message of reconciliation. While comparing the DPRK to Nazi Germany and referring to Chairman Kim Jong Un as a "brutal dictator," the American outlet could not help but note the powerful impact Kim Il Sung's charismatic granddaughter appeared to have by visiting Seoul alongside the head of state, stating: "If 'diplomatic dance' were an event at the Winter Olympics, Kim Jong Un's younger sister would be favoured to win gold. With a smile, a handshake and a warm message in South Korea's presidential guest book, Kim Yo Jong has struck a chord with the public just one day into the PyeongChang Games."[19] A North Korean cheerleading team with unification flags, described by the *BBC* as "mesmerising"[20] and elsewhere as an "army of beauties," also stole the show and was described by *USA*

Today as "one of the most indelible memories of these Olympics."[21] South Korean President Moon Jae In was personally presented with a hand written invitation to North Korea by Chairman Kim, handed over by his sister at the Blue House, and an exchange of envoys and symbolic gifts began soon afterwards, from pine mushrooms and Pungsan dogs to 200 tons of tangerines. Plans for high level meetings and a joint bid for the 2032 Olympics were also made.

Despite an air of reconciliation in early 2018, some more hawkish elements in Washington appeared intent to undermine it—perhaps in spite of the wishes of the presidency. Side discussions between North Korean and American delegations had been expected to take place at the Olympics, but the fact that the latter was led by Vice President Mike Pence, perhaps the most hawkish member of the administration and strongest advocate of preventative war, ended such hopes. The vice president repeatedly stressed a hard line, promising "the toughest and most aggressive round of economic sanctions on North Korea ever" in a stop in Japan on his way to the Olympics.[22] He proceeded to invite the father of Otto Warmbier, an American student who Washington accused North Korea of killing in its custody a year prior, to the Olympic games' opening ceremony (see Appendix II), repeatedly denounced Pyongyang, visited the memorial to the ROKS Cheonan and gave prolific audiences to anti-DPRK defectors. Pence had reportedly intended to use a meeting with the DPRK delegation as an opportunity to issue threats to the country's representatives in person, rather than to hold negotiations, and the North Korean side promptly cancelled the meeting.

Pence's chief of staff referred to the inter-Korean reconciliation in the harshest terms as a "world stage for their [DPRK] propaganda" and an attempt to "whitewash their murderous regime with nice photo ops at the Olympics."[23] The opening weeks of 2018 were a turning point in the DPRK's relations with its adversaries which many were attempting to forestall, the vice president being but one. CIA Director Pompeo again strongly implied the possibility of an American attack on the DPRK,[24] while other influential individuals such as John Bolton and Edward Luttwak, published prominent articles which respectively attempted to legally justify[25] and openly called for[26] an immediate American attack on North Korea. The latter, as previously mentioned, was particularly harsh to the point of being distasteful in its assertions. Further B-2 and B-52H nuclear capable intercontinental range bombers were meanwhile deployed to Guam—the former directly coinciding with sensitive inter-Korean talks.[27]

President Trump himself, to the contrary, appeared happy to accept praise for the success of the Olympic detente, possibly with some basis, given his rumoured behind the scenes role in the inter-Korean reconciliation. He subsequently ended his harsh criticisms of the DPRK—apparently much to the chagrin of hawks in his administration. It is notable that while Moon Jae In had been elected largely due to his promises of reconciliation with North Korea, which he had touted since he was elected president in early May 2017, he had been dissuaded from pursuing this further throughout the year by the United States and had made little to no ground. Thus the sudden success of his new policy indicated a green light had been given by elements in the American leadership to go ahead. Had Trump's administration been unified in drawing a harder line against Moon's initiative, as the George W. Bush administration had against the Kim Dae Jung government's reconciliatory policy in the early 2000s, it could have derailed it with little difficulty.

Seoul's Tightly Managed Mediation: The Complex Position of South Korea

President Moon's envoys, Chung Eui Yong and Suh Hoon, were dispatched to North Korea shortly after the Olympics, and immediately afterwards flew to Washington to meet with President Trump. While enroute to the United States, the Blue House issued the following statement based on the results of their meetings with DPRK officials:

> The North Korean side clearly stated its willingness to denuclearise… It made it clear that it would have no reason to keep nuclear weapons if the military threat to the North was eliminated and its security guaranteed… The North expressed its willingness to hold heartfelt dialogue with the United States on the issues of denuclearisation and normalizing relations with the United States…while dialogue is continuing, it will not attempt any strategic provocations, such as nuclear and ballistic missile tests.[28]

It is notable that nothing of the kind was reported by North Korean media, and Pyongyang had reportedly implied "denuclearisation of the Korean Peninsula" rather than its own unilateral denuclearisation. The willingness to denuclearise under the right conditions had been expressed since the early 1990s, and these yet unspecified conditions could have been purely theoretical. Thus while there was no genuine commitment to anything concrete, it remained strongly in the interests of both Washington and Seoul to ignore this detail—and to present Pyongyang's theoretical commitment to denuclearisation of the Korean Peninsula as a concession by the DPRK in order to meet a key U.S. precondition for talks. While it was the United States which was being forced by trying circumstance to change its position, and that of North Korea remained effectively unaltered, a spin on Pyongyang's statement could allow the U.S. to begin negotiations without it looking like an American defeat. These would be one-to-one negotiations, and they would take place without precondition—a major concession. While the United States, and the wider Western Bloc which had been heavily involved in the "Maximum Pressure" campaign, were allowed to save face, the opening for dialogue facilitated a move away from harsh rhetoric and an easing of tensions. By providing some room for inter-Korean reconciliation, however small, South Korea's Moon Jae In administration also gained more leeway to implement its own agenda.

As part of its effort to spin a failure to coerce North Korea into a victory for the policy of economic sanctions and military pressure, the White House claimed that the opening of talks served as "further evidence that our campaign of maximum pressure is creating the appropriate atmosphere for dialogue with North Korea."[29] Statements by a number of other prominent Western sources quickly followed suit. Even UN Secretary-General António Guterres, a Portuguese politician who repeatedly criticised the DPRK on a unilateral basis and strongly endorsed the Western engineered economic warfare efforts through the UN, praised the Western-drafted sanctions as the facilitator of peace. He stated that the DPRK's peaceful denuclearisation was "on track" because the Security Council "was able to come together and to have a very strong and meaningful set of sanctions."[30] While this interpretation suited Western interests at the time, and was key to their saving face after an effective defeat in 2017, it did not stand up to scrutiny based on an assessment of Pyongyang's actions and the influences of Western pressure on them. Indeed, "Maximum Pressure" and the harsh sanctions the Secretary General was backing were widely credited with forcing Pyongyang to accelerate its deterrence program.[31]

The importance of allowing the Trump administration to spin talks with the DPRK as the result of a successful American-led pressure campaign, rather than a lack of options forced by the Korean deterrence program, would remain a significant factor in ensuring the talks' success. It was increasingly recognised that attempts to dictate terms to Pyongyang were unrealistic, and that while forcing full denuclearisation increasingly appeared unachievable the administration could not politically afford to concede defeat on this major issue. As the Centre for the National Interest's Director of Korea Studies Harry J. Kazianis observed, referring to a North Korea which would remain a nuclear power for the foreseeable future:

> There are domestic politics, which make facing reality a nearly thankless task. No U.S. politician wants to go down in history as the one who admitted America has failed to stop North Korea from building nuclear weapons, as the damage to one's own reputation, political capital, and ammunition you would hand to your political enemies is obvious. Even though no one single administration, policy or person deserves such blame, the fallout—pardon the term—would be immense.[32]

Thus, both Washington and Pyongyang appeared aware than any moves by the U.S. to make concessions and tacitly recognise the DPRK's nuclear status would need to be subtle, gradual and implicit rather than explicit.

The arrival of envoys Chung and Suh in Washington again revealed sharp contrasts in the positions of President Trump and the hawks in his administration. The president on Twitter hailed: "Possible progress being made in talks with North Korea. For the first time in many years, a serious effort is being made by all parties concerned. The World is watching and waiting! May be false hope, but the U.S. is ready to go hard in either direction."[33] Trump quickly moved to distance himself from the hawks, accepting a letter from Chairman Kim Jong Un the contents of which remain unknown—but were speculated to promise the early release of three Americans being held in North Korean prisons. His tone and his actions were once again strongly contradicted by his vice, with Pence's office stating shortly after the envoys' arrival: "All options are on the table and our posture on the regime will not change until we see credible, verifiable, and concrete steps toward denuclearization."[34] This may have been wishful thinking on Pence's part, and the president appeared not to share this hardline approach and took a more realistic position based on the circumstances the U.S. now faced.

A separate statement from the White House may well have been intended to pre-empt moves towards diplomacy by President Trump. It claimed regarding a potential meeting with the DPRK leader: "The President will not have the meeting without seeing concrete steps and concrete actions [towards unilateral disarmament] take place by North Korea."[35] Attempts to move the U.S. back towards confrontation and "Maximum Pressure" appear to have been thwarted by the president himself, who actively moved to build very high expectations for a meeting with Chairman Kim. He tweeted on March 9: "Kim Jong Un talked about denuclearization with South Korean representatives, not just a freeze. Also, no missile testing by North Korea during this period of time. Great progress being made but sanctions will remain until an agreement is reached. Meeting being planned!"[36]

President Trump contradicted the previous line set by his vice president when he very quickly agreed to a meeting with Chairman Kim, and reportedly would have scheduled it immediately were it not for advice to allow for the planned Kim-Moon summit to take place first. Seemingly exuberant about the meeting, he made an unprecedented entry into the White House press room and told the media to expect a "major announcement" soon. "Hopefully you [the press] will give me credit,"[37] he said, and an hour later an official statement to the press revealed his intentions. To what extent Trump's decision was motivated by his need to boost his own image domestically, his awareness of the extremely limited options the U.S. had been left with after 2017, and according to some critics even the need to deflect media attention from a number of personal scandals which were then surfacing,[38] remains uncertain. A possible combination of these factors led to a strong willingness to seek out such a high-level meeting—an unprecedented event in the history of the two nations' decades long conflict.

Pyongyang for its part appeared to capitalise on the momentum building towards peace, and on April 21 after an almost five month pause in missile and nuclear testing Chairman Kim Jong Un announced a permanent end to such tests and immediate closure of the country's nuclear test centre. He stated regarding this development: "under the proven condition of complete nuclear weapons, we no longer need any nuclear tests, mid-range and intercontinental ballistic rocket tests, and that the nuclear test site in northern area has also completed its mission." The Korean leader further declared that the country would never use its nuclear arsenal unless there was a "nuclear threat or nuclear provocation" against it—an effective commitment to a no-first-use policy—and that the DPRK "in no case will proliferate nuclear weapons and nuclear technology."[39] This statement appeared to be an attempt to further legitimise Pyongyang's claim to be a responsible nuclear power, which would potentially facilitate easier recognition of its nuclear status. Chairman Kim also drew a line under the previous phase of intensive weapons testing, announcing a new focus on economic development and a raising of living standards.[40] The DPRK's ability to so clearly state its threshold for nuclear retaliation, and to place it so high with a no first use policy, demonstrated an unprecedented level of confidence in the country's strength and security—in contrast to the near total ambiguity of the Kim Jong Il years when the state's nuclear arsenal and delivery capabilities were still immature. Perhaps the most critical implication of the announcement for the emerging rapprochement between Pyongyang and its adversaries, however, was that an official halt to nuclear and missile testing could be spun as a victory by the Trump administration—allowing it to pursue talks without losing face.

President Moon met with Chairman Kim on April 27 in a moving but almost purely symbolic event. Each standing on his own soil, the two shook hands across the Military Demarcation Line at Panmunjom just a few meters from where the Korean War armistice had been signed. "(You) are coming to the South, when will I be able to visit the North?" President Moon asked. "Let's step over now," Kim replied, leading his counterpart by hand into the DPRK—a wholly unprecedented gesture.[41]

Following subsequent discussions the two Koreas made commitments in the interest of peace and cooperation—although there was little specificity to what they implied or when or how they would be implemented. Thus, the meeting appeared to have been very much for show, a way of easing tensions and symbolising an intention to pursue friendship. Commitments made included aspiring to peaceful reunification "led by Koreans," fulfilling joint economic projects including joint infrastructure modernisation, making joint efforts to alleviate military tensions, cooperating to establish a peace regime and working towards the common goal of realising the Korean Peninsula's denuclearisation.

It was in the U.S. interest to use Moon's South Korea as a pivot with which to turn its relations with North Korea around. Beyond this, however, efforts towards genuine inter-Korean cooperation and reconciliation undermined the American position in Northeast Asia, reducing the adversary's isolation, reducing the client state's dependence on the West and undermining the pretext for U.S. command over the South Korean military and a permanent presence in the country.[i] This was perhaps best demonstrated by President Trump's response to later South Korean moves to lift its unilateral economic sanctions on the DPRK, harshly rebuking the move and stating: "They won't do it without our approval. They do nothing without our approval." Seoul was forced to almost immediately stand down—a testament to the degree of independence the client state enjoyed from its former ruler.[42]

Other examples where the Moon administration attempted to step out of line with U.S. demands—from opposing further THAAD missile deployments to withdrawing from the GOSMIA intelligence pact and expressing reservations regarding making a military commitment in the Persian Gulf—consistently showed that Washington's tremendous leverage was sufficient to ensure it always had its way.[43] Accordingly, an article published by the prominent defence analysts in *Military Watch Magazine* the day after the inter-Korean summit highlighted the potential risks posed to U.S. interests should the ROK and DPRK take cooperation too far. Titled "Goodbye to America's 4 Million Man Army? Inter-Korean Summit Risks Compromising U.S.' Most Formidable Pacific Asset," it highlighted the significant benefits America derived from command over South Korea's armed forces in the event of a war in Northeast Asia and the threat a more comprehensive inter-Korean rapprochement posed to this. The article stated:

> While U.S. troops deployed to East Asia number less than 100,000, South Korea retains one of the largest and most powerful military forces in the world which in wartime would field close to 4 million men. The military is renowned for its high levels of training, maintains a high defence

---

i As attested to multiple times by U.S. officials, the American interest in maintaining the status quo in its military relations with South Korea went far beyond issues pertaining to the DPRK, with a strong military presence on the Asian mainland seen as invaluable to countering China and any other potential challengers to U.S. hegemony over the Asia-Pacific region. (Hwang, Joon-bum, 'American troops in Korea advance US interests, Biegun says,' *Hankyoreh,* July 24, 2020.)

> budget of almost $50 billion annually, and deploys some of the world's most sophisticated weapons systems from Sejong the Great Class destroyers to K2 Black Panther battle tanks, K9 Thunder Artillery Pieces and F-15K strike fighters. Indeed, South Korea's armed forces may well be among the top five most capable in the world, ranking behind only the U.S., Russia, China and India,[44] and combines scale and modernity in a way few others can match. The United States currently retains wartime operational command over the South Korean military, meaning that should war break out in the region the U.S. would be in full command of one of the largest armed forces in the world—and could theoretically order a joint offensive against Chinese targets, a full scale invasion of North Korea or any other action which would suit U.S. interests in the Pacific. The value of this asset cannot be overstated, and could well be key to success in any war effort waged in the region and do much to minimise the United States Military's own losses.[45]

President Moon had previously indicated a strong interest in ending U.S. command of his country's armed forces,[46] and should his reconciliation initiative gain momentum this remained a possibility. As such, moves towards further inter-Korean cooperation would be blocked at all turns. Harsh Western-drafted economic sanctions, including those passed through the UNSC and unilateral secondary sanctions, as well as extensive U.S. influence over South Korea, prevented genuine moves towards meaningful economic ties.[47] As Bruce Cumings observed: "The United States has been a force for division for 75 years, trying in vain to isolate and punish North Korea, and trying to keep South Korea in line—following American policy. The United States is the only major power that keeps interfering in Korean affairs—other countries do not do this," noting as a result that Seoul's peace initiatives "can't get anywhere without American support."[48] This was perhaps best symbolised by American intervention to stop a joint railway infrastructure project in August of that year,[49] and its later moves to block a lifting of South Korean sanctions on Pyongyang imposed in 2010 over the *Cheonan* incident.[50]

Korea's Second Armistice: Summit Meeting and an End to the Standoff

The inter-Korean summit laid the ground for a meeting between President Trump and Chairman Kim, which was preceded in early April by a visit by Mike Pompeo to Pyongyang for preliminary discussions. Pompeo at the time served as both acting CIA Director and Secretary of State due to Secretary Tillerson's unexpected dismissal, and appeared at least publicly to have revised his hawkish position supporting preventative action to now fully support President Trump's new strategy. He would meet with North Korean officials on several subsequent occasions as the Trump administration's new point man for the issue. While in Pyongyang Pompeo reportedly requested that the DPRK unilaterally relinquish five nuclear warheads—if not to American custody then to European allies—and release American prisoners.[51] The first condition was flatly refused as unacceptable, but in a sign of good will the prisoners were released early shortly after the meeting. Secretary Pompeo subsequently issued statements confirming North Korea's intention to denuclearise, which was key to facilitating the subsequent Trump-Kim meeting.

While most of President Trump's foreign policy team appeared to outright oppose a meeting with the North Korea leader, as did his opposition in the Democratic Party, others appeared to be seeking to derail the peace process by turning the beginnings of a peace accord into a surrender—under which the DPRK was expected to make rapid, unrealistic and unilateral concessions. Whether such terms were introduced with the intention of undermining peace talks, or whether those who introduced them genuinely misunderstood the new balance of power and the strength of Pyongyang's position, remains unclear. It was at this stage that the president's new National Security Advisor, John Bolton, who had replaced H. R. McMaster on April 9, came to the fore as a key figure in the administration. Formerly Secretary of State and later UN ambassador under the George W. Bush administration, Bolton strongly favoured a hard line and advocated preventative warfare much like McMaster had. What perhaps distinguished him from other hawks in the United States was his frank and exceptionally honest demeanour—his hardline positions and simplistic assessments were not disguised but stated plainly and openly.

John Bolton's agenda towards the DPRK was clear from the outset, and although it was hardly unique, he was uniquely blunt and clear in stating it. When asked by a *New York Times* reporter during the Bush years what the administration's North Korea policy was, he reportedly handed him a copy of the book *The End of North Korea* by fellow neo-conservative Nicholas Eberstadt and said "that's our policy."[52] The complete destruction of the Korean republic had long been seen as a goal by the large majority of the American foreign policy community –they only differed on the means of bringing it about, whether it would happen by itself, and over what time period it would occur. The Korean successes of 2017, however, meant that this long-term goal was superseded by the immediate need to draw a line under those events and present a reduction in tensions as something other than a failure by the United States to coerce its East Asian adversary into halting its deterrence program before completion.

Plans for a summit between the American and North Korean leaders were temporarily cancelled by Washington, following a diplomatic rift and considerable Korean displeasure with the U.S. position. This came after John Bolton reportedly said the U.S. would look to a "Libya Model" for the denuclearisation of North Korea—terms akin to a surrender under which the DPRK would send its entire nuclear arsenal to the United States and accept intrusive inspections not only of its nuclear facilities, but its military bases as well, by American personnel. All ballistic missiles including short-range missiles would also likely need to be relinquished—as had been the case with Libya.[53] This was a non-starter for the Korean side, not only because the victors were being treated as the vanquished but also due to the considerable implications which came with a "Libya model." Some speculated that by adopting such a hard line, which made a failure in negotiations inevitable, the United States seriously risked alienating much of the international community, and particularly China, Russia and South Korea which sought to reduce tensions and facilitate a U.S.-DPRK agreement quickly. Reducing tensions was strongly in line with the security and economic interests of all three neighbouring states.[54] Thus John Bolton may well have inadvertently worked against the American interest, had his "Libya model" become official U.S. policy—potentially creating a significant rift between the U.S. and those whose support it had sought to put pressure on Pyongyang.

Planning for a summit resumed within 48 hours of its cancellation, and significant preparatory measures were undertaken throughout the prior month. On May 10, three U.S. citizens previously serving prison sentences in the DPRK arrived in the Washington D.C. after an early release was granted. President Trump portrayed the release as a major achievement for his administration and did not miss the opportunity to greet the released prisoners in person at the airport and pose for photos. Alluding to a major turning point in relations with the DPRK, he stated: "We're starting off on a new footing. This is a wonderful thing that he [Chairman Kim] released the folks early."[55]

North Korea's release of the American prisoners was more significant than it may have first appeared. Allegations that Korean-American pastor Kim Dong Chul had been involved in espionage targeting the country's military and nuclear program, while long ridiculed in the West, were confirmed by his own admission two years after his release.[56] Espionage had been the cited cause for his sentencing, and Chul's later confirmation lent credibility to allegations that the other two prisoners had been involved in "hostile acts"[57] and "hostile criminal activities with an aim to subvert the country."[58]

On May 12th Pyongyang announced the closure of the Punggye Ri nuclear test site and invited foreign journalists to witness its demolition, which took place 12 days later. This again represented a largely symbolic gesture rather than a major concession. With a miniaturised thermonuclear warhead already developed, there was no need for further nuclear tests. The extent of destruction caused by the demolition was also uncertain and remained unverified, although journalists witnessed and filmed the destruction of the portals of several test tunnels. Some reports also indicated that the test site was already seriously damaged and its value, even if the DPRK did for some reason seek to resume nuclear testing, may thus have been limited.[59] North Korea would later pledge to dismantle a test site for long range missile engines—although this too was widely seen as a symbolic gesture not only due to the existence of other similar sites, but also because the deterrence program had already passed the testing phase for such missiles.[60] On the 22nd, President Moon visited the United States to assist the Trump administration's preparations for the joint summit.

On June 12th President Trump and Chairman Kim met on Sentosa Island in Singapore. This was an unprecedented event, and the first ever meeting between holders of their two respective offices. The summit meeting could be seen as a "second armistice"—an informal agreement to conclude the hostilities of the previous year and move towards a new phase of less antagonistic relations, whatever this might entail. The extent to which the balance of power had shifted was evidenced by the format of the meetings themselves—in neutral territory, one-to-one between the highest authorities of the two states, and without preconditions from either side. This was previously unthinkable considering the extensive preconditions Washington had demanded and its repeated refusal to hold official meetings in anything other than a multi-party forum. Where the U.S. had gone to great lengths to deny the DPRK any official recognition in the past, as best demonstrated by the format of the aforementioned Korean War armistice negotiations, this too appeared to have been tacitly conceded. It was notable the extent to which the DPRK was able to assert its interests and deter the U.S. from making unilateral demands, a sharp contrast to the case during the Korean War armistice negotiations with American options for coercion now far more limited—and after 2017 increasingly appearing ineffective.

The two leaders met one-to-one with interpreters for 45 minutes and held subsequent meetings for several hours with the participation of other officials. President Trump reportedly presented a film which showed the chairman two paths for the DPRK's future—one bleak one depicting poverty and war and another prosperous one under which Pyongyang denuclearised and embraced a more Western-style economic model. The simplistic and reportedly almost caricaturish film was unlikely to have moved the Korean leadership but avoiding any direct objections and playing along to Trump's line without actually yielding nuclear weapons or altering policy stances proved an effective tactic for Pyongyang. Allowing the American president to spin a public victory out of defeat suited Korean interests well, and ensured not only a relaxation of pressure but also that the status quo of a nuclear DPRK would gradually be normalised.

In perhaps the most important statement of the summit President Trump alluded to at least a partial end of "Maximum Pressure," addressing his thanks to "a very special person. President Xi [Jinping] of China. He has really closed up that border. Maybe a little less the last couple of months. That's okay."[61] Though largely overlooked, it was arguably the most important statement of the summit considering the centrality of sanctions to the Trump strategy the previous year, the cruciality repeatedly alluded to of Chinese participation to the overall success of the sanctions regime, and the parallel moves announced by the president to relax military pressure. A relaxation of sanctions enforcement by third parties such as China, precisely the opposite of what the Obama administration, the CFR and others had so strongly advocated, was now "okay" by the President. This relaxation was later confirmed by a U.S. congressional commission in November and marked an effective end to maximum pressure on the DPRK.[62]

Much like the inter-Korean summit, what was symbolised and implied was far more significant than what was agreed to in writing—with both parties agreeing to general statements with no time period for implementation or explicit details. These included establishment of "new U.S.-North Korea relations" in pursuit of a "peace regime," provision of (unspecified) American "security guarantees" to the DPRK and Pyongyang's affirming of "firm and unwavering commitment to the complete denuclearisation of the Korean Peninsula." It was notable that the United States had accepted the DPRK's wording—"denuclearisation of the Korean Peninsula" rather than "complete irreversible and verifiable denuclearisation of North Korea"—which had very different implications and demonstrated the East Asian state's position of strength at this time. The DPRK had called for "denuclearisation of the Korean Peninsula" for decades and had not altered its terms—but the U.S. had been forced for the first time to amend its position. This bore strong testament to the result of the conflict of the previous year—an effective Korean victory. The language used by President Trump at a joint press conference with Chairman Kim at the closing of the summit further revealed that it had been the United States that had been won over to the Korean position—not the other way around. The president unprecedentedly referred to joint exercises with South Korea in typically North Korean terms—criticising the "war games" as "very provocative."[63] Both leaders also reaffirmed the declarations of the Inter-Korean summit, themselves similarly vague and adding little to the Singapore summit's own terms, and pledges to continue low level meetings were also made.

The Trump-Kim summit drew a line under the tensions of the previous year and facilitated the DPRK's removal from headlines and from the top of the U.S. policy agenda. President Trump would write on Twitter the following day: "There is No Longer a Nuclear Threat from North Korea,"[64] and five minutes later: "President Obama Said that North Korea was our biggest and most dangerous problem. No longer—sleep well tonight!"[65] Secretary Pompeo, too, insisted that there was no longer any nuclear threat from the DPRK—deflecting journalists' questions seeking specific details of how denuclearisation would be achieved or material progress would be made as "silly" or "insulting and ridiculous, and frankly ludicrous."[66] Thus the U.S. could change course without admitting the obvious—it had failed to prevent North Korea from holding American cities in the firing line of its nuclear arsenal.

Much like the tacit agreement reached in the final two years of the Bush administration, North Korea would keep a lower profile and avoid showing up the U.S. with high profile weapons testing, and would in turn benefit from the relaxing of "Maximum Pressure" and receive some form of sanctions relief. This came in the form of reduced American pressure on third parties, mainly on China, to enforce sanctions against the DPRK. These were supplemented by a reduction of military pressure, which most significantly materialised in the suspension of joint military exercises in South Korea—as per the "Freeze for Freeze" which Ambassador Haley had called an "insulting" proposition less than a year prior.[67] With prospects for pressuring Pyongyang to meet Western terms unilaterally having faded, the U.S. now had little choice but to make these concessions.

North Korea would not test any new nuclear delivery systems—but with the new intercontinental and intermediate range platforms declared combat ready the year prior there was no immediate need to do so. Its ballistic missile arsenal was already the most diverse in the world other than that of China,[ii] and included advanced tactical and strategic systems suitable for striking all manner of targets from American cities on the East Coast to small bases in South Korea—and anything in between. The KPA would thus devote its efforts towards manufacturing existing designs for missiles, warheads and launch vehicles[68] on a large scale—with the Hwasong-15[69] and Pukkuksong-2[70] reported by U.S. intelligence to be in mass production in 2018. The location of production facilities underground made confirmation of the types of missiles being produced difficult, but considering the significant efforts made to develop these and other platforms, it followed that investments would go into building an arsenal after three years of intensive testing. Possible inspections of nuclear sites and a freeze of enrichment and reprocessing activities under a potential future deal for further sanctions relief provided a strong incentive to continue production of warheads as quickly as Korean facilities could manage.

---

ii The United States and Russia were at this time seriously constrained in the diversity of their ballistic missile arsenals by the Intermediate Range Nuclear Forces treaty, which prohibited either from deploying ground-based platforms with ranges between 500km and 5,500km.

Consolidating Victory and a New Status Quo

On September 9, the DPRK held large scale celebrations for the 70th anniversary of its founding—hosting a large parade in central Pyongyang with mixed civilian and military elements. The parade was the second of that year, with the first in February celebrating 70 years since the formation of the Korean People's Army. While newly tested ballistic missiles had taken centre stage in the February parade, the military element of the second was overall less emphasized and ballistic missiles were notably absent. Although the DPRK was continuing to manufacture missiles and their warheads at a considerable pace, the state was increasingly evolving into a more mature and stable nuclear power. The KPA's capabilities for massive retaliation were now well known by its adversaries, and there was little need to reemphasize them at a time of détente. Doing so would have empowered hawks in Western world who opposed Donald Trump's new line and called for a return to maximum pressure, and it was thus important for Pyongyang to keep quiet about its deterrent capabilities to effectively support Trump's position. A return to high tensions was strongly against the interests of both countries. North Korea further removed references to its ballistic missile capabilities from tourist areas, and online Korean media outlets even removed clips of the test launches from patriotic music videos.[iii]

Instead of ballistic missiles, the military elements of the September parade focused on new high-tech conventional assets which had recently entered service—emphasizing that modernisation had taken place across the spectrum and not just for the country's strategic forces. Of note were Pyongae-5 (KN-06) air defence systems, Kumsong-3 (KN-19) cruise missile systems, new armoured personnel carriers, anti-tank missile carriers, battle tanks, rifles, and short ranged anti-aircraft systems among other assets. A new variant of the KN-09 rocket artillery system was also on display, and set a world record for its strike range with the ability to bombard targets up to 200km away with 300mm calibre munitions.[71] This would allow Korean artillery units to engage targets far deeper into South Korean territory, with the KN-09's range covering most of the country. Presidium President Kim Yong Nam subsequently gave a lengthy speech acknowledging that the country had achieved its goal of developing significant military capabilities and emphasizing a new focus on economic modernisation.

iii Parts of Pyongyang less commonly visited by or off limits to foreigners continued to display images of ballistic missiles, as observed by the writer.

The Trump administration through its actions appeared to be acknowledging that bringing about Complete Irreversible Verifiable Denuclearisation (CIVD), or any significant denuclearisation at all, would not have been possible at least in the near term. While this had been apparent for some years, and particularly evident after 2017, this reality had to be revealed gradually so as to avoid depicting the administration as defeated, failing or yielding to foreign pressure. In fact, if CIVD was the end goal, the administration appeared to have attempted in its first year to do all possibly could to achieve it short of exposing its own territory to nuclear attack—including contemplating placing its East Asian allies in the firing line of a nuclear war. The reality was, however, that by January 20, 2017 when the new administration was inaugurated, the possibility of achieving denuclearisation had long since passed. Arguably the last real opportunity to achieve it had been forfeited when the George W. Bush administration entered the Iraq War in 2003, allowing the DPRK to continue its deterrence program. As former State Secretary Warren Christopher had predicted, the opportunity costs of that war were high—likely far exceeding even his expectations, considering the massive increase in Korean deterrence capabilities which it facilitated by diverting American attentions towards a costly but relatively inconsequential quagmire in the Middle East.

An effective "freeze for freeze" would continue for the remainder of 2018, with no notable moves towards either disarmament of North Korea or the lifting of Western-drafted sanctions, which were the respective next steps Washington and Pyongyang sought. A summit meeting in Hanoi on February 27, 2019 saw President Trump and Chairman Kim meet for a second time. While both maintained amicable postures and Trump referred to a strong and positive relationship, attempts to reach a concrete agreement ultimately failed. North Korea had reportedly initially proposed a partial lifting of economic sanctions imposed through the United Nations, in exchange for allowing inspections of the Yongbyon nuclear site to confirm its freezing of operations, but appeared amenable to compromise on the basis that both sides would take gradual and reciprocal steps. While the U.S initially appeared to accept such an approach, which had been strongly supported by experienced negotiators,[72] terms were reportedly drastically altered at the eleventh hour and a hard line was again adopted.

At the close of the talks, President Trump handed Chairman Kim a piece of paper calling bluntly for a full transfer of the entire Korean nuclear arsenal and all the country's nuclear fuel to the United States—with a further demand that Pyongyang declare all its chemical and biological weapons inventories before an agreement could be reached. According to South Korean sources, this came as a result of an intervention from John Bolton, who strongly advocated this hard line roughly in accordance with the "Libya Model."[73] This was done either in the knowledge that it would cause the summit to collapse, or in ignorance as to the strong position of the DPRK and the unacceptable nature of the deal. Such terms were, inevitably, flatly rejected. A lunch between the two leaders was subsequently cancelled and both parties departed early, although both ensured openness to the initiation of future talks and neither issued public criticism of the other. While President Trump stated that the talks had collapsed because the DPRK had demanded total sanctions relief in exchange for only some limited moves towards denuclearisation,[74] this was contradicted by multiple sources on both sides and would have been totally out of line with Pyongyang's previous highly consistent negotiating position.[75]

While President Trump portrayed the summit as ending because of his decision to "walk away from a bad deal," several American analysts would conclude, when assessing his statements and the Korean leader's absence from the final press conference, that "it certainly looked as if Kim Jong Un had walked away." It was Washington, not Pyongyang, which would be expected to change its position for subsequent meetings.[76]

Although the Hanoi summit had failed, the Trump administration appeared eager to prevent further damage to its relationship with Pyongyang. In March Trump personally vetoed a set of unilateral economic sanctions by the U.S. Treasury targeting the DPRK,[77] which hardliners had reportedly intended as punishment for Pyongyang's unwillingness to comply with the harsh terms offered at Hanoi. Contrary to the president's veto, the State Department would issue an official statement to the press on March 7 effectively rolling back the American position to what it had been a year prior—namely that a step by step approach of reciprocal concessions was off the table and that no American concessions would be made until the DPRK had unilaterally completely denuclearised first.[78]

Pyongyang for its part moved to increase pressure on Washington to return to the negotiating table quickly and propose more reasonable terms—or else face a complete breakdown in the negotiating process and a return to high profile missile tests.[79] Chairman Kim in early April issued an ultimatum regarding the dragged-out negotiation process, warning that the hardline American position raised the risk of a return to high tensions, while implying that his country could resume conspicuous strategic weapons testing if necessary. "What is needed is for the U.S. to stop its current way of calculation, and come to us with a new calculation," he stated, further setting an ultimatum "until the end of this year"—after which the window for negotiation would close and consequences would be forthcoming.[80] Exactly what path Pyongyang would pursue should the U.S. fail to reopen negotiations with better terms was uncertain, but analysts speculated that demonstrations of the capabilities of previously tested missiles or the testing of new submarine launched missiles were a possibility.[81] Reports citing satellite imagery had indicated since 2016 that a new heavier class of ballistic missile submarine was under development,[82] and the first of these warships would likely be ready for testing by early 2020 alongside a new class of submarine launched missile.[83]

Chairman Kim's ultimatum held powerful implications not only for the future of the bilateral relationship, but also for the legacy of the Donald Trump administration and its electoral success the following year. The administration notably prided itself on diffusing the Korean crisis and building a strong rapport with Pyongyang, which was central to its claim to an effective and successful foreign policy amidst failure in multiple other theatres from Venezuela[84] to Syria[85] to the trade war with China.[86] Considering this, months of high profile North Korean missile tests and a return to high tensions leading up to elections in November 2020 would represent an overwhelming failure—robbing the administration of its much needed claim to victory. The ruling Korean Worker's Party had the cards in their hands needed to seriously jeopardise Trump's ability to remain in power, while the American president's leverage was far more limited. If Trump wanted a deal, the Korean ultimatum and its implications could perhaps convince hardliners in his administration that if they did not adopt a more compromising stance, the entire administration could face electoral defeat the following year. A subsequent change in the attitude of even the most hawkish individuals, John Bolton included, indicated this very well may have worked.

The DPRK backed its threats with swift action, and on April 17 *KCNA* announced the testing of an unnamed new "tactical weapon" which had a "peculiar mode of guiding flight" and deployed "a powerful warhead." The announcement emphasized the weapon's non-strategic nature, and speculation as to what it might be (new guided artillery, a cruise missile?) was answered the following month with the revelation that it was a new short-range ballistic missile. Designated KN-23 by United States Forces Korea, the solid-fuelled missile demonstrated a 700km range and the ability to follow irregular flight trajectories and perform complex in-flight manoeuvres, which combined with a high speed made it near-impossible to intercept.[87]

The KN-23 placed U.S. and ROK military facilities across South Korea in range of strikes with much greater speed and precision than anything North Korea had deployed previously. South Korean sources reported that the ROKAF's AEGIS air defence system, the most advanced Western anti-missile system in service, was unable to even track the KN-23.[88] It was later reported in September that Japan's own U.S. provided radar systems had failed to detect the newly developed Korean missiles.[89] Launches of short-range ballistic missiles, while banned by Western-drafted UN Security Council resolutions,[90] had long been perceived as more acceptable than longer ranged missiles capable of hitting targets beyond the Korean Peninsula.[91] By launching such missiles after an almost 18 month freeze on all testing, Pyongyang appeared to be seeking to apply pressure and reiterate the serious nature of its ultimatum—but without collapsing the detente entirely.

President Trump quickly responded with a statement to protect his administration's standing and its considerable stake in the negotiating process. He did so by playing down the seriousness of the new tests and denying that they were a threat at all. This would have been unthinkable just two years prior or under any administration since the Cold War's end, and again demonstrated Pyongyang's new position of strength. The president stressed that the DPRK had ceased nuclear testing, had returned American prisoners and was returning the remains of fallen American soldiers from the Korean War, while also emphasizing his own faith that Chairman Kim was looking towards Western-style economic reform and eventual denuclearisation. "I am in no rush," he said, seemingly avoiding the issue of the recent missile test entirely. "I am very happy with the way it's going, and intelligence people agree with me," he concluded. A reporter quickly interjected: "you're not bothered *at all* by the small missiles?" to which he replied in the negative.[92]

The Korean ultimatum and missile test appeared to prompt the Trump administration to again accelerate talks with the DPRK. There were suspicions in Pyongyang, and speculations among analysts, that

Washington was playing the DPRK for time. By freezing KPA missile testing it had ended the embarrassment which came from its inability to force unilateral disarmament, while Korean economic growth and modernisation of the civilian economy continued to be slowed by harsh economic sanctions—a favourable status-quo for the U.S. While realistically Western sanctions were expected to remain in place indefinitely, the lifting of the final rounds of sanctions imposed through the United Nations in 2016 and 2017 would be a major boon for Korean exports, and this had reportedly been precisely what Chairman Kim's delegation had sought during the Hanoi summit.[93] By issuing an ultimatum and testing short-range missiles, it was made evident that there was a limit to Pyongyang's patience and that retaliation would be forthcoming if the U.S. did not act quickly.

President Trump's weak position forced him to continue to downplay the seriousness of Korean missile tests, and he stated later in the month: "My people think it could have been a violation, as you know. I view it differently. I view it as a man, perhaps he wants to get attention, and perhaps not. Who knows? It doesn't matter. All I know is that there have been no nuclear tests. There have been no ballistic missiles going out. There have been no long-range missiles going out. And I think that someday we'll have a deal."[94] Secretary Pompeo again backed the president, apparently shifting the terms of the unwritten peace agreement to deny that the DPRK had violated it. He stated: "The moratorium was focused, very focused, on intercontinental missile systems, the ones that threaten the United States."[95] This implied that all the DPRK's missiles, other than the Hwasong-14 and Hwasong-15, could be tested without violating the agreement or requiring a U.S. response—pre-empting future tests of short-, medium- or even intermediate-range missiles which could further embarrass the administration.[iv]

For North Korea, missile tests in early May were only the beginning of its new phase of pressure on the U.S. In the final week of that month, responding to criticisms of its missile tests by John Bolton,[96] *KCNA* quoted a foreign ministry official slamming Bolton as "ignorant" and a "warmonger" and equating the right to launch tactical missiles as part of the state's right to self-defence—therefore a non-negotiable right.[97] One month later on June 28, Director General for U.S. affairs at

iv It was notable that intermediate range systems such as the Musudan and Hwasong-12 were in fact capable of striking the United States—but only its overseas territories such as Hawaii and Guam. Interpretations of the Trump administration's line and whether these were now acceptable too appeared very fluid.

North Korea's Ministry of Foreign Affairs Kwon Jong Gun warned that the country would not wait indefinitely for new negotiations, stating: "The dialogue would not open by itself, though the United States repeatedly talks about resumption of dialogue like a parrot without considering any realistic proposal that would fully conform with the interests of both sides. If the United States is to move towards producing a result, time will not be enough." He further noted that the United States was "becoming more and more desperate in its hostile acts,"[98] likely a reference to moves by the U.S. Senate to approve new economic sanctions against Pyongyang.[99]

Director General Kwon expressed growing frustration with the American negotiators, particularly with Secretary Pompeo[v] who the DPRK Foreign Ministry had previously requested be replaced on the negotiating team with someone "more careful and mature in communicating."[100] The Director General stated: "It would be difficult to look forward to the improvement of bilateral relations and denuclearization of the Korean Peninsula as long as American politics are dominated by the policy-makers who have an inveterate antagonism towards the DPRK. If anyone dares to trample over our sovereignty and the right to existence, we will never hesitate to pull a muscle-flexing trigger in order to defend ourselves." He was particularly critical of Pompeo's position, accusing him of "sophistry" and of "viciously slandering" the DPRK.[101]

Facing a potential breakdown in the peace process, President Trump appeared to respond quickly and effectively by organising a new high-profile meeting on short notice with Chairman Kim Jong Un. Just hours after Director General Kwon's statement, President Trump tweeted from Japan in the early hours of June 29 that he hoped he could meet the Korean leader at the inter-Korean demilitarised zone. He stated: "After some very important meetings, including my meeting with President Xi of China, I will be leaving Japan for South Korea (with President Moon). While there, if Chairman Kim of North Korea sees this, I would meet him at the Border/DMZ just to shake his hand and say Hello(?)!"[102] Though few analysts highlighted it, it appeared the North

v The U.S. Senate Foreign Relations Committee, and the President of the Council on Foreign Relations, separately came to very similar conclusions regarding Pompeo's character and his performance as the country's chief diplomat. (Gaouette, Nicole, 'Democratic report claims staff in Pompeo's State Department are demoralized and afraid,' *CNN,* July 28, 2020. and Hass, Richard N., 'What Mike Pompeo doesn't understand about China, Richard Nixon and U.S. foreign policy,' *New York Times,* July 25, 2020.)

Korea side's harsh words and ultimatums were behind the subsequent meeting between the American and Korean leaders at the DMZ.

The following day the Korean leader accepted Trump's invitation, and an apparently impromptu third meeting was held at Panmunjom on that day. While the body language contrasted strongly to that of the meeting between Kim and Moon a year prior at that same place, and neither led the other by the hand, President Trump described stepping across the border into the DPRK as "a great honour"—the first sitting U.S. president in history to enter North Korea. President Moon attended the meeting but was visibly side-lined—left sitting outside while the two leaders held one-to-one talks. He stated that the event was "a significant milestone in the peace process on the Korean peninsula," referring to "the flower of peace truly blossoming on the Korean Peninsula." President Trump reportedly invited Chairman Kim to visit Washington "when the time is right," and used unprecedently conciliatory language towards the DPRK and its leadership in strong contrast to all of his predecessors.[103]

It was notable that when the two leaders met there was no mention of the nuclear issue or denuclearisation whatsoever—representing a considerable step towards normalisation of North Korea as a nuclear power and away from the previous hard line under which denuclearisation was a precondition for any kind of talks. The major shift this implied in the administration's position was picked up on by a number of American media outlets, with *The Atlantic* referring to the meeting as "The Day Denuclearisation Died."[104] President Trump's position on the kind of deal that would be agreed had also changed markedly after the Hanoi summit. Rather than attempting to dictate terms for full denuclearisation in return for partial sanctions relief, which had been firmly rebuffed the first time, he stated that step for step measures could be taken to ease sanctions as Pyongyang took steps towards freezing nuclear development. Such an agreement suited North Korea well, and if reached it would allow the U.S. president to claim success in diffusing a major crisis—boosting his credibility and placing him in a strong position to contest upcoming elections.

While the Korean position remained unchanged, the Trump administration appeared to have again shifted further towards meeting Pyongyang's terms. This can be partially explained by the fact that Washington had taken a far harder and less compromising line to begin with, while North Korea had not tried to make unilateral or uncompromising demands of the United States in a comparable way. The most significant factors at play, however, appeared to be the imbalance in the strength of their positions strongly favouring the East Asian state, with Pyongyang holding considerable leverage over the Trump administration through its ability to resume conspicuous full-scale demonstrations of its strategic missile and nuclear capabilities. North Korea could survive and its economy and deterrence capabilities were both continuing to grow even with sanctions fully in place[105]—but whether the Donald Trump administration could remain in power if North Korea staged strategic weapons tests in the leadup to the elections was highly questionable.

Pyongyang's apparent stake in the 2020 U.S. election further complicated the tense U.S. DPRK relationship. The Democratic Party's general position on the DPRK appeared as hawkish as before—reflecting a conceited attitude towards the East Asian state under which any dialogue or agreement short of bringing about Pyongyang's utter capitulation was seen as unacceptable. Hillary Clinton referred to the Trump administration's moves towards a deal with Pyongyang as putting "lipstick on a pig,"[106] while frontrunner Joe Biden echoed discourse prevalent throughout the opposition by slamming Trump for having "rushed to legitimise a dictator."[107] Biden advocated cutting all dialogue until Pyongyang first made unilateral concessions towards denuclearisation, referring to dialogue as a "reward" for North Korea rather than a means for resolving issues. This led to comparisons of his hard line as "virtually indistinguishable" from that of John Bolton.[108] More harshly still, Biden had strongly advocated for unprovoked preventative attacks on Korean targets to prevent the KPA from developing a long-range missile capability.[109] Other Democratic Party frontrunners did not appear much more conciliatory.[110] The Democrats themselves had no alternative to negotiations, but by consistently taking a more self-righteous position on an ideological basis from the outset it may have taken them far longer to reach this conclusion for themselves if they came to power—to the detriment of both U.S. and DPRK interests. Thus, Pyongyang had an interest in seeing President Trump retain power, and in providing him with a deal which he could spin for political capital.

The Trump administration would continue to downplay the importance of Korean ballistic missiles as a new, heavier class of ballistic missile submarine was unveiled in late July, or when a second class of shorter range tactical missile was tested in August.[111] Its responses were similarly muted when new longer range rocket artillery systems were tested successfully every month for four months from late August. Dubbed KN-25, these systems improved on the global record for range previously set by the KN-09,[112] and were estimated to be able to strike targets up to 400km away—possibly much further.[113] The KPA's launch of the Pukkuksong-3, an entirely new submarine-launched intermediate-range ballistic missile tested in the first week of October, saw a similarly muted American response. It demonstrated that the KPA now had an increasingly modern and survivable second stage deterrent capable of threatening U.S. territory. The lack of an American response or even denunciation, despite the Pukkuksong-3's strategic role and much longer range than the tactical systems tested since 2017, provided another indicator as to how much had really changed and how strong the Korean position was at the time.[114]

NOTES

1 Warrick, Joby and Nakashima, Ellen and Fifield, Anna, 'North Korea now making missile-ready nuclear weapons, U.S. analysts say,' *Washington Post,* August 8, 2017.

2 Lewis, Jeffrey, 'The Game Is Over, and North Korea Has Won,' *Foreign Policy,* August 9, 2017.

3 Macdonald, Hamish, 'Putin praises Kim Jong Un, says N. Korean leader has "won this round,"' *NK News,* January 11, 2018.

4 'North Korea's Stable Exchange Rates Confound Economists,' *Associated Press,* November 16, 2018.

5 Nephew, Richard, *The Art of Sanctions: A View from the Field,* New York, Colombia University Press, 2018 (Chapter 1: Defining Terms, Section 1: Why Impose Sanctions?).

6 'How Sanctions Affect Iran's Economy,' *Council on Foreign Relations,* May 22, 2012.
Crossette, Barbara, 'Iraq Sanctions Kill Children, U.N. Reports,' *New York Times,* December 1, 1995.
Sachs, Jeffrey and Weisbrot, Mark, 'Economic Sanctions as Collective Punishment: The Case of Venezuela,' *Center for Economic and Policy Research,* April 2019.
Selby-Green, Michael, 'Venezuela crisis: Former UN rapporteur says US sanctions are killing citizens,' *The Independent,* January 26, 2019.

7 Dorell, Oren, 'North Korean Economy Keeps Humming Despite Ever-Tighter Sanctions,' *USA Today,* November 24, 2017.
Kim, Christine and Chung, Jane, 'North Korea 2016 economic growth at 17-year high despite sanctions: South Korea,' *Reuters,* July 21, 2017.

8 Ansley, Rachel, 'Tillerson's Take on US. Foreign Policy: A Year in Review,' *New Atlantacist,* December 13, 2017.

9 Cha, Victor D., 'Hawk Engagement and Preventive Defense on the Korean Peninsula,' *International Security,* vol. 27, no. 1, 2002 (p. 4).

10 Riley-Smith, Ben, 'Exclusive: US Making Plans for "Bloody Nose" Military Attack on North Korea,' *The Telegraph,* December 20, 2017.
Seib, Gerald F., 'Amid Signs of Thaw in North Korea, Tensions Bubble Up,' *Wall Street Journal,* January 9, 2018.

11 Beavers, Olivia, 'Graham: 30 percent chance Trump attacks North Korea if it conducts another missile test,' *The Hill,* December 14, 2017.

12 Jackson, Van, *On the Brink,* Cambridge, Cambridge University Press, 2018 (pp. 163, 228).

13 'Tillerson a voice of reason in Trump's Cabinet,' *Los Angeles Times,* December 12, 2017.
Von Nahmen, Alexandra, 'With Tillerson's firing, White House loses a voice of reason,' *Deutsche Welle,* March 13, 2018.

14 'White House Contradicts Tillerson on North Korea,' *BBC News*, December. 14, 2017.

15 Kim Jong Un's 2018 New Year's Address, January 1, 2018.

16 Ibid.

17 Anderson, Carl, 'Don't call it the Trump administration. Call it a regime,' *Guardian,* July 3, 2017.
'Is it the Trump administration or the Trump regime?,' *Washington Post,* May 4, 2017.

18 O'Connor, Tom, 'Kim Jong Un is Now Officially Head of North Korea,' *Newsweek,* July 11, 2019.
'North Korean President Steps Down at 91: Kim Yong Nam's 21 Years in Power,' *Military Watch Magazine*, April 14, 2019.

19 Sterling, Joe and McKenzie, Sheena and Todd, Brian, 'Kim Jong Un's sister is stealing the show at the Winter Olympics,' *CNN,* February. 10, 2018.

20 'Winter Olympics: North Korean cheerleaders mesmerise crowds,' *BBC News,* February 10, 2018.

21 Madhani, Aamer and Rogers, Martin, 'North Korea cheerleaders making quite an impression at Winter Olympics,' *USA Today*, March 2, 2018.

22 Kim, Christine and Shin, Hyonhee, 'North Korea Says No U.S. Talks Planned at Olympics, Pence Vows. Continued Pressure,' *Reuters*, February 8, 2018.

23 Parker, Ashely, 'Pence Was Set to Meet North Korean Officials During the Olympics Before Last-Minute Cancellation,' *Washington Post*, February 9, 2018.

24 Sciutto, Jim and Bash, Dana, 'Nuclear Missile Threat a "Red Line" for Trump on North Korea,' *CNN*, March 1, 2018.

25 Bolton, John, 'The Legal Case for Striking North Korea First,' *Wall Street Journal,* February 28, 2018.

26 Luttwak, Edward, 'It's Time to Bomb North Korea,' *Foreign Policy*, January 8, 2018.

27 'Air Force deployed B-2 stealth bombers to Guam as sensitive talks involving North Korea commenced,' *Washington Post,* January 11, 2018.
Johnson, Jesse, 'Nuclear-capable B-52 bombers join B-2s, B-1Bs on Guam amid tensions with North Korea,' *Japan Times,* January 16, 2018.

28 Choe, Sang-hun and Landler, Mark, 'North Korea Signals Willingness to "Denuclearize," South says,' *New York Times,* March 6, 2018.

29 Sanchez, Luis, 'White House: "Maximum Pressure" Campaign on North Korea is Working,' *The Hill*, March 27, 2018.

30 'Transcript of the Press Conference by the Secretary-General with the Prime Minister of Sweden,' Stockholm, April 23, 2018.

31 Jackson, Van, *On the Brink,* Cambridge, Cambridge University Press, 2018 (p. 201).

32 Kazianis, Harry J., 'America Must Move Past Its "Sputnik" Moment on North Korea—Or Else,' *National Interest,* March 4, 2019.

33 Donald J. Trump on Twitter, 'Possible progress being made in talks with North Korea. For the first time in many years, a serious effort is being made by all parties concerned. The World is watching and waiting! May be false hope, but the U.S. is ready to go hard in either direction,' March 6, 2018.

34 'Statement from Vice President Mike Pence on North Korea,' *The White House,* March 6, 2018.

35 Karl, Jonathan and Phelps, Jordyn and Faulders, Katherin, 'Trump Agrees to Meeting with North Korean Leader Kim Jong Un on Denuclearisation,' *ABC News,* March 9, 2018.

36 Donald J. Trump on Twitter, 'Kim Jong Un talked about denuclearization with the South Korean Representatives, not just a freeze. Also, no missile testing by North Korea during this period of time. Great progress being made but sanctions will remain until an agreement is reached. Meeting being planned!' March 6, 2018.

37 Michael DelMoro on Twitter, 'So the President himself just popped into the WH briefing room and told reporters there is a "major announcement" coming from South Korea on North Korea. He told @jonkarl it was "beyond" talks, and said "hopefully, you will give me credit,' March 8, 2018.

38 Jackson, Van, 'The Trump-Kim Summit Is WrestleMania for Pundits,' *Foreign Policy,* June 11, 2018.

39 Jeong, Sophie and Ripley, Will and McKirdy, Euan, 'Kim Jong Un: North Korea no longer needs nuclear tests,' *CNN*, April 22, 2018.

40 'A New Era Begins in North Korea? Pyongyang Declares the Successful Completion of its Deterrence Program,' *Military Watch Magazine,* April 21, 2018.

41 Choi, He-suk, '[2018 Inter-Korean summit] Conversation between Moon Jae-in and Kim Jong-un,' *The Jakarta Post,* April 28, 2018.

42 Kim, Bo-eun, 'Trump's remarks infringe national sovereignty,' *Korea Times,* October 11, 2018.
Choe, Sang-Hun, 'South Korea Backtracks on Easing Sanctions After Trump Comment,' *New York Times,* October 11, 2018.

43 Asmolov, Konstantin, 'North Korea: What Is and What Should Never Be,' *Vladai,* June 19, 2020.
'"Shocked" S.Korea leader Moon orders probe into extra U.S. THAAD launchers,' *Reuters*, May 30, 2017.

44 Military Watch Force Comparison, National Rankings by Military Strength (2018) (http://militarywatchmagazine.com/forceApp/countries/) (accessed December 31, 2019).

45 'Goodbye to America's 4 Million Man Army? Inter-Korean Summit Risks Compromising U.S.' Most Formidable Pacific Asset,' *Military Watch Magazine,* April 28, 2018.

46 Kang, Hyunmin Michael, 'Is it Time for South Korea to Regain Wartime Operational Control?,' *The Diplomat,* October 20, 2017.

47 'Inter-Korean relations will never progress if they are subordinate to N. Korea-US relations,' *Hankyoreh,* May 27, 2020.

48 'Moon has done more for inter-Korean peace than any other president, US professor says,' *Hankyoreh,* June 29, 2020.

49 Hass, Benjamin, 'Train project linking North and South Korea stopped in its tracks by US,' *The Guardian,* August 21, 2018.

50 Asmolov Konstantin, 'South Korea: "They Do Nothing Without Our Approval!,"' *NEO*, October 27, 2018.
Choe, Sang-Hun, 'South Korea Backtracks on Easing Sanctions After Trump Comment,' *New York Times*, October 11, 2018.

51 Shim, Elizabeth, 'Report: North Korea weapons could be flown to France,' *UPI,* May 11, 2018.

52 Kim, Suk Hi, *The Survival of North Korea: Essays on Strategy, Economics and International Relations*, Jefferson, NC, McFarland, 2011 (p. 46).
Funabashi, Yoichi, *The Peninsula Question: A Chronicle of the Second Korean Nuclear Crisis*, Washington D.C., Brookings Institution Press, 2007 (p. 143).

53 Miller, Judith, 'U.S. Says Libya Will Convert Missiles to Defensive Weapons,' *New York Times,* April 11, 2004.

54 'Is John Bolton Playing Right into North Korea's Hands? How a Hard Line Against Pyongyang Could Alienate Allies and Undermine the U.S. Led International Front,' *Military Watch Magazine,* May 2, 2018.
55 Rampton, Roberta and Brunnstrom, David, 'Upbeat Trump welcomes U.S. prisoners released by North Korea,' *Reuters,* May 10, 2018.
56 Kim, So-hyun, 'Korean American pastor says he was spying in NK,' *Korea Herald,* July 30, 2019.
57 Lee, Taehoon, 'North Korea Detains Fourth U.S. Citizen,' *CNN,* May 8, 2017.
58 Park, Ju-min, 'North Korea says American was detained for "attempted subversion,"' *Reuters*, May 3, 2017.
59 Page, Jeremy, 'Damage to North Korea's Nuclear Test Site Worse Than Previously Thought,' *Wall Street Journal,* May 10, 2018.
60 Sabur, Rozina, 'North Korea's "dismantling of ballistic missile test site facilities" draws wary response from experts,' *Telegraph,* July 24, 2018.
61 Press Conference by President Trump, Capella Hotel, Singapore, June 12, 2018.
62 Brunnstrom, David, 'China appears to relax North Korea sanctions: report to U.S. Congress,' *Reuters,* November 15, 2018.
63 Press Conference by President Trump, Capella Hotel, Singapore, June 12, 2018.
64 Donald J. Trump on Twitter, 'Just landed—a long trip, but everybody can now feel much safer than the day I took office. There is no longer a Nuclear Threat from North Korea. Meeting with Kim Jong Un was an interesting and very positive experience. North Korea has great potential for the future!,' June 13, 2018.
65 Donald J. Trump on Twitter, 'Before taking office people were assuming that we were going to War with North Korea. President Obama said that North Korea was our biggest and most dangerous problem. No longer—sleep well tonight!,' June 13, 2018.
66 Jackson, Van, *On the Brink,* Cambridge, Cambridge University Press, 2018 (p. 187).
Crowley, Michael and Nelson, Louis, '"Ludicrous": Pompeo Snaps at Reporters Seeking Clarity on North Korea Deal,' *Politico*, June 13, 2018.
67 Shinkman, Paul D., 'China's "Freeze for Freeze" Plan for North Korea Gets Chilly Reception in U.S.,' *U.S. News*, September 5, 2017.
68 Panda, Ankit, 'Exclusive: North Korea Has Continued Ballistic Missile Launcher Production in 2018, Per US Intelligence,' *The Diplomat,* June 30, 2018.
69 Panda, Ankit, 'US Intelligence: North Korea Is Continuing to Produce ICBMs,' *The Diplomat,* July 31, 2018.
70 Cheng, Jonathan, 'North Korea Expands Key Missile-Manufacturing Plant,' *Wall Street Journal*, July 1, 2018.
71 Joseph Dempsey on Twitter, 'For reference this #NorthKorea 300mm MRL system conducted three separate multiple firings in March 2016, the latter two including reported ranges of ~200km (124miles),' May 27, 2018.
Choi, Ha-young, 'North Korea reveals pictures of multiple rocket launch test,' *NK News*, March 22, 2016.
72 Oberdorfer, Don, *The Two Koreas: A Contemporary History*, Boston, Addison-Wesley, 1997 (p. 352).
73 Shorrock, Tim and Richards, Kathleen Ok Soo, 'The Trump-Kim Talks Ended Abruptly—but Negotiations Will Continue,' *The Nation*, February 18, 2019.
정세현 "합의문 괄호만 메우면 됐는데..볼턴때문에 사달난 듯" [Jeong Se Hyun, All I had to do was fill in the parenthesis of the agreement], 노컷뉴스, February 28, 2019.
74 Taylor, Adam, 'Nukes and sanctions: What actually went wrong for Trump and Kim Jong Un,' *Washington Post,* March 1, 2019.
75 Wroughton, Lesley and Brunnstrom, David, 'Exclusive: With a piece of paper, Trump called on Kim to hand over nuclear weapons,' *Reuters,* March 29, 2019.
Byrne, Leo, 'North Korean FM says Pyongyang asked for "partial" sanctions relief,' *NK News,* February 28, 2019.

76 LeTourneau, Nancy, 'Kim Jong Un Played Trump Like a Fiddle,' *Washington Monthly,* February 28, 2019.

77 Rampton, Roberta, 'Trump decides against more North Korea sanctions at this time—source,' *Reuters,* March 22, 2019.

78 Ward, Alex, 'A top Trump official may have just doomed US-North Korea talks,' *Vox,* March 8, 2019.

Johnson, Jesse, 'North Korean denuclearization possible during Trump's first term: U.S. official,' *Japan Times,* March 8, 2019.

79 Wroughton, Lesley and Brunnstrom, David, 'Exclusive: With a piece of paper, Trump called on Kim to hand over nuclear weapons,' *Reuters,* March 29, 2019.

80 Smith, Josh and Lee, Joyce, 'North Korea's Kim Jong Un gives U.S. to year-end to become more flexible,' *Reuters*, April 12, 2019.

81 'North Korea Sets Ultimatum for U.S. to Return to Negotiating Table; Continues to Modernise Military,' *Military Watch Magazine,* April 13, 2019.

82 Bermudez Jr., Joseph S., 'Is North Korea Building a New Submarine?,' *38 North,* September 30, 2016.

83 Roblin, Sebastian, 'Coming Soon: North Korea's Nukes Could Go Underwater,' *National Interest,* July 29, 2018.

84 Friedman, Uri, 'How an Elaborate Plan to Topple Venezuela's President Went Wrong,' *The Atlantic,* May 1, 2019.

85 Cook, Steven A., 'The Syrian War Is Over, and America Lost,' *Foreign Policy,* July 23, 2018.

86 Krugman, Paul, 'Trump Is Losing His Trade Wars,' *New York Times,* July 4, 2019.

'Trump's Tariffs Have Fully Kicked In—Yet China's Exports Grow,' *Wall Street Journal*, November 8, 2018.

87 'New North Korean Projectiles Could Reach Japan Without Being Intercepted—Military,' *Sputnik,* July 27, 2019.

88 'Radar Evading Ballistic Missiles from North Korea? AEGIS Air Defence System Fails to Track New Projectiles,' *Military Watch Magazine,* May 15, 2019.

Shim, Elizabeth, 'Report: Radar in South Korea network could not track missiles,' *UPI,* May 13, 2019.

89 'Japanese radar stations and MSDF crews failed to track recent North Korean missiles launches,' *Japan Times*, September 23, 2019.

90 Gale, Alasdair, 'Bolton Says North Korea Missile Tests Broke U.N. Ban,' *Wall Street Journal*, May 25, 2019.

91 Mullen, Mike and Nunn, Sam and Mount, Adam, *A Sharper Choice on North Korea: Engaging China for a Stable Northeast Asia*, Council on Foreign Relations, Independent Task Force Report No. 74, September 2016.

92 Remarks by President Trump and Prime Minister Abe of Japan in Joint Press Conference, Akasaka Palace, Tokyo, Japan, 3.02PM. JST, May 27, 2019.

93 Byrne, Leo, 'North Korean FM says Pyongyang asked for "partial" sanctions relief,' *NK News,* February 28, 2019.

94 McGraw, Meridith and Scott, Rachel, 'Trump backs Kim Jong Un's attacks on Biden, dismisses North Korea missile tests,' *ABC News,* May 27, 2019.

95 Johnson, Jesse, 'North Korea calls Bolton "warmonger" and says halting missile tests means giving up right to self-defense,' *Japan Times,* May 27, 2019.

96 Gale, Alasdair, 'Bolton Says North Korea Missile Tests Broke U.N. Ban,' *Wall Street Journal*, May 25, 2019.

97 Johnson, Jesse, 'North Korea calls Bolton "warmonger" and says halting missile tests means giving up right to self-defense,' *Japan Times,* May 27, 2019.

98 Shin, Hyonhee, 'North Korea says time running out for talks as U.S. envoy due in South,' *Reuters,* June 27, 2019.

99 Bowman, Michael, 'US Senate Approves New North Korea Sanctions,' *Voice of Asia,* June 27, 2019.

100 'North Korea rejects Pompeo from nuclear dialogue: KCNA,' *Reuters,* April 18, 2019.
101 'Tick Tock: Pyongyang Warns Time is Running Out For Denuclearization Deal with US,' *Sputnik,* June 27, 2019.
102 Donald J. Trump on Twitter, 'After some very important meetings, including my meeting with President Xi of China, I will be leaving Japan for South Korea (with President Moon). While there, if Chairman Kim of North Korea sees this, I would meet him at the Border/DMZ just to shake his hand and say Hello(?)!,' June 28, 2018.
103 McCurry, Justin, 'Donald Trump invites Kim Jong-un to US after entering North Korea,' *The Guardian,* June 30, 2019.
104 Friedman, Uri, 'The Day Denuclearisation Died,' *The Atlantic,* July 2, 2019.
105 Maresca, Thomas, 'Report: North Korea economy developing dramatically despite sanctions,' *UPI,* December 4, 2019.
106 Oprysko, Caitlin, 'Clinton predicts Trump's North Korea deal will be like putting "lipstick on a pig,"' *Politico,* February 26, 2019.
107 Oprysko, Caitlin, 'Biden dings Trump for his handling of North Korea and Iran,' *Politico,* July 1, 2019.
108 DePetris, Daniel R., 'How Joe Biden Became John Bolton on North Korea,' *National Interest,* July 15, 2019.
109 DePetris, Daniel R., 'Watch the Video: Would Joe Biden Launch a War Against North Korea?,' *National Interest,* May 7, 2019.
110 Sganga, Nicole and O'Keefe, Ed, 'Potential 2020 Democratic hopefuls are biggest skeptics of North Korea deal,' *CBS,* June 13, 2018.
111 Panda, Ankit, 'North Korea Tests New Type of Short-Range Ballistic Missile,' *The Diplomat,* August 12, 2019.
112 'North Korea Tests New "Super Large" Multiple Rocket Launcher,' *KCNA*, August 25, 2019.
113 Elleman, Michael, 'North Korea's New Short-Range Missiles: A Technical Evaluation,' *38 North*, October 9, 2019.
114 Regan, Helen and Ripley, Will and Browne, Ryan and Kwon, Jake, 'North Korea says it test fired a new type of submarine-launched ballistic missile,' *CNN,* October 3, 2019.

Chapter 17
THE ART OF THE DEAL

The End of Détente

As North Korea's ultimatum approached for the U.S. to reach a deal by the end of 2019, the country appeared to enjoy growing support for its position internationally,[1] particularly from neighbouring China. The deadline marked 25 months without a test of a ground-based strategic weapons system—the first 17 of which had seen no ballistic missile testing at all. If North Korea were to resume tests of strategic weapons, Moscow, Beijing and many others appeared increasingly inclined to blame Washington for refusing a deal for mutual concessions despite a two year testing freeze, several opportunities to make a deal and multiple warnings that it was critical to provide some sanctions relief before the new year. Chinese and Russian moves to relax sanctions previously imposed through the UN Security Council in both 2018[2] and 2019[3] were flatly rejected by the U.S. and its Western allies. The two in turn blocked the passing of Western-drafted resolutions accusing Pyongyang of violating the sanctions regime.[4] Growing support for the Korean position from Moscow and Beijing led many Western analysts to conclude that maximum pressure could never be restored to its former levels,[5] and signs of both parties' unwillingness to enforce the Western-drafted UN sanctions only grew.[6]

China would show increasingly overt support for Pyongyang, and in August 2019 the country's Central Military Commission announced that the People's Liberation Army (PLA) would boost defence ties with North Korea and that both were "ready to contribute to peace and stability in the region together."[7] This followed high level meetings between the KPA and PLA leaderships in Beijing.[8] The announcement came amid signs of growing ties in other fields, from major concerts by Korean artists performed in Beijing in January 2019, one of which was attended by Premier Xi Jinping,[9] to the premier and first lady's high profile visit to Pyongyang in June. Xi was treated to a special Chinese version of the Arirang Mass games, the largest show on earth performed in the world's largest stadium, which saw classical Chinese songs, costumes and the five starred red flag given pride of place alongside their Korean counterparts. Massive human collages of the Chinese flag, and of Premier Xi himself, were made to honour them alongside the usual collages of the three Korean leaders, and multiple statements were made regarding agreements to further improve bilateral ties.[10] This support and signs of very considerable Chinese investment placed Pyongyang in a strong position to endure a new period of high tensions with the United States should Washington fail to reach a negotiated settlement.

As North Korea's new year deadline approached, and Washington appeared to take no steps towards altering its negotiating position, signs of escalating tensions began to emerge. The North Korean Foreign Ministry's U.S. Affairs Bureau issued a statement on September 16 slamming continued U.S. pressure and "the twisted view regarding that sanctions led the DPRK to dialogue," and warning that there were serious doubts regarding whether a breakthrough in relations could be achieved from these premises.[11] The Foreign Ministry stated on September 27 that the U.S. had failed to follow through on the summit agreements, but that Pyongyang hoped President Trump would personally take a wise and bold decision.[12] At the United Nations General Assembly three days later, the DPRK's ambassador placed the blame fully on the U.S. for failing to negotiate in good faith, stating: "The situation on the Korean peninsula has not come out of the vicious cycle of increased tension, which is entirely attributable to the political and military provocations perpetrated by the U.S."[13]

Little seemed to improve, and tensions between the two adversaries continued to escalate both leading up to and following the new year. On December 4, America's Deputy Assistant Secretary of Defense for East Asia, Heino Klinck, confirmed that the U.S. maintained military options on the table for dealing with Pyongyang—further warning that the Pentagon, rather than the State Department, could be tasked with disarming the adversary.[14] Four days later a spokesperson for North Korea's Academy of National Defense Science announced that a major test "of great significance" had taken place at the country's Sohae Satellite Launching Ground. "The results of the recent important test will have an important effect on changing the strategic position of the DPRK once again in the near future," he stated, leading to speculation that a new long range ballistic missile engine was under development. It was also speculated that the country may have been preparing for a satellite launch—a means of further placing pressure on the U.S. without escalation directly to the level of a strategic weapons test.[15] Satellite images showed work simultaneously underway at the "March 16 Factory" for long range ballistic missiles—possibly in preparation for an upcoming test.[16] Under considerable pressure from members of the Senate from both political parties to get tougher on Korea, President Trump signed a new round of unilateral sanctions into law on December 20th.[17]

As both countries celebrated the new year, and fears in the West that North Korea would mark the occasion or even Christmas day itself with a major strategic weapons test[18] increasingly subsided,[19] a shift in the Korean position was increasingly evident. On December 21, Pyongyang hosted a high-level meeting of Korean People's Army headed by Chairman Kim Jong Un to discuss improving the country's security,[20] which was followed by a rare convening of the Korean Workers' Party Plenary on the 28th.[21] After high level meetings of both the KPA and the Workers' Party—what appeared to be a charting of a new course for the country by its two major leadership bodies—Chairman Kim announced the DPRK's new policy line in his new year's address. Addressing over 300 officials at the party plenary on its final day, the chairman announced a lifting of the self-imposed and unilateral freeze on the testing of strategic weapons, stating: "There is no ground for us to get unilaterally bound to the commitment any longer… The world will witness a new strategic weapon to be possessed by the DPRK in the near future."[22] Such steps had previously been warned both by the chairman[23] and the Foreign Ministry.[24]

Rather than addressing the camera directly from his office as he had the previous year, the chairman's 2020 address took a more impersonal style and saw his address to the party from the main hall of the workers' party headquarters televised in its stead. He pledged a "new path" for the country, and appeared to officially abandon hopes for a breakthrough in relations with either the United States or South Korea, in sharp contrast to his addresses the previous two years, indicating Western-drafted sanctions could be expected to remain in place indefinitely. "We can never sell our dignity, which we have so far defended as something as valuable as our own lives, in the hope of a brilliant transformation… The DPRK-U.S. standoff, which has lasted for generations, has now been compressed into a clear standoff between self-reliance and sanctions," he stated, which was consistent with prior statements at times of high tension in the prominence it gave to economic warfare in particular. He continued: "Nothing has changed between the days when we maintained the line of simultaneously pushing forward the economic construction and building of nuclear force and now when we struggle to direct our efforts to the economic construction due to the U.S.'s gangster-like acts… There is no need to hesitate with any expectations of the U.S. lifting sanctions."

Giving further insight into the nature of the country's "new direction," state newspaper *Rodong Sinmun* wrote the following Monday:

> As a leopard cannot change its spots, the aggressive nature of imperialism can never change. So is the U.S. behaviour today. The real intention of the U.S. is to seek its own political and diplomatic interests while wasting time away under the signboard of dialogue and negotiations and at the same time keep sanctions so as to gradually reduce our strength. The reality shows that now that the ambition of the enemy to stifle our system remains unchanged, it is foolish to dream of the ease of situation and the lift of sanctions.[25]

The shift in the North Korean position was notably also reflected in the performing arts. At a prominent new year's national concert by the Samjiyon Orchestra, the song "Our Peace is on Our Bayonets" was performed in prime position among the pieces. A remix of the classic in new style, the song's chorus read: *"However precious is peace. We will not beg for it. On our bayonets. On our bayonets. Peace—peace is there."* Peace through strength was the obvious message. This song had been popular in 2017, particularly after the first ICBM tests, but had not featured prominently in televised performances since.

On January 10, the state media outlet KCTV released a statement by Chairman Kim, reportedly made to President Trump during their meeting in June the previous year, stressing that Pyongyang would only accept negotiations on equal terms. It stated:

> We consider it important to resolve problems through dialogue and negotiation and hope true peace will descend as soon as possible. But we cannot comply with the American style of dialogue, which unilaterally pushes for its demands. We do not want to beg for peace at the dialogue table or trade it for something. Our future is what we choose and we make, not what you guarantee and point to. The obvious thing is

> that if the United States insists on the current political calculations, the prospect of resolution will be murky and very dangerous.[26]

U.S. Defence Secretary Mark Esper had responded to the potential resumption of Korean strategic weapons testing with a warning on January 3 that America was ready to take military action against the DPRK if necessary.[27] This warning appeared particularly serious given its timing, just hours after the CIA oversaw[28] an airstrike personally authorised by President Trump[29] to assassinate Iranian Quds Force Commander and Revolutionary Guards Lieutenant General Qasem Soleimani—Iran's foremost military leader considered the second most powerful many in the country.[30] The attack was not provoked[31] and took place near Baghdad International Airport. The commander was in the country legally and was scheduled to hold a meeting with the Iraqi Prime Minister later that day.[32] Analysts both in the United States and internationally widely concluded that the assassination was illegal,[33] if not a war crime.[34]

The Soleimani assassination appeared to have been staged at least in part as a warning to other U.S. adversaries that even against its four declared "great power adversaries"—Iran, China, North Korea and Russia—the country was willing to risk serious escalation and act well outside the boundaries of international law. This was stressed by State Secretary Mike Pompeo, who warned that the attack was part of "a bigger strategy" involving "the restoration of deterrence"—noting that this was not confined to Iran but had implications for other leading American adversaries.[35] Former CIA Director and Commander of the U.S. Central Command David Petraeus similarly referred to the attack as intended to "re-establish deterrence," noting that it could be a precursor to threats to strike Iranian oil fields and other vital infrastructure if Tehran did not meet American terms.[36] President Trump for his part warned that Iranian cultural heritage could be the next target for American attacks—another serious war crime.[37] As the U.S. would later again demonstrate by repeatedly commandeering Iranian civilian shipping in international waters, the degree to which it was willing to brazenly violate both the law and international norms in seeking to undermine targeted states was now unprecedented.[38] As a number of analysts observed, the assassination had considerable implications for the security of North Korea and other U.S. adversaries[39]—strongly signalling that Washington was willing and ready to act offensively and unimpeded by the confines of international law. With Pompeo having previously stated that North Korea had to be dealt with in an entirely different way to Iran due to its possession of a nuclear strike capability against the U.S. mainland, American conduct towards and threats against an adversary which lacked such capabilities arguably fully vindicated Pyongyang's pursuit of this deterrence capability.[40]

Pyongyang the following week slammed perceived U.S. intransigence in negotiations, with the Foreign Ministry's First Vice Minister Kim Kye Gwan stating:

> We have been deceived by the U.S., being caught in the dialogue with it for over one year and a half, and that was the lost time for us… Although Chairman Kim Jong Un has good personal feelings about President Trump, they are, in the true sense of the word, "personal"… There will never be such negotiations as that in Vietnam, in which we proposed exchanging a core nuclear facility of the country for the lift of some UN sanctions in a bid to lessen the sufferings of the peaceable people even a bit.[41]

The Korean side appeared to be seeking to place further pressure on Washington by warning that its negotiating position was only going to become harsher with time. Its ability to sustain living standards and economic growth under sanctions, and its wide range of options for non-violent escalation up to and including strategic weapons demonstrations, placed it in a strong position. As senior adviser at the International Crisis Group and expert on the DPRK, Duyeon Kim, noted: "Pyongyang has raised the price for even resuming talks… Negotiations, if they ever resume, will be much more difficult. They're trying to make it sound like they're not desperate for talks and that they can survive without Washington's help. Unfortunately, this is quite true—North Korea has proven to be very resilient and they can trudge along and work towards their economic and nuclear objectives."[42]

South Korea's Moon Jae In administration for its part, having failed to make any tangible gains in its own relations with the north, appeared to be doing whatever it could to prevent a deterioration of relations between Washington and Pyongyang. While South Korea had featured prominently in Chairman Kim Jong Un's 2018 and 2019 new year's addresses, it was conspicuous by its absence from that in 2020—which was widely interpreted by analysts as a sign that Pyongyang had given up on Seoul as either a channel for normalisation of relations with the U.S. or an independent economic partner.[43] The writer's conversations with North Korean officials near the end of 2019 indicated that disappointment in Seoul and in President Moon were widespread. With the possibility of a rapid end to the U.S.-DPRK détente, should Pyongyang carrying out a strategic weapons test, the Moon administration's flurry of actions included inviting Chairman Kim Jong Un to visit Seoul,[44] conveying birthday wishes from President Trump,[45] considering seeking exemptions from UN sanctions for inter-Korean projects,[46] and considering allowing a resumption of tourism by South Koreans to the DPRK.[47] These all occurred within the first two weeks of January, 2020.

Seoul was blocked by UN sanctions from fully opening trade relations with North Korea and had been harshly warned by Washington against even a partial opening through relaxation of unilateral sanctions, which effectively closed options for economic cooperation. Inter-Korean railway projects, too, had been blocked by the U.S.—with the U.S.-led UN command still maintaining control of the inter-Korean border. Moon's plane had even been blacklisted by the U.S. Military for entering North Korea on a diplomatic visit.[48]

While President Moon had stated that he would consider seeking exemptions from UN sanctions, the chances of these being granted by the Council's permanent Western members remained slim. Resumption of tourism, the only major field of the North Korean economy not covered by UN sanctions, was thus possibly the only means of offering Pyongyang some form of economic benefit—which needed to be given and soon to ensure its continued commitment to the détente. North Korea's concessions were otherwise almost entirely unilateral—which Pyongyang had reiterated would not be the case indefinitely. The DPRK's tourism industry was otherwise booming,[49] and considerable investments had been made in further expansion of tourist activities, beach resorts,[50] ski resorts[51] and other facilities[52] to capitalise on the one unsanctioned part of its economy. Demand was such that airlines were seeking to open a number of new flight routes to the country—with Pyongyang increasingly suffering from a shortage of hotels in high season.[53] Lifting the ban on tourism from South Korea had the potential to provide a boost to the industry, particularly if later announced plans to allow individual as well as group tours were implemented.[54] Seoul's ability to lift the ban without

Washington's consent, and whether this would be enough to placate Pyongyang in the long term, both remained highly questionable.

Pyongyang would go on to carry out record levels of testing to refine its tactical deterrence capabilities, including the new KN-25 rocket artillery system which broke a world record by a considerable margin for its engagement range[55] alongside the KN-24 ballistic missile—both of which placed American military bases across South Korea in the firing line.[56] Signs of continued work on the development of a more advanced submarine-launched missile capability,[57] and warnings from the U.S. Military leadership and from prominent analysts of future strategic weapons tests,[58] showed that Pyongyang retained options to place pressure on the increasingly overwhelmed Donald Trump administration in its election year. Signs at the beginning of the year showed that Korean pressure could be yielding results, with conservatives in the United States leadership increasingly favouring a softer stance in negotiations and a possible loosening of the sanctions regime which could pave the way to a deal, ensuring both a much needed foreign policy win for Trump and assurances that no new long range missile tests would scupper their electoral prospects.[59] The alienation of South Korea through the administration's hard line has only been cause for further concern and given additional stimulus to change course.[60] A further indicator of the shift in Washington's position on North Korea came at the United Nations, with American criticism of Pyongyang's tactical weapons tests having softened considerably and the Trump administration having blocked a European-backed hearing on alleged Korean human rights abuses. Such moves were described by the New York Times as the administration "trying to preserve a diplomatic opening," but were roundly criticised by both leftist media in the U.S and by European officials. The United States under Donald Trump appeared to have the most interest in diplomacy and détente with Pyongyang among the major Western powers, placing it at odds with European members of the Security Council[i] which took a much harder line against Pyongyang.[61]

---

i The aforementioned divisions over the Korean peace process between the Trump administration and the U.S. intelligence, foreign policy and defence establishments, as well as with European allies, raised the question of whether the administration could soften UN sanctions even if it wanted to. Lacking full internal support, the administration could struggle to bring the European UNSC members into line with its policy, meaning European states could, with the approval of elements in the U.S. leadership, threaten to veto a Trump administration sponsored Security Council motion relaxing sanctions if it is believed to be against the interests of the Western world as a whole.

Amid growing unrest domestically and an ongoing economic crisis unprecedented since the Second World War,[62] if not ever,[63] the need for a quick deal or some sign of progress on the Korean issue appeared increasingly urgent as the Trump administration drew closer to the November elections. American officials would request a reopening of dialogue with unprecedented frequency and at almost every occasion,[64] with Pyongyang giving very cold responses, repeatedly referring to prior American diplomatic efforts as ploys to buy time without making concessions,[65] and reiterating that it had no interest in another "useless" summit meeting.[66] Alluding to its very considerable leverage in the leadup to the elections, Pyongyang referred to the summit meetings as publicity stunts intended to boost the Trump administration's standing domestically,[67] and sent a clear message that it would expect concrete concessions and an entirely different format for dialogue.

Further driving home that it was fully aware of the card it had to play in determining the outcome of what was widely considered President Trump's most prolific foreign policy initiative and thus holding significant influence over public perceptions of the American administration, First Vice Department Director of Central Committee of Workers' Party of Korea Kim Yo Jong warned on July 10 that the previously mentioned "Christmas gift," which the U.S. "hasn't received so far," could arrive "on the eve of the presidential elections." This was widely seen to be an allusion to Pyongyang's ability to show up the Trump administration by testing an ICBM or nuclear warhead—underscoring the president's failure to uphold his red line and prevent Korea from being able to target the U.S. with thermonuclear strikes.[68] It was clear that Pyongyang sought to use its leverage to gain meaningful concessions—likely ones a subsequent administration could not reverse, such as a rolling back of at least some sanctions at the United Nations—and that the pre-election months provided the optimal time to push for such a deal.

What Might a DPRK-U.S. Deal Look Like?

While considerable emphasis was placed on denuclearisation as the end goal of negotiations between the United States and North Korea, realistically the prospects for both states agreeing to sufficient stages of concessions to bring this about remain extremely slim. On October 25, 2016, the Obama administration's Director of National Intelligence James Clapper stated: "I think the notion of getting the North Koreans to denuclearize is probably a lost cause." The best the U.S. could settle for, he believed, was a negotiated limit on the types of nuclear weapons the DPRK could deploy.[69] This had been the first such admission by a senior U.S. official, who proved to be well ahead of his time—if not in his conclusions then in his willingness to publicly admit to the reality of the situation. North Korea is set to remain a nuclear power indefinitely, with nuclear weapons written into the constitution and their possession seen as inseparable from the state's right to independence and self-defence. How a process of normalising the state's nuclear capabilities can commence, both internationally but most critically in the Western world where it is most stringently opposed, remains to be seen.

The difficulties for the Western psyche in accepting North Korea as a nuclear power have been and will continue to be considerable. The emergence of this reality represents perhaps the most direct contradiction to the idea of a new world order centred on the economic and military power of the Western world—under which the global triumph of Western values over others was seen as an inevitability. The DPRK provided the greatest contradiction to a world order built in the image of the West, next to which even China and Iran appeared somewhat Westphilian, and its political philosophy and social system were firmly rooted in Asian values. This state, described by its leading American critics as the "ultimate outlier in world order"[70] and an imminent threat to "the moral structure on which global order is built,"[71] has despite its meagre size gained the military capacity to devastate cities across the Western world with thermonuclear strikes. Under the protection of this nuclear deterrent, a growing economy independent of Western trade or investment and a society almost untouched by Western values can continue to exist and grow stronger seemingly indefinitely.

Regarding the difficulties American society specifically would face in coming to terms with a nuclear North Korea, the Center for the National Interest's Director of Korea Studies, Harry J. Kazianis, observed:

> Our own national psychology that reinforces over and over our own need for primacy in all parts of the world and our "exceptional" nature surely means we should not have to accept a nuclear North Korea. That psychology declares that we can make Pyongyang bend to our will and that the Kim regime simply has no way to resist our demands. And yet, every intelligence report that breaks puts cracks in our own collective sense of invulnerability. Those reports that a nation

> as economically backward such as North Korea can kill millions of Americans rocks us to our core and challenges how Americans think of themselves. That might explain why so many of us here in Washington—including yours truly—reacted with such shock and anger over North Korea's nuclear weapons and missile tests back in 2017. It was, and still is, our twenty-first-century "Sputnik" moment, a series of events that shattered our sense of security, our perceptions of how powerful our nation is mixed with the dreadful realization that a country with the human rights record such as North Korea has and will continue to build even more dangerous weapons of mass destruction. We want to believe that this is unacceptable, and yet the facts tell us otherwise.

Referring indirectly to a strong case of cognitive dissonance, Director Kazianis referred to the constant denial of both North Korea's capabilities and its newfound position of strength as a "foreign policy fantasyland."[72]

Providing some insight into what a deal between the DPRK and the U.S. could look like, leading negotiator under the Clinton administration Robert Gallucci observed that "there wasn't sufficient trust for one to take a very large step assuming the other would take the compensator counter step. There had to be a series of smaller steps."[73] For North Korea's part, it appears the state is looking for a partial lifting of economic sanctions in return for limitations on its nuclear activities—possibly including freezes on its production of nuclear materials, the expansion of its arsenal or the testing of new strategic systems. It is possible that as a second stage, some types of ballistic missile could be decommissioned in return for more comprehensive sanctions relief—perhaps the lifting of earlier rounds of UN sanctions. However, as covered below, unilateral economic sanctions from the Western Bloc can be expected to remain in place indefinitely, and these are unlikely to be included in the negotiating process.

North Korea is unlikely to relinquish its intercontinental range ballistic missile capability, which for aforementioned reasons of national security as well as historic reasons remains particularly vital. Restrictions on the ranges of its intermediate-range missiles—possibly resembling the previous Intermediate-Range Nuclear Forces (INF) treaty between the U.S. and Russia—remains a possibility, however. Elimination of the Hwasong-12 and Musudan from active service, for example, would remove one of the primary threats to an American war effort in the Pacific—the threat to Guam, which is set to become increasingly important in the 2020s as a hub of U.S. military forces in the region. Guam could still be targeted by ballistic missile submarines, but removal of upper-intermediate range land-based missiles would still represent a major concession. The likelihood of such concessions may diminish should the U.S. see through plans to deploy similar intermediate-range missiles of its own to Northeast Asia.[74]

While it would be extremely difficult to monitor considering the tightness of the security system in the DPRK and the KPA's tendency to store the bulk of its arms underground, a cap on the number of ICBMs and nuclear warheads deployed could also be presented as a major concession in exchange for sanctions relief, as could a show of handing over and destroying a portion of the Korean nuclear arsenal. These are all concessions which would not significantly compromise Korean security but would help the United States come to terms with its overall inability to impose total denuclearisation and thereby facilitate a rolling back of sanctions at the United Nations.

It is important when considering the possibilities for a future deal to observe one key impediment to major concessions by Pyongyang—even if offered highly favourable terms. That is the nature of the political system in the United States, and the consistent tendency for administrations to annul, withdraw from or simply ignore commitments made by their predecessors from the opposing political party. Indeed, every single administration since the end of the Cold War has broken a major security related agreement made by its immediate predecessor from the opposing party—and thereby seriously compromised the interests of a country which had previously placed a degree of trust in the United States. In the 1990s the Bill Clinton administration[ii] chose to ignore "iron clad guarantees" its predecessor had made to Moscow that NATO's expansion would go "not one inch eastward"—taking advantage of the Soviet trust and renunciation of its sphere of influence in Eastern Europe made on these grounds to rapidly expand the U.S.-led alliance and bring hostile troops ever closer to Moscow.[75] The George W. Bush administration in the early 2000s subsequently abandoned the Agreed Framework and ongoing denuclearisation talks with the DPRK for a hard line on regime

ii The Clinton administration notably also initiated a major bombing campaign against Yugoslavia just four years after Belgrade signed the Dayton Agreement, a peace deal in which it made major concessions to Western interests.

change. Had Pyongyang made concessions which were not so easily reversible on its nuclear activities under the Clinton administration, it would have been in a far worse position under Bush.

The Barack Obama administration in the early 2010s in turn entirely ignored security guarantees provided by its predecessor to the government of Libya. The state had disarmed its missiles and weapons of mass destruction, and even allowed for intrusive inspections of its military facilities, and in return Western sanctions had been lifted and relations were temporarily normalised. Sanctions were re-imposed under Obama, with Libyan assets across the Western world seized, and the now near-defenceless state was devastated by Western air attacks. The trust placed in the U.S. and its European allies was directly cited by Libyan officials as the cause of the state's downfall.[76] The formerly stable and wealthy African state is unlikely to recover for the foreseeable future—and consequences of the Western attack have included the emergence of Islamic terrorism, civil war and open slave markets.[77] In 2018 the Donald Trump administration would unilaterally withdraw from the Joint Comprehensive Plan of Action (JCPOA), a multilateral agreement with the Islamic Republic of Iran limiting its nuclear program in exchange for sanctions relief. The new U.S. administration demanded a renegotiation of terms, imposing harsh economic sanctions and threatening military action. Had Iran's Supreme Leader not personally insisted that any deal should not encompass the state's ballistic missile capabilities,[78] or personally overseen a massive expansion in missile deterrent capabilities with North Korean support, the possibility of U.S. military action against the denuclearised state would have been considerable.

An understanding of the nature of American politics and foreign seriously limits the extent to which Pyongyang can afford to roll back its deterrence program—even if presented with full sanctions relief and full normalisation of relations. While a number of analysts pointed to individual cases of the United States withdrawing from agreements, and how they undermined prospects for a comprehensive deal with the DPRK,[79] it was rarely noted that these withdrawals were part of a greater trend—or the way the American political system effectively ensured such policy. An analysis of the statements of the DPRK's leadership and foreign ministry indicates that Pyongyang remains painfully aware of the nature of its adversary and the fate of those parties which had placed trust in peace agreements with and security guarantees from the U.S. and the Western Bloc,[80] with Pyongyang's policies appearing fully consistent with this understanding.

Concerning the risks of disarmament through negotiation, North Korea's Foreign Ministry stated regarding the valuable lessons learned from Tripoli's example: "Libya's nuclear dismantlement much touted by the U.S. in the past turned out to be a mode of aggression by which the latter coaxed the former with such sweet words as 'guarantee of security' and 'improvement of relations' to disarm and then swallow it up by force." In exchange for a lifting of sanctions and normalisation of diplomatic ties, Libya "took the economic bait, foolishly disarmed themselves, and once they were defenceless, were mercilessly punished by the West."[81] Referring earlier to the example of Iraq, which partially disarmed and allowed Western inspectors extensive access to its facilities, the DPRK Foreign Ministry stated on a separate occasion: "The Iraqi war shows that to allow disarming through inspection does not help avert a war but rather sparks it."[82] A similar awareness of the risks of comprehensive disarmament were expressed on several other occasions.

Perhaps one of the most ominous warnings directed towards the DPRK came from the son of Libyan leader Muammar Gaddafi, Saif Al Islam Gaddafi, who while naming North Korea and Iran specifically, referred to the circumstances of Libya's downfall and Tripoli's mistakes as "a good lesson for everybody." Noting that the country had agreed to disarm despite warnings from Pyongyang, he stated in a televised interview in 2011 while his country was under Western bombardment:

> you give up your weapons of mass destruction, you stop developing long range missiles, you become very friendly with the West and this is the result. So what does this mean, it means this is a message to everybody that you have to be strong. You never trust them, and you have to be always on alert. Otherwise those people [Western Bloc], they don't have friends. Overnight they change their mind and they start bombing us, and the same thing could happen to any other country… One of our big mistakes was that we delayed buying new weapons, especially from Russia, it was a big mistake. And we delayed building a strong army because we thought that we will not fight again, the Americans, the Europeans are our friends [since disarming and normalising relations in 2003.][83]

The Trump Administration's Director of National Intelligence Daniel R. Coats appeared to reach the very same conclusion as the Libyans and the Koreans, affirming that it was strongly against the DPRK's national security interests to disarm. He stated that the North Korean leadership

> has watched, I think, what has happened around the world relative to nations that possess nuclear capabilities and the leverage they have and seen that having the nuclear card in your pocket results in a lot of deterrence capability… The lessons that we learned out of Libya giving up its nukes…is, unfortunately: If you had nukes, never give them up. If you don't have them, get them.[84]

Coats' predecessor under Barack Obama, James Clapper, in much the same vein referred to the Korean deterrent as "their ticket to survival"—one which Pyongyang was not realistically going to yield.[85] While the DPRK appears willing to negotiate compromises to its deterrent capability, these will be limited and, much like those agreed to under the Agreed Framework in 1994, they will not be irreversible. Pyongyang's awareness of the nature of the American political system and its often extremely dire consequences for those parties which put their faith in a deal with a particular administration will guarantee this. The DPRK's first-hand experience in its two major deals with the United States—the Korean War armistice and the Agreed Framework—further this awareness. It has not been forgotten that the U.S. unilaterally abrogated article 13(d) of the former without legal pretext in order to unilaterally nuclearize the Korean Peninsula, and failed to meet its terms for the latter after which it withdrew following a change in administration.

Ultimately the only thing that can realistically be verified in a Korean disarmament process other than an end to testing is a cessation of production of further nuclear warheads through monitoring of Korean nuclear facilities—like that which occurred for eight years from 1994. With perhaps the world's largest network of underground military bases and the ability to store nuclear warheads, manufacture more missiles or store existing ones undetected, a cap on the number of nuclear warheads or the types of missiles the KPA deploys can never be absolutely verified. As noted repeatedly by U.S. officials, nothing short of an invasion and destruction of the state can fully verify Pyongyang's complete disarmament of any of the assets it already has. Even if a portion of its miniaturised warheads or IRBMs were turned over for destruction, the state's security system and the "intelligence black hole" faced by Western agencies ensures that the total number the country possessed in the first place remains completely unknown—with estimates ranging very widely.

The DPRK has a further card to play in negotiations for sanctions relief, a latent capability which could be used to press for concessions without directly affecting Korean security, which is its ability to proliferate advanced missile and even nuclear technologies. Indeed, the announcement by Chairman Kim Jong Un in April 2018 that North Korea would not proliferate its new technologies appeared to come as part of a package which could lead to the Western Bloc, however reluctantly, accepting North Korea as a nuclear state. One could interpret the implication therefore being that North Korea will renege on some of these pledges if moves towards acceptance of its nuclear status and at least a partial lifting of sanctions are not forthcoming.

Iran in particular remains a potential recipient of highly advanced Korean systems well ahead of those currently in its arsenal should talks between Pyongyang and the U.S. collapse entirely, and funds from major weapons sales to the oil rich state could be seen as a means of compensating for the economic losses caused by Western sanctions on the DPRK. When the Musudan was sold to Iran in the mid-2000s it represented the most advanced ballistic missile design in the Korean arsenal, and remains, by a considerable margin, the most capable in Iranian hands. The very same was true for the Rodong-1 and before it the Hwasong-6 and Hwasong-5, which like the Musudan in later years all incrementally increased the range and sophistication of Iran's ballistic missile deterrent.

With relations between Iran and the United States likely to remain hostile for the foreseeable future, the ability to arm Iran with Korean technologies is a game changer for the balance of power in the Middle East—and has been for decades. Given Iran's lagging conventional capabilities, North Korean missiles provide Iran with its most important deterrent capability. Should Iran be equipped with the Hwasong-12, Pukkuksong-2 or even an ICBM, or provided the technologies, components and assistance needed to manufacture similar systems domestically, it would profoundly shift the regional balance of power against the interests of the Western Bloc. The fact that Iran increased uranium enrichment in 2019 and has threatened multiple times to withdraw from the NPT[86] in response to U.S. pressure means it could potentially look to mount nuclear warheads on these missiles. For this too, North Korean technologies and experience could fast track the development of a miniaturised warhead and potentially avoid the need for high profile nuclear weapons tests altogether.

Ultimately while technology transfers between the two states are difficult to monitor, and new Iranian missile designs such as the Sejil are set to continue to rely heavily on technologies and components sourced from the DPRK, a pledge not to sell Iran more advanced missiles in completed form as it had done with the Musudan or to transfer nuclear technologies remains a valuable concession Pyongyang could offer in exchange for sanctions relief. Expert on North Korean arms sales, American professor Bruce E. Bechtol, indicated that proliferation of new capabilities including an ICBM and possibly a nuclear warhead from the DPRK to Iran was highly likely, and that this would be a game changer for Iranian power in the Middle East. Citing a number of reputable sources, Bechtol referred to the Hwasong-15 ICBM in particular, either as a finished product or as a set of constituent technologies, as likely to end up in Iranian hands—a catastrophe for Western interests in the region if it did occur.[87] Some Western concessions to Pyongyang could be the only effective means of forestalling such transfers.

A major sticking point in previous negotiations between the U.S. and the DPRK was the issue of satellite launches, and American concessions on this issue can be expected. The pretext for Western opposition to Korean satellite launches in the past was that its Unha rockets were said to be technology demonstrators which advanced the country's ICBM program. Using engines based on those of the Rodong-1, these launchers are today almost thirty years behind existing Korean ICBM technology. Testing such engines cannot benefit the Korean deterrence program in its current form, and the fact that satellite launchers do not re-enter the atmosphere with their payload means they cannot be used to test re-entry vehicle technologies. The primitive nature of the satellite launch rockets relative to North Korea's far more advanced missile technologies developed since the rockets were first tested, effectively nullifies claims that satellite launches are a cover for missile testing. This was used as a pretext in the past to effectively deny North Korea its rights under the Outer Space Treaty. The possibility remains, therefore, that satellite launches will be condoned under a deal which bans ICBM and/or IRBM testing.

The Long Shadow of Regime Change: A Look to the Future

Ultimately the Western world, in seeking to remake global order in its own image, cannot accept an Asian nationalist state with a degree of political, military, economic and ideological independence like North Korea. The eventual goal of the Western Bloc is regime change in North Korea, but as the country's capabilities have repeatedly exceeded all Western expectations, from the performance of the KPA in the Korean War to the state's survival in the 1990s through the Arduous March and the rapid development of a sophisticated deterrent capabilities from the mid-2000s, the strategy and timeline for bringing this about has repeatedly been altered.

All parties remain aware during current negotiations that a full lifting of Western economic sanctions against the DPRK remains effectively impossible. Hypothetically, even if the state were to fully and verifiably denuclearise and disarm, other pretexts for continued economic warfare efforts would be found. Indeed, the testing of nuclear weapons and ballistic missiles may in the long-term result in less rather than more Western sanctions as it provides some leverage for pursuing sanctions relief. Many other Western target states with no long or medium-range missile capability and no weapons of mass destruction have failed to gain such leverage and are sanctioned extremely harshly by the Western Bloc partly as a result. Venezuela, Syria, Zimbabwe, Myanmar, and Cuba are a few among many examples. Should the DPRK denuclearise fully, the state of the country's domestic politics, its economic system, or its willingness to trade and maintain relations with other Western adversaries such as Syria and Russia can all be used as pretexts for the imposition of Western economic sanctions—and have been against other states in the past.[88]

A significant indicator of the prospects for future Western relations with the DPRK was a statement in a September 2016 report by a task force from the highly influential Council on Foreign Relations (CFR) think tank. It stated regarding prospects for relations if the DPRK fully denuclearised:

> Full normalization of relations and sanctions relief will require major progress on North Korea's human rights position, including the release of all political prisoners and their families, a full accounting and voluntary repatriation of all persons abducted from foreign countries, nondiscriminatory

> food aid distribution monitored by aid workers who are guaranteed full nationwide access, freedom to leave the country and return without punishment, and ending the information blockade imposed on North Korea's citizens by the government.[89]

These conditions were broadly consistent with those listed in Sec. 402 of the North Korea Sanctions and Policy Enhancement Act of 2016, HR 757. The CFR's statement itself appeared to be closely based on Title III of the North Korea Sanctions and Policy Enhancement Act of 2016, which enshrined the fulfilment of unrealistic demands for domestic changes in and Western penetration of the DPRK into U.S. law as necessary preconditions for any relief of American unilateral sanctions. While many of the allegations made by the CFR and the Policy Enhancement Act have little evidence behind them and are based on highly questionable defector testimonies (see Chapter 19), maintaining these allegations and this narrative provides the Western Bloc with pretext for continued sanctions and pressure on the DPRK indefinitely—or at least until its territory is governed in compliance with Western interests. By depicting itself as a champion of human rights with global jurisdiction, the Western world can assert it has the right to delegitimise and economically strangle any state which does not comply with the Western-led order.

The CFR paper further emphasized the final goal of the Western Bloc—beyond denuclearisation:

> Finally, let us be clear about the essence of the North Korean nuclear threat: that threat is the North Korean government itself. So long as the real existing North Korean government holds power, that threat will continue. It is therefore incumbent upon the United States and its allies to plan for a successful Korean reunification that does not include the DPRK.[90]

The CFR was hardly alone among leading think tanks and prominent analysts in explicitly stating that the hostile agenda towards the DPRK went far beyond its deterrence program—and that the final goal for the Western Bloc was imposing change and remaking the Northeast Asian state in line with its own vision and interests. Head of the CIA's Korea Mission Centre Andrew Kim, for example, emphasized this shortly after the second Trump-Kim summit meeting in Hanoi in February 2019, stating: "The conflict is not only about denuclearization, it is also about redrawing the geopolitical and geo-economic map for North Korea."[91] Senior fellow at the Foreign Policy Research Institute, Yale University Professor Paul Bracken, similarly previously noted that U.S. moves to impose intrusive inspection and force denuclearisation: "must surely be seen as only the first moves to open up the entire North Korean state." He stated regarding this further objective:

> There are two "games" being played on the Korean peninsula. The first game is non-zero sum in character. It amounts to bargaining around a military and nuclear negotiation where the gains of one side do not necessarily come at the expense of the other. The second, and more important game, is zero sum. It is a game of control, and only one state can gain control of the entire Korean peninsula…it is the state-survival competition, rather than one concerning non-proliferation and arms control, that shapes the dynamics of inter-state relations among all affected parties.[92]

A further example came in September 2019, at a time of détente between Pyongyang and Washington and a pause in the former's strategic weapons testing, when the Center For Strategic and International Studies (CSIS) published a paper strongly calling for the United States to seek to impose further sanctions through the UNSC over allegations of Korean human rights abuses.[93] Mark Fitzpatrick, associate fellow and Executive Director of the International Institute for Strategic Studies (IISS) in North America and Director of the IISS Non-Proliferation and Disarmament Programme, was one of many influential figures who stressed that bringing about regime change and forced reunification of the Korean Peninsula under a Western aligned and Westphilian government was the final endgame of policy towards the state. He noted, however, that the Korean deterrence program and the nature of tensions meant regime change could no longer be an "immediate answer"—but rather was a long-term goal. In an influential paper titled "North Korea: Is Regime Change the Answer?" he stated: "There is only one happy ending to this long-running tragedy: unification of the Korean Peninsula as a democratic, free-enterprise-based republic that would be free of nuclear weapons."[94]

Somewhat in contradiction to his initial statement which showed the DPRK's abolition to be the end goal, Director Fitzpatrick claimed that Pyongyang—despite being so targeted—would be better off without nuclear weapons on the following basis: "The sad irony for North Korea is that the strategic-weapons programmes undermine regime survival because they hamper prospects for economic development. The trade, aid and investment from South Korea, Japan and the West that could help North Korea escape its poverty trap and dependence on China will not be forthcoming as long as Pyongyang wields a nuclear threat."[95] An assessment of the Western agenda towards the DPRK, nuclear armed or otherwise, as attested to by Fitzpatrick himself among others, indicates precisely the opposite. As has been repeatedly demonstrated by Western sanctions regimes against multiple other targets, it is highly unrealistic for the DPRK to expect anything near full sanctions relief, should it denuclearise.[96] The idea that the Western world would lift economic sanctions against and end pressure on the DPRK in exchange for anything less than a complete remaking of the country in the West's own image does not stand up to scrutiny. A dozen pretexts beyond nuclear weapons can and will be found for placing economic pressure on the state and denying it recognition. The prevailing Western position in this regard, rooted in ideology (see Chapter 18), seriously limits the extent to which a lasting détente can be reached.

North Korea for its part remains aware of this reality but, using its considerable leverage, it has continued to press for a de-escalation of hostilities, even if temporary, which is in the interests of both itself and the United States. While President Trump, a businessman and outsider to the American foreign policy establishment, may not personally believe in imposing regime change on North Korea, this remains the prevailing view from the intelligence community to the State Department to the members of his own administration. The fact that the long-term American goal is regime change is beyond question, but with military options realistically off the table at least for the foreseeable future the question remains to what extent the DPRK can press the United States to loosen economic sanctions in the short term.

A Change in World Order

The balance of power in North Korea's conflict with the United States has long been heavily influenced by the balance of forces globally. When the Soviet Union was a thriving power in the 1950s and closely allied with China, Pyongyang had enjoyed a position of considerable strength—its trading partners were some of the healthiest economies in the world and Soviet arms were generally equal to if not superior to their Western counterparts. The subsequent fall of the communist bloc, from the Sino-Soviet split to the stagnation of the Soviet economy and the USSR's eventual collapse, weakened Pyongyang's position considerably—leaving it extremely vulnerable. Its enduring of extreme pressure in the period of "New World Order" and unchallenged Western hegemony in the 1990s was a direct result. In much the same way, however, the shift in world order from the mid 2000s away from complete Western control bodes well for the DPRK and will increasingly place it in a strong position vis-à-vis the United States. From stronger Chinese and Russian diplomatic and economic support to an increasingly overstretched American military, the emergence of a world order in which the West is less powerful and less central in the global economy gives Pyongyang a much stronger chance of prevailing in the long term.

The emergence of the novel Coronavirus (COVID-19) in November 2019 was initially widely interpreted in the Western world as a tool to "correct" the balance of power globally by weakening China and other developed East Asian economies and thus comparatively strengthening the Western powers. President Trump initially appeared confident, stating on January 30 without further elaboration that the crisis would have "a very good ending" for the United States. U.S. Commerce Secretary Wilbur Ross stated on the same day that the fallout from the virus in China "will help to accelerate the return of jobs to North America" with millions at the time placed under lockdown in China.[97] Western publications from the *New York Times* to *Forbes* to the *Guardian* hailed the virus as bringing an end to decades of rapid Chinese economic growth and to its position as the world's leading manufacturing power.[98] While China locked down major cities, North Korea would close its borders on January 22, which was hailed in the West s bringing about an end to cross-border trade with China and Russia and thus isolating and placing pressure on the Korean economy as the Western powers had long sought. The *New York Times* on March 13 stated to this effect:

> President Trump has called the coronavirus "the invisible enemy." But when it comes to sanctions on North Korea, the pathogen may turn out to be his administration's most effective ally. North Korea's fear of coronavirus infection appears

> to have achieved what Mr. Trump's "maximum pressure" campaign against North Korean nuclear and missile work has not: choking the North's economy...[99]

As it turned out, rather than "rebalancing" the centre of world power towards the West by undermining East Asian rivals, the Western world would prove far less resilient to the crisis and would come to bear the brunt of its fallout. By April all of the top sufferers from the Coronavirus were Western states, with the U.S., Spain and Italy in particular seeing an uncontrolled spread and thousands of deaths per day. The U.S. would turn to seizing masks and ventilators from other countries,[100] as many of those in its own stores were found to be filled with rot or broken,[101] with CNN referring to the chaos as a "war for masks."[102] Across the Western world, only New Zealand could be called a success story in dealing with the virus with results remotely comparable to those in Northeast Asia. China, South Korea, Vietnam and others were meanwhile hailed by the World Health Organisation[103] and increasingly by global media as models for the world in responding to the crisis—which was attributed both to cultural factors, including high general hygiene standards, and to superior organisation.[104] Western media, inevitably, would praise responses in Asian territories with westernised political systems such as South Korea, Taiwan and Hong Kong while criticising or ignoring those in China and Vietnam—although the factors which had led to success in all of them were very similar. North Korea appeared to follow the general trend in Northeast Asia, and the fallout from the virus was minimal. While the state's report of no deaths from the virus were difficult to believe, the early closing of borders and the very limited deaths in other East Asian states—none in Vietnam and less than a dozen in Taiwan—made this claim at least somewhat credible. The country would carry out intensive testing in June and July, with the World Health Organisation confirming at the end of the second month that there were no cases of COVD-19.[105]

It was notable that not only were widespread calls for a temporary humanitarian relaxation of Western economic sanctions on target states such as the DPRK for the duration of the pandemic flatly rejected, with further rounds of sanctions even passed during it, but Western analysts continued to warn against allowing North Korea to access medical supplies. These warnings were made on the basis that, although it was admitted there was no evidence of a Korean biological weapons program, medical supplies could contribute to such a program if there turned out to be one.[106]

The Coronavirus crisis will very likely accelerate the trend towards a decline in American[107] and European[108] power relative to East Asia and China in particular, which in turn will cause a long term strengthening of the North Korean position. A weaker Western world will have far less leverage to pressure potential North Korean trading partners, from Taipei and Seoul to Delhi and Riyadh, not to trade with the DPRK. An end of the Western-led order will thus likely see the DPRK's integration into the world economy and even more impressive economic growth rates than those witnessed in the past. The West's ability to project power and fight wars as far away from their own territory as East Africa and East Asia was facilitated primarily by how much larger their economies were than those of rival powers—allowing them to bear the burdens of maintaining long supply lines and fighting so far from home while still retaining an advantage. As this economic disparity diminishes, the West will not be able to fight and win "away games" as easily—particularly in Northeast Asia. With the China's People's Liberation Army Navy expected to overtake the U.S. Navy before 2030 in overall combat capacity, and already far outmatching American assets deployed to Northeast Asia,[109] the Western world's capacity to bring war to the region is today lower than it has been since at least the 18th century. These trends are all strongly in Pyongyang's favour.

It is important not to overstate the impact of the Coronavirus crisis in bringing about a Western decline; that trend was already strong long before the crisis began, but the virus has done a great deal to expose the extent of the East Asian political and social advantages[110] which presage the region's emergence as the new centre of the global economy. When the Cold War ended the U.S. and wider Western world were certain that, with enough time and economic pressure and with sustained information warfare operations, North Korea would collapse, a Western economic and political system would be imposed and Western militaries would be able to base their soldiers north of the 38th parallel. With these hopes dashed, increasingly so from the mid 2010s as Pyongyang emerged from crisis and began to conspicuously modernise both its economy and its defences, the Northeast Asian state itself is now poised to prevail. The "tide of history," as it was widely referred to after the Soviet collapse, is now firmly on the DPRK's side as the balance of global power—both military and economic—shifts away from its adversaries.

Increasingly unable to achieve its objectives militarily or diplomatically, the western world's extreme reliance on economic sanctions and unsustainably rapid expansion of their use—threatening states from India and Indonesia to China and Russia—is in the long run expected to seriously limit their effectiveness while side-lining the West in global trade[111] and fuelling the rise in increasingly sophisticated means of evasion.[112] Meanwhile the growing availability of cost-effective high-end technologies from friendly non-Western sources such as China to raise living standards—from vertical farming to solar energy—are increasingly providing Pyongyang with a means of realising its long-frustrated goals for economic modernisation. Global economic and power trends thus strongly favour the DPRK's position.

The West's dominance in many key areas of high technology and its central position in the global economy have for decades been key to facilitating efforts to place extreme downward pressure on living standards in North Korea. As this dominance and centrality diminish rapidly a Korean economic boom can be expected. Signs of this boom—from the fast growing number of local consumer brands available to major construction and infrastructure projects—are evident today with conspicuous changes every year. Having survived the most extreme pressure at a time when the Western world was at the height of its power, and having considerably reduced the threat of attack from 2017 by developing nuclear-tipped ICBMs, North Korea's economic and security situations are set to only improve as its adversaries continue to decline and as non-Western actors play an increasingly dominant role in both the global economy and in determining the future of world order.

NOTES

1 'Lee Jong-seok calls for easing of sanctions under "snapback" provision,' *Hankyoreh,* January 21, 2020.
Bernama, 'Dr M hails Seoul's "Look South" policy; affirms rapprochement with Pyongyang,' *New Straits Times,* November 26, 2019.

2 Alexander, Harriet, 'Russia and China's calls to lift North Korea sanctions rejected by Mike Pompeo,' *Telegraph*, September 27, 2018.
Smith, Josh, 'U.S.-led pressure fractures as China, Russia push for North Korea sanctions relief,' *Reuters*, December 17, 2019.

3 'U.S. rejects sanctions relief for North Korea as Trump says he will 'take care of' Pyongyang's plans,' *Japan Times,* December 17, 2019.

4 Lederer, Edith M., 'Russia, China block UN from saying N Korea violated sanctions,' *Associated Press,* June 19, 2019.

5 Smith, Josh, 'U.S.-led pressure fractures as China, Russia push for North Korea sanctions relief,' *Reuters,* December 17, 2019.

6 Watanabe, Shin, 'Sanctions on North Korean migrant workers undermined by "interns,"' *Nikkei Asian Review,* November 15, 2019.
'N Korean workers in China and Russia look set to defy sanctions,' *Financial Times,* December 18, 2019.
7 'N. Korea, China demonstrate military ties in high-level talks,' *Yonhap*, August 18, 2019.
8 'Top. Chinese, North Korean generals meet in Beijing,' *Associated Press,* August 18, 2019.
9 Shin, Elizabeth, 'North Korean performers feted after China concert, state media says,' *UPI,* January 31, 2019.
Lee, Jeong-ho, 'What Xi Jinping attending North Korean pop concert signals to Donald Trump,' *South China Morning Post,* January 28, 2019.
10 Goldman, Russel, 'In Pictures: For Kim Jong-un and Xi Jinping, Small Talk and Mass Games,' *New York Times,* June 21, 2019.
11 'N. Korean foreign ministry advisor calls on Trump to make "bold decision,"' *Hankyoreh,* September 30, 2019.
12 Ibid.
13 Peltz, Jennifer, 'North Korea complains at UN about US "provocations,"' *Associated Press*, September 30, 2019.
14 Lee, Haye-ah, 'U.S. has never abandoned military options for N. Korea: Pentagon official,' *Yonhap*, December 5, 2019.
15 Panda, Ankit, 'North Korea Announces Completion of "Very Important" Test at Satellite Launching Ground,' *The Diplomat*, December 8, 2019.
16 Dilanian, Ken, 'Satellite photos show work on North Korean site linked to long-range missiles,' *NBC News,* December 22, 2019.
17 Nakamura, David, 'Senators ramp up pressure on Trump over North Korea, warning that his policy of engagement is "on the brink of failure",' *Washington Post,* December 18, 2019.
18 Fredericks, Bob, 'US spy planes fly near North Korea after "Christmas gift" missile threat,' *New York Post,* December 25, 2019.
19 Elbaum, Rachel, 'Christmas Day passes with no sign of "gift" that North Korea warned of,' *NBC News,* December 26, 2019.
Frazin, Rachel, 'Christmas Day passes with no sign of North Korea "gift" to US,' *The Hill,* December 25, 2019.
20 'North Korea's Kim holds military meeting as tension rises under looming deadline,' *Reuters,* December 22, 2019.
21 'North Korea's Kim convenes party plenary as deadline looms,' *Al Jazeera,* December 29, 2019.
22 Millward, David, 'Kim Jong-un says North Korea ending moratoriums on tests—and touts "new strategic weapon,"' *Telegraph*, January 1, 2020.
23 Martin, Timothy W., 'North Korea's Kim Gives U.S. End-of-Year Deadline on Nuclear Talks,' *Wall Street Journal,* April 13, 2019.
24 'North Korea suggests it might lift weapons test moratorium,' *Politico,* July 16, 2019.
25 Jo, Hak Chol, 'Basic Idea and Spirit of the 5th Plenary Meeting of the 7th C.C., WPK,' *Rodong Sinmun,* January 6, 2019.
26 'In June summit, Kim told Trump he won't make unilateral concession: N.K. TV,' *Yonhap,* January 10, 2020.
27 Manning, Ellen, 'US says it's ready for conflict with North Korea if necessary,' *Yahoo News*, January 3, 2020.
28 Read, Russ, 'World's most feared drone: CIA's MQ-9 Reaper killed Soleimani,' *Washington Examiner,* January 3, 2020.
29 'New details about Soleimani killing further undercut Trump's lies,' *Washington Post,* January 13, 2020.

30 Nakhoul, Samia, 'U.S. killing of Iran's second most powerful man risks regional conflagration,' *Reuters,* January 3, 2020.
Burgess, Sanya, 'The second most powerful person in Iran: A profile of Qassem Soleimani,' *Sky News,* January 8, 2020.
31 'New details about Soleimani killing further undercut Trump's lies,' *Washington Post,* January 13, 2020.
32 Tawfeeq, Mohammed and Humayun, Hira, 'Iraqi Prime Minister was scheduled to meet Soleimani the morning he was killed,' *CNN*, January 6, 2020.
33 Nebehay, Stephanie, 'U.N. expert deems U.S. drone strike on Iran's Soleimani an 'unlawful' killing,' *Reuters*, July 6, 2020.
Brennan, David, 'Killing Soleimani was a "Violation of National and International Law," Former Nuremberg War Crimes Prosecutor Says,' *News Week,* January 17, 2020.
'Consequences of America's Assassination of General Qasem Soleimani: Everything That Has Happened Since,' *Military Watch Magazine*, January 4, 2020.
Korso, Tim, 'Putin, Erdogan See US Actions in Persian Gulf, Soleimani Assassination as Illegal—Lavrov,' *Sputnik*, January 8, 2020.
34 Gamp, Joseph, 'Iran has a 'shockingly strong' war crimes case against Trump over Soleimani's killing, NATO military attache warns,' *The Sun,* January 15, 2020.
35 Pamuk, Humeyra and Landay, Jonathan, 'Pompeo says Soleimani killing part of new strategy to deter U.S. foes,' *Reuters,* January 14, 2020.
36 Seligman, Lara, 'Petraeus Says Trump May Have Helped "Reestablish Deterrence" by Killing Suleimani,' *Foreign Policy,* January 3, 2020.
37 Levenson, Eric, 'Trump's threatened attack on Iranian cultural sites could be a war crime if carried out,' *CNN,* January 6, 2020.
38 'US Seizes Ship Carrying Zeolite for Production of Oxygen Concentrator for Coronavirus Patients in Iran,' *Fars News,* August 5, 2020.
'Freedom of Navigation? Why is America Seizing Civilian Tankers in International Waters,' *Military Watch Magazine,* August 16, 2020.
39 Borowiec, Steven, 'As Iran-US drama plays out, North Korea leader Kim Jong Un takes notes,' *Channel News Asia,* January 11, 2020.
Friedman, Uri, 'A New Nuclear Era Is Coming,' *The Atlantic,* January 9, 2020.
Chandran, Nyshka, 'What do tense US-Iranian relations mean for China, North Korea?,' *Al Jazeera,* January 13, 2020.
Johnson, Jesse, 'How the U.S. killing of a top Iranian general rekindled Kim Jong Un's worst fears,' *Japan Times,* January 7, 2020.
40 'Pompeo calls Iran more destabilizing than N. Korea,' *France 24*, February 14, 2019.
41 Panda, Ankit, 'Trump-Kim Relationship No Longer Sufficient for US-North Korea Diplomacy: NK Official,' *The Diplomat,* January 14, 2020.
42 Berlinger, Joshua, 'North Korea says US "deceived" Pyongyang on nuclear talks after Trump sends Kim birthday letter,' *CNN*, January 11, 2020.
43 'Kim Jong-un makes no mention of inter-Korean relations in 2020 vision,' *Hankyoreh,* January 2, 2020.
44 'South Korea's Moon seeks Kim Jong Un visit to Seoul,' *Bankok Post,* January 7, 2020.
45 'South Korean president takes heart from Trump's birthday wishes to North Korea's Kim,' *Reuters,* January 14, 2020.
46 Kim, Hyung-Jin, 'SKorea's Moon could seek exemption of UN sanctions on NKorea,' *Associated Press,* January 14, 2020.
47 'South Korean Leader Considers Letting Its Tourists Visit North Korea,' *New York Times,* January 14, 2020.
48 Joyce, Kathleen, 'South Korea president's plane blacklisted by US after North Korea flight, reports say,' *Fox News,* December 14, 2018.

49 O'Carroll, Chad, 'How a massive influx of Chinese visitors is changing North Korean tourism,' *NK News,* November 1, 2019.
'North Korea enjoying tourism boom after summit between Kim Jong-un and Moon Jae-in in April,' *South China Morning Post,* July 29, 2018.
Jang, Seul Gi, 'Has thriving Chinese tourism emboldened North Korea?,' *Daily NK,* October 28, 2019.
O'Carroll, Chad, 'As Chinese tourism to North Korea soars, local operators feel the strain,' *NK News,* October 31, 2019.

50 'North Korea's new beach resort will soon be ready for tourists,' *South China Morning Post,* January 17, 2019.

51 Choe, Sang-Hun, 'North Korea Touts New Resort, Seeking to Blunt U.N. Sanctions,' *New York Times*, December 3, 2019.

52 Choe, Sang-Hun, 'Kim Jong-un Orders "Shabby" South Korean Hotels in Resort Town Destroyed,' *New York Times*, October 23, 2019.

53 Zwirko, Colin, 'Qingdao Airlines awaiting approval to run three new routes to Pyongyang,' *NK News,* January 16, 2020.
Zwirko, Colin, 'North Korean airline begins twice-weekly Pyongyang-Macau route following delay,' *NK News,* October 1, 2019.

54 Marcus, Lilit and Seo, Yoonjung, 'South Korea says it may be open to solo travel for its citizens to North Korea,' *CNN,* January 15, 2019.

55 'Thanksgiving Warning: North Korea Confirms Successful Test of Superheavy Rocket Artillery System,' *Military Watch Magazine,* November 29, 2019.

56 Smith, Josh, 'North Korea fires more missiles than ever amid coronavirus outbreak,' *Reuters,* March 28, 2020.
Dempsey, Joseph, 'Assessment of the March 9 KN-25 Test Launch,' *38 North,* March 10, 2020.

57 Makowsky, Peter, 'North Korea's Sinpo South Shipyard: Probable Ejection Testing,' *38 North,* April 8, 2020.

58 Lee, Haye-ah, 'N. Korea may be ready to test more advanced ICBM: U.S. general,' *Yonhap,* March 13, 2020.
Cotton, Shea, 'Expect a surge in North Korean missile tests, and of greater range,' *Defense News,* March 10, 2020.

59 Shorrock, Tim, 'Washington Hawks Are Softening Their Hard Line on Sanctions Against North Korea,' *The Nation,* March 5, 2020.

60 Ibid.

61 Nichols, Michelle, 'Europeans, Britain raise North Korea missile launches at U.N. Security Council,' *Reuters,* March 5, 2020.
Lederer, Edith M., '6 European nations condemn North Korean missile launches,' *Associated Press,* April 1, 2020.
Wong, Edward and Choe, Sang-Hun, 'Trump Officials Block U.N. Meeting on Human Rights Abuses in North Korea,' *New York Times,* December 9, 2019.
Lynch, Colum and Gramer, Robbie, 'Desperate to Save Diplomacy, White House Blocks U.N. Meeting on North Korean Atrocities,' *Foreign Policy,* December 9, 2019.

62 Cox, Jeff, 'Second-quarter GDP plunged by worst-ever 32.9% amid virus-induced shutdown,' *CNBC,* July 30, 2020.
Cox, Jeff, 'Goldman says downturn will be 4 times worse than housing crisis, then an 'unprecedented' recovery,' *CNBC,* April 14, 2020.

63 'COVID-19 to Plunge Global Economy into Worst Recession since World War II,' *The World Bank,* June 8, 2020.

64 Ahn, Sung-mi, 'Trump says open to third summit with Kim: report,' *The Korea Herald,* July 8, 2020.

Kim, Jeongmin, 'U.S. committed to renewed diplomacy with North Korea, envoy says,' NK News, July 9, 2020.

65 Johnson, Jesse, 'North Korea says U.S. is seeking December nuclear talks, warns of "trick" to buy time,' *Japan Timies*, November 15, 2019.

66 Zwirko, Colin, 'North Korean leader's sister rules out another "useless" summit with U.S.,' *NK News,* July 9, 2019.

'New Department Director General of DPRK Foreign Ministry for Negotiations with U.S. Issues Statement,' *KCNA*, March 30, 2020.

Hotham, Oliver, 'North Korea has no interest in more talks with the U.S., senior diplomat says,' *NK News,* July 4, 2020.

67 'North Korea says no more photo ops for Donald Trump,' *Nikkei Asian Review*, November 19, 2019.

Taylor, Adam, 'North Korea says it doesn't want Trump meeting if it's just something to brag about,' *Washington Post*, November 18, 2019.

68 'Press Statement by Kim Yo Jong, First Vice Department Director of Central Committee of Workers' Party of Korea, *KCNA*, July 10, 2020.

69 Brunnstrom, David, 'Getting North Korea to Give Up Nuclear Weapons Probably "Lost Cause": U.S. Spy Chief,' *Reuters*, October 26, 2016.

70 Lindsey Graham on Twitter, 'North Korea is the ultimate outlier in world order. It is a country built around the philosophy of the divinity of a family. And the person who's inherited the mantle is, on a good day, unstable,' December. 15, 2017.

71 Mullen, Mike and Nunn, Sam and Mount, Adam, *A Sharper Choice on North Korea: Engaging China for a Stable Northeast Asia*, Council on Foreign Relations, Independent Task Force Report No. 74, September 2016 (p. xiii).

72 Kazianis, Harry J., 'America Must Move Past Its "Sputnik" Moment on North Korea—Or Else,' *National Interest,* March 4, 2019.

73 Oberdorfer, Don, *The Two Koreas: A Contemporary History*, Boston, Addison-Wesley, 1997 (p. 352).

74 'US considers intermediate-range missiles in Asia,' *Financial Times,* August 3, 2019.

Karlik, Evan, 'Where Will the US Base Intermediate-Range Missiles in the Pacific?,' *The Diplomat,* August 30, 2019.

'Rumors of S. Korea hosting the US' intermediate-range missiles are hopefully false,' *Hankyoreh,* January 2, 2020.

75 Itzkowitz Shifrinson, Joshua R., 'Op-Ed: Russia's got a point: The U.S. broke a NATO promise,' *Los Angeles Times,* May 30, 2016.

76 'Gaddafi's son: Libya like McDonald's for NATO—fast war as fast food,' *RT,* Interview with Saif Al Islam Published on July 1, 2011.

77 'African migrants raped & murdered after being sold in Libyan "slave markets"—UN,' *RT*, April 11, 2017.

Osborne, Samuel, 'Libya: African refugees being sold at "regular public slave auctions,"' *The Independent*, April 11, 2017.

78 Karami, Arash, 'Rafsanjani missile tweet draws fire from Khamenei,' *Al Monitor*, March 31, 2016.

79 Toosi, Nahal, 'Nixed Iran nuclear deal looms over Trump's North Korea talks,' *Politico,* June 10, 2018.

Schwarz, Jon, 'Trump Intel Chief: North Korea Learned From Libya War to "Never" Give Up Nukes,' *The Intercept*, July 29, 2017.

80 'North Korea cites "tragedy" of countries that give up nuclear programs,' *Reuters,* February 21, 2013.

'North Korea cites Muammar Gaddafi's "destruction" in nuclear test defence,' *Reuters*, January 9, 2016.

81 Bandow, Doug, 'Thanks to Libya, North Korea Might Never Negotiate on Nuclear Weapons,' *The National Interest*, September 2, 2015.

82 French, Howards W., 'A Nation At War: Nuclear Standoff; North Korea Says Its Arms Will Deter U.S. Attack,' *New York Times*, April 7, 2003.

83 'Gaddafi's son: Libya like McDonald's for NATO—fast war as fast food,' *RT,* Interview with Saif Al Islam Published on July 1, 2011.

84 Schwarz, Jon, 'Trump Intel Chief: North Korea Learned From Libya War to "Never" Give Up Nukes,' *The Intercept*, July 29, 2017.

85 Snaith, Emma, 'Trump claim Obama begged for Kim Jong Un meeting dismissed by former US intelligence chief: "I don't know where he's getting that,"' *Independent,* July 1, 2019.

86 Goodenough, Patrick, 'Zarif: Iran May Withdraw From Nuclear Non-Proliferation Treaty,' *CNS News*, April 29, 2019.

'If nuclear issue is referred to U.N., Iran will pull out of the NPT: Iran foreign minister,' *Reuters*, January 20, 2020.

'Iran Threatens Withdrawal from Nuclear Non-Proliferation Treaty Unless West Reduces Pressure,' *Military Watch Magazine,* February 10, 2019.

87 Bechtol Jr., Bruce E., *North Korean Military Proliferation in the Middle East and Africa,* Lexington, University Press of Kentucky, 2018 (pp. 27, 92–94).

88 Cox, Christopher Nixon and Arnold, James, 'Threatening foreign states with sanctions can backfire,' *The Hill*, November 24, 2019.

89 Mullen, Mike and Nunn, Sam and Mount, Adam, *A Sharper Choice on North Korea: Engaging China for a Stable Northeast Asia*, Council on Foreign Relations, Independent Task Force Report No. 74, September 2016.

90 Ibid. (p. 46).

91 Kim, Andrew, *Remarks delivered at Stanford's Shorenstein Asia-Pacific Research Center,* February 22, 2019 (https://aparc.fsi.stanford.edu/news/transcript-andrew-kim-north-korea-denuclearization-and-us-dprk-diplomacy).

92 Bracken, Paul, The North Korean nuclear program as a problem of state survival, in: Macck, Andrew, *Asian Flashpoint: Security and the Korean Peninsula,* Canberra, Allen and Unwin, 1990

93 King, Robert R., 'New U.S. Ambassador to the UN Should Press for Security Council Discussion of North Korean Human Rights,' *CSIS,* September 5, 2019.

94 Fitzpatrick, Mark, 'North Korea: Is Regime Change the Answer?,' *Survival*, vol. 55, no. 3, May 29, 2013.

95 Ibid.

96 'U.S. Threatens Oil Embargo on Caracas: Venezuela's Example Sends a Strong Message to North Korea,' *Military Watch Magazine,* February 15, 2018.

97 Staracqualursi, Veronica and Davis, Richard, 'Commerce secretary says coronavirus will help bring jobs to North America,' *CNN,* January 30, 2020.

98 Bradsher, Keith, 'Coronavirus Could End China's Decades-Long Economic Growth Streak,' *New York Times,* March 16, 2020.

Rapoza, Kenneth, 'Coronavirus Could Be The End Of China As A Global Manufacturing Hub,' *Forbes,* March 1, 2020.

Davidson, Helen, 'Coronavirus deals China's economy a "bigger blow than global financial crisis,"' *The Guardian,* March 16, 2020.

99 Koettl, Christoph, 'Coronavirus Is Idling North Korea's Ships Achieving What Sanctions Did Not,' *New York Times,* March 26, 2020.

100 'US Seizes Ventilators Destined for Barbados,' *Telesur,* April 5, 2020.

Willsher, Kim and Holmes, Oliver and McKernan, Bethan and Tondo, Lorenzo, 'US hijacking mask shipments in rush for coronavirus protection,' *The Guardian,* April 3, 2020.

101 Chandler, Kim, 'Some states receive masks with dry rot, broken ventilators,' *Associated Press,* April 4, 2020.

102 Lister, Tim and Shukla, Sebastian and Bobille, Fanny, 'Coronavirus sparks a "war for masks" as accusations fly,' *CNN,* April 3, 2020.

103 'WHO Says China Actions Blunted Virus Spread, Leading to Drop,' *Bloomberg,* February 24, 2020.
Nebehay, Stephanie and Farge, Emma, 'WHO lauds Chinese response to virus, says world "at important juncture,"' *Reuters,* January 29, 2020.
Lau, Stuart, 'Coronavirus: WHO head stands by his praise for China and Xi Jinping on response to outbreak,' *South China Morning Post,* February 13, 2020.
104 Inkster, Ian, 'In the battle against the coronavirus, East Asian societies and cultures have the edge,' *South China Morning Post,* April 10, 2020.
Cha, Victor, 'South Korea Offers a Lesson in Best Practices,' *Foreign Affairs,* April 10, 2020.
'Once the biggest outbreak outside of China, South Korean city reports zero new coronavirus cases,' *Reuters,* April 10, 2020.
Graaham-Harrison, Emma, 'Coronavirus: how Asian countries acted while the west dithered,' *The Guardian,* March 21, 2020.
Magnier, Mark, 'Asians in the US least likely to get coronavirus infection despite racist assumptions of many, data suggests,' *South China Morning Post,* May 18, 2020.
Kim, Youn-Jong, 'Kimchi protects against COVID-19, a study says,' *Donga,* July 17, 2020.
105 Kim, So-hyun, 'N. Korea has zero confirmed cases of COVID-19: WHO,' *Korea Herald,* July 21, 2020.
Kim, Jeongmin, 'North Korea conducted more than 1,000 COVID-19 tests: All results "negative",' *NK News,* July 21, 2020.
Kim, Jeongmin, 'North Korea has now tested 922 people for COVID-19: World Health Organization,' *NK News,* June 30, 2020.
106 Ralph, Elizabeth, 'How Covid-19 Could Give Kim Jong Un a Doomsday Weapon,' *Politico,* July 28, 2020.
107 Blyth, Mark, 'The U.S. Economy Is Uniquely Vulnerable to the Coronavirus,' *Foreign Affairs,* March 30, 2020.
Schulze, Elizabeth, 'The coronavirus recession is unlike any economic downturn in US history,' *CNBC,* April 8, 2020.
Schwartz, Nelson D., 'Coronavirus Recession Looms, Its Course "Unrecognizable,"' *New York Times,* April 1, 2020.
Davies, Rob, 'Coronavirus means a bad recession—at least—says JP Morgan boss,' *The Guardian,* April 6, 2020.
Lowrey, Annie, 'Millennials Don't Stand a Chance,' *The Atlantic,* April 13, 2020.
Holcombe, Madeline, 'Expert warns the US is approaching "one of the most unstable times in the history of our country",' *CNN,* July 11, 2020.
108 Neinaber, Michael and Wagner, Rene, 'German economy could shrink by as much as 20% due to coronavirus: Ifo,' *Reuters,* March 25, 2020.
Horobin, William, 'French Economy Shrinks Most Since WW II,' *Bloomberg,* April 8, 2020.
Sylvers, Eric, 'Italy's Economic Pain Shows Burden of National Coronavirus Lockdowns,' *Wall Street Journal,* April 7, 2020.
Mammone, Andrea, 'The European Union will be destroyed by its immoral handling of the coronavirus crisis,' *The Independent,* April 1, 2020.
Rohac, Dalibor, 'Coronavirus Could Break the EU,' *Politico,* March 16, 2020.
Crisp, James, 'Will the coronavirus crisis tear the European Union apart?,' *Telegraph,* March 21, 2020.
Chapman, Ben, 'UK plunges into deepest recession on record, as economy shrinks 20 per cent in second quarter,' *The Independent,* August 12, 2020.
109 Goldstein, Lyle J., 'Naval Gazing as the World Economy Goes Up in Flames,' *National Interest,* March 29, 2020.

The Military Balance, Volume 120, International Institute for Strategic Studies, 2020.
Evans, Michael, 'US "would lose any war" fought in the Pacific with China,' *The Times,* May 16, 2020.

110 Chalabi, Mona, 'Coronavirus is revealing how broken America's economy really is,' *The Guardian,* April 6, 2020.
Wallace-Wells, David, 'America Is Broken,' *New York Magazine,* March 12, 2020.
Inkster, Ian, 'In the battle against the coronavirus, East Asian societies and cultures have the edge,' *South China Morning Post,* April 10, 2020.
Reuters on Twitter, 'The first coronavirus case in the U.S. and South Korea was detected on the same day. By late January, Seoul had medical companies starting to work on a diagnostic test—one was approved a week later. Today, the U.S. isn't even close to meeting test demand,' March 18, 2020.

111 Seib, Gerald F., 'The Risks in Overusing America's Big Economic Weapon,' *Wall Street Journal*, May 13, 2019.
Gilsinan, Kathy, 'A Boom Time for U.S. Sanctions,' *The Atlantic,* May 3, 2019.
Burns, William J. and Lew, Jacob J., 'U.S. Treasure Secretary Jacob J., Lew on the Evolution of Sanctions and Lessons for the Future,' *Carnegie Endowment for International Peace,* March 30, 2016.
'U.S. Treasury Warns Sanctions "Overreach" Will Lower Dollar's Status,' *Radio Free Europe,* March 31, 2016.
Ignatius, David, 'A grim warning against America's overuse of sanctions,' *Washington Post,* March 29, 2016.

112 Gale, Alastair, 'After Losing Cargo Ship to U.S., North Korea Found Another in Vietnam,' *Wall Street Journal,* March 5, 2020.
Gibney, James, 'Trump's Sanctions Are Losing Their Bite,' *Bloomberg*, April 2, 2020.
Brett, Jason, 'Trend Continues For Countries Looking To Evade U.S. Sanctions Using Crypto,' *Forbess,* January 29, 2020.
'Russia, China & India to set up alternative to SWIFT payment system to connect 3 billion people,' *RT,* October 28, 2019.
Lee, Liz, 'Muslim nations consider gold, barter trade to beat sanctions,' *Reuters,* December 21, 2019.
'Iranian businesses devise creative ways to evade Trump sanctions,' *Financial Times,* February 21, 2019.

Part Four

NEW BATTLEFRONTS AND THE EVOLVING NATURE OF CONFLICT

Chapter 18
A CLASH OF IDEOLOGIES:
THE RESILIENCE OF NORTH KOREA

Ideological Foundations of the Korean Republic

To fully comprehend the nature of North Korea's conflict with the United States and the wider Western world, and the persistent underlying causes of both Western hostility towards Pyongyang and the DPRK's ability to withstand immense Western pressure, an assessment of ideology remains critical. This includes both the ideological and philosophical roots of the DPRK, and the ideological basis for the predominant Western paradigms for viewing the country. The nature of both ideologies has been a leading cause of the West's hostility towards the East Asian state since its formation, and its application of massive pressure on Pyongyang to either westernise its society, politics and ideology or to collapse entirely. North Korea's almost unique resilience to such pressure is also largely shaped by its ideological roots.

During the Cold War many hardline communist groups saw the triumph of Marxism—or of their specific interpretation of Marxism—as a historical inevitability. As U.S. President Richard Nixon noted in his memoirs: "Marxism-Leninism has a determinist view of history. Its adherents believe that history will inevitably lead to world communism and that it is their job to hurry history along. By viewing themselves in this way, they sidestep all considerations of morality because all the crimes they commit are simply deemed necessary for the furtherance of history." He further noted that this ideology "inured" many of its adherents to "heartless cruelty" as a result of this view of the historical inevitability of their triumph.[1] While this was true of a number of the more radical communist figures, it was equally if not more true of the Western-led order which emerged in the 1990s under a fundamentalist ideology which saw global westernization politically, socially, economically and ideologically as a historical inevitability.[2] In contrast to the global trend towards westernization at the time, North Korea's resilience marked it as a prime target—"the country we love to hate" as some Western analysts described it [3]—and the antithesis of the Westphilian client state.

Much like hardline Marxists viewed their own system, in the West the course of history and the nature of humankind were seen to guarantee the triumph of Western economic and political ideologies. As hardline Marxists emphasized the destruction of capitalism, so too did the ideology of the West necessitate the destruction of all rival systems, whether the developmentalist state capitalism of South Korea and the other Asian Tiger economies in 1997[4]—referred to gleefully by neoliberal economists as the "collapse of a second Berlin Wall"[5]—or the nationalist state in northern Korea, which rejected the Western-centrism and perceived injustice of the new order.

The fall of all alternative political and economic systems, total triumph and imposition of the Western way globally and instating of a Western-centered and Western-led world order was widely seen in much of Europe and North America—from policymakers down to the individual as inevitable—and in many circles it still is today. This worldview stemmed from what prominent Singaporean Professor and foreign policy expert Kishore Mahbubani referred to as the West's "messianic desire" to reshape the world in its own image.[6] It is on the basis of this ideology that the DPRK's survival is referred to as "defeating the pattern of history," with its collapse widely and consistently predicted by Western intelligence analysts, think tank specialists, scholars, and officials both civilian and military among others.[7] Not only is Western triumph seen as inevitable, but it was also but it was also portrayed as benevolent meaning those actors such as the North Korean leadership which stood in its way and offered alternatives to full westernisation necessarily labelled malign actors. As Oxford University international relations expert Tom Fowdy observed regarding Western liberal ideology specifically, there existed "the simple binary within Western political thought that liberalism represents empirical truth and authenticity, and that those who purport to oppose it represent deception and inauthentic, malign purposes. In other words, nobody can seriously disagree with their ideology without being held a suspect to some sort of manipulation, evil intent, or grand scheme."[8]

Predictions of the DPRK's eventual certain destruction and furthering of the global triumph of the West have long dominated and continue to dominate Western discourse. Commander of U.S. and UN forces in South Korea General Garry Luck informed the U.S. Congress in the mid 1990s that the DPRK's disintegration was inevitable, a conclusion he was very far from alone in reaching.[9] In 2003 Assistant Secretary of Defence for International Security Policy and Senior Advisor on the North Korea policy review Ashton Carter cited the course of history and human nature as incompatible with the Korean state, and referred to its destruction as a process to "hasten this regime on in history."[10] More recently in 2015 Jamie Metzl, a prominent Senior Fellow of the Atlantic Council and former member of the U.S. National Security Council, State Department, and Senate Foreign Relations Committee, referring to the state as an "abomination" and "historical relic," stated that North Korea's disappearance and integration into the Western-led order was inevitable. He predicted the state's disappearance within a decade.[11] Fellow at the Ethics and Public Policy Center Pascal Emanuel Gobry, opening with the statement that "North Korea is easily the world's most demonic regime," came to the same conclusion that year.[12]

The Brookings Institute and the RAND Corporation were among many prominent think tanks which published several articles and papers stating that the DPRK's collapse was an inevitability. [13] The opening line of a prominent article from the former prophetically stated: "regime change in North Korea is inevitable"—adding that when this occurred it would require U.S. boots on the ground in the country.[14] Thus not only was the collapse inevitable, but an American military presence north of the 38th Parallel, so stringently opposed for 70 years and so brutal last time it occurred, was also supposedly a historical certainty. Dr. Parag Khanna, a prominent member of the Council on Foreign Relations and the International Institute for Strategic Studies, stated in March 2019 at a think tank event attended by the writer that whether North Korea was invaded and regime change brought about by force in a major war, or whether the U.S. forced an opening up of the country to impose regime change and eventual assimilation into the ROK by other means, whichever option was chosen would in ten years be inconsequential, as the inevitable result would be the same. Within a decade "what had once been North Korea will not be there anymore."[15] The same line of thought pervades in Western publications from *Bloomberg*, which called for the execution of the country's leadership to make the world a better place,[16] to *CNN*[17] to the *World Policy Journal*.[18]

North Korea, although influenced by communist ideology, was considered by U.S. sources to be one of the more ideologically moderate of the communist states, as perhaps best demonstrated by the good treatment of landlords even during the height of its revolution where in China, Vietnam, Eastern Europe and elsewhere executions were commonplace.[19] This moderation has not translated into compromises on the right to self-defense and sovereignty, in which Pyongyang has always been unyielding since the Korean War, but it means that the state has shown no ideological fundamentalisms regarding its own manifest destiny or the historical inevitability of a world order under its control or under a socialist system. Indeed, even in its calls for reunification with South Korea, Pyongyang has not called for imposition of its own economic or political systems but for a federation in which each Korean state would be free to conduct economic and domestic political affairs as they see fit.[20] President Kim Il Sung reiterated this point multiple times, stating on one occasion: "Our Party considers that the most realistic and reasonable way to reunify the country independently, peacefully and on the principle of great national unity is to draw the north and the south together into a federal state, leaving the ideas and social systems existing in the north and south as they are."[21] A similar line has been put forward repeatedly under subsequent administrations.[22] In January 2019, amid an apparent détente between the Koreas, Pyongyang reiterated: "It is necessary to pool [our] wisdom and efforts to make a nationwide proposal for reunification in line with the will and demand of the nation on a basis of recognizing ideologies and systems existing in the North and the South and allowing them."[23]

It is notable that ROK President Roh Tae Woo's 1989 "Korean Commonwealth" proposal, which envisaged coequal North-South institutions to govern the peninsula, was accepted by the DPRK under President Kim Il Sung as a basis on which to hold negotiations for reunification. Later ROK President Kim Dae Jung's plan for a loose confederation was similarly accepted under Kim Jong Il, demonstrating that Pyongyang had little issue with a unification plan even under ROK proposed frameworks so long as its sovereignty was respected.[24] Thus while the West has demonstrated an intense "messianic desire" to reshape the world, there are by contrast no signs of North Korean intentions to infringe on the sovereignty of others, including South Korea's own right to maintain its social, political and economic system.

While the DPRK has demonstrated its willingness to cooperate with the United States and the Western powers so long as demands did not infringe on its sovereignty, the Western world cannot tolerate the state's existence—an "abomination" and an anomaly in a world where its influence is near universal. A highly influential 2016 paper by the Council on Foreign Relations was one of the multiple sources attesting to this, stating: "Finally, let us be clear about the essence of the North Korean nuclear threat: that threat is the North Korean government itself. So long as the real existing North Korean government holds power, that threat will continue. It is therefore incumbent upon the United States and its allies to plan for a successful Korean reunification that does not include the DPRK." [25] Continued pressure on Pyongyang to this end is widely portrayed in the West not only as historically inevitable, but as a moral imperative.[26]

Key to North Korea's success in resisting decades of often extreme Western pressure, and complementing its considerable military capabilities, the DPRK's lack of internal weakness or divisions and the united front presented by its population have made fomenting unrest from within extremely difficult. While destabilisation strategies have proven devastating for Western adversaries elsewhere, from Libya and Syria to Yugoslavia and Afghanistan, they have repeatedly failed to yield results in Korea. Ashton Carter, who was heavily involved in the Clinton administration's negotiations with the DPRK, stated that while the administration had favoured imposing regime change from the outset, the means of bringing it about had proven elusive. He stated to this effect in an interview in 2003: "We looked very hard at the possibility of, was there some way that we could undermine the North Korean regime or get rid of it? We looked very hard at that. That didn't look very promising, and ultimately we set that aside. But it's worth asking why."[27] Carter later recalled: "I looked at the possibility of regime change in some detail, and short of conquest…there is little evidence indeed of a situation or a crack in the armour of the North Korean regime into which we could stick a crowbar and bring them down. There's no evidence that I'm aware of that a strategy of unhorsing the regime is a realistic strategy. It's a hope. The president can hope that, if he wants. But hope and a strategy are two different things. You have to have a plan for how you're going to achieve this."[28] This was supplemented by other Western sources which observed that the lack of factionalism within the Korean government ensured stability and undermined a potential avenue through which its adversaries could seek to destabilise it.[29]

Noting the strengths of the DPRK's ideology and its resulting resilience to American efforts to force change, Carter stated: "The North Koreans see themselves as a miniature Soviet Union. They believe in socialism. But they believe even more in being proud Koreans, and 'proud Koreans' means, in their view of history, that they've always been kicked around, by the Chinese, the Japanese, the Russians, the Americans. That causes their ideology to be one of absolute and total and iron self-reliance, as they call it… It's a very tough nut to crack when the definition of their state is one that is arrayed against a hostile world." He continued regarding the unified nature of society and the impacts of three generations of political education: "There was never a conspiracy, never a tremendous fear…children in North Korea have several hours of political education a day. Their parents did, and their grandparents did… If you take the other extreme, which is Afghanistan, where you go in and you stir the pot a little bit and everybody rises up against the Taliban—there [is] no evidence that we could deduce that we had any such prospect in North Korea."[30]

A number of factors have contributed to the DPRK's resilience, and the small state's ability to withstand immense pressure during more than 70 years of conflict with the world's leading superpower. Primarily, it is critical to recognize that the state represents first and foremost not the interests of global communism or any other political or economic ideology—but rather perceives itself as the protector of the Korean nation and its future. Ashton Carter's statement alluded to this, when he said: "They believe in socialism. But they believe even more in being proud Koreans." While leftist revolutions in the Soviet Union and China did at certain stages place ideology above national identity, and saw attacks on the cultural heritage of both these nations and an attempt to purge what was traditionally "Russian" or "Chinese" about them, such ideologically driven purges of national heritage never occurred and were always unthinkable in the DPRK. While the Soviet Union in its own revolution destroyed valuable cultural heritage associated with the Orthodox faith[31] and China's cultural revolution saw Confucian and other philosophical and religious treasures lost,[32] North Korea long protected such heritage and allocated significant funding to its restoration after the Korean War. A prominent example is the Pohyonsa Buddhist temple, which dates back to the 11th century and was allocated priority state funding for reconstruction after the Korean War after being targeted by American bombings. The intricacy and quality to which it was rebuilt, according to South Korean experts the writer consulted, exceeds that of temples reconstructed in South Korea and serves as an indication of the value Pyongyang has ascribed to its cultural heritage. This contrasted sharply with much of the rest of the communist world where in revolutionary periods such sites and heritage were shunned and at times destroyed.

From its formation North Korea's ideology has been influenced by and has assimilated parts of the country's traditional culture, Confucianism in particular, in a way that few if any other ideologies have in communist states. Premier Kim Il Sung's reformism *Juche* speech on December 28, 1955, which outlined the country's future ideological position to the propagandists and agitators of the Korean Workers' Party, notably stressed the need to draw inspiration from national culture, history and traditions for the ideological work of the Korean revolution. While no mention was made of Marx, Engels, Lenin, Mao or even Stalin, the Korean leader warned against the "negation of Korean history" with "foreign ideas," emphasizing above all else the importance of a Korean national identity. While the Stalinist economic model, which had rapidly industrialised the Soviet Union, would be largely adopted, this would be interpreted and applied in a way that was compatible with Korea's own culture. As the Korean leader envisioned, the "essence" and "principles" of communist ideology would be "creatively applied" in line with the needs of the Korean nation—the former would bend to the latter rather than vice versa. He thus strongly criticised "dogmatism and formalism" in ideological work and advised: "There can be no set principle that we must follow the Soviet fashion. Some advocate the Soviet way and others the Chinese but is it not high time to work out or own?"[33] Korean nationalism has thus remained central to North Korea's revolution from its inception.

Regarding the ideological foundations of the Korean state, Premier Kim stated:

> To make revolution in Korea we must know Korean history and geography and know the customs of the Korean people. Only then is it possible to educate our people in a way that suits them and to inspire in them an ardent love for their native place and their motherland. It is of paramount importance to study, and widely publicize among the working people, the history of our country and of our people's struggle, before anything else. This is not the first time we have raised this question. As far back as the autumn of 1945, that is, immediately after liberation, we emphasized the need to study the history of our nation's struggle and to inherit its fine traditions. Only when our people are educated in the history of their own struggle and its traditions, can their national

> pride be stimulated and the broad masses be aroused to the revolutionary struggle.

Criticising the Soviet Koreans in the country's government, most notably Vice Premier Pak Chang Ok who was firmly aligned with Moscow, for disregarding Korea's unique cultural identity and attempting to impose a blanket Soviet model on the country, the Korean leader further stated: "Many of our functionaries are ignorant of our country's history, and so do not strive to discover and carry forward its fine traditions. Unless this is corrected, it will lead, in the long run, to the negation of Korean history." Kim Il Sung and the ideology he sanctioned were not internationalist, instead placing the Korean nation first and socialist ideology second. Highly wary of foreign influences which infringed on the identity of the Korean nation, Premier Kim stated when addressing party members:

> What assets do we have for carrying on the revolution if the history of our people's struggle is denied? If we cast aside all these things, it would mean that our people did nothing. There are many things to be proud of in our country's peasant movements of the past. In recent years, however, no articles dealing with them have appeared in our newspapers. In schools, too, there is a tendency to neglect lectures on Korean history. During the war the curricula of the Central Party School allotted 160 hours a year to the study of world history, but very few hours were given to Korean history. This is how things were done in the Party school, and so it quite natural that our functionaries are ignorant of their own country's history. In our propaganda and agitation work, there are numerous examples of extolling only foreign things, while slighting our own.
>
> Once I visited a People's Army vacation home, where a picture of the Siberian steppe was hung. That landscape probably pleases the Russians. But the Korean people prefer the beautiful scenery of our own country. There are beautiful mountains such as Mts. Kumgang San and Myohyang San in our country; there are clear streams, the blue sea with its rolling waves and the fields with ripening crops. If we are to inspire in our People's Army men a love for their native

> place and their country, we must show them many pictures of such landscapes of our country. One day this summer when I dropped in at a local democratic publicity hall, I saw diagrams of the Soviet Union's Five-Year Plan shown there, but not a single diagram illustrating the Three-Year Plan of our country. Moreover, there were pictures of huge factories in foreign countries, but there was not a single one of the factories we were rehabilitating or building. They do not even put up any diagrams and pictures of our economic construction, let alone study the history of our country. I noticed in a primary school that all the portraits hanging on the walls were of foreigners such as Mayakovsky, Pushkin, etc., and there were none of Koreans. If children are educated in this way, how can they be expected to have national pride?

The structures of authority, bureaucracy, hierarchy, familism, filial piety, man-centeredness, mentalism, education and patriarchy promoted by the Korean state, in sharp contrast to many other socialist states, all point to the powerful influence of Northeast Asian Confucian traditions.[34] Bruce Cumings would thus refer to the Korean state's ideological position, with some basis, as "Neo-Confucianism in a Communist Bottle."[35] While traditional religious practices were strongly discouraged in revolutionary China and the USSR, North Koreans have continued to widely practice ancestor worship in line with the Confucian tradition—as is evidenced by a visit to any of its major cities on the Chuseok "autumn eve" festival, where shrines and graves are paid homage by officials and the wider population alike. The observance of this traditional Confucian custom is widely televised, as are visits by military officials to the shrines of the country's war dead. The writer has observed these Confucian traditions being practiced firsthand when spending Chuseok in North Korea—drawing a sharp contrast to other communist states. In communist Europe, for example, religious traditions such as churchgoing were not only discouraged but were often forbidden.

The DPRK's foundation as a nationalist Korean state first and a socialist state second explained this discrepancy, showing a consistent respect for tradition and national identity throughout its history which other socialist states such as China have only begun to do far more recently.[36] This ideological foundation largely explains the country's resilience—as the oldest socialist system in the world with the longest serving ruling party. Where a nation can be pressured to abandon a particular economic or political ideology, particularly an internationalist one, forcing a state to abandon its nationalism remains a considerably more difficult task.

President Richard Nixon, when commenting on his admiration for Chinese Premier Zhou Enlai and why he believed he and men like him had the potential to lead the country to a more prosperous future, emphasized the distinction between those who put the nation, its traditions and its history first and political ideology second, and those ideologues who did the opposite. He stated in his memoirs:

> A journalist once asked Zhou if, as a Chinese Communist, he was more Chinese or more Communist. Zhou replied, "I am more Chinese than Communist." Zhou's colleagues were all Chinese nationals, of course. But most of them were Communists first and Chinese second. Zhou deeply believed in his ideology as well, but it was not his nature to carry this belief to extremes. Zhou's Mandarin background also set him apart from his colleagues. His family had been rooted in the ways and manners of old China, its members maintaining their social position for centuries by training their children in the Chinese classics and placing them in positions in the imperial bureaucracy. Zhou renounced the philosophical cornerstones of Chinese society in his adolescence, but he could never rid himself of their cultural imprint, nor did he wish to. He always retained a certain respect for China's past—for those elements of the "old society" that deserved preservation. Unlike most Communist Chinese, he acknowledged repeatedly his indebtedness to his past and to his family… It may seem discordant for a Communist Chinese leader to cite Confucius as an authority, but for Zhou the incident was wholly in character. His upbringing had imbued him with the qualities Confucius ascribed to the "gentleman" or "superior man" who ruled society—intelligence, dignity, grace, kindness, resolution, and forcefulness.[37]

Nixon's observations regarding China, and more specifically regarding two paths for an Asian communist state—nation first or ideology first—have considerable implications for the DPRK and do much to explain its resilience, unity and continued successes against overwhelming pressure. Nixon stated regarding China: "Whether it will survive and in the end do more good than harm depends on whether the present Communist Chinese leaders decide, as Zhou did, that they are going to be more Chinese than Communist. If they do, China in the twenty-first century…can become not only the most populous, but also the most powerful, nation in the world." Despite his strong anticommunist leanings, Nixon's faith in the potential of Confucian culture and East Asian civilization led him to predict great things for states whose identity was rooted in such ideas, even if also communist.[38]

Those who have met North Korea's President and Head of State Kim Yong Nam, in power from 1998 and retiring in 2019 at 91 years old, have consistently described him in much the same way as Nixon described Zhou—the Confucian gentleman. Two Westerners acquainted with the president with whom the writer spoke, one a businessman and one a communist, both agreed with this characterization. Similar observations, to various extents, have been made of other senior figures in the Korean leadership.

In many of its aspects, the Korean nation north of the 38th parallel can be seen as a modern Confucian state. This is perhaps best exemplified by the symbol of the Korean Workers' Party, which alongside the hammer and sickle representing the industrial and rural workers, features a brush in its centre representing the scholars and intellectuals who are held in the highest regard in Confucian society. Placing the traditional writing instrument of Korean and East Asian scholars at the centre of the party flag gives a strong indication as to the nature of the Korean state, which differs considerably from China and the Soviet Union in the prominence it gives it cultural and historical roots. No other ruling communist or socialist party has adopted a similar symbolism—which represents a unique aspect of the DPRK's ideology in place from its outset. Confucianism was the guiding philosophy of the Choson dynasty for over 500 years, and the DPRK, unlike the ROK, continues to emphasize its connections to this dynasty in particular—calling itself "Choson" where the south in the U.S. occupation period renamed itself "Hanguk." The latter name has no similar roots. Confucianism was readily accepted by the Korean population and has profoundly influenced the nation's thought and way of life since the fourth century—arguably more so than in neighbouring China, Japan and Vietnam. Korea was thus regarded in China itself as the paragon of Confucian virtue and "the country of Eastern decorum."[39] The impact of Confucian thought on Korean society was comprehensive, influencing fields from civil administration and the judicial system to education and ceremony. The reverence for learning, culture, social stability and respect for history can all be observed in the DPRK today.

Senior fellow at the Center for International Policy and expert on U.S. foreign policy in Asia Selig S. Harrison, following multiple visits to the DPRK and meetings with high-level officials, concluded that "Confucian traditions" underlay the strength of the Korean system and were key to its continued survival long after the fall of the Soviet Bloc.[40] American scholar Bruce Cumings similarly attributed North Korea's ability to survive Western pressure in the post–Cold War world to "a combination of cultural and historical factors, including the part played by Neo-Confucianism, the principle of self-reliance (*Juche*), and the military-first policy (*Songun*)."[41] These latter two political ideologies were adopted based on the circumstances of the Cold War and the post–Cold War years respectively, and rather than contradict it they complemented the Confucian philosophical foundation of the state. Both ideologies are heavily rooted in Korean nationalism as well as socialism and have emphasized the importance of independence and the building of a robust economic and military defence independently of other nations.

The three principles of the *Juche* idea are as follows: 1) Independence in politics (*Chaju*). 2) Self sustenance in the economy (*Charip*). 3) Self-defence in national defence (*Chawi*). Adopted in 1955, the idea cemented the DPRK's independence both from the Soviet Bloc and from China—protecting the state from influences seen to be unfavourable from the neighbouring communist powers[42] be they revisionism in the former and extremism (or "unbelievable idiocy" in Kim Il Sung's words)[43] in the latter. In hindsight, this proved highly effective. The paths adopted by the Soviet Union and China in the two decades following the Korean War led to stagnation in the former and serious instability in the latter, and by the late 1980s both faced the danger of an imminent collapse. The DPRK, to the contrary, remained stable. The creation of an ideology distinct from those of its neighbours in retrospect was likely key to the survival of the state and its political and economic systems. *Juche* was also heavily rooted in the Korean people's recent historical memory of subjugation, particularly by Japan and the United States, and its emphasis on defence, independence and self-sustenance were a direct result.

Where *Juche* responded to the conditions of the Cold War, *Songun*—the ideology of "military first"—was adopted in the post–Cold War years in response to the new extreme security and economic threats the increasingly isolated country faced under the new Western dominated world order. *Songun* dates back to a visit by newly appointed leader Kim Jong Il to a military unit in 1995 and, according to North Korean media, it draws on the ideological legacy of Kim Il Sung's guerrilla struggle against Imperial Japan. With Korean resistance to external subjugation in the 1990s more isolated and vulnerable than it had been since the 1930s, a reversion to the ideology of the original independence struggle appeared to be borne out of the essential necessity for state survival. *Songun* can be seen as a direct response to efforts by the Western Bloc to bring about a collapse of the Korean state through maximum pressure and, according to a number of Western studies, its adoption made a key contribution to maintaining national security and stability during this trying time.[44]

While an ideology of "military first" was widely portrayed in the West, particularly in the 1990s, as evidence of the DPRK's aggressive intent, *Songun* appears to be firmly rooted in resistance to external pressure as a means of safeguarding Korean independence. As Leader Kim Jong Il told former president Bill Clinton when asked about *Songun*, the ideology "had nothing to do with hostility," but rather with deterrence. He stated to this effect, referring to historical examples of foreign subjugation of the Korean nation: "The DPRK was a small country surrounded by giants…the purpose of the military first policy was not to attack others but to prevent other countries from attacking the DPRK."[45]

A hallmark of *Songun*, as its meaning would suggest, was the growing power of the Korean People's Army—with General Secretary Kim Jong Il seen regularly flanked by military officials where his predecessor had more commonly surrounded himself with party members. State newspaper *Rodong Sinmun* stated regarding the new ideology in 1997: "Never before have the status and role of the People's Army been so extraordinarily elevated as today," and that the military was now "synonymous with the people, the state, and the party."[46] In accordance with this ideological shift, the National Defence Commission became the highest organ of the Korean state in 1998. The emphasis on *Songun* appears to have declined as the country emerged from its most trying period and from the early-mid 2010s the Korean Workers' Party again appears to have become the most prominent organisation in governing the country—marking an end to the effective rule of the military. Chairman Kim Jong Un, like his grandfather, appears to have comprised his inner circle primarily of party rather than military officials to this end, restoring to them the prominence of place surrounding him.

The DPRK's respect for and close identification with the historical Korean nation state distinguished it from the Soviet Union and its other Cold War allies and has served to guarantee its survival due to its very unique nature among Western adversaries. *Juche* and *Songun* have complemented the nation's cultural legacy—rather than diminishing or seeking to replace it as communism in China, the Soviet Union and elsewhere at certain stages did—and these ideas provided the DPRK with a more pragmatic and effective ideological foundation than those of its neighbours.

President Nixon referred to Zhou Enlai as "rooted in the ways and manners of old, heavily influenced by classical thought and society's philosophical cornerstones and retaining a respect for the past and for elements of the 'old society' requiring preservation"—a description apt for DPRK's leadership today. North Korea's leadership, much like the venerated Chinese premier, does not espouse Confucian thought by name, but through its actions and its behavior it is clear that this remains the primary underlying ideological influence on the state—complemented by the modern influences of *Juche* and *Songun* which were developed and adopted based on the country's revolutionary experience. Assuming Western assessments predicting regime change or collapse will continue to be proven wrong and the Korean state will prevail indefinitely, *Juche* and *Songun* may be replaced by newer policies and ideas or otherwise be adapted as the state's circumstances change. The state's Confucian roots, however, will remain central to its identity as the modern Korean civilization state.

No Shock, No Awe: Psychological Warfare and the North Korean Culture of Resistance

Western portrayals of North Korea have frequently drawn on stereotypical colonial-era concepts of "Asiatic Despotism," consistently depicting the country since the 1940s either as a one-man dictatorship or as a puppet of the Soviet Union.[47] As previously mentioned, this has led to a serious failure to understand the nature of the Korean state—and as a result to repeated underestimations of the country since its inception from battlefield performances in first days of the Korean War[48] through to technological achievements in the present day.[49] The Korean nationalist state's firm rooting in both Korean history and culture, its "culture of resistance" built on the potent historical memory of subjugation, and its firm commitment to the centrally organised party system as a secondary factor, have set the DPRK apart from other Western adversaries. These often overlooked factors do much to explain its unique ability to sustain a conflict under immense pressure for so long.

The beginnings of the West's failure to comprehend Korean resistance could be seen even before the outbreak of the Korean War, with stereotypes and propagandistic portrayals of the people and their cause hindering a possible understanding. During the American occupation of southern Korea, shortly following the forced abolition of the Korean People's Republic, the U.S. Military Government found it hard to fathom that there was genuine resistance to their rule from the Koreans themselves. A prominent example were the mass protests organised by people's committees in 1946—the Autumn Uprising—which were depicted as being organised by cells receiving orders from Moscow. There was no evidence to substantiate this, and while the circumstances strongly indicate a lack of communist ideological motive, for the Americans any resistance to their self-perceived benevolent rule had to be a Soviet conspiracy.[50] Following the outbreak of hostilities North Korean prisoners of war, when questioned, consistently surprised American interrogators by insisting that the KPA fought with determination because it was fighting for the cause of the Korean nation—not, as the Western narrative indicated, on orders from Moscow or as part of an "international communist conspiracy."[51] Thus when the DPRK failed to collapse 40 years later when the Soviet Union did, this too was extremely difficult for Western analysts to comprehend.

Korea expert Professor Bruce Cumings observed regarding the common depictions of the DPRK in the Western world:

> In nearly all Western literature North Korea has been depicted as a classic Soviet satellite and puppet… Few grant that North Korea even in the recent period has developed much independence, and until the late 1980s it was routinely called a Soviet satellite—yet more reason for the DPRK to follow the post-1989 demise of the Soviet-aligned systems. North Korean internal politics was almost thought to be as Soviet influenced as any European socialist regime ever was, a pure

> form of "Stalinism in the East." This was given an added filip with the assumption, most often tacit, that Stalinism itself was "Oriental," and that "Kimilsungism" is a wretched excess of the Stalinist-Orientalist tendency.[52]

While North Korea could no longer be depicted as a Soviet puppet after 1991, increasingly fantastical stories about an "Asiatic Despot" began to emerge. The state was depicted as undertaking extreme measures to hold back the "tide of history"—preventing its people from doing what all peoples of the world inevitably were destined to do in the eyes of Western ideologues, join the Western-led order and accept governance under a westernised and Westphilian system. Pyongyang continued to confound and frustrate Western assertions that either collapse or a drastic pivot towards westernisation were inevitable. Referring to these assertions, and their repeated thwarting over decades, associate professor of international relations at South Korea's Pusan National University Robert Kelly stated, himself seemingly perplexed: "North Korea has some hidden source of strength we don't fully understand."[53] He was far from the only one to express such sentiments.

The influences of the DPRK's culture of resistance on the state's policies can be seen to this day. This has provided the state with considerable reserves of strength to resist foreign pressure on the economic, military and information fronts which sharply contrast to other U.S. adversaries, from Panama and Guatemala to Syria, Iraq and Libya. Unlike these states, where third columns and Westphilian sentiments pervaded both in government and among the populations, Koreans' perceptions of the West are primarily influenced not by Western soft power and positive depictions of themselves through popular media, but rather by historical memory from the Korean War period and local media.[i] This may well be the singular most vital explanation for Korea's "hidden source of strength," and its significance was alluded to by a number of sources

---

i An interesting contrast to Korea's ideological strength was Syria in the 2010s, as while its government remained hostile to the West its population appeared heavily influenced by Western soft power through means such as popular media. Even Syrian soldiers on the frontlines against European backed insurgents were reported to exclaim: "Look how beautiful this land is! It is almost as beautiful as Europe!," and such sentiments were common even in wartime. The idea of Western primacy and supremacy, long engrained through centuries of colonial rule across much of the world, is notably absent from North Korea—and is arguably key to its strength and its ability to resist Western pressure in a way a Westphilian population cannot. (Quote from: Vltchk, Andre, "How Come the World is Suffering from Stockholm Syndrome," NEO, February 15, 2019.)

including Ashton Carter.[54] This has allowed the Korean state to resist Western pressure with the full support of its population—adopting a hard line against compromises to sovereignty and applying pressure of its own.

Defence & Strategy Fellow at the Centre for Strategic Studies Van Jackson observed regarding the manifestation of the DPRK's culture of resistance in its foreign policy, at a time when U.S. and North Korean goals were in direct conflict: "the more the United States brought pressure to bear on North Korea, the more North Korea responded with greater defiance and even more grandiose threats."[55] He further observed: "North Koreans would rather accept a war than capitulate—or even be seen as capitulating—to outside pressure on matters that they see as being of existential importance."[56] According to Jackson, the state emphasized this willingness to resist because Pyongyang always held true "that clear shows of hostility and resolve (i.e., a willingness to take risks and die) are necessary to deter enemy aggression. It also believes that *adversarial reputations* matter a great deal: North Korea expects that adversaries will judge its future resolve based partly on what it does in the present moment; small actions of toughness or weakness can therefore have exaggerated consequences in the future."[57]

The importance of North Korea's formidable culture of resistance is particularly apparent when considering the importance of psychosocial warfare and the intimidation of adversaries as a core facilitator of Western hegemonic ambitions. Maj. Ralph Peters, a Foreign Area Officer for Eurasia assigned responsibility for future warfare at the Office of the Deputy Chief of Staff for Intelligence, strongly alluded to this, citing its impact in the 1991 Gulf War in a prominent and highly insightful paper, stating:

> Hollywood is "preparing the battlefield"...the image of U.S. power and the U.S. military around the world is not only a deterrent, but a psychological warfare tool that is constantly at work in the minds of real or potential opponents. Saddam [Hussein, the Iraqi president] swaggered, but the image of the U.S. military crippled the Iraqi army in the field, doing more to soften them up for our ground assault than did tossing bombs into the sand. Everybody is afraid of us. They really believe we can do all the stuff in the movies. If the Trojans "saw" Athena guiding the Greeks in battle, then the Iraqis

> saw Luke Skywalker precede McCaffrey's tanks. Our unconscious alliance of culture with killing power is a combat multiplier no government, including our own, could design or afford. We are magic. And we're going to keep it that way. [58]

The image of the West as an indomitable and often ruthless force was a vital facilitator of success in Western offensive wars long before the Gulf War—and long afterwards. This image was critical to forcing adversaries, which if they had had the proper resolve may well have prevailed, to yielding quickly.[ii] Vasco da Gama may well have set the trend in this regard, committing atrocities against civilians which shocked and horrified Asian populations and were remembered for centuries afterwards—instilling fear in all who dared oppose Portuguese imperial demands. This strategy was intentional, with the Portuguese admiral sending the mutilated bodies of his captives to targeted cities as a warning of the price of resistance.[59] Francisco de Almeida, who led a Portuguese raid on the Indian trading city of Dabul six years later told his captains prior to the assault to "instil terror in the enemy that you're going after so that they remain completely traumatized."[60] The Portuguese proceeded to slaughter the civilian population indiscriminately, and then burned the city to the ground. Similar strategies were adopted by European powers throughout the colonial era, and the importance of this psychological warfare saw adversaries defeated and capitulating to the West without firing a shot.

The use of "Shock and Awe" against Iraq can be seen as a modern descendant of this strategy and saw Iraq's million-man army effectively capitulate with little resistance. Similar trends could be seen in Yugoslavia. NATO's bluff that it would invade, although most analysts agree such an operation was not feasible, was enough to force Belgrade to capitulate. After witnessing the devastation of an intensive and indiscriminate NATO bombing campaign, the Yugoslav leadership feared a

---

ii The writer has witnessed the effects of this first hand, when a militia in a certain African state the writer resided in was rumoured to have acquired American M16 rifles. The idea that the militia would be using American rifles provoked considerable terror among their potential targets, and the writer was repeatedly asked what the M16 could do. Few knew its actual performance specifications, but the fact that it was American was enough to cause terror. The M16 was first used in 1964 and had a far from exceptional combat record, with East Asian and European rifle designs produced under licence in the region boasting overall superior capabilities. But the idea of fighting American weapons was considerably more powerful than the weapons themselves and played strongly into the militia's favour.

ground invasion would if anything be more brutal.[61] Perhaps the most brutal case of this "Shock and Awe," however, was the firebombing of Tokyo on March 9, 1945. Over 300 American B-29 heavy bombers flew low over the city and targeted its most congested residential areas with incendiaries—applying what Western historians referred to as "blunt psychological trauma" to the Japanese population.[62] General Kurtis LeMay, who planned the attack, emphasized its importance as a means of waging psychological warfare against the Japanese through extreme brutality. He knew the Japanese had no experience of a low-level mass incendiary strike, and the attack's primary purpose was as a psychological warfare operation to stun the country into submission. 100,000 were killed at a conservative estimate, by far the bloodiest night in the history of war, with some estimates placing the death toll several times higher. The purpose of such attacks, according to the United States Strategic Bombing Survey, was to destroy "the basic economic and social fabric of the country"[63] and to terrorise the population into submission. "It was as though Tokyo had dropped through the floor of the world and into the mouth of hell," LeMay concluded.[64]

It was largely on the basis of the conditioning of the non-Western world to fear Western power that in the Korean War, Western sources almost unanimously predicted the KPA would flee at the first sight of American soldiers.[65] While the training and efficiency of KPA units came as a major surprise to their adversaries, it was their psychological resolve, their resilience to images of an undefeatable West, and their resulting willingness to confront the forces of the Western Bloc against overwhelming odds, which came as the greatest surprise. The result was the longest routing of the U.S. Military in its history, which brought the KPA very near to total victory in the war's initial months.

Today North Korea's greatest strength is arguably the unity of its population, and the near complete failure of Western influences to affect their thought or soften their resistance—whether it be Western portrayals of itself as a benevolent civilising and democratising force or as a ruthless and undefeatable adversary which leads the "tide of history." These propaganda assets in different but often complementary ways have been key to sustaining Western-led order across the world—and North Korea's apparent insulation from their effects explains the near uniquely formidable nature of Korean resistance. This may well explain why North Korea represents by far the longest lasting adversary with which the United States and Western world have ever been in conflict—due not to unique material assets but rather to a degree of resolve and indomitability which Ba'athist Iraq, the Soviet Union (post-1953), and even Communist China, among other adversaries and to various extents, have all lacked.

Ultimately North Korea's ability to endure seven decades of conflict with the United States cannot be understood without an understanding of the country's cultural and ideological roots and the paradigm through which it has viewed this conflict. One of the more notable assessments of impacts of the DPRK's "culture of resistance" and ideological strength on the state's power and stability was made by the former director of the South Korean Central Intelligence Agency (KCIA), Brigadier General Kim Hyong Uk, in a testimony to the U.S. Congress in 1977. At the time a larger population and greater access to foreign markets and investment were providing the ROK with considerable advantages including a larger and better funded military. According to the director, however, these were largely compensated by a stronger ideological foundation, greater perceived regime legitimacy and in some respects a superior quality of life in the DPRK. The general stated:

> The North Korean people do not suffer from a high degree of international demonstration effect. The international demonstration effect in South Korea is extremely high. There are no visible gaps between the haves and have-nots in North Korea. Therefore, I feel that the North Korean population most likely feel less relatively deprived than their southern counterparts. I estimate that the standard of living of the ordinary people in North Korea is higher than in South Korea. Even though the average standard of living in North Korea may be lower than the standard of living of South Koreans, I believe that the people of North Korea live with a greater sense of satisfaction… The discipline and the ideological zeal of the North Korean Communists is much stronger than that of the South Koreans. In fact, I feel that there is no comparison; the will of the North Koreans is almost 100 times stronger than the will of the South Koreans.

Regarding the impact of discrepancies in morale and perceived regime legitimacy would have in the military field, the director stated:

> Although North Korean troops are inferior in numbers (that is, 430,000 army, 20,000 navy, 45,000 Air Force, and total: 500,000), they are much stronger than South Korean troops on the battlefield because they are so well-disciplined both militarily and ideologically... Let's now take a look at the Vietnam War for a moment to demonstrate my point. Just before the fall of Vietnam, the ratio of the South Vietnamese to the North Vietnamese was 3 to 1 in military troop strength and 7 to 1 in weapons and equipment. But in contrast with the corruption of the ruling elite and the lack of ideological conation of the South Vietnamese soldiers, because the North Vietnamese had strong ideological convictions they defeated the South.

The director's statement was highly consistent with the performance of both Korean armies during the Korean War, and despite the considerable improvements and the success of reforms under the Park Chung Hee presidency, he predicted that the state of corruption in South Korea undermined morale to the extent that South Koreans would not fight effectively in the event of a new war.[66]

Meeting Pressure with Pressure

A key part of North Korea's foreign policy strategy for several decades has been the imperative of meeting Western pressure with pressure of its own, and the importance attributed to this has been key to the state's survival and set it apart from the majority of U.S. and Western adversaries. Statements by Korean officials at times of high tension with the United States shed considerable light on the country's position in this regard. Following the KPA Air Force's downing of an American EC-121 surveillance plane in 1969, and subsequent preparations by the Richard Nixon administration to carry out massive air and nuclear strikes on Korean targets,[67] it was Washington's awareness that Pyongyang would respond with a massive offensive of its own resulting in all-out war with the United States which ultimately deterred it from striking.[68] As DPRK deputy foreign minister Heo Dam told the Soviet ambassador to Pyongyang, Korea was "ready to respond to retaliation with retaliation, and total war with total war," referring to efforts to condition American behaviour and make them "draw the proper lesson from the [seizure of *USS*] *Pueblo*."[69]

Further to this effect, DPRK Foreign Minister Pak Seong Cheol told Soviet ambassador Sudarikov regarding the shootdown incident:

> If the Americans had decided to fight then [when the EC-121 was shot down], we would have fought…we wage firefights with the Americans in the area of the 38th parallel almost every day. When they shoot, we also shoot…But no special aggravation arises from this…we've also shot down American planes before, and similar incidents are possible in the future… It's good for them to know that we won't sit with folded arms… If we sit with folded arms when a violator intrudes into our spaces, two planes will appear tomorrow, then four, five, etc. This would lead to an increase of the danger of war. But if a firm rebuff is given, then this will diminish the danger of an outbreak of war. When the Americans understand that there is a weak enemy before them they will start a war right away. If, however, they see that there is a strong partner before them, this delays the beginning of war.[70]

This rationale has pervaded the DPRK since the Korean War and has served as a major constraint on the ability of the Western Bloc to coerce the East Asian state with the threat of military action, economic sanctions or other forms of pressure. In the 1960s actively taking to the offensive in the DMZ Conflict was reportedly also seen by North Korean officials as a way of conveying the country's resolve to the United States, which they believed forestalled prospects for a future American invasion.[71] In the 1980s, after repeated protests by Pyongyang regarding the violation of its airspace by American SR-71 surveillance aircraft, the KPA used its S-75 missile system to fire on one of the aircraft. Carried out on August 26, 1981, the strike was a near miss but served its purpose. The U.S. Air Force thereafter became much more cautious when carrying out future flights in or near DPRK airspace.[72]

Following the Soviet collapse, the knowledge that any provocation including a redeployment of U.S. assets to the region[73] would be met with a quick response deterred the Clinton administration from starting a war against the DPRK despite its offensive and highly interventionist policies across much of the rest of the world. The unique status of North Korean airspace among the "Axis of Evil" members in the 1990s and early 2000s arguably bears testament to this. While long incursions by

U.S. Military aircraft deep into Iranian and Iraqi airspace were common at this time and were met with little response, aircraft operating near North Korean airspace were frequently intercepted by KPA fighter jets—at times aggressively—with the apparent purpose of deterring the U.S. from pressing further.[74] Not only has the KPA consistently demonstrated high morale and professionalism, which even those U.S. and ROK military sources highly critical of the DPRK expressed outright confidence in,[75] but it has also demonstrated a willingness to respond to pressure with pressure and to attacks with counterattacks. The administrations of Lyndon Johnson, Richard Nixon, Bill Clinton and Donald Trump among others, when considering limited strikes on the DPRK, were well aware of the inevitable response.

The Fundamental Clash of Korean National Sovereignty and Western Global Hegemony: The DPRK's Need for Nuclear Weapons

A leading cause for conflict between the Democratic People's Republic of Korea and the United States of America has been a stark conflict in their worldviews. This does not refer to a clash of capitalist and socialist ideologies, but rather to nations' perceptions of the nature of international relations, world order and states' right to self-determination. The DPRK, like other East Asian states which won their independence in the aftermath of the Second World War, expressed a strong belief in global and regional orders comprised of nation states equal in their rights to their sovereignty, including self-defence and self-determination and prohibiting forced external interference into their domestic affairs. This is the same order enshrined in the United Nations Charter. The perceived sacredness of sovereignty and self-determination dates back to the origins of North Korea's resistance movement against Imperial Japan and forms a key part of the state's ideological foundation.

For the United States and the wider Western Bloc, a framework of international relations has long been pursued under which both the world and regional orders are centred on their own dominance, allowing the Western world to influence the affairs of all other states and retain indefinite dominion over the Asia-Pacific and the wider world. Indeed, such an order existed to a large extent before the early 20th century industrialisation of Japan, followed by the Soviet Union, began to provide non-Western parties with the economic and military might needed to protect their interests. Its reinstatement has long been central to Western foreign policy, leading to modern states independent from Western dominance from the Japanese Empire to the USSR and today China and North Korea consistently being placed under considerable economic and military pressure. Former Assistant Secretary to the U.S. Treasury under Ronald Reagan, associate editor at the *Wall Street Journal* and holder of the William E. Simon chair in economics at CSIS, Paul Craig Roberts, noted to this effect: "The United States has an ideology of world hegemony and does not accept any prospect of any country being sovereign or acting on its own. You have to be an American vassal state." According to Roberts the U.S., influenced by its own extreme ideological position, "intends to destroy" those states seeking to retain genuine sovereignty.[76] This essential clash of worldviews has been the underlying cause and the primary point of contention between Pyongyang and Washington—with each intent on and unyielding in maintaining its position and certain of the virtue of its cause.

The concept of a global Western military presence and profound Western political and economic influence over states across the world, referred to by scholars as "a historically unprecedented system of semi sovereign states,"[77] emerged in the aftermath of the Second World War in place of direct Western imperial rule—with many states granted a token independence under circumstances which ensured continued their client status to the Western world.[78] The United States has approximately 800 military bases overseas, "more bases in foreign lands than any other people, nation, or empire in history" according to the American *Nation*,[79] and these account for 95 percent of foreign military installations globally. The majority of the remaining 5 percent belong to allied Western military powers such as the United Kingdom and France. Deployments of U.S. Special Forces are even more widespread. In 2016 they were deployed to 138 nations, the only notable exceptions being China, Russia, North Korea, Iran and South Africa.[80] Special forces deployed overseas are increasingly relied on by the U.S. as a means "to maintain global dominance," a scalpel where heretofore direct colonial rule was the hammer.[81] The prevalence of U.S. and Western military units overseas is a key pillar of the Western world's ability and intent to project power globally against those parties which challenge or otherwise undermine the Western-led order, and the presence of Western soldiers in the vast majority of countries strongly indicates an order premised on Western hegemony rather than sovereignty and global consensus.

North Korea's existence is considered unacceptable because it refuses to submit to the imposition of Western leadership and become part of the Western-led order. For Pyongyang, the Western position is considered unacceptable because it is contrary to states' right to self-determination and, in North Korea's case their very right to exist, as well as contravening international law and the UN Charter. The Western Bloc are so often referred to as "the imperialists" in Korean rhetoric because they seek to impose their values, their ideologies, their economic and political systems and above all their soldiers and their governance—whether direct or indirect—on the Korean people. Many of the consequences of the imposition of Western dominance can be seen in South Korea (see Chapter 11).

Western calls for the destruction of North Korea as a state entity and the forceful integration of its population and territory into the Western-led world order have been widespread and persistent, and all number of pretexts have been put forward to justify such calls to action. Director of Korean Studies at The Center for the National Interest and Executive Editor of The National Interest, Harry J. Kazianis, noted to this effect: "Clearly North Korea is a stain on human history that needs to be expunged"[82]—a sentiment he was far from alone among Westerners in expressing. Prominent research associate at the Asian Institute for Policy Studies Ben Forney similarly noted: "it is time for the world to accept that 'peace on the Korean Peninsula' begins when the Kim regime ends"—insisting that the only solution to conflict was Western action to force the overthrow of the Korean state.[83] Whether stated directly by figures such as UN Ambassador John Bolton[84] and President Barack Obama[85] or indirectly alluded to, this has been the policy of all post–Cold War U.S. administrations at least until that of Donald Trump. The existential nature of the Western threat has directly led North Korea to seek more effective means of retaliating against efforts to end its existence—most conspicuously in recent years the thermonuclear warhead–tipped ICBM.

NOTES

1 Nixon, Richard, *Leaders*, New York, Simon & Schuster, 2013 (Chapter 7: Zhou Enlai The Mandarin Revolutionary).

2 Lukin, Alexander, *China and Russia: The New Rapprochement,* Cambridge, Polity Press, 2018 (pp. 5, 6, 15).
Fukuyama, Francis, 'The End of History?,' *National Interest*, no. 16, Summer 1989 (pp. 3–18).

Slater, Philip and Bennis, Warren, 'Democracy is Inevitable,' *Harvard Business Review*, September-October 1990.
3 Napoleoni, Loretta, *North Korea: The. Country We Love to Hate*, Perth, UWA, 2018.
4 Abrams, A. B., *Power and Primacy: The History of Western Intervention in the Asia-Pacific*, Oxford, Peter Lang, 2019 (Chapter 14: Economic War on Asia).
5 Pinera, Jose, *The 'Third Way' Keeps Countries in the Third World*, Prepared for the Cato Institute's 16th Annual Monetary Conference cosponsored with *The Economist*, Washington D.C., October 22, 1998.
Pinera, Jose, *The Fall of a Second Berlin Wall*, October 22, 1998.
6 Mahbubani, Kishore, 'Has the West Lost it?,' (Lecture), *Lee Kuan Yew School of Public Policy*, June 26, 2018.
7 Kim, Suk Hi, *The Survival of North Korea: Essays on Strategy, Economics and International Relations*, Jefferson, NC, McFarland, 2011 (p. 29).
8 Fowdy, Tom, 'How U.S. pressure is changing Silicon Valley social media firms,' *CGTN*, January 14, 2020.
9 Harrison, Selig S., 'Promoting a Soft Landing in Korea,' *Foreign Policy*, No. 106, Spring 1997 (p. 57).
10 'Interview: Ashton Carter,' *Frontline*, March 3, 2003.
11 Metzl, Jamie, 'Why North Korea Is Destined to Collapse,' *National Interest*, September 18, 2017 (first published in 2015).
12 Gobry, Pascal-Emmanuel, 'Why North Korea's collapse is inevitable,' *The Week*, August 21, 2015.
13 Trifunov, David, 'North Korea collapse inevitable, new report says,' *PRI*, September 20, 2013.
14 O'Hanlon, Michael E., 'North Korea Collapse Scenarios,' *Brookings Institute*, June 9, 2009.
15 *The Coming Asian Century: challenges for the West*, Event Hosted by LSE Ideas, March 5, 2019.
16 Lake, Eli, 'Preparing for North Korea's Inevitable Collapse,' *Bloomberg*, September 20, 2016.
17 'Warning over N. Korea collapse,' *CNN*, November 4, 2003.
18 *World Policy Journal*, Fall 1993 Issue.
19 Cumings, Bruce, *Korea's Place in the Sun: A Modern History*, New York, W. W. Norton & Company, 1997 (pp. 428–429).
Lee, Mun Woong, *Rural North Korea under Communism; A Study of Sociocultural Change*, Houston, Rice University Studies, 1976 (pp. 30–32).
20 Donahue, Ray T. and Prosser, Michael H., *International Conflict at the United Nations—Addresses and Analysis*, London, Greenwood, 1997 (p. 128).
21 Kim, Il Sung, *Let Us Reunify the Country Independently and Peacefully*, Report to the Sixth Congress of the Workers' Party of Korea on the Work of the Central Committee, October 10, 1980.
22 'Federalizing the Korean Peninsula: North Korea Calls for Unifying Confederation with South Korea,' *Xinhua*, July 7, 2014.
23 Da-min, Jung, 'North Korea calls for unification under two regimes,' *Korea Times*, January 24, 2019.
24 Harrison, Selig S., 'Promoting a Soft Landing in North Korea,' *Foreign Policy*, no. 106, Spring 1997 (p. 74).
25 Mullen, Mike and Nunn, Sam and Mount, Adam, *A Sharper Choice on North Korea: Engaging China for a Stable Northeast Asia*, Council on Foreign Relations, Independent Task Force Report No. 74, September 2016 (p. 46).
26 Fitzpatrick, Mark, 'North Korea: Is Regime Change the Answer?,' *Survival*, vol. 55, no. 3, May 29, 2013.
Mounk, Yascha, 'Before Making Peace With North Korea, Let's Not Forget the North Koreans,' *Slate*, May 3, 2018.

27 'Interview: Ashton Carter,' *Frontline*, March 3, 2003.
28 Ibid.
29 Park, Kyung-Ae, 'Regime Change in North Korea?: Economic Reform and Political Opportunity Structures,' *North Korean Review,* vol. 5, no. 1, Spring 2009 (p. 37).
30 'Interview: Ashton Carter,' *Frontline*, March 3, 2003.
31 Guzeva, Alexandra, 'How did the Soviets use captured churches?,' *Russia Beyond,* January 29, 2019.
32 Lu, Xing. *Rhetoric of the Chinese Cultural Revolution: The Impact on Chinese Thought, Culture, and Communication*, Colombia, University of South Carolina Press, 2016 (p. 61–62).
33 David-West, Alzo, 'Between Confucianism and Marxism-Leninism: Juche and the Case of Chŏng Tasan,' *Korean Studies*, vol. 35, 2011 (pp. 93–121).
Kim, Il Sung, *On eliminating dogmatism and formalism and establishing Juche in ideological work*, Speech to Party Propagandists and Agitators on December 28, 1955, Kim Il Sung Selected Works, vol. 1 (pp. 582–606).
34 Armstrong, Charles K., 'Familism, Socialism and Political Religion in North Korea,' *Totalitarian Movements and Political Religions,* vol. 6, no. 3, 2005 (pp. 383–394).
35 Cumings, Bruce, *Korea's Place in the Sun: A Modern History*, New York, W. W. Norton and Company, 2005 (p. 423).
36 Wang, Xiangwei, 'Xi Jinping endorses the promotion of Confucius,' *South China Morning Post,* September 29, 2014.
37 Nixon, Richard, *Leaders*, New York, Simon & Schuster, 2013 (Chapter 7: Zhou Enlai The Mandarin Revolutionary).
38 Ibid. (Chapter 7: Zhou Enlai The Mandarin Revolutionary).
39 Yoo, Yushin, *Korea the Beautiful: Treasures of the Hermit Kingdom,* Los Angeles, CA, Golden Pond, 1987 (p. 137).
40 Harrison, Selig S., 'Promoting a Soft Landing in North Korea,' *Foreign Policy,* no. 106, Spring 1997 (pp. 60–61).
41 Kim, Suk Hi, *The Survival of North Korea: Essays on Strategy, Economics and International Relations*, Jefferson, NC, McFarland, 2011 (pp. 49–50).
42 'Conversation between Aleksei Kosygin and Kim Il Sung,' 12 February 1965, Archive of the Central Committee of the Czechoslovak Communist Party, Collection 02/1, File 96, Archival Unit 101, Information 13, 1962–66.
43 Radchenko, Sergey S., *The Soviet Union and the North Korean Seizure of the USS Pueblo: Evidence from Russian Archives*, Woodrow Wilson International Center for Scholars, Washington D.C. (p. 11).
44 Kim, Suk Hi and Roehrig, Terrence and Seliger, Bernhard, *The Survival of North Korea: Essays on Strategy, Economics and International Relations,* Jefferson, NC, McFarland, 2011 (p. 35).
Park, Han S., 'Military-First Politics (Songun): Understanding Kim Jong Il's North Korea,' *2008 Academic Paper Series on Korea 1*, 2009 (pp. 118–130).
45 Jackson, Van, *On the Brink,* Cambridge, Cambridge University Press, 2018 (p. 40).
Osnos, Evan, 'The Risk of Nuclear War with North Korea,' *The New Yorker,* September 18, 2017.
46 Byung, Chul Koh, 'Military-First Politics and Building a "Powerful and Prosperous Nation" In North Korea,' *Nautilus Institute Policy Forum,* April 14, 2005.
47 Koo, Hagen, *State and Society in Contemporary Korea*, Ithaca, Cornell University Press, 1993 (p. 198).
48 Princeton University, Dulles Papers, John Allison oral history, April 20, 1969.
United States Army in the Korean War: Volume 4, Washington D.C., Government Printing Office, 1961 (p. 84).
49 Warrick, Joby and Nakashima, Ellen and Fifield, Anna, 'North Korea now making missile-ready nuclear weapons, U.S. analysts say,' *Washington Post,* August 8, 2017.

50 Cumings, Bruce, *Origins of the Korean War: Liberation and the Emergence of Separate Regimes, 1945–1947, Volume 1*, Yeogsabipyeongsa Publishing Co, 1981–1990 (pp. 367, 375).
51 Kim, Monica, *The Interrogation Rooms of the Korean War; The Untold History,* Princeton, NJ, Princeton University Press, 2019 (pp. 201, 203).
52 Koo, Hagen, *State and Society in Contemporary Korea*, Ithaca, Cornell University Press, 1993 (p. 198).
53 Power, John, 'The Long History of Predicting North Korea's Collapse,' *The Diplomat*, January 27, 2017.
54 'Interview: Ashton Carter,' *Frontline*, March 3, 2003.
55 Jackson, Van, *On the Brink,* Cambridge, Cambridge University Press, 2018 (p. 29).
56 Ibid. (p. 37).
57 Ibid. (p. 37).
58 Peters, Ralph, 'Constant Conflict, Parameters,' *U.S. Army War College Quarterly*, Summer 1997 (pp. 4–14).
59 Gady, Franz-Stefan, 'How Portugal Forged an Empire in Asia,' *The Diplomat,* July 11, 2019.
60 Ibid.
61 Stigler, Andrew L., 'A Clear Victory for Air Power: NATO's Empty Threat to Invade Kosovo,' *International Security*, vol. 27, no. 3, Winter 2002–2003 (pp. 124–157).
Dixon, Paul, 'Victory by Spin? Britain, the US and the Propaganda War over Kosovo' *Civil Wars,* vol. 4, issue 6, Winter 2003 (pp. 83–106).
62 Fox, Senan, 'Tokyo and the Night of the Firewind,' *The Diplomat,* February 24, 2016.
63 'United States Strategic Bombing Survey, Summary Report (Pacific War),' Washington DC, U.S. GPO, 1946, vol. 1 (p. 16).
64 Ham, Paul, *Hiroshima Nagasaki: The Real Story of the Atomic Bombings and their Aftermath*, New York, Doubleday, 2012 (pp. 59–60).
Wilson, Ward, 'The Bomb Didn't Beat Japan … Stalin Did,' *Foreign Policy*, May 30, 2017.
65 Cumings, Bruce, *The Korean War: A History*, New York, Modern Library, 2010 (p. 27).
Halberstam, David, *The Fifties*, New York, Ballantine Books, 2012 (p. 71).
66 Hearing Before the Subcommitteee on International Organisations of the Committee on International Relations, House of Representatives, Ninety-Fifth Congress, First Session, Part 1, June 22, 1977 (pp. 13–14).
67 McGreal, Chris, 'Papers reveal Nixon plan for North Korea nuclear strike,' *The Guardian*, July 7, 2010.
Foster, Peter, 'Richard Nixon planned nuclear strike on North Korea,' *Telegraph*, July 8, 2010.
68 Nixon, Richard M., *RN: The Memoirs of Richard Nixon,* New York, Warner Books, 1978 (pp. 473–475).
69 'Record of Conversation between N.G. Sudarikov and Heo Dam, the Leader of the Ministry of Foreign Affairs of DPRK,' April 16, 1969, History and Public Policy Program Digital Archive, RGANI: fond 5, opis 61, deloo 462, listy 71–74, obtained by Sergey Radchenko and translated by Gary Goldberg.
70 'Record of Conversation between N.G. Sudarikov and Pak Seong Cheol, a Member of the Political Committee of the Workers' Party of Korea,' April 16, 1969, History and Public Policy Program Digital Archive, RGANI: fond 5, opis 61, delo 466, list 199–127.
71 Jackson, Van, *On the Brink,* Cambridge, Cambridge University Press, 2018 (p. 22).
Jackson, Van, 'The EC-121 Shoot Down and North Korea's Coercive Theory of Victory,' *Wilson Centre*, April 13, 2017.
72 Graham, Richard H., *Flying the SR-71 Blackbird: In the Cockpit on a Secret Operational Mission,* Beverly, MA, Quarto Publishing, 2019 (p. 140).

73 Jackson, Van, *Rival Reputations: Coercion and Credibility in US-North Korea Relations*, Cambridge, Cambridge University Press, 2016 (p. 161).
74 Schmitt, Eric, 'North Korea Migs Intercept U.S. Jet on Spying Mission,' *New York Times,* March 4, 2003.
75 Schobell, Andrew and Sanford, John M., *North Korea's Military Threat: Pyongyang's Conventional Forces, Weapons of Mass Destruction, and Ballistic Missiles*, U.S. Army War College Strategic Studies Institute, April 2007 (pp. 63–64).
Dreazen, Yochi, 'Here's what war with North Korea would look like,' *Vox,* February 8, 2018.
76 'The U.S. govt bent on world hegemony, Russia stands in its way—Reagan economic ex-advisor,' *RT*, December 4, 2014.
77 Stone, I. F., *Hidden History of the Korean War*, Amazon Media, 2014 (Foreword).
78 Abrams, A. B., 'Power and Primacy: The History of Western Intervention in the Asia-Pacific,' Oxford, Peter Lang, 2019 (Chapter 5: America in the Philippines: How the United States Established a Colony and Later Neo-Colony in the Pacific).
Ibid. (Chapter 13: Modern Japan and Western Policy in Asia).
79 Vine, David, 'The United States Probably Has More Foreign Military Bases Than Any Other People, Nation or Empire in History,' *The Nation*, September 14, 2015.
80 Durden, Tyler, 'U.S. Special Forces Deployed To 70 Percent of The World In 2016,' *Ron Paul Institute for Peace and Prosperity*, February 11, 2017.
Turse, Nick, 'Special Ops, Shadow Wars, and the Golden Age of the Grey Zone,' *Tom Dispatch*, January 5, 2017.
81 Philips, Michael M., 'New ways the U.S. projects power around the globe: Commandoes,' *Wall Street Journal,* April 24, 2015.
82 Kazianis, Harry J., 'A U.S. Invasion of North Korea Would Be Like Opening the Gates of Hell,' *National Interest,* May 13, 2019.
83 Forney, Ben, 'Peace in Korea Begins with Regime Change,' *National Interest,* February 1, 2018.
84 Kim, Suk Hi, *The Survival of North Korea: Essays on Strategy, Economics and International Relations*, Jefferson, NC, McFarland, 2011 (p. 46).
Funabashi, Yoichi, *The Peninsula Question: A Chronicle of the Second Korean Nuclear Crisis*, Washington D.C., Brookings Institution Press, 2007 (p. 143).
85 Foster-Carter, Aidan, 'Obama Comes Out as a North Korea Collapsist,' *The Diplomat*, January 30, 2015.

Chapter 19
INFORMATION WAR:
THE FINAL FRONTIER

Information War on North Korea and the Regime Change Agenda

Looking towards the future evolution of Western policy towards and strategy against the DPRK, information warfare increasingly appears set to play a central role. For the purposes of this work, this form of warfare will be defined as the manipulation of information trusted by a target without the target's awareness leading the target to make decisions against their own interest, but in the interest of the one conducting information warfare operations. In the context of inter-state relations, information warfare has often involved the manipulation of public opinion by an enemy state in line with that offending state's interest. A notable contemporary example is the widespread Western claims of the malign influence of Russian media, including social media accounts sponsored by Moscow, on public perceptions in the Western world. Moscow has allegedly used obscurantist means to promote Russophilian narratives and undermine faith in the institutions, political systems and ideologies of the targeted Western countries with the end goal of subversion and the furthering of Moscow's interests.[1] While reports of Russian information warfare efforts have been prominent since 2016, it is notable that Western states have made effective use of media including social for similar ends since at least 2010, targeting a number of adversaries including the DPRK.

Information warfare came to the fore of America's ongoing conflict with the DPRK under the Barack Obama administration in the early 2010s, partly in response to growing limitations placed on American military options by growing KPA capabilities and the acceleration of Pyongyang's economic recovery despite Western sanctions. Western experts have continued to express considerable faith in it since as a potential means to a decisive victory over Pyongyang. With advances in North Korea's deterrence capabilities seriously limiting, and from 2017 effectively closing, military options for coercion, and with the Korean economy growing and modernising despite maximum pressure from sanctions[2] (see Chapter 22), it is logical that the DPRK's adversaries will in future look to a third front through which to exert pressure. Information warfare has proven highly successful against other Western target states in the past and provides a means of opening such a third front.

The waging of information warfare became central to American foreign policy strategies under the Barack Obama administration, and often succeeded where military options and economic warfare were not viable. This included a focus on active dissemination of obscurantist political narratives supporting Western objectives—most often by demonising Western target governments, delegitimising their institutions and political systems, and promoting narratives which were both pro-Western and favourable in their coverage of Western-sponsored political actors in the targeted countries. Social media emerged as a key tool to promote such narratives, and Western governments maintained close cooperation with internet and social media companies such as Google and Twitter which often directly supported such efforts.[3] This was coupled with provision of funding and training for pro-Western and anti-state activists and organisations through Western non-governmental organisations, which maintained very close cooperation with the CIA and other Western intelligence agencies.[4]

As a prominent 2015 paper on information warfare from the NATO Cooperative Cyber Defence Centre of Excellence noted, citing Russian sources: "information can be used to disorganise governance, organise anti-government protests, delude adversaries, influence public opinion, and reduce an opponent's will to resist." This could be coupled with other forms of warfare, perhaps preceding a ground invasion, but it could equally prove effective on its own.[5] The results of Western information warfare efforts, which escalated significantly during Obama years, could be seen in Ukraine,[6] Hong Kong,[7] Libya[8] and much of the Middle East[9]—destabilizing and in many cases toppling governments outside the Western sphere of influence. Senator John McCain, who would soon afterwards become Chairman of Senate Joint House Services Committee, referred in 2011 to the weaponization of information targeting a number of the Western Bloc's adversaries as "a virus that will attack Moscow and Beijing," following its success against Western adversaries in the Arab World.[10] President of Joseon Institute and founder of Liberty in North Korea and Pegasus Strategies Adrian Hong, who later led a violent attack on the Korean embassy in Spain and worked in close cooperation with U.S. intelligence,[11] stated in much the same vein that the rapid and successive overthrow of independent Arab governments by Western backed groups was "a dress rehearsal for North Korea."[12] It is notable that shortly after these successes, attempts to penetrate North Korea's tight security system with Western state-funded propaganda supporting Western favored political narratives also escalated. Korean language radio broadcasts and the smuggling of USB drives with political content were all supported to this end.[13]

President Obama strongly alluded to using information as a weapon to target North Korea specifically and accelerate what he believed, at least until his final eighteen months in office, to be the inevitability of a state collapse. "Over time you will see a regime like this collapse. We will keep on ratcheting the pressure, but part of what's happening is that the Internet, over time is going to be penetrating this country. And it is very hard to sustain that kind of brutal authoritarian regime in this modern world. Information ends up seeping in over time and bringing about change, and that's something that we are *constantly looking for ways to accelerate*."[14] [italics added] Where offensive actions under the George W. Bush administration can be characterised by tens of thousands of boots on the ground and two large scale invasions, Obama's can be characterised by presidentially sponsored kill lists, under which drones would extrajudicially assassinate American enemies across the world including U.S. citizens,[15] and perhaps more significantly by major investments in information warfare.

The president was hardly alone in calling for a focus on information war, using state-funded assets both to shape the perceptions of the Korean population in line with Western approved political and historical narratives and to undermine faith in and support for the Korean government. The Council on Foreign Relations repeatedly alluded to the benefits of such a strategy and the means by which a spread of Western supported political and historical narratives among the population could be used to undermine unity, weaken the nation as a whole and potentially lay the ground for regime change. The growing informal market system in particular was cited as a potential medium through which to spread such information. The CFR's highly influential 2016 paper stated: "North Korean citizens' increasing access to information from the outside world, as well as growing internal markets, could form the basis for a gradual transformation of the totalitarian system.... U.S. policymakers should facilitate governmental and nongovernmental efforts to allow information about the outside world to reach the North Korean people."[16] The report emphasized that the strength of the state and its tight security system meant that such plans for subversion would need to plan for long term rather than immediate results.[17]

A paper for the Korea Institute for National Unification, a prominent Seoul-based government-funded think tank in South Korea, stated regarding the centrality of information war to new strategies for undermining the DPRK and means by which to carry it out: "If Pyongyang's grip on the weakening North Korean economy gets loosened, informal markets such as Jangmadang may thrive further. Popularity of Jangmadang can facilitate the spread of outside information. Through Jangmadang, information can *and should* be spread out that people's suffering is not caused by international sanctions but the wrong policy decisions made by their nuclear-obsessed leaders; that the suffering is unavoidable for a considerable period of time unless the regime's mindset and policy shift; and that the consequences of their leaders' bad decisions will fall upon them, not the regime."[18]

Such narratives attempted to shift the blame for the effects of Western sanctions against the Korean population onto the Korean government for failing to comply with Western demands for unilateral disarmament. They fail, however, to mention that it is the Western world which has chosen to strongly push for a sanctions regime against the DPRK, rather than Pyongyang's own actions which are no more provocative than those of the world's other eight nuclear powers—none of them comparably sanctioned. This was one of a number of obscurantist narratives used to promote anti-government and pro-Western sentiments. Reports from agents actively engaged in information warfare operations noted that narratives blaming North Korea for starting the Korean War were also common among the materials disseminated by foreign agencies.[19]

A significant part of the information warfare effort has centred around shifting blame for the Korean population's hardships, including the Korean War, the Arduous March and the impacts of the Western sanctions regime, onto the government in Pyongyang and away from external actors. Western and South Korean reports have appeared increasingly frustrated, however, by the "failure" of North Korea's population to draw the "right conclusions" regarding their government. President of the Association of Korean Political Studies in North America Park Kyung Ae, an expert on North Korean politics, noted regarding the absence of anti-government sentiments among the DPRK's population following a period of popular protests:

> Protests were mostly triggered by food shortages, rather than by people's political consciousness or their demands for participatory values. One Korean-Chinese hotel worker in Yanji remarked: "Even though they go hungry, North Korean [economic] refugees still continue to praise the Great Leader." North Koreans appear to attribute their economic difficulties to outside forces such as the collapse of the socialist market, economic sanctions by the U.S., and natural disasters, rather than to Kim Jong Il's leadership itself.

She noted that only a very small minority of defectors, under 10%, cited political dissatisfaction as their reason for leaving the country. The expert stressed the importance of actions by the West and South Korea to artificially create political opposition and dissatisfaction within the DPRK as a path to regime change.[20]

Among the most vocal in their calls to use growing informal markets in the DPRK as a medium to wage information war were Lee Myung Bak, National Security Advisor to the President and Chief Negotiator for South Korea during the Six Party Talks, and Chun Yung Woo, founder of the Korean Peninsula Future Forum.[21] This strategy being advocated by Western and some South Korean sources presents Pyongyang with a dilemma. A clamp down on market activities for the sake of security would undermine the economic gains made as a result of partial marketisation, weakening the country's position in the long term and leaving it more vulnerable to Western economic warfare efforts. A failure to counter the use of markets for subversive purposes by external actors, however, presents other possibly more immediate risks. This explains what appears to be the DPRK's current policy, coupling allowances for controlled and gradual marketisation of parts of the economy with extensive efforts to thwart efforts by adversaries to use markets as a medium for subversion.

Associate fellow and Executive Director of the International Institute for Strategic Studies (IISS) in North America and Director of the IISS Non-Proliferation and Disarmament Programme, Mark Fitzpatrick, referred to the infiltration of foreign media into the DPRK as "a cost-effective and non-kinetic way of encouraging conditions for change"—by which he referred to state collapse. In his paper titled "North Korea: Is

Regime Change the Answer?," in which he concluded decisively in the affirmative, he stressed that the U.S. could "hasten the day of Korean unification" through information warfare, stating: "Balloons carrying information pamphlets can be quietly launched at night. Powerful radio signals can be beamed in, using domestic frequencies so they can be picked up by local radios. Overseas North Korean workers can be targeted for political proselytising."[22] By reunification, Director Fitzpatrick was not referring to a consensual or reciprocal process—but a unilateral one through which the system of the Western-aligned state would be forcefully imposed north of the 38th parallel through the undermining of the people's republic.

In a paper published by the Council on Foreign Relations in 2009, written by prominent North Korea expert and director of the Korea Risk Group Andrei Lankov, information warfare was identified and strongly advocated as a means of toppling the Korean state. In the article support for radio broadcasts, funding of documentaries specifically targeting the North Korean population with pro-Western narratives on political and historical issues, and infiltration of Western popular media, were all strongly advocated by Lankov as a means by which the U.S. could undermine and eventually bring about the end of the DPRK. He also advocated policies to "help create an environment in which unauthorised information spread faster and more easily" in the DPRK, and finally advised: "the United States should be cultivating a political opposition and alternative elite that could one day replace the fallen Kim regime."[23]

A comprehensive and extremely detailed study of media in North Korea and the influences of Western media on the population was authored by the associate director of the Washington D.C. based research consultancy Intermedia, Nat Kretchun, and the Korea projects coordinator at the New York based NGO EastWest Coalition, Jane Kim, in 2012. Like other reports, it emphasised the role of the United States government in particular in bringing change to North Korea through information warfare efforts, emphasising the long-term nature of such a campaign to undermine the state. The study also highlighted the importance of NGOs actively working to infiltrate media into the country, and alluded to creating "significant pushback against the regime from the ground up" and "laying the ground for a more open North Korea" as long term objectives. It also emphasised the benefits of popular media such as soap operas over other forms of media, and equated progress and positive developments with the emergence among the North Korean population of positive attitudes towards the United States and South Korea and negative attitudes towards their own government and political system. The paper also showed a strong interest in and highlighted the importance of tracking social change in the country through a variety of means to monitor the success of information warfare efforts over time.[24]

President of the Association of Korean Political Studies in North America Park Kyung Ae strongly alluded to the opening provided by partial marketisation of the Korean economy for an external push for regime change. She referred to marketisation as a potential "Trojan Horse" to force political change and stated, while alluding to this possibility: "Rather than through war, many argue that North Korea's regime change could be brought about through an implosion." Park further noted that the economic hardship could be leveraged to bring about the state's overthrow. Alluding to this possibility, Park stated: "a failure of a national economy undermines the legitimacy of an authoritarian regime and triggers a transition to democracy, resulting in the termination of authoritarianism or socialism. Economic crisis has been widely accepted as the catalyst of regime collapse." Citing the continuities in policy under leaders Kim Il Sung and Kim Jong Il, Park stressed regarding the end goal of the Western-led push for forced regime change through non-military means: "Any efforts to change the North Korea regime should involve attempts to destroy the fundamental values and structures of Kim's government, and alter the governing principles and norms, including the socialist values and the *Juche* (self-reliance) ideology." Park expressed what appeared to be a consensus in the West—the regime change agenda pertained not only to removing the heads of state but to a full debellatio—forcing the complete ideological, economic, social and cultural remaking of the country in the West's own image.[25]

As early as 1997 Major Ralph Peters, a Foreign Area Officer for Eurasia assigned responsibility for future warfare at the Office of the Deputy Chief of Staff for Intelligence, had written a prominent and highly insightful paper detailing how penetration of information from the Western Bloc into non-Western societies across the world served as an effective means for the West to undermine potential adversaries and guarantee its own continued primacy. "The number one priority of non-Western governments in the coming decades will be to find acceptable terms for the flow of information within their societies," he observed, further elaborating that the citizen of a non-Western nation faced:

> a deluge of information telling him, exaggeratedly and dishonestly, how well the West lives. In this age of television-series franchising, videos, and satellite dishes, this young, embittered male gets his skewed view of us from reruns of Dynasty and Dallas, or from satellite links beaming down Baywatch, sources we dismiss too quickly as laughable and unworthy of serious consideration as factors influencing world affairs. But their effect is destructive beyond the power of words to describe. Hollywood goes where Harvard never penetrated, and the foreigner, unable to touch the reality of America, is touched by America's irresponsible fantasies of itself; he sees a devilishly enchanting, bluntly sexual, terrifying world from which he is excluded, a world of wealth he can judge only in terms of his own poverty.

Regarding the weaponization of Western information superiority, Peters observed:

> There is no "peer competitor" in the cultural (or military) department. Our cultural empire has the addicted—men and women everywhere—clamoring for more. And they pay for the privilege of their disillusionment. American culture is infectious, a plague of pleasure, and you don't have to die of it to be hindered or crippled in your integrity or competitiveness. The very struggle of other cultures to resist American cultural intrusion fatefully diverts their energies from the pursuit of the future. We should not fear the advent of fundamentalist or rejectionist regimes. They are simply guaranteeing their peoples' failure, while further increasing our relative strength.... Hollywood is "preparing the battlefield," and burgers precede bullets.

Regarding the challenges facing those non-Western states targeted by information war, Peters further noted: "Information is at once our core commodity and the most destabilizing factor of our time. Until now, history has been a quest to acquire information; today, the challenge lies in managing information.... One of the defining bifurcations of the future will be the conflict between information masters [U.S.] and information victims." Elaborating on the fates of "victims" of the U.S. information war, he stated: "For those individuals and cultures that cannot join or compete with our information empire, there is only inevitable failure... Information, from the internet to rock videos, will not be contained...our victims volunteer."[26]

The North Korea Strategy Center, which established its first international office in New York in 2015—the year President Obama called for escalated information warfare efforts against the DPRK—has led efforts to alter North Korean society and subvert the unity of the state along lines highly similar to those laid out by Major Peters. An anti-DPRK NGO with the stated goal of regime change, it invested heavily in the smuggling of flash drives into the country and their dissemination through black markets. Alongside an encyclopedia co-developed by the Wikimedia foundation promoting Western-favored political narratives, the Strategy Center has focused heavily on Western popular media—pictures such as *Friends*, *Superbad* and *Sex and the City*. Such media represent what Major Peters referred to as: "America's irresponsible fantasies of itself; [which] he [the non-Westerner—the target] sees a devilishly enchanting, bluntly sexual, terrifying world from which he is excluded."[27] The strategy group notably held screenings of different types of media in South Korea to test the reactions of North Korean defectors living there and see which would have the greatest psychological impacts. They reported, as an example, regarding one North Korean viewer of *Superbad* at such a screening: "She would later explain to me that she 'had never seen a movie on that scale of filthiness before,' and she doesn't hide her reaction; she spends most of the 113-minute barrage of adolescent sexual angst and dick jokes covering her face with the backs of her hands, as if to cool off her burning cheeks.... [she] starts by listing the most astonishing elements from a North Korean perspective: the frank sex talk, constant genitalia references, underage drinking, cops crashing their car, teenage McLovin shooting a gun. All would be seen as indescribably alien, she says. 'Even watching it now, I find it vulgar and shocking,' she says. 'If I were still in North Korea, it would blow my mind.'" This "shock factor" was key to Western efforts to force a societal change in the country.[28]

Peters' claim, that Western popular media "that feature extreme violence and to-the-victors-the-spoils sex—are our most popular cultural weapon, bought or bootlegged nearly everywhere,"[29] corresponds closely to the strategy of anti-DPRK organizations attempting to infiltrate such media into the country. Such media provide North Koreans with images of sex and violence to which they are not accustomed in a country where pornography is banned, media is conservative and television violence is moderate. This, according to organizations targeting the country, is seen as a potential basis for forcing social change and starting a revolution—if not a political one then a social and cultural one with very significant political implications in the medium-long term.[30] Those Koreans exposed to such media are referred to by such NGOs as the "enlightened"—a testament to the self-righteous and self-congratulatory nature of the propaganda campaign.[31]

The North Korea Strategy Center was just one of several Western NGOs involved in information efforts against the DPRK. The New York-based Human Rights Foundation sought to infiltrate information into the country with the stated aim of promoting public dissent to subvert the state.[32] The foundation's activities were described as "initiatives that disrupt the North Korean regime" under the "Disrupt North Korea" program.[33] One of the foundation's more notable programs saw the organisation drop 10,000 copies of the film *The Interview* into the DPRK by balloon.[34] Bruce Bennett, an ardently anti–North Korean expert from the RAND Corporation think tank, had strongly advised Sony Pictures to maintain the gore-filled execution of Chairman Kim Jong Un at the end of the film for political reasons as it was "something Koreans needed to see" on both sides of the 38th parallel.[35] He had stated: "I believe that a story that talks about the removal of the Kim family regime and the creation of a new government by the North Korean people (well, at least the elites) will start some real thinking in South Korea and, I believe, in the North once the DVD leaks into the North (which it almost certainly will)."[36] It was thus to be expected that, with the film altered specifically to bring about a political impact in North Korea, efforts would be undertaken by hostile actors to propagate it.

Some anti-North Korean, Western-backed NGOs and self-proclaimed human rights groups have gone so far as to drop pornographic materials into the country by balloon, which in 2020 included professionally photoshopped leaflets showing the First Lady Ri Sol Ju, formerly a much-celebrated singer and national icon, performing sexual acts on South Korean politicians. A leading organiser of the campaign, Hong Gang Cheol, stated in an interview with South Korean media in June 2020 that human rights groups received considerable funding for such activities from sponsors in the U.S., and were "paid about 1.5 million won (US$1,234) for launching a single balloon. But the actual cost for a balloon is between 80,000 and 120,000 won (US$65.81–98.21) These groups are getting credit for launching balloons that bring in 10 times their cost." Regarding the considerable threat these launches posed to North Korea, he stated that members had "suggested filling the balloons bound for North Korea with dollar bills smeared with stuff that COVID-19 patients had breathed on," noting that such measures had been actively discussed at a time when the DPRK was going to considerable lengths to contain the outbreak.[37] Escalated launches at the time, which the South Korean government was allowing to take place from restricted areas,[38] led Pyongyang to issue a harsh response, downgrading ties to Seoul, destroying the inter-Korean liaison office, and warning that such actions would not be tolerated.

The human rights groups and their American sponsors could thus have been seen to have succeeded, in that their actions undermined the détente between the two Koreas, which had been stringently opposed by hardliners in both Washington and Seoul. As Co-founder and International Director of the Atlas Network NGO Casey Lartigue said to the writer in person in 2017, the goal of promoting human rights in North Korea, in the eyes of the West, equates to nothing less than the total destruction of North Korea's political system, remaking of its society and punishment of its leadership—presumably to be done by the United States. Lartigue was the host of *North Korea Today,* and his NGO is funded by the U.S. State Department and by Congress and itself directly funds defectors such as Park Yeonmi (see below) and defector groups to promote anti-North Korean narratives. The resulting campaigns can be seen as a wholesale assault on North Korean society carried out with a degree of zeal and self-righteousness that is outstanding, even when compared to other Western campaigns against defiant non-Western states.

Other prominent NGOs targeting the DPRK by using information warfare included North Korean Intellectuals Solidarity and the Fighters for a Free North Korea, both of which strongly advocated forced regime change and are reported to have worked closely with Western intelligence organisations. Radio broadcasts into North Korea have provided another means to further such efforts, and several Western state-funded initiatives have been launched for this purpose. The more prominent among them are Radio Free Chosun, North Korea Reform Radio, Free North Korea Radio, the North Korea Development Institute and Save North Korea—all directly funded by the U.S. Congress through the National Endowment for Democracy (NED).[39] The NED itself has been closely affiliated with the CIA since its foundation, carrying out overtly what the agency had formerly done alone, and more covertly.[40] Other notable broadcasters included Voice of America[41] and Radio Free Asia—part of the state-funded U.S. Agency for Global Media, and the British BBC.

Forcing a westernization of North Korea society through Western popular media, in what may be deemed the ultimate case of cultural imperialism, does pose a potential threat to the DPRK. Western state-funded broadcasts into the country promoting Western narratives on historical or political affairs, or infiltration of films depicting the execution of the Korean leader by Westerners, can be termed propaganda by foreign agents. This is in contrast to state propaganda to which North Koreans are exposed through state media outlets such as *Rodong Sinmun.* The difference is that one is funded by the Korean state, which is tasked with protecting the interests of the Korean nation and holds this as its primary agenda, and the other funded by hostile Western states which have demonstrated ill intentions towards the Korean people multiple times including a history of severe war crimes against them. The responsibility of Western propaganda outlets, for which they receive state funding, is to further the interests of their respective governments—which in the case of broadcasts into the DPRK involves undermining an independent non-Western actor. The final goal is this actor's destruction and the annexation of its territory and population into the Western sphere of influence.

Counteroffensive: Pyongyang Responds to Information War

North Korea's security system has shielded it from many potentially destabilizing influences, and among the targets for Western information warfare efforts it has been and arguably remains today the most secure. The strong cultural, national and ethnic identity of the Korean nation plays a large part in galvanizing the population, as does the historical memory of Western atrocities against the Korean people—reinforced by more recent Western military threats and economic warfare efforts. Much as was the case in Israel in the 25 years following the Holocaust,[42] this historical memory and sense of imminent threat has fostered ideological unity, allowing the North Korean state and society to withstand enormous external pressures. It is notable that Major Ralph Peters singled out "cultures of East Asia" as a minority which "appear strong enough to survive the onslaught" of "contemporary American culture, the most destructive of competitor cultures." While he believed that America's "most popular cultural weapon" would leave adversaries in the Middle East and the Islamic world in chaos and inevitably bring about their defeat, he strongly implied that East Asian civilisation states could potentially prove more resilient and ultimately survive.[43]

Pyongyang for its part has been far from passive in its efforts to strengthen its defenses against information warfare efforts, and the Obama administration was not the only party in the 2010s to show awareness of the growing importance of this form of warfare and its potential to prove decisive in conflict. Under the new leadership of Kim Jong Un and the reorganized Korean Workers' Party from December 2011, Pyongyang began to place its own emphasis on improving both the state's ideological unity and its prosperity. One prominent means for doing so has been by considerable investment in improving the quality and appeal of the country's own popular media. The Moranbong Band—which made its debut in July 2012, and the Chongbong Band—which formed three years later, were two of the foremost manifestations of this, both introducing entirely new styles to classical songs and new songs entirely. These promoted themes from the nobility of studying hard for the sake of the country to the pride of satellite launches and missile tests. Public musical and artistic performances meanwhile not only adopted new and more modern styles, but were also far larger, more ambitious and more spectacular—among them the massive Great Party Rosy Korea performance in 2015 featuring over 1000 artists on a specially built floating stage on the Daedong River in central Pyongyang.

While the Korean state had always prized music and the arts, stylistically these new performances were considerably more widely appealing and perhaps "catchy," than what had come in prior years—a trend which only accelerated throughout the 2010s. As politics professor Pekka Korhonen from Finland's University of Jyväskylä, in one of the few Western analyses made of the considerable changes to musical style in the DPRK at the time, observed of the Moranbong Band in particular in 2014: "Moranbong Band has to be regarded as a symbol of a new era…the real audience has been the whole population with an access to a TV set. The band, an object of talk and admiration, became immediately extremely popular with the North Korean population. The band had style, it promised something new, had a foreign aura even when playing familiar military marches, and made music that truly inspired people. Visitors tell about people dancing in public while listening to Moranbong Band DVDs, or shops closing and streets becoming deserted when the group's concerts were broadcast on national TV." Referring to "the distinct Moranbong Band style, simultaneously catchy and intricate," he observed that the music was working "at a more popular level" than older Korean works. "This poetic creation is continuous. Practically all of their versions of the national hymn *Aegukka* are different, although there would be no ethical social realist reason for this. They simply create art."[44]

Chairman Kim Jong Un from the outset appeared intent on focusing on strengthening the unity of the population and countering external information warfare efforts. This was perhaps most strongly alluded to in his speech on February 25, 2014, in which he addressed the Ideological Workers of the Workers' Party of Korea. The chairman stressed the importance of "an information offensive to ideologically and morally overpower the imperialist reactionary forces who are trying to stamp out socialism by all means," and warned that the Western Bloc were "persisting in their attempts to infiltrate corrupt reactionary ideology and culture into our country with our service personnel and young people as the target, while clinging to manoeuvres to apply sanctions against our country and stifle it."[45] When considered as a response to the paper of Major Ralph Peters, which articulated with considerable accuracy the future of information warfare, and taking into account the centrality of information warfare to Obama administration's strategy for targeting the DPRK, the implications of Chairman Kim's speech appear very significant. It also came at a time of the aforementioned calls by leading experts and a number of highly prominent think tank papers to focus heavily on information warfare as central aspects of a subversion strategy.

The Korean leader advocated:

> an offensive operation to, outwardly, gain the political and ideological upper hand over the imperialists that hinder our onward movement and, inwardly, sweep up non-socialist practices and decadent ideology and culture by means of the revolutionary ideology and culture. Ideological workers should dishearten the enemy by launching a skilful anti-enemy media warfare, radio warfare, which is aimed at giving wide publicity to the validity of our ideology and cause and at laying bare the vulnerability and foul nature of the imperialists. They should make ideological "missiles" in larger numbers that can deal a heavy blow at the enemy and instil

firm confidence in victory in our service personnel and people. They should take the initiative in launching operations to make the imperialist moves for ideological and cultural infiltration end in smoke, while putting up a double and triple "mosquito net" to prevent the viruses of capitalist ideology which the enemy is persistently attempting to spread from infiltrating across our border.

By nature, the working masses reject the bourgeois ideology and culture which preach the money-is-almighty principle and the law of jungle. We need to create and propagate larger numbers of wholesome and revolutionary works of art and literature, articles and presentations of our own style which contain the beautiful dreams and ideals of the masses and which brim over with national flavour, so as to make the people turn their backs on the bourgeois ideology and culture of their own accord. A decisive measure should be taken to use the Internet as a medium for giving publicity to our ideology and culture in order to cope with the enemy's moves to widely propagate their reactionary ideology and culture by misusing the latest scientific and technological achievements made by mankind.

The sector of ideological work and related units should work out elaborate plans for putting mass media and external publicity means on a modern and IT basis and make persevering efforts to carry them out. The ideological work of the Party should be conducted in an aggressive manner. Our Party's strategy and tactics in ideological work is to make the whole country seethe with a revolutionary leap forward by making the flames of ideological offensive flare up fiercely in the attack spirit of advancing against all odds. The ideological position of our Party should be arranged in the form for attack, not for defence.

We should also conduct the ideological education aimed at imbuing the whole society with the red ideology of the Workers' Party in a proactive way, the political work aimed at calling forth the mental strength of all the service personnel and people as it is done on the frontline and the struggle to sweep away all shades of evil ideas and spirits at a lightning speed. In order to conduct ideological work in an aggressive

> manner, it is necessary, above all, to root out the defeatist view revealed among ideological workers. The ideological workers infected with such a view cannot take even a single step by themselves even if they are put forward in the van of the ideological offensive.[46]

In the first years of the new government, the DPRK did indeed appear to be waging an "ideological offensive" to counter the information war against it. While "ideological work" is extremely difficult to quantify or assess, particularly from outside North Korea, considerable investments in new mediums for such work give a significant indication as to its perceived importance at the time. In 2013 the world's largest stadium, the Rungrado 1st of May Stadium on Pyongyang's Rungra Island,[47] underwent an extensive two-year renovation to prepare it for major future events such as the Pyongyang Marathons—intended to display Korean modernity to athletes from across the world, as well as the Arirang Mass Games. Chairman Kim Jong Un personally oversaw changes to the artistic style of these games. The writer viewed footage of the Mass Games performance attended by leader Kim Jong Un and Chinese Premier Xi Jinping at the stadium June 21, 2019 with Chinese artists, who informed him that their own country had yet to put on a comparably enthralling performance

The importance of passing historical memory on to new generations of Koreans, particularly those of revolution and struggle against U.S. invasion, were also emphasized under the new campaign. In 2013 the Victorious Fatherland Liberation War Museum commemorating the Korean War effort was expanded and thoroughly refurbished. In July 2015 the Sinchon Museum of American War Atrocities was rebuilt, and the previously bland and unimposing structure was replaced by an imposing and spectacular monument—intended to educate the population and in particular the military on the events of the past and the nature of the country's enemy.[i] Eleven months later, in July 2016, the state opened the National House of Class Education to educate its population on the "History of Aggression" against the state. The facility was

i For a society unaccustomed to televised violence, the displays are graphic and extremely striking. On the writer's first visit to the museum, several of the preceding tour group of around two dozen soldiers were seen vomiting in the bathrooms after seeing displays on methods used by Americans for torture and execution. The writer could later verify the large majority of claims made at the museum using official South Korean and Western sources—on the whole they were not fabricated or exaggerated.

intended particularly for younger Koreans who, having not experienced the Korean War or Japanese occupation themselves, lacked first-hand knowledge of the nature of the country's adversaries or the necessity of the military and Workers' Party struggles. Korean media stated that the facility would help the people of the DPRK to clearly realize who its enemies were.[48] Awareness of the nation's history, not through the narrative of its Western adversaries but through the population's own experiences, is seen as vital to both galvanising society against current threats and to prevent repetition of the same atrocities by the same perpetrators. As head of the National House of Class Education Kim Hyong Chol said shortly after its opening in regard to its purpose: "If we forget the history of aggression, it can be repeated. We need to teach a new generation not to forget it."[49]

Complementing efforts to counter information warfare through ideology and popular media, the Korean government in the 2010s increasingly emphasized the importance of economic modernization and improvement of the population's quality of life.[50] Investments in new forms of agriculture,[51] electronics,[52] and infrastructure[53] and renewed efforts to attract foreign investment all served to improve the population's living standards. Pristine new water parks, theme parks and beach resorts began to open across the country and were accessible at low prices, while everything from architecture to flower arrangements and police uniforms have emphasized good aesthetics. This was a polar opposite to the archetypal image of a drab Soviet-style socialist state, epitomized by the appearance of Moscow in the USSR's final decade, and images of Pyongyang, Kaesong and the Korean countryside have thus repeatedly surprised those who previously visited or lived in the Soviet Union and expected a similar style in the DPRK. Progress in these fields to beautify the country and raise living standards can serve to undermine hostile information warfare efforts targeting the Korean citizen with what Major Peters referred to as "a deluge of information telling him, exaggeratedly and dishonestly, how well the West lives."[54]

While outlining measures to counter hostile information warfare efforts domestically, the Korean leader notably also mentioned plans to counter negative coverage of the state abroad in his February 2014 address, stating: "A decisive measure should be taken to use the Internet as a medium for giving publicity to our ideology and culture in order to cope with the enemy's moves to widely propagate their reactionary ideology and culture by misusing the latest scientific and technological achievements made by mankind."[55] The DPRK subsequently began to host websites on its own newly established server in Pyongyang—rather than relying on those in China and Japan—and the number of websites managed by the state and the quantity and quality of their content began to grow rapidly.[56] Efforts to promote pro-Korean material on the internet such as films, music videos, performing arts and documentaries have made extensive use of social media channels such as YouTube.

The aforementioned study by director Nat Kretchun and project coordinator Jane Kim noted regarding the growing sophistication of North Korea's use of new forms of media in the early 2010s:

> North Korea is beginning to develop a more sophisticated internet strategy—specifically, one that reflects a clear understanding of the internet's economic potential and the importance of strategic marketing. Close examination of North Korea's websites reveals something of a two-pronged approach of targeting consumers according to purchasing power. Commercial websites show strong determination to attract investors and acquire foreign capital by promoting North Korea as an attractive investment opportunity while noncommercial websites appear to target individuals to market North Korean ideology and culture.[57]

Efforts by the DPRK to promote its image overseas overall appear to have been less successful than efforts to counter offensive Western information warfare efforts domestically.[ii] This can be attributed to a number of factors, including the overwhelmingly greater power of Western media and soft power internationally building on several decades of investment in the field, compared to negligible funding for Korean programs, language and cultural barriers and active moves by Western social media companies such as YouTube to ban highly popular channels and pages deemed "pro-North Korean" and purge their content. This has occurred on multiple occasions without explanation, which has been labelled by some analysts as a form of censorship. Such targeting

ii The reason the writer refers to Western efforts as "information war," but not to those of the DPRK, is the fundamentally different agendas of efforts to promote narratives and images overseas. The stated purpose of the Western Bloc in its campaign has been to bring about the destruction and westernisation of the Korean state, whereas the DPRK's efforts to promote its image abroad appear intended to attract investment and tourism and undermine hostile narratives—not to force cultural or societal changes or to overthrow governments overseas.

has not been unique to North Korea, and similar measures by Western social media companies such as Google and Twitter have very frequently arbitrarily targeted information sources associated with Western adversaries such as Russia,[58] China,[59] Cuba,[60] Syria[61] and Iran.[62] These sources—from the Twitter accounts of leaders such as First Secretary Raoul Castro[63] and Supreme Leader Ali Khamenei[64] to state run media outlets such as RT—are often blocked entirely or artificially "de-ranked" by search engines.

There is a reason that the embassies of Iran and the U.S. trade words and argue various issues on Chinese social media platforms—that is that the predominant Western platforms such as Twitter and Facebook come under tremendous pressure to impose censorship, erasing posts and deleting accounts such as that of the Iranian Foreign Minister and a wide range of other officials which give voice to the thoughts and opinions of those being targeted by the West.[65] North Korean efforts to create an overseas media presence have inevitably similarly suffered. Korean channels blocked have included Chosun TV, KCTV, StimmeKoreas, Tonpomail, and Uriminzokkiri among others.[66] The last three are thought to be run by Korean supporters or Korean diaspora communities overseas, rather than the Korean state itself, and their targeting indicates that the source of their content was not the cause for their censorship—but rather the pro-DPRK messages themselves. The Facebook page Beauty of DPRK North Korea, which posted apolitical footage of the North Korean countryside, architecture and scenery and at its peak reached hundreds of thousands with its videos, was similarly inexplicably terminated in October 2019. Again these were hardly isolated instances—with Facebook, for example, in January 2020 announcing measures to delete content sympathetic to American adversaries.[67] The internet servers set up in Pyongyang from which Korean media is hosted have also come under multiple cyberattacks, which the DPRK blamed on the United States. The source of the attacks remains unconfirmed, however, and North Korea has yet to provide evidence for its claim.[68]

While the West and those who believe in the universalism of Western values may exaggerate the universal appeal of their ideology, and thereby overestimate the potency of their attempts at quiet revolution through flash drives and other means of information warfare, a potential danger does remain to the Korean state. The Korean leadership however, particularly under Chairman Kim Jong Un and the again dominant Korean Workers' Party, have through their statements and actions demonstrated a high level of awareness regarding this threat. The country remains perhaps the most challenging target for information warfare however, due to both effective state responses and the resilience of North Korean society and ideology based on both its East Asian civilizational roots and the strong "culture of resistance" encouraging unity among the population. Historical memory of the constant struggle for survival forms a significant part of the foundation of this culture and continues to shape North Korean society. Nevertheless, with options increasingly limited for economic or military pressure, the Western Bloc is likely to continue to rely heavily on information warfare to exploit any possible chink in the nation's defences. Relative to the maintenance of the considerable arsenal of U.S. and allied military assets aimed at Pyongyang, this remains a very low cost and potentially far more dangerous means of waging war.

Atrocities, Human Rights, Propaganda and Intelligence Failures: How the West Understands the DPRK

As with all major conflicts, a critical aspect of the confrontation between Washington and Pyongyang has been the struggle to influence narratives and win global support—to have "history on one's side" not only in the eyes of one's own people, but in those of the international community. When U.S. troops first landed in Korea in September 1945 the United States accounted for half of the world economy and was investing heavily in enhancing its soft power globally on a scale with which the Korean nationalist movement, or any world power for that matter, could not hope to compete.[69] The use of propaganda took on a newfound importance following outbreak of the Korean War, with public support in America and morale in the military reaching historic lows and Washington's justifications for intervention increasingly being questioned.[70] This led the United States to place greater emphasis on demonization of its adversary and delegitimization of its cause to compensate for waning public and international support for its own actions.[71]

One of the most prolific examples of the use of wartime propaganda was the American response to the return of significant numbers of its servicemen who made public statements in support of the Korean and Chinese adversaries—often strongly criticising the conduct of the U.S.-led coalition and alleging that war crimes were committed. The creation of the myth of "brainwashing," a term first coined by the CIA, was thus intended to delegitimise these servicemen and their testimonies—supposedly the soldiers were not criticising U.S. policy of their own volition, but were doing so under some mysterious form of Asiatic mind control. Although seemingly ridiculous, racial sentiments against East Asians and the atmosphere of "Yellow Peril" at the time, combined with the narrative's endorsement by respected sources in media and the intelligence community, led to its widespread acceptance. As New York University professor of history and prominent Korea expert, Monica Kim, noted: "'Brainwashing' became the perfect trope with which to render these American POW's 'desires'—or politics, to be more exact—into a more familiar racialised narrative of the unwitting, innocent American being seduced by the mysterious 'Oriental.'"[72] "Brainwashing" allowed America and the wider Western world to rest assured in the righteousness of their cause, neutralising as contradictions to this narrative not only the former servicemen who spoke against their government, but also those who defected to or collaborated with the East Asian allies, and even the Chinese and North Korean prisoners of war who refused to see the light and defect to the "free world" rather than return home.

Kim described "A process of fashioning the Korean Communist POW into an ideological figure—or more specifically, a "fanatic"—a phrase used extensively by U.S. military personnel to describe the Communist POWs in both their statements for the case file and administrative memos passed from higher command to the camps."[73] These individuals, Western and allied populations were assured, were not acting of their own free will—and fantastical stories of communist Asiatic mind control were commonplace to explain their actions.[74] Thus those whose first-hand experience of the war led them to dispute the narrative of a Western good against an Asian communist evil were stripped of their voices—it was the Asian communist propagandists speaking through them, not the people themselves, be they freed American soldiers or East Asian prisoners.

Use of propaganda also proved highly effective to delegitimise DPRK's struggle for Korean self-determination. Depictions of the "fanatic Oriental Communist," rather than simply the enemy nation or the adversary, made anything from Pyongyang's requests that its borders be respected to demands by North Korean prisoners in Western run camps for basic rights appear illegitimate.[75] Korean nationalism, the Korean People's Republic in southern Korea and opposition to U.S. Military occupation and the policies of the U.S. imposed government of Syngman

Rhee had in much the same way been delegitimized by depicting them as puppets of the USSR—not a genuine aspiration of the Korean people.[76] The same was true of the North Koreans and the Democratic People's Republic—depicted as a proxy of Moscow[77]—despite the roots of the Korean nationalist movement and Korean resistance long predating a Soviet presence on the peninsula. Propagandistic depictions nevertheless afforded the U.S. and its allies the right to blanketly dismiss opposition to its designs for the Korean nation.

Efforts to delegitimize and silence voices undermining the narrative of a "good West" against an "Asian communist evil" would persist long after the Korean War and appear to have redoubled following the Cold War's end. As perceptions of a global communist menace, of which the DPRK was previously portrayed as a fanatical puppet, have faded, demonization of the state has increasingly come to focus on allegations of major human rights abuses. North Korea's population are portrayed as oppressed or even enslaved, and the state's collapse, westernisation and integration into the Western-led order is depicted not only as an inevitability—but as a fate desired by and strongly in the interest of its people. Such a narrative depicts the benevolent Western world's actions against the northeast Asian state largely as altruistic—emphasizing the interests not of Western governments but rather of the supposedly enslaved Korean people themselves.

To further this narrative, atrocity fabrications and horror stories regarding life in North Korea are vital. The accounts of a small number of defectors from the DPRK residing in South Korea and the West have served as the most essential source of such stories—although a significant number of the most influential and best publicised testimonies have proven to be highly dubious. Several North Korean defectors have been able to derive significant financial benefits from denouncing their former homeland, some of the most prominent gaining celebrity status in the West in the process while giving inconsistent or otherwise unreliable testimonies. Shin Dong Hyuk was one such defector, whose allegations of severe human rights abuses were widely accepted as fact in the West despite a lack of evidence. Shin's life story, *Escape from Camp 14: One Man's Remarkable Journey from North Korea to Freedom in the West*, was authored by former *Washington Post* journalist Blaine Harden, based on his narration. The book's title was notably indicative of the agenda it represented—the story of "Western good" against "Asian communist evil"—and it became a bestseller promoted in Western countries as a key reference for understanding the DPRK. The book was translated into 27 languages and sold worldwide—while Western human rights organizations heavily based several of their reports on the DPRK on Shin's testimony. This testimony was then used as a pretext for further Western economic sanctions against the DPRK, and was said to have "shifted the global discourse about North Korea."[78] A Western-led United Nations commission on North Korean human rights would base its reporting and positions almost exclusively on Shin's testimony, with a member of the commission referring to him as the world's "single strongest voice" on Pyongyang's abuses.[79]

Several years after Shin's testimony was published, the author, Blaine Harden, himself revealed that Shin had fabricated much of his story while the book was being written.[80] Shin later admitted to having "altered details" of his testimony. Harden stated that Shin was an "unreliable narrator" and re-emphasized that "Shin was the only source of information about his early life," allowing him to alter his testimonies as they would be accepted without the need for evidence.[81] Harden also said he would not be surprised if Shin made further alternations to his testimony in future.[82] Other North Korean defectors interviewed by South Korean media notably referred to Shin's testimony as "complete lies,"[83] while Korea expert Andrei Lankov, despite being a strong critic who had called for regime change in Pyongyang,[84] stated that Shin's testimony was unreliable—noting that defectors faced considerable pressure to exaggerate their stories.[85] Western sanctions on Pyongyang and UN reports made on the basis of Shin's testimony notably were not reviewed, much less changed.[86] What the DPRK's adversaries needed was not necessarily a verifiable story—but rather an emotional and horrifying one which could be used to demonise the Korean state before the world and serve as a pretext for further hostile actions towards it. Shin's testimony filled this role perfectly—and it didn't have to be even remotely true to do so.

Another highly prominent defector whose fame went on to eclipse that of Shin was Park Yeonmi, who was strongly endorsed and widely promoted in the West in much the same way as her predecessor shortly after the flaws in Shin's testimony were revealed. It has been widely reported by other North Korean defectors, and even by some prominent Western reporters with a basic knowledge of the DPRK, that Park's stories were highly inconsistent with reality and at times nonsensical. Award-winning documentary producer Mary Ann Jolley, having interviewed Park several times, noted telling inconsistencies in her stories.

In an article for *The Diplomat* Jolley details how interviews Park gave changed completely depending on when she told her story. She also noted that several facts Park gave did not stand up to reason; for example, Jolley wrote: "In telling of her escape from North Korea, Park often says she crossed three or even four mountains during the night to get to the border and describes the pain she endured because her shoes had holes in them. However, Hyesan where Park was living is right on the river that divides the two countries and there are no mountains to cross."[87] This was but one of many impossible claims that Park made, added to a list of severe contradictions between her different interviews. Several other observers, including journalist Michael Basset, concluded that Park's statements regarding the DPRK were not synonymous with the reality in the country, and that she was using outright lies to gain fame and, in the process, tarnish the country's image. Park has meanwhile reaped a small fortune from her "sensationalized" speeches, from which she earns over $12,500 per speech according to her agent.[88]

Je Son Lee, a North Korean defector, noted that several facts about Park's story were clearly fabricated. Regarding some of Park's claims she commented "no one would believe this unless they were an idiot."[89] South Korea professors Shi Eun Yu and Kim Hyun Ah, who worked at the ROK's processing sector for North Korean defectors, strongly refuted several of Park's statements. "It's not possible" they commented outright .[90] Swiss businessman Felix Abt, who had worked and travelled extensively in North Korea for seven years, strongly refuted Park's claims as "obviously exaggerated or plain false," noting multiple significant inconsistencies.[91]

Stories such as those of Shin and Park have been endorsed and promoted because they suit the Western agenda towards North Korea. They are able to gain such traction because of the general ignorance about the DPRK around the world and the country's lack of global media with which to counter this misrepresentation. Among those with even a basic understanding of the country, however, there is generally a consensus that the narratives endorsed in the West and on which Western human rights organizations and reports have based their testimonies are unreliable—often bordering on absurd.

While the allure of fame and fortune may motivate some to seek celebrity status, the need to subsist in the ROK where defectors face discrimination, earn significantly less money than South Koreans and often struggle to adapt to life is another key motivating factor. The fact that defectors and their children residing in Seoul have been known in extreme cases to die of starvation alone says much regarding their plight.[92] Statistics from defectors' unemployment rates to high school dropout rates among their children[93] further demonstrate this, which leaves resorting to sensationalist reporting as one of their few avenues to escape poverty and provide better for themselves and their families. Dr. Konstantin Asmolov was among several scholars who noted that defectors had a strong financial incentive to fabricate testimonies that were as gruesome as possible—with Western and South Korean media prizing such stories highly. He stated to this effect: "The media has enough materials about how difficult they find it to adapt in the South and that they are considered second-class citizens there. One of the few ways to get more is to actively participate in propaganda against the North Korea, telling the public not so much what is really going on, but what is desired to be heard. And as the competition is high, it is necessary to tell something particularly terrible and become the author of an 'exclusive rumor.'"[94] Interviews with defectors living in Seoul strongly indicate that there is a strong tendency towards fabrication of testimonies which are particularly gruesome or horrific regarding life in the DPRK—and that the financial incentive for doing so can be very considerable.[95]

While defectors are a prominent source of horror stories regarding life in the DPRK, Western media outlets and human rights organisations have repeatedly been found to have themselves entirely fabricated accounts to demonise the state. Several Western journalists have attested to the unreliability of major outlets' reporting on the DPRK. *The Telegraph* wrote: "when it comes to covering news about the 'Hermit Kingdom' it seems that sometimes the rule book is thrown out the window."[96] A report from *Business Insider* came to much the same conclusion.[97] Max Fisher from the *Washington Post* wrote that regarding North Korea: "almost any story is treated as broadly credible, no matter how outlandish or thinly sourced."[98] Isaac Stone-Fish wrote in *Foreign Policy* that: "as an American journalist you can write almost anything you want about North Korea and people will just accept it." He admitted to having done the same himself, detailing a severe "North Korean Drug Epidemic" without evidence, which later proved to be entirely false.[99] Almost any story depicting the country negatively is generally accepted.

Korean Studies professor and prominent expert on the DPRK Charles Armstrong referred to North Korea's isolation as having "served in the West as a blank screen on which many—often mutually contradictory—fears and fantasies have been projected."[100] A prominent example was a report shortly after Kim Jong Un's accession to leadership that all men in the DPRK were required by law to get his exact haircut. This was first reported by *Radio Free Asia* (RFA),[101] a U.S.-based and government-funded nonprofit broadcasting corporation with the stated purpose of "advancing the goals of U.S. foreign policy."[102] RFA retained close ties to U.S. intelligence from its foundation, and was referred to by the *New York Times* as a "CIA broadcasting venture"—established during the Cold War as part of a generously funded agency propaganda network alongside Radio Free Europe, Radio Liberty, Free Cuba Radio and several others.[103] The purported law's absurdity reinforced the image of a repressive and farcical leadership in Pyongyang, and the story was re-reported by major news outlets such the BBC as fact without evidence or fact-checking.[104] As was so often the case with such stories, those from RFA in particular,[105] it turned out to be entirely false. Foreign businessmen and NGO workers in Pyongyang at the time all contradicted the seemingly fabricated story—it was "just stupid" in the words of the director of Singapore-based NGO Choson Exchange.[106]

By using false information to demonize the DPRK, *Radio Free Asia* fulfils the purpose for which it receives its government funding—advancing the goals of U.S. foreign policy by depicting North Korea as a pariah state and exacerbating tensions around the country. In 2017 *RFA* reported that China's Foreign Ministry had advised all Chinese citizens to immediately evacuate the DPRK for their safety, at a time of high military tensions with the United States.[107] While some Chinese citizens who heard the broadcast did evacuate, there was no record of such a warning[108] and the Chinese Foreign Ministry had to release a statement denying the report—which it referred to as Fake News.[109] This case was far from isolated—and represented part of a wider trend in Western reporting on the DPRK. Other prominent examples included the report that Chairman Kim Jong Un "fed his uncle to dogs,"[110] a story widely reported by Western media, which proved to be entirely fabricated,[111] and a report that Pyongyang claimed to have discovered a "unicorn lair."[112] This was again widely re-reported by Western sources, from news outlets to the *New York Times*-endorsed bestselling guide to the country: *North Korea, Unmasking Three Generations of Madmen*. The original Korean statement announced the discovery of an archaeological site associated with the ancient capital of King Dongmyeong of Goguryeo—a poetic term for which is "kiringul," a unicorn lair. The report represented a combination of cultural ignorance and a willingness to depict the country negatively.

Fabricated reports of executions carried out by the Korean state have been similarly common. Serbian volleyball coach Branislav Moro, who trained North Korea's national team, noted as an example of the near complete detachment of Western reporting from reality that major Western media outlets had reported on the executions of North Korean athletes as punishment for their poor performance at international competitions. Moro stated: "for example, I sit right next to one of those 'killed' athletes and I'm too ashamed to tell him that he's supposed to be dead. I even used my cellphone to check on the internet to confirm his identity. Basically there is very little truthful information out there." Moro noted that this was indicative of a wider phenomenon of demonizing misreporting on the country.[113] Indeed, Western reports of "executions" of high profile North Korean figures,[114] from leading pop singers[115] to generals,[116] have more often than not turned out to be entirely false, with these same supposedly dead figures reappearing on camera. A short disappearance from high profile meetings or television is very often treated as an opportunity by Western journalists to write a sensationalist piece depicting a brutal purge by an erratic leadership.

While Western human rights organisations frequently cite unreliable sources, Shin Dong Hyuk's testimony being a prominent example, as the basis to impose economic sanctions—such organisations have been found to directly fabricate horror stories themselves. Notable examples were the reports by a number of Western organisations, most prominently the Washington-based organisation Human Rights without Frontiers, regarding the fate of Korean defector Yu Tae Jun. Yu had left the DPRK and received South Korean citizenship, but later returned to find his wife. The report stated: "In June of last year he is known to have been executed in South Hamyong Province in North Korea. It is known that the North Korean government executed many former North Koreans, however this is the first time that the victim has actually been identified. In addition, due to the fact that Mr. Yu was a South Korean citizen, the repercussions for this incident are expected to be large. Mr. Yu was publicly executed in front of a group of North Korean citizens. It is known that he was charged with going to South Korea and committing treason against the Pyongyang government."[117] "By all accounts," noted prominent British Korea expert Aidan Foster-Carter, "he's now very dead—at just 33."[118] Western and South Korean media were quick to pick up on this execution, and the prominent paper *Chosun Ilbo* notably reported on it on ten separate occasions.

After reports on his public execution had circulated in Western press for some months, the "now very dead" Yu Tae Jun gave a press conference in the DPRK on June 12, 2001.[119] He subsequently returned to South Korea in 2002, having been fully pardoned for his defection by Pyongyang. Yu's mother, Ahn Chong Suk, stated regarding the circumstances of his return: "I heard from my son that the North Korean leader directed my son's pardon on April 30 last year by saying that a man who loves his wife also loves the fatherland." She nevertheless cautioned her son to lie about the circumstances of his return because otherwise "it might make Kim Jong Il look good."[120] Yu's case was far from an exceptional one, and such reporting by Western human rights groups has not been restricted to the DPRK exclusively, with such organisations found to have similarly fabricated reports on other states targeted by the West.

Examples of atrocity fabrication by Western press and Western human rights organisations to demonise and provide pretext for action against Western target states are many, and the targeting of the DPRK can thus be seen as part of a much wider phenomenon. Western intelligence agencies, for their part, have played a role in planting such stories to justify economic sanctions and military action against their targets. A recent example was the testimony of German journalist and editor Udo Ulfkotte, who stated that intelligence agents frequently forced journalists to publish agency-approved articles under their own names. He testified to this effect:

> I ended up publishing articles under my own name written by agents of the CIA and other intelligence services, especially the German secret service… One day the BND [German foreign intelligence agency] came to my office at the *Frankfurter Allgemeine* in Frankfurt. They wanted me to write an article about Libya and Colonel Muammar Gaddafi… They gave me all this secret information and they just wanted me to sign the article with my name. That article was how Gaddafi tried to secretly build a poison gas factory. It was a story that was printed worldwide two days later.

Ulfkotte went into considerable further detail regarding the means by which Western intelligence agencies would contact journalists and use them to plant stories, the risks of non-compliance and the perks that came with supporting their stories.[121] Stories such as that of a Libyan poison gas factory provided key pretext for hostile policies towards the state—including economic sanctions and eventually an intensive U.S. and European bombing campaign and Western-imposed regime change. Reports from a number of sources including British intelligence revealed only after the Libyan government's overthrow and assassination of its leader that this information had been largely fabricated.[122]

Ulfkotte's allegations were hardly isolated or without precedent. Previously in the Cold War years one of the more prominent operations for this purpose was the CIA's Operation Mockingbird—under which American journalists were recruited to publish articles dictated by the agency.[123] The agency also funded student and cultural organizations and magazines as fronts for spreading propaganda.[124] A report from a congressional investigation in the early 1970s revealed the extent of these operations and their global reach—influencing reporting not only in the United States but across much of the world in line with American foreign policy objectives. The report concluded regarding influence over foreign media in particular:

> The CIA currently maintains a network of several hundred foreign individuals around the world who provide intelligence for the CIA and at times attempt to influence opinion through the use of covert propaganda. These individuals provide the CIA with direct access to a large number of newspapers and periodicals, scores of press services and news agencies, radio and television stations, commercial book publishers, and other foreign media outlets.[125]

The report further noted that agents were placed undercover in key management positions in major media organisations in the United States to ensure that publications were in line with the agency's agenda—a key asset to influence public opinion in a time of Cold War.[126] Former CIA employee William Bader supported the conclusions of the report, stating as an example of the means by which media was influenced by the agency: "You don't need to manipulate *Time* magazine, for example, because there are agency people at the management level."[127]

The CIA's propaganda efforts were described by the *Washington Post* as "a fascinatingly byzantine effort to turn the world to the American way of thinking," and alongside hundreds of media outlets the agency funded and heavily influenced globally hundreds of films and "at least a thousand books" for publication and distribution. The intention was to create anti-Soviet, anti-Chinese and Westphilian content and ideas which would influence populations globally.[128] The *New York Times* noted in its own more extensive report that "in its persistent efforts to shape world opinion, the CIA has been able to call upon a separate and far more extensive network of newspapers, news services, magazines, publishing houses, broadcasting stations and other entities over which it has at various times had some control. The *Times* referred to CIA's "communications Empire" as having "embraced more than 500 news and public information organisations and individuals. According to one CIA official, they ranged in importance 'from Radio Free Europe to a third-string guy in Quito who could get something in the local paper'… the network was known officially as the 'Propaganda Assets Inventory.'" It also noted that the CIA maintained extensive "financial ties to academic, cultural and publishing organisations" globally for much the same purpose. Operations were extremely effective and truly worldwide in their scale, with millions of dollars in subsidies paid to influence media in Cuba alone and other large scale and long-term operations from Kenya and India to Taiwan and South Vietnam.[129]

Tactics for influencing media included funding existing publications, but "in some instances the CIA simply created a newspaper or news service and paid the bills through a bogus corporation." A number of front groups were set up for the CIA to fund media outlets worldwide, the Congress of Cultural Freedom being one example named in the *New York Times* report. "In the United States, the Asia Foundation published newspaper, *The Asian Student*, that was distributed to students from the Far East who were attending American universities" the *Times* noted as an example, with this foundation having been established and run by former CIA members.[130]

More recently the formerly secret Office of Strategic Influence was authorised to plant stories including feeding false reports to journalists to influence public opinion globally, and while the Pentagon was forced to disband the office shortly after its existence became known, later comments by high level officials indicate that such operations have continued under different bodies. The value of this "black propaganda," as it was referred to repeatedly by the *BBC*, was extremely high as a means to target U.S. adversaries.[131]

To take Iraq as an example of the use of "black propaganda," the most prominent atrocities supposedly committed by the Ba'athist state reported to foster anti-Iraqi sentiments in the West and globally turned out to be fabrications. This was aside from allegations of its development of weapons of mass destruction in the late 1990s and early 2000s, which were also revealed to have been fabricated but proved invaluable as a pretext for hostile policies towards Baghdad.[132] One prominent example of this "black propaganda" during the First Gulf War was the claim that Iraqi soldiers had killed several hundred Kuwaiti babies by throwing them out of incubators, based on testimony given to the U.S. Congressional Human Rights Caucus which was cited by both the presidency and by a number of senators as additional pretext for an attack on Iraq. The testimony was strongly supported by the prominent British human rights NGO Amnesty International, an organisation that had itself worked closely with British and U.S. intelligence agencies,[133] which published multiple reports to this effect citing a range of sources.[134] Only once the war was over and Iraq thoroughly ravaged was the incident confirmed to have been completely false—the girl who testified was the daughter of the Kuwaiti ambassador to the U.S., had not been in Kuwait since the Iraqi invasion and had fabricated the story with the cooperation of the Bush administration.[135]

While an illegal U.S. and British-led invasion in 2003 was based on the pretext of halting Iraqi development of weapons of mass destruction, when this narrative had been fully debunked the poor human rights record of the Ba'athist government was used to retrospectively justify the attack. Thus, a figure of 400,000 Iraqis killed and buried in mass graves by the "Saddam regime" was widely circled in U.S. and British media and cited by a number of prominent sources. Amid mounting criticism of the invasion and its lack of legal or even moral pretext, British Prime Minister Tony Blair stated: "400,000 bodies *had been found* in Iraqi mass graves." He was later forced to amend his statement—saying only five thousand had been found—although given the degree of veracity of his previous claims this too remains doubtful. Since the Prime Minister alleged that the larger number of bodies *had* been found, rather than asserting that they *would* be found, it appeared a very deliberate falsification intended to vilify the Iraqi state and justify Western use of force to reshape the country in line with the interests of Washington and London.[136]

In the months preceding the 2003 Iraq War similar horror stories were widely publicised to demonise the Iraqi state—perhaps the most prominent being the "human shredder." This was a plastic shredding machine into which President Saddam Hussein reportedly fed his enemies feet first as a particularly brutal form of execution—described in graphic detail. According to these reports, the remains of the victims were subsequently used as fish food. "See men shredded, then say you don't back war," headlines read, and the story itself originated in an address to the British House of Commons. Although this story too proved a baseless fabrication it proved invaluable in justifying an invasion. As the British paper *The Sun* noted regarding the Prime Minister's campaign to gain support for an invasion: "Public opinion swung behind Tony Blair as voters learned how Saddam fed dissidents feet first into industrial shredders." The story proved to have a similarly strong impact in the United States, and was part of a far larger trend of Western atrocity fabrication which in this case was used to justify the serious violation of international law through unprovoked attack on a UN member state.[137] Iraq presents only one example of how atrocity fabrication and demonization have been used to further aggressive designs against Western adversaries, and of the Iraqi atrocities flagged by Western media and rights groups and later debunked only a few examples are mentioned here. Yugoslavia was another prominent example where atrocities, later proven to be entirely fabricated, were used as pretexts for hostile policy, in this case an illegal Western military intervention in 1999.[138] An understanding of the ability of the West to demonise its adversaries with impunity for political gain, and the frequency with which this is done as a tool of foreign policy, is vital to understanding the nature of Western coverage of North Korea and other targeted states.

Complementing efforts to demonise North Korea in Western reporting, positive imagery of the state is consistently depicted either as a façade or else is censored entirely. Aforementioned efforts to block Korean run or pro-North Korean media by U.S. social media companies represent only part of the picture. A prominent article for the German Institute of Global Area Studies by researchers David Shim and Dirk Nabers regarding portrayals of North Korea in the Western world concluded that positive images were tightly and effectively censored. Depictions of the DPRK were made to simultaneously alienate its people and present them as a threat, with the researchers concluding:

> Images of North Korea showing its military "strength" and internal "weakness" are highlighted as idiosyncratic aspects to emphasize its Otherness. The use of images marks North Korea in particular ways, which separate "them" from "us"… A good example of what is made almost invisible in Western representations of North Korea is smiling or joyful ordinary North Korean people.[139]

Positive imagery of the country is almost always dismissed or otherwise interpreted negatively ("they are being forced to applaud for their leader or to cry for his death,"[140] etc.).

Assessment of one seemingly trivial example of suppression of positive imagery, the response to the popular video blog by British traveller Louis Cole, provides a valuable indicator of this wider trend. Cole's apolitical video on North Korea focused on the quality of attractions such as fun karaoke and water parks and the kind local people, and due to its popularity, the footage risked undermining predominant and overwhelmingly negative Western portrayals of the country. Cole was heavily criticized by organizations such as the American NGO Human Rights Watch for failing to mention the "true North Korea"—the invisible one that is never seen on camera but which Western sources insist represents the true nature of the country:[141] one where seemingly happy and well fed people are, if Western reports are to be believed,[142] secretly starving and miserable behind closed doors. Cole was even widely accused of being a paid agent of the DPRK's government,[143] and although his trip and coverage were entirely apolitical he was strongly expected to take a political stance against the state despite seeing nothing which would prompt this.

As a result of the way the DPRK has been depicted in the West for several decades, and the creation of a social consensus which exists to varying degrees throughout the Western world that the state is a negative presence in the international community—or in more extreme terms "a stain on human history that needs to be expunged"[144]—the ability to objectively analyse North Korea has very often eluded Western analysts and policymakers. CIA analyst John Nixon, who worked on cases for both North Korea and Iraq, noted that the U.S. leadership would consistently put their own prejudices and preconceptions above what intelligence and evidence on the countries actually indicated even if it was in complete contradiction—an extreme case of cognitive dissonance. Nixon noted regarding the way this restricted policymakers' ability to objectively analyse states which they had been conditioned to see as "evil," stating after several meetings in the White House and with military and intelligence officials: "I can conclude that U.S. policymakers were prisoners of what they thought they knew…countervailing intelligence be damned." Regarding prejudices towards these states, policymakers were "convinced it was right, no matter what the intelligence showed."[145]

Nixon recounted that intelligence reports on either Iraq or North Korea which did not fit in with their images as maniacal and essentially evil regimes were consistently dismissed. In North Korea's case, when working for the CIA, he noted that "The Agency seemed completely locked into its interpretations of Kim [Jong Il]," and evidence which contradicted their preconceived ideas was never accepted.[146] The impact of this phenomenon on Western intelligence at the highest levels was exemplified by the testimony of former U.S. Secretary of State Madeleine Albright, who indicated that when visiting Pyongyang in 2000 she had been seriously misinformed by anti-North Korean propaganda and prejudices. She said: "I went having been briefed on what kind of a weirdo he [Kim Jong Il] was from our own people. He was portrayed as reclusive-like with many girlfriends and watching porno movies—basically a very weird kind of person." After meeting him she expressed her surprise that the way he had been portrayed to her had been completely wrong. "He was actually quite charming… He was very, very well prepared, responded without notes, was not only respectful but also interested in what I had to say." To her complete surprise the talks were a success.[147] In an interview nineteen years later, the former State Secretary's impression remained unchanged, stating:

> I do think that what is interesting is how smart and informed Kim Jong Il was…he technically knew an awful lot of things. We were actually talking about missile limits at the time. He did not consult his experts. He really was able to talk about various aspects of the programs. And he spent a lot of time on it. It was very interesting. He also could be very gracious. I mean, it was all kinds of dinners and all kinds of things. But I think that he was determined to make some progress…. I was surprised by how technically adept and smart he was.[148]

According to Albright, the success of future negotiations would rely heavily on whether or not American leaders would recognise how adept and capable the North Korean leadership was—in sharp contrast to what briefings based on U.S. intelligence had led her to believe.[149]

Dr Konstantin Asmolov, leading fellow at the RAS Institute for Far Eastern Studies' Korean Studies Center, noted based on his extensive research of the DPRK both extensive demonization by its adversaries and cognitive dissonance in the West when analysing developments in the country—under which all positive aspects and achievements of the state are denied based entirely on speculation. Asmolov stated:

> the author sees one more aspect associated with the fundamental demonization of the DPRK as the Land of Darkness. After all, from the standpoint of the demonizing propagandists, such a state is fundamentally unable to create something positive, especially something aimed at improving the living standards of the population… If something is noticed there which is along the lines of improving the living standards of the population, it is propaganda, and the actual situation does not work that way. If they invent something useful, that is not actually their own invention, they just stole it. If something is built there, then the building has been erected on the bones of countless prisoners, or it has something to do with the Potemkin village [a term for façade or "show city" unrepresentative of the "true reality"].[150]

In sharp contrast to Western depictions and understandings of the DPRK, impartial non-Western sources have repeatedly reported highly positively on North Korea—as doing so does not so starkly contradict their preconceived worldviews. Japanese citizens of Korean origin of all ages can be seen in their hundreds in Pyongyang in the summertime—and although fully exposed to Western and ROK media they still maintain their close cultural and educational ties to and prefer to visit the north. As one 22-year-old Japanese student of Korean origin studying a summer course in Pyongyang in 2017 told the writer on the flight out of the country: "life is much better here, food is better. There is more of the traditional Korean culture. There are less social issues and people are far more open and welcoming than in the south." When asked, she said she had visited the south before.

The Japanese Koreans, coming from a country with among the highest living standards in the world, live among the North Korean people as Koreans for extended periods and choose to return for study, work and tourism regularly in large numbers. Were the country's virtues truly a complete illusion as consistently claimed by Western media, this could not explain such actions. Koreans of Chinese, Russian and Central Asian origin were encountered by the writer in Pyongyang and other cities in smaller but still considerable numbers and were also frequent visitors who reflected highly positively on life there. The UN workers, telecommunications executives, sports coaches and embassy staff from non-Western backgrounds with whom the writer interacted while studying in and visiting North Korea, all of whom had spent an extended time there, were almost all full of praise for a country many of them had previously known little about. Ambassadors and visiting government officials of non-aligned countries have consistently come to similar conclusions. This is not to say that the DPRK is necessarily better than the ROK—only that it is a far cry from the hell on earth it is described as in the West. Nevertheless, the cognitive dissonance which colours Western assessments of the country as a result of over seven decades of effective propaganda leads to such extreme and often nonsensical assessments.

NOTES

1 Richter, Monika L., 'The Kremlin's Platform for "Useful Idiots" in the West: An Overview of RT's Editorial Strategy and Evidence of Impact,' *European Values: Protecting Freedom,* September 18, 2019.
'America's exposure to Russian information warfare,' *Financial Times,* December 19, 2018.
Putin's Asymmetric Assault on Democracy in Russia and Europe: Implications for U.S. National Security, A Minority Staff Report Prepared for the Use of the Committee on Foreign Relations, United States Senate, One Hundred and Fifteenth Congress, Second Session, January 10, 2018.

2 'North Korea's Stable Exchange Rates Confound Economists,' *Associated Press*, November 16, 2018.
Dorell, Oren, 'North Korean Economy Keeps Humming Despite Ever-Tighter Sanctions,' *USA Today*, November 24, 2017.

3 Assange, Julian, 'Google Is Not What It Seems,' *Wikileaks*.

4 Nixon, Ron, 'U.S. Groups Helped Nurture Arab Uprisings,' *New York Times,* April 14, 2011.
Cartalucci, Tony, 'Twitter Targets Hong Kong in US-backed Regime Change Operation,' *Ron Paul Institute for Peace and Prosperity*, October 15, 2019.
Blum, William, *Rogue State: A Guide to the World's Only Superpower,* London, Zed Books, 2006 (Chapter 19: Trojan Horse: The National Endowment for Democracy).

5 Geers, Kenneth, *Cyber War in Perspective: Russian Aggression against Ukraine*, Tallinn, NATO CCD COE Publications, 2015 (Chapter 10: Russian Information Warfare: Lessons from Ukraine).

6 Soloviev, Andrei, 'NED, просто NED. США вложили в "печеньки" на Майдане почти $14 млн,' *Sputnik,* July 15, 2015.

Moniz Bandeira, Luiz Alberto, *The World Disorder: US Hegemony, Proxy Wars, Terrorism and Humanitarian Catastrophes,* Cham, Springer, 2019 (pp. 191–192).

7 Wei, Xinyan and Zhong, Weiping, 'Who is behind Hong Kong protests?,' *China Daily,* August 17, 2019.

Cartalucci, Tony, 'Twitter Targets Hong Kong in US-backed Regime Change Operation,' *Ron Paul Institute for Peace and Prosperity,* October 15, 2019.

8 *Libya: Examination of intervention and collapse and the UK's future policy options,* House of Commons Foreign Affairs Committee, Third Report of Session 2016–17, September 14, 2016.

9 Nixon, Ron, 'U.S. Groups Helped Nurture Arab Uprisings,' *New York Times,* April 14, 2011.

10 Clemons, Steve, 'The Arab Spring: "A Virus That Will Attack Moscow and Beijing,"' *The Atlantic,* November 19, 2011.

11 Shorrock, Tim, 'Did the CIA Orchestrate an Attack on the North Korean Embassy in Spain?,' *Foreign Policy,* May 2, 2019.

Cho, Yi Jun, 'Who Is Anti-N.Korean Guerrilla Leader?,' *Chosun Ilbo,* April 4, 2019.

12 Taylor, Adam and Kim, Min Joo, 'The covert group that carried out a brazen raid on a North Korean embassy now fears exposure,' *Washington Post,* March 28, 2019.

13 Epstein, Susan B., 'CRS: Radio Free Asia: Background, Funding, and Policy Issues, July 21, 1999,' *Wikileaks,* February 2, 2009.

Graham Ruddick, 'BBC braces for backlash over North Korea service,' *The Guardian,* August 20, 2017.

'30–40% of NK thought to be tuning into pirate radio: how do we reach more?,' *Daily NK,* September 14, 2015.

14 Foster-Carter, Aidan, 'Obama Comes Out as a North Korea Collapsist,' *The Diplomat,* January 20, 2015.

15 Becker, Jo and Shane, Scott, 'Secret "Kill List" Proves a Test of Obama's Principles and Will,' *New York Times*, May 29, 2012.

Bauman, Nick, 'The American Teen Whose Death-by-Drone Obama Won't Explain,' *Mother Jones,* April 23, 2015.

Silverglate, Harvey, 'Obama Crosses the Rubicon: The Killing of Anwar al-Awlaki,' *Forbes,* October 6, 2011.

16 Mullen, Mike and Nunn, Sam and Mount, Adam, *A Sharper Choice on North Korea: Engaging China for a Stable Northeast Asia*, Council on Foreign Relations, Independent Task Force Report No. 74, September 2016.

17 Mullen, Mike and Nunn, Sam and Mount, Adam, *A Sharper Choice on North Korea: Engaging China for a Stable Northeast Asia*, Council on Foreign Relations, Independent Task Force Report No. 74, September 2016.

18 Chung, Sung-Yoon, *Implications of North Korea's Nuclear Advancement and Response Measures,* Seoul, Korea Institute for National Unification, 2017 (pp. 45–46).

19 Greenburg, Andy, 'The Plot to Free North Korea with Smuggled Episodes of "Friends,"' *Wired*, March 1, 2015.

20 Park, Kyung-Ae, 'Regime Change in North Korea?: Economic Reform and Political Opportunity Structures,' *North Korean Review,* vol. 5, no. 1, Spring 2009 (pp. 23–45).

21 Chun, Yung Woo, 'Examining the North Korean Paradox', *International Institute for Strategic Studies*, March 26, 2013.

22 Fitzpatrick, Mark, 'North Korea: Is Regime Change the Answer?,' *Survival*, vol. 55, no. 3, May 29, 2013.

23 Lankov, Andrei, Changing North Korea: An Information Campaign Can Beat the Regime, *Foreign Affairs,* vol. 88, no. 6, November/December 2009 (pp. 95–105).

24 Kretchun, Nat and Kim, Jane, *A Quiet Opening: North Koreans in a Changing Media Environment*, Washington D.C., Intermedia, May 2012.

25 Park, Kyung-Ae, 'Regime Change in North Korea?: Economic Reform and Political

Opportunity Structures,' *North Korean Review,* vol. 5, no. 1, Spring 2009 (pp. 23–45).
26 Peters, Ralph, 'Constant Conflict, Parameters,' *U.S. Army War College Quarterly*, Summer 1997 (pp. 4–14).
27 Ibid. (pp. 4–14).
28 Greenburg, Andy, 'The Plot to Free North Korea with Smuggled Episodes of "Friends,"' *Wired*, March 1, 2015.
29 Peters, Ralph, 'Constant Conflict, Parameters,' *U.S. Army War College Quarterly*, Summer 1997 (pp. 4–14).
30 Greenburg, Andy, 'The Plot to Free North Korea with Smuggled Episodes of "Friends,"' *Wired*, March 1, 2015.
31 Ibid.
32 Flashdrives for Freedom, (website homepage: flashdrivesforfreedom.org) (Accessed August 2, 2017).
33 'Disrupt North Korea,' *Human Rights Foundation* (website. Politics/Causes), June 21, 2017.
34 Bond, Paul, 'Largest Balloon Drop of "The Interview" Underway Over North Korea,' *Hollywood Reporter,* April 15, 2020.
35 De Moraes, Lisa, '"The Interview" Release Would Have Damaged Kim Jong Un Internally, Says Rand Expert Who Saw Movie At Sony's Request,' *Yahoo News*, December 19, 2014.
36 Hornaday, Ann, 'Sony, "The Interview," and the unspoken truth: All movies are political,' *Washington Post,* December 18, 2014.
37 'Defector groups get paid to launch propaganda balloons, former N. Korean soldier says,' *Hankyoreh,* June 15, 2020.
38 Asmolov, Konstantin, 'North Korea: What Is and What Should Never Be,' *Vladai*, June 19, 2020.
'"Shocked" S.Korea leader Moon orders probe into extra U.S. THAAD launchers,' *Reuters*, May 30, 2017.
39 Chun, Susan 'Radio gives hope to North and South Koreans,' *CNN*, Feb. 27, 2008.
40 Blum, William, *Rogue State: A Guide to the World's Only Superpower,* London, Zed Books, 2006 (Chapter 19: Trojan Horse: The National Endowment for Democracy).
41 VOA Broadcasting in Korean, Voice of Asia Public Relations (website: https://www.insidevoa.com/p/6438.html), (accessed August 3, 2019).
42 Tidy, Joanna, *The Social Construction of Identity: Israeli Foreign Policy and the 2006 War in Lebanon*, University of Bristol, Working Paper No. 05-08, 2007.
43 Peters, Ralph, 'Constant Conflict, Parameters,' *U.S. Army War College Quarterly*, Summer 1997 (pp. 4–14).
44 Korhonen, Pekka, 'Rock Gospels: Analyzing the Artistic Style of Moranbong Band,' *SinoNK,* March 4, 2014.
45 Kim, Jong Un, *Let Us Hasten Final Victory Through a Revolutionary Ideological Offensive,* Speech Delivered at the Eight Conference of Ideological Workers of the Workers' Party of Korea, February 25, 2014.
46 Ibid.
47 'Biggest Stadiums In The World By Capacity,' *World Atlas* (accessed August 3, 2019).
48 'North Korea unveils study facility dedicated to anti-Japan, anti-U.S. education,' *Japan Times*, August 14, 2016.
49 Ibid.
50 'Kim Jong-un highlights economic development in Supreme People's Assembly,' *Hankyoreh,* April 15, 2019.
51 Bermudez, Joseph and DuMond, Marie, 'Examining the Modernization and Expansion Project at the Korean People's Army Fishery Station No. 15,' *Beyond the Parallel,* September 19, 2018.
'Kim Jong-un conducts on-the-spot guidance at agricultural modernization facility,' *Hankyoreh,* October 10, 2019.

52 Ji, Dagyum, 'North Korean electronics corporation launches new smartphone brand,' *NK News*, June 7, 2018.
53 'Inside North Korea's shiny new international airport … but where are all the passengers?,' *South China Morning Post,* July 2, 2015.
54 Peters, Ralph, 'Constant Conflict, Parameters,' *U.S. Army War College Quarterly*, Summer 1997 (pp. 4–14).
55 Kim, Jong Un, *Let Us Hasten Final Victory Through a Revolutionary Ideological Offensive,* Speech Delivered at the Eight Conference of Ideological Workers of the Workers' Party of Korea, February 25, 2014.
56 Kretchun, Nat and Kim, Jane, *A Quiet Opening: North Koreans in a Changing Media Environment*, Washington D.C., Intermedia, May 2012 (p. 77).
57 Ibid. (p. 78).
58 Sabur, Rozina, 'Google to "de-rank" stories from Russia Today and Sputnik,' *Telegraph,* November 21, 2017.
'Twitter Suspends Russian Embassy in Syria's Account,' *Moscow Times,* July 31, 2019.
59 'British scholar tells the truth about deleted social media accounts related to Hong Kong issues,' *CTGN,* September 18, 2019.
60 'Twitter blocks accounts of Raúl Castro and Cuban state-run media outlets,' *The Guardian*, September 12, 2019.
Sweeney, Steve, 'Cuban journalists condemn Twitter's mass blocking of their accounts,' *Morning Star,* September 12, 2019.
61 'YouTube shuts down pro-Syrian government channels,' *Al Jazeera,* September 10, 2018.
'YouTube Offers Cryptic Explanation on Shutdown of Syrian Government Accounts,' *Sputnik*, September 12, 2018.
62 'YouTube Censors Iranian Press, HispanTV, Press TV Targeted,' *Telesur,* April 19, 2019.
'Google "disables" Press TV's YouTube account,' *Islamic Republic News Agency,* April 19, 2019.
63 Marsh, Sarah, 'Twitter blocks accounts of Raul Castro and Cuban state-run media,' *Reuters,* September 12, 2019.
64 'Twitter suspends Iran Leader's accounts,' *Press TV,* March 31, 2020.
65 Hernandez, Javier C., 'U.S. and Iran Are Trolling Each Other—in China,' *New York Times,* January 16, 2020.
66 Solon, Olivia, 'YouTube shuts down North Korean propaganda channels,' *The Guardian,* September 9, 2017.
Macdonald, Hamish, 'YouTube continues to terminate North Korea-related channels,' *NK News,* September 8, 2017.
Fifield, Anna, 'YouTube has shut down more North Korean channels—and researchers are livid,' *Washington Post,* September 14, 2017.
67 Zimmerman, Max, 'Facebook to Remove Pro-Soleimani Posts on Instagram, CNN Reports,' *Bloomberg*, January 11, 2020.
68 Kim, Jack, 'North Korea accuses U.S. of cyber attack "sabotage,"' *Reuters*, March 15, 2013.
69 Parmar, Inderjeet and Cox, Michael, *Soft Power and U.S. Foreign Policy,* Abingdon, Routledge, 2010.
70 Muller, John E., 'Trends in Popular Support for the Wars in Korea and Vietnam,' *The American Political Science Review*, vol. 65, no. 2, 1971 (pp. 358–375).
Crabtree, Steve, 'The Gallup Brain: Americans and the Korean War,' *Gallup,* February 4, 2003.
Jones, Jeffrey M, 'Who Had the Lowest Gallup Presidential Job Approval Rating?,' *Gallup*, December 26, 2019.
71 Stone, I. F., *Hidden History of the Korean War*, Amazon Media, 2014 (Chapter 45: Atrocities to the Rescue).

72 Kim, Monica, *The Interrogation Rooms of the Korean War; The Untold History*, Princeton, NJ, Princeton University Press, 2019. (p. 335).
73 Ibid. (pp. 205–206).
74 Ibid. (p. 306).
75 Ibid. (pp. 203–204).
76 Cumings, Bruce, *Origins of the Korean War: Liberation and the Emergence of Separate Regimes, 1945–1947, Volume 1*, Yeogsabipyeongsa Publishing Co, 1981–1990 (pp. 367, 375).
77 Lowe, Peter, *The Origins of the Korean War*, London, Routledge, 1997 (p. 180).
78 Donghyuk, Shin, Dalhousie University, Academics, Convocation, Ceremonies, Honorary Degree Recipients, Honorary Degree 2014.
79 Pilling, David, 'Lunch with the FT: Shin Dong-hyuk,' *Financial Times*, August 30, 2013.
80 Fifield, Anna, 'Prominent N. Korean defector Shin Dong-hyuk admits parts of story are inaccurate,' *Washington Post*, January 17, 2015.
81 Harden, Blaine, *Escape from Camp 14: One Man's Remarkable Odyssey from North Korea to Freedom in the West*, New York, Viking, 2012 (p. 46).
82 Power, John, 'Author of book on North Korea's founding addresses Shin controversy,' *NK News*, March 18, 2015.
83 '그는 처음부터 18호 수용소에서 살았다' [He Lived in Camp 18 From the Beginning], *Hankyoreh*, April 1, 2016.
84 Lankov, Andrei, 'Changing North Korea: An Information Campaign Can Beat the Regime,' *Foreign Affairs*, vol. 88, no. 6, November/December 2009 (pp. 95–105).
85 Lankov, Andrei, 'After the Shin Dong-hyuk affair: Separating fact, fiction,' *NK News*, February 3, 2015.
86 Dorell, Oren, 'U.S. puts N. K. leader Kim Jong Un on sanctions list for human rights abuses,' *USA Today* July 6, 2016.
87 Jolley, Mary Ann, 'The Strange Tale of Yeonmi Park,' *The Diplomat*, December 10, 2014.
88 O'Carroll, Chad, 'Claims N. Korean defector earns $41k per speech "completely incorrect",' *NK News*, June 30, 2015.
89 Lee, Je Son, 'Why defectors change their stories,' *NK News*, January 21, 2015.
90 Jolley, Mary Ann, 'The Strange Tale of Yeonmi Park,' *The Diplomat*, December 10, 2014.
91 Power, John, 'North Korea: Defectors and Their Sceptics,' *The Diplomat*, October 29, 2014.
92 Lee, Hakyung Kate, 'North Korean mother and son defectors die of suspected starvation in Seoul,' *ABC*, September 22, 2019.
93 Go, Myong-Hyun, 'Resettling in South Korea: Challenges for Young North Korean Refugees,' *The Asan Institute for Policy Studies*, vol. 4, no. 26, September 12–29, 2019.
'Report to Congressional Requesters, Humanitarian Assistance: Status of North Korean Refugee Resettlement and Asylum in the United States,' *United States Government Accountability Office* (GAO-10-691), June 2010 (p. 44).
94 Asmolov, Konstantin, 'On the Fate of Thae Yong-ho,' *New Eastern Outlook*, January 28, 2017.
95 Yun, David, 'Loyal Citizens of Pyongyang in Seoul,' (Documentary), October 16, 2018.
96 O'Carroll, Chad, 'North Korea's invisible phone, killer dogs and other such stories—why the world is transfixed,' *The Telegraph*, January 6, 2014.
97 Taylor, Adam, 'Why You Shouldn't Necessarily Trust Those Reports Of Kim Jong-un Executing His Ex-Girlfriend,' *Business Insider*, August 29, 2013.
98 Fisher, Max, 'No, Kim Jong Un probably didn't feed his uncle to 120 hungry dogs,' *Washington Post*, January 3, 2014.

99 Stone Fish, Isaac, 'The Black Hole of North Korea,' *New York Times*, August 8, 2011.
100 Armstrong, Charles K., 'Korea and its Futures: Unification and the Unfinished War, Review,' *The Journal of Asian Studies*, vol. 60, no. 1, February 2001.
101 'North Korean University Students Copy Kim Jong Un's Hairstyle,' *Radio Free Asia*, March 25, 2014.
102 Welch, David, *Propaganda, power and persuasion from World War I to Wikileaks*, London, New York, I. B. Tauris, 2014.
Sosin, Gene, *Sparks of Liberty: an insider's memoir of Radio Liberty*, University Park, Pennsylvania State University Press, 1999 (p. 257).
Radio Free Asia, 'About,' Broadcasting Board of Governors. n.d. (Retrieved June 5, 2016).
103 'Worldwide Propaganda Network Built by the C.I.A.,' *New York Times,* December 26, 1977.
104 'North Korea: Students required to get Kim Jong-un haircut,' *BBC*, March 26, 2014.
105 Asmolov, Konstantin, 'How the Radio Free Asia released the whole set of baloney,' *New Eastern Outlook*, November 26, 2016.
106 Macdonald, Hamish, 'Why men's Kim Jong Un hairstyle requirement is unlikely true,' *NK News*, March 26, 2014.
107 'China Warns its Citizens in North Korea to Leave as Conflict with U.S. Looms,' *Sputnik*, May 2, 2017.
108 Ibid.
109 Ministry of Foreign Affairs of the People's Republic of China, Foreign Ministry Spokesperson Geng Shuang's Regular Press Conference on May 2, 2017, *USA Today*.
110 Dier, Arden, 'Report: Kim Jong Un fed uncle alive to 120 starved dogs,' *USA Today*, January 3, 2014.
111 Kaiman, Jonathan, 'Story about Kim Jong-un's uncle being fed to dogs originated with satirist,' *The Guardian*, January 6, 2014.
112 'North Korea Says It's Found a "Unicorn Lair,"' *U.S. News*, November 30, 2012.
'Unicorns' Existence Proven, Says North Korea,' *Time*, November 30, 2012.
113 'Serbian Coach Reveals How Mainstream Media "Kills" North Korean Athletes,' *Sputnik*, September 16, 2017.
114 Hancocks, Paula, 'North Korean leader ordered aunt to be poisoned, defector says,' *CNN,* May 12, 2015.
Hotham, Oliver, 'Kim Jong Un's aunt, once reported killed, makes first appearance in six years,' *NK News,* January 25, 2020.
115 'Kim Jong Un's Ex-Lover Hyon Song-Wol "Executed By North Korean Firing Squad After Making Sex Tape,"' *Huffington Post*, August 23, 2018.
'Kim Jong Un's "executed" ex-girlfriend comes back from the dead with appearance on state TV,' *Mirror*, May 17, 2014.
116 'Former North Korean general believed executed turns up alive,' *Fox News*, May 10, 2016.
117 'Former North Korean was "publicly executed,"' *Human Rights Without Frontiers*.
118 Foster-Carter, Aidan, 'They shoot people, don't they?,' *Asia Times,* March 22, 2001.
119 Seo, Soo-min, 'Video footage shows defector alive in NK,' *Korea Times*, August 21, 2001.
120 'Defector pardoned by NK leader, mother says,' *Korea Times,* August 31, 2002.
121 'German journo: European media writing pro-US stories under CIA pressure,' *RT*, October 18, 2014.
122 *Libya: Examination of intervention and collapse and the UK's future policy options,* House of Commons Foreign Affairs Committee, Third Report of Session 2016–17, September 14, 2016.
123 Davis, Deborah, *Katharine the Great: Katharine Graham and the Washington post,* New York, Harcourt Brace Jovanovich, 1979 (p. 137–138).

124 Bernstein, Carl, 'CIA and the Media,' *Rolling Stone Magazine*, October 20, 1977.
125 *Church Committee Final Report, Vol 1: Foreign and Military Intelligence* (p. 455).
126 Ibid. (p. 455).
127 Davies, Nick, *Flat Earth News: An Award-Winning Reporter Exposes Falsehood, Distortion and Propaganda in the Global Media,* New York, Vintage, 2009 (p.228)
128 Bunch, Sonny, 'The CIA funded a culture war against communism. It should do so again.,' *Washington Post,* August 22, 2018.
129 'Worldwide Propaganda Network Built by the C.I.A.,' *New York Times,* December 26, 1977.
130 Ibid.
131 Carver, Tom, 'Pentagon plans propaganda war,' *BBC*, February 20, 2002.
Beal, Tim, *North Korea: The Struggle Against American Power,* London, Pluto Press, 2005 (p. 133).
Krakauer, Jon, *Where Men Win Glory*, New York, Doubleday, 2009 (p.238).
132 Schwarz, Jon, 'Lie After Lie: What Colin Powell Knew About Iraq 15 Years Ago and What He Told the U.N.,' *The Intercept,* February 6, 2018.
Matthews, Dylan, 'No, really, George W. Bush lied about WMDs,' *Vox*, July 9, 2016.
133 Rubinstein, Alexander, 'Amnesty International's Troubling Collaboration with UK & US Intelligence,' *Ron Paul Institute for Peace and Prosperity,* January 19, 2019.
134 Cockburn, Alexander, 'Sifting for the Truth on Both Sides: War brings propaganda, all designed to protect government,' *Los Angeles Times,* January 17, 1991.
135 'Deception on Capitol Hill,' *New York Times,* January 15, 1992.
MacArthur, John R., 'Remember Nayirah, Witness for Kuwait?,' *New York Times,* January 6, 1992.
136 Beaumont, Peter, 'PM admits graves claim "untrue,"' *Observer,* July 18, 2004.
Beal, Tim, *North Korea: The Struggle Against American Power,* London, Pluto Press, 2005 (p. 129).
137 O'Neill, Brendan, 'Not a shred of evidence,' *Spectator,* February 21, 2004.
138 Pilger, John, 'Calling the humanitarian bombers to account,' *Counterpunch,* December 11–12, 2004.
139 Shim, David and Nabers, Dirk, *North Korea and the Politics of Visual Representation,* German Institute of Global and Area Studies, GIGA Research Programme: Power, Norms and Governance in International Relations, April 2011.
140 Sifton, John, 'North Korean mourners, crying to survive?,' *CNN*, December 22, 2011.
141 Robertson, Phil, 'Louis Cole's Merry North Korea Adventure,' *Human Rights Watch,* September 20, 2016.
142 Anderson, David, 'Useful Idiots: Tourism in North Korea,' *Forbes*, March 6, 2017.
143 Butterly, Amelia, 'Vlogger Louis Cole Denies North Korea Paid for Videos of his Trip,' *BBC*, August 18, 2016.
144 Kazianis, Harry J., 'A U.S. Invasion of North Korea Would Be Like Opening the Gates of Hell,' *National Interest,* May 13, 2019.
145 Nixon, John, *Debriefing the President; The Interrogation of Saddam Hussein,* London, Bantam Press, 2016 (pp. 204–205, 220).
146 Ibid. (pp. 204–205, 220).
147 'Nuclear Nightmare: Understanding North Korea,' *Discovery Times*, (Documentary), 2003 (00:35:50–00:37:42).
Gender in Mediation: An Exercise for Trainers, CSS Mediation Resources, ETH Zurich Centre for Security Studies and Swisspeace 2015 (p. 59).
148 'Transcript: Securing Tomorrow with Madeleine Albright,' *Washington Post,* May 31, 2018.
149 Ibid.
150 Asmolov, Konstantin, 'Korea: Large Construction Baloney,' *New Eastern Outlook* August 21, 2016.

Chapter 20

ECONOMIC WARFARE

Sanctions and the Targeting of Korean Living Standards

One increasingly critical front of non-kinetic warfare in recent years, particularly between states deterred from direct military confrontation by mutual vulnerability and the sheer destructive potential of their arsenals, is economic warfare. Indeed, if miniaturised thermonuclear warheads and long-range ballistic missiles had been invented and proliferated 20 years earlier, the Second World War may have been fought very differently—with greater emphasis on blocking an enemy's access to overseas trade and resources, crippling its economy and otherwise driving down living standards. During the Cold War this form of warfare was at the forefront of the Ronald Reagan administration's offensive against the Soviet Union—what prominent expert on this offensive Fu Ruihong referred to as the use of "economic tools to attack the USSR… use [of] offensive and destructive economic means to destroy the Soviet economy and financial structure."[1] Central to this strategy was maintaining Soviet isolation from the majority of the world economy, including not only the Western world but also Latin America, Japan and much of Africa and Asia. Considerable economic pressure was placed on states in the Western sphere of influence to eschew strong political and trading relations with Moscow, and harsh punishment including secondary sanctions were applied against state and non-state entities which undermined this directive.[2] Other more overt initiatives, such as the effort to drive down global oil prices and strip Moscow of a key source of revenue,[3] were also undertaken with varying levels of success. Although economic warfare cannot exclusively be credited for the Soviet collapse,[4] with complementary Western military and information warfare initiatives also having strong effects while internal mismanagement, growing ideological uncertainty and deficiencies in political leadership undermined the state's ability to resist, the role it played was not insignificant.

As the global economy has grown increasingly interconnected, the ability of powers at its centre—the Western states through which the majority of the "wiring" of the global financial system passes—to inflict damage comparable to wartime destruction on other parties has grown significantly. Continued use of economic warfare could be seen in the immediate post–Cold War years. The Western sanctions regime against Iraq under the Bill Clinton presidency killed many more people than the military campaigns of the administration, its predecessor or its successor ever would—devastating sectors from sewage treatment to medicine.[5] Economic warfare on rising Asia-Pacific economies in the mid-1990s served not only to enrich the Western world, but caused a collapse in living standards in the targeted countries—what *The Economist* referred to as "a destruction of savings on a scale more usually associated with a full-scale war."[6] This represented warfare not through sanctions and isolation, but rather through a combination of political pressure to instigate economic reforms, such as the lifting of capital controls, followed by what came to be known as "speculative attacks" by Western firms, complemented by the efforts of Western-led financial institutions.[7]

For North Korea the end of the Cold War saw severe restrictions on its trade with the vast majority of the world economy continue to be imposed by the United States, with prominent means including state listing under the Trading with the Enemy Act and considerable pressure on parties such as Japan not to normalise trading relations.[8] As covered in Chapter 12, the Korean economy was left in an extremely fragile state following the collapse of the Soviet Bloc, and the loss of the vast majority of its trading relationships including its access to cheap oil, on which its mechanised agriculture and fertiliser industries relied heavily, undermined what little economic growth there had been. This was compounded by two years of flooding of "biblical proportions," the worst the country had seen in over a century,[9] followed by a year of drought. The resulting crisis was exacerbated by continuing sanctions, which the United States notably maintained indefinitely, despite its pledge under the Agreed Framework in 1994 to lift them within three months.[10]

While it was widely believed that North Korea's collapse was inevitable, economic pressure was seen as a means of speeding up this process—ensuring the state remained isolated and placing further downward pressure on living standards. The connection between economic pressure and regime change was widely alluded to, with the president of the Association of Korean Political Studies in North America and a strong advocate of forced regime change, Pak Kyung Ae, stating: "a failure of a national economy undermines the legitimacy of an authoritarian regime and triggers a transition to democracy, resulting in the termination of authoritarianism or socialism. Economic catalyst has been widely accepted as the catalyst of regime collapse."[11]

Senior fellow at the Center for International Policy and expert on U.S. foreign policy in East Asia Selig S. Harrison, who played a leading role in high-level U.S. negotiations with the DPRK under the Bill Clinton administration, noted regarding the impact of sanctions:

> While the North Korean system is not likely to "implode" or "explode" in the foreseeable future, as General [Gary E.] Luck predicts, it could well erode over a period of five to 10 years if the United States and its allies remain wedded to policies that exacerbate the economic problems facing the Kim Jong Il regime. In particular, the continuance of economic sanctions and a failure to give support to the U.N. food aid program [vital in the immediate post–Arduous March years] in Pyongyang would undermine the prospects for a "soft landing."

The "soft landing" referred to a smooth recovery from the Soviet collapse and subsequent turbulence.[12] Harrison made this assessment in 1997 at a time when both the power transition after Kim Il Sung's death and the worst of the Korean economic crisis had passed—when optimism in the West regarding a Korean collapse had begun to ebb. He further stressed the importance of American sanctions in preventing the full normalisation of the DPRK's economic relations with Japan and South Korea, which in the case of the former in particular was expected to provide a major boost to the North Korean economy.[13]

Economic sanctions continued to be widely advocated under the George W. Bush administration, which oversaw their escalation and multiple threats to illegally interdict Korean shipping acted on in at least one instance.[14] While the United States had previously sought to impose economic sanctions on the DPRK through the United Nations Security Council, China and increasingly Russia began to oppose U.S. use of the Council to achieve its own foreign policy objectives and threatened to veto Western-drafted resolutions targeting small third world states. The Korean nuclear test in 2006, however, forced the two powers to comply, for reasons covered later, and Resolution 1718 adopted on October 14 of that year banned imports and exports of major armaments, forced a freezing of the overseas assets of all Koreans connected to the weapons program, allowed for legal interdiction of Korean shipping and forced the DPRK to unilaterally suspend its ballistic missile and nuclear weapons programs and return to the Six Party Talks without precondition. A further ban on the export of "luxury goods" to the DPRK was open to interpretation and caused considerable difficulties for North Koreans across the world—from the ice hockey team that couldn't acquire training equipment[15] to the musicians forced to rely on illicit channels to smuggle instruments. The final resolution was notably delayed due to Chinese insistence that the terms of the resolution be relaxed, albeit very slightly, for Beijing to approve its passage.[16]

Chapter VII of the United Nations Charter was cited as the pretext for sanctions—which obliged the Council to "determine the existence of any threat to the peace, breach of the peace, or act of aggression" and to take action to "restore international peace and security." This was central to the purpose for which the UN was founded—to prevent member states from attacking one another and to thereby to avert war. While there appeared little possibility of the Korean nuclear program starting a war however, the UN had failed to prevent the U.S. from starting multiple unprovoked and illegal invasions from Guatemala and Panama to Iraq. The failure of the Council to do so while sanctioning North Korea—despite the fact that Pyongyang had not breached customary international law, the UN Charter or any of its treaty obligations—set a dangerous precedent for gross double standards and unilateralism. Indeed, North Korea's pursuit of a deterrent against U.S. attack could be seen as a direct result of the failure of the UN to prevent powerful states from attacking weaker ones—with a deterrent upholding the organisation's core founding principle and mission where the Security Council had not.

The Western Bloc notably failed to significantly expand the scope of UN sanctions against the DPRK, with China and Russia insisting that sanctions remained "clearly tied to ending the DPRK programme to create nuclear missiles" and did not target the Korean population indiscriminately.[17] Russian and Chinese vetoes on the UNSC ensured that subsequent rounds of Western-drafted resolutions sanctioning the DPRK could only be passed immediately after a nuclear test—which occurred in May 2009 and February 2013. These led to resolutions 1874 and 2094 respectively, the former which tightened the arms embargo on the DPRK and targeted potential sources of financing for its missile and nuclear programs while the latter reiterated previous resolutions, imposed sanctions on a number of individuals linked to the nuclear program and restricted financial transfers by diplomats. Attempts by the Obama administration to use satellite launches as a pretext to pass further sanctions resolutions ultimately failed, although resolutions condemning the launches were passed.

In 2016 rapid progress in North Korea's deterrence program led the Obama administration for the first time to begin to prioritise the targeting of the country above other foreign policy concerns, with the complacency of earlier years beginning to fade. The commander of the U.S. Strategic Command had referred to the Korean missile program in 2015—in particular the new prototype ICBM Hwasong-13 (KN-08) which appeared to be a two-stage derivative of the Musudan—as "a threat we can't ignore as a country."[18] Similar assessments began to be made by a wide range of sources, with the U.S. Northern Command NORTHCOM responsible for protecting the U.S. mainland going so far as to state: "Our assessment is that they have the ability to put a nuclear weapon on a KN-08 and shoot it at the homeland."[19] JCS Vice Chairman Admiral Hames Winnefeld had previously stated regarding the missile: "we believe the KN-08 does have the range to reach the United States… The Korean threat went just a little bit faster than we might have expected."[20] These conclusions regarding the Hwasong-13 and the Korean deterrence capability appeared to represent a minority view at the time and were based purely on the design's theoretical specifications as an extended-range Musudan derivative, as the missile had yet to be tested and there was no evidence that complex re-entry vehicle technologies had been mastered. Nevertheless, they signified the state of growing concern in the United States at the time which, alongside considerations for military action, led the Obama administration to press harder on the sanctions front.

UNSC Resolution 2270 was passed two months after the DPRK's fourth nuclear test in January 2016, and this length of time indicates the complexity of negotiations which were likely taking place to get the resolution approved by Moscow and Beijing. The resolution's stipulations were unprecedented and appeared to blur the line between targeting the missile programs and targeting the Korean economy as a whole—which had long been the purpose of unilateral Western sanctions imposed outside the UN. Its target was specifically products and activities "used by DPRK individuals or entities to generate revenue." The Obama administration appeared willing to place more pressure on China and Russia over the Korean issue due to the issue's growing importance. It is possible, as would be the case the following year, that presenting unilateral military options as an alternative should Western-drafted sanctions fail to pass may have spurred Beijing and Moscow to act. The resolution targeted Korean exports such as rare earths, iron and gold—with an exemption for transactions for "livelihood purposes." Bodies such as the National Aerospace Development Administration were also targeted; providing weapons maintenance service either by or for the KPA was banned and financial transactions, aviation and shipping were also heavily sanctioned. Joint ventures, ownership interest and establishment of relations with Korean banks were banned and all existing ventures were to be immediately terminated. Travel bans and asset freezes further targeted a number of individuals including those involved in the scientific, mining, shipping, space exploration, trading and financial sectors.

The resolution also sought to force the DPRK to become a party to the Convention on the Prohibition of Chemical Weapons and the Convention on the Prohibition of Biological Weapons and abandon all chemical and biological weapons. Egypt, which was a member of and had recently chaired the UNSC and voted for the resolution, was itself a non-signatory of the former convention, while the U.S. and Russia held two of the largest chemical weapons stockpiles in the world and both had shown only limited compliance.[21] The DPRK had already acceded to the latter convention and denied having a biological weapons program, but there was no legal pretext or even a consistent standard under which the Council could force Pyongyang to accede to the former. A number of additional stipulations, including a global ban on teaching Koreans "advanced physics, advanced computer simulation and related computer sciences, geospatial navigation, nuclear engineering, aerospace engineering, aeronautical engineering and related disciplines" was also put in place. The resolution was accompanied by an escalation in unilateral sanctions by the United States, the European Union and other Western parties as well as Japan. While sanctions had already been comprehensive, they began to target almost anything which could be sanctioned in an attempt to cripple the Korean economy. The United States Treasury Department notably used the Patriot Act Title III: Anti-Money Laundering to Prevent Terrorism to pass particularly harsh restrictions on the DPRK's access to the international financial system—despite Pyongyang not being designated a "State Sponsor of Terror" at the time.[22]

Four subsequent rounds of Western-drafted sanctions were passed by the Security Council in November 2016 and in August, September and

December 2017—resolutions 2321, 2371, 2375 and 2397 respectively. These built on resolution 2270 by further isolating the North Korean economy from international trade, cutting its exports and imposing asset freezes on prominent individuals in various sectors. One of the most significant restrictions was a cap on Korean oil imports to just 500,000 barrels (59,172 metric tons) per year. To place this in perspective for the country's industries and its fuel intensive agricultural sector, before the Arduous March and loss of trade with the Soviet Bloc, North Korean oil consumption in 1991 had been 3.8 million metric tons—or 64 times greater than the limit the Western-drafted sanctions were imposing.[23] While industry was beginning to recover from the crisis of the 1990s, new sanctions appeared to be intended to almost completely deindustrialise the country, including its agriculture sector. Oil consumption per capita under this resolution would make North Korea one of the very lowest consumers in the world—with gross consumption among the world's twelve lowest below that of sparsely populated deindustrialised island nations such as the Solomon Islands and St Vincent and the Grenadine with populations of well under 1 million. For an industrial and resource-scarce country of over 24 million—this was effectively a death sentence.[24]

Further stipulations of the sanctions regime included blanket bans on all joint ventures with Korean companies, over 90% of Korean exports including textiles, food, machinery and coal, all imports of natural gas and the vast majority of petroleum imports. Koreans were further restricted from working overseas, which alongside other measures meant sanctions now covered all major sectors of the Korean economy other than tourism. Western countries meanwhile moved to escalate use of secondary economic sanctions against parties suspected of doing any form of business with the DPRK. As one European official told the writer in 2017: "they are sending North Korea into a black hole."

Weathering Economic Sanctions

Assessing the impact of Western-drafted sanctions against the DPRK, including those imposed both unilaterally and through the UN, it appears that the country's economy overall has proved extremely resilient. Indeed, North Korea's economic performance has drawn a stark contrast to other states with far greater endowments of natural resources which have been placed under far lighter sanctions such as Iran,[25] Iraq[26] and Russia.[27] Despite their severity and wholly indiscriminate nature, the primary impact of sanctions appears not to have been the undercutting of North Korean living standards, but rather the undercutting of its significant potential to use exports to stimulate growth—as repeatedly alluded to by President Trump among others.[28] It is notable that, in sharp contrast to other sanctioned states, the DPRK has sustained economic growth[29] and kept both exchange rates[30] and prices for most basic goods stable.[31] Indeed, as *USA Today* reported at the end of 2017, despite the unprecedented economic pressure brought to bear that year both unilaterally from the West and through the UNSC: "North Korea's economy has proven resilient and seems to have fended off the suffering President Trump has sought to halt the country's nuclear program." This was in reference to the DPRK's stable living standards and continued, albeit slower, rate of growth.[32]

Western sources have consistently reported on the state of North Korea's economy with a degree of surprise and at times amazement, particularly since 2016 as new rounds of economic sanctions were meant to drive the state into an Iranian or Iraqi-style economic crisis. Reuters reported in late 2016, three years after the implementation of the new indiscriminate UNSC sanctions resolutions that "the price of rice, corn, pork, petrol and diesel remained relatively stable over the past year, demonstrating resilience to domestic and outside events." The absence of crisis where one was expected would "help strengthen Kim's grip on power," the article noted, citing growing production of consumer items domestically "from toothpaste to perfume" as a possible factor which may have helped stabilise the value of the North Korean won.[33] The stability of the exchange rate between the won and the U.S. dollar was "a bit of a mystery to everyone," according to Stephan Haggard, an American expert on the DPRK's economy at the University of California.[34] The economic situation was expected to worsen over the following year as sanctions had time to further wear out the Korean economy. As expert Andrei Lankov noted, citing "easily traceable macro-economic indicators" such as the price of rice and corn and exchange rates, reports "do not indicate any deterioration in the economic situation.... it is still remarkable that the sanctions regime has failed to produce any noticeable impact on any major economic indicators."[35]

Citing South Korean official figures, Reuters, the following year, reported North Korean growth rates "at 17-year high despite sanctions" at 3.9 percent. Again it was predicted that new rounds of sanctions would begin to show a greater effect by the following year.[36] Later in November

2017, *USA Today* reported, citing experts, that North Korea's economy was "beating sanctions" and "kept humming despite ever-tighter sanctions," stressing "no shortage of imported goods or of foreign currency needed to buy them."[37]

In November 2018, the Associated Press published an article titled "North Korea's Stable Exchange Rates Confound Economists," in which the country's ability to withstand tremendous economic pressure as no other target had was examined. "It's a question that nags at North Korea economy watchers: How has the country been able to maintain stable exchange rates—and avert hyper-inflation—despite intense sanctions, political tensions and a swelling trade imbalance?" Such questions were widely raised by Western analysts.[38] A number of analysts including the ROK's former Unification Minister, Lee Jong Seok, noted that South Korean figures on the DPRK's growth rates were "unrealistic and unbelievable"—citing among other things massive construction projects across the country and the proliferation of automobiles, which indicate a rate of growth far faster than that reported.[39] Expectations that sanctions would have a sharper effect on the Korean economy as time passed appear to have also been disappointed. A report in December 2019 by the prominent South Korean think tank, the Sejong Institute, was among several to indicate the North Korean economy had sustained a strong performance. The economy was found to be undergoing a construction boom and a boom in the production of consumer goods, maintaining stable prices and exchange rates, and set to improve its performance in coming years.[40] Visits to North Korean shopping centres, outdoor markets and convenience stores as late as 2018 and 2019 appear to show a fast-growing selection of domestically produced consumer goods—rather than a decline as would be the case for a shrinking or stagnating economy.

North Korea's ability to weather the impact of sanctions can be attributed to a number of factors. The country's economy had never fully adopted an export-led growth model and relied heavily on domestic consumption, which increased self-reliance and lessened the impact of a cutting of exports. Ri Ki Song, a leading economist with the Economic Institute of the DPRK's Academy of Social Sciences, stated to this effect: "Our economy is not an economy that relies on exports.… Due to the sanctions, we are not making a lot of trade or financial dealings with other countries, so there will be not so many changes in the exchange rates."[41] Investment in independent domestic manufacturing also appears to have increased from the 2010s, from catfish and goat farming to floating rice paddies and other means of producing crops without the need for extensive farmland. Increasingly efficient food production, and greater production of quality consumer goods from smartphones to violins, contributes to the state's ability to maintain or even increase living standards despite the undermining of foreign trade. Growing marketisation of some sectors of the economy, which complements state planning in other sectors, is also seen as a means of increasing efficiency. Senior researcher at Japan's Economic Research Institute for Northeast Asia (ERINA) and North Korea expert Mitsuhiro Mimura, who had visited the country over 45 times, was one of a number of analysts to stress the importance of this.[42] The fact that market activities are not taxed by the state, ever since the Supreme People's Assembly passed the law "On Completely Abolishing Taxes,"[43] has very likely allowed them to grow considerably faster.

The Council on Foreign Relations noted in their influential 2016 paper on the DPRK, which strongly advocated a harsher sanctions regime: "the increasing complexity of its economy affords North Korea greater ability to resist and circumvent the international sanctions regime."[44] Many other Western assessments came to similar conclusions. Combining a highly educated and professional workforce and a remarkable work ethic, which has made North Korean workers highly sought after across much of the world, with a resourceful and adaptive leadership, the DPRK's economic situation will likely continue to improve.

It is also possible that Pyongyang leverages the close link between sanctions, downward pressure on living standards, and Western designs for forced regime change to press neighbouring China to provide economic support. Loans, direct aid, technical assistance for increasingly complex and ambitious agricultural projects, and lax enforcement of trading restrictions are all possible avenues for this. Indeed, China has been seen directly bolstering the economies of Iran[45] and Venezuela,[46] where the United States has made no secret of its intention to force regime change through harsh sanctions regimes and impoverishment of their populations. Although these petroleum-based rentier economies were far less developed or resilient, and the impact of sanctions was only worsened by severe corruption, Chinese intervention prevented economic disaster by softening the impact of the American attacks. It is far from inconceivable that Beijing would take a similar approach to the DPRK—albeit less overtly.

Does a Nuclear Deterrent Help North Korea's Economy?

While North Korea's nuclear and missile programs have been cited by a number of Western sources, President Donald Trump among them,[47] as a key impediment to the country's potential for economic growth, an assessment of the impacts of these programs on the state's economy may indicate otherwise. First, as previously elaborated on in Chapter 17, it is unrealistic to think that Western economic sanctions would be lifted even if the DPRK were to fully denuclearize and scrap its missile deterrent capability. As repeatedly stated by a wide range of sources from the CFR to various U.S. officials, the DPRK is targeted by Western sanctions due to far more fundamental aspects of its nature as a state and society than its nuclear program. Sanctions are guaranteed to remain in place after a theoretical denuclearization just as they were in place for over 60 years before the country fully nuclearized.

Advocates of sanctions against the DPRK have notably repeatedly alluded not to any realistic means by which this could force the state to denuclearize, but rather to their usefulness in weakening the state as a whole. For example Professor Lee Sung Yoon and activist Joshua Stanton, prominent supporters of the sanctions regime, jointly referred not to denuclearization as the primary benefit of UN sanctions resolutions, but rather that sanctions "would significantly diminish, if not altogether deny, Kim the means to pay his military, security forces and elites that repress the North Korean public." This would potentially lead to instability, a state collapse and what Stanton referred to as "One Free Korea"—forced unification on Western terms. The target, according to these individuals who represented a very widespread viewpoint in the Western world, was the Korean state itself—not the nuclear program.[48] The CFR's prolific 2016 paper on the DPRK similarly alluded to the purpose of sanctions being an anti-state rather than a specifically anti-nuclear measure, stating regarding potential for relaxation after denuclearization: "Let us be clear about the essence of the North Korean nuclear threat: that threat is the North Korean government itself. So long as the real existing North Korean government holds power, that threat will continue." It emphasized that even a fully denuclearised Korea would still be targeted by Western sanctions, and that forced regime change remained the final goal.[49]

Nuclear weapons provide the Western Bloc with a valuable pretext to sanction the DPRK and to further internationalize economic warfare efforts against it, but they are not the fundamental cause for the state's targeting which would only end with its complete capitulation and westernization. Sanctions on Iran provide a key example, in that even after their relaxation following major concessions by Tehran on its nuclear program, U.S. sanctions were partially re-imposed under different pretexts within 24 hours[50]—and were later fully re-imposed and strengthened, despite Tehran's full compliance with the nuclear agreement.[51] It was evident that the nuclear program was not the cause for Iran's targeting, but rather its existence as a non-Westphilian state which was not in compliance with the designs of the Western-led order.

While nuclearization has not caused North Korea's targeting by Western sanctions, it has the potential to help seriously undermine their effects and thereby benefit the DPRK's economy. It is notable that nuclear weapons have facilitated a reduction[52] in conventional defense spending, which in turn has been cited as a contributing factor to the country's ability to weather Western-drafted sanctions.[53] A smaller and more elite and high-tech military is likely to be the result in the long term, signs of which began to emerge in the mid-2010s, while redirection of government spending to civilian sectors of the economy will promote growth in the long term. The need to deter a nuclear armed superpower with an extremely large conventional force had previously imposed a very large burden on the Korean state budget, which the development of a nuclear deterrent has gradually lifted. It was as a result of this that after several decades of mandatory conscription, mandatory military service was for the first time abolished in 2009[54]—shortly after the country's second nuclear test and international confirmation of its status as a "fully fledged nuclear power."[55]

There are significant historical precedents of states using nuclear weapons as a more cost-effective deterrent to reduce the burden of high conventional spending—both superpowers took this route during the Cold War. After 1945 the Soviet Union was forced to retain a significantly larger conventional force in Europe than the United States or its Western allies due to its lack of nuclear weapons—where its adversaries had demonstrated both an advanced nuclear capability and a reliable long range-delivery system. The USSR was thus forced to compensate by maintaining more numerous ground forces which were, in terms of their deterrence value, far less cost effective than nuclear warheads.[56] It was only when the USSR began to deploy large numbers of its own nuclear weapons with diverse payloads and delivery vehicles that cuts to Soviet spending on vast conventional forces could be made without compromising security. The funds made available were subsequently redirected towards the civilian economy with a focus on increased production of consumer goods.[57]

Throughout the mid-1950s the United States faced a significant spending deficit and sought to reduce expenditure on its conventional forces through greater reliance on nuclear assets for deterrence. In Korea alone the U.S. had deployed over 300,000 military personnel while financially supporting a vast South Korean army of 720,000—over twice the size of the KPA.[58] In 1956 President Eisenhower declared his intention to reduce the deficit by reducing military spending, which required deployment of nuclear weapons to Korea to facilitate the scaling down of conventional forces. A similar pattern of reduced defence spending, in this case relative to the size of GDP rather than in absolute terms, could be seen in Israel following the country's obtaining of a nuclear deterrent in the late 1960s and the subsequent reduction of threats from neighbouring Arab states.[59]

In North Korea the development of a nuclear deterrent has been directly tied to economic development under the Byungjin policy—which prioritises the two programs in parallel, implicitly at the expense of conventional military spending. This policy was first announced in 2013 and was particularly emphasized at the 7th Congress of the Workers' Party of Korea in May 2016. The first significant signs of reduced overall defence spending came that year.[60] The DPRK's ability to increasingly focus on improving its civilian economy from the early 2010s has thus directly resulted from the country's development of a nuclear deterrent.[61]

Regarding the costs of developing a nuclear capability, it is important to take into account the fact that the program has overwhelmingly relied on workers and manufacturing from the DPRK itself and has been pursued at a very low cost—particularly when considering the importance of the security benefits it had provided. This was attested to by former North Korean diplomat Kim Min Gyu, who defected in 2009. Kim stated regarding the cost of the program: "actually, what they spend isn't that much. Their workforce works for free[i] and, except for a few key

i Since the state guarantees the right to a job, and provides the majority of the workforce with employment, there is a large surplus of already paid labour available to commit to new projects. This often includes military personnel which, much like in China before 1990, are used for work on state infrastructure projects. This makes the labour costs the government pays for new projects negligible—essentially free—since the soldiers and workers remain in the state's employ regardless of whether a project is being pursued or not.

imported parts, they make everything else."[62] Nuclear weapons can thus be said to offer, literally, more "bang for the buck" than conventional spending, making them key facilitators of security, lower military spending and a stronger economy.

A secondary economic benefit of the North Korean deterrence program, particularly in its development of advanced ballistic missile technologies, is its ability to earn considerable revenues from exports. The Hwasong-5, Hwasong-6 and Rodong-1 programs were effectively subsidised by exports to Egypt, Iran, Pakistan, Libya and other parties. By offering technologies which few others were able to provide, North Korea's missile deterrent program effectively paid for itself. Licenced production of these missiles in Iran and Egypt using facilities set up by the Koreans, and technology transfers to the former, were very significant further sources of continuous revenue which seriously undermined Western economic warfare efforts against the (then non-nuclear) state at the time. As the DPRK has developed more advanced technologies, these have remained in high demand—from the solid-fuelled Toksa missiles sold to Syria to the Musudan sold to Iran—while other high-end Iranian missiles such as the Sejil[63] continue to make extensive use of Korean technologies and components. Although the North Korean economy as a whole does not rely on an export-led growth model, the country's missile program at several stages appears to have done so.[64]

Ultimately while the proportion of the North Korean state budget allocated to defence is likely to continue to decline in the short term, net defence spending may well grow in the long term as reinvestment in the civilian economy continues to fuel economic growth and thereby facilitates a state budget which is overall considerably larger. Nuclear weapons serving as a facilitator of lower defence spending can thus in the long term also boost conventional capabilities.

Humanitarian Impacts of Economic Warfare Against the DPRK

Although the vast majority of reports have concurred that North Korea's economy has remained healthy despite considerable economic sanctions, Western-drafted sanctions imposed through the UN and unilaterally have served to limit access to specialist products which could not be developed domestically. Foremost among these have been chemical and medical products, the lack of which has had seriously detrimental impacts for many of the more vulnerable segments of the Korean population. In 2013 the UN Food and Agricultural Organization (FAO), which had a representation in the DPRK for over a decade, reported, following a tightening of unilateral U.S. economic sanctions, that "the precarious foreign exchange situation combined with international restrictions on trade has not allowed adequate commercial imports of much needed agricultural inputs such as fertilizer, pesticides…over the years, domestic production of fertilizer has declined to a level of about 10 percent of total requirement, increasing dependence on imported fertilizer and reducing its overall use."[65] This notably affected food production for a brief period in the mid-2010s, although North Korean sources report that the domestic producers have since increased production of fertilisers to compensate for this.[66]

UNICEF and the World Food Programme, which had previously provided medical assistance to North Korean children such as vitamin A supplementation, was prevented from providing this to tens of thousands of children as a result of economic sanctions. An estimated 2,772 had died as a result—a far cry from the figure of "over 500,000 children" who died as a direct result of sanctions on Iraq[67] but still a significant number. Citing the Western-drafted sanctions regime, a subsequent cutting of funds for aid programs, and delays in the UN Security Council's allowances for humanitarian exemptions to the sanctions regime, director of the North Korea Programs at the Korean American Medical Association Kee B. Pak noted: "The lives of ordinary North Korean people, as seen here with children under 5, should never be placed at risk when trying to achieve political objectives. The UN's appeal for urgent humanitarian needs in North Korea should be fully funded."[68] Pierre Peron, spokesperson for the UN Office for the Coordination of Humanitarian Affairs, similarly noted that sanctions had caused serious complications for humanitarian agencies, including "lack of funding, the absence of a banking channel for humanitarian transfers and challenges to the delivery of humanitarian supplies."[69]

A number of workers in various aid agencies who had witnessed the impact of sanctions on the ground strongly condemned their implementation, with humanitarian aid falling 63% in four years from $117.8 million in 2012 to $43.8 million in 2016. The primary impact of this was in treating illnesses which North Korea's medical sector could not itself provide. Founder and director of KorAid, Katharina Zellweger was among many who stressed that it was primarily sick and elderly people in the DPRK who suffered from the sanctions regime, and citing tuberculosis treatment as an example, she reported: "The global fund has stopped [a tuberculosis] programme…thousands of people do not get medicine any more and there is a higher risk that [tuberculosis] may spread much wider." An estimated 130,000 North Koreans suffered from the disease in 2016, according to the World Health Organization, with sanctions limiting options for treatment and containment.[70] Workers from other NGOs noted that channels for supplies into the DPRK were blocked by the sanctions regime, which resulted in some of the most vulnerable in Korean society losing their access to much needed aid.[71] A 2019 report from the United Nations Development Program reached similar conclusions,[72] as did a report the same year from panel of experts established by the UN Security Council to report on the sanctions regime.[73] The impact of sanctions on medical equipment related to reproductive health alone was estimated to have killed 72 pregnant women and 1,200 infants.[74]

Similar conclusions regarding the humanitarian impact of the Western-drafted sanctions, imposed both through the United Nations Security Council and unilaterally, were reached by a number of analysts. Nobel laureates who visited the DPRK in 2016 came to this conclusion. Israeli laureate Aaron Ciechanover observed regarding the nature of sanctions, which targeted the population indiscriminately rather than the nuclear program specifically: "You cannot turn penicillin into a nuclear bomb… You don't pressurise via making people sicker. That's not the right way to go." British laurate Richard Roberts stated that he was "quite impressed" with the country's scientific achievements despite harsh economic sanctions, but nevertheless noted that "this embargo is really hurting the scientists and that's a great shame… Many of the things the doctors would like, the professors would like, they just can't have them because of the embargo."[75]

The North Korean government itself echoed these complaints, with Han Tae Song, ambassador to the United Nations in Geneva, stating: "Due to these inhumane economic sanctions, vulnerable peoples like women and children are becoming…victims." He added: "Such sanctions against humanity which block even the delivery of the medical equipment and medicines for maternal and child health and the basic goods for daily life including even children's bicycles threaten the protection and promotion of our women's rights and even the right to survival of the children."[76]

The implications of economic sanctions on the DPRK was often greater than the texts of the resolutions themselves may have indicated. A prominent study by a Council on Foreign Relations task force, for example, noted that stipulations for intrusive cargo inspections targeting shipping moving into and out of the DPRK presented "a significant barrier…to North Korea's few remaining legitimate exports." Even for exports and imports not covered at the time by UN sanctions, intrusive inspections and resulting delays can deter clients and suppliers from trading in even unsanctioned materials.[77] KorAid Director Zellweger was among those who attested to this, stating: "It's become much harder to find suppliers…and shipping companies as they don't want to do business in North Korea. Everything has become much more complicated." Kim Soon Kwon, who set up a directed NGO providing higher-yield corn to the DPRK, similarly observed: "After the sanctions were imposed, the negative sentiment about helping North Korea started building and we saw a dramatic decline in donations…NGOs are run and maintained on donations from ordinary people." He added that many other NGOs operating in North Korea had the same experience. [78]

Responding to the defection of a KPA soldier across the 38th parallel in November 2017, and widespread publicization by Western sources of reports that he was infected with parasitic worms, Swiss businessman Felix Abt elaborated on possible causes. A resident in the DPRK from 2002 to 2009, Abt attributed deteriorating medical conditions in the country to the harsh Western-drafted economic sanctions imposed both unilaterally and through the United Nations. Abt had worked as managing director of the Pyongsu Joint Venture Company, the first foreign-invested joint venture in the pharmaceutical field in the DPRK, and thus had considerable knowledge of the practical effect of sanctions. Abt noted that when he first ran PyongSu he had invested in production of Mebendazole—a treatment for parasitic worm infections. He stated:

> Despite being competitors, we also shared our management and production know-how with other pharmaceutical factories in the country to contribute to a more efficient fight against disease across the country. North Korea had then over two dozen smaller and larger pharmaceutical factories, about half of them operating under the Ministry of Public Health. As we were the first pharmaceutical company to achieve WHO recognition as fully compliant with its Good Manufacturing Practices (GMP) the cabinet (council of ministers presided over by the Prime Minister) declared our company then as one of North Korea's five best joint ventures and the model

> company for the entire upcoming pharmaceutical industry. Shortly thereafter I signed the first two contracts with the WHO for the production of Mebendazole for distribution to hospitals across the country and I expected regular repeat orders.

Abt noted that production of anti-helminthic drugs was carried out at very low prices, but as the sanctions continued to escalate both investors and NGOs such as the World Health Organisation, Red Cross and Red Crescent struggled to continue their initial support for their manufacturing. Abt referred to the result of this economic warfare effort as "a continuation of the Korean War by other means," stating:

> The rising geopolitical tensions and more and more weaponized sanctions including serious obstacles for foreign businesses and NGOs to operate in the country (e.g. financial sanctions making money transfers into and out of the country impossible) led to a noticeable donor fatigue: Instead of maintaining or even increasing budgets to purchase the amount of drugs necessary to minimize important diseases from worm infestations to respiratory tract infections to tuberculosis and malaria the procurement budgets were slashed. Manufacturers of pharmaceuticals and foodstuff items in North Korea which all depend on the import of unavoidable items such as laboratory equipment and consumables (to identify and fix contaminations in the production and the end products) were not able to uphold the newly achieved "good manufacturing practices" (GMP) when these items were also banned by sanctions. Subsequent sanction rounds banned ever more products.

Emphasizing the destructive impact of economic sanctions, Abt stated:

> But even items that were not yet banned in the mid-2000s, such as a power back-up system or a multi-stage water purification system, which nobody produced in North Korea and which we needed to import in order to make our factory fully compliant with international Good Manufacturing Practices

(GMP) as defined by the WHO could not be purchased directly from foreign suppliers. The demonization of North Korea and the threat of being sanctioned post-festum at some point frightened foreign suppliers, including Chinese ones, to sell [from selling] equipment to a North Korean pharmaceutical factory. Many industries such as the pharmaceutical industry and the garment industry are heavily import-dependent. North Korea's pharmaceutical industry is a formulation industry, which means it processes imported active and other ingredients; the textile industry processes the cloth and other materials and semi-finished products, which it is almost entirely importing too. North Korean industries and its agriculture also use imported machines and other equipment which need spare parts or replacement when worn out.

Since the U.N. Security Council banned 90% of North Korea's exports (coal generating more than one third of the country's income, textile products, the second largest hard currency earner, iron, iron ore, lead, lead ore, and seafood) there won't be any more hard currency left to buy and pay for imports. As a consequence, entire industries, certainly the pharmaceutical industry and the garment industry (which has been exporting most of its production, which is now also prohibited from doing so) will come to a standstill. Even fishermen are not allowed to sell fish to Chinese customers any longer, artists are prohibited to sell their paintings abroad, sailors transporting fish or textiles are "punished" with a global port ban and tens of thousands of workers abroad who are forced to return to North Korea (many of which could make savings with which they bought a front store, opened a restaurant or started a small garment enterprise upon their return in the past) will lose their livelihood.[79] Local sub-suppliers and service providers of the manufacturing industry will suffer the same fate. North Korea's garment industry alone employs 200,000 workers.[80]

Why Do China and Russia Support Western Sanctions Resolutions at the United Nations

While the powers of the Western Bloc have imposed harsh unilateral economic sanctions against North Korea for decades, which in the case of the United States have been in place for over 70 years, the ability to pass Western-drafted economic sanctions through the United Nations Security Council has provided a key boost to Western economic warfare efforts against the East Asian state. Although Western sources have long been vocal in criticizing the veto system, the right of all five permanent Security Council members, including the two non-Western members China and Russia, to block any resolution with a single vote, these two states have since 2006 approved several successive rounds of sanctions against the DPRK. Beijing and Moscow have been able to prevent the Western Bloc from targeting a number of small non-Westphilian states either militarily or economically through the United Nations—Syria,[81] Sudan,[82] Yugoslavia,[83] Iraq (2003),[84] Myanmar[85] and Zimbabwe[86] being among the many examples. This use of the veto forced the Western Bloc to either back down or take unilateral action—which fueled Western calls for a reform of the Security Council to annul the veto system and facilitate easier passage of Western-drafted resolutions.[87] China and Russia have been pressed, however, to support sanctions against those states which are seen to undermine the global nuclear non-proliferation regime—namely Iran and, from 2006, the DPRK.[88]

While there is no legal prohibition on non-signatories of the Nuclear Non-proliferation Treaty preventing them from pursuing a nuclear deterrent, and the right to self-defence is guaranteed under the UN charter which can be interpreted to imply a right to pursue deterrence and military parity, neither Beijing nor Moscow can afford to be seen as in any way endorsing the nuclearization of a small Western adversary. An understanding emerged following the Cuban Missile Crisis in the 1960s, when nuclear proliferation brought the world to the brink of nuclear war, which stipulates that major powers will not proliferate nuclear arms to their defence partners to aim at other powers. Moscow's reversal of plans to arm Cuba was a case in point.[89]

While China and Russia's relationship with the Western Bloc has grown increasingly antagonistic since the mid-2000s, their relationship is far from a state of total war and several mutual understandings remain, particularly in the field of nuclear proliferation. Thus, should either Beijing or Moscow be perceived to be in any way facilitating a Korean nuclear program aimed at the United States or shielding Pyongyang from reprimand at the United Nations, this understanding may well be broken, leading to reprisals from the Western Bloc. It was notable that intervention by the United States was responsible for cutting short the

South Korean[90] and Taiwanese[91] nuclear programs, both of which posed significant threats to Chinese security. Should Beijing be seen to allow North Korea to nuclearize the U.S. is likely to reciprocate and assist Japan, South Korea and perhaps even Taiwan and Australia to do the same.[92] The U.S. could even potentially facilitate the nuclearization of states neighbouring Russia, perhaps Poland or the Baltic States, which could in turn provoke a cycle of escalation and nuclear proliferation unfavourable to all parties.

Only when the North Korean issue became a nuclear issue were Beijing and Moscow forced to support UN resolutions targeting the country. Sanctions have not passed due to any particular objections either China or Russia have to a nuclear North Korea per-se, which both have repeatedly indicated does not threaten their security in and of itself, but rather due to the potential consequences of condoning nuclearization. In 2016 and 2017 in particular, the stakes were raised as the Barack Obama and Donald Trump administrations both seriously considered military action against the DPRK. The latter appeared particularly adept at tying Chinese compliance on the sanctions issue to its other security interests—presenting Beijing with alternatives potentially far more dangerous than sanctions on its neighbour should it fail to comply including the possibility that America would provoke a major nuclear war on its border by attacking North Korea.

In April 2016 Chinese Premier Xi Jinping told a group of foreign (non-Korean) diplomats that his country "will never allow war or chaos on the peninsula," a statement seemingly directed at the West more than at either of the Koreas. "As a permanent member of the United Nations Security Council, China has implemented relevant Security Council resolutions fully and faithfully. As a close neighbour, we will never allow war or chaos on the Korean peninsula, as this serves nobody's interests. We hope that various parties will exercise restraint, avoid mutual provocation and escalation of tension and make a joint effort to bring the nuclear issue back to the track of dialogue and negotiations as early as possible and walk towards peace and security in northeast Asia."[93] Xi appeared to be implying what had been widely suspected: that China was acquiescing to Western demands for sanctions on the DPRK as a means of venting Western hostility towards Pyongyang, and in return expected that the U.S. would continue down the road of economic pressure and would not consider military action or armed provocation in Korea.

Beijing allowed for sanctions only as long as military options remained off the table—something it would not tolerate.

China would again come under pressure to support further sanctions—or else—under the Donald Trump administration. President Trump implied a policy of presenting China with a stark choice over Korea in his interview with the *Financial Times* on April 3 of his first year in office, stating: "China has great influence over North Korea. And China will either decide to help us with North Korea or they won't... If they do, that will be very good for China, and if they don't, it won't be good for anyone...if China is not going to solve North Korea, we will. That is all I am telling you."[94] In the run up to Premier Xi's visit to Trump's resort in Mar-a-Lago in April there were signs that the new American president would offer a serious warning to Beijing, and that China's economy would suffer both due to a harder line on a trade agreement should it fail to comply and due to secondary economic sanctions increasingly imposed on Chinese companies and banks trading with North Korea.[95] Such sanctions also applied from 2018 to limit Chinese cooperation with Russia[96] and shortly afterwards to target Chinese companies trading with Iran[97]—countries also targeted by Western economic warfare campaigns. Beyond sanctions, the threat of a U.S. attack on China's neighbor remained.

President Trump tweeted on March 31: "The meeting with China next week will be a very difficult one," and he proceeded to send a strong signal to Beijing regarding the Korean issue at the meeting. As Xi and Trump dined at Mar-a-Lago, the U.S. Navy launched 59 cruise missiles in an illegal strike on Syrian military sites—which according to American sources housed chemical weapons. Syria was a close economic and defence partner of both China and North Korea, and Beijing had repeatedly closed the only legal avenue for strikes or sanctions on the country by vetoing Western-drafted resolutions at the UNSC. President Trump was thus demonstrating his willingness to launch attacks on Chinese defense partners without UNSC approval and in direct and brazen violation of international law—an action which had serious implications for the Korean Peninsula where American attentions were already focused. President Trump reportedly leaned over to Xi mid-meal and informed him that a strike which he had ordered was currently underway.[98]

Premier Xi succeeded in convincing President Trump at Mar-a-Lago, at least temporarily, that China was not in a position to influence Pyongyang. The president stated in an interview the following week:

"After listening for 10 minutes, I realized it's not so easy… I felt pretty strongly that they had tremendous power over North Korea. But it's not what you would think."[99] This was a rare admission by the president that he had in fact been mistaken. Whatever words were exchanged between the leaders of the world's most powerful nations, China appeared to emerge in a considerably stronger position facing no further threats to increase military deployments or employ secondary sanctions by the U.S., while it appeared there were no expectations for Beijing to immediately increase pressure on the DPRK as the American side had initially demanded.

China had found a way not to pressure North Korea as the Western Bloc had desired—while also avoiding the harsh repercussions promised by the United States should it fail to apply pressure—by somehow convincing the Trump administration that its options for applying such pressure and its leverage over Pyongyang were limited. Vetoing Western-drafted resolutions targeting the DPRK, however, would be seen as openly siding with North Korea and would potentially jeopardize the Chinese position. Of course, China remained relatively free in the extent to which it would enforce sanctions once such resolutions were passed, and as the state conducting the vast majority of trade with the DPRK the effectiveness of the sanctions regime was overwhelmingly dependent on China's internal policies—which the West had few options to monitor or influence. China did not present Western intelligence agencies with the "intelligence black hole" that North Korea did, but it retained a reasonably tight security system on the mainland which made it one of the most challenging targets for Western parties to collect intelligence on.[100]

President Trump would notably again change tone in late July, stating following a second test of the Hwasong-14 ICBM on July 28: "I am very disappointed in China. Our foolish past leaders have allowed them to make hundreds of billions of dollars a year in trade, yet they do NOTHING for us with North Korea, just talk… We will no longer allow this to continue. China could easily solve this problem!"[101] This was likely not in relation to China's enforcement of sanctions domestically, where nothing significant had changed, but rather due to Beijing's refusal to agree to new rounds of particularly harsh Western-drafted economic sanctions at the United Nations. These new sanctions were less disguised in their indiscriminate nature, and targeted Korean exports and access to foreign currency in what appeared to be an attempt to force the East Asian state into economic crisis. A new round of sanctions was passed on August 5, but the draft was altered by the Chinese and Russian delegations to lessen its severity relative to what the Western powers had originally intended. This potentially seriously restricted Korean trade with the wider world—but enforcement on the borders with China and Russia still remained a key weakness in Western efforts to undermine the Korean economy.

On August 22, as part of a comprehensive effort to further tighten economic pressure on North Korea, the U.S. Treasury Department announced that it would impose secondary economic sanctions on firms which did business with North Korea—and would particularly target Korean expat workers.[102] China, and to a lesser extent Russia, inevitably bore the brunt of this as the DPRK's largest trading partners. On September 3, in his response to a Korean test of a thermonuclear warhead, President Trump again struck a less hostile tone towards the Chinese position on the Korean issue. The president tweeted: "North Korea is a rogue nation which has become a great threat and embarrassment to China, which is trying to help but with little success."[103] Three months later National Security Advisor McMaster again urged countries across the world to fully break ties with and isolate the DPRK on the United States' behalf—or else the United States would need to consider military options. This thinly veiled threat, aimed primarily at North Korea's neighbors, raised the prospect of war on their borders if they did not comply more fully with the Western-led economic warfare effort.[104]

Arguably the primary issue which resulted from North Korean nuclear and long range missile development for China, Russia and all northeast Asian actors is that testing caused a major increase in tensions between Pyongyang and Washington—and each time posed a risk, however small, that the U.S. could launch a military response and bring war to the region. These tensions were not due to the inherent nature of Korean weapons testing, with very similar tests being carried out by other non-NPT members India[105] and Pakistan[106] at the same time, but rather due to the arbitrarily hostile response by Washington and the wider Western world towards the Korean tests. It thus remained strongly within the interests of both Beijing and Moscow to reduce the number of North Korean nuclear and long-range missile tests or end them entirely. While forcing the country to abandon its deterrence program would be seen by Pyongyang as a fundamental infringement on its sovereignty, speeding up the deterrence program and reducing the need for testing presented another possible means of achieving an end to testing. Technology transfers to North Korea relating to miniaturised thermonuclear warheads, ballistic missile re-entry vehicles and fuel composites among other things could have provided a serious enhancement to the Korean deterrence program and reduced both the duration of testing and the frequency of tests—although allegations to this effect remain unproven.[107]

While Western analysts have had a strong incentive to underestimate North Korean technological capabilities, and have often levelled allegations of Russian or Chinese provision of certain advanced technologies which later turned out to be fully indigenous,[108] the possibility of their provision of some support to speed up the Korean deterrence program cannot be ruled out. Had the Hwasong-14 and Hwasong-15 and miniaturised thermonuclear bomb not been successfully tested in 2017, but 1–2 years afterwards, not only would the chances of American military action have been higher but the duration of a period of high tensions in the region would have been considerably longer. There was thus a strong incentive for Beijing and Moscow to act to speed up the testing period. Since the détente on the Korean Peninsula which emerged from early 2018, as Pyongyang introduced a self-imposed moratorium on strategic weapons testing, Russia and China have repeatedly called for a relaxation of economic sanctions targeting the DPRK.[109]

NOTES

1 Fu, Ruihong [付瑞红], 里根政府对苏联的 "经济战": 基于目标和过程的分析 [Reagan Administration's "Economic War" with the Soviet Union: An Analysis Based on Objectives and Processes], *Chinese Academy of Social Sciences*.

2 Yaqub, Salim. Containing Arab Nationalism, Chapel Hill, University of North Carolina Press, 2004 (Chapter 2).
Jameson, Sam, 'Shock Waves From Toshiba-Soviet Deal Still Rattle Japan,' *Los Angeles. Times,* August 11, 1987.

3 Busch, Andrew E., 'Ronald Reagan and the Defeat of the Soviet Empire,' *Presidential Studies Quarterly*, vol. 27, no. 3, Summer 1997 (pp. 451–466).

4 'Former Congressman Ron Paul Debates Former CIA Officer Mike Baker,' *Fox Business Network, Kennedy*, 25 April 2017.

5 'Sanctions Blamed for Deaths of Children,' *Lewiston Morning Tribune*, December 2, 1995.
Stahl, Lesley, 'Interview with Madeline Albright,' *60 Minutes*, May 12, 1996.

6 'The Weakest Link,' *The Economist*, February 6, 2003.

7 Abrams, A. B., 'Power and Primacy: The History of Western Intervention in the Asia-Pacific,' Oxford, Peter Lang, 2019 (Chapter 14: Economic War on Asia: South Korea and the Asian Tigers).
Klein, Naomi, *The Shock Doctrine: The Rise of Disaster Capitalism*, London, Penguin, 2008 (Chapter 13: Let it Burn: The Looting of Asia and the 'Fall of a Second Berlin Wall').

8 Cronin, Richard P., 'The North Korean Nuclear Threat and the U.S.-Japan Security Alliance: Perceived Interests, Approaches, and Prospects,' *The Fletcher Forum of World Affairs*, vol. 29, issue 1, Winter 2005 (p. 54).

9 Park, Kyung-Ae, 'Regime Change in North Korea?: Economic Reform and Political Opportunity Structures,' *North Korean Review*, vol. 5, no. 1, Spring 2009 (p. 27).

10 Harrison, Selig S., 'Promoting a Soft Landing in North Korea,' *Foreign Policy*, no. 106, Spring 1997 (p. 65).

11 Park, Kyung-Ae, 'Regime Change in North Korea?: Economic Reform and Political Opportunity Structures,' *North Korean Review*, vol. 5, no. 1, Spring 2009 (pp. 23–45).

12 Harrison, Selig S., 'Promoting a Soft Landing in North Korea,' *Foreign Policy*, no. 106, Spring 1997 (p. 60).

13 Ibid. (p. 65).

14 'Sailing on, the ship with a hold full of Scud missiles,' *The Guardian*, December 12, 2002.

15 'Not so jolly for North Korean sports when hockey sticks are banned luxury goods,' *Straits Times*, August 3, 2017.

16 'Haggling delays N Korea sanctions vote,' *Daily Telegraph*, October 15, 2006.

17 Varner, Bill and Green, Peter S., 'UN Votes to Punish North Korea for Nuclear Test,' *Bloomberg*, June 12, 2009.

18 News transcript: Department of Defense Press Briefing by Admiral Cecil Haney in the Pentagon Briefing Room, March 24, 2015.

19 Capaccio, Tony, 'North Korea Can Miniaturise Nuclear Weapon, U.S. Says,' *Bloomberg*, April 8, 2015.

20 Park, Hyun, 'US to Boost Missile Defense in Response to North Korea Threats,' *Hankyoreh*, March 18, 2013.

21 'Russian Government: Violation by the US of its Obligations in the Sphere of Nonproliferation of WMD,' *Global Research*, August 7, 2010.
Columbus, Frank, *Russia in Transition: Volume 2*, New York, Nova Science Publishers, 2003 (p. 47).

22 'Treasury Takes Actions to Further Restrict North Korea's Access to the U.S. Financial System,' *U.S. Department of the Treasury* (press release), June 1, 2016.

23 Democratic People's Republic of Korea, Food and Agriculture Organization of the United Nations World Food Program Joint Rapid Food Security Assessment, May 2019 (p. 14).
'United Nations Security Council Resolution 2397,' 8151st meeting of UNSC, Adopted on December 22, 2017.

24 Crude Oil Consumption by Country, *Index Mundi* (accessed September 14, 2019).

25 'How Sanctions Affect Iran's Economy,' *Council on Foreign Relations*, May 22, 2012.
Peterson, Sabrina M., 'Iran's Deteriorating Economy: An Analysis of the Economic Impact of Western Sanctions,' *International Affairs Review*, July 1, 2012.

26 Crossette, Barbara, 'Iraq Sanctions Kill Children, U.N. Reports,' *New York Times*, December 1, 1995.

27 'Russia Economic Report 34: Balancing Economic Adjustment and Transformation,' *World Bank*, September 30, 2015.

28 'Trump says North Korea has "tremendous potential" to become "absolute economic power,"' *RT*, February 28, 2019.

29 Kim, Christine, and Chung, Jane, 'North Korea 2016 economic growth at 17-year high despite sanctions: South Korea,' *Reuters*, July 21, 2017.
Lankov, Andrei, 'Sanctions working? Not yet …,' *Korea Times*, May 29, 2016.
Pearson, James and Park, Ju-Min, 'Despite sanctions, North Korea prices steady as Kim leaves markets alone,' *Reuters*, August 8, 2016.

Maresca, Thomas, 'Report: North Korea economy developing dramatically despite sanctions,' *UPI,* December 4, 2019.

30 'North Korea's Stable Exchange Rates Confound Economists,' *Associated Press*, November 16, 2018.

31 Kim, Christine and Chung, Jane, 'North Korea 2016 economic growth at 17-year high despite sanctions: South Korea,' *Reuters*, July 21, 2017.

32 Dorell, Oren, 'North Korean Economy Keeps Humming Despite Ever-Tighter Sanctions,' *USA Today*, November 24, 2017.

33 Pearson, James and Park, Ju-Min, 'Despite sanctions, North Korea prices steady as Kim leaves markets alone,' *Reuters*, August 8, 2016.

34 Ibid.

35 Lankov, Andrei, 'Sanctions working? Not yet …,' *Korea Times*, May 29, 2016.

36 Kim, Christine and Chung, Jane, 'North Korea 2016 economic growth at 17-year high despite sanctions: South Korea,' *Reuters*, July 21, 2017.

37 Dorell, Oren, 'North Korean Economy Keeps Humming Despite Ever-Tighter Sanctions,' *USA Today*, November 24, 2017.

38 'North Korea's Stable Exchange Rates Confound Economists,' *Associated Press*, November 16, 2018.

39 'Former unification minister criticizes Bank of Korea statistics on North Korean growth rate,' *Hankyoreh,* January 1, 2019.

40 Maresca, Thomas, 'Report: North Korea economy developing dramatically despite sanctions,' *UPI,* December 4, 2019.
Choi, Eun-joo, '21st Colloquium of 2019: Changes in the North Korean Economy Observed at Field Investigation of 2019 to China-North Korea Borders,' *Sejong Institute,* November 12, 2019.
Féron, Henri, 'Pyongyang's Construction Boom: Is North Korea Beating Sanctions?,' *38 North,* July 18, 2017.

41 'North Korea's Stable Exchange Rates Confound Economists,' *Associated Press*, November 16, 2018.

42 Baron, Jeff, 'What if Sanctions Brought North Korea to the Brink? "Well, in 1941…,"' *38 North*, September 7, 2017.

43 Kim, Il Sung, 'On Abolishing the Tax System,' Fifth Supreme People's Assembly of the Democratic People's Republic of Korea at its Third Session, March 21, 1974.

44 Mullen, Mike and Nunn, Sam and Mount, Adam, *A Sharper Choice on North Korea: Engaging China for a Stable Northeast Asia*, Council on Foreign Relations, Independent Task Force Report No. 74, September 2016 (p. 14).

45 Fassihi, Farnaz and Lee Myers, Steven, 'Defying U.S., China and Iran Near Trade and Military Partnership,' *New York Times*, July 11, 2020.
Esfandiary, Dina and Tabatabai, Arinae M., 'Will China Undermine Trump's Iran Strategy?,' *Foreign Affairs,* July 20, 2018.
Downs, Erica S. and Maloney, Suzanne, 'Getting China to Sanction Iran,' *Brookings Institute*, February 23, 2011.
Richter, Paul, 'West worries China may undermine Iran sanctions efforts,' *Los Angeles Times*, June 28, 2010.

46 'Venezuela: China's Support is Essential Against the US Blockade,' *Orinoco Tribune*, June 29, 2020.
Zerpa, Fabiola and Recht, Hannah, 'Venezuela's Choking Points: Here's Where Maduro Gets His Revenue,' *Bloomberg*, January 29, 2019.
Salama, Vivian, 'U.S. Expands Sanctions Against Venezuela Into an Embargo,' *Wall Street Journal*, August 5, 2019.

47 Lee, Yen Nee, 'Trump says there is "AWESOME" economic potential for North Korea—if Kim abandons nukes,' *CNBC,* February 26, 2019.

48 Lee, Sung-Yoon and Stanton, Joshua, 'How to Get Serious with North Korea,' *CNN*, January 15, 2016.
49 Mullen, Mike and Nunn, Sam and Mount, Adam, *A Sharper Choice on North Korea: Engaging China for a Stable Northeast Asia*, Council on Foreign Relations, Independent Task Force Report No. 74, September 2016.
50 'Iran condemns new US sanctions over missile test,' *BBC*, January 18, 2016.
51 Murphy, Francois and Emmott, Robin, 'Iran is complying with nuclear deal restrictions: IAEA report,' *Reuters*, August 30, 2018.
52 Ha-young, Choi, 'North Korea to decrease national defense proportion this year,' *NK News*, March 31, 2016.
53 Dorell, Oren, 'North Korean economy keeps humming despite ever-tighter sanctions,' *USA Today*, November 26, 2017.
54 Conversation with retired Korean People's Army serviceman (anonymous), September 10, 2019.
Conversation with conscription age male university graduate in Pyongyang (anonymous), September 8, 2019.
Conversation with overseas diplomat from DPRK (anonymous), November 7, 2019.
55 Moore, Malcolm, 'North Korea now "fully fledged nuclear power,"' *The Telegraph*, April 24, 2009.
56 Calvocoressi, Peter. *World Politics Since 1945*, Abingdon, Routledge, 2008 (p. 18).
57 Mathers, Jennifer G., *The Russian Nuclear Shield from Stalin to Yeltsin: The Cold War and Beyond*, London, Palgrave Macmillan, 2000 (pp. 220–224).
58 United States of America Department of State, Office of the Historian, Foreign Relations of the United States, 1955–1957, Korea, Volume XXIII, Part 2, *162. Progress Report Prepared by the Operations Coordinating Board*, July 18, 1956.
59 Beinin, Joel, 'Challenge from Israel's Military,' *MERIP Reports*, no. 92, November–December 1980 (p. 7).
60 Ha-young, Choi, 'North Korea to decrease national defense proportion this year,' *NK News*, March 31, 2016.
61 Cordesman, Anthony H. and Colley, Steven, *Chinese Strategy and Military Modernization in 2015: A Comparative Analysis*, Washington D.C., Centre for Strategic and International Studies, 2016 (p. 377).
'Less than one aircraft carrier? The cost of North Korea's nukes,' *CNBC*, July 20, 2017.
62 Pearson, James and Park, Ju-min, 'North Korea overcomes poverty, sanctions with cut-price nukes,' *Reuters*, January 11, 2016
63 Crail, Peter, 'Iran Lauds Development of Solid Fuel Missile,' *Arms Control Today*, vol. 38, no. 1, January/ February 2008.
'Iran-Bound Rocket Fuel Component Seized in Singapore,' *Iran Watch*, 1 September 2010.
64 Crail, Peter, 'Iran Lauds Development of Solid Fuel Missile,' *Arms Control Today*, vol. 38, no. 1, January/ February 2008.
'Iran-Bound Rocket Fuel Component Seized in Singapore,' *Iran Watch*, 1 September 2010.
65 Gunjal, Kisan and Goodbody, Swithun and Hollema, Siemon and Ghoos, Katrien and Wanmali, Samir and Krishnamurthy, Krishna and Turano, Emily, *Special Report, FAO/WFP Crop and Food Security Assessment Mission to the Democratic People's Republic of Korea*, November 28, 2013.
66 Writer's Conversations with Industrialists when Visiting the Hungnam Fertiliser Factory in Wonsan, July 2017.
'Supreme Leader Kim Jong Un Cuts Tape for Completion of Sunchon Phosphatic Fertilizer Factory,' *Rodong Sinmun*, May 2, 2020.

Katzeff Silbersttein, Benjamin, 'North Korea's Chemical and Coal Liquefaction Industries: The Difficult Path Ahead to Self-Reliance,' *38 North,* July 9, 2020.
'Political Bureau of C.C., WPK Meets under Guidance of Supreme Leader Kim Jong Un,' *KNCA,* June 8, 2020.
'Kim Jae Ryong Inspects Chemical Industrial Units in South Hamgyong Province,' *KCNA,* June 23, 2020.

67 Gordon, Joy, *Invisible War: The United States and the Iraq Sanctions*, Cambridge, MS, Harvard University Press, 2010 (p. 87).
'Sanctions Blamed for Deaths of Children,' *Lewiston Morning Tribune*, December 2, 1995.
Stahl, Lesley, 'Interview with Madeline Albright,' *60 Minutes*, May 12, 1996.

68 Kim, Joengyon and Park, Kee B., 'How Sanctions Hurt North Korea's Children,' *Global Health Now,* August 5, 2019.

69 Lee, Christy, 'Humanitarian Groups Say Sanctions Impede Aid to North Koreans,' *VOA*, March 26, 2019.

70 Lee, Jeong-ho, 'North Korea UN sanctions are hurting the vulnerable, aid workers say,' *South China Morning Post,* June 26, 2018.

71 Ibid.

72 'DPR Korea: Needs and Priorities,' *United Nations Development Program*, March 2019.

73 Letter dated 21 February 2019 from the Panel of Experts established pursuant to resolution 1874 (2009) addressed to the President of the Security Council, United Nations Security Council (pp. 66–67).

74 Park, Kee and Kim, Miles, 'Underfunded: the urgent need for emergency reproductive health kits in N. Korea,' *NK News*, July 3, 2019,

75 'Israeli Nobel laureate calls for easing North Korea sanctions,' *Times of Israel,* August 17, 2019.
'North Korea sanctions should be eased, say Nobel laureates,' *BBC News*, May 7, 2016.

76 Nebehay, Stephanie, 'North Korea says sanctions hurting women, children,' *Reuters*, November 8, 2017.

77 Mullen, Mike and Nunn, Sam and Mount, Adam, *A Sharper Choice on North Korea: Engaging China for a Stable Northeast Asia*, Council on Foreign Relations, Independent Task Force Report No. 74, September 2016 (p. 23).

78 Lee, Jeong-ho, 'North Korea UN sanctions are hurting the vulnerable, aid workers say,' *South China Morning Post,* June 26, 2018.

79 Lankov, Andrei, 'The Real Story of North Korean Labor Camps in Russia,' *Carnegie Moscow Center*, July 10, 2017.

80 Abt, Felix, 'Sanctions and the Targeting of a Population: The Continuation of the Korean War By Other Means And Its Impact On Ordinary North Koreans,' *Military Watch Magazine,* January 27, 2018.

81 'Syria war: Russia and China veto sanctions,' *BBC,* February 28, 2017.

82 Charbonneau, Louis, 'China, Russia resist West's sanctions push for Sudan, South Sudan,' *Reuters,* May 1, 2012.

83 Lauria, Joe, 'Yugoslavia: China, Russia Threaten To Block UN Kosovo Resolution,' *Radio Free Europe,* June 9, 1999.

84 'Russia Hints at U.N. Veto On Iraq,' *CBS*, February 28, 2003.

85 'China, Russia block UN statement on Myanmar,' *South China Morning Post,* March 18, 2017.

86 Nasaw, Daniel, 'China and Russia veto Zimbabwe sanctions,' *The Guardian*, July 11, 2008.

87 Sheeran, Scott, 'The U.N. Security Council veto is literally killing people,' *Washington Post*, August 11, 2014.

'The Security Council's sine qua non: The Veto Power,' *Rutgers Global Policy Roundtable,* Occasional Paper Eight, 2018.

Akin, David, 'In bid for UN Security Council seat, Canada's position on reform could be a barrier: analyst,' *Global News*, January 3, 2020.

88 Mu, Ren, 'China's Non-intervention Policy in UNSC Sanctions in the 21st Century: The Cases of Libya, North Korea, and Zimbabwe,' *Ritsumeikan International Affairs,* vol.12, 2014 (p.101–134).

89 Savaranskaya, Svetlana, 'Cuba Almost Became a Nuclear Power in 1962,' *Foreign Policy*, October 10, 2012.

90 Kim, Byung-Kook and Vogel, Ezra, *The Park Chung Hee Era, The Transformation of South Korea*, Cambridge, MA, Harvard University Press, 2011 (pp. 483–510).

Burr, William, 'Stopping Korea from Going Nuclear, Part I,' *National Security Archive,* March 22, 2017.

91 Ide, William, 'How the US stopped Taiwan's bomb,' *Taipei Times*, October 14, 1999.

Weiner, Tim, 'How a Spy Left Taiwan in the Cold,' *New York Times,* Dec. 20, 1997.

92 Rubin, Michael, 'Why Taiwan needs nuclear weapons,' *The National Interest,* May 31, 2020.

Lyon, Rod, 'The Next Nuclear Weapons State: Australia?,' *National Interest,* October 27, 2019.

'Australia debates developing nuclear weapons,' *Bangkok Post*, July 8, 2019.

Stangarone, Troy, 'Is Trump Right to Suggest that South Korea and Japan Should Go Nuclear?,' *Korea Economic Institute of America.*

93 "China to Never Allow War or Chaos on Korean Peninsula: Xi," *China Radio International Online*, April 28, 2016.

94 'Donald Trump Warns China the US Is Ready to Tackle North Korea,' *Financial Times*, April 3, 2017.

95 'U.S. appeals court upholds ruling against Chinese banks in North Korea sanctions probe,' *Reuters,* July 31, 2019.

96 Wroughton, Lesley and Zengerle, Patricia, 'U.S. sanctions China for buying Russian fighter jets, missiles,' *Reuters,* September 20, 2018.

97 Talley, Ian and McBride, Courtney, 'U.S. Sanctions Chinese Firms for Allegedly Shipping Iranian Oil,' *Wall Street Journal,* September 25, 2019.

98 Alexander, Harriet and Boyle, Danny and Henderson, Barney, 'US Launches Strike on Syria—How it Unfolded,' *The Telegraph*, April 7, 2017.

99 Baker, Gerard and Lee, Carol and Bender, Michael, 'Trump Says He Offered China Better Trade Terms in Exchange for Help on North Korea,' *Wall Street Journal,* April 22, 2017.

100 'Western spy agencies being outgunned by "bad actors," ex-CIA operative James Olson warns,' *ABC News*, July 29, 2019.

'Killing CIA Informants, China Crippled US Spying Operations,' *New York Times*, May 20, 2017.

Mai, Jun, 'CIA spy-killing claims "show China's strength in counter-espionage,"' *South China Morning Post,* May 22, 2017.

Murphy, Margi, 'Dozens of US spies killed after Iran and China uncovered CIA messaging service using Google,' *Telegraph,* November 3, 2018.

101 Yi, Yang, 'Commentary: U.S. should stop blaming China for trade deficit, Korean nuclear issue,' *Xinhua,* July 31, 2017.

102 'Treasury Targets Chinese and Russian Entities and Individuals Supporting the North Korean Regime,' *US Department of Treasury*, Press Center, Washington D.C., August 22, 2017.

103 Donald J. Trump on Twitter, *North Korea is a rogue nation which has become a great threat and embarrassment to China, which is trying to help but with little success*, September 3, 2017.

104 'World Faces "Last Best Chance" to. Avoid War with North Korea, US General Warns.' *Sky News*, December 13, 2017.

105 'India conducts fourth test launch of Agni-V missile,' *BBC News*, December 26, 2016.

106 Panda, Ankit, 'Pakistan Tests New Sub-Launched Nuclear-Capable Cruise Missile. What Now?,' *The Diplomat,* January 10, 2017.

107 Chang, Gordon C., 'Did North Korea Just Launch a Chinese Missile?,' *National Interest,* February 15, 2017.
Goncharenko, Roman, 'Where did North Korea get its missile technology?,' *Deutsche Welle,* August 15, 2017.

108 Fisher, Max, 'Remote Textile Plant May Secretly Fuel North Korea's Weapons,' *New York Times,* September 27, 2017.
Panda, Ankit, 'No, North Korea Isn't Dependent on Russia and China For Its Rocket Fuel,' *The Diplomat,* September 28, 2017.

109 Lee, Jeong-ho, 'China, Russia, North Korea call for adjusted sanctions ahead of denuclearisation,' *South China Morning Post,* October 10, 2018.
Nichols, Michelle, 'Russia, China to hold more U.N. talks on lifting North Korea sanctions: diplomats,' *Reuters,* December 30, 2019.

Appendices

MAJOR INCIDENTS IN THE 2010s

APPENDIX I

THE KIM JONG NAM ASSASSINATION

On February 13, 2017, Kim Jong Nam, the half-brother of DPRK Chairman Kim Jong Un, was assassinated at Kuala Lumpur International Airport in Malaysia. The assassins, two women of Indonesian and Vietnamese origin, reportedly used a VX nerve agent, and within hours South Korea's ruling party had stated with certainty that Pyongyang was responsible—terming it a "naked example of Kim Jong Un's reign of terror."[1] Western sources were quick to follow, despite no investigation having taken place, and the incident was used as a pretext to swiftly apply further economic sanctions against North Korea. The extent of Western speculation was overwhelming, and leading media outlets had the influence needed to turn this theory into an effective fact—regardless of what the Malaysian investigators themselves would come to conclude. Reports in Western media and subsequent accusations by Western experts and officials focused overwhelmingly on what Western and South Korean sources had to say—not on what Malaysia, a relatively neutral party with good relations with both the Western world and the DPRK, concluded from its investigation.

In sharp contrast to the Western press, official Malaysian sources never directly accused the DPRK of masterminding the assassination. The only statements from the Malaysian investigation were to the effect that South Korea and the United States had accused the DPRK of masterminding the attack, without an investigation of their own or presentation of evidence, and that North Korean had denied this. South Korean media were quick to depict Ri Jong Chol, a North Korean residing in Malaysia, as the mastermind behind the attack. Ri was subsequently arrested by Malaysian police for questioning but was later released due to a lack of evidence against him. Staff at the North Korean embassy in Malaysia were also cleared of all suspicion and, after questioning by Malaysian police, were no longer mentioned in the investigation. The case was effectively closed in April 2019 with light sentences given to both the women on the basis that neither were aware of what they were doing, as both thought they had been carrying out a televised prank. The official result of the investigation did not state that the DPRK was the perpetrator.[2] Claims of North Korean culpability were later dismissed as pure speculation by the Malaysian Prime Minister.[3]

The purpose of highlighting that there was no evidence North Korea was the perpetrator is not to rule out the possibility of its responsibility, but rather to highlight the means by which the country's adversaries are able to create facts and thereby manipulate global opinion in accordance with their interests. There were considerable incentives for multiple parties, including hardline anti-North Korean elements in the ROK and the Western world, as well as the DPRK itself, to have organised the assassination. The newly inaugurated Donald Trump administration at the time was conducting a thorough review of its North Korea policy, and much to the chagrin of hardline elements in the foreign policy and the intelligence communities in the U.S., in Europe and in South Korea, the new president appeared set to adopt a more conciliatory line. No hostile statements towards the DPRK had been issued before the assassination took place. This quickly changed, and many prominent analysts concluded that the assassination was key to setting the Trump administration on a collision course with the East Asian state.[4]

North Korea too had an incentive to carry out the killing, although why it would have done it so publicly when Kim Jong Nam had regularly stayed at the country's embassy, and at a time of potential détente with the U.S. under a new administration, remains unclear. Reports which emerged in 2019 revealed that Kim Jong Nam had begun working as a CIA informant, and some sources indicate he could have been instrumental in Western plans to overthrow the Korean government. It is hardly unheard of for such assets to be targeted for assassination overseas—not by North Korea but by a number of other states including the United States itself—which has used chemical or biological substances for such purposes in the past.[5] Another possible incentive for the DPRK, which would explain the public setting of the assassination and the means used, would be to demonstrate the reach of its operatives and its expertise in deploying chemical agents. This show of force could have been intended to complement ongoing missile and nuclear testing—with Korean special operatives potentially able to carry out far larger chemical attacks overseas, striking American assets should the U.S. launch a war against it. Ultimately the perpetrator of the attack and the motivations behind it, at present, can only be speculated.

NOTES

1 Choe, Sang-hun, 'Kim Jong-un's Half Brother Is Reported Assassinated in Malaysia,' *The New York Times,* February 14, 2017.
2 Asmolov, Konstantin, 'Kim Jong-nam Murder Case is Closed, or More Precisely Falls Apart,' *New Eastern Outlook,* April 16, 2019.
3 Bernama, 'Dr M hails Seoul's "Look South" policy; affirms rapprochement with Pyongyang,' *New Straits Times,* November 26, 2019.
4 Jackson, Van, *On the Brink,* Cambridge, Cambridge University Press, 2018 (pp. 100–102).
5 'The C.I.A. and Lumumba,' *New York Times,* August 2, 1981.
Norton, Roy, 'The CIA's Worldwide Kill Squads,' CIA-DRP84-00409R001000080001-7, Approved For Release on March 6, 2001.

APPENDIX II

DEATH OF AN AMERICAN STUDENT

On January 2, 2016, American student Otto Warmbier was arrested in Pyongyang after entering as a tourist. He was accused of carrying out a "hostile act against the state" after attempting to steal a poster from a restricted area of the Yanggakdo Hotel, and two months later was convicted under Article 60 of the DPRK's Criminal Code. His court case cited his confession, CCTV footage, forensic evidence, and witness testimonies, and sentenced him to 15 years of hard labour. The sentence was near unanimously criticised by Western sources, although it was in fact no harsher to that he could have received in the United States for a similar act and or in several Western aligned states. A notable example was that of a Hispanic American man, Adolfo Martinez, who was sentenced to 16 years in prison in the state of Ohio in December 2019 for tearing down an LGBT flag outside a church and destroying it. Unlike Warmbier, he was not a foreign citizen and did not enter a restricted area to access the flag.[1] In Thailand, considerably harsher sentences have repeatedly been issued against those disrespecting symbols of its monarchy, including foreigners, but like the Martinez case, their coverage in the Western press was far more nuanced than that of Warmbier's own trial.[2]

On June 13, 2017, 15 months after his sentencing, U.S. Secretary of State Rex Tillerson announced that the DPRK had released Warmbier to American custody. U.S. media reported that the State Department had been informed Warmbier had fallen into a coma and was seriously ill, and he was hospitalised as soon as he returned to the United States.[3] Warmbier died six days later, although the cause of his illness was unclear. Damage to his brain tissues from suffocation and reports of hypoxia alongside the total lack of trauma or injury on the rest of his body was consistent with an attempted suicide by hanging, which a number of analysts speculated was the likely cause.[4] A blood clot, pneumonia, sepsis, kidney failure, and sleeping pills were also cited as potential causes of Warmbier's injury, and could have caused him to stop breathing if he had botulism and was paralyzed from it.[5] The Director of the University of Cincinnati Medical Center's Neurocritical Care Program, Dr. Daniel Kanter, stated regarding the student's condition:

> We have no certain or verifiable knowledge of the cause or circumstances of his neurological injury… This pattern of injury, however, is usually seen as the result of cardiopulmonary arrest, where the blood supply to the brain is inadequate for a period of time, resulting in the death of brain tissue.

He further noted that there was no trauma to the head or skull.[6] Warmbier reportedly had had a neurological injury "for 15 months or so" according to U.S. sources, indicating he may have been in poor health before entering Korean custody.[7] CNN Chief Medical Correspondent Dr. Sanjay Gupta speculated that medication given to Warmbier after his arrival in the U.S. could have directly caused his situation to deteriorate, leading to his eventual death.[8]

Shortly after his death, Warmbier's parents alleged that their son's passing was the result of torture in the DPRK—something widely picked up on by Western media at a time of high tensions with the East Asian state. This account not only strongly contradicted the results of medical examination carried out, but also the experiences of previous American prisoners held in Korean custody. American citizen Matthew Todd Miller, for example, was sentenced to six years of prison labour in April 2014 for committing acts hostile to the state. While in custody, he repeatedly alluded to his good treatment at the hands of his captors—which led Western sources to widely speculate that he had been coerced to make such claims. Miller was released early after 212 days in custody, and confirmed he was surprised at his good treatment—citing permission to listen to music on his iPad and iPhone in prison. Upon returning to the United States he described his transformed perception of the country, stating regarding his time in prison: "This might sound strange, but I was prepared for the 'torture.' But instead of that I was killed with kindness, and with that my mind folded."[9] Miller also denied widespread speculation in Western reports that his public apology for his crimes in the DPRK was coerced, stating that he had been entirely sincere.[10]

Hamilton County Coroner's Office carried out an external examination of Warmbier's body, which, according to CNN and other media reports, contradicted the account of his parents. For example, Warmbier's father had made an emotionally charged statement that: "His bottom teeth look like they had taken a pair of pliers and rearranged them." Directly contradicting this, the coroner's report stated: "the teeth are natural and in good repair." Addressing the statements by Warmbier's parents, which were widely re-reported by a number of media outlets and used as a basis for further economic sanctions on and justification of hostile policy towards the DPRK, Coroner Dr. Lakshmi Kode Sammarco stated addressing the claim of forced rearranging of Otto's teeth: "I felt very comfortable that there wasn't any evidence of trauma. We were surprised at the [parents'] statement." She said her team, which included a forensic dentist, thoroughly evaluated the body and assessed various scans of his body.[11]

Warmbier's parents declined to comment on the coroner's report, and notably refused to allow an autopsy which could determine the cause of their son's death. They instead continued to support a narrative blaming the North Korean government for torture, and subsequently sought through an American federal court to obtain half a billion dollars in compensation from the East Asian state.[12] Forensic scientists were highly critical of the unusual and unexpected decision not to perform an autopsy, which Warmbier's parents did not explain, and by doing so it was ensured that the cause of the student's death would remain undetermined.[13] This decision led to speculation that Warmbier's parents sought to protect their narrative blaming the Korean government, which not only supported hardline positions of many in the U.S. government against and further demonised the country, but also could potentially have won them very significant financial rewards. Subsequent moves by the United States Navy to seize a North Korean cargo ship in 2018 and escort it to U.S. territory, where it was prepared for sale at auction, were followed by reports that the U.S. Marshals Service was considering providing the full value of the Korean ship to Warmbier's parents.[14] They were later provided with part of the ship's value, which represented a major loss to the Korean merchant shipping fleet.[15] The legality of the seizure remains hotly disputed.

NOTES

1 Knox, Patrick, 'Bigot Caged: Homophobe jailed for 16 YEARS for tearing down LGBTQ flag and setting fire to it in Iowa,' *The Sun,* December 20, 2019.
2 'Man jailed for 35 years in Thailand for insulting monarchy on Facebook,' *The Guardian*, June 9, 2017.
3 Shesgree, Deirdre and Dorell, Oren, 'U.S. college student released by North Korea arrives back in Ohio,' *USA Today,* June 14, 2017.
4 Lockett, Jon, 'Tragic student Otto Warmbier 'may have attempted suicide' in North Korean prison after being sentenced to 15 years for stealing poster,' *The Sun*, July 28, 2018.
Basu, Zachary, 'What we're reading: What happened to Otto Warmbier in North Korea,' *Axios*, July 25, 2018.
Tingle, Rory, 'Otto Warmbier's brain damage that led to his death was caused by a SUICIDE ATTEMPT rather than torture by North Korean prison guards, report claims,' *Daily Mail,* July 25, 2018.
5 Fox, Maggie, 'What killed Otto Warmbier?' *NBC News,* June 20, 2017.
6 Tinker, Ben, 'What an autopsy may (or may not) have revealed about Otto Warmbier's death,' *CNN,* June 22, 2017.
7 Ibid.
8 Nedelman, Michael, 'Coroner found no obvious signs of torture on Otto Warmbier,' *CNN,* September 29, 2017.
9 'Freed American Matthew Miller: "I wanted to stay in North Korea,"' *The Guardian,* November 20, 2014.
10 Nate Thayer, 'Matthew Miller's excellent adventure in North Korea,' *NK News*, November 14, 2014.
11 Nedelman, Michael, 'Coroner found no obvious signs of torture on Otto Warmbier,' *CNN,* September 29, 2017.
12 'US court orders North Korea to pay $500 million for Otto Warmbier's death,' *Deutsche Welle,* December 24, 2018.
13 Tinker, Ben, 'What an autopsy may (or may not) have revealed about Otto Warmbier's death,' *CNN,* June 22, 2017.
Nedelman, Michael, 'Coroner found no obvious signs of torture on Otto Warmbier,' *CNN,* September 29, 2017.
14 Lee, Christy, 'U.S. Marshals to Sell Seized North Korean Cargo Ship,' *VOA,* July 27, 2019.
15 'Seized North Korean cargo ship sold to compensate parents of Otto Warmbier, others,' *Navy Times,* October 9, 2019.

APPENDIX III

STORMING THE NORTH KOREAN EMBASSY

Five days before the second summit meeting between President Donald Trump and Chairman Kim Jong Un scheduled for February 27, 2019, the DPRK's Embassy in Madrid was attacked. Armed men broke into the embassy, beat and tied up the diplomats and their families, and seized computers which reportedly held highly sensitive information. Bags were placed over the captives' heads, and the Korean commercial attaché was reportedly taken into the bathroom and threatened with iron bars and imitation handguns to defect.[1] Spain's national police and the CNI foreign intelligence unit of its National Intelligence Centre reportedly examined a number of possibilities and concluded that the means by which the embassy was attacked resembled the "method of work" of the American intelligence services—citing the "perfectly coordinated" military precision of the operation. The attackers were "professionals, and were responsible for lowering the power, dimming the street lights on the road in front of the embassy and neutralising other security systems around the building without raising an alarm."[2] While the involvement of U.S. intelligence was widely suspected, Spanish government sources admitted that proving this in court would be extremely difficult.[3]

Computers, encryption equipment and other systems taken by the attackers would reportedly provide a "treasure trove" of information to Western intelligence services and would have been "eagerly sought after" by such services.[4] Embassies' use of non-electronic communications methods and encrypted communications meant that some particularly sensitive information could only be obtained by gaining forced physical access to the facility in such a way. Decryption devices could furthermore potentially allow Western intelligence agencies to monitor communications between the DPRK and its embassies across the world.[5] Access to private information on former North Korean ambassador to Spain, Kim Hyok Chol, who was playing a central role in ongoing negotiations with the United States, was speculated to be the reason why the embassy in Spain had been chosen as the target of the attack at this time. Such information could assist the U.S. in understanding the DPRK's long term negotiating strategy and prove highly valuable for the talks which would ensue in Hanoi five days later.

The Cheollima Civil Defense group, an organisation devoted to the forced overthrow of the Korean state with close ties to the CIA, was found to have carried out the attack and later accepted responsibility. Perpetrators included Adrian Hong, President of Joseon Institute and founder of the anti-Korean organisations Liberty in North Korea and Pegasus Strategies. These organisations were heavily involved in information warfare efforts against the state. Christopher Ahn, a former U.S. Marine who served in Iraq as deputy chief of intelligence for his battalion, also participated in the raid. The subsequent Spanish investigation found at least two of the perpetrators had direct links to the CIA. The *Financial Times* was among the sources which noted that the CIA maintained close ties with such anti-Pyongyang non-government organisations.[6] Spanish media indicated that such an operation would most likely have been carried out in conjunction with other Western intelligence agencies.[7]

Andrei Lankov, a prominent Korea expert who had in the past strongly advocated forced regime change in the DPRK,[8] himself observed that it was: "inconceivable to imagine how such an operation could be planned and successfully executed without the prior knowledge of those government agencies whose job is to watch for exactly these types of activities."[9] Spanish officials were reported to have "solid proof" that Hong had met with CIA officials in Spain including photographs and communication records—although this may not be publicised.[10] The South Korean conservative newspaper *Chosun Ilbo*, known for its close contacts with ROK intelligence agencies, attested to Hong's close ties to the CIA.[11] Hong reportedly had at least one meeting in Washington at the Office of the Director of National Intelligence in 2018.[12]

Regarding the possible incentives for the attack, the U.S. Military establishment and intelligence community were notably highly sceptical of President Trump's peace initiatives,[13] repeatedly contradicting him regarding the chances of achieving denuclearisation through meetings with the Korean leadership. Just ten days before the attack on February 12th the Chief of the U.S. Indo-Pacific Command, Navy Admiral Philip Davidson, stressed that North Korea "remains the most immediate challenge…we think it is unlikely that North Korea will give up all of its nuclear weapons or production capabilities, but seeks to negotiate partial denuclearization in exchange for U.S. and international concessions."[14] Daniel Coats, Director of National Intelligence, stated on the same day that the DPRK was "unlikely to completely give up its nuclear weapons and production capabilities."[15] These were two of several indications of widespread disagreement with the president's policies, which were contrary to the preceding Maximum Pressure policy and to the policies of the previous two administrations for dealing with the country. It remains a possibility, given its sensitive timing, that the attack was staged so overtly in order to undermine the Trump administration's upcoming summit meeting. The *Washington Post* noted to this effect: "Any hint of U.S. involvement in an assault on a diplomatic compound could have derailed the talks, a prospect of which American intelligence would likely be mindful."[16]

The DPRK, apparently eager not to see talks sabotaged, waited until one month after the summit meeting in Hanoi before commenting on the attack, and suggested involvement of American intelligence behind it. Later confirmation from the perpetrators that the equipment stolen in the raid was turned over to American intelligence by Hong and his associates further supported this assessment.[17] The operation may have been intended to send a signal to Pyongyang before the summit that, while the country may think itself safe from a direct military action after 2017, it could still be targeted through attacks on its overseas interests. While an assessment of the nature of the participants and their organisations, the divisions within the U.S. leadership over Korea policies, and the timing and purposes of the attack, can give some indication as to its nature and the likely perpetrators, the extent of official involvement by the United States is unlikely to be confirmed for the foreseeable future.

NOTES

1 Shorrock, Tim, 'Did the CIA Orchestrate an Attack on the North Korean Embassy in Spain?,' *Foreign Policy,* May 2, 2019.

2 Ryall, Julian and Badcock, James, 'Was North Korea's vital "transformation computer" taken in raid on Madrid embassy?,' *The Telegraph*, March 26, 2019. Dolz, Patricia Ortega, 'Spain investigates alleged attack on North Korean embassy in Madrid,' *El Pais,* February 27, 2019.

3 González, Miguel and Dolz, Patricia Ortega, 'CIA implicated in attack on North Korean embassy in Madrid,' *El Pais*, March 13, 2019.

4 Hudson, John, 'A shadowy group trying to overthrow Kim Jong Un allegedly raided a North Korean embassy in broad daylight,' *Washington Post*, March 15, 2019.

5 Dilanian, Ken and De Luce, Dan and Lederman, Josh, 'FBI has data stolen from North Korea embassy by anti-regime group,' *NBC News*, March 29, 2019.

6 'A tale of daring, violence and intrigue from a North Korea embassy,' *Financial Times*, March 29, 2019.

7 Fernandez, David and Ballesteros, Roberto B., 'Asalto a la embajada de Corea: Policía y CNI sospechan del servicio secreto de EEUU,' ['Assault on the Korean embassy: Police and CNI suspect US secret service'], *El Confidencial*, March 10, 2019.

8 Lankov, Andrei, 'Changing North Korea: An Information Campaign Can Beat the Regime,' *Foreign Affairs,* vol. 88, no. 6, November/December 2009 (pp. 95–105).

9 Lankov, Andrei, 'What to make of a mysterious break-in at the North Korean embassy in Madrid,' *NK News,* March 20, 2019.

10 Shorrock, Tim, 'Did the CIA Orchestrate an Attack on the North Korean Embassy in Spain?,' *Foreign Policy,* May 2, 2019.

11 Cho, Yi Jun, 'Who Is Anti-N.Korean Guerrilla Leader?,' *Chosun Ilbo,* April 4, 2019.

12 Taylor, Adam and Kim, Min Joo, 'The covert group that carried out a brazen raid on a North Korean embassy now fears exposure,' *Washington Post*, March 28, 2019.

13 Krawchenko, Katiana, 'Former CIA analyst: U.S. must remain "very, very sceptical" of North Korea,' *CBS,* June 1, 2018.
Bechtol, Bruce and Maxwell, David, 'North Korean Military Proliferation in the Middle East and Africa: A Book Launch' Presentation at the Korea Economic Institute of America, September 25, 2018.

14 Brunnstrom, David, 'U.S. commander says North Korea unlikely to give up all nuclear weapons,' *Reuters,* February 12, 2019.

15 O'Brien, Connor, 'North Korea remains a top threat despite diplomatic thaw, U.S. commanders say,' *Politico,* February 12, 2019.

16 Hudson, John, 'A shadowy group trying to overthrow Kim Jong Un allegedly raided a North Korean embassy in broad daylight,' *Washington Post*, March 15, 2019.

17 'North Korea says Madrid embassy raid was "grave terror attack,"' *BBC News*, March 31, 2019.
Dilanian, Ken and De Luce, Dan and Lederman, Josh, 'FBI has data stolen from North Korea embassy by anti-regime group,' *NBC News*, March 29, 2019.

INDEX

Index

Index

Z